Karen Wagner

PETER BISKIND is the acclaimed author of *Easy Riders, Raging Bulls*; *Down and Dirty Pictures*; and *Star*, among other books. His work has appeared in *The New York Times*, the *Los Angeles Times*, *The Washington Post*, *The Nation*, and *Rolling Stone*. He is the former executive editor of *Premiere* and the former editor in chief of *American Film*, and is a contributing editor to *Vanity Fair*. He lives in the Hudson Valley.

Additional Praise for *My Lunches with Orson*

"What makes *My Lunches with Orson* appealing is the piquancy of the much younger, skinnier [Jaglom] taking on the Sisyphean job of reviving the Falstaffian outcast."
—*The New York Times Book Review*

"Riveting . . . This is Welles riffing uninhibitedly on his life and times, lurching from mischief to melancholy. . . . I defy anyone not to feel moved by the narrative arc of greatness laid low by its own luminosity."
—*Financial Times*

"Enthralling . . . loaded with hilarious digressions and old showbiz tales related by Welles with hugely articulate relish."
—*The Hollywood Reporter*

"If you love old movies, *My Lunches with Orson* is like being handed a big tin of macadamia nuts—you just keep devouring it."
—*NPR*

"*My Lunches with Orson* offers the experience of sitting in on a particular historical-cultural moment. Read with your Netflix on hand, as Welles's wealth of knowledge inspires re-viewings of both his own films and those of his favorite actors like Buster Keaton and Carole Lombard."
—*The Christian Science Monitor*

"A wonderfully fluid peek into Welles's mind. Rich with acerbic observations about cinema, theater, filmmakers, actors, politics, and the essence of storytelling, *My Lunches with Orson* might be the elephantine storyteller's last great work."
—*Indiewire*

"It's time to add another line of adjectives to our descriptions of Orson Welles. In this remarkable collection of conversations, we come upon Welles the conversationalist provocateur who can't open his mouth without saying something outrageously funny, fiercely opinionated, and always off-center about the men and women he claims to have known, played with, worked for, slept with, been courted and betrayed by, and admired or detested (often simultaneously) during his half century in show business. I laughed so hard I had an asthma attack."

—David Nasaw, author of *The Patriarch*

"We don't often get close to a legend, but here we have lunch with one week by week, in the last years of his life. Welles's conversations with Henry Jaglom glitter with memory, intelligence, and malice, and above all offer a magnificent act of self-impersonation: Orson Welles playing Orson Welles."

—Michael Wood, author of *Film: A Very Short Introduction*

"When Henry Jaglom sent me the galleys, I was skeptical about their entertainment value. But as soon as I picked them up, I was hooked. Welles was an ornery, sometimes unpleasant genius, but his opinions on just about everything and everyone were unvarnished. You can almost hear the silverware clinking and the waiters delivering lunch as the likes of Richard Burton drop by to pay their respects. . . . For those not fortunate enough to have Hollywood running through their family tree, this book may be the next best thing."   —Ralph Gardner Jr., *The Wall Street Journal*

My Lunches with Orson

Conversations between

Henry Jaglom and Orson Welles

Edited and with an Introduction by

Peter Biskind

Picador

A Metropolitan Book
Henry Holt and Company
New York

www.picadorusa.com
www.twitter.com/picadorusa • www.facebook.com/picadorusa
picadorbookroom.tumblr.com

Picador® is a U.S. registered trademark and is used by Henry Holt and Company under license from Pan Books Limited.

For book club information, please visit www.facebook.com/picadorbookclub or e-mail marketing@picadorusa.com.

Photographs courtesy of Rainbow Film Company

Designed by Meryl Sussman Levavi

The Library of Congress has cataloged the Henry Holt hardcover edition as follows:

Jaglom, Henry, 1939–
    My lunches with Orson : conversations between Henry Jaglom and Orson Welles / edited by Peter Biskind.— First edition.
        p. cm.
    ISBN 978-0-8050-9725-2 (hardcover)
    ISBN 978-0-8050-9726-9 (e-book)
  1. Jaglom, Henry, 1939—Anecdotes. 2. Welles, Orson, 1915–1985—Anecdotes.
3. Motion picture producers and directors—United States—Anecdotes. I. Welles, Orson, 1915–1985. II. Biskind, Peter. III. Title.
    PN1998.3.J276A5 2013
    791.4302'33092—dc23

                                                                            2013000291

Picador Paperback ISBN 978-1-250-05170-7

Picador books may be purchased for educational, business, or promotional use. For information on bulk purchases, please contact Macmillan Corporate and Premium Sales Department at 1-800-221-7945, extension 5442, or write specialmarkets@macmillan.com.

First published in the United States by Metropolitan Books, an imprint of Henry Holt and Company

First Picador Edition: July 2014

10 9 8 7 6 5 4 3 2 1

For Steve Bloom

Contents

Introduction

How Henry Met Orson
by Peter Biskind

ORSON WELLES has long been regarded as one of the greatest film-makers of all time, more specifically, the most gifted of a long line of gifted Hollywood mavericks that started with D. W. Griffith, or perhaps Erich von Stroheim. Today, his *Citizen Kane*, over seventy years after it was released in 1941, still finds a place on every Ten Best list. It topped the British Film Institute's *Sight & Sound* magazine's survey for fifty years in a row, only to be toppled in 2012 by Alfred Hitchcock's *Vertigo*, a picture that Welles despised.

But we all know lists and such mean next to nothing in our awards-obsessed, rankings-ridden culture, and there's a much easier and infinitely more pleasurable way to judge the stature of Welles and his films: just watch them, starting with *Citizen Kane*. The opening, a dark and doomy shot of the massive iron gates of Xanadu capped by a gigantic K, with the Transylvanian ruins of Kane's folly looming above and behind it, grabs our attention, but at the same time warns us that there is more going on than meets the eye, so to speak, because it's all too much, drama shading into melodrama, undermining itself with irony and camp.

Welles had a genius for the dramatic; he was a master of shock and awe long before they were turned to other, considerably less noble ends, but at the same time he was a skilled miniaturist who worked just as easily on a small canvas with lightness and subtlety. Above all, it was his wizardry with time, space, and light, along with the exquisite tension between his furious, operatic imagination and the elegant, meticulous design and execution of the film— the deep focus, extreme camera angles, striking dissolves, ingenious transitions—that make it crackle with electricity. After *Kane*, movies were never the same. When asked to describe Welles's influence, Jean-Luc Godard remarked, simply, "Everyone will always owe him everything."

Welles was not only a director, but a producer, a skilled actor and screenwriter, and a prolific author of essays, plays, stories, even a newspaper column. More often than not, he wore several of these hats at once, making him a veritable Bartholomew Cubbins of the arts. One finds oneself reaching in vain for adjectives adequate to describe him. As considerable as his gifts were, he himself was more than the sum of his parts, his own greatest production, a commanding, larger-than-life figure of equatorial girth who in later years sported a beard of biblical proportions that made him every casting director's first choice for deities and gurus of all sorts, from Jor-El (Marlon Brando eventually got the role) to God.

George Orson Welles was born on May 6, 1915, in Kenosha, Wisconsin. His parents, Richard Welles, an inventor, and Beatrice Ives, a pianist, artist, and suffragette, were a mismatched couple with a stormy marriage. Eventually, they separated, and his mother, who raised him, died at an early age. Dr. Maurice "Dadda" Bernstein, Beatrice's close friend and rumored lover, became his guardian.

Welles was fiercely precocious. Even as a child, he read widely, showed a keen interest in music, and even became an amateur magician. He finished high school in two years, and got a scholarship to Harvard. He had a prodigious intellect, and was on intimate terms with the great literature of the Western canon, able to recite lengthy swatches of prose and poetry. But he preferred experience to book learning, and persuaded Dadda Bernstein to send him on a walking tour of Ireland when he was only sixteen. Aided by raw talent and boyish good looks—he was over six feet tall, with blond hair and a face like a baby with a little snub nose that always embarrassed him—he talked his way into a small part in a play at the Gate Theatre in Dublin, run by Hilton Edwards and Micheál Mac Liammóir, that started him on his way.

Returning to the States, he soared through New York's theater world and was dubbed "the boy wonder" before he was out of his teens. In 1936, Welles was hired by the Federal Theatre. Fascinated by modernist figures like Max Reinhardt and Bertolt Brecht, he was unafraid to surprise the classics by putting them in contemporary settings, like his triumphant so-called "Voodoo" *Macbeth*, that he produced that year when he was only twenty-one, with an all-black cast. Although he venerated the classics, no text was so sacrosanct that Welles wouldn't or couldn't have his way with it. The following year, he produced his "Blackshirt" *Julius Caesar*, which he turned into an allegory of fascism. (He played Brutus.)

Although he never swallowed the Stalinist line, Welles breathed the heady fervor of those Popular Front years. He considered himself a New Deal liberal, and later would brush up against President Franklin D. Roosevelt, who used him in various ways, taking full advantage of his rhetorical and oratorical skills, most famously his booming voice that sounded like the rumble of not-so-distant thunder.

In between *Macbeth* and *Caesar*, Welles created a scandal with Marc Blitzstein's operetta *The Cradle Will Rock* in 1937. The feds padlocked the doors of the theater where it was set to open, apparently because FDR and/or his advisors feared that its full-throated defense of unions in general and striking workers at Republic Steel in particular (ten were shot by Chicago police in the so-called Memorial Day Massacre), would provoke their enemies in Congress to further slash funding for the Federal Theatre and its parent, the Works Progress Administration. On June 16, 1937, amid a firestorm of press, hundreds of ticket holders marched twenty blocks to New York's Venice Theatre, where they were treated to a bare-bones production in which Blitzstein played the piano on stage while the cast, scattered about the audience, performed the songs. That same year, Welles founded the Mercury Theatre, another successful enterprise. It seemed that he could do no wrong. Three days after his twenty-third birthday, on May 9, 1938, *TIME* magazine put him on the cover.

Controversy—welcome and unwelcome—continued to dog Welles's footsteps. After creating a name for himself in radio, most famously playing Lamont Cranston, or "the Shadow," in the series of the same name, he was given his own show on CBS. His Halloween broadcast on October 30, 1938, adapted from H. G. Wells's *War of the Worlds*, panicked millions of Americans with its urgent, you-are-there style coverage of a Martian invasion, although the target of the ostensible attack, not Washington, D.C., not New York City, but Grover's Mill, New Jersey, should have given listeners pause.

Two years later, the new head of RKO, George Schaefer, gave Welles an unprecedented two-film contract with final cut that shocked and angered the industry. Welles embarked on *Citizen Kane*, which he wrote (with Herman J. Mankiewicz), directed, and headlined. The picture earned him the enmity of news baron William Randolph Hearst, on whose life it was loosely based, and whose *petit nom d'amour* for his lover Marion Davies's nether part—Rosebud— the picture made famous, although, to be sure, there are other claimants to that particular honor.

Kane premiered on May Day, 1941, when Welles was all of twenty-five years old. Hearst made a feverish attempt to block the release of the movie. According to Hearst columnist Louella Parsons in her autobiography, several studio heads, including L. B. Mayer and Jack Warner refused to book the picture in their theaters. Hearst also threatened to decline ads from RKO. Schaefer held fast, but Hearst did manage to force *Kane* into smaller, independent, and therefore less profitable venues, damaging the box office. In the last analysis, though, *Kane* was just too sophisticated for a mass audience, and RKO lost an estimated $150,000 on the picture.

Before Welles started his next movie, the studio insisted that he sign a new contract that revoked his final cut. *The Magnificent Ambersons* (1942) was based on a novel by Booth Tarkington. Production proceeded relatively smoothly, but after he completed part of a rough cut of *Ambersons*, America entered World War II, and Welles abruptly left for Brazil at the behest of President Roosevelt on a goodwill mission, leaving that cut in the hands of editor Robert Wise to finish according to his instructions, to be delivered via phone calls and telegrams. Wise was then to carry it down to Rio for the director to polish. Welles agreed to do yet another film, *It's All True*, in Brazil, at the same time he was busy sampling the pleasures afforded by Rio's louche lifestyle, for which he confessed more than a passing interest. The war interfered with his plans to polish the film in Brazil himself, and his idyll turned to ashes when unbeknown to him, the studio sneak-previewed *Ambersons* at the Fox Theater in Pomona, California, on March 17, 1942. The screening turned into a fiasco when a flock of ticket holders walked out, leaving scathing comments on the cards. Running scared, RKO slashed 45 minutes out of Welles's original 132-minute cut, without consulting him. Then as now, unhappy endings were taboo, so the studio took it upon itself to shoot a new, happier one. What was supposed to be a dark saga of the rise and fall of a wealthy family, left behind by an America forever changed by industrialization, was turned into an inane, maudlin, and totally preposterous tale of reconciliation. The film flopped.

Welles never entirely recovered his footing. With his directing career sidelined, he found work as an actor, performing in pictures such as *Journey into Fear* (1943), *Jane Eyre* (1943), and *The Stranger* (1946), much of which he unofficially directed, while pursuing an active social life. He eventually married three times—to Virginia Nicholson, Rita Hayworth, and Paola Mori—and fathered three daughters, one by each wife. Welles spent the last twenty-four years of his life with Oja Kodar, a stunning Croatian-Hungarian artist, actress, and collaborator, twenty-six years his junior, although he never divorced Mori. He couldn't have been an easy man to live with, considering his roving eye and what Nicholson called his "crushing ego."

Hayworth, the former Margarita Carmen Cansino, was, of course, one of the brightest stars of the forties and early fifties, so much so that the crew of the *Enola Gay* is rumored to have used her pinup decal as "nose art" for either the bomber or its payload, Little Boy, before dropping it on Hiroshima. Welles whimsically fell in love with her, so the story goes, when he saw her picture on the cover of *LIFE* magazine, and then and there decided to marry her. Which he did, only to discover that she was, with much justification, insanely jealous, as well as morbidly insecure and depressed. After a few turbulent years, she kicked him out, married Prince Aly Khan, and gave birth to a daughter, Yasmin. Before the divorce was finalized, Hayworth and Welles did a movie together, *The Lady from Shanghai* (1947).

The Lady from Shanghai does not, of course, take place in Shanghai, nor is the femme fatale Hayworth plays exactly a lady. It is classic film noir with an absurdly intricate plot featuring a dizzying array of twists and turns. The picture ends with a justly celebrated face-off between Welles and Hayworth in the Magic Mirror Maze, inside a fun house. And like *Ambersons*, it was mutilated by the studio.

Welles followed up *The Lady from Shanghai* with one of his most successful turns in front of the camera, in *The Third Man*, which won the Palme d'Or at the 1949 Cannes Film Festival. Directed by Carol Reed, in part from a script by Graham Greene, it is a dark and moody specimen of its kind, shot on actual locations in rubble-strewn, postwar Vienna. An unremittingly grim picture, it is notable not only for the location work, but for Welles's diamond-hard performance as a contemptible black marketeer named Harry Lime who makes his living stealing, diluting, and selling penicillin. It also boasts of a wonderful set piece on Vienna's outsized Ferris wheel, the *Wiener Riesenrad*; a climactic manhunt in the city's sewers, anticipating Andrzej Wajda's *Kanal* by nearly a decade; and a distinctive score, performed exclusively on the zither.

His last studio movie, *Touch of Evil* (1958), was also recut. It is too much of a mixed bag to be considered one of his best efforts. It features Charlton Heston at his most wooden and Janet Leigh playing a character so repellent that it's hard not to root for the ridiculous, black leather jacket clad delinquent refugees from *The Wild One* who menace her with dope-filled needles and worse. On the other hand, the picture can boast of an extraordinary performance by Welles as a border town cop so degenerate he makes Harry Lime look good, an all-too-brief appearance by Marlene Dietrich, lots of vintage Wellesian dialogue, and a bravura opening: a heart-stopping, three-minute-and-twenty-second tracking shot that follows a car as it meanders across the border from Mexico into Texas, where it explodes in a spectacular inferno of fire and smoke. If you can ignore Heston and Leigh, these gems alone are worth the price of admission, not to mention the entire careers of many directors. No exaggeration.

Despite his fitful success behind the camera, Welles directed eleven or so feature-length movies in the course of his career, including his outstanding Shakespeare trilogy—*Macbeth* (1948), *Othello* (1952), and *Chimes at Midnight* (1965), his tribute to Falstaff. The last feature-length picture he made, *F for Fake*, finished in 1973, and not released in the United States until four years later, was financed by Welles himself when he was unable to find backing elsewhere. Both fish and fowl, fiction and documentary, he called it an "essay film," which meant that it was a melange of everything he could lay his hands on in the vicinity of art forger extraordinaire Elmyr de Hory and faux Howard Hughes biographer Clifford Irving in sun-drenched Ibiza, as well as found footage of Picasso standing in a room behind a venetian blind, edited so that it appears that the artist is ogling Kodar as she parades up and down the street in a variety of chic outfits. Last but not least was Welles himself, dramatically draped in his signature black magician's cape skewering critics, while sharing his thoughts on illusion, art, and authenticity. *F for Fake* is an original, ingenious film, in which Welles bends the medium to his own ends and foreshadows pictures like Chris Marker's *Sans Soleil* (1983) and Banksy's *Exit Through the Gift Shop* (2010) that blur the lines between fact and fiction, but it was all too clever for its own good. However, the public never even got the opportunity to judge for itself since the distributor dumped the film.

These years, despite his more than respectable track record against daunting odds, tell a depressing tale of frustration, often featuring Welles as his own worst enemy. Like Kane, whose Xanadu was never finished, he accumulated a collection of incomplete pictures, earning him a reputation for walking away from his own movies before they were finished. True or false, the bad rap was impossible to shake, and made it difficult—not to say impossible—for Welles to raise money for his films.

Desperate for cash to complete old projects and/or launch new ones, he cobbled together an income by means of his performances in innumerable pictures, some very good and many very bad, ranging from B movies produced by fly-by-night producers in no-name countries to odds and ends like soaps, game shows, and TV commercials. It didn't seem to matter to him, so long as they put money in the bank, although hustling like this took its toll. He made Paul Masson a household name by intoning the slogan, "We will sell no wine before its time." (Outtakes of an inebriated Welles slurring his way through one of these commercials can be seen on YouTube.) But even Paul Masson turned him out when a slimmed down Welles reportedly explained on a talk show that he had given up snacks—and wine.

Henry Jaglom was born into a family of wealthy German and Russian émigrés. His father, Simon, was imprisoned after the 1917

Russian revolution for being a "capitalist," and left the Soviet Union with his brothers shortly thereafter, eventually making his way to London, where Henry was born in 1941, and then to New York City, where he grew up. He never knew exactly what his father did for a living, but when he applied to the University of Pennsylvania and was asked his father's occupation, Simon told him, "Write international commerce and finance."

Jaglom studied at the Actors Studio, and then joined the mid-1960s migration from New York to Los Angeles, where his friend Peter Bogdanovich had promised him the lead in his first feature, *Targets* (1968), a role Bogdanovich later decided to play himself. His acting career ended abruptly when he was washing his feet in the sink of his apartment and the phone rang, the caller notifying him that Dustin Hoffman had gotten the lead in *The Graduate* (1967), a role he was convinced he was born to play. He muttered an epithet and turned his attention to writing and directing.

In the wake of a worldwide explosion of film culture in the 1960s, movies became the medium of choice for aspiring artists. Under the sway of the French, Jaglom, like many of his contemporaries, wanted to do it all: not just act or write, but edit, direct, and produce as well. They didn't want to be directors for hire by some baboon in the front office with a big, fat cigar; they wanted to be filmmakers or, as the French would have it, *auteurs*, a term popularized in America by Andrew Sarris in the sixties. Simply put, an *auteur* was to a film what a poet was to poetry or a painter was to painting. Sarris argued, controversially, that even studio directors such as Howard Hawks, John Ford, and Alfred Hitchcock, or bottom-of-the-bill toilers like Sam Fuller, displayed personal styles, were the sole authors of their pictures, and were therefore authentic artists. Welles, of course, was the very avatar of an *auteur*. Jaglom and his friends venerated him as the godfather of the so-called New Hollywood. He recalls, "We used to talk about him as the patron saint of this new wave of filmmaking."

Partial to long, colorful scarves and floppy hats, Jaglom swiftly fell into bad company. He smoked dope at the Old World Restaurant on Sunset Boulevard with Jack Nicholson and was drawn into the orbit of Bert Schneider. Schneider, along with Bob Rafelson, had made a lot of money off the Monkees, and with the addition of Steve Blauner, ran a small production company called BBS. Schneider gave Jaglom a crack at editing the company's second picture, Dennis Hopper and Peter Fonda's *Easy Rider* (1969).

Easy Rider was a hit, and BBS was on its way. Jaglom discovered in himself the ability to talk people into things they didn't want to do. On the basis of his work on *Easy Rider*, he convinced Schneider to allow him to finance his first feature, *A Safe Place* (1971), with Nicholson and Tuesday Weld. Jaglom was desperate to add Welles to the cast. Bogdanovich was conducting a series of exhaustive interviews with Welles that would become a book and had become very friendly with him. Jaglom asked his friend to introduce the two of them. Bogdanovich warned him, "He won't do it."

"Well, tell me where he is, and I'll go meet him."

"He's in New York at the Plaza Hotel. But you musn't go to him without a script. He hates that. And you don't have a script."

Welles was an intimidating presence with an imperious manner, a slashing wit, and a reputation for not suffering fools. Jaglom was no fool, but he didn't have a clue how he was going to persuade the great man to join his cast. Undeterred, he flew to New York and went up to his hotel room. Welles opened the door wearing purple silk pajamas. Jaglom remembers, "He looked like this huge grape." Welles demanded, "What do you want?" in an unwelcoming way.

"I'm Henry Jaglom."

"Yes, but does that tell me what you want?"

"It should, if Peter Bogdanovich has spoken to you."

"Peter speaks to me often."

"The reason I'm here is because I'm making a film for Bert Schneider who Peter is making a film for. Which I arranged."

"I know who Bert Schneider is."

"Peter is making *The Last Picture Show*—"

"Yes, good for him."

"And I want to make my film, *A Safe Place*. With you in it."

"Where's the script?"

"I don't have a script."

"Why not?"

"Because if you're going to be in it, it's going to be completely different than if somebody else is going to be in it."

"No script? No interest."

"Your character is a magician."

"A magician? I'm a magician. An amateur magician, of course. But I don't do first scripts by first-time directors."

"What do you mean you don't do them? *Citizen Kane* was your first script."

"Did you really say 'A magician'?"

"Yeah. And I think I want him with a little Jewish accent. I know you go to lunch in London at that Jewish restaurant all the time. There are rumors that you think you're Jewish—"

"I am Jewish. Dr. Bernstein was probably my real father." He thought for a moment and then said, "Can I wear a cape?"

"Sure, wear a cape."

"OK, I'll do it."

Needless to say, the old-timers on the set, which meant most of the crew, looked askance at the young director, whose hair was gathered in a long pony tail and whose feet were squeezed into white Capezio dancing shoes. The second day of shooting, they all turned up wearing American flag lapel pins. (This was, after all, 1971, the middle of the Vietnam war.) During a lunch break, Jaglom was sitting with Schneider, Nicholson, and Weld. Welles joined them, saying, "You're the arrogant kid who pushed me into this. How's your arrogance doing?"

"Not very well. The crew hates me. They're totally negative. Everything I tell them to shoot, they say, 'It won't cut,' or 'it's not in the script.' I have to fight to get every single shot. I'm exhausted."

Jaglom talked a reluctant Welles into appearing in A Safe Place, *his first film. Here, he directs Welles and Tuesday Weld in Central Park, c. 1971.*

"Oh, my God, I should have prepared you. Tell 'em it's a dream sequence."

"What?"

"Just do as I tell you. Trust me. You trusted me enough to hire me. Do it." After lunch, they returned to the set. Jaglom had mapped out an intricate shot. The cameraman said, "Can't do it."

"Why?"

"It won't cut."

"It's a dream sequence."

"A dream sequence? Why didn't you say so? I'll get on my back and do it like this. It will be psychedelic." Jaglom went to Welles that night, and said, "What the fuck is this? Everything I want to do, I say, 'Dream sequence,' and they're pussycats."

"You have to understand, these are people who work hard for a living. They have tough lives. Structured lives. They work all day, then they have dinner, put their kids to bed, go to sleep, and get back to the set at five o'clock the next morning. Everything else in life except for dreams has rules. The only place they're truly free is when they fall asleep and dream. If you tell them it's a dream sequence, they will be freed of those rules to be creative, imaginative, and give you all kinds of stuff that they've got inside of them." That was the best advice Jaglom would ever get.

Welles taught Jaglom two other lessons: First, "Make movies for yourself. Never compromise, because those compromises are going to haunt you for the rest of your life." And second, "Never give Hollywood control over your tools because sooner or later, they will take them away from you."

When Jaglom screened *A Safe Place* for Schneider, the lights came up and Schneider was crying. Jaglom thought, "Oh, that's great, I moved him." Schneider said, "Yeah, I'm very moved. I'm also an asshole."

"Whaddya mean?"

"This movie can't possibly make a penny. Too abstract and poetic. The only person more self-indulgent than you in making this picture is me, for letting you. Why? Because it made me cry."

Jaglom was cutting his second film, *Tracks*, with Dennis Hopper when he ran into Welles in 1978 at Ma Maison, where the great man was having lunch with Warren Beatty. Now no more than a tarnished monument to an illustrious but checkered career, pursued by creditors, overweight and afflicted with depression—the "black dog" as he called it—Welles had pretty much given up. Schneider had been willing to finance a picture for him early in the decade, starring Jack Nicholson. As he put it, "Jack was ready to work for nothing, but when push came to shove, Orson just didn't have the courage to work anymore. It didn't matter what you put on his plate. He was frozen." Schneider was right. Welles's high hopes for *F for Fake* had been dashed on the rocks of public indifference.

As he himself explained, "I had begun to think I should stop and write my memoirs of twenty volumes so I could be paid for something and stop this misery." Or, as he put it to Jaglom, rather more succinctly, "I've lost my girlish enthusiasm."

Still, much as he might have wanted to, Welles couldn't or wouldn't give up. Welles's attitude toward the studios was ambivalent. He admitted to Jaglom that he had something to prove to a Hollywood that had turned its back on him. And vanity aside, he had an expensive imagination, and he was eager to take advantage of the resources only the studios could provide. On the other hand, he knew that he was temperamentally and aesthetically unsuited to the factory filmmaking practiced by the studios. He was forced to work as an independent filmmaker outside the system even in the late sixties and early seventies, when mavericks were courted, if only momentarily. But by the late seventies and eighties, when the studio system reasserted itself, his chances of finding a studio home vanished entirely.

Welles and Jaglom became fast friends. They were an odd couple, to say the least. Their backgrounds, personalities, ages (Jaglom was in his late thirties, Welles in his mid-sixties)—even their films were discrepant. What they did have in common was a fierce desire to go their own way. Moreover, the relationship was mutually advantageous. Jaglom was dazzled by the legend and seduced by the reality of Welles. Who wouldn't have been? He treasured his friend's advice, basked in his reflected glow, relished the role of Welles's gatekeeper. He also realized that he had something that Welles needed—energy, enthusiasm, and viability as a working filmmaker. He had bankrolled his own films by selling off the rights for foreign territories to a patchwork of overseas distributors and investors in much the same way American independents would do a decade later, and so he was perfectly positioned to navigate the maze of European financing to Welles's benefit. Although Jaglom had only a few films to his credit at the time he started to help Welles, he went on to make many more.

Welles blossomed in the warmth of Jaglom's admiration. As he put it, in the flush of a new optimism, "Henry has brought me back to life. Nothing can stop me now." With new movies in limbo and mired in unfinished projects, Welles had to know Jaglom was his best bet. More, Welles took a real interest in his friend's films, spending hours hunched over the flatbed editing machine with him, giving him the benefit of the narrative genius that lived inside him, and in fact, working vicariously through Jaglom.

Eventually, the younger man became Welles's sounding board, confessor, producer, agent, and biggest fan. He was the magician's magician who was going to turn the dross that Welles's career had become into gold, even if he had—figuratively speaking, more or less—to steal, cheat, and lie to do it.

Jaglom picked him up and dusted him off, set about buffing his image and laundering his legend. Using the playbook he had followed himself, Jaglom began lining up backers for Welles's various films. He got him good press, arranging interviews in which both men spoke enthusiastically about the projects on Welles's plate, many of which were so, so close to production, already cast, just waiting for the check to clear the bank. He energetically rebutted the conventional wisdom, that his friend suffered from cinematic ADD: "It's not that he didn't finish the movies. He ran out of money, somebody gave him more money to do something else, but he always planned to go back to everything." Admit it or not, however, Jaglom had set for himself a Sisyphean task. True, it's impossible to exaggerate the difficulties facing a filmmaker like Welles trying to get traction in a business dominated by a handful of powerful studios. There were more than enough extenuating circumstances to get Welles off the hook for the butchery of *Ambersons*, but even Barbara Leaming, his best and friendliest biographer, admits he had little excuse for disappearing to Europe before *Macbeth* was edited, replicating almost to the letter the *Amberson* fiasco. And doubly so, after he had made a point of coming in early and under budget to confound the doubters. It was the same old song. Victim of his own prodigious gifts, he was the man who did too much, and thus did, in the end, too little. Not even he—writer, actor, producer, and director—could execute all the films, plays, radio shows, and miscellaneous projects that popped into his head, especially while aiding the war effort and carrying on an energetic love life. His brain was like a boiling cauldron filled with bubbles that rose to the surface and burst—into thin air. He needed someone to yell, "Focus!" and this was the mantle Jaglom assumed.

Regardless of the reasons for Welles's spotty, post-*Kane* record, Jaglom discovered that indeed, none of the deep pockets that flapped about the Wellesian flame were willing to drop cash on the table. Welles found himself in the paradoxical position of being honored as America's greatest filmmaker yet unable to get backing for his projects. Buffeted by a blizzard of rejections, he struggled like any neophyte filmmaker just out of film school. "Orson couldn't get a movie done," says Jaglom. "He wanted to do this wonderful adaptation of these Isak Dinesen stories, *The Dreamers*. I went around to every studio, every producer, and I couldn't get him money. So I said, 'Orson, they don't want to do an adaptation. But I can sell you with a new movie, and new script. Tell me some stories.' He said, 'I can't write anymore, I'm no longer capable of writing.'

" 'That's bullshit. Just put it down on paper. Or just tell it to me; I'll put it down on paper.'

" 'I can't. I know what I can do, I know what I can't do.' Then "three weeks later, the phone rang at four in the morning," Jaglom continues. " 'I don't know what the fuck you're making me do this for. I can't sleep, but I've written three pages. They're terrible!'

" 'Read them to me.' Of course they were great. So for the next three or four months, I got him to write this whole script." It was called *The Big Brass Ring*, and it was about an old political advisor to Roosevelt, a homosexual named Kimball Menaker, who has mentored a young, Kennedy-esque senator from Texas with presidential ambitions named Blake Pellerin, who runs against Ronald Reagan and loses. Pellerin, according to Welles, as if describing himself, "is a man who has within him the devil of self-destruction that lives in every genius . . . Like all great men he is never sure that he has chosen the right path in life. Even being president, he feels, may somehow not be right: 'Should I be a monk? Should I jerk off in the park? Should I just fuck everybody and forget about everything else?' *That* is what *The Big Brass Ring* is all about."

Adds Jaglom, "*The Big Brass Ring* was about America at the end of the century, the way *Kane* was America at the beginning of the century. I couldn't fuckin' believe it—I've got the bookend to *Kane*." Now Jaglom was sure the wallets would open. "I told Orson, 'You know, all the people I came up with and struggled side by side with have become stars and production heads. I know them; they're my friends. They all worship you.' I went around to everybody, and I couldn't get anyone to do it. Every studio turned it down. The times had changed. Instead of talking about Orson Welles, they were talking about grosses. Orson understood this. He said, 'I expected the studios to turn me down. Why wouldn't they? I've never made any money for them.'"

After Jaglom failed to get the studios to show even a glimmer of interest in *The Big Brass Ring*, producer Arnon Milchan agreed to give Welles $8 million and final cut—for the first time since *Kane*—"if I got one of six or seven A-list actors to agree to play Blake Pellerin," Jaglom continues. "We celebrated, opened a big bottle of Cristal, because one thing Orson thought was that actors wouldn't betray him. He said, 'I know actors.'" But apparently not well enough. Clint Eastwood turned down the film because it was too left wing for him. Robert Redford said he already had another political thriller lined up. Burt Reynolds's person just said, "No." "Orson was really pissed about that," Jaglom continues. "He said, 'Burt Reynolds owes me so much, I wrote the foreword to a book about him, and he didn't have the guts to phone me himself and simply say, "It's not for me." His agent told me. Big money is the problem with these stars. When they get too rich, they behave badly.'

"One by one each of these actors came up with reasons, including my two friends Warren and Jack. Warren behaved better than anybody. He was very honorable, and Orson never blamed him. He had just come off of *Reds*, which Orson thought was the stupidest idea for a movie he'd ever heard. Warren said to me, 'Oh, God, tell Orson it's like coming out of a whorehouse after being there all night fucking, you're exhausted, and you walk out in the sunlight, and there's Marilyn Monroe with her arms out. I'd love to, but I just can't.'"

The best bet was Nicholson. Welles was ready to go in July 1982. He had a budget and a shooting schedule, as well as a crew and locations. Half a million dollars was slated to go to Nicholson. But the bigger the stars, the slower they are to respond, and by 1984, Welles still hadn't gotten an answer from him.

Welles was disappointed, but Jaglom refused to give up. In his words, unlike Hannibal, "he needed to bring the elephants over the mountains to Rome." Jaglom arranged a "coming out" press conference for Welles on the terrace of the Carlton Hotel at the Cannes Film Festival in 1983. Within ten minutes the great man had attracted a flock of journalists. To demonstrate that Welles was ambulatory, Jaglom hid his wheelchair.

Welles's unveiling was a success, generating a flurry of good press, but in some ways, the trip to Cannes was too much of a good thing. His diet had been drastically restricted by his doctor. Dining with his friend at L'Oasis, Welles ordered a salad, a light fish with lemon, and Perrier. "Then he made me order everything, three entrees, six desserts," Jaglom recalls. "'Just take a bite, and describe the taste to me,' he told me. What I didn't know was that he was going back to the hotel, waking up the chef, and ordering four steaks, seven baked potatoes, and a whole lot more in the middle of the night."

Beginning in 1978, Welles and Jaglom had lunch nearly every week—sometimes more often—at Welles's regular hangout, Ma Maison, where he ate almost every day. A celebrated French restaurant owned by Patrick Terrail, Ma Maison was located at 8360 Melrose Avenue, near Kings Road, in West Hollywood. It opened its doors in 1975 in a tiny, worn, and very unprepossessing bungalow formerly owned by a carpet company. It was set far back from the street, so that the area in between served as a "garden room," covered with leaky plastic that Terrail fondly referred to as a "shower curtain," and carpeted by Astroturf, colored a bilious green. The decor of the interior was nothing to speak of either; one critic mocked it as "the fanciest French restaurant in Kingman, Arizona."

But none of that mattered. Ma Maison quickly became the hottest restaurant in Hollywood. The kitchen served French cuisine with a nouvelle California accent and was the home of Wolfgang Puck for its first six years. It was so chic that it didn't even publish its phone number. It was a place where deals were made, where agents conned producers and producers conned agents.

Welles, who had ballooned to the size of a baby elephant, customarily ditched his wheelchair at the back door and entered the establishment through the kitchen. He used to sit in a mammoth chair to the right of the entrance at one of Ma Maison's few indoor tables. According to Gore Vidal, who also dined regularly with Welles, he draped himself in "bifurcated tents to which, rather idly, lapels, pocket flaps, buttons were attached in order to suggest a conventional suit."

Welles and Terrail were great friends, and Welles used to call upon Terrail to perform every sort of impossible, last-minute service. "The restaurant had become his office," he recalls. "We used to get all his mail and a lot of his phone calls." Terrail relayed messages from people who wanted to contact him, like George Stevens, Jr., who produced the telecast of the Kennedy Center Honors, and wanted to know if Welles would accept one of its distinguished awards, which usually meant the recipient was ready for the form- aldehyde. Terrail told Welles, "They'll fly you to Washington. Do you want to do it?" Welles replied, "No. I would have to sit next to Reagan in the box up there." On one occasion, the archbishop of the Greek Orthodox Church, dining at Ma Maison, asked to be introduced to Welles. As he reached over to shake his hand, Welles's constant companion, an ill-tempered toy poodle named Kiki that was no bigger than a box of Kleenex, leaped up from his master's ample "crotch," as Terrail puts it, and went for his arm. Neverthe- less, the orthodox pope invited the portly filmmaker to a high mass he was conducting at the Cathedral of Saint Sophia the following day, offering to dedicate the ceremony to him. Welles replied, "I am flattered by the invitation, but I must decline. I'm an atheist."

People of all sorts—friends, fans, and strangers—stopped by his table hoping for a golden word or two. Welles would roar at them, in his resonant, Orsonian voice, "HELLO, HOW ARE YOU?!" But he could also be rude. Recalls Jaglom, "People would say, 'So nice to see you.' He would say, 'So nice to see you too, but that's enough.' He would try to intimidate them." Jaglom asked him why. Pointing at his pug nose, he would answer, "You have to do something to let them know that you're not just a little creature. You have to be the ruler of the forest. People want me to be 'Orson Welles.' They want the dancing bear show."

"You don't need that. You're not so insecure that—"

"I'm much more insecure than even you know, Henry."

"I don't believe that. You're arrogant and sure of yourself."

"Yes, I'm sure of myself, but I'm not sure of anybody else."

According to Vidal, Welles's conversation "was often surreal and always cryptic. Either you picked up on it or you were left out." With Jaglom, he seemed to find a comfort zone that enabled him to show his vulnerabilities. His exchanges with his friend roamed over many subjects—movies, theater, literature, music, politics—of which Welles demonstrated an alarming mastery. There was no topic too insignificant or esoteric for Welles to weigh in on. The words he put in the mouth of Menaker in *The Big Brass Ring* suited him as well: "I am an authority on everything." Movies? "Ballet— that's the only thing less interesting." Eisenhower? "Underrated." Art Deco? "I deeply hate it." Kiwis? "Ruined by all the French chefs."

Although Welles was generous with his praise for people he respected, he invariably peppered his conversation with amusing if often unflattering anecdotes about those he didn't. He was particularly biting when his attention was directed toward former friends and enemies. Welles's outsized personality, as well as his early, dazzling success in the theater, radio, and movies, made him the envy of everyone in the arts, and a target of more than a few. Rightly or wrongly, and in the course of the lunches, he settled scores with those he thought had done him wrong. One of them was Pauline Kael, who became something of a celebrity in the sixties and seventies for her movie reviews in the *New Yorker*. Kael engaged in a decade-long feud with fellow critic Andrew Sarris. *Pace* Sarris, Kael argued that film is a collective art form, the fruit of a collaboration among many talents. A writer herself, she particularly lavished praise on the long-suffering screenwriter. Kael knew that if she could chip away at Welles's credit block, she could reduce the *auteur* theory– and Sarris–to a pile of rubble. In a notorious two-part essay published in the *New Yorker* in 1971 called "Raising Kane," she made the case that Herman J. Mankiewicz, not Welles, was largely responsible for the script of *Citizen Kane*. (On the film itself, both men are credited with the script.) To add insult to injury, the essay, since discredited, was republished that same year in *The Citizen Kane Book* as the introduction to the shooting script. Welles was deeply wounded. As Jaglom put it, "Everyone treated Orson badly, but the one thing that he had was that he made the greatest movie ever made, and she tried to undermine that by creating this mythology that he had nothing to do with the script, that he was taking false credit. He was furious."

Ironically, even Bogdanovich, who was a confirmed *auteurist*, was not proof against his ire. He had followed up *The Last Picture Show* with *What's Up Doc*, starring Barbra Streisand in 1972, and *Paper Moon*, featuring Ryan O'Neal and his daughter, Tatum, in 1973. With three hits in a row, he could have filmed the phone book and still found studio backing. His friendship with Welles endured throughout this period, but in the late seventies, it cooled. Welles complained that Bogdanovich never helped him when he was riding high and had the power to do so.

After his trifecta of hits, Bogdanovich went into a dramatic decline. Welles took a dim view of his late-seventies tabloid romance with Dorothy Stratten, a former *Playboy* centerfold, as well as the book he wrote about her, titled *The Killing of the Unicorn*, after she was shot to death by her estranged husband.

John Houseman, whom Bogdanovich called his "single most destructive enemy," was the target of Welles's most venomous barbs. He felt that his former partner had built his reputation with bits and pieces scavenged from the wreckage of his own. It was Houseman who had brought Welles into the Federal Theatre in 1934, where Welles quickly eclipsed his benefactor. "Houseman started out being in love with me, and then turned to hate," he once said. For the next decade or so, the two, like the proverbial scorpions in a bottle, were uneasily paired in a variety of projects, including the Mercury Theatre, until the ill will between them boiled over while Welles was at RKO. At a dinner at Chasen's, Houseman claimed Welles threw plates of food at him, including "two dishes of flaming methylated spirits," and accused him of stealing money.

In later years, when Welles's career went into free fall, Houseman's soared. After a lengthy career as a producer and director on both stage and screen, he won a Best Supporting Actor Oscar for *The Paper Chase* (1973) and segued into the long-running TV series of the same name. Houseman published several volumes of memoirs that to some degree framed the accounts of Welles's career thereafter, not to his benefit. The two remained enemies for the rest of their lives.

With Bogdanovich unable or unwilling to help him, Welles found himself only fitfully employed throughout much of the post-*Kane* period. He had decades to contemplate his mistakes and missed opportunities. He was never comfortable in Hollywood. Or perhaps it was the other way around: he was too comfortable, and despised himself for it. He loved to instruct Jaglom in the subtle ways the town distorted the values of the people who lived and worked there. A week or so after Welles delivered a tribute to Natalie Wood, Robert Wagner came up to the table. Welles asked, "Are you OK?"

"Yes, fine."

"Such a terrible thing."

"But you know, you were great."

"I was?"

"You were the best one."

"Thank you."

"The best one. It had so many elements. You were strong; you were poignant." After Wagner left, Welles turned to Jaglom and said, "You understand? You have just seen what Hollywood is really about. The man is in tears, he feels the tragedy, but he is so inured to reality, that for him it's a show. And I gave the best performance. He's giving me a review." Says Jaglom, "Even Orson was shocked."

In the spring of 1984, the movie version of *The Cradle Will Rock*, which Welles was slated to direct, and which was already cast, came crashing down when the main backer withdrew. Welles was desolate. He told Barbara Leaming, "It just shows me that I really shouldn't have stayed in this business . . . We live in a snake pit here. I've been keeping a secret from myself for forty years—from myself, not from the world—which is that I hate it."

Welles knew that Jaglom had recorded his own father's reminiscences for thirty years, and asked him to record their conversations as well. His only proviso was that the recorder be out of sight, concealed in Jaglom's bag, so he didn't have to look at it. Jaglom began taping the conversations in 1983 and continued until Welles was struck down by a fatal heart attack in the middle of the night of October 10, 1985. He died with a typewriter on his lap, working on a script. The conversations survived. Jaglom stashed the tapes—about forty of them—in a shoebox where they gathered dust for almost three decades.

I first met Jaglom in the early 1990s, when he shared his recollections and diaries with me while I was researching my history of the New Hollywood of the seventies, *Easy Riders, Raging Bulls*. He told me about these tapes, and I urged him to have them transcribed, but there was always another film to make, and of course that took precedence. The tapes sat and sat, even though he was eager for them to see the light of day. Eventually, they did. I read the transcripts with an eye to whether or not there was a book in them, and decided that there most definitely was.

Jaglom's tapes, a record of the last three years of Welles's life, may be the last undiscovered trove of Welles on Welles. Eavesdropping on Welles and Jaglom is the next best thing to sitting at the table. And what a table it was. Welles comes off as a fascinating bundle of contradictions, at once belligerent and almost childishly vulnerable, a schemer who often behaved impetuously at great cost to himself, a shy man who hid behind an endless array of masks but loved to display himself and liked nothing better than the thunderous roar of applause. He was forgiving and generous but tenaciously held grudges against those he felt had done him wrong. He could roar with anger one minute and laughter the next. Who knows to what darkness he was prey in moments of depression, but he rarely gave in to self-pity, at least not in these conversations with his friend.

The Welles who emerges here is a different Welles from either the fraud his detractors pilloried in their biographies or the genius his admirers enshrined in theirs. Because Jaglom was not interviewing Welles, but conversing with him, we have a Welles unguarded and relaxed, with his hair down, unplugged, if you will, willing to let fly with all manner of politically incorrect opinions—sexist, racist, homophobic, vulgar (let's be kind, call it "Rabelaisian")—driven, perhaps, by the impish pleasure he took in baiting his liberal friend, offending his progressive susceptibilities, or just by native, irrepressible ebullience. The more perverse Welles's views, the more fiercely he argued them. His antic wit, stringent irony, and enormous intelligence shine through these conversations and animate every word, making it difficult not to love the man.

"Orson is an enigmatic figure to most people," Jaglom wrote. "He presents a compelling challenge: how to reconcile the brilliant child prodigy, the precedent-shattering stage director, the iconoclastic radio figure, the celebrated Shakespearean artist, the groundbreaking filmmaker credited by almost everyone with having made the greatest movie of all time with the TV talk show buffoon, the corny wine commercial huckster, the willing participant in tasteless low-comedy "roasts," the bloated, seemingly self-destructive outcast whose unfinished works and aborted projects became legendary?"

These two may never be reconciled. And unplugged or not, this book makes no claim to discover the "real" Welles. There may never have been a real Welles. As Jaglom puts it, "The final scene of *The Lady from Shanghai* is perhaps the most autobiographically truthful metaphor in all of his work. It is ultimately impossible to find the real Orson Welles among all the fun-house mirrors he so energetically set in place." Welles appeared to prefer it that way. "Wait till I die," he once told Jaglom at lunch. "They'll write all kinds of things about me. They'll just pick my bones dry. You won't recognize me and if I came back to life and read them, I wouldn't recognize me myself. I've told so many stories, you know, just to get out of situations, or out of boredom or just to entertain! Who can remember them all, but I'm sure they'll come back to haunt me. Or rather, my ghost. Don't set them right, Henry. They don't want to know. Let them have their fantasies about me."

Welles's final turn in front of the camera occurred in Jaglom's *Someone to Love* (1987). Jaglom played the lead, a filmmaker, and Welles's character is known only as "the friend." "I gave him his farewell to the audience," Jaglom recalls. "He wouldn't let me ever show him laughing on screen, because he insisted, 'Fat men shouldn't laugh. It is very unattractive.' Once I caught him laughing, and he actually said, 'Cut,' to my cameraman. And my cameraman stopped the camera. 'What are you doing?'

" 'Orson Welles told me to cut.'

" 'Turn it right back on.' He turned it back on, and Orson, thinking that it was off, reached behind him, somehow producing a lit cigar. He puffed on it, and started to laugh, a roaring, embracing, wonderful laugh. I knew I wouldn't be able to get it in the film because he would have hated it. When he died, I felt the least I could do was give them his one last laugh."

Patrick Terrail closed Ma Maison in the autumn of 1985, a month or so after Welles's death. The decision had been made before Welles's heart attack, but regardless, the timing was appropriate. Generally, life goes on when one or another of us sheds this mortal coil, but in this case, the restaurant that was his second home, which sustained him in so many ways, died with him. It did survive, under new ownership in a different location, but in the absence of its most famous patron at his regular table, it was never the same.

A Note on the Text

My Lunches with Orson is divided into two parts, 1983, the year in which most of these conversations took place, and then 1984 and 1985. The organization is roughly, but not strictly, chronological. Welles's ruminations on like subjects, in fact separated by months or even years, have been grouped together. The quality of the tapes varies drastically. Many of them are clear, but some, with the recorder lying muffled in Jaglom's bag, are indistinct, and so I have taken occasional liberties with the text—adding or subtracting phrases, smoothing out syntax—for the purpose of making the conversations more concise and intelligible. Occasionally, I have attributed material to Welles that is quoted in Jaglom's diaries or was furnished by him in interviews with me. With his permission, I have sometimes altered his comments with an eye to furnishing context. Welles was, above all, a great entertainer, a fabulator who, like Scheherazade, learned early to sing for his supper. Some of the stories he tells in these conversations will have a familiar ring, and indeed, they have been told elsewhere, but they were too good to go unrepeated, and since he always provided fresh details or new twists in every telling, I have included them.

PART ONE

1983

Lunch companions at a star-studded reception c. 1983, thrown by the Hollywood Foreign Press Association, organized by Jaglom to show potential backers that Welles was still viable. Guests included Warren Beatty, Jack Nicholson, Jack Lemmon, and Michael Caine.

At lunch at Ma Maison, I encountered Orson standing with difficulty to embrace me after several months with great warmth (or what seems like great warmth, I have never been quite sure), and I am always moved, as I was today. And as always, amazingly for me, I was somewhat at a loss for what to say, and all I came up with was some general pleasantry/banality on the order of, "How is everything?" Orson answered me with, "Oh, I don't know, do you?" And I, acknowledging that my question had been excessive in scope, reduced it to, "How is everything today?" To which he answered, happy that he had forced greater specificity: "Fine . . . as of this hour."

Then tonight, two hours ago as I twirled the television dial, I was astonished to find myself watching the opening newsreel segment of Citizen Kane. *I have just finished watching him grow old with makeup and acting skill on a body in its twenties, in a film designed by his mind in its twenties, and the film—and he in it—are so affecting and so near-perfect that the idea of watching anything else after seemed incomprehensible. I wonder, Was there nothing for him to do with the rest of his life after making it, is that his secret and does he know it? Is* Citizen Kane *his "rosebud"?*

—HENRY JAGLOM, Journal Entry, April 2, 1978

1. "Everybody should be bigoted."

In which Orson turns restaurant reviewer, confesses that he never understood why Katharine Hepburn disliked him, but knew why he disliked Spencer Tracy. He detested the Irish, despite his friendship with John Ford, and liked right-wingers better than left-wingers.

(Jaglom enters, Welles struggles out of his chair to greet him. They embrace, kissing each other on the cheek in the European way.)

HENRY JAGLOM: *(To Kiki)* How are you, Kiki?

ORSON WELLES: Look out—she'll bite you . . . All right, what are we gonna eat?

HJ: I'm going to try the chicken salad.

OW: No, you aren't! You don't like it with all those capers.

HJ: I'm going to ask them to scrape the capers away.

OW: Then let me tell you what they have on their hands in the kitchen.

HJ: It must be nuts in the kitchen. I've never seen it this packed.

OW: They're so busy, this would be a great day to send a dish back to the chef.

HJ: You know, Ma Maison is not my idea of the legendary restaurants of Hollywood. The romance for me was Romanoff's. And then I got here and there was no Romanoff's.

OW: Yeah! Romanoff's only stayed open until forty-three or forty-four. It had a short life. Romanoff's and Ciro's were the two restaurants that we did all the romancing in, and they both closed. Everybody was photographed with the wrong person coming out, you know? Romanoff's is a parking lot now, and when it was going broke, Sinatra came with sixteen violins and sang every night for three weeks for free, to try and help the business. We all went every night. It was sensational. Don the Beachcombers was another great place to take the wrong girl because it was dark. Nobody could see anybody.

HJ: What about Chasen's?

OW: Chasen's was a barbecue place, originally. I was one of the original backers of Chasen's—and Romanoff's.

HJ: You owned Romanoff's?

OW: Yes, and he never gave me anything. Nor did Chasen. I was a founder of both those restaurants. Me and a lot of suckers. We didn't expect anything from Romanoff because he was a crook. And Dave Chasen somehow forgot the original barbecue backers when his became a big restaurant.

Ma Maison was started in 1973, and continues. I wouldn't go for a long time because of the unlisted phone number. It irritated me so. It's a snobbish business not having a phone number. Somebody gave the number out on television, just to be bitchy. I don't envy these guys, though. It's a tough, tough business to run a restaurant.

WAITER: Going to have a little lunch today? We have scallops, if you want, Mr. Welles. Plain, or we have them prepared with a petite legume.

OW: No, it would have to be plain. Let's see what other choices I have.

W: Just in case, no more crab salad.

OW: No more crab salad. Wish you hadn't mentioned it. I wouldn't have known what I wasn't gonna get!

W: Would you wish the salad with grapefruit and orange?

OW: That's a terrible idea. A weird mixture. It's awful—typically German. We're having the chicken salad without . . . without capers.

HJ: They ruined the chicken salad when they started using that mustard. It's a whole different chicken salad.

OW: They have a new chef.

W: And roast pork?

OW: Oh, my God. On a hot day, roast pork? I can't eat pork. My diet. But I'll order it, just to smell pork. Bassanio says to Shylock: "If it please you to dine with us." And Shylock says: "Yes, to smell pork; to eat of the habitation which your prophet the Nazarite conjured the devil into. I will buy with you, sell with you, talk with you, walk with you, and so following, but I will not eat with you, drink with you, nor pray with you."

HJ: Isn't there something about the devil taking the shape of a pig in the Bible? Or did Shakespeare invent that?

OW: No, Jesus did put a whole group of devils into the Gadarene swine. Shakespeare was just trying to give Shylock a reason for not eating with them.

HJ: I would like the grilled chicken.

W: Okay.

OW: And a cup of capers.

W: Capers?

HJ: No, no—that's his joke.

OW: So I'll have a soft-shell crab. Alas, he breads it. I wish he didn't, but he does. I'll eat it anyway. *Est-que vous avez l'aspirine?* Have you any aspirin?

W: Of course. Here you are, Monsieur Welles.

HJ: Do you have some pain or something?

OW: I have all kinds of rheumatic pains today. The knees. I always say it's my back, because I get more sympathy. But I've got a bad right knee, which is what makes me limp and walk badly. The weather must be changing. I never believed that, until I became arthritic. I just started to ache the last half hour. I think it's gonna rain or something. Aspirin is great stuff. I have no stomach problems, and no allergy to it.

(Waiter exits.)

HJ: Isn't that terrible, the Tennessee Williams thing? Did you hear how he died?

OW: Only that he died last night. How did he die?

HJ: There was a special kind of pipe that he used to inhale something. And it stopped him from being able to swallow or breathe, or . . .

OW: Some dope? Or maybe a roast beef sandwich.

HJ: "Natural causes." Then they went to "unknown causes." So mysterious.

OW: I'd like to be somebody who died alone in a hotel room—just keel over, the way people used to.

Ken Tynan had the funniest story he never printed. He and Tennessee went to Cuba together as guests of [Fidel] Castro. And they were in the massimo leader's office, and there are several other people there, people close to El Jefe, including Che Guevara. Tynan spoke a little fractured Spanish, and Castro spoke quite good English, and they were deep in conversation. But Tennessee had gotten a little bored. He was sitting off, kind of by himself. And he motioned over to Guevara, and said (in a Southern accent), "Would you mind running out and getting me a couple of tamales?"

HJ: Do you think Tynan made it up?

OW: Tynan wasn't a fantasist. Tennessee certainly said it to somebody. But I've suspected that he improved it, maybe, by making it Guevara.

Did I ever tell you about the play of his I lost, like a fool, to [Elia] Kazan? Eddie Dowling, who used to be a producer on Broadway, sent me a play by a writer called Tennessee Williams. I didn't even read it. I said, "I can't do this; I just can't consider a play now." It was called *The Glass Menagerie*.

HJ: *The Glass Menagerie*—my God.

OW: If I had done *The Glass Menagerie*, I would have done all those others. A big dumb mistake.

HJ: A pity . . . By the way, I was just reading Garson Kanin's book on Tracy and Hepburn.

OW: I blurbed that book. I thought if I wrote something, I'd finally make it with Katie! But instead, I found out it was the worst thing I could have done!

HJ: I must say, reading it, I didn't understand why she was so upset about it.

OW: I think it was that he said she and Tracy lived together that—

HJ: A lot of people knew that.

OW: Particularly since she laid around the town like nobody's business.

HJ: Hepburn?

OW: Hoo boy! I sat in makeup during *Kane*, and she was next to me, being made up for *A Bill of Divorcement*. And she was describing how she was fucked by Howard Hughes, using all the four-letter words. Most people didn't talk like that then. Except Carole Lombard. It came naturally to her. She couldn't talk any other way. With Katie, though, who spoke in this high-class girl's finishing-school accent, you thought that she had made a decision to talk that way. Grace Kelly also slept around, in the dressing room when nobody was looking, but she never said anything. Katie was different. She was a free woman when she was young. Very much what the girls are now.

HJ: I wonder what she's got against you. Did you ever do anything to Tracy, or say anything about him?

OW: I was never a fan of his. When I was a young man, I got up and made a fuss at *Captain Outrageous*—uh, *Courageous*.

HJ: Well, you see, that probably got back to Hepburn at some point, and that's why she doesn't like you.

OW: Come on. Nobody knew who I was when I did that. I was nineteen years old. I stood up in the Paramount Theater and said, "You ought to be ashamed of yourself!" when he was doing the Portuguese accent. With the curled hair! The usher told me to get out because I was making such fun of his performance.

HJ: Did you bark?

OW: No, I was imitating his accent as he went along.

HJ: The single lapse in his career.

OW: That was not the only one. He had several. I'm having a hard time trying to think of a great Tracy performance. Well, he was gigantic in *Judgment at Nuremberg*, although it is not a great picture, but I couldn't stand him in those romantic things with Hepburn.

HJ: You didn't find him charming as hell?

OW: No, no charm. To me, he was just a hateful, hateful man. Tracy hated me, but he hated everybody. Once I picked him up in London, in a bar, to take him out to Nutley Abbey, which was Larry [Olivier] and Vivien [Leigh]'s place in the country. Everybody came up to me and asked for autographs and didn't notice him at all. I was the Third Man, for God's sake, and he had white hair. What did he expect? And then he sat there at the table saying, "Everybody looks at you, and nobody looks at me." All day long, he was just raging. Because he was the big movie star, you know. When he was on the set it was, "Why is that actor distracting everyone while I'm talking?"

But I don't think that's it, really. I think Katie just doesn't like me. She doesn't like the way I look. Don't you know there's such a thing as physical dislike? Europeans know that about other Europeans. If I don't like somebody's looks, I don't like them. See, I believe that it is not true that different races and nations are alike. I'm profoundly convinced that that's a total lie. I think people are different. Sardinians, for example, have stubby little fingers. Bosnians have short necks.

HJ: Orson, that's ridiculous.

OW: Measure them. Measure them! I never could stand looking at Bette Davis, so I don't want to see her act, you see. I hate Woody Allen physically, I dislike that kind of man.

HJ: I've never understood why. Have you met him?

OW: Oh, yes. I can hardly bear to talk to him. He has the Chaplin disease. That particular combination of arrogance and timidity sets my teeth on edge.

HJ: He's not arrogant; he's shy.

OW: He *is* arrogant. Like all people with timid personalities, his arrogance is unlimited. Anybody who speaks quietly and shrivels up in company is unbelievably arrogant. He acts shy, but he's not. He's scared. He hates himself, and he loves himself, a very tense situation. It's people like me who have to carry on and pretend to be modest.

HJ: Does he take himself very seriously?

OW: Very seriously. I think his movies show it. To me it's the most embarrassing thing in the world—a man who presents himself at his worst to get laughs, in order to free himself from his hang-ups. Everything he does on the screen is therapeutic.

HJ: That's why you don't like [Bob] Fosse either—*All That Jazz*.

OW: Yes, that's right. I don't like that kind of therapeutic movie. I'm pretty catholic in my taste, but there are some things I can't stand.

HJ: I love Woody's movies. That we disagree on. We disagree on actors too. I can never get over what you said about Brando.

OW: It's that neck. Which is like a huge sausage, a shoe made of flesh.

HJ: People say Brando isn't very bright.

OW: Well, most great actors aren't. Larry [Olivier] is very—I mean, seriously—stupid. I believe that intelligence is a handicap in an actor. Because it means that you're not naturally emotive, but rather cerebral. The cerebral fellow *can* be a great actor, but it's harder. Of performing artists, actors and musicians are about equally bright. I'm very fond of musicians. Not so much of singers. All singers think about is their throats, you know? You go through twenty years of that, what have you got to say? They're prisoners of their vocal cords. So singers are the bottom; actors are at the top. There are exceptions. Leo Slezak, the father of Walter Slezak the actor, made the best theater joke of all time, you know? He was the greatest Wagnerian tenor of his era. And the king—the uncrowned king—of Vienna. He was singing *Lohengrin*—if you're a Wagnerian, you know that he enters standing on a swan that floats on the river, onto the stage. He gets off, sings, and at the end of his last aria, is supposed to get back on the swan boat and float off. But one night the swan just went off by itself before he could get on it. Without missing a beat, he turned to the audience and ad libbed, "What time does the next swan leave?"

HJ: How can those people have such charm without any intelligence? I've never understood that.

OW: Well, it's like talent without intelligence. It happens.

HJ: If Tracy was hateful, none of that comes across in the work.

OW: To me it does. I *hate* him so. Because he's one of those bitchy Irishmen.

HJ: One of those what?

OW: One of those bitchy Irishmen.

HJ: I can't believe you said that.

OW: I'm a racist, you know. Here's the Hungarian recipe for making an omelet. First, steal two eggs. [Alexander] Korda told me that.

HJ: But you liked Korda.

OW: I love Hungarians to the point of sex! I almost get a hard-on when I hear a Hungarian accent, I'm so crazy about them.

HJ: I don't understand why you're saying that about the Irish.

OW: I know them; you don't. They hate themselves. I lived for years in Ireland. The majority of intelligent Irishmen dislike Irishmen, and they're right.

HJ: All these groups dislike themselves. Jews dislike themselves.

OW: Nothing like Irishmen.

HJ: That doesn't make them right, Orson, and you know that. And I don't accept this prejudice from you. I know that you don't really have it.

OW: I do have it. I do have it. Particularly against Irish-Americans. I much prefer Irishmen from Ireland. If I have to have an Irishman, I'll take one of those. And Irishmen in England are quite good. All the great Irish writers mostly left and went to England, except for [George William] Russell and [William Butler] Yeats. Yeats makes me shiver. I was in Dublin at the time when he was still—

HJ: I didn't realize he was still around in the thirties.

OW: Yeah. He was at every party, and you could see him walking in the park. And Lady Gregory. All those people were still around—the famous Gaelic nationalists. I got to know them all. And you know, some of my best friends are Irishmen.

HJ: Oh, God!

OW: But when I look at Tracy, I see that everything that's hateful about him is Irish. Everything that's mean. Every Irishman will tell you that. Seven hundred years of bitter oppression changed their character, gave them that passive meanness and cunning. All I can say is what Micheál Mac Liammóir said when we were making *Othello*, and I asked him, "Describe the Irish in one word." He said, "Malice." Look, I love Ireland, I love Irish literature, I love everything they do, you know. But the Irish-Americans have invented an imitation Ireland which is unspeakable. The wearin' o' the green. Oh, my God, to vomit!

HJ: That's boring and silly, and—

OW: No, it's to vomit. Not boring and silly. Don't argue with me. You're such a liberal! Of course there's no proof. It's the way I feel! You don't want me to feel that, but I do! I think everybody should be bigoted. I don't think you're human if you don't acknowledge some prejudice.

HJ: Yes. But acknowledging some prejudice and really having full-out hate, like you have against the Irish—

OW: Well, not so much that I'm rude to them or would bar them from my house. It doesn't *mean* anything, it's just a perception of their character. Or of the majority of them.

HJ: Okay. But if that's true, then all it means is that there's cultural conditioning.

OW: Well, of course there is!

HJ: So when they come to America, that changes them.

OW: Yes, they become a new and terrible race. Which is called "Irish-Americans." They're fine in Australia; they're fine in England; they do well in Latin America. It's in New York and Boston that they became so frightful. You know, the old Kennedy was a real Irish-American. That's what I mean.

HJ: But his kids weren't?

OW: No. They escaped it. You can see the Irish ancestry, but their character wasn't Irish. Their life wasn't based on malice. You know, if you're here in America long enough, you lose the faults and the virtues of your original culture. The Italians will lose the sense of family when they finally get to the next generation. They won't hang together, the way they still do now.

HJ: It's like in Israel, where there's no art now. All these Jews, they thought they were gonna have a renaissance, and suddenly, they're producing a great air force, but no artists. All those incredible virtues of the centuries—

OW: They left all that in Europe. Who needs it? They get to Israel, and they sort of go into retirement.

HJ: Their theater is boring; their film is boring. Painting and sculpture—

OW: Boring. You know, the only time they make good music is when Zubin Mehta, a Hindu, comes to conduct.

HJ: It's amazing. When the Jews were in Poland, every pianist in the world—

OW: Every fiddler who ever lived was Jewish. It was a total Russian-Jewish, Polish-Jewish monopoly. Now they're all Japanese and Orientals. [Arthur] Rubinstein is gone.

HJ: Last year.

OW: I knew Rubinstein for forty years, very well. I told you his greatest line. I was with him at a concert in Albert Hall, and I had no seat, so I listened to the concert sitting in the wings. He finished. Wild applause. And as he walked into the wings to mop his face off, he said to me, "You know, they applauded just as loudly last Thursday, when I played well."

HJ: Dying at ninety-five is not bad. He had a full life.

OW: Did he ever.

HJ: It's true, all that, then? That he fucked everybody?

OW: He was the greatest cocksman of the nineteenth century. Of the twentieth century. The greatest charmer, linguist, socialite, raconteur. Never practiced. He always used to say, "You know, I'm not nearly as good a pianist technically, as many of my rivals, because I am too lazy to practice. I just don't like to. [Vladimir] Horowitz can do more than I can. He sits there and works. I like to enjoy life. I play clinkers all the time." But, he says, "I play it better with the clinkers."

HJ: And Horowitz hates his life, and for fifteen years hasn't been able to play or even move.

OW: Rubinstein walked through life as though it was one big party.

HJ: And then ended it with this young girl. Didn't he leave his wife after forty-five years when he was ninety to run off with a thirty-one-year-old woman?

OW: Like Casals. Who suddenly, at the age of eighty-seven or something, came up with a Lolita.

HJ: Getting back to the Irish, some are liberals, like Robert Ryan. He was a brave man, politically and socially. Tell me Robert Ryan was not a decent man.

OW: He's a wonderful actor. I don't think of him as Irish; he just has an Irish name. He must be fourth-generation.

HJ: Now, Ford you liked. He was an Irishman.

OW: We were very good friends, and he always wanted to do a picture with me. He was a pretty mean son-of-a-bitch Irishman. But I loved him anyway.

HJ: When did you first meet him?

OW: When I was shooting *Kane*, he came to the set on the first day of shooting.

HJ: Just to wish you well?

OW: No, for a reason. He pointed to the assistant director, a fellow called Ed Donahue, who was in the pay of my enemies at RKO, and said, "I see you got snake-in-the-grass Donahue on the picture." And left. He came to warn me that my assistant was a fink.

HJ: I've always heard that Ford was a drunk.

OW: Never when he was working. Not a drop. Just the last day of a picture. And he'd be drunk for weeks. Serious, serious drunk. But for him, drinking was fun. In other words, he wasn't an alcoholic. Went out with all the boys. Irishmen, get drunk and fight. Everybody gets beat up in the pub, you know? I've lived through all that. Went to jail in Ireland for rowdyism. It was a culture where nobody got married until they were thirty-five, because they were always dreaming of emigrating, and they didn't want to be stuck with the kids, financially. So all these poor virgin ladies sat around waiting to get married, and the guys are all swinging at each other, reverting to the bestiality of the male.

HJ: There was not much fucking around, I would imagine, because it was a Catholic culture?

OW: Oh, my God, yes. By the girls. I could hardly draw a breath when I visited the Aran Islands. I was all of seventeen. And these great, marvelous girls in their white petticoats, they'd grab me. Off the petticoats would go. It was as close to male rape as you could imagine. And all with husbands out in their skin-covered canoes. All day, while I had nothing to do. Then the girls would go and confess it all to the priest, who finally said to me, "I had another confession this morning. When are you leaving?" He was protecting the virtue of his flock. When I told that story, there was tremendous excitement in America from the clergy, who said it could never have happened.

HJ: Wasn't Ford very reactionary, politically? Like his pals John Wayne and Ward Bond?

OW: Yes, but all those guys loved me, for some reason. And I loved them. I have a beer bottle that was put together on Ford's yacht, with different Mexican and American beer labels signed by that gang of people, all dedicated to me. Now this was at a time when I was a well-known Hollywood Red.

HJ: And their reactionary positions came from what?

OW: Irish, Irish, Irish. The Irish were taught, "Kill the kikes," you know. I really loved John Wayne. He had some of the best manners of almost any actor I've ever met in Hollywood.

HJ: Did you ever speak to him about politics at all?

OW: Why would I? I'm not like you. I'm not gonna set John Wayne straight. I never had any trouble with extreme right-wingers. I've always found them tremendously likeable in every respect, except their politics. They're usually nicer people than left-wingers.

HJ: Easy for you to say. You were in Europe in the fifties, during the blacklist, when all that shit happened.

OW: Yes, I was lucky. I wasn't in America during the McCarthy era. I was on every list in the world. Every time they asked for help for whatever cause, I said, "Sign me up." But in my *New York Post* column, all during the forties, I was in print attacking Stalinist Russia at a time when everybody thought God was smiling on Stalin. I wanted to explain to HUAC the difference between a Communist and a liberal, so I kept begging, "May I please go to Washington to testify?" But they didn't dare ask me.

HJ: But you're so forgiving about these kinds of very dangerous—

OW: Forgiving!? Supposing you go to the Amazon, and you live in a village of headhunters. Now, if you're an anthropologist, you can become very fond of those headhunters, but you're not gonna argue about head-hunting with them.

HJ: I don't understand how somebody with liberal feelings would not discuss politics with Wayne or Bond or Adolphe Menjou at a time when they had the power to hurt people, and in fact did a lot of damage.

OW: Well, Menjou was so fighting mad that you couldn't talk to him. But Noël Coward took care of him wonderfully. Menjou was heading a USO troupe. Noël Coward was heading the equivalent of the USO—whatever it was called in England—you know, entertaining the troops. And they met in Casablanca. And they were eating in the mess. Menjou was talking about how terrible it was in England, that those "nigger" soldiers were fucking all the English girls, and you didn't know what kind of race it was gonna be: "Isn't that true, Noël?" And Noël said, "Well, I think it's perfectly marvelous." Menjou said, "What?" Noël said, "At last there'll be a race of Englishmen with good teeth." No, with Menjou you couldn't talk. He was a raving maniac.

2. "Thalberg was Satan!"

In which Orson is rude to Richard Burton, was bored by Meyer Lansky, and argues that Irving "the Boy Wonder" Thalberg invented factory filmmaking with his producer system.

HENRY JAGLOM: During these last two weeks, two studios have been taken over by their distribution chiefs.

ORSON WELLES: Well, if RKO hadn't been taken over by a distribution head, I would never have made *Citizen Kane*. That's why I got that contract with final cut. Because George Schaefer didn't know any better! None of the other guys would ever have given me a contract like that.

HJ: Were things really better in the old days?

OW: It's terrible for older people to say that, because they always say things were better, but they really were. What was so good about it was just the quantity of movies that were made. If you were Darryl Zanuck, and you were producing eighty moving pictures under your direct supervision, how much attention could you pay to any one picture? Somebody was gonna slip something in that's good.

I got along well with even the worst of the old moguls, like Harry Cohn. They were all easier to deal with than these college-educated, market-conscious people. I never really suffered from the "bad old boys." I've only suffered from lawyers and agents. Wasn't it Norman Mailer who said that the great new art form in Hollywood is the deal? Everybody's energy goes into the deal. Forty-five years I have been doing business with agents, as a performer and a director. As a producer, sitting on the other side of the desk, I have never once had an agent go out on a limb for his client and fight for him. I've never heard one say, "No, just a minute! This is the actor you should use." They will always say, "You don't like him? I've got somebody else." They're totally spineless.

HJ: In the old days, all those big deals were made on a handshake. With no contract. And they were all honored.

OW: In common with all Protestant or Jewish cultures, America was developed on the idea that your word is your bond. Otherwise, the frontier could never have been opened, 'cause it was lawless. A man's word had to mean something. My theory is that everything went to hell with Prohibition, because it was a law nobody could obey. So the whole concept of the rule of law was corrupted at that moment. Then came Vietnam, and marijuana, which clearly shouldn't be illegal, but is. If you go to jail for ten years in Texas when you light up a joint, who are you? You're a lawbreaker. It's just like Prohibition was. When people accept breaking the law as normal, something happens to the whole society. You see?

(Richard Burton comes to the table.)

RICHARD BURTON: Orson, how good to see you. It's been too long. You're looking fine. Elizabeth is with me. She so much wants to meet you. Can I bring her over to your table?

OW: No. As you can see, I'm in the middle of my lunch. I'll stop by on my way out.

(Burton exits.)

HJ: Orson, you're behaving like an asshole. That was so rude. He actually backed away, like a whipped puppy.

OW: Do not kick me under the table. I hate that. I don't need you as my conscience, my Jewish Jiminy Cricket. Especially do not kick my boots. You know they protect my ankles. Richard Burton had great talent. He's ruined his great gifts. He's become a joke with a celebrity wife. Now he just works for money, does the worst shit. And I wasn't rude. To quote Carl Laemmle, "I gave him an evasive answer. I told him, 'Go fuck yourself.'"

HJ: So you're saying he sold out, and you didn't.

OW: If I would have gone and done their scripts, I could've worked for any of the big studios. I was perfectly bankable even when the bad Welles legend was at its most virulent. I could still make pictures.

HJ: As long as it was somebody else's picture, and not an "Orson Welles picture." So would you have made a movie based on one of their scripts?

OW: No. I wouldn't. I was offered *Porgy and Bess* and—Sam Goldwyn offered me two or three pictures.

HJ: What was he like?

OW: In his time, he was considered a classy producer. Because he never deliberately did anything that wasn't his idea of the best quality goods. I respected him for that. He was an honest merchant. He may have made a bad picture, but he didn't know it was a bad picture. And he was funny. He made me laugh. He actually once said to me, in that high voice of his, "Orson, for you I'd write a blanket check." He said, "With Warner Brothers, a verbal commitment isn't worth the paper it's written on." He was there for me all the time. But Gregg Toland, who shot so many Goldwyn pictures, told me that in Russia, if you didn't see every actor's face brilliantly, they had to go back and reshoot it. Sam was the same way. Whenever there wasn't a bright light on a star's face for thirty seconds he went nuts: "I'm paying for that face! I want to see the actor!" Long shots, all right, but no shadows. It was all too much for me. I was just not constituted to deal with him.

HJ: You were never tempted?

OW: Never. To go through what Willie Wyler went through with him? Life is too short. Charlie MacArthur and Ben Hecht wrote *Wuthering Heights* in my house in Sneden's Landing, and Goldwyn was with 'em all the time. I was trying to sleep in the afternoon, before my radio show. And I heard the way Sam behaved with them. And I thought, "Never will I put myself through that."

He was really a monster. The last night I ever spent with him turned me against him forever. He was a guest at my house. I had come back to Hollywood, after years away, and I invited all these old dinosaurs, who were still around, and some other people. And he left right after dessert, because there were a number of guests who weren't on the A list. You know, he wouldn't have done that before. He got old.

HJ: Did anyone else offer you movies besides Goldwyn?

OW: [Louis B.] Mayer offered me his studio! He was madly in love with me, because I wouldn't have anything to do with him, you know? Twice he brought me over—spent all day wooing me. He called me "Orse." Whenever he sent for me, he burst into tears, and once he fainted. To get his way. It was fake, absolutely fake. The deal was, I'd have the studio but I'd have to stop acting, directing, and writing—making pictures.

HJ: Why wouldn't you have anything to do with him?

OW: Because he was the worst of them all. The rest of them were just what they were. The thing about Harry Cohn was: he looked like such a villainous Hollywood producer, there was nothing he could do that would surprise you. But L.B. was worse than Harry Cohn. He was self-righteous, smarmy, waving the American flag, doing deals with the Purple Gang in Detroit—

HJ: The Purple Gang in Detroit?

OW: Before the unions, it was all Mafia. But no one called it the Mafia. Just said "the mob." And, mainly, the Purple Gang. They controlled all the blue-collar guys who projected the movies, pushed the dollies, swept the floors. They controlled the Teamsters. They didn't control directors or anything—didn't need to. And when L.B. needed extra money, he got it from the Purple Gang. When he wanted strong-arm work, he'd call the Purple Gang, who'd send their tough guys into town.

HJ: Louis B. Mayer had people hit?

OW: Beat up. I wouldn't put it past him to have people killed. He liked to think of himself as a founding father and capo of the Mafia.

HJ: Did you know any of them? Meyer Lansky?

OW: Very well. He was probably the number-one gangster in America. I knew them all. You had to. If you lived, as I did, on Broadway during that period, if you lived in nightclubs, you could not not know them. I liked screwing the chorus girls and I liked meeting all the different people who would come in, and I liked staying up until five in the morning, and they used to love to go to nightclubs. They would come and sit at your table.

HJ: How did Lee Strasberg do with Hyman Roth, remember, in *Godfather II*?

OW: Much better than the real thing. Meyer Lansky was a boring man. Hyman Roth is who he should have been! They all should have been like that and none of them were. *The Godfather* was the glorification of a bunch of bums who never existed. The best of them were the kind of people you'd expect to drive a beer truck. They had no class. The classy gangster is a Hollywood invention. The classy gangster was the ideal of every real gangster, who then started to dress like George Raft, and tried to behave like George Raft, and so on.

HJ: They must have had something to get to the top.

OW: Energy, guts, luck, and the willingness to kill your friends in the interest of business. All this code of honor, and all that shit— pure invention. There was a famous cop on Broadway called Brannigan. I think I've got his name right, because his name was slightly changed by Damon Runyon and used as a character in *Guys and Dolls*. He used to go down Broadway every few weeks with a baseball bat, and I went with him a couple times, to watch it happen. Followed him, not went with him. He'd come into Lindy's—"Mindy's" to Runyon—and places like that, late at night. And if he'd see anybody, no matter who, he'd grab him, take him out in the street, and beat him up. Meaning: Get out of town. Don't sit around here—you make the town look bad. I saw him put Charlie Luciano, head first, into a garbage can outside of Reuben's, at five thirty in the morning.

HJ: "Lucky" Luciano?

OW: Yeah. He was never called "Lucky," except by the press.

HJ: In my mind, Luciano had forty people around him who would kill anyone who came near him.

OW: Not Brannigan—they all ran. They all had to go to the men's room when he came in with a baseball bat. He was just a tough Irishman. He said, "Fuck 'em."

HJ: But on the plus side, didn't Mayer create Thalberg, the greatest producer who ever lived?

OW: Thalberg was the biggest single villain in the history of Hollywood. Before him, a producer made the *least* contribution, by necessity. The producer didn't direct, he didn't act, he didn't write—so, therefore, all he could do was either (A) mess it up, which he didn't do very often, or (B) tenderly caress it. Support it. Producers would only go to the set to see that you were on budget, and that you didn't burn down the scenery. But Mayer made way for the producer system. He created the fellow who decides, who makes the directors' decisions, which had never existed before.

HJ: Didn't the other studio heads interfere with their directors?

OW: None of the old hustlers did that much harm. If they saw somebody good, they hired him. They tried to screw it up afterwards, but there was still a kind of dialogue between talent and the fellow up there in the front office. They had that old Russian-Jewish respect for the artist. All they did was say what they liked, and what they didn't like, and argue with you. That's easy to deal with. And sometimes the talent won. But once you got the educated producer, he has a desk, he's gotta have a function, he's gotta do something. He's not running the studio and counting the money—he's gotta be creative. That was Thalberg. The director became the fellow whose only job was to say, "Action" and "Cut." Suddenly, you were "just a director" on a "Thalberg production." Don't you see? A role had been created in the world. Just as there used to be no conductor of symphonies.

HJ: There was no conductor?

OW: No. The *konzertmeister*, first violinist, gave the beat. The conductor's job was invented. Like the theater director, a role that is only 150, 200 years old. Nobody directed plays before then. The stage manager said, "Walk left on that line." The German, what's his name, Saxe-Meiningen, invented directing in the theater. And Thalberg invented producing in movies. He persuaded all the writers that they couldn't write without him, because he was the great man.

HJ: F. Scott Fitzgerald must have been impressed by him, to make him the model for *The Last Tycoon*.

OW: Writers always fell for his shtick, knowing better. Writers are so insecure that when he said, "I don't write, but I'll tell you what's wrong with this," they just lapped it up. He could cut them off at the knees with all his "genius" stuff, and making them sit for three hours before he allowed them to come in to see him, and all that. By the way, there were better scripts written, on the whole—this is a generalization, but it's my opinion—even when writers considered that they were slumming by coming out here. Faulkner and everybody. "We're going out there to get some money." Still, they did an honest job for that money, because instead of going back to their little place up in the Hollywood hills to write their scripts, they had to eat with each other every day in the studio commissary, which made for a competitive situation. It was collegial—"What are you working on?"—and they shared funny stories about how dumb the producer was, how bad the director was, and all that. But they didn't want their peers to do better than they did, so they worked hard. Harder than these people now who want to be directors, who have done nothing but look at movies since they were eight years old, who have never had an experience in their lives. Or experienced any culture beyond movie culture.

HJ: But Thalberg was also creative. At least from Fitzgerald's point of view.

OW: Well, that's my definition of "villain." He obviously had this power. He convinced Mayer that without him, his movies wouldn't have any class. Remember that quote Mayer gave? All the other moguls were "dirty kikes making nickelodeon movies." He used to say that to me all the time.

HJ: When Mayer found you, you were very young, and very attractive, very magnetic.

OW: That's why he loved me; he thought I was another Thalberg.

HJ: Did you know Thalberg?

OW: I didn't know him. I was out here, playing in the theater, when he was alive, but I didn't meet him. Then he died.

HJ: Irene Mayer Selznick says in her book about L.B., her father, that everybody knew Thalberg had this sort of death sentence hanging over him from the beginning. He started at MGM knowing that at thirty he was gonna die. He had rheumatic fever. A bad heart.

OW: I know a lot of people who expect to die early. Thalberg turned it to his advantage.

HJ: He must have been incredibly skillful at manipulating Mayer.

OW: Thalberg used to manipulate everybody, brilliantly. Not only Mayer, but actors, directors, writers. He used his death sentence, his beauty, everything.

HJ: He was also beautiful, apparently, yeah?

OW: Yeah. Enormously charming and persuasive. Thalberg was Satan! You know, the classic Satan. And, of course, Norman worked around the clock.

HJ: Irving.

OW: Irving, yeah. I always think of him as Norman, and I don't know why. He would reduce people; and, having reduced them, flatter them. He was obviously a weaver of spells who was able to convince everyone that he was the artist. Thalberg was way up here, and the director was way down there. The result was that he negated the personal motion picture in favor of the manufactured movie. He was responsible for the bad product of Metro, and the style which continued afterwards: the Thalberg style.

HJ: That's true. Nobody knows who directed *Gone With the Wind*. Or, there were many directors on the same movie, like *The Wizard of Oz*. Metro's great, great movies somehow just happened.

OW: Yes. And they still look like any one of the Metro directors could have made them. At lunch in the commissary, you could play musical chairs with every movie—move every director to another movie—and you would not be able to tell the difference in the rushes the next day. Now, Warner's made the good pictures. It was rough there. Jack Warner tortured and murdered everybody, but he got great pictures out of them, obviously.

HJ: What directors managed to work under Thalberg that way?

OW: Vic Fleming, or Woody Van Dyke, whoever.

HJ: Were any of them gifted?

OW: George Cukor was.

HJ: Not as much as they say. His films were signature-less. Even the good ones.

OW: He was a very competent stage director. But it's true, you can't tell a Cukor picture.

HJ: *Holiday, Philadelphia Story.*

OW: Writers' pictures.

HJ: Or Tracy pictures, or Hepburn pictures; they're star pictures.

OW: Exactly—all of them. That's why, to me, Thalberg is the number-one villain. I think he was a real destroyer.

HJ: Okay. But, he didn't do anything to hurt people.

OW: Well, he destroyed [Erich] von Stroheim, as a man and as an artist. Literally destroyed him. And von Stroheim at that moment was, I think, demonstrably the most gifted director in Hollywood. Von Stroheim was the greatest argument against the producer. He was so clearly a genius, and so clearly should have been left alone—no matter what crazy thing he did—

HJ: But he was so extravagant that he reached the point where economically, it was impossible. If the stories about him are true. Or was he just so original he threatened everyone?

OW: They had to make him into a monster. I had a very interesting experience when I was making *Touch of Evil*. I had a scene in a police archive, and they let me shoot it in the real archive of Universal. And while they were setting the lights, I looked up von Stroheim, the budgets of his movies. They weren't that high. The idea that he was so extravagant was nonsense. Anita Loos wrote a brilliant book about Hollywood—*Kiss Hollywood Goodbye*. And she thinks [Josef] von Sternberg is a marvelous man. Sorry, not von Sternberg. Von Stroheim. Von Sternberg was a real louse. But nevertheless, the portrait of von Stroheim was a hatchet job. She said, "We all loved Von," and then she presents a picture of this terrible Prussian. Once she said to me, "The nicest Jewish actor you ever met in your life." You know?

HJ: Did you know von Stroheim?

OW: Yes, very well. But later, when he had become an actor and was living in France, Charlie Lederer and I wrote a movie for him in Paris, with Pierre Brasseur, and Arletty. It was called *Portrait of an Assassin.* It was about those guys that ride around on motorcycles inside a cage, going faster and faster. Kind of carny shit. They didn't use one word we wrote. But we wrote the story, which they did use. And we got paid by a black-market producer who came to the Lancaster Hotel with the money wrapped in newspapers— soaking wet; it was always raining in Paris. That's how we got to live it up in Paris, writing this story.

HJ: And you liked von Stroheim?

OW: Loved him. He was a terribly nice fellow. A French script girl who worked on *Grand Illusion* told me that he was the greatest prop actor she'd ever known. Because he'd have a newspaper, a swagger stick, a monocle, a cigarette—all of these things. And he would do a scene where he would put them down and pick them up on certain lines. You can't have that number of props and get it all right. But every time [Jean] Renoir would shoot a take, he'd do it right. On the syllable.

HJ: Did von Stroheim direct any movies in his later life?

OW: No, he didn't. He became purely an actor. He became a star in France in the thirties, but in bad pictures. A terrible loss. 'Cause there was a gigantic gift, really. No question.

HJ: Was he very frustrated? Was he very angry or sad?

OW: He didn't seem to be. By the time I knew him, he'd come to terms with it, so he didn't treat people badly out of his frustration. He was not a jolly fellow, but he was not brooding. He was very fond of being a star. And even after the war, he was still a star. That compensated a lot for him.

HJ: And he did that wonderful turn in *Sunset Boulevard.* That brought him back.

OW: Only in terms of Hollywood. In America it seemed as though he'd been reclaimed from obscurity, when the reality was he was coming from continuous stardom in France. But the success of *Sunset Boulevard* meant nothing to him, because it was Swanson's picture, and Billy Wilder's—compared to what he was getting in France. VON STROHEIM on top of every marquee.

HJ: So all the stories about von Stroheim were made up?

OW: He did some crazy things, but he didn't do anything as crazy as the young directors of the fifty-million-dollar pictures do today.

HJ: But his pictures were without precedent—eight hours long.

OW: Yes, they were, but Thalberg was the one without precedent. Without him, von Stroheim would never have been ruined. D. W. Griffith did much crazier things. But he was in charge, because he was the director, and "D. W. Griffith."

3. "FDR used to say, 'You and I are the two best actors in America.' "

In which Orson recalls sabotaging David O. Selznick's charades, claims that Carole Lombard's plane was shot down by Nazis, and says FDR's biggest regret was not having intervened in the Spanish Civil War.

HENRY JAGLOM: You were trashing Thalberg the other day. It's funny, because the myth gets handed down that Thalberg had great taste and culture.

ORSON WELLES: In his whole career he didn't make a picture that will last fifty years from now, and still he's revered. *Romeo and Juliet*, as produced by Thalberg, and directed by Cukor, was the cultural high point of his ten years of moviemaking. Now, you cannot sit through four minutes of it, it's so terrible. Norma Shearer with those tiny eyes, and Leslie Howard, a Hungarian Jew, as Veronese teenagers?

HJ: But he was so foppish, and so, so British. God, Hungarians made great Englishmen, didn't they? I wonder why.

OW: Well, there was a period during the Austro-Hungarian empire when the older aristocracy had all their clothes made in London. They spoke French with great chic, but their shoes were made in London; their hats were made in London; the nanny who raised their children was from London—and the greatest thing to be was an English gentleman. And I'm sure that's why Lord Leslie Howard, as Sir Winston [Churchill] used to call him, trilling his *r*'s, was such a good Englishman. And then to die in a plane crash, because of Churchill . . . Not killed by some angry Magyar peasant.

HJ: That was the incident where Churchill couldn't reveal that they'd broken the German code, so he let the Nazis shoot down the plane? Wasn't that the same plane that Norma Shearer was on? Thalberg's widow?

OW: No, no. Norma Shearer wasn't killed in a plane. That was another thing that is amazing. After Thalberg died, Norma Shearer— one of the most minimally talented ladies ever to appear on the silver screen, and who looked like nothing, with one eye crossed over the other—went right on being the queen of Hollywood, and getting one role after another.

HJ: Marie Antoinette.

OW: The biggest bust ever made, you know? And everybody used to say, "Miss Thalberg is coming," "Miss Shearer is arriving," and all that, as though they were talking about Sarah Bernhardt. You know, while there were Garbo and Dietrich and Lombard and all the good people. It was a continuation of the magic of this man.

HJ: But Thalberg was also responsible for careers of people like David O. Selznick, who came after him and who managed to make some extraordinary films.

OW: They would have been made by the directors, anyway—and better. The man was a simple pain in the ass! I knew him as well as I know you. He was a total monster, the worst of them all.

HJ: He has the image of somehow being elegant and classy.

OW: He wasn't elegant. He was gross. Tremendous energy and very intelligent. And very bad taste. He thought he was the greatest thing since Jesus. His job, like Thalberg's, was to efface the signature of the director. The man had a tremendous drive to be more than Thalberg. And he had no conscience. Selznick wanted to be the greatest producer in the world—and would have been happy to do anything to achieve it. It was unbelievable. Once I was on David's yacht, and we were all gathered together after dinner. He said, "We can either go back to Miami tonight, or we can go to Havana. I'd like to see a show of hands. Who wants to go to Havana?" Everybody's hands went up. We all went to bed, woke up in Miami.

HJ: That's what happens if you own the boat.

OW: I was close to David because friends of mine liked him. I used to go to his house on Sunday nights. Everybody in Hollywood would be there, and we'd play "The Game," which was just charades, you know. But Selznick played to *win*. Week after week after week. If our team lost, he would follow us in our cars down the driveway, screaming insults at us for having been such idiots, with his voice echoing through the canyons as we drove away. He would become so violent that it was worth it. It was funny just to watch him. And then he had us back the next week. "Now we're gonna win," you see?

Once Selznick wanted to have a fight with me. This was at Walter Wanger's house. After the ladies had left, the gentlemen sat around drinking port. He said how disappointed he was not to have Ronald Colman in *Rebecca*. Because he had this fellow Olivier. That irritated me. I said, "What's wrong with Olivier?" He said, "He's no gentleman." And I said, "David, what kind of shit is this? What are you talking about, 'no gentleman?'" "Well, he just isn't. You can tell that. But with Ronnie you know right away—he's a gentleman." And I said, "Why, you pious old fart." So David stood up, took off his glasses, and assumed the fighting position. We went out into the backyard, and everybody held us back.

HJ: You were really going to fight?

OW: Oh, yes. We used to do that all the time in Hollywood, always stepping out into the garden and fighting. While everybody held you, and nothing ever happened.

HJ: Bogart was always beating up guys, wasn't he?

OW: Now, Bogart, who was both a coward and a very bad fighter, was always picking fights in nightclubs, in sure knowledge that the waiters would stop him. Making fearless remarks to people in his cups, when he knew he was well covered by the busboys.

The great fistfight of the prewar days, though, was between John Huston and—who was the other fellow? It lasted a long time, and they kept running at each other, but neither one of them ever landed a blow. I only saw one great fighter in my life. I was sitting in Harry's Bar in Venice, in the afternoon, and there were four GIs, and their sergeant. Another soldier came in and made a remark, and the sergeant just turned to the soldier and knocked him out with the neatness of a John Ford movie, and they carried him away. Then another soldier made a remark, and he knocked him out. Now, you know, it is *impossible* to do that. But he did it, right in front of me, and each time the sergeant turned to me and said, "I'm very sorry, sir."

HJ: So if it wasn't Norma Shearer, who was killed in the plane crash?

OW: You're thinking of what's-her-name—the good one. I can't think of anybody's name, ever. Terrible.

HJ: Gable's girlfriend—Carole Lombard.

OW: His wife. I adored her. She was a very close friend of mine. And I don't mean to imply that we were ever lovers. I remember when Gable made a picture called *Parnell*, a costume picture. Nineteen thirty-seven, with Myrna Loy. Nobody came. They released it to *empty* theaters! Proving that there's no such thing as the star who can't empty a theater. I think it was the only MGM film that lost money. Not that it mattered to Mayer. Money was almost no object to Metro, 'cause they couldn't lose money.

HJ: You mean the way they had the distribution set up, owning the theaters, they were so locked in that—

OW: And when I learned to fly, I flew with Carole over Metro, at lunchtime. We buzzed the commissary, just as everyone was coming out, and she dropped leaflets that said, "Remember Parnell"! That's the kind of girl she was.

HJ: She looked to me like kind of a road-company Garbo.

OW: Not at all Garboesque! My God, she was earthy. She looked like a great beauty, but she behaved like a waitress in a hash house. That was her style of acting, too, and it had a great allure. She wasn't vulgar; she was just . . . I got to know her when I had to make peace between her and Charles Laughton. I was sort of an emissary for Laughton. They were making a picture called *They Knew What They Wanted*, about an Italian vintner who gets a mail-order wife, played by Lombard, you know? The movie was directed by Garson Kanin. Laughton was the simple Italian peasant. He would come to my office, and sit down across the desk from me, and put his head on the desk and cry.

HJ: Laughton?

OW: In the middle of the day. Said, "I can't go on the way they're making fun of me on the set." 'Cause they were sending him up so. And then I would go and talk to Gar, and talk to Carole, and say, "You know, he is a great actor. Take it easy with him. You're gonna ruin your own picture." Laughton was beside himself. Because he had been such a star in England with Korda. When he played Rembrandt for Korda, years before—a wonderful performance, one of the only times an actor has ever persuaded you he's a genius—he asked to be taken by Alex's brother, the art director, to Holland, to the museum in Amsterdam, to see *The Night Watch*, and other Rembrandt pictures. They arrived on Sunday, and the museum was opened just for Laughton. He walked up to *The Night Watch*, looked at it, and fell into a faint. From the beauty of it all. When he'd make an entrance, they had little sets built for him where he would be sitting, doing what he was doing just before he came on. You see?

HJ: A very Method actor for his time.

OW: Well, his own method.

HJ: Now, Lombard could not have been very bright.

OW: *Very* bright. Brighter than any director she ever worked with. She had all the ideas. Jack Barrymore told me the same thing. He said, "I've never played with an actress so intelligent in my life."

HJ: But Gable was certainly not bright.

OW: No, but terribly nice. Just a nice big hunk of man. If you're working hard that long—if you have to be in makeup at five fifteen, and you get home at seven o'clock—how much brightness do you want? The guys just wanted to stagger home—and, if they could, get laid. Otherwise, a happy smile and get ready for the next day's work.

HJ: So Lombard was also killed in a plane crash?

OW: Yes. You know why her plane went down?

HJ: Why?

OW: It was full of big-time American physicists, shot down by the Nazis. She was one of the only civilians on the plane. The plane was filled with bullet holes.

HJ: It was shot down by who?

OW: Nazi agents in America. It's a real thriller story.

HJ: That's preposterous. What was she doing on a plane full of physicists? Do people know this?

OW: The people who know it, know it. It was greatly hushed up. The official story was that it ran into the mountain.

HJ: The agents had antiaircraft guns?

OW: No. In those days, the planes couldn't get up that high. They'd just clear the mountains. The bad guys knew the exact route that the plane had to take. They were standing on a ridge, which was the toughest thing for the plane to get over. One person can shoot a plane down, and if they had five or six people there, they couldn't miss. Now, I cannot swear it's true. I've been told this by people who swear it's true, who I happen to believe. But that's the closest you can get, without having some kind of security clearance.

No one wanted to admit that we had people in the middle of America who could shoot down a plane for the Nazis. Because then everybody would start denouncing anybody with a German grandmother. Which Roosevelt was very worried about. The First World War had only happened some twenty-odd years before. He'd seen the riots against Germans. No one could play Wagner—or Beethoven, even. Germans weren't safe on the street. They were getting lynched. And he was very anxious for nothing like that to be repeated. He was really scared about what would happen to the Japanese if all the rednecks got started. Especially in California, with its coastline on the Pacific.

HJ: So his idea was to protect them? That's why he rounded them up and put them in camps?

OW: Yes. That was the motivation in his mind. But it was a ghastly mistake. Now, other people—the Pentagon types—thought we were riddled with spies. But his concern was the safety of the Japanese who lived here. Of course, they didn't know that. They're quite rightly indignant. They would never agree that it was a good thing.

HJ: You knew Roosevelt, right? Were you ever alone with him?

OW: Yes, several times. And then Missy [LeHand] would come in. And she hated it when I visited the White House.

HJ: Why?

OW: Because I kept him up too late. He liked to stay up and talk, you see. He was free with me. I didn't need to be manipulated. He didn't need my vote. It was a release for him, and he enjoyed my company. He used to say, "You and I are the two best actors in America."

HJ: Was he bright?

OW: Very bright.

HJ: What was that letter he wrote you about Spain?

OW: A four-page letter out of the blue, only a few months before he died, about the state of the world. It was lost in a fire. I never knew why he'd written it to me. He just sort of sat and dictated it one night.

HJ: He wrote he felt bad about Spain?

OW: Oh, no, he didn't write that. That's what he said to me. It was on the campaign train, not in the White House. We were talking about mistakes that other people had made—that [Woodrow] Wilson had made, that [Georges] Clemenceau had made. Yes, Spain. The neutrality with Spain was a big mistake. "That comes back to me all the time," he said.

HJ: It always struck me that the fact that some of our more progressive presidents—the Roosevelts and the Kennedys—came from wealthier backgrounds meant that they were less intimidated by other rich people, and therefore, less susceptible to special interests. The poor kids are the more dangerous ones—Reagan is so impressed with rich people—it is such an important part of his life.

OW: And they had Nixon in their pocket when he was still a congressman. From the beginning. But I still don't think your point is right. It's because of the old tradition of the Whig—of the liberal rich, the old tradition of public service and of liberalism—Roosevelt was a genuine, old-fashioned American Whig. The last and best example of it. And—

HJ: But I still say you can't be a poor person in the presidency and be surrounded by wealthy people.

OW: Well, a senator can be a poor person, but it's true, eventually he'll become a puppet of the rich. A senator used to be a tremendous office. Now it's really, more than it's ever been, what the money buys. The special-interest thing.

HJ: We always heard that Roosevelt really wanted [Henry] Wallace in '44 to run as his vice president again, and it was the reactionary Southern Democrats who forced Truman on him.

OW: He would have liked to have had a better Wallace.

HJ: William O. Douglas or someone.

OW: Yeah. He would have loved to have Douglas. But they did force Truman on him, and he didn't give Truman any kind of break. Roosevelt didn't think much of him. None of us did.

HJ: Were your sympathies with Wallace when he ran for president in '48 on the Progressive Party ticket?

OW: Oh, no. I thought it was just fatal. He was a prisoner of the Communist Party. He would never do anything to upset them. Not that I thought that in itself would make him a bad president. But it showed his weakness. I was very, very passionately against him. The left thought I was a real traitor. Had he won, I think we would have had a much bigger reaction after him.

HJ: Bigger McCarthyism?

OW: More dangerous, and more venomous, and more long-lived.

4. "I fucked around on everyone."

In which Orson and Rita Hayworth, who were separated, were reunited to make *The Lady from Shanghai*. He recalls that she stuck by him when he tried to leave Hollywood to do good works.

——————

HENRY JAGLOM: Rita worked for Harry Cohn at Columbia, didn't she?

ORSON WELLES: Yes, he thought he was a great lover. He chased Rita around the desk all the years she was there. She was always going on suspension.

HJ: I just saw *Lady from Shanghai* again. She's so good in it.

OW: Are you kidding? She was magnificent! And she thought she wasn't. And nobody in the town would give her any credit for it.

HJ: It makes you realize what a waste her career was.

OW: She was a really talented actress who never got a chance.

HJ: They say that you ruined her in that film. Cut off her famous red locks, dyed what was left blond without telling Harry Cohn.

OW: Yes, that was supposed to be my vengeance on her for leaving me. I made her character a killer and cut off her hair, and all that. That's pretty profound psychological work, isn't it? Why would I want vengeance? I fucked around on everyone. And that's hard on a girl, very hard.

HJ: Did she believe that vengeance business?

OW: No, never. She always thought it was the best picture of her life. Defended me, and it. I was gonna make a nice little B picture with a girl I brought over from Paris—and get out, you know, in twenty days. I wasn't gonna get any money for it. So Rita came and cried, begged to do it. Of course, I said, "Yes." So suddenly, I'm stuck with the studio's bread-and-butter girl, from whom I've been separated for a year. I was dragged back into the marriage and the movie.

HJ: You were not divorced yet?

OW: No. So then we were reunited. Had to be, no other way to direct the picture. I moved back in with her. It wasn't really like working with an ex-wife, because we still loved each other. Then the hairdressers and people got after her. They worked her up with stories about who I was screwing. It's a regular Hollywood thing— all those people who live off of stars. She was deeply suspicious of everybody. She'd been so terribly hurt in her life, she wouldn't believe that I would not do that to her. So she threw me out. I was devastated.

HJ: Had you the intention of staying with her? Even though she was an alcoholic? And depressed?

OW: Forever? Yeah. 'Cause I knew she needed me desperately. I would have stayed with her till she died. There was nobody else who would have taken care of her like I would. I didn't know that she would be that sick.

HJ: And you didn't mind that?

OW: It doesn't matter whether you mind it or not—you do it.

HJ: Some people do it, and some don't.

OW: Yes. But I'm a terribly guilty-conscience person.

HJ: Yet you loved her, also.

OW: I loved her, yeah. Very much. But, by that time, not sexually.

I had to work myself up to fuck her. She had become so—such a figure of lust, and she just wanted to be a housewife. Marlene called her the perfect hausfrau. You know what Rita used to say: "They go to sleep with Rita Hayworth and wake up with Margarita Carmen Cansino." And she'd been so wonderful to me, absolutely wonderful. When I almost died of hepatitis, she spent five months with me while I recovered. And she never did anything except take care of me. When I said to her, "I want to give up the movies and theater. Will you do that with me?" She said, "Yes."

Later, when I was in Rome working on *Othello*, she sent for me. She said, "Come tonight." To Antibes. She didn't say why, and I thought something terrible had happened to her. There was no space on a commercial flight, so I flew in a cargo plane, standing up, with a lot of boxes. I arrived at the hotel, you know, *that* hotel, went up to the one great suite, you know, *that* suite. She opened the door, stood there in a negligee, hair flowing, gorgeous. The suite was full of flowers. The doors opened out onto the terrace, overlooking the Mediterranean. The smell, you know *that* smell. It was overpowering. Rita looked at me, tears in her eyes, said, "You were right; we belong together; I was wrong." But by then I was crazy for this ugly, little Italian girl who gave me so much shit, but I just had to have her.

HJ: The one with the face like a spoon.

OJ: I had to tell Rita, so I said, "I'm so sorry, but there's this girl. I'm in love; it's too late." She cried and said sadly, "OK. Then just be with me tonight, just hold me while I sleep." And I did. I held her. And nothing else. My arm was falling asleep. I was looking at my watch out of the corner of my eye to see when I could catch the morning flight back to Rome. I left the next day. Five days later Rita married Aly Khan. She was *dying* to stop being a movie actor. That's why she ran to him.

HJ: Relationships are so crazy. I'm devastated that Patrice [Townsend] has left me. I thought we had the perfect marriage.

OW: Women are another race. They're like the moon, always changing. You can only win by being the cool center of their being. You have to represent something solid and loving. The anchor. Even if you're not. You can't tell them the truth. You have to lie and play games. I've never in my entire life been with someone with whom I didn't have to play a game. I've never been with anyone with whom I could be exactly who I am.

HJ: Did you really want to give up the movies and the theater?

OW: Yes, at one point I decided that the best thing I could do, the most use I could get out of what I was born with, for my fellow man—unselfish use—would be in education. So I spent five months going to every big foundation, saying, "I'm going to give up my entire career." I was then very famous and very successful. I thought to myself, "I'll discuss with these people how to educate the younger generations, so that they know what's happening in the world, and the world will be a better place for it. We will use every method we can think of, and I will belong to you." Nobody wanted it. I got out of that by nobody taking me up on it. But I would have been very happy to do it. I had exhausted my real fire. I'm essentially an adventurer. I'd done all the things I wanted to do, and now I wanted to be of use. You know what I did instead? I made another movie.

HJ: Do you feel guilty for leading the good life in Hollywood while there are so many starving people in the world?

OW: I think most people here are bothered by the fact that in America we are incredibly fortunate. There are lots who have a bad conscience. A romantic conscience, depending on the person.

HJ: If they do, they don't talk about it.

OW: Because it sounds pompous. How can I sit at the table here with lunch and say, "I was talking to Henry in Ma Maison about these people who are starving in Africa, and thinking how I ought to be in Africa helping out." The answer is, "Go to Africa and shut up! Nobody is going to sympathize with you when you say that your problem is that you *aren't* going."

HJ: Has it occurred to you that if you went and did certain things, you'd be so caught up in it that you'd have to make dramatic changes in your life?

OW: It occurs to me every day. I am tormented by it. I live with it. The way I live with death, the way I live with old age, all those things.

HJ: What do you say to yourself about it?

OW: Well, you see, I'm not like you. I'm not judgmental. With me, it's, "Here I am, not going to Africa." I don't say to myself, "Why don't you go to Africa?" I don't discuss it with myself. Because if I did, I would go to Africa. So it is the self-indulgent devil in me that stops the dialogue.

HJ: I've been saying that to myself since I was seventeen, eighteen years old. That is the time you really feel it.

OW: That's the voice that should be leading you. It takes all the peer pressure and your self-indulgence and everything else to suppress that voice.

HJ: Isn't it shocking that we all do so little to alleviate all this incredible suffering?

OW: No. No, because it's only one aspect of our essential sinfulness. We are sinful in so many ways.

HJ: I never want to believe you have a religious bent, but, actually, you do.

OW: I know. I believe that we're much healthier if we think of our selfishness as sin. Which is what it is: a sin. Even if there is nothing out there except a random movement of untold gases and objects, sin still exists. You don't need a devil with horns. It's a social definition of sin. Everything we do that is self-indulgent, and that is selfish, and that turns us away from our dignity as human beings is a sin against what we were born with, the capacities we have, what we *could* make of this planet. Our whole age has taken the line that if you feel bad about yourself, it's something that you can be relieved of by your goddamn analyst. Psst!—it's gone! And then you'll be happy, you know? But that feeling is not something you should be relieved of. It's something you should *deal* with. And there's no remission for what I mean by "sin," except doing something useful. The confessional does the same thing as the shrink, rather more quickly and cheaper. Three "Hail Mary"s, and you're out. But I've never been the kind of religious person that thinks saying "Hail Mary" is gonna get me out of it.

HJ: The concept of sin is a difficult one for me, because it implies something other than our animal, material existence. I think we just have impulses, good ones and bad ones.

OW: Yes. But those impulses are *controlled* by us. I believe in free will. I believe that we are the masters of our fate.

HJ: But that means you do believe in some kind of a plan.

OW: That's right. You see, I'm religious, but you don't need God and his angels to feel that way. "The fault, dear Brutus, lies not in our stars, but in ourselves."

HJ: Well, we have the appearance of free will. But—

OW: It's real. With my history, why shouldn't I become a drunk, and a pathetic figure sitting around Hollywood, if there isn't such a thing as free will?

HJ: Because of, well, chemical balances, which are predetermined.

OW: If they are *truly* predetermined, you're more religious than I am. You're a fatalist. Every moment of life is a choice. I don't think it is possible to live a moral and civil life unless we accept the possibility of choice.

HJ: That I have never understood. Why do you need the belief in choice? Morality comes from your understanding of what is good.

I know it's good to help people. I know it's wrong to hurt other people. I don't need to believe that I have free will in order to be a decent human being.

OW: You think our lives are just ruled by chance? You think that if you want to make this movie and not that one, it's because of a series of chemical imbalances?

HJ: You're reducing it. I'm saying that I think that we are all the product of a long, long history of genetic construction that—

OW: But none of that eliminates free will.

HJ: Whether you get struck by lightning or not is—has nothing to do with your free will.

OW: Free will doesn't mean I can stop the lightning. Free will simply means that I can decide whether I'm going to go to Africa or not! It's demeaning if you think it's all a chemical accident.

There can be nothing more sterile than an extended conversation between two people who basically agree. If we basically disagreed we'd be getting somewhere.

(Waiter arrives.)

OW: I'd like a café espresso.

W: *Décaféiné?*

OW: *Oui, décaféiné—oui.*

HJ: And I would like a cup . . . uh . . .

W: Café au lait.

HJ: Café au lait. Please. With a little steamed milk on the side, as well. Thank you. *(To OW)* Um . . . do you want some berries?

OW: *(To Kiki)* Do you want a little sweet?

Oh, the irony of these kinds of conversations is that they end with: "Do you want some berries?"

HJ: I'm just not clear about why I am so good at doing nothing for those less fortunate than I. I guess it's because if I did anything, it would be a total commitment. And that would make my life something else.

OW: You see, I'm very clear. I have people whose lives depend on me. If I became some kind of fucking secular saint, I would strew misery among all the people who are close to me. Is the cry of the starving child in Africa louder than the people near me, who depend on me? That's an interesting moral question.

HJ: I've been involved in a lot of political things, and I tend to meet people who are fully involved. And I always find them very neurotic, disturbed . . .

OW: Politics is *always* corrupting. Even saints in politics. The political world, in itself, is corrupt. You're not going to satisfy that urge to spiritual perfection in *any* political movement without being betrayed and without betraying others. Only service, direct service, say, helping a lot of starving kids in a Third World country, is impeccable."

HJ: I should feel guiltier than I do.

OW: Guilt is an entirely masculine invention. No female has guilt. And that's why the Bible is so true!

HJ: How can you say that? The Bible was written by men!

OW: Yeah, I know. But the Garden of Eden story is such a perfect embodiment of the fact that—who feels guilty? Adam!

HJ: Yeah. But the men who wrote the Bible make Eve give him the apple.

OW: Sure. But she doesn't mind it!

HJ: Because it's a male's idea of a female.

OW: No, I think it's true. I think guilt is a vice, to a large extent, and I think it is a typically masculine vice. You may find it in women, but rarely. If you were religious, your absence of guilt would be a crippling thing.

5. "Such a good Catholic that I wanted to kick her."

In which Orson remembers entertaining the troops with Marlene Dietrich, explains why he detested Irene Dunne, and why movie-going in the thirties was like watching television today.

HENRY JAGLOM: You toured for the USO during the war? With Marlene?

ORSON WELLES: Yeah. I said, "Why don't we have you do a song? And she said, "Oh, I'll play my musical saw." "Play what, Marlene?" "My musical saw." I said, "Well, all right."

HJ: She knew how to play the saw?

OW: Very well. It was the funniest thing. And she didn't do it to be funny. Toward the end of the war, I went to the South Pacific, and she went to Europe. She felt so lost being alone—"How can I go on without you?" and so on—so she began to sing, and that's how her cabaret act was born. Though she never sang with me.

HJ: And is it true that she's gained so much weight that she won't let anybody see her now?

OW: No, she won't. Not even her close friends. She makes dates to see people and breaks them. I made six trips to Paris to see her, and ended up talking to her from a phone booth. Every time she said she was ill. Once she said she had typhus!

HJ: Oh, so she probably plans and prepares—

OW: And then looks at herself and feels terrible. I'm sure Max Schell will never speak to me again. I'm going to have him as an enemy forever. He's doing a documentary about Marlene, and he has got all this audio of her on tape. But, then, when it came time to photograph her, she stalled and finally refused. So he built a set of her apartment in Paris. It's all about him—the director—in an empty apartment, with her voice piped in. And then I'm supposed to come as some kind of apparition—I think in double exposure. Well, when I heard that, I suddenly got awfully busy in another movie, you know? I sent word to him that I had a job that was too good to turn down, and I couldn't do this three-day appearance. He'll know that I was just pretending. But this movie can't be any good. It's a terrible idea for a picture. I admire him very much. But he's making a big mistake. It's not like him to be that nutty.

HJ: I like Schell as a filmmaker. Serious, you know? Very serious.

OW: Too serious. Too Swiss. He's a Swiss. He's not a Kraut. He and Yul Brynner are the two leading Swiss actors. Yul Brynner, however, seems to have—let's say—gone out to the Caucasus for a few years after leaving Zurich.

HJ: You mean all those biographies where he was supposed to have been born on—

OW: The steppes. Half gypsy, half Mongol! He had too much to drink on this long trip he took with me through the snow in Yugoslavia, and late one night he blurted out that his hometown was Brenner near Zurich, where everybody's name is Brenner. And he should never have said that, because there goes the whole story.

HJ: He only created one character, but he did it absolutely wonderfully. *The King and I.* I can't get over the fact you were offered the role in the earlier version, *Anna and the King of Siam*, instead of Rex Harrison.

OW: That's why he got it. Because I suggested him. Rex made pictures that only played in England, teacup comedies and things. The studio people had never heard of him. Sitting in the steam room at Twentieth? Rex Harrison, who's that?

HJ: Did you, by any chance, see *The Kingfisher* on cable, with him?

OW: Where he looks as though he's been on cortisone for eight years.

HJ: What was your reason for being so sure you didn't want to do *Anna and the King of Siam*?

OW: Because I couldn't stand Irene Dunne, who had already been cast. That's why I turned down *Gaslight*, too. She was going to do it. And then after I turned it down, they got Bergman and I was out. Irene Dunne. Dumb. Dumb, dumb.

HJ: Why did you have this terrible antipathy toward Dunne?

OW: You must stop trying to figure out why I have antipathies. Don't waste our time.

HJ: You mean just accept them?

OW: Yeah. That's right. Yeah. Irene Dunne was so dry-toothed and such a good fucking Catholic that I wanted to kick her in the crotch. Such a goody-goody. And she was always heading the censorship groups, and all that. Conservative, in a terrible Catholic-Christian way that I found peculiarly offensive. To me, she was the nonsinging Jeanette MacDonald, you know. And I hated her as an actress. She was so ladylike that I knew there wouldn't be any electricity between us.

HJ: Irene was in *A Guy Named Joe* with Spencer Tracy and Van Johnson. What do you think of Van Johnson?

OW: Well, I was responsible for his coming to Hollywood. I never told him that, so he doesn't know. He was a chorus boy in *Pal Joey*, and he was such a terrific personality I sent a wire to George Schaefer at RKO and said, "Get this guy Van Johnson," and they sent for him. They didn't like him, and didn't use him. And then he went to MGM and—

HJ: He wasn't a great actor or anything.

OW: Pitiable now. Most men get better looking when they get old. He's a kind of queen that doesn't. He had to be young to be attractive.

HJ: His movies are terrible.

OW: Oja [Kodar] won't go to the movies with me; she says that if I stay, I'm making groans, these awful noises.

HJ: Sitting in front of the television you don't have that experience?

OW: No. Total idiot. Other people want to switch channels. I don't. I'd much rather see junk on the TV than bad movies because bad movies stay with me for too long. And if they get a little good, then they're gonna haunt me. And who needs to be haunted?

HJ: Warren Beatty was just saying that TV has changed movies, because for most of us, once you're in a movie theater, you commit, whether you like it or not. You want to see what they've done, while at home . . .

OW: I'm the opposite. It's a question of age. In my real movie-going days, which were the thirties, you didn't stand in line. You strolled down the street and sallied into the theater at any hour of the day or night. Like you'd go in to have a drink at a bar. Every movie theater was partially empty. We never asked what time the movie began. We used to go after we went to the theater. We'd go down to the Paramount where they had a double bill, and see the B picture, and go to laugh at bad acting in the Bs. You know, childish, stupid things. There was an actor called J. Carrol Naish. Anything he did, we'd laugh at. I didn't like the screwball comedies, at all, with the exception of Carole Lombard. Anything with her—that was fine.

HJ: You didn't feel you had to see a movie from the start?

OW: No. We'd leave when we'd realize, "This is where we came in." Everybody said that. I loved movies for that reason. They didn't cost that much, so if you didn't like one, it was, "Let's do something else.

Go to another movie." And that's what made it habitual to such an extent that walking out of a movie was what for people now is like turning off the television set. Oja and I do it still. Last time we were in Paris, we saw five movies, one or two reels of each one.

HJ: There was entertainment between the features in those days?

OW: Sure. There was Kate Smith and travelogues and the newsreel and an *Our Gang* comedy, you know.

HJ: So, for people like you, it's very important that filmmakers grab you in the first reel. The first ten to twenty minutes.

OW: If not, I'm up the aisle.

HJ: Up and out. No slow and leisurely getting into it, no misdirections?

OW: No. If you stand in line, of course, you want to see what you were standing in line for. But in those days, we only ever committed like that for Sinatra when he was singing at the Paramount. No movie ever had that kind of business. The truth is, I was not very fond of the movies of the late thirties, the few years just before I went to Hollywood. The so-called "Golden Age."

HJ: I'm reading Budd Schulberg's autobiography, called *Moving Pictures*. It introduced me to the world of silent movies that I didn't know anything about.

OW: I'd rather not read it. I don't read books on film at all, or theater. I'm not very interested in movies. I keep telling people that, and they don't believe me. I *genuinely* am not very interested! For me, it's only interesting to do. You know, I'm not interested in other filmmakers—and that's a terribly arrogant thing to say—or in the medium. It's the least interesting art medium for me to watch that there is. Except ballet—that's the only thing less interesting. I just like to *make* movies, you know? And that's the truth!

But I do know quite a bit about early movies, because I was interested in movies before I made them. And I was interested in the theater before I went into it. There is something in me that turns off once I start to do it myself. It's some weakness. In other words, I read *everything* about the theater before I became a theater director. After that, I never went to plays or read anything. Same thing with movies. I believe that I was threatened, personally threatened, by every other movie, and by every criticism—that it would affect the purity of my vision. And I think the younger generation of filmmakers has seen too many movies.

6. "Nobody even glanced at Marilyn."

In which Orson greets Swifty Lazar, remembers dating Marilyn Monroe when she was just another pretty face and failing to interest Zanuck in her career, even though the mogul's weakness for starlets nearly wrecked his.

———————

(Swifty Lazar enters.)

SWIFTY LAZAR: Just wanted to say, "Hello."

ORSON WELLES: You look wonderful.

SL: I feel good. I'm good. Orson, see you Wednesday. You take care of yourself.

OW: What, do you think I look badly?

SL: No, you look great.

(Lazar exits.)

OW: I don't like people to say, "Take care of yourself." He hasn't changed in thirty years. Lives in a hotel. Orders a whole lot of towels, and when he goes from the bathroom to his bed, he lays down a path of towels.

HENRY JAGLOM: So he doesn't have to walk on the carpets? He's that nuts about germs?

OW: Yes.

HJ: And what if he wants to go to the closet?

OW: Then he'll make another path. I've seen it. With my own eyes.

HJ: What does he think he'll get through his feet?

OW: Hookworm. From the Ritz, you know? Mania.

HJ: I was going to ask you about Zanuck when Swifty interrupted us. What did you think of his movies when he headed Fox?

OW: He was the greatest editor who ever lived. But only for his kind of pictures. In other words, he was at a loss if a picture got too good. But he could save any standard picture. He would automatically make it better. He was awfully good making the corniest pictures—which I didn't like, for the most part. I think the musicals were awful. But if he knew he had an art film on his hands, he left it alone. Including pictures we don't think are art films, like what is that hanging picture? The western that was considered very high art at the time.

HJ: Henry Fonda?

OW: Yeah. And a lot of other good actors, standing around kind of projecting gloom. The lynching. *The Ox-Bow Incident*!

HJ: Did Fox make any good pictures during that period?

OW: Yes. A few. A very few. They made *How Green Was My Valley*.

HJ: What was he like?

OW: Zanuck was a great polo player. When I first came out here, he was using the old polo grounds by the Palisades. It was funny, the head of the studio playing polo. I had the usual New York sneer. You know that for years, on the drive to work and back, he had a French teacher with him? Imagine a movie head wanting to learn something!

HJ: Why, if Zanuck had that quality as a human being, was that not reflected in the films?

OW: Because he wanted to be a successful head of a studio, and he was. Until he fell in love with that terrible Juliette Gréco. I made two pictures with her.

HJ: That *Crack in the Mirror* picture.

OW: And another one, that I've forgotten. He lost everything over her, his power, left his wife—everything.

HJ: For Juliette Gréco?

OW: To serve her. He'd take her little dog and walk it around the lot while we were shooting. So help me, it was awful. I don't believe a director should ever fall in love with his leading lady. Or at least show it.

HJ: He had Marilyn Monroe under contract, didn't he?

OW: She was a girlfriend of mine. I used to take her to parties before she was a star.

HJ: I didn't know that!

OW: I wanted to try and promote her career. Nobody even glanced at Marilyn. You'd see these beautiful girls, the most chic girls in town, who spent a fortune at the beauty parlor and on their clothes, and everybody said, "Darling, you're looking wonderful!" And then they'd ignore them. The men, not the women. The men would gather in the corner and start telling jokes or talking deals. The only time they talked about the girls was to say whether they scored with them the night before. I would point Marilyn out to Darryl, and say, "What a sensational girl." He would answer, "She's just another stock player. We've got a hundred of them. Stop trying to push these cunts on me. We've got her on for $125 a week." And then, about six months later, Darryl was paying Marilyn $400,000, and the men were looking at her—because some stamp had been put on her.

HJ: God, that's amazing.

OW: Then Darryl disappeared to Europe with Juliette Gréco. We thought we'd never hear from him again.

HJ: When I arrived, in the mid-sixties, in the later part of his career, he was trying to put together a big war movie in Paris, *The Longest Day*.

OW: Twentieth was in terrible trouble.

HJ: With *Cleopatra*.

OW: He heard about it, so he rolled up his sleeves and made *The Longest Day*, which got them out from under—like that, you see. It made a fortune, and brought him back as president of Fox, because he had become a figure of fun, you see. Then his son and another group maneuvered him out.

HJ: Richard Zanuck maneuvered him out? Richard, who's partnered with David Brown?

OW: Yeah. He was the front man for those who were trying to get rid of him.

HJ: His own son? Not Jewish, in other words. It's not like Jews to—

OW: Zanuck? Everybody thought Darryl was Jewish, because Zanuck is sort of a foreign name. He was Christian. The only Christian head of a studio.

HJ: Except for his boss, [Spyros] Skouras.

OW: If you could call him Christian. He's Greek Orthodox. Twentieth was the only Christian studio. It was the worst studio in town. Yes. Zanuck is Czech, from Nebraska. He had begun his career by publishing, at his own cost, a novel. And putting it on the desks of the various producers. At nineteen he became the white-haired boy by writing the Rin Tin Tin movies, which, of course, made a fortune.

HJ: Isn't *Jane Eyre* a Zanuck movie? I watched it last night. You put on a nose for *Jane Eyre*.

OW: Yes.

HJ: Why?

OW: Because I was so baby-faced. I looked sixteen years old. How was I gonna be Mr. Rochester with this baby face? I had a nose in *Kane*. Then we made it longer as I got older. Noses do get longer.

HJ: I didn't like the acting at all.

OW: What acting?

HJ: In *Jane Eyre*.

OW: My acting?

HJ: No, I like your acting immensely.

OW: Oh, her. Joan Fontaine. No, she's no good in it. She's just a plain old bad actor. She's got four readings, and two expressions, and that's it. And she was busy being the humble governess—so fucking humble. Which is a great mistake. Because she's supposed to be a proud little woman who, in spite of her position, stands up for herself. That's why she interests this bastard of a man.

HJ: I guess that's the thing that I always have trouble with in the film, that she looks so mousy and unappealing. And I can't understand why she appeals to him.

OW: You should get the feeling that this mouse roars, but you don't. The trick of the story is that she is, by virtue of the nature of society as it was then, doomed to a position of total servility. But because of her tremendous independence of spirit, she causes the man to become interested in her. Even though she's not a beauty. It's her *character* that makes the impression on him. And that's why he loves her, finally.

HJ: What you see is an actress trying to play not a beauty.

OW: Yeah, that's all you see. The whole point of the story is ruined by that. Because you're supposed to see that the visiting lady— what's her name?—is the great beauty. And that's the sort of pearl that he ought to have, and all that. And here is this girl who not only is in a position of being a mere hired servant, but she's not even a beauty. But she finally commands this man's whole life. Because of her character. Standing up for herself. Being a fierce little girl. And that isn't the movie at all! It isn't even indicated. Nobody told her that, you know.

HJ: Neither she nor her sister Olivia de Havilland could act. I never understood their careers.

OW: Yes, you do. There are always jobs for pretty girls who speak semi-educated English. I don't think either one of 'em is worth much—

HJ: I understand their careers, but I don't understand how some people hold them in such high regard.

OW: There are a lot of bad actors.

HJ: It's like Merle Oberon is another one for me.

OW: Yeah. But very beautiful. She was mainly wonderful in one movie, but wonderful because she was not asked to do any acting. It was a very strange French movie. She played a Japanese—before she ever came to Hollywood. I've forgotten what it was called. *Sayonara 1*, or something. Now there's a bad picture for you—*Sayonara 2*.

HJ: Poor Marlon.

OW: Anybody who was trapped in that movie would have been at a loss. Yet, he got an Academy Award for it. That shows you where we were then. The picture was, on every level, an abomination. It looked like a musical that didn't have any numbers in it. The Orient is the graveyard of American directors. The only really bad [Frank] Capra picture I've ever seen is this *Shangri-La*. It's terrible—terrible. Absurd! I screamed with laughter! Shangri-La, where they were kept, was this sort of Oriental country club. Still, I was a great Capra fan.

HJ: *It's a Wonderful Life.* You want to hate it, but—

OW: Well, yes—hokey. It is sheer Norman Rockwell, from the beginning to the end. But you cannot resist it! There's no way of hating that movie.

7. "*The Blue Angel* is a big piece of shlock."

In which Orson mocks the excesses of *auteurism*, and Peter Bogdanovich in particular for falling at the feet of studio directors such as Howard Hawks. He recounts his adventures with the kings and queens of the Bs, who churned out bottom-of-the bill fillers.

ORSON WELLES: I'm going on ABC-TV this afternoon. Just before the Oscars. That's why I'm made up. Myself and Peter Bogdanovich. And Hal Roach. I suggested Hal Roach. Because I saw him on TV the other night. He's eighty-six, but he still makes great sense! He's cute as hell. They wanted Capra, and I said, "Capra may be the best living director, but he's the worst living guest. He'll talk about how beautiful America is, and so on. Forget him—get Hal Roach!" They'd already gotten Bogdanovich, and they were angling for Francis Ford [Coppola]. I said, "You have too many people—I don't really want to go. You won't have any time for any of us to say anything. All you'll get is Bogdanovich."

HENRY JAGLOM: So Bogdanovich is gonna be on this show today.

OW: He's good on TV.

HJ: Yeah, but he antagonizes a lot of people. Cynical.

OW: That makes me look better. Always nice to have a heavy man.

HJ: When I first met Bogdanovich—

OW: You thought he was nuts.

HJ: He was always finding great virtues in all of those studio directors.

OW: Unwatchable.

HJ: What's the name of that stupid director?

OW: Sam Fuller. Peter gets furious with me for not expressing enthusiasm for Fuller. Fritz Lang, you know? He thinks is great. Lang, whose mother was Jewish, told me that Goebbels, who was trying to get him to head up the Nazi movie industry, offered to make him an honorary Aryan, of which there were only a handful. Lang said, "But I'm Jewish," and Goebbels replied, "*I* decide who is Jewish!" *That* was when Lang knew it was time to leave Germany. What were we talking about? Peter also thinks von Sternberg is great. Von Sternberg never made a good picture.

HJ: What about *The Blue Angel*?

OW: It's a big piece of shlock. Painted on velvet. Like you buy in Honolulu. Peter stopped talking to me for several days when I said von Sternberg was no good. Then Hawks, Howard Hawks. The so-called greatest ever. Hawks is number one, and all the rest ate the scraps from his table.

HJ: Yeah. Yeah, *Bringing Up Baby*.

OW: Yes, the greatest picture ever made. I recently saw what I've always been told was Jack [Ford's] greatest movie, and it's terrible. *The Searchers*. He made many very bad pictures.

HJ: You're talking about *The Horse Soldiers* and stupid *Sergeant Rutledge*.

OW: I was in Peter's house one night, and he ran some John Ford picture. During the first reel I said, "Isn't it funny how incapable even Ford—and all American directors are—of making women look in period? You can always tell which decade a costume picture was made in—the twenties, the thirties, the forties, or the fifties— even if it's supposed to be in the seventeenth century." I said, "Look at those two girls who are supposed to be out in the covered wagon."

Their hairdos and their costumes are really what the actresses in the fifties thought was good taste. Otherwise, they're gonna say, "I can't come out in this." Peter flew into a rage, turned off the projector, and wouldn't let us see the rest of the movie because I didn't have enough respect for Ford. But Jack made some of the best ever.

HJ: When I first met Bogdanovich, I was very snide about John Ford movies. I made fun of them. When I grew up, I realized that they were perfectly good. Say hello to Peter if you see him. Is that book on Dorothy Stratten ever gonna come out?

OW: I have a terrible fear that it'll be a runaway best seller. Really, I have a dread! He'll behave so badly. He'll become such a pompous ass again. Right after *The Last Picture Show* he came out to Arizona to play his part in *The Other Side of the Wind*—and sat for five hours at the table talking to me, with his back turned to [my cinematographer] Gary Graver, whom he knew very well. He never said hello or goodbye to him. You want to know about your friend Peter?"

HJ: He was your friend, too.

OW: You know when vaudeville died, and all the great vaudeville performers—the comics, the singers—were thrown out of work. They couldn't make the move to radio or film. They used to huddle around these barrels in Times Square, where they made fires, and ate roasted potatoes off sticks. Then television arrived, and the TV producers came looking for these guys to use them in their variety shows. One of them was the biggest star of vaudeville. While he was on top, he treated everybody like shit. So when the bad times came, they wouldn't share their fires with him, or their food. But gradually they started to feel sorry for him. Years passed. They all forgave him. Now, the *Ed Sullivan Show* is going to do the best of vaudeville, at the Palace Theater. This guy gets a plum part. He tells all his friends, who didn't get chosen, "Guys, I just got lucky. I'll never forget you. You can't imagine what you mean to me; you've saved my life; here are some tickets, front row; come backstage afterwards; we'll go out for drinks, celebrate. I've learned my lesson." The show goes on, this guy is sensational, he's going to be a big TV star now. All his friends come backstage, knock on the door. He comes out in a velvet robe, says, "Fellas, I've got that old shitty feeling coming over me again." And he slams the door in their faces. That's Peter.

HJ: Nonetheless, say hello for me.

OW: Yeah—if I get a chance to say anything.

HJ: You'll have a few moments before, in the dressing room.

OW: Oh, but by then he'll be telling me about himself, you know. He knows that I'll listen to it all.

HJ: By the way, before I forget, I got your contract for *Two of a Kind.* John Travolta and Olivia Newton-John are set, along with your favorite, Oliver Reed, playing the devil. They want you for the voice of God, for two consecutive days. I love playing your agent. They said to me originally, "What kind of price do you think would be right?" I said, "If he does it at all, it's because he's interested in the work. The money is not what he would do it for. But, of course, you can't make it an insulting offer." And they said, "Well, we were thinking ten, fifteen . . ." I said, "Really. For the voice of *God?* Maybe you should get somebody else. I don't even want to submit that to him. I don't think it's fair. Why don't you round it out at $25,000." And they did. Now I have this agent's fantasy, which is: Could I have gone to thirty-five?

OW: Well, I once had a radio director get mad at me. Sent me a wire saying, "When I want God, I'll call heaven!"

HJ: What is it with Oliver Reed, that you like him so much? Weren't you stuck in Greece with him on some B movies?

OW: A movie, for which the money never arrived. It was a Harry Alan Towers production. 1974. Harry Alan Towers is a famous crook.

HJ: He's the guy who was charged with running a vice ring out of a New York hotel in the sixties, and also of being a Soviet agent!

OW: I worked for him for years. He always took the money and ran. He once fled Tehran, leaving a mountain of unpaid bills. When we made *Ten Little Indians*, Towers stuck Oliver Reed with the hotel bill. Oliver went down to the nightclub at the Hilton, which was in the basement, and broke it up. All the mirrors, chandeliers; wrecked the whole place. Destroyed the whole nightclub. Everyone was in such awe of the violence that they all just stood back in horror, including the police. And he just walked out—and went to the airport. Nobody ever laid a hand on him! I admire him greatly!

Then there were the Salkinds, who produced *The Trial*, that I directed. I ended up paying the actors out of my own pocket to stop them from walking off the set all the time. About seventy thousand bucks.

HJ: The Salkinds? I assume this was way before they made *Superman*?

OW: Yeah. Oh, they were broke, they had nothing. To this day, I can never go to the Meurice, in Paris. I can't go to Zagreb because the Salkinds never paid my hotel bill for *The Trial*. I was in Belgrade, making a terrible version of *Marco the Magnificent* with Tony Webb—a whole lot of tatterdemalion actors of that sort. There was a big snowstorm. And word came that the manager of the Esplanade Hotel in Zagreb was on his way to Belgrade to get me for my hotel bill on *The Trial*. But he was stuck in the snow. And I managed to finish the picture and fly out before he arrived!

HJ: You'd think, after *Superman*, they could retroactively take care of these things.

OW: Not for a minute. Not for a minute. And when they did those all-star *Three Musketeers*, I was the only star from *The Trial* not in those. They could've given me a job, at least, for all the money I'd put into *The Trial*.

This kind of thing happened to me all the time. My Spanish producer never paid my hotel bill for the three months that he kept me waiting in Madrid for the money for *The Other Side of the Wind*. So I'm scared to death to be in Madrid. I know they're going to come after me with that bill.

HJ: Why do they go after actors? You'd think it would be good for business to have them stay at their hotels.

OW: Actually, actors are rather well thought of in Spain. Particularly in the theater. Although, how theater actors manage to get along in Spain I don't know, because they do two shows a night. Same thing in a lot of Latin American countries, still—two shows a night. I had a friend who was the last really great illusionist, whose stage name was Fu Manchu. His real name was Bamberg, and he came from seven generations of great magicians. Born in Brooklyn, played a Chinese magician, with a Chinese accent in Spanish, you know? He had to finish a movie he was making. And he said, "I've got this show. And if I close it, I'll never get it open again with any business. Will you do it? What'll you take?" And I said, "I'll do it for free." So for a week I did his show, while he finished his movie, but there were two performances a night. And at the end of that week, I didn't know how I—or he—lived through it. He died at seventy-five last year. His father, who worked silently, was a famous magician called Okito, and played as a Japanese.

HJ: All these Jews from Brooklyn playing Japanese and Chinese!

OW: Dutchmen—Dutch Jews. The father was born in Holland, and a great variety-hall star. And he had the most ter—

HJ: *(Calls out)* Excuse me! Waiter! Can I talk to you?

WAITER: Talk to me, monsieur.

HJ: Uh, you gave me cold chicken. And I wanted warm chicken salad, like it's advertised—and it's cold chicken. The plate is very good and hot—the plate is excellent. If I were eating the plate, I would have been happy. But the chicken—

OW: Terrible thing happened to him. Whenever I have any trouble professionally, I remember Okito, 'cause I know that I will never be in the trouble he was in. He and his father and his grandfather had all been magicians to the court of Holland. And he was playing a show for the King and Queen of Holland, as well as the visiting King and Queen of Denmark. And his opening trick was producing a large bowl of water from a cloth—no, a large duck from a cloth. To complicate the story, even though he worked under the name of Okito, he wore Chinese clothes.

And he had that Chinese robe that's open here, and the duck was between his legs, in a sack. And on this occasion, the duck got its head out of the sack and grabbed him by his jewels. A death grip. Just as he made his entrance. Now that is what I call being in trouble. He said, "I did a lot of jumping around. I acted like a sort of crazy Chinaman."

(To waiter) He's looking for capers in his chicken salad.

HJ: To make sure that they gave me the right—

OW: He looks like a customs inspector. Is there a caper in it?

HJ: It's the exact same as when they had the capers in and took them out. After all this discussion, there is the same taste of caper. Here are capers. They lied to me.

OW: Don't get tiresome about the chicken salad.

HJ: Why am I being tiresome, Orson? I want to get it the way it always is, without the capers. The waiter doesn't understand.

OW: This is the way this chef makes it now.

HJ: They keep writing in the papers that, ever since Wolfgang left, this place has gone downhill. And his restaurant, in turn, has become the number-one one. He's begging me to get you to come to it.

OW: I'll never go.

HJ: Why?

OW: I don't like Wolfgang. He's a little shit. I think he's a terrible little man.

HJ: Why?

OW: I don't know. God made him that way. What do you mean, "Why"?

HJ: Well, I mean, what makes him terrible?

OW: I don't need to explain that. It's a free country. Anybody who sits down at my table without being invited is a shit.

HJ: Wolf did that?

OW: Yes.

HJ: You wouldn't want to call him just "informal," rather than "a shit"?

OW: What?

HJ: You wouldn't want to refer to that as informality, rather than being a shit?

OW: No. Shitty, shitty. A self-promoting little shit. And I'm very sorry he has all this success, because I'm very fond of Patrick. And I wouldn't do that to him.

HJ: What is wrong with your *moules*?

OW: It's not what I had yesterday.

HJ: You want to try to explain this to the waiter?

OW: No, no, no. One complaint per table is all, unless you want them to spit in the food. Let me tell you a story about George Jean Nathan, America's great drama critic. George Jean Nathan was the tightest man who ever lived, even tighter than Charles Chaplin. And he lived for forty years in the Hotel Royalton, which is across from the Algonquin. He fancied himself a great bon vivant— ladies' man and everything. I heard him say to a girl—as he was dancing by me in the old Cub Room at the Stork Club a thousand years ago—after she laughed at something he said, "I can be just as funny in German and French." And away he went, you know? He never tipped anybody in the Royalton, not even when they brought the breakfast, and not at Christmastime. After about ten years of never getting tipped, the room-service waiter peed slightly in his tea. *Everybody* in New York knew it but him. The waiters hurried across the street and told the waiters at Algonquin, who were waiting to see when it would finally dawn on him what he was drinking! And as the years went by, there got to be more and more urine and less and less tea. And it was a great pleasure for us in the theater to look at a leading critic and *know* that he was full of piss. And I, with my own ears, heard him at the 21 complaining to a waiter, saying, "Why can't I get tea here as good as it is at The Royalton?" That's when I fell on the floor, you know.

It'd be a wonderful thing to tell somebody you hated, when it isn't true. To say, "Don't you know that the waiters are doing that to your tea?" Then you don't have to even do it! You could drive a man mad! A real Iago thing to do. Better than the handkerchief, you know. I've remembered it, probably, because he was no admirer of mine. He was very anxious for you to know that he'd seen everything ever done in Europe. So whatever I did was done better in Prague in 1929. Those kinds of notices. It probably was better, but he was showing off, too.

8. "*Kane* is a comedy."

In which Orson speculates on why Jean-Paul Sartre disliked *Kane* and snubbed him, remarks on the great number of novelists who wrote film reviews, and recalls that he got his best notice from John O'Hara.

HENRY JAGLOM: I just saw a Renoir film I had never seen. I don't understand why there is such unevenness to the work of—

ORSON WELLES: He actually made bad movies.

HJ: It was a sweet little film, but terribly acted, called *The River.*

OW: Very bad picture. It's considered one of the great monuments of film. Greatly overpraised. When he isn't on pitch, Renoir comes off as an amateur. It's always mystified me. I have nothing to explain it. I don't talk about it, because it just irritates people.

HJ: What do you feel about *Grand Illusion?*

OW: Probably one of the three or four best ever. I burst into tears at *Grand Illusion* every time. When they stand up and sing "The Marseillaise." And [Pierre] Fresnay is so wonderful—all the performances are divine.

HJ: What about *Rules of the Game?*

OW: I love it, too—but, to me, it's a lesser work, by just a tiny bit. I think *Rules of the Game* is a better picture. It's like listening to Mozart. Nothing can be better than that. But I don't like the love story. And *Grand Illusion* just simply grabs me.

HJ: Did the French know about *Kane*?

OW: I thought it had been a big success in Paris. When I arrived there, I found that it had not been. They didn't know who I was. They didn't know about the Mercury Theatre, my troupe, which I thought they would, because I knew about their theater. And I was snubbed terribly by them. *Kane* only got to be a famous picture later. And then a lot of people really hated it. Americans got it, but not Europe. The first thing they heard about it was the violent attack by Jean-Paul Sartre. Wrote a long piece, forty thousand words on it or something.

HJ: Well, maybe it politically offended him in some way.

OW: No. I think it was because, basically, *Kane* is a comedy.

HJ: It is?

OW: Sure. In the classic sense of the word. Not a fall-in-the-aisles laughing comedy, but because the tragic trappings are parodied.

HJ: I never thought of *Kane* as a comedy. It's profoundly moving.

OW: It's moving, but so can comedies be moving. There is a slight camp to all the great Xanadu business. And Sartre, who has no sense of humor, couldn't react to it at all.

HJ: Was that really why?

OW: When he wasn't being a German philosopher, which he was good at—late Heidegger—most of what he wrote as a critic of the modern scene, political or otherwise, was full of shit.

HJ: And as a playwright he wasn't very hot, either.

OW: Very overrated. But he was such a god at that time. My friends forbade me to go into the Café Philippe, where he used to hang out. They said it would be unpleasant. "Go across the street to Le Dôme, where your people are, the Americans."

Years later, I was visiting Dubrovnik with one of my dearest friends in the world, Vladimir Dedijer, who was the number-three man to Tito during World War II. At that moment in the Vietnam

War, a group in Europe headed by Sartre, Bertrand Russell, and Vladimir Dedijer had formed a committee to bring the Americans to trial for war crimes. The three of them were there for a high-level meeting before going to Paris. As we approached, Dedijer and I saw Sartre and Russell sitting in a café. Dedijer said to me, "Don't go any closer." He was one of those fuck-you kind of fellows, who could have just as easily have said, "Come on, Sartre, don't be an asshole, you're gonna like Orson." But no, he says, "Don't go any closer." It was strange. I never understood it. As though Sartre was going to take off his kid glove and slap me, invite me to a duel. This wasn't 1890, you know. You can't imagine Sartre challenging anybody to a duel.

HJ: Sartre was profoundly anti-American. I wonder what the roots of that were.

OW: Well, most Frenchmen are, especially the brighter ones, so his was more carefully worked out. He thought up a lot of reasons.

HJ: Did you ever know Simone de Beauvoir?

OW: No, I never met her. How could I? We would have had to meet in secrecy.

HJ: Maybe that's the reason. That would have been the way to get even. Maybe she saw the movie, loved it, loved you, and said something like, "I think he's very attractive."

OW: Like Peter Sellers. That was the reason I could never act on the same set together with what's-her-name, that pinup he was married to, Britt Ekland, during *Casino Royale*. Because she apparently said, "Look at that Orson. That's the sexiest man I've ever seen." And someone told him.

HJ: What did they think of *Kane* in England?

OW: It was not gigantically big in England. Auden didn't like it. Nor *Ambersons*.

Some people called it warmed-over Borges, and attacked it. I always knew that Borges himself hadn't liked it. He said that it was pedantic, which is a very strange thing to say about it, and that it was a labyrinth. And that the worst thing about a labyrinth is when there's no way out. And this is a labyrinth of a movie with no way out. Borges is half-blind. Never forget that. But you know, I could take it that he and Sartre simply hated *Kane*. In their minds, they were seeing—and attacking—something else. It's them, not my work. I'm more upset by the regular, average, just-plain critics.

HJ: How did you feel about James Agee?

OW: He didn't like me. He and Dwight Macdonald, who just died.

HJ: Didn't Agee write a negative review of *Citizen Kane*?

OW: Yeah.

HJ: Why did he dislike it?

OW: I don't know. Who cares? I don't want to go into it, you know. He didn't attack it. He just didn't like it. Do you know who Indio Fernández was?

HJ: He was the guy who posed naked for the Oscar statuette?

OW: Yes. He was the only Mexican director worth anything. While cutting a movie, he once sent an invitation to the critics to see a rough cut. Told them, "Why should I only hear what you people have to say after it's too late to do anything about it? Come to the rough cut and tell me what you think, while there's still time for me to do something about it, to improve the film." So Indio Fernández ran his rough cut for the critics. Asked them afterwards to tell him what they thought. They all liked it except one critic. This guy stood up, said, "It's no good." So Indio Fernández pulled out a gun and shot the critic.

HJ: I can understand that.

OW: For a couple of years after *Kane*, every time I walked in the streets in New York they shouted at me, "Hey! What the hell is that movie of yours about? What does it mean?" Not, "What is Rosebud?" but always "what does it mean?" The Archie Bunkers. It was

[Michelangelo] Antonioni to them. All those mixtures of things—
"What kind of thing is that?" Nobody says that now. Everybody
understands.

I told you about John O'Hara's review of *Kane*? In *Newsweek*.
He was the movie critic. You'd be amazed how many novelists
wanted to be movie critics. Graham Greene was a movie critic for
about six years. His reviews were not very good. They were neither
witty, amusing, nor original. They were just intelligent, plain, ordinary reviews. If you're going to be an interesting critic, you've got
to have a little zing. It's all right to be wrong, but you've got to be
interesting. We're all in the same business. We're entertaining the
public.

HJ: What about O'Hara?

OW: He wrote the greatest review that anybody ever had. He said,
"This is not only the best picture that has ever been made, it is the
best picture that will ever be made."

HJ: What do you do after that?

OW: Nothing. I should've retired.

9. "There's no such thing as a friendly biographer."

In which Orson says he doesn't want to know about the lives of his favorite writers. He mourns *F for Fake*, denies he tried to steal sole writing credit for *Kane* from Herman J. Mankiewicz, as Pauline Kael said he did, and speculates about his parentage and progeny.

HENRY JAGLOM: Orson, there's a wonderful writer, Barbara Leaming, who has written a book about Roman Polanski, among other people, who wants to write a book about you. She says it's going to be a critical biography—your life in relationship to your works, not gossipy.

ORSON WELLES: God help us. I have turned so against biographies in the last few weeks, because I read the great biography of [Isak] Dinesen and the great biography of Robert Graves—both brilliantly written and very sympathetic. Two of my gods, you see, and Graves's is written by an *adoring* biographer, who was close to him for twenty-five years. But I learned a lot of things about him I didn't want to know. If you do the warts, the warts are gonna look bigger than they were in life. If these people were my friends, the warts wouldn't be as important to me as they seem in the book. We all have people that we know are drunks, or dopeheads or have bad tempers or whatever, and they're still our friends, you know? But in a book you focus on it. And these biographies have diminished those two people so much in my mind, I wish I had never read them. They deny me somebody who I've loved always. I like Dinesen a lot less, now. In other words, Dinesen was brilliantly careful to present herself as the person I wanted to love. And if she was somebody else, really, I'm sorry to know it. And I suddenly think to myself, "You know, there's no such thing as a friendly biographer."

If it were a military leader or a politician, or somebody who didn't write—if it were a director—it wouldn't matter so much. But with writers, they become my friends from the testimony of the pages that they have written. And anything else diminishes what I feel. If I'm enraptured by any writer's work, I don't want to know about him. Somebody's come out with a snide biography of [Joseph] Conrad now. Just reading the review of it made me sick.

HJ: But doesn't it add another dimension that—

OW: Nothing. I know everybody thinks that way, but I don't believe it. I don't want to keep hearing that [Charles] Dickens was a lousy son of a bitch. The hateful Dickens, you know. I'm very glad I don't know anything about Shakespeare as a man. I think it's all there in what he wrote. All that counts, anyway.

HJ: I'm constantly trying to understand: why has there been nobody since Shakespeare who has approached his genius? And how is it possible that one individual, three hundred years ago—

OW: Definitively, he wrote all the plays that we need. And he knew it. He knew it. He wrote a short verse in which he said that nobody would match him. He was apparently an enormously charming man. Nobody ever spoke against him. Everybody loved him. And what's interesting are the new discoveries about his acting career, that he probably played much bigger parts than we had heretofore thought. It's now almost certain that he played Iago. It was [Richard] Burbage who played Othello. Burbage must have been wonderful, because you don't get those plays written for somebody who can't do it. We know he was chubby, of course, to the point of fatness, because of the line in *Hamlet*, when the queen says, "Our Hamlet is fat and short of breath."

The mystery surrounding Shakespeare is greatly exaggerated. We know a lot about his financial dealings, for example. He was brilliant in arranging his finances, you see. He died very rich from real-estate investments. The son of a bitch did everything! And finally he got what his father had always wanted—a coat of arms. His father was a butcher. And a mayor of Stratford.

HJ: Wouldn't that make an incredible film, a biography of him? Or is it impossible? 'Cause there's just too much—

OW: They hate movies about geniuses. *Rembrandt*, the only one I ever liked, emptied the theaters, a total failure.

HJ: Do you read the books about yourself?

OW: No. They make me wince. Either because they're too nice, or not nice enough. I'm terribly thin-skinned. I believe everything bad that I read about myself. And even if I reject it, it remains in my mind as probably true. So I protect myself by reading as little about myself as I can, out of cowardice.

I had to go to court in France this year to stop a book in which that old fellow—Maurice Bessy—who's always been a kind of professional friend of mine, wrote that I was an impotent latent homosexual.

HJ: How would he know that?

OW: Turns out he's my intimate friend, you know? I never laid a hand on him! He's a mean, little, crooked fairy. And he's one of those people who declares himself your friend, follows you everywhere, saying, "I'm a devoted friend." So he's *made* himself your friend, and you can't say, "No, you're not a friend."

HJ: Is Bessy a homosexual?

OW: No. Well, it never occurred to me. Maybe he is. What probably happened is that when I was making *Othello*, I was based in Paris for about six weeks, rehearsing with Micheál Mac Liammóir. And Bessy used to join us for meals. Well, when I am with a homosexual, I get a little homosexual. To make them feel at home, you see? Just to keep Michael comfortable, I kind of camped a little. To bring him out. So he wouldn't feel he was with a terrible straight. Bessy may have seen that.

HJ: Homosexuals and Jews both have one thing in common. They want everybody else to be Jewish, or everybody else to be homosexual. I was eavesdropping in a restaurant once and the people at the next table were insisting you were Jewish because—"He has a Jewish father, Bernstein."

OW: My biggest success was with *Jew Süss*, the first play I ever did. In Dublin. And somebody overheard a couple of Dubliners—women—saying, "Orson Welles. Oh, he's a Jewman, too." And they all thought Hilton Edwards was, 'cause he had a splendid hook nose. He wasn't. He was Anglo to the marrow of his bones, but to them he was a "Jewman." They liked that. A Jewman is a clever fella, you know.

HJ: So if you went to court to stop Bessy, why didn't you try to prevent Pauline Kael from using *Raising Kane* as the introduction to the script in *The Citizen Kane Book*?

OW: How could I? You see, I had held out and refused to have the script published for years. But then I was so poor that I couldn't turn it down—I just had to have some money. And it never occurred to me to think about who would write an introduction. I should have said, "I must have approval of the introduction." Or, "Let me write it." But I just took the money and ran, you see?

I love Pauline, because she writes at length about actors. Which nobody writing about movies does. I think she's wrong a lot of the time, but she's always interesting. I wish she hadn't attacked me, because I've studied her, and I'd like to attack her, but now it will be seen as payback. She has a couple of extraordinary bad habits. First of all, she's spoiled by [William] Shawn, the editor of the *New Yorker*, and given more space to talk about movies than anybody gets for the theater, or for art, or for music. She's allowed to go on and on, and she abuses the privilege. Secondly, she misuses "we" and "us": "We" feel that, and so on, for entirely subjective criticisms, which are nothing more than her own personal opinions. And she has a third thing, which is a schoolgirl use of language. Everything is "glitzy" and all kinds of things that you'd hear in a girls' boarding school. That's the voice she's developed for herself. It doesn't work. But I've never understood the *New Yorker*, anyway. The *things* that they give length to have always amazed me. Like somebody's memories of a middle-class childhood in Bombay gets a full book-length article.

You know, four pieces on me were written and not printed before they finally ran the fifth, written by Wolcott Gibbs. And you know why they wouldn't print the first four? Because they were too sympathetic to me. Harold Ross told me that. One guy wrote a rave review about me. So Ross said, "That's no good." And he gave it to another fellow. Finally Ross just gave up and ran Gibbs's very nice piece. When I was writing a column in the *New York Post*, Ross used to write me criticisms of the column all the time, as though I were sending it to the *New Yorker*. In a sort of friendly but hostile way. His basic feeling was, "He's an actor. What's he doing writing?"

HJ: You may not read all this stuff about you, but other people do. When Diane Sawyer interviewed you on TV she asked—

OW: She was very scared of me for a long time.

HJ: Yes, because of the mythology around you. That's what scares the money people away, too. You have to debunk it.

OW: She said, "In the world, there are only four or five with your kind of legendary—" While I'm trying to think, "Who are they?" This at the beginning. And finally she got to her prepared dirty question, which she held for the end. She looked at me in a hurt way and said, "Why did you try to take Mankiewicz's name off the credits?" She'd just read Kael.

HJ: Of course that's ridiculous. You should have set the record straight. But you can't if you're not even interested in your own biography!

OW: There are a lot of things I don't remember, you know. I got a letter three days ago from a woman who says that her mother and I had a great love affair. Absolutely no recollection. According to this woman, she is the issue of this affair, and she claims that I offered to support her when she was born, but the mother said, "No." Nevertheless, she says, I bought a perambulator for her. She has enclosed photographs of what she claims is my grandson. I know it's a fantasy.

HJ: You don't know anything about this?

OW: Clearly a disturbed woman. Did I ever tell you, once after a matinee performance, I was visited in my dressing room by a beautiful, exquisitely dressed, extremely elegant young woman. She said: "I just wanted to see you . . . because we are brother and sister." And then she left. I've always wondered about that—about who she was, what she meant. I've told you about my doubts about my parentage, who my father really was. I really think it was Feodor Chaliapin, I really do.

HJ: You mean the Russian opera singer?

OW: He had an affair with my mother, at just the right time.

HJ: In England, you know, you have a man named Michael Lindsay-Hogg, of quite considerable stature and prominence, going around insisting that he's your son. Says that on television.

OW: It's extremely unlikely, which I've never told anyone, because I never slept with his mother, Geraldine [Fitzgerald], all the time she was staying with me. She lived in my house when I was divorced from my first wife, for the first six months I was in Hollywood. She was not my type.

HJ: It's true, you like the dark, Mediterranean types. People say, "I didn't know that he was such an extraordinary Don Juan."

OW: I used to love everybody thinking I was having sex with everyone. But in this case it would have had to be an immaculate conception. That's the reason I've always said no, and she's always said no.

HJ: Maybe you just forgot.

OW: Well, the dates are right. So there's just a chance that he is. He believes it. I have no idea. He's a talented fellow. He acted in a play that I did in Dublin when he was a young boy. I also saw a television movie he made. Awfully well done. He's a very good director. And he smokes cigars well.

HJ: He made the first few of those *Brideshead Revisited* episodes that I like very much. The pilot, and about six others—the best ones.

OW: Really? I didn't know that. *Brideshead* is the only [Evelyn] Waugh novel I don't like. Waugh was my idea of the greatest writer of the century. I read Waugh through, all the works, except *Brideshead*, once a year. That's how much I like him. It's the greatest therapy. *Black Mischief* and *A Handful of Dust* and *Vile Bodies*.

HJ: Back to artists showing themselves in their work, isn't *F for Fake* at least partially biographical or autobiographical? Don't you reveal yourself there? At least it poses as a confessional film. Within which Elmyr de Hory, the art forger, is the fake. And then, on the second level, Clifford Irving is the fake, for having fabricated that biography of Howard Hughes, and then written a biography of de Hory called *Fake*. And, finally, the filmmaker—you—is the fake.

OW: Not at all. It's a fake confessional. I'm not really confessing. The fact that I confess to be a fraud is a fraud. It is just as deliberate and manipulative as that. No, I think I'm absolutely genuine— that's a lie. I *never* tell the truth.

HJ: So, you're not really beating your breast in *F for Fake*?

OW: I don't get anything off my chest. That's a kind of romanticism that I don't like. The personal aspect of romanticism. I don't want to know about the hang-ups of the writers or movie people, either. I'm not interested in the artist; I'm interested in his work. And the more he reveals, the less I like it. Proust holds me by his enormous skill. But the subject matter is not that interesting. He wants us— It's not—he's being— I don't know how to explain it. Here's a way to put it: I do not mind seeing the artist naked, but I hate to see him undressing. Show me your cock. That's all right with me. But don't striptease.

HJ: So in real life, how can we trust you when you say favorable things? Or unfavorable things, for that matter.

OW: You can't. You have to ask me to repeat it. I never lie twice about the same thing. What I hate is when filmmakers ask my opinion, saying to me, "We know that you wouldn't say anything but the truth. That's why we're asking." At that moment, I'm preparing the biggest lie in the world, you know. They're going to ask about some piece of *merde*—always. I've come up with one good answer, at least, which is this: "There are no words . . ."

HJ: And your other one, that I've heard you say, is, "You've done it again."

OW: I never lie with a laugh. It's much easier to lie about an intense tragedy than about a comedy. It's very hard to sit and go, "Ha ha ha ha." It's easier to say, "It's too touching, isn't it?"

HJ: I'll never understand why *F for Fake* didn't do better here.

OW: The tragedy of my life is that I can't get the Americans to like it. Outside of New York, the critics hated it. In Chicago, Cleveland, St. Louis—they were *furious* with it. They seemed to think I was attacking critics. Which I wasn't, but why not? It did make fools of them. In France, for instance, all the art critics denounced it. That's what happens when you show a [Kees] Van Dongen that Van Dongen didn't paint, and the critics say that he did. The great Andre Malraux, with tears coursing down his face in the Museum of Tokyo where there were five Modiglianis, came up to one of them and said, "At last the true essence of Modigliani has been revealed to me." All five of them were fakes, painted by de Hory. Who should go down in art history as a serious forger. But you can't *say* that to critics, you know. Anyway, I think, *F for Fake* is the only really original movie I've made since *Kane*. You see, everything else is only carrying movies a little further along the same path. I believe that the movies—I'll say a terrible thing—have never gone beyond *Kane*. That doesn't mean that there haven't been good movies, or great movies. But everything has been done now in movies, to the point of fatigue. You can do it better, but it's always gonna be the same grammar, you know? Every artistic form—the blank-verse drama, the Greek plays, the novel—has only so many possibilities and only so long a life. And I have a feeling that in movies, until we break completely, we are only increasing the library of good works. I know that as a director of movie actors in front of the camera, I have nowhere to move forward. I can only make another good work.

HJ: *F for Fake* is a new form, film in the form of an essay, which is one of the things that appeals to me. You created a new language.

OW: I hoped *F for Fake* would be the beginning of a new language that other people would take up.

HJ: I wish you had done more films in that format.

OW: I wish so, too.

HJ: Maybe the critics' scorn for Clifford Irving damaged the film itself.

OW: He's the unsympathetic fellow in this film. But he's kind of fascinating, sitting there and talking about what makes a poseur.

HJ: And what makes something art.

OW: And, really, what is art? It's a very interesting question, you know? One that has never been sufficiently answered. I'm deeply suspicious of the unanimity that people have about the whole range of art and music. Because I don't think it's humanly possible for everybody to have the right opinion about something. Therefore, some of it must be wrong. I wish some critics would say, "You know, this is all trash!" But nobody has.

HJ: Do you mean that the reputations of Beethoven or Picasso should be challenged?

OW: Yes. Why are we admiring some painters now, like [Barto-lome] Morillo, who are going to disappear? Conversely, nobody took El Greco seriously until seventy-five years ago. Why is there this absolute unanimity and certainty that everybody has not only about painting, but about everything—movies; anything you want to name. Everyone agrees on what is classic and what is not.

HJ: But don't you think there are some works that transcend—

OW: That's the question. Are there? I'd like to think so, but I'm not—

HJ: You've made one, arguably two. The fact is that everyone agrees about *Kane*. It's on everybody's list.

OW: Who knows how it will fare in thirty years?

HJ: It's already withstood the test of time. I don't know why, because I don't think *Kane* is better than *F for Fake*.

OW: I think we can't pursue this conversation if we do it around my work. Because I get coy.

HJ: I don't think we can question a Beethoven symphony as being anything less than—

OW: One would think not. And I would personally die for Bach and Mozart, Bartók, Beethoven. I'm sure I'm right about them—and about Velázquez, too—but what troubles me is when people accept the whole edifice—the movies, the books, the paintings, what's in, what's out—just because it's already been accepted. That arouses my suspicion. Even if it's right. I also don't believe, in litera-ture, that anybody can have taste so catholic that he genuinely likes Joyce and Eliot—and Céline. And yet, many people accept *all* of them. I say there's a point where somebody can't really dig that other fellow if they dig this one. Our eyes, our sensibilities, are only so wide.

HJ: But I wonder if you and I are defining art in the same way. Because, for instance, Beckett, for me, who I consider a great—

OW: I agree that he probably is. But I don't understand it—the greatness. I believe that people are right when they say he's great. But I cannot find it, and I—

HJ: Why do you believe it, then?

OW: Because I suspect that I'm tone-deaf to it. Just like I think there is music that I don't understand. I know when I sense something is wrong. I know when I think something is a fake. I know when the emperor has no clothes. But I don't see a naked emperor with Beckett. He's just opaque to me. I think [Francis] Bacon is a great painter, but I hate his paintings. I don't really question his reputation; I just keep walking, rather than stopping and staring, you know. I believe that there is no law, and should be no law under the heavens that tells an artist what he ought to be. But my point of view, my idea of art—which I do not propose to be universal—is that it must be affirmative.

HJ: Really?

OW: Life-affirming. I reject everything that is negative. You know, I just don't like Dostoevsky. Tolstoy is my writer. Gogol is my writer. I'm not a Joyce guy, though I see that he's one of the great writers of this century.

HJ: God knows, he's not affirmative.

OW: No, and that's why I don't like him.

HJ: But, wait a minute, Orson, what are you talking about? This is a stupid conversation. *Touch of Evil* is not affirmative.

OW: Listen, none of my reactions about art have anything to do with what *I* do. I'm the exception!

HJ: Oh, my God.

OW: It doesn't bother me, because it comes out of me. I'm dark as hell. My films are as black as the black hole. *Ambersons.* Oh, boy, was that dark. I break all my rules.

HJ: What about film versus theater?

OW: Films are either superior to or inferior to the theater. The battle between the two will always exist. The lack of live actors will always be to the advantage of movies and to its disadvantage. There are things you can do in movies that *require* the absence of live actors. Therefore, it's a more versatile medium. But theater, which requires live actors, can achieve things that films can never reach, because what's up on the screen is dead. It's only an image—there are no people there. Nobody who didn't see him in the theater will ever know how great W. C. Fields was. He was a *shadow* of himself in films. A shadow! A *tenth* as funny as he was on the stage. [Al] Jolson, too.

HJ: But that's performance you're talking about. Not filmmaking.

OW: Yes. Well, that's all that's important. The making of a film is secondary to the performance.

HJ: Oh, how can you say that? You, the man who made *F for Fake*! Your own work belies that.

OW: Basically, when you speak about the performing arts, the most important thing is the performer, even if he is the *result* of the director. What you are looking at is a performance. That's my point.

HJ: Wait a minute. In *F for Fake*, it's not the performance—it's the *form* you create.

OW: The hell it's not the performance.

HJ: You center it on the performance, but it's the form! The best indication of it is that whole section where you use a still photograph of Picasso's eyes behind the images, where Oja is walking in the streets while his eyes flick up. It's you, the filmmaker, who created that!

OW: I don't argue with this at all. I don't say that the filmmaker can't be the most important thing. But, *basically*, in the great mass of films, it is the performance in the film as photographed that we see. That performance may be the result of the director or may not! And when it's at its best, it's both.

HJ: But I think film is more analogous to music than to theater.

OW: I do, too. But I wasn't talking about analogous. I was talking about the battle, the curious tension between the two performing media. I agree that film is more musical than theater—and more literary. It's more narrative than drama. A real movie is a narrative— it's a story. For [Sergei] Eisenstein, on the other hand, montage is the essence of cinema. But he is the most overrated great, great director of them all.

HJ: He doesn't value actors or performance. He's the exact opposite of you. I'm not surprised that you gave *Ivan the Terrible* an unflattering review in your *New York Post* column.

OW: Yeah. It didn't bring the hands together. And he then wrote me letters month after month. Hundreds and hundreds of words each time. Until he went into hiding.

HJ: What happened to those letters?

OW: They burnt up. I felt badly about that review. It was a stupid thing to do. I published it when I was in San Francisco where the charter of the United Nations was being written. But I was spending so much time with Yugoslav partisans who were there, in San Francisco, that I felt—and with Harry Bridges, and other known card-carrying members of the Communist Party—that I thought I could attack Soviet art with a good conscience, you see?

HJ: Stalin didn't dare touch Eisenstein, did he?

OW: He apparently was touched. He was hiding in phone booths at the end, and he was very badly off. He was not allowed to release the third part of *Ivan the Terrible*. Because it suddenly occurred to Stalin, who thought he was going to be glorified, that in *Ivan the Terrible* you couldn't help but see that he was terrible. So, of course, Stalin's displeasure then moved to Eisenstein. Who should have anticipated that at the beginning. If he was so good at dialectical materialism, he should have looked around him and said, "I think I'm going to do a pastoral story of a happy collective farm," you know?

HJ: He died in forty-eight. The time of the Doctors' Trials. All the Jews were being purged.

OW: The theater suffered much more than film. All the good theater people got it. You know, Meyerhold—

HJ: Meyerhold was shot in an earlier purge in 1940 . . .

OW: I don't know why they were persecuted more severely. Maybe because all these terrible functionaries had the habit of going to the theater as a sort of official event. So they saw all the plays. The Russians have terrible taste. I saw it at its worst when they came here to buy films while the war was still on in the Pacific. I was talking to them about Eisenstein and all that. So certain was I that my work would be taken back to Russia that I took the commissar, who'd been given the job, to all the Hollywood parties, and to Romanoff's, and poured champagne down his throat. And he went home with a list that began with *Sun Valley Serenade*, a bunch of pictures like that, mostly with Don Ameche. Crummy musicals. Not even the good ones. Just dumb. Peasant dumb. Idiots that I wasted my time on. You know, not one movie of mine has ever been shown in any theater in the Soviet Union.

HJ: You would think they would love *Kane*, because they could interpret it as a big attack on capitalism.

OW: But they don't have enough sense to understand it. The critics frothed at the mouth, because it shows the good side of the oppressor.

HJ: They thought you admired Kane? And his opulence?

OW: The truth is, if any of them got to be the premier of Russia, they would be living in Xanadu themselves. The one they really couldn't stand was *Touch of Evil*, because that showed the final decadence of the capitalist world.

HJ: That's why they should love it!

OW: But they thought it was *my* decadence. The Russians are a people of genius, you know, in every department. But instead of it flowering under this great revolution, it all withered. And they're very literal. What we used to think the German mind was like. People who don't really understand German culture always think Germans are very literal. But they're not literal at all. They're mystics—you know, hysterics. The Russians are "machine-made," "tractor-made." Poor people.

None of this is true of the satellite countries. In Yugoslavia, for example, *F for Fake* has run three times on prime-time television with Yugoslav subtitles. Here, the film is almost unknown. It just broke my heart that it never caught on. Because that would have solved my old age. I could have made an essay movie—two of 'em a year, you see? On different subjects. Various variations of that form.

HJ: Weren't you thinking of making *Don Quixote* as an essay film?

OW: That was the way I wanted to finally get it done, with the title *When Are You Going to Finish Don Quixote?* That would be the name of the movie. And it would be all about Spain, a country I've known since I was a boy. What's happened to it, and why *Quixote* is still important. That film would be much more expensive than *F for Fake*, because I'd need to shoot footage in modern Spain. You know, de-Francoed Spain. But how to sell *Quixote* without having sold *F for Fake*? It's hard if you haven't got in the door with your first Fuller brush.

10. "The Cannes people are my slaves."

In which Orson perks up when he hears there is interest in Lear *and* The Dreamers. *He plans to "come out" at Cannes, where he always traveled under a foreign flag because the French hated to give Americans the Palme d'Or.*

HENRY JAGLOM: Speaking of unfinished and new films, did you read that article about you that Mary Blume wrote in the *International Herald Tribune* I gave you?

ORSON WELLES: Yeah, sort of. You know, I don't read those things very carefully. I read the end to see how they sum it up. I'm always afraid of reading something bad along the way. It's not arrogance on my part, but cowardice, sheer funk that keeps me from reading the articles. I should, but I don't. I will.

HJ: That one's significant, because I've gotten a great many calls from Europe. They all want to be your hero. As if Hollywood didn't understand, or appreciate you, and they want to show them up. Germany, now, is back in the picture. They were mad, because they hadn't heard directly from me since *The Dreamers*, which I had offered them, and they had proposed, remember, good partial financing.

OW: Yes.

HJ: And we ended up thinking it wasn't enough. I don't recall what it was. Now they're saying, "*The Dreamers*, is that still available?" And they said, "Why didn't you come to us about *Lear*? Welles and *Lear*."

OW: Yes, I do remember.

HJ: I have reason to believe that, for the German-speaking countries, I could get a million dollars. And now they're not demanding stars.

OW: In other words, the game has changed since what's-his-name told us, "Without stars, nothing doing"? We don't need A-list actors? That's progress. *Lear* must be done. I work on it all the time. I would feel very unfulfilled if I couldn't bring this one off. And I think it is a dream tax-shelter thing.

HJ: So let's talk about *Lear*.

OW: If God gives me basic health, I can go on to make several pictures over the upcoming few years. But because I'm increasingly arthritic, I must play *Lear* in the next year. I'm worried about doing it after that. Just sheer getting around.

HJ: The energy of that part.

OW: Not so much the energy of the part, but the physical moving around. Which is fine for me to do and use as the old man. But I must be *able* to. And who knows, with arthritis, when the moment comes when I really can't get around? You see? I have to be realistic about that.

HJ: So if you can't do *Lear*—

OW: I can do *The Dreamers*, for which I almost have a new script. Which I don't want to show you, because you'll love it, and then you won't want to do anything else, it's so good. I've rewritten it and completely sharpened it and made it—

HJ: You can't do this! You're not allowed to do this to me! You say that I'll love it, I won't want to do anything else, so you won't show it to me?

OW: No, I will, I will. I'll send it to you today. And when you get it, be sure you have time to read it. Try to read it as though you never read it before. Oja thinks that it should be the second picture, because even if the knee should get worse and I can't move around in that part, I don't have to. I can do *The Dreamers* even if I can't move.

HJ: I want to talk about your knees, also, though, because I have an idea.

OW: My knees?

HJ: Knees.

OW: Knees.

HJ: Knees. Do you rub anything into your knees?

OW: Never mind. Let's talk about the medical part of it later.

HJ: I just found something very interesting.

OW: Give it to me. I'll rub anything in. But let's not talk about my knees; let's talk about *Lear*. If there is real interest in it, I really must do it.

HJ: The hardest thing for me has been to pin you down about the budget. How much money do you really require to do it?

OW: Well, I'll tell you. Because of the constant changes in rentals— When I first talked to you, the rentals of studios in Hollywood were 40 percent less than they are now for independent productions. And Italy has a new production agreement that has raised the rates 30 percent. In other words, nothing is fixed. We have to decide at what moment we're really going to go after it, and make the budget then.

HJ: Well, which budget do we work from?

OW: The budget I sent you. That is the budget that allows me shorter working hours, and addresses the problem of the five- as opposed to six-day shooting week that is routine throughout Europe.

HJ: That's a doable budget. We could get that money.

OW: I also need to have some money for myself, as an actor. I want to play the part that I was born to play. And I cannot bear to lose it. And I've done the script for it already. Big job, making a movie of Shakespeare. Because you have to take terrible risks, do things that people don't like you to do. And always criticize you for it. But I think it's what he . . . would do.

HJ: Sure, if film had existed then.

OW: For one thing, his stage at the Globe Theatre was very big—people forget that. The distance from the inner theater out to that platform was a long way. And he had to march these armies on and write these boring speeches to give them the time to get off again. He turns into a different kind of writer when he's moving armies. You could almost write the stuff yourself, the level is so mundane. Now, in a movie you don't have to do that.

I'm gonna do it in 16 millimeter black-and-white. The camera is so small that you can carry it like a typewriter. If only the people who put up money didn't turn white with terror when you say "16 millimeter." It's the only way to go. Even though it still has to be turned into 35 millimeter.

HJ: Which makes no sense.

OW: Especially in an age when most of your public is gonna see it on a television screen anyway, and the other people are gonna see it on a small screen in these smaller theaters.

HJ: Regular 16? Not Super 16? It'll have to be mostly close-ups.

OW: It will be mostly close-ups. With my little machine, I can cut in my bedroom. You know, just get out of bed and—

HJ: I don't even think it's necessary to tell people you're going to shoot in 16.

OW: But how do you do that? Unless we made a 35 millimeter blimp and hide the 16 millimeter camera inside it. And never say a word about it.

HJ: And use the money we save for . . .

OW: Just leave the word *35* out of the contract. When I think that in the last decade of my career I have to make pictures which are essentially much cheaper—require more ingenuity and faking around than when I started—and yet, they will be judged by the standards of the time when I had more money, I don't like that at all, you know.

HJ: Do you want to finance *Lear* through any of these cable people who have been interested?

OW: I don't think so. It should be a small movie that plays in small theaters everyplace in the world. And then there's the casting. I'll have to do it with people who are eager to work with me, you know. They'll share a piece of it—or nothing, or whatever.

HJ: I think you should make the rounds in Europe again, to take advantage of the interest that article has stirred up.

OW: I think that I should consider, very seriously, going to Cannes this year. The cultural importance of the festival vanished years ago. It's now ceased to be anything except a market. But if you get one of the top prizes, it helps your business.

HJ: We should make arrangements.

OW: Oh, there's nothing to arrange. You know, the Cannes people are my slaves, pretty much. But I don't want to go as a guest of the festival, if I can help it. I'll let 'em pay for the hotel, as long as I'm not obligated to do anything. They'll probably want me to do some things that I don't want to do. And if there are too many of them, I'll pay my own hotel bill.

HJ: I bet they want to give you some award or something.

OW: It's a disadvantage to be an American there. They don't *like* to give the Palme d'Or to Americans. I experienced that several times. The most notable time was with *Othello* in 1952. I didn't know whether I was getting the prize or not. Because they never tell you, you see, that you've won it, until the very last minute. And the way I learned it was when they came to my room in the Carlton, desperate, and said, "We can't find anybody who knows the national anthem of Morocco." Because I had entered the picture as a Moroccan picture! The Moor of Venice, you know? All the things I've entered in Cannes for prizes have always been as Italian or Spanish—or Moroccan.

HJ: Didn't you get some kind of consolation prize for *Chimes at Midnight*?

OW: That one was nominated for the Palme d'Or in 1966, and it was "the" picture that year because the competition was so weak. All my old French friends were on the jury: Marcel Achard, Marcel Pagnol, somebody else, I've forgotten. And it was that thing of [Claude] Lelouche, his first movie, *Un Homme et Une Femme*, that got it.

When I got word that I was being given a special prize, I said, "I don't want to come to the ceremony." Because it's very undignified. But then I thought, "If I don't show up, it'll look like I'm a sorehead." So I went. And it was the greatest triumph of my life. Because when they announced that *Un Homme et Une Femme* had won the Palme d'Or, the audience stood up, booed and yelled for ten minutes. Then they said, "We're giving a special prize to Orson Welles," and there was a fifteen-minute ovation. So it was clear what everybody thought—except the jury, you know.

HJ: And did you ever get an explanation from people like Pagnol?

OW: No. It was a French thing. To promote their industry. I hadn't figured on that. I should have insisted that *Chimes at Midnight* be shown out of competition. Instead of enduring the humiliation. The year you make your masterpiece, the Rumanians will get it, you know. I was in Cannes the year of the revolution. In '68. When all the leading directors withdrew from the festival. And I joined them. It was "to the barricades!" They all said to me, "We don't even think of you as an American." But I'm very American! My pictures are very American! All they mean is that they like them.

HJ: And you're content to let them think your pictures are un-American because it helps you there?

OW: I'm a hypocrite. A sellout. You know, Louise de Vilmorin told me a story about Malraux.

HJ: De Vilmorin. You mean the writer? *Madame de . . .* , from which [Max] Ophuls made *The Earrings of Madame de . . .* ? She was Malraux's mistress, called herself Marilyn Malraux, was she not?

OW: The very same. You know, de Gaulle made Malraux Minister of Cultural Affairs. She told me, "The limousine meets him in the morning and takes him to the ministry."

HJ: My God! A hero of the Spanish Civil War, of the French Resistance, in a limo? With a driver?

OW: And then he ended up a stooge. There was a picture in *Paris Match* at the height of the '68—the "troubles," as we called them in Dublin—in which there was a great right-wing demonstration in Paris where they all filled the Champs-Élysées right up to the Arc de Triomphe. And there was de Gaulle, standing by the Unknown Soldier, with a flame coming out. And there was Malraux, with his head leaning over onto de Gaulle, with tears running down his cheeks. That's what can happen to intellectuals, you know? They are the biggest pushovers. They love power. They cluster around whatever golden boy, or man, is in power and begin to justify it.

HJ: I wonder if it's because they feel that sense of being an outsider so early in life . . .

OW: Yes. And suddenly they have access to power. We saw that with Kennedy. It was such a beehive. I got a letter from Arthur Schlesinger, who wrote an article in a magazine called *Show* in which he talked about me as a person who inexplicably had a certain cult following. Now he's forgotten all that, and wants me to be a member of the Academy of Arts and Letters. They can't do better than make me an honorary one, because there is no category for films. And I am rather tempted to say, "Create one or do without me." They're all feebly trying to imitate the Académie française, which is a useless institution, anyway.

HJ: I wonder why they don't have a category for film.

OW: They're the last holdouts. Because when I was young, the movies were considered to be not quite serious. The theater critic is what mattered. The movie critic was a little fellow who covered hockey or the dog show.

HJ: Does the Académie française have a category for film?

OW: They do. René Clair. Pagnol. Cocteau. By the way, when is Cannes this year?

HJ: May something—tenth? To the seventeenth. In that week or so. When are you going to Paris?

OW: I go to Paris for the show at the Louvre. I'm committed to that.

11. "De Mille invented the fascist salute."

In which Orson displays his grasp of ancient history, art history, and French history, venturing several dubious theories while scheming to hijack an ambitious French television series on the Louvre.

Henry JAGLOM: What are you going to do at the Louvre?

ORSON WELLES: Between the Socialists and TV, the French have put up an enormous sum of money for thirty hours of programming on the Louvre.

HJ: What do they want you to do?

OW: To rewrite the thing. Not wanting to do it much, what I did was to make conditions that I thought rendered it impossible for them to say yes. It was a little bit like my contract for *Kane*. They asked me, "What are you interested in, what subjects?" So I said, "Well, considering it's the Louvre, I would like to do the Egyptian collection, because I have a particular thing I'd like to say about it in France." To my great astonishment, they said yes. The scripts only arrived the day before yesterday. You've never read anything so terrible in your life.

HJ: Why am I not surprised?

OW: The director of the whole show is also the writer, thus making it impossible to argue, because he's the one who calls the shots. A voice from heaven, never explained, delivers the commentary, and two people—Elle et Lui—go trotting around the Louvre. Saying banal things like, "Oh . . . the Egyptians, I believe? They're the people who invented a writing called hieroglyphs," and, "Then the mummy is placed in a coffin, which is called a sarcophagus." Any intelligent fifth-grader knows what a sarcophagus is. Every once in a while there's a little spirited remark, such as—they've been look-ing at the zodiac things and Elle says to Lui, "What's your sign?" So much for the great patrimony of Egyptian art. There's no story; there's no theme, no revelation, no point of view, just a number of stupid statements that aren't true, beginning with, "Like all ancient religions, the Egyptians were obsessed with death." So I immedi-ately said, "I will name you several ancient religions in which death is incidental: Judaism, to begin with. Confucianism. Tao-ism. Shintoism."

So I thought to myself, legally I can say, "I don't like the script," and everybody goes home. The French will be deeply embarrassed by this, and it'll look like I'm being capricious. So I decided, I won't attack the director and his script. I'll say what I want to do, and ask to write it, not just rewrite it.

WAITER: Gentlemen, bon appetit. How is everything?

HJ: Thank you.

OW: We're talking, thank you. *(Waiter leaves.)* I wish they wouldn't do that. If I ever own a restaurant, I will never allow the waiters to ask if the diners like their dishes. Particularly when they're talking.

HJ: You were saying?

OW: The great story is that Egypt was an incredibly closed society, which lasted longer than any other society in the Mediterranean world, in a state of total rigidity. Egypt is like the Japan of the Mediterranean, elegant, cruel, inexplicable, and then suddenly opened up. Who by? Napoleon. That's why the story of the Egyptian col-lection is fascinating. That never occurred to these French people. It's also very nice, because it's the one moment in Napoleon's career when it's possible to speak well of him without reservations. So the half of the population that adores him is not gonna hiss me off the screen. Napoleon in Egypt is beyond criticism.

And I pointed out that not only did Napoleon give us all these savants and the Rosetta Stone and [Jean-François] Champollion, who broke the code and therefore opened up Egyptian art and culture to the world, but Egyptian art and culture dominated the aesthetics of the First Empire.

HJ: I didn't know that.

OW: Study the interior decoration. It's full of Egyptian elements, just as the Deuxième Empire of Louis Napoleon drew on Arabic and Algerian sources for exoticism. Just as the English used India for exoticism. Paris is full of imitation Arabic places left over from the Second Empire. To which was then added Caesarism—Roman elements—foreshadowing Mussolini. Because every dictatorship has always adapted the gestures and costumes of an ancient nation. That's the kind of thing I would like to do on TV, to take people through all these kinds of connections. Including when you go into the Caesarism of Mussolini, there is the fascist salute. [Cecil B.] DeMille invented it. He had to come up with something for the crowd, all those extras, to do, and Mussolini picked it up from there. Then it went to Hitler. And everybody else has been doing it ever since.

HJ: So Mussolini sees DeMille's version of ancient Rome, and . . .

OW: Oh, you'll get historians who'll scream about it and say it isn't true, but I've never been able to find one who could *dis*prove it. And I've had some arguments in Rome with historians. I said, "Come back to me when you can show me that everybody always saluted like that." They weren't doing this at the beginning of the fascist era; it only started after the movie came out. They took up Caesarism, because it was the era, in both Italy and America, of big Roman spectacles.

HJ: And why did Napoleon stand like that?

OW: A great actor of the time instructed him, "You're an Italian, and you're very short. You look ridiculous. And when you talk you wave your arms about. Keep your hand tucked under your tunic." This was still in the days of the Directory, when it was possible to talk to him like that. And Napoleon added, "Never wear a uniform higher than a corporal."

HJ: You're making this up. Why did he say that?

OW: You know his saying. "Every French soldier carries a marshal's baton in his knapsack." In other words, they could all rise to this, you see. But what he gave the marshals was everything except final power. And since they had all the gold braid that has ever been put on a uniform, what could this little dago dress up like that would make him stand out? Leave the marshals to have their gold braid. Of course, the French hate that story, because they don't even like to hear that he's Italian. Corsican. Straight from Genoa, on both sides of the family. And the behavior—the loyalty to the family, you know? It's just like the Mafia. With the old woman running the whole thing in the back room, you know?

HJ: Which old woman?

OW: The mother.

HJ: And he puts the brother—

OW: Sure. Take care of Giuseppe, you know? Makes him King of Naples. It's a real, real Mafia story.

Anyway, I told the French, "You have two choices: either accept my proposal, or pay me $5,000 and give me the rights to what I wrote. Because I cannot do your script. I am somebody who is supposed to know something—whether it's true or not, it's a certain image—and that is greatly reduced when I become a fool, and in that case, I am done an injury. And furthermore, if I don't do your show, you won't be able to sell it in the English-speaking market." They might, but I tell 'em that to scare the shit out of 'em. Then I throw in the blackmail: "I will show my tape to the press in Paris, and explain to them what I wanted to do. On the other hand, if you do like it, I'll give it to you for free, but your director is working for me. And it has to be "Orson Welles Goes to the Louvre." Half an hour ago they got back to me. I won the point. I said, "You were gonna use Charlotte Rampling with Dirk Bogarde, but it's going to be me and Oja."

HJ: You know, in Jewish history Napoleon is quite a hero.

OW: Yes. My Dadda Bernstein taught me, as a child, that he was a great man. He had rows of books on Napoleon.

HJ: He freed the Jews in France. And in all of the French Empire. Took 'em out of the ghettoes. He was the first person to consider the Jews citizens of the country, and treated them accordingly.

OW: He did all kinds of admirable things. I'm not a mad Napoleon fan, but there's no denying his genius. A very complicated man. But had he never been born, there are millions of people who wouldn't have died. There were unnecessary wars that he fought for his own glorification, which makes him a villain in the last analysis.

HJ: That's terrible, of course. But, at least, he was good for the Jews.

OW: It's like older Hungarian Jews still worshipping Franz Joseph because he was the only king who didn't make pogroms. He wasn't a liberal, but at least he didn't go out and beat the Jews over the head! Did I tell you the story of his visit to the provinces? It's a great movie story. You can use it on a set almost any day with an assistant director.

HJ: What is it?

OW: Franz Joseph is riding in his carriage through this tiny provincial town, plumes and all. The trembling mayor is sitting next to him. He says, "Your Imperial Highness, I have to apologize to you in the profoundest terms for the fact that the bells are not ringing in the steeple. There are three reasons. First, there are no bells in the steeple—" And Franz Joseph interrupts him and says, "Please don't tell me the other two reasons." Now, that's a good answer for every assistant director, everyone in the world that you've had working for you in any capacity.

HJ: Where you just want to get a straight answer. But clearly, it's apocryphal. I mean, it can't . . . Who could have been there?

OW: He told it to his mistress, said, "I got off a pretty good one the other day, with a moronic mayor," and she told it—

HJ: To her lover, who was a writer.

OW: And somebody improved it, some Jewish writer . . . I tell that story when I make a movie, always. When somebody starts with the excuses, I say, "Bells in the steeple." It stops them every time. That's one of those you can die with, you know. Like Alex Korda's "any bloody duke," you know?

HJ: No, you never told me that one.

OW: Well, I've ruined it, 'cause that's the tag line. It won't be as funny, but it's still funny. I heard it only a few months ago, in Paris. Well, Douglas Fairbanks, Jr., was asking to see Korda.

HJ: Which Korda?

OW: Alex.

HJ: The director, or producer, or whatever he was.

OW: And Korda said, "My God, he's such a snob and a bore." But his secretary says, "Please see Douglas. You know, you've been refusing to see him and giving him evasive answers. And it's rude." So Douglas Fairbanks, Jr., comes in and sits down. There's a long silence, and then Douglas says, "Well, I think it's going to clear up." Or, "Even for England it's been raining an awful lot. But, still, when you see that green . . ." Another moment of silence. Suddenly Korda says, "Tell me, how's the duke?" And Fairbanks replies, "Which duke?" Korda says, "Any bloody duke," to this famous snob.

12. "Comics are frightening people."

In which Orson suggests that John Huston was little more than a hack, and recalls Olivier and John Barrymore. When Jack Lemmon pulls up a chair, he describes his encounters with Johnny Carson and Joan Rivers.

HENRY JAGLOM: You know, Miloš [Forman] is making *Amadeus* into a movie. I don't know why he wants to do that. It's the stupidest play in the world.

ORSON WELLES: Well, you know, it's been a worldwide hit. Paris, London, New York.

HJ: People are describing Roman [Polanski]'s performance in Paris as Mozart as—

OW: It's terrible. Embarrassing. He's a bad actor.

HJ: I liked him when he cut Jack's nose in that movie that I didn't care for, *Chinatown*.

OW: He was all right in that. Because he did nothing but stand still, you know. I hated the movie. That's John [Huston] at his worst. I have to make the big speech for him at his tribute. He's been campaigning for four years now for the AFI Life Achievement Award, and he's got it.

HJ: Did he ask for you specifically?

OW: Probably. I'm almost sure. After all, I've acted in four or five movies of his, and he's acted in some of mine. So—

HJ: And he's stolen from you so liberally.

OW: His first picture, *The Maltese Falcon*, was totally borrowed from *Kane*. It was made the next year, you know.

HJ: It's hard to look at it now without thinking of your shots. I mean, the lighting; the angles; the setups; the ceilings . . .

OW: For three or four years, everybody was doing that.

HJ: I just saw *Annie* yesterday, with Huston directing.

OW: It's really bad. On every level, I think. Don't you?

HJ: No—I was entertained, in some way.

OW: I wasn't. I thought it missed all over the place.

HJ: But the real point is, how can he bring himself to work with the studios?

OW: What you don't understand is that he doesn't. He just knows how to make a picture without directing it. He just sits and lets the choreographer or somebody else do it. He stays up and plays poker all night, and when he's shooting, *that's* when he's resting.

HJ: You mean he's able to step back, because he doesn't have a need to really be the creative artist. The fact that you've not been able to do that is testimony, in many people's minds, to a kind of—you're gonna hate the word—*purity*. It comes from a kind of insistence on making your own films . . . I'm disgusting you with my effusiveness . . . All right, so what are you reading?

OW: I was reading Montaigne last night again. I was reading the great passage where he says something like, "If you walk on stilts, you're still walking on your feet. If you sit on the highest throne in the world, you're still sitting on your ass." He was a beautiful, beautiful man.

HJ: You have an actor's memory.

OW: Not really. I can read any detective story a year later with perfect pleasure, because I totally forget the plot. So I never have to buy another book. I don't even remember the names of the characters in my own scripts, you know? I say "the girl," or whoever is playing the part. I have a terrible time with fictitious names.

HJ: You have a bad time with the names of real people, too.

OW: No. I just have a selective— It's usually the one I know best whose name I can't remember. That's what really drove me out of the theater, because of the way you're trapped in the dressing room. People come backstage—and they come from every period of your life and they're all gathered together. There's dear old Pete—or whatever his name is—and his wife, standing there, waiting to be introduced to the celebrity who's next to them. And waiting to be shown that you're a snob and won't introduce them. I've perfected the mumbling now. "You all know each other"—all that.

What I do like is when they come up to me and don't know who *I* am. I was in the airport in Las Vegas last year, and a man on crutches, an older man, looked at me with that finally-found-his-favorite-movie-star expression, and started limping toward me. Of course, I met him halfway, and he said, "Milton Berle! I'd know you anywhere." So I signed *Milton Berle* for him. True story. I swear. I finally figured out that he meant Burl Ives, who is a big fat bearded fellow. And out came "Milton Berle."

(Jack Lemmon enters.)

OW: THERE HE IS!

JACK LEMMON: May I invade for a moment?

OW: Please.

JL: You know, if I had to pick a single moment of any performance— let alone just a reading—of anything that Shakespeare ever wrote, that was you one night on the *Johnny Carson Show*, a number of years ago. Now, you take an average, goddamn audience of the *Johnny Carson Show*, and you have a knowledge of Shakespeare that is that of a newt. But you were reading, and, bang! The fucking place gave you an ovation! And I was sitting at home applauding. It was brilliant—it was fucking brilliant! And I don't remember what you were reading.

OW: I remember what it was—it was the speech to the players from *Hamlet*.

JL: Fucking wonderful.

OW: I screwed it up in the middle.

JL: Nobody realized it. And there was a great lesson in it. Because, you know, most actors create characters they want you to identify with, and all of that shit. But you just did it like you were talking to Johnny. I think it was Johnny.

OW: Yes, it was Johnny. That was just before Ken Tynan wrote a profile of Johnny in the *New Yorker*, in which he quoted somebody on Johnny's show—one of the assistants—as saying there was only one guest that Johnny was visibly in awe of, and that was Orson Welles. Since then, I haven't been on the show. For five years. There goes two million copies of my autobiography when I publish it, because I can't even get on to plug it!

HJ: Well, you can if somebody else hosts. Joan Rivers.

OW: I did go on once with "John Rivers," as she ought to be called, when she was replacing Carson. After four and a half years. Obviously, just so that I couldn't go around Beverly Hills saying I was blackballed by Carson. And I knew she was all set for me; I knew. Before I even sat down I began telling her how my wife thought she was the best-dressed woman in show business. And so on. Cut her right off at the knees. She couldn't do a fat joke to save her life.

HJ: So she was on good behavior.

OW: She had to be, after that! How could she sail into me?

JL: She runs on impulse. God knows, she's got balls. And talent. Very, very bright and talented.

OW: Yes, I'm sorry to say. In her terrible way, she's very talented.

HJ: I just heard her do this incredible line. I couldn't believe I was hearing it on television: "Brooke Shields is so dumb, she flunked her Pap test."

OW: To me it sounds like you're bugging the girls' bathroom in a particularly low-class establishment.

HJ: She really makes incredible reaches, and has no sense of limits, of stopping before—

OW: Well, she has a sense—she senses it's gold! That's the trick.

HJ: You know, the talk shows have really gone down tremendously.

OW: In the days when there were four talk shows, and I was on *Carson* every other week, and I was approached for magazine interviews, who needed an interview? I used to say, "I don't give interviews. You want to know about me, tune in to Carson." Now I'm getting in a tough spot with this line. Today, tune into what? I better start getting nice to these cocksuckers with typewriters.

I saw a very long interview with your friend Richard Pryor. Interviewed by a not stupid, but rather square and dull, black man. Pryor had decided to open up and talk. He is very moving. I've always been very fond of him as a person, without knowing him.

HJ: I used to sit with Richard Pryor every night at the Improv in New York when we were starting out, and we had a game, which was that one of us had to make the other laugh. And you couldn't go to the bathroom, you couldn't go home, you couldn't do anything until the other person laughed. So I did something, and then it was his turn to do something. It was very funny, but I didn't laugh. An hour went by, and a second hour. By then we had a crowd around us, a third hour, and he was doing everything he could think of. Richie is brilliant, but fuck it, I was refusing even to smile. There was a relish tray on each one of the tables. He took the mustard. Poured it on his head. He took the ketchup and splashed it on his face. It was a horrible mess. He had every possible color of condiment dripping down his face. Hysterically funny, but I was able to control myself until he took a napkin and with infinite delicacy, dabbed the corner of his mouth. Just like Charlie Chaplin. That got me. Five hours. He ran to the bathroom—he'd been waiting all that time to go—and I realized I would never be a standup comic.

JL: I've always been fascinated by the phrases that we all used, that are so destructive, like "I killed them!"

OW: "I murdered 'em."

HJ: "Destroyed them."

OW: It shows the hostility of the comic. Comics are frightening people. Do you know the story about the comedians sitting around the table at Lindy's? They're all telling jokes. A fellow comes in very sad. He just sits there. He says, "Well, I just finished three weeks at the Paramount—held over another week—and they booked me down in Philadelphia. I guess I shouldn't complain, but, you know, everything I earn goes to my poor kid, who's been in a wheelchair all of his life. He has polio." There's a long silence. Then somebody said, "That's good. Have you heard this one?"

HJ: I remember in childhood, when I was really lonely and scared, I fell off chairs in school to get laughs. The harder I fell, and the more I hurt myself, the bigger the laugh. There's such a clear relationship between getting attention, getting that laughter, and hurting yourself. I used to be compelled by Jerry Lewis for that reason.

OW: He plays a spastic. And he will die to make you laugh. He will do anything! Cut his head off if he needs to, you know. The speech to the players, where Shakespeare has Hamlet say, "Let not those that play your clowns speak no more than is set down for them"—he must have had a big problem with some of his successful clowns. With his Jerry Lewises. Got on there in *Macbeth* as the porter and wouldn't get off. Right in the middle of the murder.

HJ: I remember seeing Milton Berle take bow after bow after bow. He had the world at his feet. Then he came on for his last bow, and he blew his nose on the curtain. He just couldn't not do it, that's all. And he didn't even get a laugh!

JL: Yeah, that's the thing of it: the tremendous need to get the attention of the audience.

OW: But, also, you know, with a comic it's different than any other form of show business, because you are instantly rewarded by laughter. You are on the greatest high in the world. And if you are not rewarded, you're dying. Even playing in a comedy, getting a good laugh on Thursday, is not the same thing as being a comic.

HJ: *(To Lemmon)* You did the TV version of *The Entertainer*?

JL: Yes, I did.

OW: I loved it. But it's an overrated play. You would be astonished at what a rattletrap piece of crap it is. It does not hold up at all! It's all vehicle.

HJ: It was Americanized, right?

OW: No—yeah. But that wasn't important—it was essentially the same play. Fakey and off-pitch. Like Larry. The thing that was better about Jack's performance, and the great mistake that Larry made— You see, Larry can't bear to fail, even if he's supposed to fail. So when he played the comic onstage, he played for real laughs from the paying audience, instead of giving the feeling that he was in a half-empty theater where nobody was laughing. He did not play a failed comedian. Success to Larry demanded being an effective comedian, even though it made no sense! Because if he was that good, what was he doing out in a Brighton theater? What was his problem? But Jack played it like the theater was empty and nobody was laughing. A couple of guys with raincoats on, and that was it, you know?

HJ: Did you see Olivier's *Lear* on the BBC?

OW: The first two scenes are the worst things I ever saw in my life, bar none. Remember, this is the man who, when he played *Hamlet*, began the movie saying, "This is the story of a man who could not make up his mind."

HJ: I understand that Olivier plays Lear as senile in the first scene.

OW: And he mustn't be senile in the first scene! He has to *fall* from grace, you see. Such a vulgar conception. You know, Larry is in competition even with the people who were doing Shakespeare *before* he was doing it.

HJ: Dead actors! Your Jack Barrymore did Hamlet.

OW: When Larry talks about Jack Barrymore, he says, "That ham." But Jack is wonderful! There's nothing *remotely* hammy about him. He was the greatest Hamlet of the century, and the greatest Richard the Third, without any doubt. I can still hear it. And I've heard his records, too. *(As Barrymore)*:

> "Ay, Edward will use Women honourably:
> Would he were wasted, Marrow, Bones, and all,
> That from his Loynes no hopefull Branch may spring,
> To crosse me from the Golden time I looke for . . ."

Jack never intended to be an actor. He began as a newspaper cartoonist, you know, and he was just a guy around town. And Arthur Hopkins said, "You're it."

HJ: Arthur Hopkins the director?

OW: Yes. And they did *The Jest*, the Sam Benelli play. He and Lionel did *Richard III* and *Hamlet*, and they did *Justice* by [John] Galsworthy. Those were the great years of acting in the American theater. In order for Jack to play *Richard III*, Hopkins sent him to Margaret Carrington, who had been the first singer of [Claude] Debussy's songs and was a great authority on voice production. She was a millionaire and the aunt of John Huston. Jack spent four months, summer months, with her, every day, saying, "Mee, mee, mam, mum," and, suddenly, this great organ was born, you see.

HJ: How did you first meet Olivier?

OW: We met when he was playing in the *The Green Bay Tree*, in

New York, and I had just finished playing Mercutio in *Romeo and Juliet*. It was a very nice gathering of people, and we were sitting talking together. The hostess was Margaret Carrington, who had been my voice teacher as well as Jack's. That's why I can imitate Barrymore, because I took lessons from her. She charged neither Barrymore nor me, and ruined me and made Barrymore. It took me years to recover. But anyway, she came up to us and, according to me, said, "Mr. Olivier, you must stop boring Mr. Welles." And, according to Larry, she said, "Mr. Welles, you must stop boring Mr. Olivier." And both of us believe that our version is right! To this day, I honestly don't know who is right.

HJ: How is Larry? Has anybody heard anything more about his health?

OW: I hear all kinds of stories, none of them very cheerful. He has three kinds of cancer. It's particularly a shame, because Larry wanted to be so beautiful. I caught him once, when I came backstage to his dressing room after a performance, he was staring at himself with such love, such ardor, in the mirror. He saw me over his shoulder, embarrassed at my catching him in such an intimate moment. Without losing a beat, though, and without taking his eyes off himself, he told me that when he looked at himself in the mirror, he was so in love with his own image it was terribly hard for him to resist going down on himself. That was his great regret, he said. Not to be able to go down on himself!

He was supposed to be in this last movie I was in, and he couldn't make it. And he's supposed to be in another movie they want me in, and they guess he won't be able to do that, either. And that's rough on him, because he has to act. He doesn't care if it's a bad movie or a bad play. He has to work. Which is admirable. That's why he went so far beyond me as an actor. I envied him that so much, but that was the great difference between us. He was—and is—a professional, whereas I don't see acting as a profession, as a job, never have. I am an amateur. An amateur is a lover—*amateur*, the word, comes from "love"—with all the caprices and the difficulties of love. I don't feel compelled to work. And Larry does. A professional turns up on Wednesday afternoons.

HJ: I never asked you—how did you get into acting in the first place?

OW: I finished high school in two years and had a scholarship to Harvard. I *hated* school! *Hated* school! The trouble with school is that it's very good for some minds, and very bad for others. It's giving you opinions. All the time, opinions about history, opinions about people, opinions about everything. Schools are opinion factories. So I went into the theater so as not to go to Harvard!

HJ: Candice Bergen has just finished her book on growing up as the daughter of a ventriloquist. I don't know what reminded me.

OW: Edgar Bergen was an ice-cold fellow.

HJ: He never told her, "I love you."

OW: I believe that. I knew him very well, because we were fellow magicians. We went every Thursday night to the same magic club! Here's a story about him. We were in a show—I was doing a run-through with him—he was up there with a dummy. And his two leading writers were sitting in front of me in the CBS Theater, which was empty. They didn't know that anybody was behind them. One of 'em turned to the other and said, "You know, to look at him, you'd swear that Bergen was real."

HJ: You know, for the first three years of her life, Candice had breakfast with Edgar and Charlie McCarthy, and thought Charlie was her brother? Charlie would sit there and talk to her: "Drink your milk." Her father never spoke directly to her. Till one day she opened a closet she wasn't supposed to open and found five of her brothers hanging there.

JL: Have to leave. It's been fun.

OW: Bye, Jack.

13. "Avez-vous scurf?"

In which Orson claims Chaplin "stole" *Monsieur Verdoux* from him, or at least the writing credit, and explains how the Tramp wore out his welcome with the Hollywood set, compares him invidiously to Keaton, and recalls Garbo snubbing Dietrich.

HENRY JAGLOM: Orson, speaking of comics, I'm dying to hear about Charlie Chaplin. He was the hero of my youth, and I still adore his movies. Do you know whether he planned his jokes in advance, or mainly improvised?

ORSON WELLES: No. He didn't improvise much, but he wasn't the one who planned the jokes, either. He had six gagmen.

HJ: Chaplin had *six* gagmen?

OW: Yes. Oh, yes, of course. I'll tell you a story. There was a fellow who later became a director, called Mal St. Clair, and he was one of the gagmen. This was a day when Rebecca West, Aldous Huxley, and H. G. Wells were coming to watch the shooting of *City Lights*.

HJ: My God.

OW: And Chaplin has the chairs out, ready for them, and they sit down. He starts his scene, something they had been shooting the night before and hadn't finished. He has a brick. And he's going to throw it through the window of a shop to take something—because he's hungry or whatever it is—and then realizes a policeman is standing behind him. They start to roll. And Mal comes into the studio and says, "Charlie, I've got it! None of us could figure out what to do in that scene you were shooting last night, but I've got—" Chaplin says, "Go away." Mal says, "Charlie, I'm telling you, I've got it. What you do with the brick—" Chaplin says, "Get out, please. I told you not to come in." Mal says, "But we were all trying to find a kicker for this scene last night, and I've got it!" Chaplin's really angry now, says, "Listen, will you get out?" And Mal says, "As you start to raise the brick—" Charlie yells, "Get out of my studio!! I never want to see you again!!" So Mal says, "Yes, I'm going." Just as he reaches the exit, he turns around, and adds, "You are nothing but a no-good quidnunc."

HJ: Quidnuck?

OW: Quidnunc. Don't interrupt. Listen to the story. "No good quidnunc." Now, Charlie, every day after lunch, went to the can, his private can. And there he had the short Oxford dictionary, and he read a page of it to improve his mind. On this day he turns to Q. He sees that it's circled, and Mal has written, "I knew you'd look it up."

HJ: So it doesn't matter what it means.

OW: Exactly. That has nothing to do with it.

HJ: He did it in advance, was sort of saving it up, to humiliate Chaplin?

OW: Charlie was uneducated, you see, and embarrassed about his vocabulary.

HJ: Right. And he didn't want anybody to know that he had gag-men.

OW: That's why he fired Mal St. Clair. Never allowed him on the set again! Because he was blowing it in front of these highbrow, grand people, who thought he was the genius of comedy—

HJ: I'm completely stunned. It makes him Johnny Carson to me.

OW: Of course. He was Johnny Carson! He did think up gags, but he also had gagmen. The only one who didn't was Harold Lloyd, who was the greatest gagman in the history of movies. If you look at his movies, the gags are the most inventive—the most original, the most visual—of any of the silent comics.

HJ: But they weren't touching like Chaplin's were.

OW: C'mon, who's talking about touching? We're talking about gags! A gag isn't supposed to be touching.

HJ: I'm trying to talk about Chaplin's special genius . . .

OW: We're not talking about Chaplin's genius, we're not talking about his art, or whether Lloyd is better than Chaplin. We're talking about gags. The joke. You've got to separate jokes from beauty and all that. Chaplin had too much beauty. He drenched his pictures with it. That's why [Buster] Keaton is finally giving him the bath, and will, historically, forever. Oh, yes, he's so much greater.

HJ: Because he was not as schmaltzy.

OW: Because he was better—more versatile, more, finally, original. Some of the things that Keaton thought up to do are incredible.

HJ: I feel like a little child told there's no Santa Claus.

OW: But think what gags are. They're essential in a slapstick comedy. A picture has to be full of them. Chaplin had a guy who wrote better gags than he did, you see? But still, he made the pictures you admire. With his sensibility, plus all the things he did around the gags.

HJ: To me, nobody else is diminished by having writers, but it's different with Chaplin.

OW: He understood that. That's why he wanted people to think that he composed, directed, designed—everything. The day he ran *Monsieur Verdoux* for me—you know I wrote it—the credits said, "Charles Chaplin presents *Monsieur Verdoux*, produced by Charles Chaplin, directed by Charles Chaplin, music created by Charles Chaplin, executive producer Charles Chaplin." And then it said, "Screenplay—Orson Welles." Story and screenplay. And he said, "Don't you find it monotonous, my name all those times?" Not thinking he's being funny.

HJ: I don't understand. Was that his way of saying he didn't want Orson Welles?

OW: No. My name had to stay. It was in the contract. He was already being sued for plagiarism by Konrad Bercovici over *The Great Dictator*—and he did steal. So he came to me, and he said, "I have to, for my defense, say that I've written everything I ever did. And if I put it in the credits that you wrote the story and the screenplay, there goes my case. I'll put you back the minute the case is over.

HJ: But he never did.

OW: Never meant to. But I said, "Okay," and it opened in New York without my name at all. And all the papers said, as their chief criticism of *Monsieur Verdoux*, "Whoever put it into Chaplin's head to do such a thing?"

HJ: You mean to make such a dark movie about a bluebeard?

OW: Of course. So one day later the credits say, "Based on a suggestion by Orson Welles." Or "a story suggested," something like that. "Suggest" is in it. In other words, something I said to him one night over dinner. And it has said that ever since! But I wrote the whole script, which he then—

HJ: You wrote the whole script of *Verdoux*?

OW: I had a script, and I was gonna direct him in it. For two years. And he kept stalling, and finally he said, "I can't. I have to do it myself." He didn't want to be directed. He said, "I want to buy it from you." I said, "Of course, Charlie. I just want it to happen." I practically gave it to him. I said, "I'll leave the price to you." So a check came for $1,500—something like that. Cheapest man who ever lived. You love him, and I don't. And you wouldn't have loved him if you'd been through what I went through with him. It was really rough, and I have real contempt for him, because I worked very hard. Offered him something out of my love for him. It was not a suggestion, it was a *screenplay*. Do you know why I thought of Chaplin? There used to be an ad in the subways for something called Eau de Pinot. Which was the sort of thing that barbers put on, that smelled a little, and was supposed to stop dandruff. French. And they had a fellow with a little mustache saying, "Avez-vous scurf?"

HJ: Scurf?

OW: Flaky skin. And I looked at that, and I said, "Chaplin! Got to play [Henri-Désiré] Landru," you know, the real Bluebeard, eleven killings, all women except one, during World War I. Of course, Chaplin changed the script. Mine was called "The Lady-killer." Based on Landru, and I called the character Landru. He called him Verdoux. And he had to make it socially conscious, have Hitler, and so he changed the period.

HJ: So you had set it twenty years earlier, World War I?

OW: Yes. I've told you about the great sequence in the Alps that he cut out. Landru finally finds a woman whose profession is killing her husbands. His equal. And they go on a honeymoon together, a walking trip in the Alps. And each one wants to kill the other. And he cut it out, 'cause it was too good a part for the woman.

HJ: Oh, my God. Really? Who was gonna play it?

OW: It didn't matter. Because even those who loved him, and were close to him, have said, "You know Charlie will never let another actor be good on the screen with him, not for one minute." So he changed the script and came up with what was a very funny scene, but nothing like mine. His was the scene in the rowboat, in the Bois de Boulogne. If you listen carefully, you will hear yodeling in the distance. Because, in my script, I accompanied this scene in the mountains with yodeling, and he never stopped to wonder why the yodeling. That's how dumb he was!

Actually, Chaplin was deeply dumb in many ways. That's what's so strange, great hunks of sentimental dumbness with these shafts of genius. And he blew it, too. He performed *Verdoux* for two years in everybody's drawing room, so that there was nothing left when it came time to shoot it. He did the same thing with *The Great Dictator*. But he didn't get invited out that often. Because, after a point, people didn't want their whole party taken over by one entertainer. They knew he'd come, and he'd totally dominate—if you had Chaplin, you had Chaplin performing. That limited his social life terribly.

HJ: He was that insecure, that he had the need to prove himself?

OW: Or had that much pleasure in performing, whatever. He may just have enjoyed showing off. Chaplin showed me the rushes of the original *Limelight* scene with Keaton, before it was cut.

HJ: Keaton had more to do, I presume.

OW: Not only more to do, but he gave the bath to Chaplin! Washed him right off the screen. You saw who was the best. Just no argument.

HJ: And you think the reason Chaplin cut it was 'cause he was jealous of Keaton?

OW: There's no "thinking." I can't blame him, because it was almost embarrassing.

HJ: You would think that the brilliance of Chaplin would give him the generosity of spirit to recognize—

OW: I don't think *brilliance* is the word, *genius* is.

HJ: His creative brilliance, I mean. I never have understood the word *genius*.

OW: Well, you can't—any more than you'd understand *soul*, *love*. They're all the big words that no one understands.

HJ: I mean, he was some kind of genius. Right?

OW: No, not some kind of genius—he was absolutely a genius. But so was Keaton. There's nothing Chaplin ever made that's as good as *The General*. I think *The General* is almost the greatest movie ever made. The most poetic movie I've ever seen. To my great sorrow, I've got to the age now where all my old minority opinions are ceasing to be minority. I spent all my life saying, "You're all crazy—it's Keaton!" And now I've got nothing to argue about! Now Keaton is coming in. I used to say, "What are they doing all that Wagner for? Why don't they do *Don Giovanni*? Now everybody's doing it.

HJ: I don't know why Keaton to me is more farcical, broader, not as real as Chaplin.

OW: But Chaplin isn't real. He's—

HJ: Oh, how can you say Chaplin isn't real?

OW: Chaplin is sheer poetry, if you want, but it's not real.

HJ: But it's poetry based upon reality, a heightened form of reality.

OW: Not for me, no. What Chaplin did is—there are two basic kinds of clown. In the classic circus, there's the clown who is white-faced, with a white cap, short trousers, and silk stockings. He has beautiful legs, and is very elegant. Every move he makes is perfect. The other clown, who works with him, is called an *auguste*, and he has baggy pants and big feet. What Chaplin did was to marry them, these two classic clowns, and create a new clown. That was his secret—that's my theory.

HJ: You look at some of Chaplin's shorts, and they don't feel dated.

OW: They don't date because they were dated then. They were period pieces when they were made. The silent pictures always look as though they happened in a world earlier than they did when they were shot. They all derive from the nineteenth century.

HJ: That must be why, when he tried to tackle anything contemporary it was so bad. That's why there was such a gulf between his silents and his talking pictures. *Limelight* is a fake, sentimental film, but I happen to like it very much.

OW: Yeah. Well, as I said, you love him, and I don't. The visual difference between *City Lights* and the movie he made with Paulette Goddard is extraordinary.

HJ: *City Lights* is still the greatest Chaplin film.

OW: No question. But that other film is bad. From that time on, he went down so fast that he's almost unrecognizable . . . *Limelight!*

HJ: *Limelight* didn't have Paulette Goddard.

OW: No, no, the picture I'm talking about was made before, when I was still a boy.

HJ: *Gold Rush?*

OW: No, no.

HJ: No. Which one was it with her? I forget. *(Pause)* Not *Modern Times*.

OW: *Modern Times!* That's the bad picture. I saw it again just six weeks ago. It doesn't have a good moment in it. It is so coarse, it is so vulgar. It doesn't touch—I knew Paulette well.

HJ: So you knew her when she was going down on people at Ciro's, or was it Anatole Litvak going down on her under the table? Or something like that.

OW: She's a wonderful girl, but she's a living cash register, you know.

HJ: You should see Chaplin's female impersonation movie, *The Woman*, it was called. A short, about twenty minutes. He was wearing a fur muff and a fur hat.

OW: He looked terrific as a woman.

HJ: He looked gorgeous and he was so incredible and touching and flirtatious and charming and romantic and teasing. And sexual . . .

OW: He wasn't effeminate, just totally female as a performer. There was no masculine element there. And he was like that as a man, too, terribly female as a man. It's that smile, that little female smile. He was so beautiful when he was young. And he didn't want any of us not to notice it. He beaded his eyelashes. You know how long that takes? He made himself up to be the most beautiful fellow in the world, and then put that little mustache on. Vanity is very much part of that character. He didn't think he made himself look prissy. He thought he looked beautiful, and delicate and sensitive, and so did all the world. They took it on his terms. I never thought he was funny. I thought he was wonderful—wonderful—but not funny. I thought he was sinister. That's why I thought of him for *Verdoux*. I had another idea for Chaplin—with Garbo—but neither one of them would touch it. A farce. They're in the maze in Hampton Court, and he deliberately loses her.

HJ: Could she have played farce, do you think?

OW: Yes. Well, she played comedy wonderfully. I wouldn't have made her ridiculous, but I would have made her herself. I would have made her the distinguished actress that she was. I told it first to her, and then to him, and they were just—nothing. So that went nowhere.

HJ: Why did she stop acting? Was it just because of the bad reviews?

OW: Of *Two-Faced Woman*. No business.

HJ: You mean she was that unprepared for a flop? She must have, somewhere along the line, figured that, eventually, one of her pictures wouldn't work.

OW: No, I think she was getting older, and I think she hated to act. And I think she was waiting for the flop.

HJ: To go out with.

OW: I think so. I was always a wild Garbo fan. But when I saw her in *Grand Hotel*, at first I thought it was somebody else making fun of her, like somebody taking off on Garbo. She was totally miscast as a ballerina. She's a big-boned cow. She did everything that you would do if you were a drag queen doing an imitation of Garbo, you know.

Did I ever tell you about the time I introduced Marlene to

Garbo? Marlene was my house guest, and for some unaccountable reason had never met Garbo, and she was her hero. I arranged for Clifton Webb to give a party for Garbo so I could bring Marlene. I was living with Rita at the time, and she didn't want to go. That was very much like her. She never wanted to go anywhere, just stay home. So Marlene and I went without her. Garbo was sitting on a raised platform in the middle of the living room, so that everybody had to stand and look up at her. I introduced them. I said, "Greta, it's unbelievable that you two have never met—Greta, Marlene. Marlene, Greta." Marlene started to gush, which was not like her at all. Looking up at Garbo, she said, "You're the most beautiful woman I've ever seen, it's such a pleasure to meet you, I'm humble in your presence," and on and on. Garbo said, "Thank you very much. Next?" And turned away to somebody else. Marlene was crushed.

14. "Art Buchwald drove it up Ronnie's ass and broke it off."

In which Orson ridicules Ronald Reagan, explains why he lost his respect for Elia "Gadge" Kazan, and argues that old people, especially macho men like Norman Mailer, come to look like their Jewish mothers.

ORSON WELLES: Did you see the tribute to the five distinguished people at the Kennedy Center the other night?

HENRY JAGLOM: No. I missed it.

OW: I saw it. It was a riot. Art Buchwald came on, and for seven minutes drove it up Ronnie's ass and broke it off. He didn't have one joke that Ronnie could even laugh at. He said, "And Mr. Reagan . . ." you know, with that voice of his, "We have to be careful. We ought not to treat the arts the way you treat Central America." And he said, "Because, if the Kennedy Center goes Communist, the next thing is the Hollywood Bowl!" You could see the audience wondering whether they'd be photographed by the FBI on their way out if they laughed too hard.

HJ: Did they cut to Reagan at all?

OW: At the very beginning, doing a kind of wince, and then never again. The whole dressed-up audience had these frozen smiles. Art was the licensed jester. They couldn't cut. I wanted to see how Old Blue Eyes was taking it. But we didn't even get to see that.

HJ: Who else was there?

OW: It was a great group. Besides Sinatra—Kazan, Katherine Dunham, Jimmy Stewart, and Virgil Thompson. First we had a speech by Reagan, from the White House, instead of his speaking from his box or coming on the stage. They'd written a very short, gracious speech, which he read with that Reagan skill, which can be very good. Followed by Warren Beatty, who introduced Kazan, calling him "our greatest living film director." A very bad speech. And badly delivered. He looked terrible. Any thought that he's gonna be president was written off last night. Katherine Dunham is a fake dancer if ever there was one. And Virgil Thomson, introduced by John Houseman. I didn't stay for that. They roomed together—they were lovers. Why shouldn't he introduce him?

HJ: Yeah, yeah. They were lovers, really?

OW: Oh, yes.

HJ: Is he that old?

OW: Houseman is eighty-one. Something that gives me comfort every night. Every night when I get a twinge of rheumatism. He's holding up awfully well, though.

HJ: More extraordinary, that Warren would choose to introduce Kazan!

OW: Kazan gave Warren his first job, *Splendor in the Grass*. Why couldn't he have pretended that he wasn't in town, or something? When I saw Gadge it made me sick. I still can't forgive him. The people I got most mad at were people from my side who gave names. And he was one of the biggest sellers of people up the river in the whole bunch. I am not a vengeful person, but Kazan is one of the people that I feel really badly about. I was—in fact, in a terrible way, I'm still fond of him—I like Gadge. But I think he behaved so badly that it's just inexcusable. I cannot honor him. Or sit with him.

HJ: You won't give anything to *On the Waterfront*?

OW: Nothing. Because it's so immoral.

HJ: Forgetting the politics for a moment . . .

OW: I wish I could. But that was made at a time when I was very sensitive on those subjects, and it was an excuse for all those people who gave names. All those collabos with McCarthy, of which Kazan was one. And this film was to show that the hero is the man who tells.

HJ: And Budd Schulberg, who wrote it, was another.

OW: That's right—all that. So I'm bigoted. Then we had Zorba the Greek. Straight from Broadway. Tony Quinn came out and neither danced nor sang. But kind of stood there, as though we're all supposed to think that this is the biggest set of balls that's ever been seen in New York. And then he told us that he loved Kazan more than any man alive. Zorba the Testicle, to Gadge.

HJ: I'm trying to think when they even worked together.

OW: In *Viva Zapata!* He played Zapata's brother. He was quite good.

HJ: I love that movie.

OW: Above all, not a good movie. Zapata is so important to me, and I have such a clear picture of what the story is, that I was profoundly offended by the movie. On the grounds of its—

HJ: I just took it as a progressive fairy tale.

OW: I was not free to appreciate it on those terms. And it wasn't progressive. Zapata—here's a true story. Did I ever tell you what happened when he heard about the trouble Lenin was in? Because at one point Lenin had said, "If we can hold out another sixty days, the revolution is won. If we don't, it's lost." And word of this got to Mexico, where Zapata was fighting. So Zapata says, "Where is he? We will ride over and help him." He thought Moscow was somewhere over the hill.

HJ: I guess *Viva Zapata!* was another anti-left film, if you think about it. Because the revolution is betrayed by the arch revolutionary, the Lenin figure. And better to have had no revolution at all. Do you think *Streetcar Named Desire* is a good film?

OW: No. I think Gadge did it better in the theater. I don't think he's a very good filmmaker compared to his work in the theater.

HJ: You don't make allowances for people with talent, like Kazan?

OW: Let me tell you the story of Emil Jannings.

HJ: I know who he is. He played opposite Marlene in *The Blue Angel*. He won a Best Actor Oscar for something or other, I think the first one ever awarded. Not only did he collaborate with the Nazis, Joseph Goebbels named him "Artist of the State."

OW: When the allies got to Berlin in the last days of the war, he fled to his hometown. As the American troops entered the town with their tanks looking for collaborators, he stood in front of his little house waving his Oscar over his head, yelling, "Artiste, artiste!"

You know, Gadge has begun to look like a minor figure in a Dostoevsky novel. His face has become long, like a junior inquisitor. And he was standing on that stage like some terrible bird. The face he deserves, with a beak, a beak—it's a beak. A face that turns into a beak.

HJ: My mother once said, "All old people look Jewish."

OW: True. You either look Jewish or you look Irish—you have your choice. It has nothing to do with the nose. It's an expression that happens to people when they get past sixty—they usually look like their Jewish or Irish mother. Like Mailer, who looks exactly like his Jewish mother. He never looked Jewish before at all! He looked like an Irishman, if anything. If you met him and his name had been Reilly, you would have said, "Sure—that's Reilly." And Lenny Bernstein is getting to look like his mother, too, you know.

HJ: I just saw him in New York. He conducted—

OW: They don't look like their fathers, they look like their mothers! Lenny's really—I mean, he's developed this flourish with the baton, that he started a couple years ago.

HJ: His pinkie is up?

OW: Way up all the time. And he can't jump as high anymore. It's as if he's announcing to the world that he can still jump, but he doesn't really leave the floor! He used to leave the floor!

HJ: He did the most extraordinary thing. I went to a concert at Carnegie Hall and it started with Bernstein playing some Chopin. And he started crying in the middle of playing. I never saw him do that before—he just wept.

OW: Yes, he's very emotional—genuinely.

HJ: It was incredibly touching. It made the music stronger, in some way. He's so theatrical. Does he know? He must know.

OW: Of course he knew he was going to choke back the tears. He's a ham. I've known him since he started.

HJ: He's still a wonderful-looking man.

OW: Less so now. More and more like his mother. The last couple of years have been very cruel to him. Have really made him look like the old lady, you know. And, brashly, he's cut his hair shorter, hoping to look less like her.

HJ: And it doesn't work.

OW: No, now Lenny looks more like Gertrude Stein. It's a terrible fate that comes to men—and, particularly, very masculine men. And that's the cruelty, you see? You could see him in a dress, without any trouble at all, you know? . . . Oh, Kiki.

HJ: What's the matter?

OW: It's Kiki. She's forgotten herself.

HJ: She's farting?

OW: Oh, yes. Ooh, yes—oooh! Isn't that terrible?

WAITER: Shall we show you desserts?

HJ: *(To waiter)* It's not us—it's the dog. We just want you to know.

OW: Don't bring us a dessert for the next two minutes.

HJ: Oooh! That one came clear across the table.

OW: This is a real . . . like atomic warfare. Mmm, boy—that was one.

HJ: It's great to have a dog around in case one ever does it oneself.

OW: Well, in the eighteenth century, they always did.

HJ: For that reason?

OW: Yes. Do you know the *Arabian Nights* story?

HJ: No.

OW: A young man goes to a wedding feast, the most important wedding feast in the village. Everyone is on their best behavior. And just when the mullah is about to pronounce his blessing, and everything is quiet, he lets rip the loudest fart that's ever been heard. He is so embarrassed that he turns and flees. He steals a camel, and rides away from the village, out of the kingdom, and goes to the farthest reaches of the known world. And there, over the years, he prospers. Finally, as a rich old man, he comes back to the village with a great caravan. As he approaches it, a couple of women are working in the fields. They look up and say, "Look, there's the man who farted at the wedding."

HJ: Oh, God!

Part Two

1984–1985

Welles and Jaglom in Someone to Love, *Welles's final screen appearance.*

"*I always acted as if everything was going to go great for him. I needed to act that way to feel that way, so that I could make him feel that way, and hopefully make someone else, or some combination of many someone elses, give him the money to work, to live. I was hustling me and him, and hopefully them, into a self-fulfilling prophecy. I told him deals were done, all that was needed was for so and so to fly in and confirm them, when it wasn't true. I didn't make it up out of whole cloth, but where things were iffy, I made them sound much less iffy.*"

—HENRY JAGLOM, e-mail, June 8, 2012

15. "It was my one moment of being a traffic-stopping superstar."

In which Orson recalls that director Carol Reed wanted him for *The Third Man*. He reflects on Joseph Cotten's career, and wonders what the excitement over Alfred Hitchcock was all about.

Orson Welles: You're eating already. Your mouth is full, which is a disgusting sight.

Henry Jaglom: And how are you today? You're late. That's why I ordered.

OW: Angry at a lot of things going on in my household. You know those wild stupidities that happen to everybody who lives longer than they should. I have a thing I have to put on my leg that compresses it, and I put it on at night. Somebody has to get me out of it in twenty minutes or I go nuts. But somebody went to sleep, and there was no getting out, and I had to fight my way out of this machine. It took me about forty minutes to get untangled. I'm a little out of breath from rage. You know, simple, quiet, domestic rage.

HJ: I saw *The Third Man* last night. I don't think there's another movie of Carol Reed's that's in its class.

OW: I think *Odd Man Out* is close to it.

HJ: That's a good movie. But James Mason's performance is weak.

OW: Well, Carol didn't think he was good enough. He talked me out of using Mason in something I wanted to do. He said, "Mason hasn't got the range. He drove me crazy in *Odd Man Out*. He can't do from here to there. He can only do from here to here." So I believed him, because he really knew acting. Loved actors.

HJ: The longer you look at Mason's performance—

OW: The less and less good it gets.

HJ: The character of Harry Lime fit you like a glove.

OW: It's a hell of a picture. Alida Valli. Boy, she's great. She's Austrian, you know, raised in Italy. She started very young.

HJ: What happened to her?

OW: She was the biggest star in Europe. She was huge during the fascist period, all through the war. In Rome. Then she was taken up by Selznick. Selznick destroyed her. He brought her to America, tried to make a big star out of her here, thought he'd have another Bergman, and put her in three—

HJ: After *The Third Man*?

OW: No, *The Third Man* was in the middle. He loaned her and [Joseph] Cotten to Alex Korda, who produced it. Alex had to have two American stars besides me to sell the picture. So he made this deal with Selznick, giving him all American rights. That's the only good picture she made here. You can't look at the others.

HJ: What else did he put her in?

OW: A terrible trial movie, Hitchcock, *The Paradine Case*. And something else terrible. She came back to Europe, and nobody would hire her. They said, "She can't be any good. She failed in Hollywood." After that, it was just, "A special appearance by Alida Valli." She should never have come here in the first place.

HJ: Carol Reed had never directed you before. Were you his idea?

OW: Yes. Selznick had bitterly fought against having me in it. He was so dumb. He wanted Noël Coward for the part. He was impressed by Noël. And not by me. Noël was a little mysterious, but he saw me around all the time.

HJ: Well, you did fuck up his charades.

OW: Alex held out, said it had to be me, and so did Gregg Toland. I took the Orient Express from Venice or from Paris, I don't remember which, and arrived in the morning in Vienna at about eight o'clock. I had my wardrobe. We went right out to the Ferris wheel, and by nine o'clock I had shot a scene. Then we shot for six days, five in Vienna and one in London. There were three complete A-film units shooting at once. Because Carol needed an entire crew to shoot one huge scene, where you saw down four blocks at night, and then, in another part of Vienna, the second crew was working. And a third was down in the sewer. That's how come we got it done so fast.

HJ: You don't appear until near the end.

OW: All the characters do is talk about Harry Lime. Until the last reel. Then I come on.

HJ: But it's not the last reel.

OW: Yes, it is the last reel.

HJ: No.

OW: I have one appearance—a silent appearance—in the reel before. I'm in shadow, and the light suddenly hits me when the window is opened. Jo Cotten sees the cat sitting on my shoe. That was the greatest entrance there ever was. We did it in Vienna, but not in a real location. Carol had a little set built just for that, on which we shot at the end of every day, towards dusk. We would look at the rushes, and then Carol would say, "Not yet," and we'd do it again, to get it perfect.

HJ: How much of *The Third Man* was Grahame Greene's, how much was Korda's?

OW: The real makers of that film were Carol Reed and Korda. Greene was nowhere near it. His authorship is greatly exaggerated. The idea for the plot was Alex's.

HJ: Really? Everyone assumes, automatically, that the Graham Greene novel came first, and then somebody adapted— It's not from Graham Greene?

OW: Korda gave him the basic idea. Said, "Go and write a movie script set in a bombed-out, nightmare city after the war, with the black market and all that. He just wrote a rough-draft sketch for the movie, and Carol did the rest of it. There's an example of a producer being a producer. Carol deserves much more credit than people give him. Graham wrote the novel *after* the movie was made. Also, he conceived the character as one of those burnt-out cases, one of the Graham Greene empty men, which was not my vision of him at all.

HJ: Maybe that's why Selznick thought of Noël Coward for the character that Greene wrote.

OW: Maybe. But I said, "No, he has to be fascinating. You must understand why he's got this city in his hand." And Carol took a flyer on that idea and changed the character completely. Greene's Harry Lime was nothing like the way I played it. Every word that I spoke, all my dialogue, I wrote, because Carol wanted me to. Including the "cuckoo clock."

HJ: I remember that verbatim. Lime says, "In Italy, for thirty years under the Borgias, they had warfare, terror, murder, and bloodshed, but they produced Michelangelo, Leonardo da Vinci, and the Renaissance. In Switzerland, they had brotherly love, they have five hundred years of democracy and peace—and what did that produce? The cuckoo clock!"

OW: I have to admit that it's unfair, because the cuckoo clock is made in the Schwarzwald, which is not in Switzerland at all! And I knew it when I wrote the line! And did the Swiss send me letters!

HJ: You have a generation of Swiss hating you because of that.

OW: But pretending to laugh. You know how the Swiss laugh, when they want to show they have a sense of humor? It's like the Swedes.

They go, "Ho ho ho. Ho ho—your joke about the cuckoo clock. You know, the cuckoo clock is not made in Switzerland." I say, "I know, I know." It was as misleading a statement as has ever been made for a laugh in a movie. I came to Carol the morning we shot it and said, "How about this?" And he said, "Yes! And so we did it."

HJ: Greene has script credit. Did he give you any problems about your writing your lines?

OW: No. Because he didn't take the movie seriously. It wasn't a "Graham Greene" work. He gave me a line that I was supposed to say from atop the Wiener Riesenrad, the Ferris wheel: "Look at those people down there—they look like ants." Well, that's about as clichéd as you can get.

HJ: So how much of *The Third Man* is Korda, and how much is Reed?

OW: It's full of ideas that everybody thought up on the set. Because Carol was the kind of person who didn't feel threatened by ideas from other people. A wonderful director. I really worshipped him.

HJ: How was *The Third Man* received?

OW: In Europe, the picture was a hundred times bigger than it was here. It was the biggest hit since the war. It corresponded to something the Europeans could understand in a way the Americans didn't. The Europeans had been through hell, the war, the cynicism, the black market, all that. Harry Lime represented their past, in a way, the dark side of them. Yet attractive, you know.

You cannot imagine what it was, a kind of mania. When I came into a restaurant, the people went crazy. At the hotel I was staying in, police had to come to quiet the fans. It was my one moment of being a superstar, a traffic-stopping superstar. The best part ever written for an actor. Had I not been trying to finish *Othello*, I could have made a career out of that picture. From all the offers I got. But by the time I finished *Othello*, the fever was over, you see.

Now, after this huge European success, it comes out in America—Selznick's version—saying: "David O. Selznick presents *The Third Man*. Produced by David O. Selznick." About three of those credits.

HJ: It was Chaplin all over again.

OW: I took Alex and David to dinner one night in Paris, right after it opened, and Alex said, "My dear David. I have seen the American titles." And David started to hem and haw, "Well, you know . . ." Alex said, "I only hope that I don't die before you do." David said, "What do you mean?" Alex replied, "I don't want to think of you sneaking into the cemetery and scratching my name off my tombstone."

When I was up for Best Actor for *The Third Man*, I was nearby, in Italy, a few hours away from Cannes. Alex called me and said, "If you'll come to Cannes, you'll get the prize." That's the way it works. I said, "Why don't I stay here and get the prize?" And he said, "If you don't come, they'll have to give it to Eddie Robinson, because he's been here the whole two weeks." I didn't believe him. And then I talked to [Robert] Favre Le Bret, who was president of the festival in those days, who said, "Yes, you come and you've got it. You don't come—" So I said, "Give it to him," and didn't go. And Eddie Robinson won.

HJ: Joseph Cotten is rather amazing in *The Third Man*.

OW: He was very good.

HJ: I've never particularly liked him, except in *Kane* and *Ambersons*.

OW: *Shadow of a Doubt.* He's awfully good in that.

HJ: Oh, my God! He's great in that. I completely forgot about it.

OW: That's the one good Hitchcock picture made in America. Hitchcock himself said it was his best. The English ones are better than the American pictures, the very early ones, like *The 39 Steps*. Oh, my God, what a masterpiece. Those pictures had a little foreign charm, because we didn't know the actors very well. But I've never understood the cult of Hitchcock. Particularly the late American movies. I don't recognize the same director!

HJ: He decided to become popular.

OW: Egotism and laziness. And they're all lit like television shows. About the time he started to use color, he stopped looking through the camera. I saw one of the worst movies I've ever seen the other night. Hitchcock's movie where Jimmy Stewart looks through the window?

HJ: *Rear Window.*

OW: Everything is stupid about it. Complete insensitivity to what a story about voyeurism could be. I'll tell you what is astonishing. To discover that Jimmy Stewart can be a bad actor. But *really* bad. Even Grace Kelly is better than Jimmy, who's overacting. He's kind of looking to the left and giving as bad a performance as he ever gave. But, then, you see, the world was so much at Hitch's feet that the actors just thought, "Do what he says and it's gonna be great."

HJ: If you think that one is bad, there's another terrible one with Jimmy Stewart and Kim Novak.

OW: *Vertigo.* That's worse.

HJ: And then the other one—what was the other one? His much praised comedy, *The Trouble with Harry.*

OW: By then it was senility.

HJ: No, it wasn't senility—that movie came earlier.

OW: I think he was senile a long time before he died. He was in life, you know. He kept falling asleep while you were talking to him. When I would go to Jo's, Hitchcock would be there for dinner. I'd go because Jo was fond of him, not because he was interesting. When he first came to America, I looked him up and took him to lunch at 21.

HJ: He must have been a different person then.

OW: No, he wasn't very interesting then, either. I was disappointed.

HJ: There's a movie I know you would hate that Jo's in with Jennifer Jones.

OW: *Portrait of Jennie.* He and I laughed at it when it was being made!

HJ: Jennifer Jones really could not act. Would you agree with me about that?

OW: Yes. She was hopeless. But the poor girl is nuts, you know. Something is wrong there.

HJ: So how did you know Reed could get that kind of a performance out of Cotten?

OW: Because I thought he was wonderful.

HJ: From something you saw him in?

OW: No, no. He'd been with me for years in the theater! He was a great farceur. His character was funny, and that's Jo's thing. He was brilliant at that! *Brilliant!* The problem with Jo was that he was never a romantic leading man. He was a character actor. Nothing could make him a leading man. And that's all he played in Hollywood. He looked stiff and wooden. Uncomfortable. It wasn't because he got bad, it was because he was doing something outside his range. And the fact that he was attractive and looked like he could play a leading man, made them think he must be one. Plus he had this big success in *Philadelphia Story* on Broadway, so they thought that would translate to screen. Jo's career was made not by *Citizen Kane* but by *Philadelphia Story.* Selznick picked him up and said, "We'll have another Cary Grant." But nobody ever wrote him another part like that, you see. So that was his career—doing what he couldn't do.

HJ: Did he know that he was unsuited for this?

OW: No. If he did, he wouldn't tell me. And why should he—he was a success. Remember, he started as a professional football player, and then became a stage manager for Belasco, and then a radio actor. We shared this one job—on a radio show called *School of the Air*. It was a show for children in the morning, and it paid $32 a week. So we were both living on this—both married. Then one day we did an episode that broke us up. It was on the Olympic Games. And we had to say things like, "Let me see your javelin. It is by far the biggest in all Athens." We couldn't stop laughing. The word went out that we couldn't be in the show at the same time. So that meant $32 every second week for each of us.

I had one radio job, a show called *Big Sister*—God, I loved it. I was the cad. And I had this girl in the rumble seat. And the suspense was, was I gonna make her? And it went on for about three months. That's the longest session in a rumble seat, you know. We had to do two shows, one in the morning, at ten, and one in the afternoon—for the different time zones. One day I was sitting in the barbershop, and I heard the theme song come on, and Martin Gabel was playing my part. I'd forgotten about the second show! That was the end of that job! But soon I got my own radio show and then my own theater.

HJ: What happened to Cotten when you made it?

OW: That was a difficult period for me, as a friend, at least, because suddenly I was making a fortune. Jo was still making those smaller salaries, and I was big stuff. I felt uncomfortable, because he hadn't got up there with me. Here I was in a country house, with a chauffeur and a Rolls-Royce, and Jo was still in the—you know. So I helped him, a good turn that many people would have regarded as an unforgivable thing to do. But he wasn't uncomfortable, he was delightful about it. I was the one who felt bad. So I was thrilled about *Philadelphia Story*, because it reduced the distance between us.

HJ: I think it's always harder for the one who's moving on.

16. "God save me from my friends."

In which Orson battles his reputation, talks about the importance of casting fresh faces in *Kane*. He explains that he never shot coverage so that the studio couldn't recut his films, although that didn't stop RKO from mutilating *The Magnificent Ambersons*.

HENRY JAGLOM: I just saw *Othello* again, in New York, in a theater, the Thalia, on the Upper West Side. The audience was standing and cheering. Kids, twenty-year-olds, thirty-year-olds. It's superb. It doesn't look dated, like so much Shakespeare does, because of the way you did it. It's not a costume fifties movie, or a sixties movie. I know that's why you didn't like Brando in *Julius Caesar*, for instance, because it looks like a picture that was made—

ORSON WELLES: At Metro in 1950, yeah.

HJ: The togas, and the haircuts and the makeup were . . .

OW: So Max Factor.

HJ: Exactly. But you so rooted your *Othello* in some imaginary ancestral land that—

OW: Because a funny thing happens in costume pictures. You sense the lunch wagon next to the set.

HJ: You should see *Othello* now. I think you'd feel very good about it.

OW: I'd rather hear about how good it is than see it.

HJ: Right. If you saw it, you'd find things you don't like.

OW: I know one thing that's no good, which is the first sequence in Venice after the crawl. I think it doesn't have the same authority as the rest of the film. It's because that's where we ran out of dough. That's the reel of "no dough." The film is good again the minute we're in Cyprus.

HJ: There's a soap opera—*All My Children*—do you know it? Your lady from *Citizen Kane* is in it.

OW: Which one?

HJ: The one who played Kane's first wife, Emily, Ruth Warrick. She's incredibly bad.

OW: She looked the part of Emily. And I'm one of those fellows who thinks, if they look it, then you can make them act it. Particularly a small part.

HJ: The breakfast scene, my favorite, she was wonderful in that.

OW: She was!

HJ: Wonderful. By the time it was all finished, the editing, and so on.

OW: There was nothing to edit. It was just cut from shot to shot. Because after each shot I went and changed my makeup, and she changed her dress. Then we came back again, and did the next line. They'd all been rehearsed. There was nothing to monkey around with. The camera never moved. It just waited.

HJ: Did you use master shots?

OW: I never shot a master in my life. Gregg told me that Jack Ford never did it, so I never did it, either. I stop where I know I'm going to cut. I don't ever shoot through it and then go back for cuts.

HJ: You stop shooting and do the close-up?

OW: Yeah, I stop. I don't give myself anything to play with.

HJ: How do you know what you're going to need?

OW: Because I decide what I want. In advance. In the areas I don't decide, then I shoot all kinds of things, but I still don't shoot a master. There's no protection, ever.

HJ: So the studio can't fuck with you, cut it without you?

OW: That's what Jack Ford told me. What can they do? They don't have anything to go to.

HJ: Is that why he did it?

OW: Sure. But of course he had a cutter. He never cut a picture himself. Never paid any attention to it. Could not give a shit.

HJ: How long did the breakfast scene take?

OW: Less than a day. Starting in the morning. I'd say we were done about three in the afternoon. Because there were no light changes, you see? Or only very slight ones. Ruth was a wonderful girl. And when she was young, she was quite sexy.

HJ: I didn't see that in her. In *Kane* you didn't emphasize it at all.

OW: No. Nor did I notice it. Only a couple years later when she came and visited me on the set.

HJ: You never noticed she was attractive when you were working together?

OW: I never allow myself to notice any of that.

HJ: Smart, yeah. That's not the time to let yourself be distracted.

OW: No. Particularly not if you're, by accident, successful. Because then everybody hates you. All the other girls, and their friends.

HJ: Dorothy Comingore, another fresh face, was so great as Susan Alexander, Kane's mistress and second wife, the one based on Marion Davies. How did you find her?

OW: Chaplin, you know, told me about her.

HJ: What was she in?

OW: Nothing. He just found her. He'd seen her in some little play or something. Her singing "Come and Go" was a real fabricated performance, because we sprayed her throat before every take with some dangerous chemical that made her hoarse. Her performance as the younger version of the wife was herself. The older one was chemical. That scene with her singing in the nightclub was the first shot I ever made in a movie. That's what we began with.

HJ: That's the first thing you shot? When she was supposed to be older, and her throat was sprayed?

OW: Yes, we began with that. Because we had the nightclub set which had been built for some B movie. So we pretended I was shooting tests, practicing how to make movies, for ten or twelve days.

HJ: That's great. And you learned everything you needed to know.

OW: Yeah.

HJ: And how much of that did you use, actually?

OW: Everything. We were really shooting the movie. It was a trick. We weren't testing anything. It was Gregg's idea. But I made one mistake. I was stuck with one terrible piece of casting that broke my heart, because none of the faces in the movie had ever been seen before on a screen. But in that nightclub scene they gave me a waiter from New York who had been seen in every movie for twenty years, completely ruining my dream of total . . .

HJ: I can't even remember his face.

OW: Oh, you wouldn't. But if you'd been going to movies at that time, you would have recognized him. He was *the* waiter, you know?

HJ: RKO's waiter.

OW: No, not just RKO's, he was everybody's waiter.

HJ: So what happened to Comingore?

OW: For two or three years she just refused everything, waiting for another Susan Alexander. Well, you know, those parts don't come along so often.

HJ: God, in a way, it's the worst thing that can happen, to get that at the beginning of your career, isn't it?

OW: It's the old, old problem in show business. Once you're a hit as the Irish busboy, nobody wants you as the gangster. Everybody loved her in *Kane*, so she was in a good situation. She had that pathos that could turn into bitchiness because it came from insecurity and vulgarity. She ended up, you know, being arrested for prostitution. She was picking people up in bars. It was tragic.

HJ: I recall she was married to screenwriter Richard Collins, who told HUAC he divorced her because she refused to name names. She was blacklisted in 1951, which ended her career.

OW: Speaking of Ruth Warrick, yesterday I was being interviewed by David Hartman, by satellite. For *Good Morning America*. With her and Paul Stewart. God save me from my friends.

HJ: Stewart played Raymond, the slippery valet in *Kane*, yes?

OW: Yes, and he's telling Hartman how much the picture cost. He's got it wrong, of course. And sounding as though he were associate producer, whereas he was brought in for a week's work as an actor. And Ruth Warrick is saying that I'm the greatest thing since Jesus, and that I walk on water, and all of this. And I'm trying to shut her up, because I know she's wrecking the show by going on and on. And after we're off the air she gives me her book, in which she writes all these wonderful things about me, like, "He was terrific to all the actors. And we all loved him—we were a family," and all that. "Except for Dorothy Comingore. He was terrible to her." So I said, "This is all invented." Because I hardly knew Ruth Warrick, but Comingore and I were great friends. And according to Ruth I was cruel to her. Now, this is one actress in a movie talking about another. It gets worse. A little later, she writes that I abandoned *Ambersons*, which I was editing, and went off to South America to make *Journey into Fear*, which Ruth was in, and *It's All True*. And that I had already begun that wastefulness which . . . And then she says, "Poor Orson." In fact, I went to South America right after Pearl Harbor, because Nelson Rockefeller, whom Roosevelt had named head of Inter-American Affairs, sent me down there. So here was Ruth Warrick overpraising me on the show, and then giving me the book to sign! What is interesting about her book is that the reader is likely to think that we had a love affair. She's practically saying it.

I don't know how many ways there are to direct a movie, but let's say there are a hundred. And mine happens to be, I direct a movie by making love to everybody involved in it. I'm not running for office—I don't want to be popular with the crew—but I make love to every actor. Then, when they're no longer working for me, it's like they've been abandoned, like I've betrayed them.

HJ: Do those last reels of *Ambersons* exist anywhere, do you think?

OW: Somebody told me the big scene in the boardinghouse with Aggie [Moorehead] and Jo has been found, but I've never tracked it down.

HJ: How many reels were missing?

OW: It would've played another fifteen minutes.

HJ: You know the guy who books the Z Channel is trying to get permission to show *Ambersons* without all that nonsense RKO stuck on to the end of the film.

OW: We had shot one complete reel—the party scene, without a cut. RKO chopped two minutes out of the middle of it, because it didn't further the plot. This little thing about olives, and people not being used to them. A cut in the middle of a one-reel shot. It's a very skillful cut—it plays all right—but the scene was much better before. And, of course, nobody can find the two minutes they cut out of the reel. It's a bit of sour grapes, because I did it before Hitchcock did it in *Rope*. The first reel in the history of movies made without a cut was in *Ambersons*.

HJ: And that's the only change, besides all the stuff at the end?

OW: No, there're other changes, but very few in the beginning and the middle. It's only when the story begins to get too dark. I don't know when I found the letter sent me by George Schaefer, who'd been to the preview in Pomona where they laughed at Agnes Moorehead. Half of her scene is cut forever, because the audience fell on the floor laughing.

HJ: That was the test in front of the Esther Williams audience in the Valley.

OW: And Schaefer said, "We really have to make it more commercial." Poor guy—he was in a terrible spot.

HJ: So they added their new ending.

OW: By the way, somebody's published a new *Kane* book and sent it to me, with a lot of essays and criticism written around the time it was being released. I realized that I've misquoted O'Hara all my life. He didn't say, "This is the best picture ever made. And the best picture that will ever be made."

HJ: Really?

OW: Yeah. He didn't say anything as good as that. I made it better. What he said was, "This is the best picture ever made, and Orson Welles is the best actor alive." I know why I changed it. Because he said the other to a lot of people at the Stork Club in my presence. So I pasted it onto the review, the way one does.

17. "I can make a case for all the points of view."

In which Orson waits on Jack Nicholson, looks for financing for *Lear*, explains why he dropped his knee-jerk contempt for Nazi collaborators and became friends with Oswald Mosley, and recalls that General Charles de Gaulle was a brave but pompous fool.

HENRY JAGLOM: I spoke to Jack about *The Big Brass Ring*. He was up in Aspen with Bob Rafelson. I said, "Have you read it yet?" And he said, "No." But with great cheeriness, despite not adding anything more; just, "No." It's clearly on the agenda, though. I just don't know when he's going to read it. I have my fingers crossed. I'm worried about Jack. He's the last one. Even if he says, "Yes," he won't want to reduce his asking price . . . Any news on *Lear*?

ORSON WELLES: Just to keep you up on all the different situations, we now have the French. This fellow sends me almost daily wires, saying, "If wanted, we'll give you a million dollars of our money, and then go into an arrangement with other people, and so on, anything you want to do." A million dollars! And begging me to take it. Begging me, wiring me.

HJ: Well, you were awarded the Légion d'honneur, after all. Did you see [James] Cagney receiving the Presidential Medal of Freedom from Ronnie?

OW: He didn't even seem pleased, you know? He looked like he'd been dragged screaming, out of bed. Very hard to have an award in a republic. A decoration really needs a king. It's like a title. You need a fellow up there with a crown on. The only reason the Légion d'honneur works is that it's old. It goes back to Napoleon. What was so smart about Napoleon was that he realized the necessity of creating a new aristocracy. And he set up the Légion d'honneur for that. He knew his Frenchmen.

HJ: You and Jerry Lewis are the two American film stars who the French have given this award to. I remember when you said, "They give you good reviews and then you see what else they like and it takes away all the value of it." They've given Jerry Lewis every award you can imagine.

OW: Yes, every award that I've gotten. And he got all the publicity. I got no publicity at all. But he didn't get his award from the president.

HJ: It's probably your Légion d'honneur, probably, that has finally awakened the French to your *Lear.*

OW: Yes. And for *Lear*—they want to be the patrons that make it happen. They say they'll do anything. I said, "There're two parts for French actors: the King of France and the Duke of Burgundy, but only if they speak English. That's all. The grips—head grip, head cameraman, sound, all of that—my choice. Any nationality." They said, "Fine, we don't care."

HJ: So what's stopping you from saying yes?

OW: The fact that I don't know all that goes with "yes." So I keep saying to them, "Wonderful! Delighted! We're willing to let you be the central producing outfit, but please remember that you have to agree in return that none of our key people are French, unless we want them to be," and so on.

We also have another firm offer of $350,000 from Italy. Of course that doesn't begin to make the picture, but it's a terribly good cornerstone. Because it's government money set aside for the *Com-*

media dell'Arte. If they don't spend it, the government takes it back. And the reason why it's so great is that we get it in dollars, and we get the tremendous exchange advantage against the lira.

HJ: So the total figure that you'd be most comfortable with is what? Can you give me that?

OW: Supposing that, as I think, the most efficient and cheapest way to make the picture, is in Italy or France, bringing in the whole English cast. It is three million four. Something like that. That includes money for contingencies. If you take out contingencies, it's a lot less. Nobody gets rich, but that isn't the point.

HJ: Right. At Cannes, everybody hears "Welles-*Lear*" and they go crazy. If I knew who to talk to, I know I could get a small fortune from China. It seems to me that the way to complete the picture would be to have an American nontheatrical sale in advance, cable and so on. And then put that together with a combination of Italy, France, and Germany, and maybe Spain, and maybe somebody else. But if Spain is only putting in fifty or seventy-five thousand, no opening night in Madrid. If Germany puts up a million dollars, and they want a big thing at the Berlin Film Festival, why not?

OW: A festival is not an opening.

HJ: Right. We reserve the opening for whoever gives us the most money.

OW: That's a very important distinction.

HJ: So, we should put all the energy now into getting *Lear*.

OW: My energy is being put into it. There's nothing I can do now, except react warmly to these people as they come in. I think we have to have every kind of gun cocked and ready now, so that one of them will go off. Otherwise, we'll just go on talking forever.

HJ: Not just one, we need three or four of them to go off, so we can get to three and a half million dollars.

OW: The French—there's no doubt that the French—

HJ: Also, there's no reason not to film in France. There are ideal locations.

OW: That is the great argument *against* it for me. That's why I wish we *didn't* have the French money. I don't want France to be so attractive. Because living in Paris is so expensive. Whereas if we shoot in Cinecittà, we don't have to live in Rome. Here is Rome, and here is Cinecittà—and we can live out here, outside of Rome. We just go to the studio and back. I dread spending four or five months of my life living in Paris and driving through the traffic to work and back. The thought of it gives me the willies, because it's forty-five minutes of hell before you get to work and forty-five more for the return. And where would the actors stay? We know what the hotel bills will be for everybody. You can't live in Paris for less than two thousand a week. So the actors will object, saying they're slaves. They'll get so angry that I won't be able to work with them. They'll work for five hundred a week—

HJ: But they won't put up with cheap accommodations.

OW: I see the whole budget going to hell. You blow it on hotels alone; that's what scares me. There's no use saying we'll get great prices, and Jack Lang loves me and all that.

HJ: You're absolutely right. Jack Lang may be the Minister of Culture and [François] Mitterand's favorite puppy, but even he can't do anything about the prices of hotels.

OW: That's why I have always been nervous about it, but they have been battering the door down. And there's no place else in France to shoot! There's a big studio in Nice, but it's built right next to the airport.

HJ: Which makes it impossible to record sound.

OW: The planes fly in every two minutes. You couldn't get through one Shakespeare speech.

HJ: Oh, you mean the Victorine studio? They built it knowing the airport was there? Knowing—

OW: No, Victorine is a very old studio. It was built years before there was an airport, or when the airport was very little—no more than four flights a day. And now, of course, people fly direct from New York to Nice. It's a great location, and you can make wonderful deals, but only if you're making a silent picture. Or else dub it afterwards which, if you do that with Shakespeare, it comes off as totally fake. You simply cannot do it.

HJ: Cinecittà is fine.

OW: Well, it's the best bargain in the world, and the best studio in the world. Built by Mussolini, you know.

HJ: The French deal doesn't prohibit shooting in Cinecittà, does it? Or it's not clear?

OW: We're trying to get that clear. I think they're hurt, because it seems to imply that Italy is better suited for movie production. And the Italians, who always despised me, are now for some reason particularly anxious to be nice. They want to give me the highest award known to Italy. Whatever that is. The something or other, that makes me an honorary citizen of Rome.

HJ: It could still be a French movie, because it'll open in France.

OW: Maybe we could just get on the train from Rome to France, and shoot there for three weeks, just to get that French money, even though it will cost a little more. But you see how all these things are interdependent. You can't nail down one without having the others in hand. I think I'll make another phone call to France, to see how everything stands. I've made all my conditions as tough as I could, on the theory that there's no use going ahead and then being disappointed afterwards.

HJ: I sent you something about the reorganization of Gaumont. They're saying they want to be the home for all the great international directors.

OW: Well, they were talking about that four years ago, in this restaurant. I say, "Let's see some action." They told me once, "We are aristocrats. We simply don't breathe the same air." It's impossible to talk to somebody like that. "We don't breathe the same air"! Another thing is a French deal would have to be in the Common Market. The Common Market, in my opinion, is about to collapse. I think, seriously. Thanks to Mrs. Thatcher and—

HJ: You're talking about two different—

OW: No, I'm not. I'm telling you the different things that I know.

HJ: Well, we'll hear from Paris within a week.

OW: We'll proceed with them or without them. In the meantime, we keep anybody who is cooking warm on the stove. I don't care who it is. Even the Chinese—we can do it in Peking. And we'd certainly have all the right equipment, and serious assistants.

HJ: You know, I'm going to meet the Chinese representatives in Berlin.

OW: Let's make a deal.

HJ: Who said to me that *Lear* is one of the few things they know they want. "We only charge twenty-five cents a ticket. But we have a billion people." He actually said, "Rear."

OW: Rear. King Rear! And his daughter Legan.

HJ: I don't know what they can give us. I'll listen.

OW: Who cares?

HJ: Huh?

OW: Who cares? Just to have it in Red China.

(The check arrives.)

HJ: Here, I've got this.

OW: No, you don't.

HJ: That means I'm next.

OW: What? What about your neck?

HJ: I said, "That means I'm next."

OW: I thought you said, "That means my neck." You know, despite all of the telegrams from France, I would be happier with the Germans in the driver's seat than the French. I just don't trust that whole Lang situation.

HJ: You think the French offer is gonna disappear?

OW: I think the government is gonna keep on cutting Lang's funds for the arts. Not the way Reagan is—

HJ: You mean for ideological reasons . . .

OW: But out of economic necessity. In other words, we're gonna find ourselves enmeshed in French politics, in situations we can't resolve. Whereas, Italy has somehow pulled itself out of near bankruptcy, and now they're in great shape again, making movies like mad! I would be much happier if this could be done without the French.

HJ: Really? Because I would love France to be involved. The film would get a real boost from opening in Paris as a French co-production.

OW: It'll still get that. I'm just scared. Because you don't make arrangements with the French. But the Italians, you can always make an arrangement with them. In other words, if I went in with dollars into Cinecittà—oh, boy. On the other hand, I must tell you an interesting thing about Italy. It's a country that has never had an old star. Never a Wallace Beery. Never. The Italians don't support anybody over forty years old. They're like America. Everything must be about young people. So they may change their minds about a movie about an old man. *Lear* is about old age. And France is actually the only country in the world where old, ugly actors are stars. Everywhere else, they have to become supporting players.

HJ: Raimu.

OW: Yeah, Raimu. And that awful actor that they all love. Michel Simon. Jean Gabin, even when he was too feeble to move. He was wonderful doing nothing. There's another one, earlier than him. Baur—Harry Baur.

HJ: Was Harry Baur any good?

OW: He had four eyebrows over each eye, and he could work each of them separately.

HJ: He was killed by the Nazis, right? In a concentration camp?

OW: He came to some bad end, yeah—because he always talked about how he was Jewish—so, of course, they grabbed him quick. The French police did it all. The Germans didn't have to lift a finger. Horrifying, when you realize that. The French made a lot of movies during the war. The Germans, too. And a lot of French actors who would rather not be reminded of it went to Berlin.

When I visited France and Italy right after the war, I was full of that righteous antifascist feeling that we all had in the safety of America. I didn't want to meet the people who had, if not exactly collaborated, certainly had not fought the Nazis. I was too prissy. And then, as I began to learn more about Europe under the occupation, and what it was like, and to compare it to us, I became less prissy about it. Because the people who were defending their children and their lives were in a different situation from the people who were defending their swimming pools and their contracts at Metro. They weren't brave enough to be partisans, but they hadn't sent any Jews to Auschwitz, either. I wasn't gonna be the one from America to tell them they were wrong. Of course, I never forgave the people who sent Jews to the camps. But I did get so I could forgive the people who entertained the German troops. What else were they gonna do—not entertain them? Not entertain, and go where? If you had no group, if you were a group of one, what could you do? I can make a case for all the points of view.

HJ: [Maurice] Chevalier entertained the German troops . . .

OW: That was mild. He was really very little tainted compared to the people who made propaganda movies. I don't think what he did was noble, I don't like him for it, but I wouldn't say, "I won't talk to Chevalier because he—" That changed in me. And then I found myself getting to know well so many famous villains from my earlier time. You know, I spent a long, four-day weekend at a country house in England, and realized only at the end of the weekend that this man I'd become so fond of and interested in was Oswald Mosley.

HJ: Did you know he used to be a leftist, a Fabian? Then he went all the way over to the right and founded the British Union of Fascists.

OW: A complicated thing. Louis Aragon was also at that house party.

HJ: He didn't mind being there with Mosley? He fought in the Resistance and was a staunch Communist his whole life.

OW: No. He just said Mosley was a damn fool.

HJ: A lot of the French fled, but some stayed and fought.

OW: Very few, very few.

HJ: There were two Frances, though. There was Vichy, and there was the group of French who were fighting.

OW: Not in Paris. They were all in the Southwest. An old radical stronghold.

HJ: Except that, if it's true, in all of Europe—aside from Denmark—proportionately, only one-quarter—"only" is a tragic number—of French Jews died. So the other three-quarters survived because of individual Frenchmen who performed great acts of courage.

OW: There were such acts in Belgium and Holland as well. And Italy—enormous quantities. You really can't give the French credit for that, any more than the other European countries.

HJ: I always have thought of it as two Frances, somehow, occupied and unoccupied.

OW: There's one France—and in a certain mood, collaboration happens.

HJ: What about the underground and the Resistance? There was Jean Moulin, as well as—

OW: I used to write them a newsletter every two weeks during the war. To the Free French, and to the underground. So I really know a lot about them. Very few of the French resisted. We didn't hear a moment of courage from the Communists until the invasion of Russia. And then they were as harmful to the underground as they were helpful. Because they were divisive. When the Freemasons and the Catholics were fighting side by side, the Communists wouldn't stand for it, and turned them against each other. It was only by the end of 1941, when Hitler was bogged down in Russia, and it was clear to the entire world that he hadn't a chance in hell. It was then that you saw these brave movements. Not just in France; I'm talking all over the place. What was surprising was the large number of aristocrats in the Resistance. More than the bourgeois. They weren't thinking Nazi, fascist. It wasn't political for them. They were thinking, "Here come the goddamn *Boche* again," you know, the Germans again.

HJ: Foreigners.

OW: Not foreigners—Germans in particular. From all the old wars with the Germans.

HJ: They're very nationalistic.

OW: No, aristocrats are never nationalistic. Because they're all related to one another. They never have a sense of nation. That's a typically bourgeois attitude.

HJ: But it's nationalism. The Germans, *Boche* or not, are foreigners.

OW: As I was saying, generally, the French were particularly bad. They had the worst history of resistance. And think about the last fifty years of French history? Leon Blum being neutral towards Spain? That was inexcusable. From a Socialist, from the Popular Front? So shameful, really. [Pierre] Mendès France was the exception, and he lasted all of nine months. I told you what de Gaulle said about Mendès France, who was his greatest enemy. De Gaulle said he was the other great man of France—besides himself. De

Gaulle was very hard to like. God, how Roosevelt hated him. Roosevelt spoke fluent French, but with an American accent, you see. Roosevelt said to him, *"Je suis très heureux d'être avec vous, mon Général,"* you know. And de Gaulle said, *"Comment?"* Constantly. He was so snobbish it was, "If you don't speak perfectly, don't attempt it at all." So they had to translate what Roosevelt said. And this was when de Gaulle was hanging by a thread! He was always a pain in the ass, and he ended very badly. He had plans to run to Germany—to *Germany!* with his paratroopers—during the so-called revolution in '68, which he took very seriously, too seriously. After all, the kids were just throwing stones, and all that.

HJ: He was going to go to Germany? How do you know that?

OW: It was in the papers. He was gonna go with paras, and two or three planes, escape the country. And this is the man who was known for being fearless. When they liberated Paris, he walked the whole length of the Champs-Élysées from the Arc de Triomphe to the cathedral of Notre Dame. With everybody on the roofs with guns. And he never ducked when they were shooting, and he was eight feet higher than anybody else in Paris. And yet, he was ready to flee to Germany. It just shows how easily you get disoriented once you are in power if the people seem to be turning against you.

Of course, Nixon also thought that the kids were gonna come and throw him out. I saw a little tribute to him on CBS the other night, saying he's coming back, becoming a great commentator and elder statesman. I wish they'd stop interviewing him on great world topics. Because Nixon is a sort of semicomic Dickensian villain. But he's become the only man who's making sense! It drives me *crazy*! Of course, it's easy to sound sane if you've got Ronnie to criticize.

All Nixon and Reagan do is make me revise my judgment of the Eisenhower years. The economy was great. Eisenhower made the right decision on Suez. And Korea. Got us out. And at the end said, "Beware of the military-industrial complex." And he turned over the country, at peace, in 1960. Despite that, we were all groaning, "Get us rid of this terrible president!" We've just got to admit that was a great eight years, you know?

HJ: There were all the jokes about Eisenhower going off to play golf.

OW: We underrated Eisenhower. We've got a president now who works much less hard than he did. Who doesn't even know what's going on. Unless it's written on a card.

HJ: I remember being shocked at the U-2 incident, Gary Powers, the pilot, remember? When Eisenhower said it wasn't a spy plane. I didn't think he would lie to the American people.

OW: Every president lies. The spy plane didn't bother me so much, because it seemed so obvious that we had spy planes. And it's not like shooting somebody. What I couldn't believe was the CIA stuff, the plot against Castro. In my innocence, I didn't think that America, as a nation, was capable of planning murder as an instrument of policy. I didn't think that was in our character!

HJ: Well, now we know. We've lost some serious innocence. Is it true you considered running for office?

OW: I have all the equipment to be a politician. Total shamelessness. But it's lucky I never ran. In the years from [Joseph] McCarthy to now, I would have either been destroyed or reduced. I was lucky that Alan Cranston discouraged me from running for the Senate.

HJ: Cranston discouraged you? I didn't know that.

OW: Yes. He was my man, given to me by Washington, to be sure that I could get the nomination in California. The year of McCarthy.

HJ: '52.

OW: And it was Cranston who told me, "Not a chance. You'll carry northern California, but never the Hollywood community." Then I found out he had ambitions himself. That's why, when I saw him run for senator, I always thought, "That's my seat!"

HJ: Now he's busily running for president. Who do you think the Democratic candidate will be?

OW: I would vote for John Glenn just because I think he'd win, and I believe in voting for who I think will win.

I've just read Caro's new biography of [Lyndon] Johnson, which will destroy him because it tells everything. It's exhaustive to the point of—you know, when he put on his left shoe on Thursday, the twelfth of May, 1946. But there isn't one good word about him in the book. He comes out of it a total monster. There's gonna be three more volumes. This one only takes him up to getting into Congress, and he's already a prick. He has very few defenders. There's me and somebody out in Kansas, who I don't know. But I think LBJ was a great tragic figure. That's what interests me. A very tragic figure, with his monstrosity, and his energy, and his desire to be a president who counted. He gets almost no credit for the things he did domestically, because of his gross behavior. After the Kennedys, everybody in Washington was so used to Casals scratching on the cello that Johnson's act didn't go over. And he was haunted by Jack. And then Bobby coming up. But what could he do, other than be president? It was the *only* thing for him.

HJ: I'm convinced Johnson would have made a great president had he run and won . . . Not like Roosevelt, but—

OW: I don't believe there could have been a great president in those years, only a good one. I think the presidential situation now is such that until there's a hopeless crisis, and you have a semidictatorship, like Roosevelt's, then we won't see what we call a great president.

HJ: Glenn is very Eisenhower-esque. But I don't think he's committed to very much. I mean, he's just moderate—he's just really moderate on everything.

OW: That's why I'm for him. I hate to think of myself as fighting for a moderate, but a moderate is what is desperately needed for this next period. We need antipolarization, you know. After Bonny Prince Ronnie.

HJ: Is it just the nostalgia that makes the Roosevelt years seem so glorious?

OW: No. They were glorious. Because you had a president who had made a hundred mistakes and never pretended he didn't, and who was ready to try anything. And you had a fascinating cabinet, great personalities—everybody around him. And it was a happy time, even with all the misery. People were starving, but he pulled the country together. That's when the labor movement really became a wonderful thing in America. We never crossed a picket line. Now the unions have no power. They're nothing. Reactionary, even, corrupt and weak. But then they were a wonderful thing.

You know Kissinger also believed that America was on the brink of civil war during the Vietnam years. Who was gonna make a civil war? How can an educated man permit himself to put that down on paper?

HJ: You think he really believed it? He's too smart to be so stupid.

OW: I hate Kissinger even more than I hate Nixon, because I just can't get over the feeling that he knows better, somehow. He must have talked himself into it. But he's a selfish, self-serving shit.

HJ: They've all forgotten Cambodia. They've forgotten the whole thing. It's really amazing.

OW: And the fact that Kissinger got free of Watergate, walked away without a scratch! Without a scratch! No wonder he worships Mitterand.

HJ: Metternich.

OW: Metternich.

18. Charles "Laughton couldn't bear the fact he was a homosexual."

In which Orson fondly remembers his friend, who lived in terror that he would be outed. He recalls that on London's West End, actors had to be gay or pretend to be gay to get parts. Orson would have liked to have made his own version of The Dresser.

HENRY JAGLOM: Tell me more about Charles Laughton.

ORSON WELLES: During the war, there was a great bond rally in Texarkana, Texas, with every known star in Hollywood. Charlie was going to do his well-known Gettysburg Address, which he made famous in *Ruggles of Red Gap* on the radio. I was the producer and director of that show. So I said to Buster—that's what I called him— "Is there anything special that you would like?" He said, "I want a divan." I said, "What?" He said, "Don't be ignorant. You know what I want, a chaise lounge."

HJ: That's great. He was so gay.

OW: I said, "Buster, you can't mean that. You're not going to lie down on a couch like Madame Recamier and do the Gettysburg Address in front of all these people. Do you know where you are?" He said, "Yes. But that's the way I feel." So out of vengeance, I said, "All right, I'll give it to you." So he came out, lay down, delivered the address, "Fawr scawr . . . fawr scawr and seven years ago our fathers brought forth unto this continent a new nation based on the proposition that all men are created equal . . ." and he killed it. When he was great, he was so great.

I was very fond of him. He was a sweet man. It was absolutely terrible what Larry did to him. Larry was sharing a season with him at Stratford. Larry was doing—what's that little-known Shakespearean play that Peter Brook directed with Larry and made a big success? Not *Timon of Athens . . . Pericles* maybe, and Laughton was doing *King Lear* and Bottom in *Midsummer Night's Dream.* And everyone said he was very interesting in both parts. But in front of the entire company in Stratford, Larry said, "Charles, you are an amateur actor and you have never been anything else in your life. Don't ask us to take you seriously." And Laughton went away and cried, wept like a child.

I told you what Larry did to Miles Malleson, the old character actor, in *Rhinoceros.* Larry put his arm around his shoulder and walked him up and down in front of the lights. And I heard him saying, "Miles . . . Miles, old boy, you know, you've had it. You're washed up." This defenseless old man. All so that Larry could take control and tell him how his part should be played.

HJ: This was his way of tearing them down, or something stupid like that?

OW: It was heartbreaking for him. Laughton never got over it. He was like a little fourteen-year-old boy, totally immature. Laughton couldn't bear the fact he was a homosexual, you know. He was so afraid the world would discover it. He believed in art, and all of that, always searching for something that went beyond what acting can be, or writing, or anything. Really, he was really looking for the bluebird.

HJ: He found it a few times.

OW: You bet he did. When he made that speech in *I, Claudius.*

HJ: For me, he was also wonderful in *The Hunchback of Notre Dame.*

OW: I can't judge that, because I am such a partisan of the Lon

Chaney performance, I just can't buy anybody else doing it. I think Chaney was one of the great movie actors. Everything he did I adore. To me, Charlie in *Hunchback* was the village idiot, the fellow where you say, "That's the unfortunate Perkins boy." You don't want to look at him.

HJ: Oh, no, he was much more than that. I felt he put all his feeling of not belonging into that role . . . And don't forget Laughton's Rembrandt.

OW: Laughton's Rembrandt has him pose as King David. He puts on this robe and he puts on a crown and he transforms himself. I still don't understand how he did it. Who played the beggar in that? I can't remember his name now. He was even better than Laughton and that's something.

HJ: Oh, my God! That's my favorite actor.

OW: He was a dear friend. He only died about four years ago. He was the leading man in a movie directed by Gregory Ratoff with Myrna Loy, *Intermezzo*.

HJ: I'm still trying to think of the man's name.

OW: He was a wild left-winger rabblerouser. He was on the barricades for forty years. So of course he only played degenerate aristocrats, and dressed like an awful-looking don at a small university with torn patches. When he arrived in Rome, Ratoff, in his Russian accent, says, "He can't play Myrna Loy's leading man looking like a bum. Take him to your tailor." So I take him to the tailor to the King of Italy. By this time, I'm speaking Italian. I say, "This is a distinguished actor from England and he is—"

HJ: Roger Livesey!

OW: Right. Mr. Roger Livesey. And I say, "He's going to play the leading role in this picture, and he has to be dressed like an English gentleman. Money is no object." The tailor looks at him like he is an insect, and he says—I'm loosely translating—"This establishment doesn't live for money. What can we do with these schmattas?"

I say, "Not what he's wearing—if you are an artist, you can make him look like a prince." So he begins to measure him. But then the tailor throws down the tape measure and says, "No I can do." So I say, "Look, you cannot put me in a position like this. I've brought you this distinguished man, and I've told you that no matter what he looks like, he's playing a principal role opposite Myrna Loy." He says, "Opposite Loy, what he play?" I say, "Her husband." And he says, "Do she betray him?" I say, "Sure, she betrays him." "She make horns on him?" "Yes, *cornuto*. He's a schmuck." And he says, "All right. I dress him!"

HJ: He's in the single most romantic movie I've ever seen. Which has the unromantic title, *The Life and Death of Colonel Blimp*. [Michael] Powell and [Emeric] Pressburger used him in everything. *Stairway to Heaven, A Matter of Life and Death*.

OW: Hated those guys. Not my cup of tea. To me, they never made a good film.

HJ: Did you know Pressburger?

OW: I know Powell better. I think Pressburger's the more talented of the two. But I don't share your admiration for either one of them.

HJ: *The Red Shoes* is kitsch to you?

OW: Yeah, total dreck. Total dreck. I even saw part of it again and switched it off.

HJ: *Stairway to Heaven? A Matter of Life and Death?*

OW: Awful.

HJ: *One of Our Aircraft is Missing?* Do you remember that? No?

OW: Yes, with Ralph [Richardson], who was very good in it, but the picture was abominable.

HJ: I'm in love with Powell. I saw all of the Powell-Pressburger films when I was a teenager.

OW: If you see them at the right age, you see them differently. You see the real value of them, what they really are.

HJ: It's true: how you feel about a film has to do with how old you are when you see it.

OW: In the theater, I can pretend that it's all happening right there in front of me. But I see movies through such a mist of years, I am incapable of feeling the thrill of them, even the greatest ones, because I cannot erase those years of experience. I'm jaded. I know I don't see movies as purely as I ought to see them. Before I started making movies, I'd get into them, lose myself. I can't do that now. That's why I don't think my opinions about movies are as good as somebody's who doesn't have to look through all those filters. I think all films are better than we think they are.

HJ: Maybe that's why Spencer Tracy is so fantastic to me, and Humphrey Bogart, too.

OW: Of course. Your age. I still see Lon Chaney as I saw him when I was eight years old. But I have had some disillusionment since I left movies, I must say.

When are you leaving for Paris?

HJ: Tomorrow night.

OW: I will give you two or three scripts. And you can drop them off where they need to go.

HJ: All right. Now, I want to be sure that I understand the sequence of—

OW: Still *Lear* first. If *Lear* collapses, *Dreamers* is always good. It doesn't date.

HJ: Is there anybody in particular you want me to see?

OW: There's a man who's head of TNF, French television. It's like the BBC. He said he would raise the three and a half million for *Lear* by selling it all over the place. But I don't know. He's no Henry Jaglom.

HJ: So this is three times the other French offer. And it has nothing to do with Lang, or the government, or anything at all?

OW: Nothing. He thinks this will be the jewel in his crown. But I still don't want to shoot in Paris. And they don't have anyplace except Victorine, although I've heard that it's been remodeled. It's now owned by Americans and is OK.

HJ: Despite the airplanes.

OW: Yes, because I now know when the air traffic is light. I would shoot from four in the afternoon until eleven at night, you see—something like that.

HJ: I can certainly find out what kind of reputation he has, what other people there think—

OW: He doesn't have a reputation. He's just got a position. I'm afraid he's never gonna sell *Lear* to anyone. Besides, he's demanding that French television must be the center of everything. And asking me to wait three months while you try to raise the money. And if he doesn't, you see, I've wasted three months. It's a real gamble. Also, I have to know that he's not going to make me cut the picture in France. And we need to negotiate how the profits are going to be dealt with. Instead of taking a salary out of the budget and taking some money after everything is paid off, I'd like to have two or three territories. In fact, I would even like to have my company or a company associated with me be a minor co-producer. He may not like it, but I don't like to have a monolithic boss.

HJ: Absolutely not. Because he could end up owning your picture and—

OW: I won't do it. And I think I can break him now, because he has nothing else. He's so hot for it that I think he'll give in.

HJ: What about England?

OW: You're big in England. I was never big in England. I'm dreaming of when I will be.

HJ: Every time I mention *Lear* to them, they say, "Oh, wouldn't that be nice." I was worried that Olivier's *Lear* would hurt us. It was on TV. But I think it helped. They don't like Olivier in England.

OW: No, they don't. They've never gone to his Shakespearean movies. 'Cause they never go to any Shakespearean movies. They want to see Shakespeare on the stage, not in a movie theater . . . You know, everybody may be interested. But are we really going to carry the movie around by bus from country to country so we can make it a national event in every country?

HJ: Do you know who Victoria Tennant is?

OW: Who?

HJ: Victoria Tennant.

OW: A member of the Tennant family?

HJ: She is a daughter of the Tennant family. Quite a beauty. Her most famous role here was in the miniseries *The Winds of War*. She played opposite [Robert] Mitchum. Anyway, she lives with Steve Martin. He's not your favorite, I know. She begged me at a party Saturday night to tell you that she believes that there's no one who could do Cordelia as well as she.

OW: Not a chance.

HJ: All right, good. I like clear answers. They make things very simple. I don't have to tell you all about her, and what she did and didn't do, and what she said and didn't say.

OW: Too bad about Steve Martin. The Tennants controlled the English theater for forty years. They had the whole West End by the short hairs. When there was a West End, that is—it was totally Tennant. But very hard to get a job there if you weren't homosexual. Really. A real Mafia working against the few straights who were around. Even Donald Wolfit couldn't get on the West End stage. Everybody, unfairly, made fun of him because he was the only non-queer actor alive in the golden age of acting.

HJ: Wolfit was Sir in *The Dresser*, [Ronald] Harwood's play. But Harwood was actually his dresser.

OW: You'd have to pretend to be homosexual to get ahead. Either be queer or act like you were queer. Larry kind of did that.

HJ: And you think it was a political move.

OW: Absolutely.

HJ: Richardson was certainly not homosexual.

OW: Well, you see, they didn't really take to him until his old age. Not when he was at the Old Vic. Not until he did his great hit, *Dangerous Corner*, written by [J. B.] Priestley. He was one of the very few straight actors flying the flag for the heteros. As was Jack Hawkins. I wanted Hawkins to play Iago for me in the theater.

HJ: That was in '51? When you were Othello?

OW: Yeah. And I would have had him. Jack would have loved to do Iago, as anybody would. But Larry didn't want him.

HJ: Because he was straight?

OW: It was Larry's theater, and the leading actors had to be approved by him. So I had to use [Peter] Finch.

HJ: He was straight.

OW: But he was fucking Vivien.

HJ: Did Larry know that?

OW: He knew it, sure. He wanted to go away on a yachting trip with Vivie, and keep Finch busy on the London stage. And Finch was a wonderful Iago. But not as good as Hawkins would have been. He played him as eaten up with bitterness. I'd rather play Iago than any part in Shakespeare, but I'm not built for Iago. That's the part, though. Not Othello. You know, everything Iago says is in prose, and everything Othello says is in poetry. Now, look at the advantage that gives the actor right there. And—did I tell you this? [Henry] Irving and [Edwin] Booth played Othello on alternate nights in London. One night Iago, one night Othello.

Booth was famous for his Iago. So they expected him to steal it. Then Irving did the same thing. Each of them stole the play as Iago. Stole it, no matter which one played it. But you need great, big actors like that.

HJ: I saw the film version of the *The Dresser* last night. At one point, Wolfit or Sir, says, "Lear is the greatest tragic part of all time."

OW: Of course. *The Dresser* is a parody of *Lear*. The dresser is the fool—

HJ: Oh, my God. You know, I never even got that. I feel stupid.

OW: It's a little clumsy, but that's what it is. The writer, Harwood, is trying to say a lot more than he needed to say to make a very good vehicle play. You mustn't look too closely at it. But that's what it is.

HJ: Albert Finney is magnificent.

OW: Stick a dagger in me! I tried so hard to get the rights to that play. You've ruined my lunch.

HJ: You'll be even more upset when you see it, because you'll think about what you could have done with it.

OW: I have no intention of seeing it. I know it'll be good, and I know Finney will be great in it—that's why I won't see it. Why should I make myself sick? If I had any hope that it was bad, I'd go. Do you know how I screwed it up? I had the idea of having the dresser played by Michael Caine, not Tom Courtenay. I thought Michael would be something. Instead of Courtenay's flagrant queen performance. But Courtenay had a kind of lock on the property. And that's how come I lost it.

HJ: The money guy who put it together was a friend of mine. I remember, he said, "It has to be Courtenay." Because he played the role on the stage.

OW: If only I had said, "Courtenay is all right with me," I might have got it. Courtenay was a friend of mine. But I was so keen on it being Michael Caine, because I don't think anybody had *any* idea how good that play would be if it were *not* played the way Courtenay plays it. If it had the kind of richness and comedy and warmth, furious tenderness mixed with bitchiness that Michael would have brought to it. Because he's maybe the best actor on the screen now, he's so good. I'm sure Finney is great as Sir, but that part should have been done by any one of a number of actors who are the right age, and don't have to act it. It would have been wonderful with Richardson. Can you imagine Michael Caine and Richardson in that thing? And it would have been a great way for Richardson to go out, you know. Because he never made it in Shakespeare, except as Falstaff, which is written in prose. It would have blown the roof off. It would have broken your heart! There wouldn't have been that slightly mean feeling that you get.

HJ: I thought you didn't see it. Oh, you've seen clips from it, you said.

OW: Long clips.

HJ: What I thought was wrong with the movie was that Finney was too good playing Sir playing Lear. He couldn't resist grabbing you, when he's supposed to be the epitome of every bad actor's need for the audience.

OW: Just like Larry was too good as *The Entertainer*. But, you see, I didn't read it as a play about a bad actor. Sir had to go on tour because he wasn't queer, you know. But *The Dresser* absolutely annihilates any possibility of my doing my movie, which is about a very different kind of actor. They wouldn't like it as much.

HJ: It doesn't annihilate it, Orson. As you say, it's completely different. Yours is an Ameri—

OW: No, in mine, Sir is not American. He's Irish. It was based on [Anew] McMaster, who was the most beautiful man who ever lived. He looked like a god! He had blond hair, and he had the most marvelous voice you ever heard in your life! McMaster really was gay. So I couldn't play him. I could only direct it. And when he was about twenty-three years old, he got panned in the West End, went back to Ireland, and played pinups—little platforms built in church halls, and so on—for the rest of his life.

HJ: So he didn't tour because he was straight, he toured because his feelings had been hurt on the stage in Lon—

OW: And each year he could go to fewer and fewer places, because he would have fucked more and more choirboys. So his tour was increasingly reduced. And then he would play four or six weeks in Dublin. He played Othello with nothing but a little G-string. Mac Liammóir, who was his brother-in-law—

HJ: Mac Liammóir was married to his sister?

OW: His sister was a bull dyke. And these two wild queens were known in Dublin as Sodom and Gomorrah. I beg your pardon, I ruined that joke. Sodom and Begorra.

HJ: I've heard about Mac Liammóir all my life. I never heard of McMaster.

OW: Nobody heard of McMaster, nobody, 'cause he stayed in the smalls of Ireland. And he had all these famous people who worked with him at one time or another, including [Harold] Pinter, who was his stage manager. And when he died, Pinter wrote a book about him. I would love to get a copy. I've never met Pinter. I saw him at the guild hall this last time when I was speaking. And he was near, and I wanted to go up to him, but no way could I push my way past His Royal Highness and say, "Mr. Pinter, how can I get a copy of your book?"

19. "Gary Cooper turns me right into a girl!"

In which Orson argues that Cooper and Humphrey Bogart are stars, not actors, and goes on to explain the difference. Bogart thought Casablanca *was the worst picture he ever did while it was in production.*

HENRY JAGLOM: Is Bogart as good as I think he is?

ORSON WELLES: No. Not nearly as good as you believe. Bogart was a second-rate actor. *Really* a second-rate actor. He was a fascinating personality who captured the imagination of the world, but he never gave a good performance in his life. Only satisfactory. Just listen to a reading of any line of his.

HJ: What about *The Caine Mutiny*?

OW: I saw Lloyd Nolan play it on the stage. He was hair-raising. He made Bogart look sick. There's no comparison. Bogart in the thirties did the worst thing with Bette Davis, when he had that Irish accent, that I've ever seen anybody do.

HJ: I think that was *Dark Victory*. To me, he gives the perfect performance in *Casablanca*. And he was good in *In a Lonely Place*.

OW: Oh, come on, he had that little lisp. Bogart was a well-educated, upper-class American trying to be tough. You didn't believe him as a tough guy. Anybody who knew him as I did . . .

HJ: Do you always have to add "as I did"?

OW: I knew him in the theater, before he went to Hollywood as just another out-of-work leading man. We were so glad he got a job, you know.

HJ: You didn't like him in *The Petrified Forest*?

OW: Well, I didn't hate him. I was glad he got by with it, but Warner Brothers had five tough-guy actors who could've done it just as well.

HJ: They had that horrible guy they offered *Casablanca* to. George Raft.

OW: Yeah, he was a terrible actor, too. What's interesting is that George Raft knew he was the world's worst actor. He told me that all the time. He'd say, "I'm just lucky, you know. I can't say a line."

HJ: I know you love Gary Cooper, but to me, he was just a very pretty George Raft. All I see is a man stumbling over his lines, trying to remember what's going on. But you're queer for him.

OW: I am. Gary Cooper turns me right into a girl! And you love Bogie. Neither one of them were much good. But we're in love with 'em.

HJ: And yet, you tell me Gary Cooper is great, and . . .

OW: Well, no, just that he's a great movie star, a great movie creation. That's the thing about a movie star. We really don't judge them as actors. They're the creatures that we fell in love with at a certain time. And that has to do with who we want to have as our heroes. It's absolutely impossible to have a serious critical discussion about enthusiasms for movie stars. Because a movie star is an animal separate from acting. Sometimes, he or she is a great actor. Sometimes a third-rate one. But the star is something that you fall in love with . . .

HJ: We don't have movie stars like that these days. I agree Bogart was lousy in *Dark Victory*.

OW: *Dark Victory* was the first Broadway play that I lit.

HJ: Lit? I didn't know you did lighting. You were a lighting director?

OW: That's why Gregg Toland wanted to do *Kane*, because he had seen my lighting and—

HJ: You always gave Toland the credit for lighting *Kane*, for being the greatest lighting director ever.

OW: Yes. But I lit it.

HJ: All right, but you have to admit Bogart is phenomenally good in *The Maltese Falcon*.

OW: Somehow we always get back to Bogart. No, for me, [Sydney] Greenstreet is the great performance. I had seen Greenstreet all my life in the theater. He was the most extraordinary supporting actor in the Theatre Guild. A short, little tubby man just right for small drama. Then, in *The Maltese Falcon* I suddenly saw this gigantic screen-filling personality, and from then on, for the rest of his career, he was wonderful in every part he did. I adored him as a person. Adorable. Adorable man.

HJ: What about that movie with [Lauren] Bacall, her first movie? *To Have and Have Not*?

OW: It's a wonderful Hemingway story that they screwed up badly. So ridiculous compared to the story.

HJ: The hurricane one was *Key Largo*, wasn't it?

OW: I like that movie better.

HJ: Do you have that in the theater, too, stars who don't necessarily act?

OW: Oh, yes. The Lunts. The last play they did was so embarrassing I didn't know where to look. When they were good, they were—you saw *The Visit*?

HJ: Yes.

OW: They were among the greatest actors I've ever seen in my life. Truly, truly. They were unbelievable.

HJ: In what way? I wish I could understand.

OW: It was like having roses thrown at you. But the Lunts got too old. They were sour toward the end. They got bad. Actors either get better or worse as they get old.

HJ: And while we're talking about this, you're not crazy about Ingrid Bergman.

OW: No, she's not an actress. Just barely able to get through a scene.

HJ: But when she and Bogart get together in *Casablanca*—

OW: I admired *Casablanca* very much. I thought it was a very well put-together piece of *Schwarmerei*, with just the right measure of every ingredient and all that crap, and of course, tremendous luck, because they were making it up as they went along. They were playing it not knowing how it was going to end. They didn't know who she was going to end up with, or why. And all of them wanted out. Bogart used to tell me, "I'm in the worst picture I've ever been in."

HJ: You liked him personally?

OW: Very much. And once he made it in movies, I saw he was a real star. Ingrid Bergman, too. And when you start to dissect a real star, one person will say they can act, another person will say they can't. What is indelible is the quality of stardom. And whether it's acting or not is a useless argument. Because the star thing is a different animal. It breaks all the rules.

HJ: Are you saying Bogart never took himself seriously as an actor?

OW: I think Bogart thought he was as good as anybody around.

HJ: And he was a decent man?

OW: I wouldn't say decent. He was a brave man. He was amusing and original. Very opinionated, with very dumb opinions and not very well read and pretending to be. You know, a lot of people who aren't interesting on the screen were very bright. Paul Henreid is very bright. He was supposed to be the star of *Casablanca*. The antifascist hero. Bogart was the second guy. The fellow who owned the restaurant, you see. But *Casablanca* ended Henreid's career.

HJ: Because everybody remembers Bogart, Bergman—and oh yeah, that other guy. After that movie, Henreid played a supporting character for the rest of his life.

OW: You know the mean joke played on him by Walter Slezak, and a bunch of other actors on a subsequent movie? Henreid is sitting there, in his chair, waiting between takes. And the other actors get into a conversation—that he can hear—saying: "It was Ralph Bellamy in *Casablanca*. "No, no, it was . . ."

HJ: Who directed *Casablanca*? Michael Curtiz?

OW: No idea about dialogue, but a very, very good visual sense. Very Hungarian. You can't imagine how Hungarian he was.

HJ: Jewish, I'm sure.

OW: No, Hungarian. Real Hungarian. One of the stories about him was when they had an extra call with some blacks in a group, he says, "All the whites over here and all the niggers over there." There was a terrible silence and the assistant director says to the director in a low voice, "Mr. Curtiz . . . you say 'all the *Negroes* or you say *colored*.' So Curtiz says, "All right, all the colored niggers over there." Tracy told me that story. He was on the picture.

HJ: What's handled so well in *Casablanca* are those big scenes in the casino where all the French are milling about and the Germans come in.

OW: Awfully well done. Curtiz used to be an assistant to Max Reinhardt, so he knew what he was doing.

HJ: Did Reinhardt deserve the reputation that he enjoyed in Europe?

OW: He deserved it. I regarded Reinhardt with awe. He was a great, great director. A great master of spectacle as well as intimate comedy. He could do anything. I saw his production of *Merchant of Venice* and *Romeo and Juliet* with Elisabeth Bergner, who was superb.

HJ: You saw *Romeo and Juliet* with Elisabeth Bergner? Oh, my God!

OW: My father took me, as a child. I also saw an [Arthur] Schnitzler comedy that Reinhardt did in a small theater in Vienna. Marvelous performances. Wonderful.

HJ: But was he as great a force as you say?

OW: You can't imagine. Nobody, before or since, has ever had such a commanding role in the theater in as many countries at once. He had four or five theaters he ran at the same time. Hugely successful, *The Miracle* made a fortune.

HJ: *The Miracle?*

OW: *The Miracle* was a huge piece of pageantry, in which the theater was totally transformed into a cathedral. In Vienna. He collapsed the proscenium long before anybody else did. He had a theater at his castle in Salzburg, and the greatest actors in Europe would come to play there every year. Bill Dieterle was one of his assistants also. And [Ernst] Lubitsch.

Reinhardt came to see my production of *Danton's Death* when he arrived in New York. I was playing a small part, about eight lines—Saint-Just. *Danton's Death* had been one of the biggest successes of his career. He did it in a sports arena with an audience of about five thousand people each night. [Vladimir] Sokoloff played Robespierre for him in Berlin and he also played it with me in New York. I was very nervous because here was a production totally unlike his, you know. Reinhardt came backstage, sat with the director, talked for a while while I waited, and then said to me, "You are the best *Schauspieler* in America. You must do the great parts."

Nothing about the production. So all he could do was tell me what a great actor I was.

HJ: So he didn't like the production.

OW: Of course not. Couldn't blame him.

When he got to Hollywood, he couldn't come to terms with the fact that he was a nobody refugee. He was lost. Probably didn't have enough respect for the medium, either, I think. Although he had the sense to know that Mickey Rooney was one of the most talented people in Hollywood and to cast him as Puck. So this man ruling over everything in *Mittel* Europe had no chance in America. None of the refugees did. Only the writers, who could just sit and write. Think, what did Brecht do? What did Kurt Weill do? What did any of them do?

HJ: Well, Weill had another career. I mean, you may not like it, but it was another career.

OW: Not much of one until just at the end. He was out of work most of the time. So was Thomas Mann, ruling over everything. You don't know what America was like during the war. It was the pits. The stage died. People flocked to the theaters, but the movies died, too. Because all you had to do was turn the projector on. No movie failed. But they got worse and worse. The war flattened everybody's taste in a very curious way. The best thing they could do in the movies was some delirious piece of fabrication like *Casablanca*. That was *the* great work of art, during the whole period of the war. Nothing else.

HJ: Why has that picture taken on such a—?

OW: It has nothing to do with anything except Hollywood's dream of the war. But that's its charm. To me, it's like *The Merry Widow*, which is a great work of its kind. There never was a Vienna like the one in *The Merry Widow*, and there never was a Casablanca like the one in *Casablanca*. But who gives a damn, you know? It was just commercial enough, so everybody was happy. And it had a wonderful cast of actors. But a great film? You can't call it that. It's not a great film. It's just great entertainment. The person who loved it when it opened, who persuaded me to take it more seriously, was Marlene. She's the one who said, "They'll be showing that thirty years from now. You listen to me." So then I had to think, and say, "I guess you're right."

20. "Jack, it's Orson fucking Welles."

In which Jack Nicholson finally responds to *The Big Brass Ring*. Orson voices his admiration for Jacobo Timerman, considers the paranoia of Jews, and laments the destruction of Paris by the automobile.

———————————

HENRY JAGLOM: I have good news and bad news. I'll tell you the good news first. Jack said yes to *The Big Brass Ring*, but he won't reduce his salary. I said, "Jack, it's Orson fucking Welles. Imagine it's 1968!" He said, "If this were 1968, I would do it for nothing. I really want to do it, but it will totally throw me into the art movie world again and I've been working to get out of that into the big, mainstream things, where they pay me millions and millions of dollars. If I do a picture for half that, how do I explain to the next person that I'm demanding four million?"

ORSON WELLES: I should have known better. They all said no, and each kept me waiting weeks before each "no." And every "no" hurts me more than I let on. They always want earth-shattering from me. They want *Touch of Evil* from me. And I'm not ready with any *Touch of Evil*. They're thinking, "Orson is old-fashioned. He's lost it. He used to be an innovator." But I tell you, every script I've ever written, if you read it before I made it into a movie, it would look straight and conservative. I've always felt there are three sexes: men, women, and actors. And actors combine the worst qualities of the other two. I can't go on waiting for stars.

HJ: I'm afraid you may be right. And it's a shocking thing to think this about my friends, you know?

OW: But that's the way friends are, if they're stars.

HJ: You said that from the beginning—and I didn't believe it. I just thought everybody would be so excited at the chance. I'd like to kill the bastards.

HJ: What about Jack Lemmon?

OW: He's old-looking.

HJ: Really? I was just thinking that he looks good. Because he's actually not. What is he? Fifty-five?

OW: Yeah. He looks good in this restaurant, under these rosy lights. But you see him on TV—he's always giving long interviews, he loves to talk, as we know—and he looks every minute of his age because they blast him with light, so we don't recognize him. Fifteen years ago, Lemmon would have looked credible as a young candidate, but Kennedy changed the image of how a presidential candidate should look.

HJ: If we don't get the response we want on *Big Brass Ring*, would you sell the script?

OW: Well, before I went to Europe, I started improving it, and I got a third of the way through. And my improvements were so great that I was sure that I should continue in case it should ever be made. I do still have doubts about it, but I would like to see Jack play the candidate, the guy who throws himself in front of the car running against Reagan. Jack is a great loser character, you know.

HJ: What about Al Pacino, Dustin Hoffman? They are two of the greatest actors of my generation, both highly respected, and excuse me, they're a lot better than Burt Reynolds and a lot of the others on your list.

OW: Not your friend Dusty Hoffman. No dwarfs. Besides, they're ethnic.

HJ: They're what?

OW: They're ethnic.

HJ: You mean, they're not Irish leading men? Aren't the Irish ethnic?

OW: You know what I mean. No dark, funny-looking guys. I want an Irish leading man like Jack, or at least an all-American WASP.

HJ: Why?

OW: It's the president of the United States. Were you born yesterday?

HJ: That's all changed. Everyone said a Catholic couldn't get elected president, then Kennedy got elected. Everyone said a divorced guy couldn't get elected, and then Reagan did.

OW: This will never change. Never. You can't do a story like this and have some Italian play that role: "Cazzo, you gotta respect-a the president, and that's-a me."

HJ: That's disgusting.

OW: Oh, you want Dusty Hoffman? "Oy, vey, don't be such a putz, kill 'em."

HJ: You've got a very fifties, fucked-up idea of what looks American.

OW: You're my bleeding heart. I was more left than you'll ever be.

HJ: What about Paul Newman?

OW: Paul Newman would work.

HJ: Newman's Jewish.

OW: He's not ethnic. I don't care if they're Jewish; I don't care if they're Italian, but they can't be ethnic. Hoffman is ethnic, Pacino is ethnic."

HJ: So no Jews, no Italians . . .

OW: No. This has to be a guy from the heartland of America. Or we don't have a movie.

HJ: The one who was totally willing to do it was De Niro, without even reading the script, and you just—

OW: Don't try to sell me on De Niro. I don't care how great you think he is.

HJ: He's too ethnic also?

OW: Not just ethnic, though that's part of it. More, it's that the great things he does on the screen . . . none of them look to me like the qualities of a candidate. You're writing off an awful lot of the country with him. My candidate is a fellow who's got to carry Kansas. I really don't see De Niro carrying Kansas.

HJ: OK. Here's more news. I don't know if it's good or bad. I had a call from *Love Boat*. They want you from May twenty-first until June twelfth, that's twenty-one days. I said to them, "Well, are you going to make an offer?" "No. We want to know his availability." I said, "Mr. Welles's availability depends on whether you make an offer. I'm not telling him anything, honestly, until you come up with a concrete offer." I also said, "You know, I'm sorry, I've never watched your program." Complete silence. They had the main man call me, because I was dismissive of the first person. So the deal is, you fly to London—shoot in London—they then fly you to Paris—shoot in Paris for a few days—then you fly back to London. And then you board a ship to Stockholm! He said, "Have you ever been through the Kiel Canal?" I said, "No." He said, "It's meant to be fabulous!"

OW: Oh, boy! You'd have to *pay* me to go through the Kiel Canal.

HJ: He was like selling a cruise. He was a cruise director. But it's not a heavy shooting schedule. In other words, it's a party—that's what it is.

OW: One big party.

HJ: I wonder what they'll offer for that?

OW: Maximum twenty-five, probably twenty. It's amazingly small money.

HJ: I assumed $100,000 for a big-name guest.

OW: Yes, well . . . Let me tell you the history of American television in a few well-chosen words. As soon as CBS and William Morris and NBC and MCA—those four—saw what television was, they made a secret pact. I don't believe in conspiracy stories, but this one is true! Which was that nobody in a series was ever going to get anything like movie money. Nobody. So that when Henry Kissinger came on, they gave him $5,000 for one day. And even if you're a top actor, and willing to do *Love Boat*—there's always somebody—for a long time the top salary for *anybody*, for any length of time, in any hour show, was $7,500. That was broken by the Beatles, when [Ed] Sullivan paid them twenty-five, or something, for their first appearance on American television. But despite that, the fee has remained low all this time. You'll find that most of the guest stars on shows like this are getting $2,500, $3,000, $3,500. And glad to get the exposure.

HJ: Why would June Allyson want to do that? Or why would—

OW: Why not? Who's hiring her for anything else?

HJ: They ask you to go on a cruise—

OW: And they think that's the payment. They don't know that I can go on any cruise in the world free, if I'll lecture, or do magic one night, and then sign autographs.

HJ: *Love Boat* has been on the air forever, hasn't it?

OW: I'm unable to watch even one segment. Because I don't like the man who plays the captain. From *Mary Tyler Moore*. He has a kind of New York accent that gets my hackles up. I can't stand it! I liked old boring—what's his name—Lou Grant. What's his real name?

HJ: Oh, Ed Asner. He's wonderful on *Mary Tyler Moore*. I spent a very interesting evening with him and Jacobo Timerman the night before last at Michael Douglas's house—it was a fundraiser for El Salvador. Timerman wrote a book critical of Israel's invasion of Lebanon, and now he says he can't stand it in Israel anymore. He said, "They were spitting at me in the streets." I said, "If you're gonna be a conscience, you're gonna have to suffer some of this."

OW: Timerman is a real conscience.

HJ: What he's lived through—jail, torture, electroshock—in Argentina where he grew up, for speaking up against the generals during the Dirty War. Now he's a man without a country.

OW: Isn't everybody? He's got a country, and it's wherever he is.

HJ: I said, "Where are you gonna live?" He said, "I'm going to see what is going on in Argentina. I want to make sure that every one of those criminals is tried."

OW: I am really in awe of him.

HJ: At Michael's, he was talking about how upset he was at the American Jewish leadership and the American Jewish community for supporting Reagan's reactionary policies in Central America. Because Israel provides arms, at America's behest, to Honduras. It was a living room full of progressive Jews, but a lot of them were very uncomfortable with being singled out. It got them worrying about anti-Semitism. And Asner did a wonderful thing. He talked about the fact that the Jews have become part of the establishment to the point where they've forgotten their whole liberal humanitarian tradition.

OW: They won't speak out about Lebanon. Or Central America. You know, there are large sections of that community who don't like the word *Jew*. *Jewish* or *Jewish persuasion*, or *Jewish culture* are fine, but not the word *Jew*! Don't call a Jew a Jew. That's really strange. And sad.

HJ: I didn't read Timerman's Lebanon book, so I don't know to what extreme he went. Is it fair? Reasonable?

OW: To me it is. From my point of view, it's saying what I would say as a non-Jew. America has missed absolutely no opportunity, not only during the Reagan administration, but in my lifetime, to render it impossible for us to be anything but the deathly enemy of all Arabs, and, of course, all Latin Americans. We can never polish that image. I don't care how much money we pour into it.

HJ: Timerman is going to cover Central America for the *New Yorker* now.

OW: Nobody's written well about Central America. Well, there's Joan Didion. She spent seven days in Central America. Wrote a best seller. It should be called *Seven Days in Central America.*

HJ: Here's Patrick [Terrail].

PATRICK TERRAIL: What's do you call a pole with a twenty-five-million-dollar mansion? The Pope.

HJ: What?

PT: The Pope.

HJ: That's a rather bigoted joke.

PT: It's sweet.

OW: What it has is that it's clean. I expected some filthy punch line.

PT: I would never tell a filthy joke to Mr. Welles. Not coming out of my mouth . . .

(PT exits.)

OW: You have no idea how close I am to signing for *Lear*. And I've got, I think, a deal in Mexico for *The Dreamers*. I don't dare believe it—you know what it's like. The world is too full of disappointments to celebrate these kinds of things till they happen. They'll probably all collapse.

HJ: They won't all collapse.

OW: I think my future is in advertising. I did Carlsberg beer in England for five years. Then they decided they could do it cheaper by getting a man who could imitate my voice. They had him for two years and I've been back for the last three years. I did one yesterday.

HJ: Have you seen [John] Gielgud's ads for Old Spice?

OW: Yes. They're not using him well at all, you know.

HJ: He plays a sort of strange butler or something.

OW: That's because of the thing he did with Dudley Moore, *Arthur*. Well, they thought, if that went well with the movie, that'll go good with Old Spice . . . Gielgud used to play Shakespeare as though he were dictating it to his secretary. I told him that myself.

HJ: You did?

OW: In *Hamlet*, when Fortinbras is marching by, it sounded particularly that way: "Witness this army . . . 'Have you got that, Miss Jones?' Such mass and charge, led by a delicate and tender prince . . . 'Am I going too fast for you?' "

HJ: Funny!

OW: I'm exchanging telegrams during the next three days with the French TV guy I told you about.

HJ: And do you have a better inkling about his capacity to raise that money?

OW: If he can't, nobody can. He has to. His job kind of depends on it. And Jack Lang has come in on it with some government money. So let's hope it works.

HJ: Well, I heard a story in Paris, from the people who seem to know what they're talking about, that Mitterand has seven or eight cassettes that he puts on at night, over and over again. Five or six of them are about very complex intellectual subjects of some sort. But there are three movies, and two of them are yours—*Kane* and *Touch of Evil*.

OW: You know that the president in France is not like a president in America. He is more like a king, you know? As somebody once said, de Gaulle established a monarchy in a republic, because the president makes the decisions. When everybody said, "We don't like that, a pyramid in the middle of the Louvre," he said, "I like it," and that's the end of it. There's a pyramid in the middle of the Louvre.

HJ: How do you feel about that pyramid?

OW: I hate it.

HJ: I'm wondering if I hate it only because I want to hold on to the past.

OW: My answer to myself, when I ask myself that question is, "Balls. It looks ridiculous!"

HJ: But maybe it's just because we want a more traditional look.

OW: But it *is* a traditional look. I just don't believe in mixing up traditional materials that way. I think if you have to have a shape there to let the light in, a box would have been less offensive. There is something assertive about that pyramid. It's making a statement. Everybody said, "You're gonna think the [Georges] Pompidou thing is beautiful. You just have to get used to it." But the more you look at it, the more impossible it is. It's a big piece of junk. But I remind myself that half of aesthetic France threatened to leave Paris when they started to build the Eiffel Tower. So maybe I'm just as reactionary. If I am, it doesn't bother me much, though. I'm perfectly content to be reactionary—to belong to my own time.

HJ: Everybody thought the Eiffel Tower was a piece of junk. Now it's something so beautiful—

OW: But, you see, the Eiffel Tower is marvelous because it has an historical meaning. It is the last great work of the Age of Iron.

HJ: Still, at the time, you can imagine people who wanted the vista uncluttered being—

OW: But now it's destroyed anyway because all the good views have been ruined by the Tour Montparnasse. If you stand and look through that small Arc de Triomphe—that little miniature, which is in front of the Louvre, and look up the Champs-Élysées, you used to be able to look right through the Arc de Triomphe into blue sky. Now what you see looks like Detroit.

HJ: But I'm curious. Is taste objective or subjective?

OW: Subjective, basically. But it's an interesting question. I remember my darling Louise de Vilmorin, who always swore that Paris was one of the ugliest cities in the world, a terrible nineteenth-century atrocity. She could only stand the things that dated from before then, and there were few enough of those. If your taste is back there in the seventeenth and eighteenth centuries, then Paris is an ugly city. The automobile did it, with all those underpasses and the highway by the Seine. Do you remember what the Seine was like when you could stroll along it with your girl? God, that was another world.

I've been asked to write some little thing in *Paris Vogue*, along with a lot of other people who don't know anything, about why I love Paris. And I can't think of anything to say. It should be "Why I Loved Paris." When I could walk on the sidewalk in Paris, I loved it, but now I have to climb over automobiles. Taking down the Halles was the beginning of the end. Les Halles was a good building. The new one is already falling apart. It looks older than Notre Dame! The paint is peeling off it. Soon there won't be any real Paris left, you know. Or real London or real Rome. Because a few untouchable monuments are not gonna keep a city . . . I think all the cities of the world are in decline. Because the idea of supporting cities has ceased to be part of world culture. We're all moving into shopping malls . . .

HJ: The old concept of the city as a cultural magnet has been abandoned. And they're overcrowded.

OW: And, of course, the traffic has ruined the sex life of the French. There's the famous *cinq à sept*. You know what that is? The businessmen, when they finished at five, before they went home to their wives had a *cinq à sept*, which was with a mistress. Now, you can't do that and get back home by seven. You can't *move* in the city. I think architects are bums nowadays. I'm convinced of it.

HJ: I. M. Pei is a bum?

OW: A show-off, anyway. I'm very interested in architecture, and I'm absolutely persuaded that I'm right. I don't have a moment's doubt. Architects have achieved marvelous theatrical effects with their mirror-glass buildings. But then you realize that they're built over volcanic earthquake faults. And that they depend on high-energy usage. You cannot open a window on a spring day. You could be locked up in there with no heat, or no air-conditioning, or whatever it is. And, therefore, these are bad buildings. For a moment, a group of people in Brazil was making interesting modern buildings with big louvers that you could open to the air, which gave them a kind of human feeling. I don't believe buildings should dehumanize us. By definition, they have to belong to us, on some level. Otherwise, they're just monuments to greed.

HJ: I love the older New York skyscrapers.

OW: I don't think that most of them are any good, either. I think they were only good at the very start, with [Louis] Sullivan. And those buildings weren't skyscrapers.

HJ: You don't think that the Chrysler Building—

OW: I like the Chrysler Building, but it's a little kitschy. A little Art Deco.

HJ: I love Art Deco.

OW: I hate it, you see? I deeply hate it.

HJ: So does my mother. She always said it was the maid's furniture.

OW: The maid's furniture is what it is. I knew that Deco was bad—let me be modest—when I was as young as fourteen! And I was so happy after the World War, when people started building other things. I said, "Oh, thank God! You know, there goes another one of those awful things down!" Deco was what I had against all the great ocean liners. I loved going on those ships, but I used to say, "What a shame that they aren't like the ones they made in 1890," you know? The older ships were wonderful to look at.

HJ: But you like Lubitsch. And he uses the Deco look.

OW: All the time. But I don't think Lubitsch has a strong visual sense. He wasn't interested in the sets. I watched him shooting, and it was all about the actors and what they're saying.

21. "Once in our lives, we had a national theater."

In which Orson is offered a job directing a feature about the contretemps over The Cradle Will Rock. *But the script, by Ring Lardner, Jr., is awash in Old Left pieties, and he wonders if he will be able to control the film.*

———————

HENRY JAGLOM: So what's new?

ORSON WELLES: There is a young man, thirty-three years old, handsome, tremendously intelligent, and rich as hell, who financed a terrible picture called *Wide Blood*.

HJ: Not *Wise Blood*?

OW: *Wise Blood*, I guess, whatever it is.

HJ: Huston's film. I know who you're talking about, Michael Fitzgerald.

OW: Yeah, for $900,000. So he tells me, "We have a script written by Ring Lardner, Jr." And I read it. Not because I really wanted to, but because I'm in it—there's a leading character named Orson Welles. It's about the night we moved *The Cradle Will Rock* from the Maxine Elliott to the Venice Theatre. It's got a very simple MGM plot. The kind with Mickey Rooney and Judy Garland, you know: What are you gonna do when the bad guys close the theater? If you knuckle under to the bad guys, aren't you gonna throw everybody out of work? The hell with that—the show is gonna go on.

Rent a theater, find a piano. Open the show. That's all the movie is. But I am shown in the worst light of any character, because the guy's source is Houseman. Offensive. I said, "This is terrible." My problem is, should I direct it?

HJ: Was Lardner's script true to what happened, aside from the fact that you're presented in a bad light?

OW: Yes, it's accurate, in fact. And they propose to start as soon as they can. I said yes, because in the last analysis, I am the hero, and a glamorous one. I sat them down at this table, and I said, "Would you sit still for my beginning the movie as I am now, saying, 'There was a young man called Orson Welles, age twenty-four, and I don't know him at all. I know his memories—the ones that have survived—but I really don't know this guy. He may have been the biggest pain in the butt, and I know what the other people who were in this story are going to tell you about him, or I think I do, but I'm going to show you what I think happened. The basic facts.'" So they agree to everything, which is a great problem for me, because I'm having second thoughts. I'm saying to myself, "This is terrible. I cannot, in my old age, live off pieces of my youth."

HJ: What budget are we talking about?

OW: Four million.

HJ: Four million! Wow! You should do it.

OW: My other problem is Ring Lardner. I don't know if I can cope with him as the author. Because I have to have a free hand, including rehearsals and everything else. I like the way the story is constructed, because it's such a clear-cut heroic story. But not the way it's written. As the movie stands now, it has a great fault. Very easy to fix. Ring Lardner's membership in the Communist Party is leaking all over the pages. People are talking about what defying the government means for the revolution of the world, and so on. And I think all that needs saying is that once in our lives, in America, we had a national theater, and that padlocking the doors was the end of it, and the end of the Depression as a subject for the American theater.

HJ: Who's the cast?

OW: Amy Irving, David Steinberg, and Rupert Everett.

HJ: Of course! Amy is married to Spielberg. What's his first name?

OW: *You* need Reagan cards.

HJ: David Spielberg? No.

OW: Steinberg—yes.

HJ: Spielberg, not Steinberg.

OW: Spielberg! . . . It's David Spiel—Steven! It's Steven!

HJ: Amy is playing Virginia Nicholson, whom you were still married to then. And Steinberg as Blitzstein, and Rupert as the young you.

OW: The starting date will be the first week in February, next year. I have no problem with Amy's pregnancy. Because I suddenly remembered that Virginia was pregnant. So if she starts to show, I'll put a line in about it. I could easily fall in love with her. But as you know, I don't believe in directors falling in love with their leading ladies. And I'm glad that I'm at an age when it would be indecent.

HJ: So you don't need any other casting for *The Cradle Will Rock*? You'll shoot at Cinecittà? And do exteriors in New York?

OW: Yes.

HJ: And what about the march?

OW: If I come back to America, I'm going to do only their feet. Because I began thinking of how these extras are going to react, and how one bad face, out of the hundreds, could be—I'm just scared that I cannot control the expressions of so many people. So I thought I'd make a little Eisenstein montage.

HJ: Are you going to be able to get the contract you want?

OW: I'm assured of it, but I haven't gotten it yet. I talked to Fitzgerald and said, "You know, your letter says I have absolute artistic control. But your two other producers are not friendly to me."

HJ: Who?

OW: You know, the asshole from *Animal House*, a real shit.

HJ: John Landis. Well, let me be of some help here. He's a person I can influence.

OW: Kill him.

HJ: No, no, I don't want to. He's a really decent guy. What's he done?

OW: Won't leave me alone. Keeps phoning me and giving me advice on how to make the movie. In a very patronizing way. Everything he says is dumb!

HJ: And who's the other? Not Folsey, George Folsey. His father shot a lot of Minnelli musicals—*Meet Me in St. Louis*. They're not coming to Rome, are they?

OW: Oh, yes, they're coming with their wives. To shop and all that. Unless they're in jail.

HJ: Oh, right, that *Twilight Zone* thing. The Vic Morrow thing, killed by a helicopter blade.

OW: You know that both of them phoned me to give me advice on the script the day they were indicted? On the *day* they were indicted!

HJ: You would think they would have better things to do than to call—

OW: Exactly. Well, anyway, I said to Michael Fitzgerald, "Pretty soon I'm going to have to have a contract, because you're making your deal. And artistic control in a note from you is not the same as a contract. I must have final cut." And he says, "No argument. I've told them." Apparently, when he told Paramount, they said, "This is a collaborative art form." And Michael said, "Not with Orson

Welles. Final cut or nothing." He claims we're set. But there may be a question about *his* authority. I have to have a commitment from everybody. I will not make the movie without it, and I know that I've got them by the balls, because of all the money they've put into it already. But unless it's in the contract, they have tricks.

HJ: I'm telling you, Landis is a good guy.

OW: I already know I'm gonna have Michael on the set from early morning till late at night every day. There was already a moment when he got mad at me. He asked me a useless question, and I said to him, "Why do you ask me that question?" So I got a letter from him saying, "I am not John Houseman. I can ask any question I want."

HJ: If he's turning it all over to you, why does he want to be on the set?

OW: Because he has nothing to do. It's fine, just as long as he doesn't sidle up to me and say, "Wouldn't it be better if you did it this way? Walk that way? Emphasize that a little more? We don't quite feel—" The answer to that always is, "That's very interesting. Yes, I'll have to think about that." Nobody has told him that the real producers, in the old days, never came on the set. Ever. Because on the set, the director is the boss. It would make the producer look like nothing. You went to their office. That was their way of showing they were somebody.

HJ: What's the status of it now?

OW: Ring Lardner is sending me, on Monday, a rewrite of his first twenty pages, based on what I've said. I, in the meantime, have knocked myself out writing the first twenty pages. And I hope my twenty pages crosses his twenty pages in the mail, so mine don't seem to be an answer to his. I cannot get the producer to understand the delicacy of a situation in which I am *not* the coauthor.

HJ: But why can't you be the coauthor?

OW: In a sense, I have to be. Having been witness to these events, and never in my life having made somebody else's script. But I can't get that through to him. And Ring with me would be like . . . you know.

HJ: So you don't want him at all. Well, what does Fitzgerald say when you talk to him about it?

OW: "Anything you want. And Ring will be there with you, and so on." What am I gonna *say* to him?

HJ: You have to persuade the producers that Ring is superfluous, without hurting his feelings.

OW: No way I can do it without hurting his feelings. I shouldn't be put in that situation. I really shouldn't.

HJ: Did you say that to Fitzgerald?

OW: I sat with him the other night, alone, and he just wouldn't listen. All he wanted to do was beg me to have Ring there. As though, just having the screenwriter and the director together, somehow—

HJ: The movie would magically come into being?

OW: Yeah, 'cause that's the way John Huston did it. In *Under the Volcano*, which Fitzgerald also produced. And I said to him, "You must understand that John and I are two different kinds of directors. He has been gainfully employed, without interruption, for all these years. Because if he doesn't get what he wants, he goes ahead with the picture anyway."

HJ: And gets what he wants on the next one.

OW: Yes. But I can't, you know?

HJ: Because there may not be a next one.

OW: The only thing I can say for myself is that I do not have on my record a single clear-cut artistic failure. And that can't be said of many people. This situation is so unfair to me! They didn't ask me who should write the script. Ring is ready to do anything I say, but, really, he ought to be paid off and leave. And they want to start now, you see. They're pushing me: "Where are your pages?" So my alternative is to have three weeks' rehearsal and improvise an awful lot of things. But it's the kind of story that I think is better planned, even if you then depart from the plan.

HJ: Can't you get them to use your twenty pages?

OW: Well, I'll see what he's done. But the first twenty pages have to be my twenty pages, unchanged. I think there's little question that mine are going to be better than his. It *must* be my picture. I cannot allow a piece of my own life to be told by somebody else. I don't even *approve* of using a piece of my life, because of my own peculiar prejudices in that regard. And here I am, being frankly autobiographical, and depending on my memory, which may be unreliable.

HJ: Why are they averse to a cowriting credit?

OW: That's been suggested. That he should come and work with me—in the traditional way of the writer with the director, you see. And I've got a great way to counter that, because I can say, "These things concern my memory of a real event." I mean, Ring Lardner? An ex-Communist, who still has his heart in the party, and a WASP. This film should be filled with Jewish-Italian ambiance. It's New York. Let's have a latinity in it, a little salsa.

HJ: They ought to be giving you a contract, because you're now actually writing without one.

OW: Or any explicit agreement on my part I want the picture made. Because if I can't correct the script and casting, I don't think the picture should be made. I started to say, "Well, to save money we should get rid of Lardner." And they said, "You mustn't think about money." And I said, "You want me to make a picture under four million. I have to think about it. No matter how smart the producers are." "You just be the artist, and direct, and Ring'll write the script." Of course, I have no idea what Ring is gonna say about my pages.

HJ: What if he says, "No, I don't like them?" Now they're confronted with the writer they've hired saying, "Orson's pages are too, uh, subjective. You need an outside—"

OW: Or he'll say, "Orson is trying to make himself look more sympathetic." I'd say, "You're goddamn right I am!"

HJ: You told me a very good thing, which you should emphasize with them, that you'll make yourself unsympathetic in those areas where it will be good theatrically.

OW: My crime, you see, according to this script, is that I was willing to risk these people, who'd been out of work for all this time, put 'em on the street, for the sake of my principles.

HJ: It's economic immorality, an artist's self-absorption.

OW: You know, at the time, everyone involved with the production expressed the automatic knee-jerk reaction of the progressive: "Free speech cannot be stopped," and so on. Marc [Blitzstein], my wife, and myself were biting our fingernails. I was saying, "We're all for moving it but are we being cruel? Nobody's stopping to think that all these people are gonna be out of work." I kept thinking we could save the situation, somehow. I said, "We don't have to make a big drama out of this. Remember, I can go to Harry Hopkins, and we can arrange something, I'm sure. The administration doesn't want this to happen. This is the Justice Department and the Congress. They're out to kill the Federal Theatre, and they're going to do it." But they padlocked the theater. And we decided.

HJ: So padlocking the theater was the last straw. You figured they were going to kill it one way or another anyway, so why not blow the whole thing up by moving the play.

OW: I have to explain, in the script, why Houseman agreed to all of this.

HJ: You mean moving the play to the Venice Theatre and—

OW: Without telling the truth, that he saw this move would make him a Broadway producer. And the hell with everybody. Because that would be really cruel. But I have very interesting proof of his thinking, because some fans have been sending me old programs of my plays. Just recently, I got one for the *Voodoo Macbeth*, in which you can only find Houseman's name on the back page, with the man who turns on the lights. All Houseman did on the original production was take care of the box office.

HJ: You mean he thought that the publicity would make his reputation.

OW: Recently, some producers who wanted me to do something or other, wrote me a letter. They planned to do a handful of plays for Home Box Office. And they said, "One of our plays for the year is the Houseman-Welles *Cradle Will Rock*." And I can't bring myself to answer them. It stops me, every time. Because I want to read them a little lecture. And I can't do that, you know. After we had moved *Cradle* to a commercial theater, we were making a fortune—we financed the Mercury Theatre with that money—you suddenly had on the first page: "Mr. John Houseman."

HJ: So his goal was really what you were accused of, exploiting the situation to forward your career, making you seem like a ruthless person.

Getting back to your contract or lack of contract, it is inevitable that what they will try to do—it's just the nature of the beast—is get you to work as long as possible without signing you. Orson, you're going to have to be a little hard-nosed now.

OW: We're talking. Fitzgerald says, "Well, I want to do what I've done on my other two pictures. Everybody who's important to the picture—sound, and executives, and the art director—will get a piece of the picture proportionate to his effort, and so on." And I said, "That's a beautiful idea. But I make a lot of money doing other things, and I have to give them up to do your picture. And I don't have any money, I don't have any assets at all. And I have an enormous amount of tension, obligations, human beings who depend on me. So I have to ask for my money up front. I'll happily lose the five million dollars that I could have made on the back end." I think he's bought that, agonized his way through it, even though it spoils his beautiful symmetry.

22. "I smell director."

In which Orson complains about the onerous demands made on directors, and helps Henry with his movie Always, understanding that his approach requires the illusion of transparency.

HENRY JAGLOM: I've just come from a three-hour meeting that totally drained me. The worst kind of boring—trailers and ads and teasers and posters. Having to pretend to listen to a lot of people's opinions. That's the thing I hate. Having to try to not get a reputation right off for being an impossible dictator. Even though I'm in the position, fortunately, where I can say no.

ORSON WELLES: In my dealings with Hollywood, I was always in charge of the trailer. I made it myself. In fact, in *Kane*, I wrote the outline of the trailer and shot stuff for it while we were still shooting the movie. Because you see something that you're doing, and you say, "That would be good for the trailer, you know?" Even if it wouldn't work for the film.

Making a picture is always a tremendous strain on a director, who is supposed to be the source of energy. And being the source of energy, he must also be a monument of patience. But I'm so impatient on a set, I always announce at the beginning, so that it's clear, that no assistant director is allowed to ask for silence, or to talk to sound, and sound is not allowed to say anything except, "Rolling," after I say, "Camera." Not another word. So then, after you get through with that, you have to wait for Joe with the hammer, or Jill with the curl—or whatever it is.

Then, after you're done with the shooting, you go into the cutting room. And that's a tremendous nervous strain, too. Editing is the other great pain of being a director, how much of your life is spent in a dark room, not creating, but waiting for someone to do something. Waiting, not for yourself to think of an idea in front of a typewriter or behind a camera, but for other people who do dumb things. And the dumber the thing is, the longer it takes. You advance the film to the place you want, then make the note and hope the cutter understands, and wait till he executes it. Because he has to roll back the film, or he puts it in backwards, or it's upside down, or there's a break in the film, and he has to go and find it.

I hate those great huge rolls of film in stacks of cans. And I have a system, which is, I always make what I call a source, for every scene. Which is another reel that includes every fragment of what I've picked out that *might* be good. Because in a bad take, there may be something I like, so I put all of them on one reel. And before I'm finished with a scene, I always run the source, to be sure I've squeezed everything I can out of it. But I have to run through the whole reel to find that one bit, so it takes forever. I spend all my time handling film. The new editing machine, which I've seen now, is the greatest step forward since I don't know what.

HJ: The flatbed?

OW: It means that three months' work can be done in ten days.

HJ: Why do I fear that something about the creative process will get lost by that expedition? I like to go back and forth, looking over everything again and again.

OW: I don't look over everything again and again. You know that I never wait until after I've looked at the rushes to begin the editing. I cut them as I'm looking at them. But I suffered agonies spending twelve hours a day on the old machines. Why not spend six?

Before, my ratio was, I figure, three days cutting to one day of shooting. Now, at most I would spend a fraction of that on the cutting. What that means is that I no longer have to be the great organist at the console, which drove me nuts. Now I can behave as if I were painting a picture or writing a script or a book. If I want to think, I just stop and think. It liberates you. Frees you from taking months out of your life, just sitting around. Now, I don't wait for the tool. The tool waits for me.

(Zsa Zsa Gabor enters.)

ZSA ZSA GABOR: How are you, darling? How wonderful to see you.

KIKI: Arf! Arf!

ZG: Whose dog is that?

OW: That's my dog, who bites.

ZG: No, no. *(To Kiki)* You bite?

OW: Yes. Especially Hungarians. How are you?

ZG: Fine, darling.

(Zsa Zsa Gabor exits.)

HJ: I see your point. I'd love to speed up my editing process, especially if I gained more time to think.

OW: But of course, it's going to be the end of the director controlling the cutting. Because the cutting will all be done by the time he gets off the set, by the editor. Who will have worked very hard for an hour and a half every day. Then the cutter really will get a credit with a card for himself for great editing. But how will anyone know who edited what? Who made what cut? It's hard enough to know what's directing, what's acting. You really don't know, in any single instance, whether it's the actor or the director. But you never can tell that to a critic.

HJ: I need help with the script of my new movie, which I'm calling *Always*. I'm going to act and direct, and I always have trouble with that. The first day is insane, every time, because I'm sitting there, in the scene, trying not to be there, so I can see what is going on.

OW: You have to be able to press a button and become the director for a certain length of time, and then become the actor. Say, "Fuck all the rest of it; now I'm gonna act."

HJ: Let me tell you the story line, which is based on my real relationship with my ex, Patrice, who's going to act in it. Prior to when the movie starts, she has come back from Santa Fe, where she's been for six months. I've called her up and asked her to come back to the house that was our house—now my house—to sign the divorce agreement. In honor of the occasion, I've decided to cook her dinner. I don't know how to cook, and I do something wrong, which results in her getting food poisoning. Either I pick mushrooms from my garden, stupidly, or I leave the fish out too long, or—

OW: May I stop you right on that point, with food poisoning?

HJ: Sure.

OW: Mushrooms are too dangerous. Mushrooms—that's like life or death. Don't call it "food poisoning." She's told you, over and over again, that she's terribly allergic to something, and you forgot it, and put it in the stew, where it's unrecognizable. It could, in a Freudian way, be interpreted as deliberate.

HJ: So, I surprise her with this lovely dinner that I've made myself. She's pleased, touched. And in the course of our two-person dinner, with elaborate silverware—

OW: Beautiful napery—it's obviously not only more than you'd ever do, but more than you could ever *conceive* of doing. It looks like a page out of "Home" in the *Los Angeles Times*.

HJ: With flowers on the table—everything.

OW: *Comme il faut.*

HJ: She's stunned, and touched and everything. In the course of the dinner, the audience learns a little bit of the background, which is that she left me two years ago, that I was devastated because I thought this marriage would last for the rest of my life. We didn't break up because of fights or arguments or incompatibility, like most people. It had more to do with today's world, where women are told, "It's not enough to be happy, it's not enough to love somebody. You've gotta find out who you are," and all of that. The point is we really love each other, despite her having done this thing. In the course of the dinner the bell rings. It's the notary who has to witness the signing of the divorce papers.

OW: Now, why did you do that? Because that's essentially gross.

HJ: Is it poor taste? I wondered. I can prepare her by saying, during dinner, "Listen. We have to sign in front of a witness who is a notary."

OW: If you say that right away, it's all right. As long as it isn't a surprise. As a surprise, it's gross. You can't really have cooked her this marvelous dinner, and then say, "And now we have the man with the notary stamp."

HJ: This is exactly what I'm asking you for, so this is marvelous. Thank you, Orson. I hope you don't mind doing this.

OW: No, I love it!

HJ: I own an old Wurlitzer jukebox. I put on a Fred Astaire tune from the thirties, and we dance. And it is during the dance that she starts feeling ill. She has to stop. I take her upstairs to bed—my bed, which was our bed—and put her to sleep there. I quietly tiptoe out and into the cutting room, which is a room around the corner in the upstairs of the house. I am a man who makes documentary films on science and science-allied fields for public broadcasting. And I'm working on a film either on time and memory, or on the relationship between men and women. Or on the chemistry of love, that pseudo-science that tries to investigate the emotional condition.

OW: What worries me about everything you've said just now about the three subjects, is they all sound like they might turn into allegories for your story. And that's bad. Bad, bad, bad.

HJ: Perhaps, more than anything else this afternoon, that's what I have to ask you about. Naturally, I admit I am tempted to use—

OW: Don't do it.

HJ: Not allegorically in an intellectual way, but in an emo—

OW: Not in *any* way.

HJ: Too heavy-handed? Too schematic? But stuff about memory, and the past, and time and loss—that's the kind of thing I've been thinking about, and I'm quite obsessed with my childhood, my past, and so on.

OW: I just don't know about the documentary.

HJ: All right, let's leave that open. I forgot to mention one thing. The very opening of the movie you're probably gonna hate. Which is, I sit in a chair, in my living room, speaking into the camera. I say I was completely happy, I was positive that I had the best relationship in the world, and there was nothing that I wanted. Then one day she came home from yoga class. And the camera whirls to the door, and Patrice comes in. This is a flashback. I see that she is worried. "What's wrong?" "Nothing." "What's wrong?" "Nothing." "Something is obviously wrong. You look upset." I keep probing, which is what actually happened in real life. And she says, "I'm thinking that I don't know if we can live together anymore."

Then the camera comes back to me in a chair—present time— and I say, "After that came the most devastating two years of my life. I cried, I experienced the most incredible pain that could be imagined. Eventually I felt better, I got stronger, I went about my life. And tonight she's coming over to sign the divorce agreement. I've gotta cook her dinner." I get up and go into the kitchen, and the doorbell rings. That kind of thing. Basically, to try to cover, in perhaps a minute and a half, the whole two years we were together. And bring it from when she says, "I can't live with you anymore," to now. Any thoughts on that?

OW: I don't like it at all.

HJ: Why?

OW: I smell director. I smell director. It's getting too neat. You're setting yourself up for a terribly tight, well-constructed piece of clockwork. You see how the whole movie could be like that.

HJ: Oh, I would hate the whole movie like that.

OW: So, don't lead us to expect it. Don't set us up for something we're *not* gonna get, and that looks cleverer than its content. The content should be more important than the ingenuity of the director.

HJ: I didn't mean to make the shot too smart. I wanted to take care of the past that way, quickly, in one setup.

OW: Now, I would suggest that the past—I don't think this is too precious—the past should have her coming in with a Chinese dinner in buckets—or you doing that. In other words, so we see how they lived. You know, they're kind of intellectual gypsies. "I went out to the Imperial Palace and got all the stuff you like." So we've seen that the happy past consisted of takeout food. And the dinner and the notarized divorce is, you know, Lubitsch. And I would suggest—only because you asked—that if you do do that dinner, when she is expressing her appreciation and surprise at this effort, that you turn against what you've done, and condemn it as a piece of Lubitsch nonsense. So, in effect, you start arguing with her about her appreciation of what you've done for her.

HJ: That's very good—very, very good.

OW: Sure. You say, "All I lack is, you know, three fiddles and a cimbalom."

HJ: Three fiddle players and a what?

OW: And a cimbalom.

HJ: What's that?

OW: That's the thing that—*(sings a few notes)*. Pronounced ZIM-ba-lom. It's a funny word.

HJ: But what about my jukebox?

OW: You shouldn't say, "I've got the jukebox." She should say, "You've got the jukebox." And she stands there. Not asking you to dance, but with her arms out. So it's the easiest thing to go and take her . . .

HJ: Now, the next day we wake up together in the same bed. I fell asleep next to her, close to her. And she wakes up shocked that I'm there.

OW: Has it been made clear to us that there's gonna be no rising magoo in the bed?

HJ: That there wasn't any what? Oh, sex, you mean? That would be clear.

OW: She sits up, maybe, because she's gotta go to the can. And she says to you, "I know that you fed me"—whatever it is—"papaya," you know? "It's all gone, and it wasn't fun getting rid of it. I've told you at least nine hundred and ninety-nine times that I'm allergic to papaya. I think I should go to the office."

HJ: She's just taken a job in Los Angeles at the Yoga Center which, in fact, is where Patrice now lives. She likes it. She feels it's part of the search.

OW: The search, the terrible search. Wait a minute. I have an idea. You must let me tell it. It has nothing to do with the plot at this point. It's an argument for you to give her, somewhere. This great search is mainly being conducted on the West Coast. And it is because people, pioneers, have been fighting their way to get here for one hundred and fifty years. Finally they're here, and there's nothing here.

23. "I've felt that cold deathly wind from the tomb."

In which Orson refuses to embrace Henry because he is afraid of catching AIDS. *Lear* is going forward, but he thinks the political situation in France is unstable. He fears *Wind* is dated. *Cradle* is stalled.

Henry Jaglom: You look troubled? What? No hug?

Orson Welles: If we could figure out a way to hug without kissing, that would be fine.

HJ: Why no kissing?

OW: You know, we could have AIDS.

HJ: Well, neither of us, as far as I know, has AIDS. Is there something I should know about you, Orson?

OW: They don't know how it's transmitted, and saliva is one of the responsible parties.

HJ: We don't drool on each other when we kiss.

OW: I'm not kissing anybody. I'm not even sure about shaking hands. But I can hug you in such a way that we each face in opposite directions.

HJ: Orson, what is this, a comedy routine?

OW: I'm deadly serious. I haven't gone through my life to be felled by some gay plague. We might be carriers. You never know.

HJ: Oh, my God. Oh, my God. If people are going to start doing that . . .

OW: I might be a carrier. For every thousand guys with AIDS, five thousand are carriers who will never have it.

HJ: Yes, but those are people who have homosexual relationships, the carriers.

OW: There are 6 percent of the people that have it for which there is no explanation.

HJ: I'm going to pee.

OW: Then what are you going to do?

HJ: Zip up, wash my hands, and come back.

OW: That's not good enough. Are you going to touch the knobs?

HJ: Orson, you're becoming a fanatic.

OW: Yes, a fanatic to save my life. Did you touch Kiki?

HJ: Yes, I petted her.

OW: I don't know if dogs can catch it.

HJ: If dogs could get it, they'd be dying. All gay guys have dogs.

WAITER: *Qu'est-ce que vous aimez manger?*

OW: *Rien.* I'm not too well. I don't think I'm going to eat.

W: Do you want a little turnip soup? Very nice.

OW: I don't like soup.

W: OK, then. Maybe a salad or something mild?

OW: Never salad in a restaurant . . . *(To HJ)* I'm determined never again to eat a salad in a restaurant. Because I've watched them in the kitchen, and I've been told that's how you get hepatitis. It's the dirty-fingers disease. The first courses are only salads. There must be something else they could come up with for a first course. God-damn nouvelle cuisine; they only think in terms of salad. They make salad out of every goddamn thing in the world—salad of roast beef. What salad generation do you belong to?

HJ: What?

OW: This emphasis on greenery, and all that. The 'sixties. The Great Health Movement. Oh, I'm sure it's done everybody good. And it's probably good that people don't drink the way they used to. Everybody was drunk when I was young. It wasn't fun. It was boring. You just got used to dealing with your drunken friends.

HJ: I came from a generation where everybody was high all the time.

OW: Equally boring. Although I think that more middle-class Americans and fewer show-business people are stuffing it up their nose these days.

HJ: What's that painting on the wall?

W: A David Hockney.

OW: Patrick asked me to do a drawing as well, and I'm ashamed that I didn't do it. I have a bad hand. For the last three months, I can hardly sign my name. I have this pinched nerve. I got it in Paris, for no reason at all. Agonizing pain. I'm crippled—these two fingers are almost dead. Oh, boy, I'm scared.

HJ: Chiropractors are good for that.

OW: Or acupuncture. I got into the hands of a fake acupuncture man in Paris who came with incense. And he said, "What house are you?" And I said, "What house?" And he said, "Astrologically." I was, already, "Goodbye." And he wasn't even Chinese or anything. On the other hand, I also think that there are many areas in medicine where the proper quack is the right fellow to go to. But I have a foolish prejudice against anybody who isn't a doctor, because my father believed in everyone who wasn't a doctor. He lived his life by his horoscope, which was done for him by very expensive people. He believed in everything—

HJ: But science.

OW: But God, you know? It's often the people who are not religious who are the most superstitious. There are more clairvoyants in Paris than in any city in the world, four clairvoyants to one doctor, even though the French don't believe in God. It's the old Chesterton remark, "If you don't believe in God, you'll believe in anything." It's true. Because if you don't believe in God, you will substitute every mystery that is outside of yourself, however nonsensical it may be. And, of course, astrology is so maddening, because it was all laid down at a time when the planets were in another position. An Aries is now actually a Pisces, and so on. I'm old enough to remember when everybody had their palms read, the way they now have their charts done. And in palmistry as practiced in the West for the last two hundred years, every line is different from the old palmistry of the Hindus. The lifeline was here, the love line there, but it's still supposed to work. The place with the greatest number of believers in this sort of thing is the Soviet Union, supposedly ruled by dialectical materialism. The hunger to believe has not been filled by Lenin, mummified in the Kremlin. The time may come when we'll be able to live without mystery, but then we'll have to question whether we'll still be capable of poetry. It's pretty hard to imagine—a world or an art without any kind of deception.

HJ: There was that rock that you brought on *Carson*.

OW: I went to a shop that sold exotic minerals. I got one of those funny-looking stones. And I came on *Carson* and I said, "There are only seven of these in the world. And I have permission, just for tonight, to show it on television, because these stones are being studied at leading universities. The writing on the spine of this stone is extraterrestrial, and we have no idea how either got there. But if you have a watch or a clock which doesn't work anywhere in your house, or on your person, this stone will make it go." At that moment, when I held up the stone, the clock in the studio at NBC, which had gone on the blink, started to tick.

HJ: Love it! . . . Bogdanovich called. He told me—

OW: Wait a minute! I'll tell you what he talked about. He talked about Bogdanovich!

HJ: He said, "I'm having a problem." He was using Springsteen for the picture he's finishing, *Mask*. "The studio made me take all my music off . . ."

OW: Yeah, I read about that.

HJ: So he's suing the studio for a couple of million dollars.

OW: It's a great thing to do after you've been out of work.

HJ: So I said, "Peter, do you really think this is a good idea?" He said, "Well, I've done it." Apparently the boy that the movie is about loves Springsteen. So he sent a letter to Frank Price at Universal, where the film is set up, demanding that he not interfere with his creative rights, that filmmakers have the right to put any music they want in their movie, and he would like you to—

OW: Fat chance.

HJ: To sign it!

OW: No.

HJ: I have to find a graceful way to decline for you.

OW: No. Ask him to call me and I'll tell him. You know, if we were in France, he'd have the law on his side. According to French law—

HJ: He'd own the movie.

OW: Here a movie is the property of the people who are hiring you. And you cannot invoke a right which doesn't exist.

HJ: They gave him final cut, so they promised him a certain kind of—

OW: A promise! Where is a letter like that gonna get you, you know? Everybody'll say he's a pain in the neck. Who'll want to work with Bogdanovich?

HJ: He can't win this. The movie's out. There're hundreds of prints going around.

OW: And good notices. First good notices he's had in years.

HJ: The movie relates to the book Peter wrote about Dorothy Stratten. You know, the Playmate he met at Hef's. Who was murdered by her husband. Peter is very emotionally involved with this material.

OW: I read that book.

HJ: I think it's called *The Killing of the Unicorn*, or something like that.

OW: For a man to betray himself that way, in front of the world, is really disturbing. She was a semihooker, you know.

HJ: Which is not Peter's thing at all.

OW: And he implicates himself as a stooge of Hefner.

HJ: He says he owes it to Dorothy.

OW: Oh, no. After I finished the book, I don't believe he was in love with her. He was in love with himself being in love with her.

HJ: You're being too hard on him. I think it's part and parcel of the *Kane* thing, the great man thing, which has been fed to him by *you*. It's all your fault.

OW: A little bit, yeah.

HJ: And it's not just him. Von Sternberg with Marlene, Hitchcock with Grace Kelly, Woody Allen with Diane Keaton, Fellini with Giulietta Masina, Bergman with Liv Ullmann. People think that part of their job now, to be a great artist, is to find one of these young ingénues and mold them. It has entered his subconscious. Because he did the exact same thing with Cybill [Shepherd]. And now he—

OW: He's never gonna get over Cybill.

HJ: Dorothy was the great romance of his life. She was a nineteen-year-old who had a brutal husband, and for the first time she was being treated nicely—by Peter.

OW: It's all so Ernest Dowson—the last of the romantic poets—who spent his life mooning around because he was hopelessly in love with a girl who served him beer in a pub. "I have been faithful to thee, Cynara! in my fashion." You know? "I called for madder music and for stronger wine, /But when the feast is finished and the lamps expire, /Then falls thy shadow, Cynara! the night is thine." And this is all about Adelaide the barmaid. Who was bored to death with it, you know? It always has to be with an unworthy object. That's a necessary part of all this. It's never with some marvelous girl who's clearly worth it. It's always somebody that you just happened on. He's gonna spend his life on this.

HJ: *Mask* is about a boy born with a deformed face. He apparently picked this subject because the first play he took Dorothy to see was *The Elephant Man*. She identified with it, because her great beauty was similar to the grotesque ugliness of the Elephant Man. In that the extremeness of each of them—extreme beauty and extreme ugliness—separated them from the common folk of the world.

OW: Shit!

HJ: This is his movie for Dorothy. It's the myth of how horrible it is to be beautiful. But despite it all, I'm very fond of Peter. He's uniquely gifted. And he's as much a victim as everyone else.

OW: But he mustn't go writing manifestos. He certainly isn't doing himself any good.

HJ: Then why is he? Why?

OW: Well, I think the chief reason for most self-destruction is the death wish, which almost everybody has, to one degree or another. And people who are actively creative, or actively and fruitfully in love, or involved in the living world, escape it. But it's always there. And people who assume attitudes of a romantic nature, that have to do with ego, are particularly prone, I think, to the death wish. Like Narcissus who drowned in his own image. The ultimate act, in some way, of self-love. I can choose the time and manner of my death. Romantic suicide. The world will be sorry it didn't treat me better. I think it's very common.

HJ: Are you conscious of it in yourself?

OW: Oh, yes. Two or three times I've thought I had a fatal disease. And I've thought of it with a certain relief. In other words, no more obligation to take care of people. I've felt that cold deathly wind from the tomb blowing over me. It's the real voice of the devil, you know? It's why people invent the red guy with the horns. It's the death wish, the opposite of life. It's surrender. Which is, I think, a very egotistical thing to do. I turned that voice off quickly, when I heard it and felt that.

HJ: Did you happen to see this six-part thing on Freud on the Arts and Entertainment Channel? Wonderful, wonderful program. And a very well-written script by the son of Rex Harrison and Lilli Palmer.

OW: Lilli Palmer is very good in *The Other Side of the Wind*. She plays Marlene. But don't let's go into that this lunch.

HJ: Well, can we just mention one thing about that? *California* magazine wants to know if you'll tell the story of what happened with *The Other Side of the Wind*. I thought that to have all of that out might help the situation in France.

OW: The opposite. It's just *because* of France that I wouldn't do it. I cannot tell the truth without attacking the French judicial system. But I am in no position right now to get the French angry at me.

HJ: But can't you give an account leading up to how it got into the vault in Paris? Pending arbitration with the Shah's brother-in-law, who is claiming he owns it, the French refusing to release it to you, all that.

OW: No, I can't. If *Lear* is off for any terrible reason, I'll do it instantly. You know, it's just a scandal . . .

HJ: I thought that you had won the rights to *The Other Side of the Wind*.

OW: Yes, I did.

HJ: But then I heard just this week that there was somebody new assigned—

OW: Yes, a new arbitrator. And it has to be all done all over again.

HJ: If you got it away from the Iranians and the French, could you finish it? The cast is dying off.

OW: Yes. Edmond O'Brien just died. Tony Selwart is blind. John Huston can't move. I don't want to think about it now. The film has become strangely dated. But in an interesting way. I'd have to turn it into an essay film on that period. Because that's when all the young movie people wanted to be *auteurs*. And not to be Spielberg, as they do now. It was a different time.

HJ: Speaking of France, Gilles Jacob, who's now the head of the Cannes Film Festival, wants to stop by and say hello to you.

OW: Sucking up to the Cannes Film Festival people, eh?

HJ: I don't have to suck up to him. They love me. Now I just want you to be nice, Orson.

OW: He's a member of the "criminal class." Anybody connected with the Cannes festival is a crook.

HJ: Please, Orson, don't be ridiculous.

OW: Don't worry, I'll be gentle. You have no idea. I'm a hypocrite. A sellout.

HJ: Michael York asked, did I convey to you what he said about his indefinite availability. Especially for *Lear*.

OW: I like him very much.

HJ: Oh, he's a fine actor. And a truly modest actor. You can do with him, more or less, what you want.

OW: English actors are more modest than Americans, because they've never had Lee Strasberg to teach 'em that they know better than the director. I'm always making fun of Method, but I used a lot of that Stanislavski stuff in my work with actors, making Iago impotent, for instance, and giving that to Mac Liammóir to "use" in *Othello*. Othello is destroyed easily because he has never understood women—like Lear. Shakespeare was clearly tremendously feminine. Every man who is any kind of artist has a great deal of female in him. I act and give of myself as a man, but I register and receive with the soul of a woman. The only really good artists are feminine. I can't admit the *existence* of an artist whose dominant personality is masculine.

HJ: So what is the status of *Lear*?

OW: They are passionately anxious to make it. But after having promised me that *I* would be the producer, I have been given, with no choice in the matter, a French producer they want, a successful and intelligent man who I dislike intensely. Very cold. The only thing in his favor is that he's producing a lot of different things— he'll be awfully busy. What I don't have yet is a contract, and that's what I have to have. I'm not just demanding that I have artistic say-so, but also that I have production say-so—if I stay within the budget. I don't want somebody telling me, as he already has, that this or that costs a lot of money. They are shocked by the fact that I want to know everything about the production. They want me to be the artist and not concern myself with all of that. Well, the first thing they did with me as the artist not concerned with all of that was to take me to an enormous studio outside of Paris and say, "This is your studio." It's the biggest studio in Europe. It was filled with a set. I said, "When is the set gonna be out?" They said, "Well, maybe in August, but we don't know." So I said, "Well, I can't make the picture in one studio. I must have two studios, because while we're shooting one scene, they have to build what's gonna be the set for the next scene." Obviously, two studios. They'd never thought of that. That's the kind of leave-it-to-us mentality.

HJ: Just like Michael Fitzgerald. Is there anything to be done about that situation, in terms of—

OW: Not with him in the Bahamas. I don't dare deal with *Cradle* without Michael. I don't want to seem to be speaking for him. But he's not gonna be trying very hard in the Bahamas.

HJ: Do you get any feel from him about where he is on *Cradle*? Is it—?

OW: He claims he's got it all together, which isn't true. He's got it all together if we're willing to shoot in Berlin, because Berlin is offering a million dollars. But it's ridiculous to shoot this picture in Berlin. I'm not gonna do it, until I've done at least one other picture. Nothing can convince me otherwise.

HJ: Is there a reason?

OW: I've told you, and you don't agree. And that's the end of it. I don't think the first thing I should do after being absent from the business for ten years should involve mining my own past. There's an inherent weakness in this as a comeback movie. Politically it's wrong.

HJ: Because it looks like, instead of plunging forward—

OW: That's right. I'm going backwards. My feeling about *Cradle* is that I'd like to do it. But I would be perfectly happy to sell the script.

HJ: It's such a brilliant script, now that you've reworked it. I'd hate to see anyone else directing it.

OW: I wish you'd be more complimentary. The truth is I haven't got anything unique to offer it as a director. I've done it as a script.

HJ: So you feel good about *Lear*? I mean, it looks good?

OW: I don't dare say. But I fear they'll never come through. They all want to have dinner with me, but when it comes time to fork over the money, they disappear. It's always the same thing—I'm unmanageable, I walk away from films before they're finished, et cetera, et cetera, et cetera. So boring. I don't want to hear about it. More disappointment. Lang, who last year was receiving people in his office in an open-necked shirt, is now dressed by [Pierre] Cardin. Has bought an apartment on Place des Vosges, which costs about a million and a half. The *Socialist* Minister of Culture! On the other hand, he's talked about *Lear* again to Mitterand, so from that point of view, it looks good. There's nobody fighting it. It's just me trying to make sense of the deal. I don't want to sign a deal in which I discover that there's any possibility of disaster, of miscalculations which put it over budget, or anything. That's why I've been difficult, because I want to know the ground I'm gonna walk on.

HJ: Have you made it clear to them that that's the reason you've been difficult?

OW: Yes. But they don't listen very much. They listen to themselves. I hope I have a contract with the *Lear* people in the next week or two. If it doesn't go first, it'll never happen. But I think the French situation is very delicate. If the people who are now in the government and television change . . . There's a real fascist element rising in France. And because this is a socialist government—and of course, it's nonsense to call him a socialist—all the centrist conservatives are afraid, as they always are, that it is the weak wall through which communism will break. The French always put the blame on their president for everything that could possibly be wrong. So they may join them, even though the Communist Party has become a joke.

HJ: *(Calls out)* Excuse me—Hello!

OW: He's not our waiter.

HJ: Oh.

WAITER: Here is your kiwi.

OW: My God, that's beautiful. It's not as beautiful as a plain peeled one, but it's beautiful. Thank you. I made a discovery about the kiwi.

HJ: Which is?

OW: That it's the greatest fruit in the universe, but it's ruined by all the French chefs of the world who cut it up into thin slices. You cannot tell what it tastes like unless you eat it in bulk. Then it is marvelous. And it has the highest vitamin content of any fruit in the world.

HJ: You look much better than when you went to France. I mean, you're looking particularly well, and healthy and fit.

OW: What's that?

HJ: That's my mint carrier. As others might have cigarettes or toothpicks, I carry mints for my coffee. It's a little eccentricity, I suppose.

OW: If Ronnie can have his jelly beans . . . God, I'm worried. I hope that his checkup turns out all right, because I'm more worried about [George H. W.] Bush than I am about Reagan! I want Reagan to live! Bush is a creep, a real creep. Especially compared to Gorbachev. Bush thinks if he doesn't ignore Gorbachev he'll lose the Jesse Helms group, so he has to kowtow. What's amazing is that not one American Kremlinologist . . . Krem . . . Krem-lin-ologist . . . had a word to say about Gorbachev. He popped out of a box.

HJ: The great thing that Reagan has is a sense of personal security about himself. God knows based upon what.

OW: But he has it, and it's absolutely genuine. He comes bouncing into the room. You know Tom Wicker's line "My favorite thing about Reagan is that he's a genuine phony." And that's what he is. But he has this security, which we haven't seen in a president in a long time. Even Eisenhower was stuttering around, not sure what it was to be a politician, you know?

HJ: People have always liked him. He knows he's a nice guy.

OW: Yeah. He made one funny joke not long ago. In the cabinet room he says, "We ought to have a plaque saying, 'Ronald Reagan slept here.'" He can make any kind of mistake. He could promise anything and have it fall apart, and the public goes right on adoring him. Anybody who could get out of that retreat from Lebanon, with two hundred eighty Americans killed for nothing, without a scratch on his popularity or anything, is amazing.

24. "Jo Cotten kicked Hedda Hopper in the ass."

In which Orson recalls his affair with Lena Horne, who was black, gifted, and radical. Hopper warned him against it. When the owner of the 21 Club told him Horne was unwelcome, he played a nasty joke on him.

ORSON WELLES: I have to go to a social event that I . . . dread.

HENRY JAGLOM: What is that?

OW: A surprise party for Jo Cotten's eightieth birthday. It's in Santa Monica, at seven thirty. Black tie. Jo has had a stroke, you know. The last time I talked to him was about four days ago, and I said, "Well, what are you reading?" He said, "I can't read. I can follow conversation; I can talk; but I cannot read." Now, that's awful. I thought you could still read after a stroke.

HJ: Depends what kind of a stroke.

OW: Every kind of a stroke.

HJ: Why can't he read? It must be—

OW: I don't know. Somehow the process of turning letters into words is blocked. You have to help him with words. And he has to have therapy four times a week to keep that up. But he has something in Pat, a very devoted, attentive wife. He's always been very lucky. He had one other wife, who died, who worshipped him for twenty-five years. He's been coddled all his life.

This evening just hangs over me now. With his stroke, and with all the people who are going to be there that I don't know, I don't really want to— All those socialites from Palm Springs and Santa Barbara. And they all hate me, because I'm the oldest friend. What I'm really gonna be doing is entertaining them. It'll be just ghastly. If I could just go and visit him on another day. But how could his best friend not be there? The feeling is not how nice that I come, but how could I *not* come.

HJ: Did you see that made-for-TV movie *Malice in Wonderland,* where Elizabeth Taylor plays Louella Parsons and Jane Alexander plays Hedda Hopper? There are two characters named Orson Welles and Joseph Cotten.

OW: You know, they sent the script to me and Jo, and they said, "What do you think of it? Do you like it?" And he said, "No." So then they called me and said, "Do you approve of this?" I hadn't read it, so I just said, "No."

HJ: There's this scene where the Cotten character gets furious, because Hedda said something about his wife.

OW: Well, no. What Hedda was doing was printing that he was balling Deanna Durbin, which he was. In cars, in daylight, where everybody could see!

HJ: There's also this wonderful, strange scene where Cotten pushes Hedda's face in a plate of food.

OW: No, he kicked Hedda Hopper in the ass. The truth is that Jo Cotten was a Southern gentleman, with extremely good manners. That's what makes this story so good. He came up to her at a party and said, "Hedda, I just want you to understand, if you say that again, I'm going to kick you in the ass." She didn't believe it. She kept talking about it, and he just came and kicked her in the ass. The last man in Hollywood that you'd think would behave that way to a woman.

HJ: They made you the more reasonable one. Which is also not your reputation.

OW: That's true. I did say, "You mustn't kick Hedda in the ass." I told him I would kick her in the ass instead. But he insisted.

HJ: And in another scene, Hedda walks in on you when you're about to screen *Kane*, and you say, "What are you doing here?" And she was the one, according to this, who tipped off Hearst. She's portrayed as this insane woman running roughshod over the whole town, terrifying everybody.

OW: She was. And she destroyed Louella. Hedda had always been my defender, because I'd hired her as an actress when she was out of work. She always said, "I know you're a dirty Commie Red. But you were good to me and good to my son, and I won't—" Then she added, "But you've got to stop fucking Lena Horne." And I said, "I don't take instruction about things like that." And she said, "You *have* to, if you care about your career, and care about your country!" Nobody who knew about it gave a damn that Lena was black. Except Hedda, you know. But what was she gonna do? Write it in a column? I didn't give a damn. So I said, "Hedda, you can go boil your head." She always laughed when I insulted her. That's show business.

HJ: She was that reactionary, that she really believed these things?

OW: Violently, much more than Louella. She was wittier. She was smarter. You know what Jack Barrymore called Louella Parsons, who was terribly ugly. He said, "Louella—that queer udder."

HJ: "Queer udder." What a horrible description!

OW: This great truck used to come up to your house, just before Christmas with gifts from her. And you must never have given the news of your divorce to anybody but Louella. She would never forgive you. She always had to have the divorce. That was hers. You don't know the *power* those two cows had in this town! People opened the paper, ignoring Hitler and everything else, and turned right to Louella and Hedda.

HJ: How did she know about things like you and Lena?

OW: She offered fifty dollars for information and people called her up. Not friends, but waiters or valet-parking people, anybody. Somebody reported that I went into Lena's house or something. She and I never went out. In those days, you didn't go out with a black woman. You could, they wouldn't stop you, but things were delicate. And I didn't want to hurt her feelings. I once took her out to the 21 Club, thinking it was safe. Jack Kreindler, who looked just like a baked potato, and owned it then with his cousin, behaved correctly. But he took me aside afterwards and said, "Next time, it would be better not to come here." So when I got back to Hollywood, I told Charlie Lederer what had happened, and said, "What are we going to do about it?" Well, Jack Kreindler used to come to Hollywood on a holiday, and everybody would entertain him. So Charlie and I stopped what we were doing for two weeks and worked night and day on this prank. I gave a party in the private room of Chasen's, honoring the "Maharani of Boroda," and invited Jack. Now, we got the Maharani from Chicago. She was a hooker. I said she couldn't be local; it would have gotten around. She couldn't even know who the people she'd be meeting were. Everybody you ever heard of was at that table. It was very grand, so that Jack would be at ease, and not get suspicious. I sat him next to the Maharani. And she began giving him a little knee thing. And then the hand on the knee, and all that. And finally she says to him, "You know, I'm here without my husband—he's coming later. But we have a special religion, and it forbids us to stay in a hotel. So we have to buy a private house wherever we go. I'm going to slip you the address. You come there at two o'clock in the morning. Scratch on the window." So he took this piece of paper. Now, for the previous ten days, we had been searching for a house down on Central Avenue. And we found a big black mammy, like Aunt Jemima, a Hattie McDaniel type, you know? Coal-black, and this big. And we had been sending her obscene letters. Calling obscene things through the window. Generally annoying this poor black woman. By the time dessert was served, the Maharani got up and said she had to leave. And she was taken by a limousine to a plane.

HJ: She was taken by a limousine to a plane from Chasen's?

OW: To an airport, so she'd be out of town and couldn't talk. Now, at two o'clock in the morning you've got Jack Kreindler, man about town, all-around American, scratching on the window of this woman's house. Ten cops rush up and grab him, because she's been complaining. They take him downtown to the station house, where they take photographs. Which were never printed, but he thought they would be, so he went through all that. Of course, his high friends got him out, and kept him out of the newspapers. He never knew who did it to him. I think it's the best practical joke I've ever played.

HJ: This is really true? How did you know, for sure, he would show up? The whole thing wouldn't have worked if he hadn't shown up.

OW: He had to. She was the greatest hooker you ever saw. You would have shown up, too. *Anybody* would have shown up. We were very sad that she had to leave. And she was very funny. She knew exactly what she had to do—she'd been pretty well educated. It was a lot of work. Very expensive, too—the dinner, everything. But we thought Jack had it coming to him. I never told Lena. I never wanted her to think that anything had ever happened. She's half-Indian, you know, red Indian. If you were black, nobody was ever luckier.

HJ: For being able to hide the fact that she was black?

OW: That was never hidden. She was black from the minute she stepped on the stage. I told you what Duke Ellington said about her to me when he introduced us. He said, "This is a girl that gives a deep suntan to the first ten rows of the theater!"

HJ: She struck me as tremendously repressed.

OW: Well, no more than any other black, except that she's the one that received storms of applause for forty years. Come on. I'll accept that any black had a rough time, but she didn't, not particularly. Nobody urged her to pass for white. She was a famous black singer her whole career, and nothing else, no matter what she says now. And her marriage, a mixed marriage, was the first famous mixed marriage. Everybody wrote about it as such.

HJ: But she said that they put makeup on her to look darker in the movies. Because they didn't want her to look white.

OW: She's leaving out the truth. The movies that they made her look darker in—those were the black movies, the race movies. You know, made only for black audiences. I was on the set, waiting to take her out to lunch, when she was doing *Cabin in the Sky*. And she was made up like she would be with her own skin color. But when she was fifteen, and sixteen and seventeen, she made a lot of those race quickies.

HJ: It's amazing, those two women, Hedda and Louella, could get that strong.

OW: And in New York, [Walter] Winchell. Winchell was terrible, but I was very fond of him, because he had great charm. And he was such an egomaniac that it was funny to be with him. As you know, after the *Kane* thing, my name was never, ever printed in a Hearst paper. The Hearst paper in New York was the *Daily Mirror*, and Winchell was forbidden to write my name. So he called me G. O. Welles, George Orson Welles, and nobody ever noticed it. He deliberately put me in almost every day, just for the fun of it. That was his idea of being cute.

HJ: "George" being your actual first name.

OW: Of course. And he was such a prominent character in the Broadway of that time that not to be friends with him was to miss a whole side of that life. And you know, it was better to be his friend than his enemy. I had a big enemy among those guys, Lee Mortimer, a sort of second-rate Winchell, who used to print awful things about me every day. And I always greeted him effusively so that he would think that I'd never read a word he wrote.

25. "You either admire my work or not."

In which Orson encounters Mrs. Vincente Minnelli. He tells stories about John Barrymore, and gets a nibble on *The Dreamers*, but his prospects for financing any of his projects are growing steadily dimmer.

———————

HENRY JAGLOM: I am just reading this book on RKO which you are prominently featured in. It's the one that Jesse Lasky's daughter wrote, *The Biggest Little Major of Them All*.

ORSON WELLES: I've heard about it.

HJ: There's a picture on the back of you and your lady of the time, and Schaefer, I guess who was head of RKO when you made *Kane*.

OW: Dolores del Rio.

HJ: Dolores—at the premiere of *Kane*.

OW: That was actually in Chicago, the one with Schaefer. The real opening was in New York. That was in the days when the crowd were still screaming, "Here comes Norma Shearer!" The days when there was that kind of opening. Jack Barrymore made the famous joke. A radio reporter announced, "And here come Mr. John Barrymore, and Orson Welles, who made this picture! What have you got to say, Mr. Barrymore?" And he said, "Now it can be revealed. Orson is, in fact, the bastard son of Ethel [Barrymore] and the Pope!" On the air, across the nation. Cold sober. Just sheer mischief.

You know, Jack was quite mad. His father died at forty-five, in an insane asylum. Jack would get drunk in order to be the drunk Barrymore, instead of the insane Barrymore. He would suddenly realize at the table that he didn't know where he was or how he got there. A tragic situation.

One day I got a call: "Jack is in Chicago, dying. Get on a train and go there." So I got on a train, went to Chicago. Went to the Ambassador East, where Jack was staying, but he wasn't there. But Ethel was there and Lionel was there. Ethel and Lionel and I went around Chicago looking for Jack. We finally located him in a whorehouse on the South Side. He wasn't dying, but God knows, we could see he was going to. And then all of us were stuck in his hotel for the weekend. I just sat there and listened to them talk, because they hadn't been together, the three of them, in forty years. Or very seldom. They began reminiscing about their childhoods, and so on, these three extraordinary people with their gargoyle laugh, like creatures on the front of a cathedral. It was unbelievable.

Did I ever tell you the story of the love affair between Jack and Katharine Hepburn? Now I've checked this story with both Jack and Katie, and it's true. Her first picture, *A Bill of Divorcement*. He was still a top-of-the-bill star. He hadn't yet descended to, you know, "Swing and Sway with Sammy Kaye." After a day's shooting, he said, in that Barrymore voice, "Miss Hepburn, would you like to come to my dressing room for lunch?" She said, "Well, I, I, I . . ." So she did. She arrived at the door and is met by Jack in a dressing gown. He opens the door, and she comes in and she looks around, and there's a couch, and nothing else. And she says, "Well, I, I think, you know . . . there must be a mistake." Jack, all very proper, said, "Oh, yes, I made a mistake." He went to the door, opened it, bowed, and she went out. That's the whole affair!

HJ: A real gentleman.

OW: Not gonna fumble around. He went on making those terrible movies, in order to pay his creditors. If he'd gone into bankruptcy, he wouldn't have had to make them. I saw *Grand Hotel* again the other day. They had it on the cable. It was almost the last picture he made, where he was still highly considered, was still "John Barrymore." You know what Garbo did the first day of shooting? When he came to work in the morning, she was waiting outside the stage. To say good morning to him, to escort him to the set. It is the only nice thing I know about her.

(Lee Minnelli enters.)

LEE MINNELLI: Orson, you're one of my favorite people in the whole world. Such a beautiful voice.

OW: Aren't you nice? Here's Mr. Jaglom . . .

HJ: How do you do. Please sit down.

LM: You know Vincente is home now.

OW: Yes, I'm so glad he's out of the hospital. Well, send him my very best wishes.

LM: The doctor said in a few weeks, he could have some friends visiting . . . If you were free?

OW: Oh, I'd be delighted . . . if I'm still in the country. We're leaving in a couple weeks . . .

LM: May I give you our address and number?

OW: Would you please? Yes. Absolutely.

LM: Because it would mean so much to him. It would be good if he could see his friends. I don't want him to think he's forgotten.

OW: Of course not.

LM: It's a right turn at the Beverly Hills Hotel.

OW: Yes.

LM: But please call me. I would be flattered. We have tea about four thirty. When will I call you?

OW: Well, I can give you my number. If that doesn't answer, I have left for Italy. Lovely to see you.

LM: Well, thank you very much. It would mean a lot to Vincente.

OW: All my best.

LM: Goodbye.

(Lee Minnelli exits.)

OW: The difficulty with this sitcom is that I've never met Vincente. Never once. Even in the golden days, even at a party, I have never met him. Maybe we may have met back in the—but no, I remember very well the people I have never met before.

By the way, some people have appeared saying that they love *The Dreamers*. First time I've ever heard that from anybody aside from you and me. Two girls and two guys. The gentlemen are 100 percent. The American girl is 100 percent, but the French girl is a bitch.

HJ: I know. I know. I don't know if it's worth it even if they come up with the money. She's the one who was looking at Oja and said, "Yes, but can she be cold?" I replied, "I didn't know *you* were casting this. Are you questioning that Orson Welles can get the performance he wants out of this person? Are you assuming the right to tell him who's right for—" I was furious at that.

OW: Now that having been settled, my dear Henry, back they came and said, "We're worried about the other parts." And I said, "We really have our choice of the best English actors of that age group, but only if they're free at the time we shoot." I'm in no position now to give those people contracts and deliver them in a package.

HJ: I told them Rupert Everett . . . Jeremy Irons . . . Michael York . . .

OW: They said, "We would like an option." And I said, "My dear friends, you pay for an option. An option means you have exclusive rights to something. Nobody in the world gets an option without any recompense." I added, "What I could do for you, if I decided it was the right thing to do—*if*—would be to write a letter of intent. I'll only do that when you give me the feeling that you're close to the money. And you are not giving me the feeling that you are close to the money, only that you would like to get close to the money. In which case, a letter of intent ties my hands.

HJ: Because you don't know that next week somebody is not going to—

OW: Drop out of the sky. Now, in fact, another group loving *The Dreamers* has shown up. And one of them is a horse's ass who lives in Hollywood.

HJ: Which horse's ass?

OW: How to distinguish? If they turn around and show their heads, I can tell better! But well meaning. And the other is an investment consultant, who has intimate contact with big money, but does not pretend to have it himself. But believes that he can raise it in short order. And they sat here and this is what the conversation was like: The horse's ass said, "I hear all these different stories." I said, "Do you expect me to sit at this table and prove to you that I'm . . . you know . . .

HJ: Stable?

OW: I said, "The biggest madman in the world could be very convincing. You either admire my work or not." And after an hour and a half, it emerged, he doesn't believe he can raise the money, pretty much because the rich guys won't like *The Dreamers*. Then the horse's ass said, "You must do *Lear*; that's the thing," so on and so on. "And have you anything else?" And I said, "Are we in a souk? I'm going to put out all my things on a rug and then you'll decide what you want to buy?"

26. "I'm in *terrible* financial trouble."

In which Orson vainly pitches a project, complains about friends who disparage him, reviews several books about his life, and bemoans the fact that he can't make a living while his bête noire Houseman, thrives.

———————————

(Susan Smith, from HBO, joins them.)

ORSON WELLES: I've been working on a book, and I've only got it in outline form, with some scenes blocked in. And as I was getting excited about it, my friend Henry here told me about you and your interest in miniseries. I have two ways I can go with what I have. One is to do it as a novel, and then sell it, and let the network development system do its thing—

SUSAN SMITH: You mean, do an injustice to the mat—

OW: Without me having anything to do with it. Because I could not stand to work under that committee system. I'd just take the money and run. But when I heard about you, I thought even though it might be economically suicidal for me, maybe I should do it directly for HBO.

SS: Tell me what you have in mind.

OW: In one sentence, it's a miniseries set in Majorca or San Tropez, where the richest people in the world go. Or better, a dictatorship in a Central American country that is overthrown by a coup d'état, and there is a revolution. Much of it offstage, but some of it is in the story as a background for all the things that happen to people in a kind of Acapulco-type place. There are two cities on the island. One is the port, and the other is the resort. The resort is on the Atlantic side, and the story is basically the life of a resort. The kind of people who are there range from [Robert] Vesco to a presidential candidate. Everybody who is anybody.

SS: I'm very interested in doing something about the Dominican Republic. Because I think that it's kind of an interesting—

OW: I wouldn't be remotely interested.

SS: Why?

OW: Because I have my own story, in my own Dominican Republic. I've *invented* my Dominican Republic. I'm not interested in real history, because I know Latin American politics to an unbelievable degree. I'm an expert on it. And you cannot tell that story using any individual country. You must combine them to do it properly, and it must be fictional.

SS: Oh, I only said Dominican Republic more than Acapulco, 'cause—

OW: I don't understand why you don't understand it, frankly.

HENRY JAGLOM: There's a resort like Acapulco in the Dominican Republic.

OW: We're not getting anywhere.

HJ: No, no. Wait, wait, wait—wait! We're just trying to understand—

OW: I'm not gonna go on. 'Cause if a resort doesn't immediately interest her, it won't, even if I go on for an hour.

HJ: Wait a minute, I don't agree. I don't agree.

OW: She doesn't like rich people! Doesn't want a story about rich people. That's what doesn't get anywhere with her, is that it?

SS: I think you should go on. I want to hear it.

OW: I can't sell it. I'm a bad seller.

HJ: No, it's not a question of selling.

OW: I quit.

HJ: Tell it, rather than selling it.

OW: No, I can't.

HJ: Okay. Well, then maybe if she could read something . . .

OW: I haven't got anything. It'll take me six months. It just didn't ring a bell with her, so no use talking about it.

SS: Well, it does interest me very much. I think you're wrong.

OW: *You're* wrong. You're really wrong! Boy, are you wrong.

HJ: You're not being fair. You're not being fair.

OW: Her eyes went dead when she heard *resort*.

HJ: Her eyes didn't go dead.

OW: Sure they did.

HJ: You're being too sensitive about that.

OW: I am, yes. I can't sell a thing. Forget it. We'll think of something else. You don't see what a resort— You didn't like *Grand Hotel?*

SS: I loved *Grand Hotel.*

OW: Well, then, that's it.

HJ: Instead of a hotel, it's in a resort.

SS: I understand that. I just want to hear the story.

OW: There isn't *a* story.

HJ: Wait a minute. Orson, there is a story. I mean, there is a story about a presidential candidate; there's a story about the revolution going on outside. The opening on the airplane.

OW: There are a lot of stories. But when I get that dead look, I'm dead! I can't do it. I begin to wonder what I'm talking about. I have to get a little spark from somebody. If I don't get it, that's it. I'm lost. Because I have nowhere else to go with it. You're my only market. You're the only game in town.

SS: There are a number of different alternatives. As I told you earlier, there are basically like six or seven half hour—

OW: I couldn't work in a half hour. You didn't tell me that.

SS: Maybe I didn't. That's why I'm telling you now.

OW: I thought you said that you told me.

SS: You're not listening, because you're so angry.

OW: Yes, I am. Oh, yes.

HJ: That's not fair, Orson!

OW: I don't like to be iced off like that.

(Smith exits.)

HJ: I'm changing the subject. The *New York Times* called me to ask me what I thought of Charles Higham's biography of you. Higham got slammed in the reviews.

OW: Higham has given interviews in which he's said that I pushed him away from my table. But I've never even met him. I did dip into his book, and I couldn't find one page that didn't have a glaring factual error, you know? So I didn't read the book. *Everything* is wrong. But who remembers anything correctly? That was what *Citizen Kane* was originally going to be, the film that Kurosawa finally made, *Rashomon*. It was going to be the same scene, played over and over from different points of view. Higham's is a book made by a crew of underpaid research people. He didn't write it. He just pasted together clippings. I don't know why they're digging it up now.

HJ: Because it just came out. It's his second book on you.

OW: I know why—because they're furious at Barbara Leaming for being so successful. And at me, because I'm the first person who has ever been on the cover of the *New York Times Magazine* who is not a personal friend of the editor-in-chief.

HJ: I hate the title they used for her excerpt: "The Unfulfilled Promise." It emphasizes the negative.

OW: They made it up before they read her book. And they wouldn't change it. There will be a review of Barbara's book in *The Saturday Review of Literature* by Houseman's boyfriend. He'll lash out at me.

HJ: The reviewers are blaming her for falling in love with you. They say that you completely captivated this woman. The only criticism I've heard of the book is that she lost her objectivity.

OW: Well, I told her that. And I warned her against exactly what the publishers wrote on the back of the book. I said, "You must not emphasize my collaboration. You must underplay that, because it's—"

HJ: She couldn't help herself. She wanted them to know that it was authorized, and that she really—

OW: It was *not* authorized. An authorized biography is when she hands me her manuscript, and chapter by chapter I say, "No, no, no, yes . . ." and I get the last word on any point of fact. But I never read a word of it. I said, "I'm saving that pleasure for my old age." But the truth is, I don't want to read it, because there'll be some things I don't like, and I don't want to feel quarrelsome. I only read the captions of the pictures. And one made me so furious that I decided that— You know, that my memory of Dolores del Rio is her underwear.

HJ: Yeah, that was a good line, something like, "It was so erotic it was indescribable."

OW: But I've got a good piece I want to write, which is a refutation of the reputation she gives me as the great lover. I'm gonna tell about all my failures.

HJ: The thing that's really great about the book is that she puts the lie to the myth of your self-destructiveness, dissecting—film by film—what happened, and really making it clear. That's something they wouldn't believe coming from you. And she does it not sounding like you.

OW: That's also something I wouldn't want to do myself. It's whining. But the other important thing is that Barbara's book kills the "Houseman-Welles production" canard, which you've read a million times. Because at the time the plays were done, they were never called the "Houseman-Welles" productions. Apparently, Houseman is trembling with rage. I think he's deeply wounded. And that's a good thing, too, after all these years.

HJ: People are saying, "I didn't know that Houseman was that insignificant."

HJ: The only thing I objected to in the whole book was the Joseph Cotten involvement—complicity, by implication—in the cutting of *Ambersons*. Where she says RKO used him to persuade you.

OW: It's going to be terrible, because he's my oldest friend. He'll never forgive me. I kept saying to her, "Put on your thinking cap. Think about my friends who are alive, and don't hurt them." The Cotten thing is very serious. I call him a "Judas," and so on. It's very unfortunate. Because Jo was acting in my best interests. But I say, "So was Judas." It's too tough. I'm going to write him about it. I can't talk to him about it, because he'll cut me off and say it doesn't matter. But it does.

I don't want to start picking at Barbara's book, you know. I'm enormously grateful. She did a nice job.

HJ: She really captures the truth. So you become this demystified . . . human, instead of all those terrible— The mythology is so destructive.

OW: Alex Trauner, the great production designer who I am very fond of, who did *Othello* for me, was quoted in a review of Higham's book, saying, "The trouble with Orson is, he's self-destructive. As soon as the picture is ready to go to the lab, he invents a reason not to send it," and so on. But Trauner wasn't around. He was only on

Othello the five weeks that we were in Morocco, not on the rest of the picture. But he saw that the picture stopped and started, so he came to a conclusion that this was my caprice.

HJ: As somebody who's been spending time going around trying to get financing for your projects, I know just how destructive that particular line is.

OW: Especially from a man of his position—he designed for Marcel Carné, Billy Wilder—*Hôtel du Nord*; *Le Jour Se Lève*; *Les Enfants du Paradis*; *Kiss Me, Stupid*—and there he was, knocking me down.

HJ: And then he's saying it with love, which is even—

OW: Worse. And admiration, which is worse yet.

HJ: Yeah, because it makes it sound like it's true!

OW: He actually told me that he's always admired me. And I said, "I believe that, but it's not the point."

HJ: He's so apologetic.

OW: An apology for something like that is worthless. He should have shut his mouth. Even supposing it's true. Say you believe it's true. That's your right. But you should shut up about it, that's all. Because my point to Alex was not, "Is it true or not?" But rather, it's not for a friend to say. *I* may be self-destructive, but I don't expect my friends to destroy me. That's the reason I got mad at Peter Brook, who gave a long interview about how I lack the epic sense in my movies. I said to Peter, "Probably I *do* lack the epic sense, but even so, I think we should leave it to the critics. We've got enough of them." If some other filmmaker says it, all right. At least I don't know him. But not my close friend. "You were the best man at my wedding! Why are you doing a long interview about my lack of epic sense?"

Now Gallimard is publishing all of Trauner's paintings for movies and they want me to write an introduction. I don't want to write the thing. So I said, "I really don't see, Alex, what I can say about you. It's not that I'm cross—we're still friends—but I can't do a heartfelt tribute to your work after what you said about mine." And that got me out of two days' work. Because introductions, to me, are the hardest things to write.

HJ: Robert Wise stood up at this big Directors Guild thing for you, and said how wonderful you were, how you had a huge impact on his life and so on, and then made some kind of negative remark, "What a shame that—"

OW: Who needed that? He was shaking when I ran into him afterwards. He wouldn't have had to shake if he hadn't said that. It's like Chuck Heston, who still claims that *Touch of Evil* is a minor film. Over and over, every time he's asked to speak, he says, "Let's not talk about *Touch of Evil* as though it's a major work." He sincerely believes that. And he's a horse's ass, because he's in a film of mine that other people think is important, so why doesn't he shut up and pretend it's important? What besides that has he made that's important, you know? He speaks wonderfully about me. He's full of admiration. But he says, "There's some side to him, that I've never seen that we must assume is very abrasive to producers." That's his other line. I've heard that over and over again. Then, when he's completely relaxed, he says, "Well, of course, we have to remember that, as it turned out, it's really Orson's film as an actor." He has a bad conscience, too, because he refused to come back to the studio and do the reshoots. He phoned me and told me, "I signed on to do a picture with Willie Wyler, *The Big Country*." So he's got that little guilt. That makes *Touch of Evil* a minor film.

HJ: He called Ed Asner "a continuation of what's been going on in Hollywood since the days of Paul Robeson." That's quite a quote. Racist, to boot.

OW: What the hell is he talking about? The left in Hollywood today is the feeblest—Heston once marched with Martin Luther

King, you know. It's a long way from marching with Martin Luther King to "a continuation of what's been going on since Paul Robeson." What a horse's ass.

HJ: You know, *Touch of Evil* is playing on cable this month.

OW: It's got all the lost stuff in it! I saw a reel and a half of it last night. And I had to quit. I got too excited. I had forgotten those scenes. I thought they were gone forever. It was such a joy. And it's so beautiful in black-and-white. Oh, my God.

HJ: What did you think of Robert Carringer's book *The Making of Citizen Kane*, the professor in Indianapolis?

OW: Houseman has claimed for twenty-five or thirty years that there *was* no second script—my script—only Mankiewicz's. He was always a jealous son of a bitch. He never got over the fact that I gave him work to get him money once when he was struggling. But this fellow Carringer found the smoking gun, the telegram from Houseman to me, telling me that my script is better than Mankiewicz's. Carringer was given the opportunity to go into the RKO archives, and he read everything. And that satisfied him that my version of the controversy is right.

But I was kind of disappointed in Carringer. He is just as harmful as Higham. He has a description of me putting my arms around him as we sat at a table. Now, I am a nontoucher. It's just a dream of his. His great discovery is that *Kane* was made by a number of people, not just by me. He begins his book by saying that "I said to Orson something about movies being a collaborative art. And he immediately flew into a tantrum." I don't fly into tantrums. It's not in my character. I simply said to him, forcefully, that the use of the word *collaborative* is no more true of films than it is of the theater. Sometimes it is, sometimes it isn't. You know what I'm saying. And as far as the credit goes, I hadn't seen the beginning of *Kane* since I made it, or the end—I had forgotten where the credits are—and I saw it yesterday morning. I saw that I shared the director's title card with Toland. It says: "Directed by Orson Welles; photography by Gregg Toland." On the same card. I don't think many people have done that. The cameramen were always listed with the make-up department. And I'm supposed to be the one who wants credit for everything? Carringer pads out his book with a little half-baked chapter on *Ambersons*, making the point that it's a failure because I didn't have the same people with me, the same art director, and the same cameraman, and so on.

HJ: You know, Houseman was Higham's source.

OW: Yes, he thanks Houseman for his collaboration. Higham is really unspeakable. He lists seventeen major untruths in a *Vogue* piece that I wrote. What are the lies that he's exploding? I was telling how hard it was for anybody to get a room in my father's hotel, that it was one of the most exclusive hotels in America. And he says, "The hotel in Grand Detour was not one of the most exclusive hotels in America."

HJ: The level of trivia is truly wonderful. Why do you suppose he hates you so? Because you are Orson Welles and he's not? I think envy of the gifted colors all these books. He's just jealous. Like Houseman.

OW: You know, in the beginning, when I should have been playing Hamlet, Houseman kept saying, "These plays are not vehicles for you. Remember, we're an ensemble company, not the Orson Welles Players." So Martin Gabel plays Danton, instead of me. And so on, you know. But in the profession which I have chosen, my only real disappointment is that I feel I've never been properly appreciated as an actor. Mostly my own fault, for giving my energy to the production, rather than to my performance. Also, my own fault for pretending I wasn't a star actor and was just there.

HJ: I've wondered about that, why you didn't capitalize on your great notices. So it was mainly Houseman, then?

OW: All Houseman. But I had no argument with that, you know? That seemed right to me.

HJ: The spirit of the times dictated a kind of group, or collective mentality.

OW: You know, Houseman's become so famous now that Rich Little does an imitation of him.

HJ: A terrible comic. Houseman is so pompous and pretentious.

OW: That's what he's like. Pomposity is his basic characteristic.

HJ: Where did that absurd accent come from?

OW: He's a Rumanian.

HJ: Jewish, right?

OW: Yeah. But a Rumanian who was born and raised in Buenos Aires.

HJ: What about that accent?

OW: In Buenos Aires, there's this whole population of people who have been speaking English for generations and have never been back to England. So they've developed their own English accent. Besides being Rumanian. Which, as Alfonso XIII said, "Being a Rumanian is not a race. It's a profession."

HJ: In the past years, have you ever found yourself in the same place with him?

OW: No. If I know he's going to be someplace, I don't go. Not because I don't want to speak to him, but because it's uncomfortable.

HJ: He's made such a reputation off you, in a way. It's infuriating when history is revised. It's not only the Stalinists in the Soviet Union. He's rewritten his whole life, using his memoires, so that he's become central to everything you've achieved. And now he's enjoying his senior citizenship as a grand old actor. He is dreadful. As an actor he can't read a line.

OW: Absolutely dreadful! And he got the Academy Award! It drove Cotten mad with rage. But he laughed all through the show. Laughing mad, you know? He was in some movie with Houseman and he said, "Jack made a tremendous fuss about where his dressing room was going to be." And Jo couldn't look at him! If a gypsy had told us, "One of you will get the Academy Award. Who will it be?" he would have been the last one any one of us would have chosen. My first wife, who was a very clever lady and understood people awfully well, said from the beginning of my partnership with Houseman that there was something of Iago in him. She said, "He's destructive! He's trying to destroy you. Listen to me!" And I said, "This is pure mischief! The malice of a wife! Houseman is my valued partner." But she was right! About three weeks after we met, he said to me, "I keep dreaming of you riding bareback on a horse." And I should have taken that more seriously. But I just laughed. Before he rose to his present eminence, he had about twenty years when he wasn't doing much of anything, except dining out and knocking me. And then he slowly built himself up to what he is now: elder statesman, Academy Award–winning actor, and leading salesman of anything you have.

HJ: Life is full of amazing turns.

OW: Houseman has had twenty commercials on camera. I've had one. I'm in *terrible* financial trouble. And I keep trying to make a decent movie that will also make me money.

HJ: I know this irritates you, but I keep getting back to the fact, Orson, that I don't fully understand why, with all the frustration that you have to deal with, you don't invent a film like *F for Fake*, which you know you can do brilliantly, while you're waiting for these projects to go forward.

OW: I need money. When I had *F for Fake*, I had money.

HJ: How much did *F for Fake* cost?

OW: Very little, but I had it. And *F for Fake* was such a flop in America, you know.

HJ: I keep thinking that whether they get it or not at the exact time that you make it, eventually, they'll get it!

OW: We don't agree, you see. Essentially, I don't believe in a film that isn't a commercial success. Film is a popular art form. It has to have at least the kind of success that European and early Woody Allen movies had. People should be in those tiny theaters, lining up to see it. And they didn't do it with *F for Fake*.

HJ: So why don't you—I hope you don't mind my bringing it up—cut one of your unfinished films and release it? Or why don't you do some commercials again?

OW: No personal essay film will make any money, you know that. *F for Fake* proved it. If Wesson Oil would let *me* say that Wesson Oil is good, instead of Houseman, I'd be delighted, but nobody will take me for a commercial. It's just a closed door, and I don't understand why. He must have made five or six million dollars. I don't understand that man's continued success. And when he isn't making a big commercial, he makes a small one. He's now selling automobiles for a local automobile dealer in New York. While I cannot seem to crack it. Why I can't, I do not know. A real mystery: why they prefer Houseman, with his petulant, arrogant, unpleasant manner. I don't know what is the matter. It's a very weird and terrible situation. I don't know where to turn. Except I can't . . . I can't . . .

HJ: During the period when you're preparing for *Lear*, or for *Dreamers*— Orson, I'm not— Please don't be mad at me.

OW: No, I'm not mad at you. I'm explaining to you that it's not like I'm just sitting around doing nothing. I'm working on scripts that might make some money. And they take all kinds of time. I've been fighting the income tax people for a long while now. The deals for *Lear*, even, include very big salaries for me that would get me out of trouble with them. And that's what I need. I can't afford to sit down in the cutting room with my old films. I have the cheapest competent editor, who's willing to work as a kind of favor for eight hundred dollars a week. But I haven't *got* eight hundred dollars a week to give the man. And I have big obligations, so that—that's the awful thing—I'm not a free soul. I'm doing the impossible thing of trying to make money off the kind of movies that don't make money.

HJ: Please understand, I don't mean to minimize your situation. I've told you that I'm working on this problem now. I know you're taking care of a lot of people, and—

OW: You know, I had it made with that damn brandy company, the French cognac.

HJ: You had it, and then it went away.

OW: Do you know why? The owner went to Hong Kong, checked into his hotel, turned on the TV, and saw an old commercial, which they were not supposed to show anymore, by contract, of me talking about Japanese whiskey. The local station figured, "Who's gonna catch us at this?" and put it on the air.

HJ: Oh, God! So they fired you.

OW: And that was five years, that contract.

HJ: Okay. We'll get another one. We'll get another one.

OW: I've worked with advertising agencies all my life. In the old days in radio, you worked for them, because they were the boss, not the network. And I have never seen more seedier, about-to-be-fired sad sacks than were responsible for those Paul Masson ads. The agency hated me because I kept trying to improve the copy.

HJ: Whoever heard of Paul Masson before you—

OW: And now we have John G.

HJ: Who is that?

OW: John Gielgud. He's doing his butler, from the little dwarf's movie.

HJ: From *Arthur*.

OW: That's one of our profound disagreements—Dudley Moore.

HJ: I don't have anything against short people.

OW: Nor do I. I just know what they have against me. There's never been a tall dictator—never.

HJ: Oh, my God.

OW: Name one. They're all under normal height.

HJ: Was Mussolini short?

OW: Very short.

HJ: Franco?

OW: Short. Hitler was short. Including those that you might feel more sympathetic to. Like Tito—tiny. Stalin—tiny.

HJ: The height theory of history.

OW: Remember that the melancholy freaks are all giants, not midgets. The midgets and dwarfs all have delusions of grandeur.

HJ: How tall are you?

OW: I used to be six-three and a half, and I'm now about six-two. Six-one and a half, maybe. My neck keeps disappearing. Gravity, you know? Like Elizabeth Taylor. She has no neck left! Her shoulders come to her ears. And she's still young! Now, look, imagine where her face will be when she's my age. In her navel, you know?

HJ: They'll have a special man in Beverly Hills who pulls—elongates necks.

OW: She had a neck like a swan when she was in *Jane Eyre*. That's how I understood *Lolita*, when I read it later. I used to offer to read lines with her. "Wouldn't you like to go through that with me?"

HJ: How old was she?

OW: Oh, something disgraceful!

HJ: You had a touch of . . . a touch of . . .

OW: Your Polish fella.

HJ: A touch of Roman. And Chaplin.

OW: More Roman. Chaplin was like that only in his old age.

HJ: Getting back to your financial situation—

OW: I'm a wage earner who— You know, I live from week to week. My wife and her establishments cost me six thousand dollars a month, apart from anything else. And I've got a daughter—one of my daughters, who has to be helped all the time, and I have, you know, every kind of obligation. And that's the hell of it. If I were free of any financial obligation, I would have done essay films, because that's what I would rather do now, more than story films. It's what I think has not been done. But essay films are like essays. They are never going to compete with fiction features, just as books of essays have not been able to compete with novels, ever.

If I got just one commercial, it would change my life! And that's why my failure as a performer in commercials hurts me so much, because of the difference it would make in my life. I don't even get the radio ones anymore! My whole income has gone from—three years ago, I made a million seven hundred thousand dollars . . . You know, I could comprehend it, in this youth-oriented world, if my ex-partner wasn't getting so rich on it.

HJ: Let me try to do what I can to find out about that. I really didn't understand. I have to assume that people don't know that you're available. In the meantime, you could—

OW: There is no "meantime." It's the grocery bill. I haven't got the money. It's that urgent. That's what drives me off my . . . nut. I can't afford to work in hopes of future profits. I have to hustle now. All I do is sweat and work. I'm imprisoned by a simple economic fact. Get me on that fuckin' screen and my life is changed.

HJ: Okay, I understand the priorities.

OW: The priorities are personal; they're not an artistic choice. For some reason, there are people all over the world who think Welles-*Lear* is a great idea. So I'll get paid big money for that. And, you know, there are five or six people scattered all over the world who think *The Dreamers* is a wonderful script. Then there's *The Big Brass Ring*. They're all things that, if they come through, there's money up front. But we haven't got the deals.

27. "Fool the old fellow with the scythe."

In which Orson realizes that his prospects will most likely evaporate, contemplates the evanescence of fame, which ebbs and flows with the regularity of the tides, and peers into the future.

———————

HENRY JAGLOM: Now, what is with *Lear* today? What's happening?

ORSON WELLES: Dead.

HJ: Well, it's not dead, because this producer is trying to come up with terms.

OW: No, no, it's dead.

HJ: Why?

OW: No way of doing it in France. He's changed every single point in the agreement that we made.

HJ: So there's no use communicating with Jack Lang?

OW: I'll tell you all about it, if you'll give me the time. Rather than answering—

HJ: Okay. Sorry.

OW: I'd rather do a monologue than submit myself to an interrogation. I have a problem with Jack Lang, of course, because he thinks his producer is the best producer in France. He'll believe the producer's side of the story, and not mine. And Lang is not putting up enough money to make the difference anyway. He's just giving his blessing. The producer, as described to me by my old cameraman, is indeed very successful and very intelligent, but he's a weather vane. He'll tell you one thing at ten in the morning, and another at noon.

The budget was five million dollars. Then they began to talk about how it was hard to get the last million. I said, "I'll give up three hundred thousand up front, and defer it." Then they wanted me to do postproduction, all the editing, in Paris. I explained to them that I have back income tax that I have to pay for another year, and that I can only do that by finding some money in America. I cannot spend a year in France cut off from my other sources of income. And since we are doing it on tape as well as film, I said I'll give them a very good rough cut before I leave, but I'll do the final cut and mix in America. They agreed to that and the compensation, so then I said, "In all of your correspondence, you have called me the producer, but now you're giving me this man." They said, "We have to, by French law." I said, "But I must have the right to decide how the money is spent within the budget. Not just artistically. If I want to spend one day on one thing and ten days on another, it's my decision. That makes me the producer." They said, "All right."

Yesterday came the telex—yesterday! My entire compensation is seven hundred thousand, instead of a million plus the cassette rights we agreed on, and I am not to get one cent of that until the entire film is delivered. Which is the first I ever heard of that. And I must do all the postproduction in Paris—a total violation of our understanding. So, there's no way of patching it up in France. My immediate problem is public relations. How is this bombshell going to go off in the French press? All the newspapers in Paris are ready to say, "He doesn't really want to make a movie. He's running away after we—a million dollars isn't good enough for him." So what I want to do is to tell Jack Lang, and the French press, that it's not that I'm walking away from *King Lear*. It's that my producer has changed the conditions under which I am to make the picture, unilaterally. It's a diktat. The telex is not, "We regret that we are forced to change—" Rather, it's take it or leave it. Now, the big money from French television had been earmarked for a miniseries called *Ali Baba*, and they had to take a big hunk from *Ali Baba* for *Lear*. So I suspect that this producer *wants* me to say no, so he can get the money back for *Ali Baba*. How do you like those apples?

HJ: Those are bad apples. Have you heard from the English about *Lear* at all?

OW: This morning I talked to the daughter of the producer, who is my liaison. She said, "Well, we have the money in London, but we have to move it to Switzerland. And until it gets to Switzerland, we'll be unable to give you a starting date." Which is about as unlikely a story as I've ever heard. Just a bad lie.

HJ: Look, this might cheer you up. Do you know about the video-disc of *Kane*? With the narration and the explanation?

OW: No, I don't know about narration and explanation. I don't like that. Why didn't they invite *me* to do it?

HJ: Every single cut you made is validated now by this professor who comments on the film. This is why you couldn't have done this.

OW: Well, theoretically, that's good for teaching movies, so long as they don't talk nonsense. "Do you see why this camera's in the wrong place? Do you see why this cut is bad? Do you see why the pace drops here?" That would really be teaching people. I could do it with somebody else's film—but you're right, I couldn't with my own. You can't say why it's good. You can only say why it's bad! You could teach the ordinary grammar of moviemaking using a fairly respectable bad film, you know. Cukor would be a very good director for that. Because he doesn't stand up under a hard look.

I noticed that the new movies for television, which are obviously made by young directors out of film school, are technically much better than they were five, six years ago. And inventive. They're just, of course, doomed, because they're for television, and these directors are being clever with garbage. But you get to a point—I have, all my life, not just now—when you make something that's really quite good, not wonderful, but a very good mediocre play or movie, and you settle for it.

HJ: The great thing about what's happening with these laser discs and video things, is that it gives film permanence. As opposed to when you started working, when you could easily expect that film would be gone twenty, thirty, forty, fifty years from now. Now you know that they're gonna last.

OW: I regard posterity as vulgar as success. I don't trust posterity. I don't think what's good is necessarily recognized in the long run. Too many good writers have disappeared.

(Gilles Jacob enters.)

GILLES JACOB: I just saw you on the French TV talking to students.

OW: It was all a little too reverent for me, you know?

GJ: You know, we have not too many people to revere. So we are not so used to revere someone.

OW: I don't know. I think it is a French instinct to revere or to neglect, with nothing in between.

GJ: Probably.

OW: The giants of French culture suddenly don't exist anymore. Nobody has attacked them; they just aren't there, you know. Look what happened to Anatole France—disappeared. Malraux—vanished.

HJ: But they're dead.

OW: Well, look at Scottie Fitzgerald here, in America. He disappeared in his own lifetime. For the last five years of his life, none of his novels was in print. You could not buy a Fitzgerald novel. Faulkner is vanishing. He used to totally dominate the whole world, not only America, but the Continent, particularly. My God, he's starting to become invisible. Steinbeck, poor fellow. He was a bigger talent than anybody gives him credit for. But his faults have over-shadowed his talent to such a point that he's vanished, you know? He was a terribly sweet man. Writers are not necessarily the sweet-est people in the world. Robert Frost was an angry man—but who knows—maybe just rude to bores. When someone came up to him, he'd say, "Yes? Get out." My trouble is that I say, "Stay another ten minutes," and people still say I'm a shit!

HJ: Their natural lives exceeded their creative lives.

OW: It's no wonder Fitzgerald and Hemingway and O'Hara hated the fact of aging. They simply couldn't bear to be forty-two years old. The fear of death. They wanted to fool the old fellow with the scythe.

HJ: Filmmakers disappear all the time.

OW: René Clair was a good friend of mine. He was very bitter at the end of his life. He used to say to me: "You know, there has never been a movie which isn't out of fashion after fifteen years. It's like journal-ism where you write on sand. It disappears; it's nothing." He was really revered, in the English-speaking world particularly. My God, René Clair was, you know, what Fellini was twenty years ago.

HJ: What was the reason for Clair's decline?

OW: He made some commercial movies at the end, which were not "René Clair" movies. So that hastened the deterioration of his reputation, until it disappeared entirely. Because we all had a picture of a "René Clair" movie. Then he began to make amusing sort of . . .

HJ: Entertainments.

OW: You couldn't tell the difference between those movies and any other well-made films. It's like Olivier choosing to make *Dracula* rather than disappear from view. That hurt him very much. If you make that choice, your reputation is gonna suffer.

GJ: Also, I have the feeling that some directors have only ten years, fifteen years, before they're finished. Don't you think so?

OW: Directors are poor fellows, carrying not much baggage. We come in with only our overnight bags, and go out with nothing. There are names in those old lists of the greatest movies that have totally vanished, you know? Now, when my career is only a memory, I'm still sitting here like some kind of monument, but the moment will come when I'll drop out of sight altogether, as though a trapdoor had opened, you know? Although I'd prefer a Verdi ending.

HJ: What's that?

OW: Verdi did great work when he was young. Very early. Highly acclaimed. Spent his middle years overseeing productions of his music, orchestrating his earlier work. Trivialities. Then, in old age, one day someone came and told him, "Wagner is dead." He lit up. Did his greatest work in the following years, after decades of nothing.

HJ: Who would your Wagner be? Who would have to die to set you free?

OW: I'm not going to answer that.

Orson Welles died on October 10, 1985, five days after his last lunch with Henry Jaglom, in the middle of the night, with his typewriter in his lap. It was a heart attack.

Epilogue

Orson's Last Laugh
by Henry Jaglom

Saturday afternoon, Oct. 5th, at lunch, Orson told me that the attacks were beginning to come in, in response to the books out on him, especially Barbara Leaming's wonderfully supportive—to his mind, largely accurate—biography. The success of the book as it was about to go into its second printing had cheered him, setting the record straight on Houseman and so many things, and he was philosophical about the attacks: "Once they decide they're for you or against you, it never changes. Hope and Crosby they always loved. Me and Sinatra they decided against early on, and they never let up." He talked of *Time, Newsweek*, the *Washington Post*.

He complained that in a year and a half, Ma Maison would be moving into a new hotel, and "What will we do then?" Kiki growled and he fed her a small cookie, while warning her that if she kept on crying he'd never take her out again.

He told me that Paul Masson wanted him back to endorse its "terrible wine again," but on a one-year contract instead of three, at lesser money and with required performances-cum-appearances around the country. He'd turn it down, but slowly, seeing how good he could make the deal.

Welles never let anyone capture his likeness, but made an exception for Jaglom, provided his friend use a grease pencil on black paperboard that Welles sent a Ma Maison waiter to procure.

We talked of Israel's raid on Tunis and Gorbachev's public relations talents as evidenced in Paris, how "Reagan was going to be made to look like an amateur," and how the French bungling of the Greenpeace ship business in New Zealand was "going to cost Mitterand his job." And what a shame that was. He made me have dessert by dramatically reading the menu and we laughed at stories of people's odd pomposity and pretensions and he let himself have a dessert plate full of lime sherbet.

A typical few hours—in short—some stories, some hopefulness, some creative ideas, some anecdotes, some sadness, some old memories, much shared understanding, many communicative smiles. As always.

But for some reason I didn't have my little tape recorder on in my bag. I remember thinking as I drove over that I'd done almost every lunch for a few years and I didn't feel I had to anymore. I remember wondering if he'd notice that it wasn't there, and what would he think it meant if he did.

The tape recorder was one of the only two things we didn't speak about. The other was his weight and its health implications. The closest we got was, "You're looking well," or "I swam my laps," or "I can't eat that anymore; you have to eat it for me and describe it to me." We did a lot of that in the south of France.

In fact, he looked a bit tired. He said, "Time is passing," but he said it lightly, sadly but lightly, in relation to our ongoing inability to get a film financed for him to direct.

This morning my phone rang; it was my office. There was a rumor he was dead; the press was calling. I called him on his private number. His man, Freddie, answered, said how sorry he was, yes it was true, he found him on the bedroom floor at ten this morning, and he couldn't rouse him. Freddie called the paramedics. He apologized to me (in lieu of Orson) for calling them, as if he had violated the trust for privacy that he still somehow felt he was expected to honor, even now.

Orson was dead.

All day the hypocrites got on radio and TV and eulogized him. I kept wanting to call him and tell him, "You won't believe what Burt Reynolds said, what Charlton Heston came up with." One by one each of those who wouldn't help him when they could, now stepped forward to praise him. I cried and tried to hear his laugh.

Even in death he did his "dancing bear" act for them. I got furious and gave a few angry interviews of my own.

Then I watched him on my editing machine in *Someone to Love*, which I am cutting together, saying that you are born, live, and die alone.

"Only through love and friendship can you create the illusion that you are not entirely alone," he said, in what turns out to be his last appearance in a movie, his last acting job.

I'm having a harder time now, creating that illusion.

"You have your ending now," he says to me, on my screen.

"Can't I have an ending after the ending?" I ask, essentially.

"No," he says.

"Why not?" I ask.

"Because," he finishes, with a smile, "this is The End."

And he blows me a kiss.

And to the cameraman he shouted, "Cut!"

And the screen went black.

Appendix

Welles had so many unfinished or unmade films, scripts, treatments, and pitches, in addition to trailers, tests, shorts, fragments, and filmlets of every sort, it's nearly impossible to determine how many there were at the end. According to Jonathan Rosenbaum's meticulous inventory of Orsoniana, *Discovering Orson Welles*, when he died, Welles left approximately nineteen projects in various states of completion. What follows are thumbnails of the four that figure in his conversations with Jaglom, as well as a partial cast of characters.

NEW OR UNFINISHED PROJECTS

Don Quixote

Welles transposed Don Quixote and Sancho Panza to Franco's Spain. The juxtaposition of the two throws into stark relief both the pathos of their quest, rendered anachronistic by the march of history, particularly the rise of fascism, as well as its timeless significance. Child actress Patty McCormack played a little girl visiting Mexico City who encounters Welles. Soon after he tells her the story of the two windmill tilters, she meets them herself. The shooting began in 1956 in France, and continued, fitfully, until the late 1960s, early 1970s. Welles kept running out of money. Over the course of lengthy production delays, McCormack grew up, and Welles had to drop her from the film. He repeatedly changed the concept, at one point exposing Quixote and Panza to a nuclear holocaust, and at another sending them to the moon. Welles claimed he originally shelved the film because he was waiting for Franco to die, saying, "It's an essay on Spain, not Don Quixote." He worked on it on and off until he himself died.

The Dreamers

The Dreamers was a script written in 1978 by Welles and his companion Oja Kodar based on two short stories by Isak Dinesen, "The Dreamers" and "Echoes." In the course of his years-long attempts to find financing, Welles shot two ten-minute segments around his home. In the first, fully made up and costumed as a nineteenth-century Dutch-Jewish merchant, Welles tells the story of Pellegrina Leoni, an opera diva who loses her voice. It was shot in black-and-white. In the second, shot in color, Leoni, played by Kodar, appears herself. She bids the merchant farewell, explaining that she is off to seek a new life.

King Lear

Welles was also anxious to put his version of *King Lear*, for which he had very definite ideas, on the screen. "Up to now, everybody, myself included, felt we had to extend the visual elements of *Lear* instead of doing what the movies make possible, which is reducing it to its essential so it becomes a more abstract and intimate *Lear*," he explained. "It's about old age and it's not about somebody trying to outsing the Metropolitan [Opera] and outshout the thunder." He intended to do a less-is-more production, shot in 16 millimeter black-and-white, mostly in close-up. He continued, "I believe the key to *Lear* and his extraordinary behavior at the beginning of the play, which is the toughest thing to swallow, is the fact that he probably had three wives, anyway probably two, and his last wife died in childbirth and he has lived for at least 25 years without the company of women. He lives with his knights, he's going to pieces. The absence of women, of the civilizing element of life, is the thing that blinds him and makes the tragedy."

The Other Side of the Wind

The Other Side of the Wind was cowritten and coproduced by Welles and Kodar. Shot between 1969 and 1976, it is Welles's satirical take on the state of film, circa 1970, and a film à clef in which he skewers his enemies, including John Houseman and Pauline Kael. It features John Huston as Jack Hannaford, an over-the-hill director trying to make a comeback with a New Wave-y film-within-a-film called *The Other Side of the Wind* that parodies fashionable European directors of the moment, such as Michelangelo Antonioni and Jean-Luc Godard. Guests are on their way to Hannaford's seventieth birthday party, staged in all its extravagant, Aquarian glory, but he is killed in a car crash immediately thereafter. The movie is a mash-up of stills; various film gauges and formats—Super 8, 16, 35 millimeter, as well as video—black-and-white and color; and different genres. Before *The Other Side of the Wind* could be completed it became embroiled in a legal fight over ownership between Welles and the brother-in-law of the Shah of Iran, who invested in it. It has not been released to this day. Henry Jaglom, Peter Bogdanovich, Oja Kodar, Susan Strasberg, Paul Mazursky, Lilli Palmer, Stephane Audran, Cameron Crowe, Dennis Hopper, Claude Chabrol, and more make appearances.

PARTIAL CAST OF CHARACTERS

Joseph Cotten, one of Welles's oldest friends, hooked up with him for the Federal Theatre production of *Horse Eats Hat*. Cotten was a founding member of the Mercury Theatre. His breakout role, playing the part that Cary Grant would later make famous in the movie, was that of C. K. Dexter Haven in *The Philadelphia Story* on Broadway opposite Katharine Hepburn. He then played Jedediah Leland in *Citizen Kane* (1941), and went on to have a long and varied career in Hollywood. He played Eugene in *The Magnificent Ambersons* (1942), and appeared in Hitchcock's *Shadow of a Doubt* (1943), as well as *Gaslight* (1944), and four movies with Jennifer Jones, including *Duel in the Sun* (1946). He also played Marilyn Monroe's husband in *Niagara* (1953), and even showed up in Michael Cimino's notorious *Heaven's Gate* (1980).

Samuel Goldwyn formed Samuel Goldwyn Pictures in 1916. In 1924, it was folded into Metro-Goldwyn-Mayer. (Roaring Leo the lion, the MGM trademark, was originally his.) He subsequently became a successful independent producer. William Wyler made his best films for Goldwyn, including *Wuthering Heights* (1939), *The Little Foxes* (1941), and *The Best Years of Our Lives* (1948). Many of Hollywood's finest writers worked for him, including Ben Hecht, Dorothy Parker, and Lillian Hellman. He was also notorious for mangling the English language, coming up with locutions affectionately known as "Goldwynisms." Trying to cheer up Billy Wilder after a flop, he once said, "You gotta take the sour with the bitter."

Charles Higham, a prolific biographer, published two books on Welles, *The Films of Orson Welles* and *Orson Welles: The Rise and Fall of an American Genius*. Welles and his admirers detested Higham for perpetuating the view that Welles was a failure. Welles delighted in mispronouncing his name "Higgam."

Lena Horne was Hollywood's Jackie Robinson, so to speak, the first black movie star, in an era when most black performers were relegated to the roles of butlers, nannies, cooks, or cannibals. She began her career in the chorus line of the legendary Cotton Club in 1933 when she was sixteen. She was known for her silken voice, and eventually replaced Dinah Shore on NBC's jazz show *The Chamber*

Music Society of Lower Basin Street. She signed with MGM, becoming the first black star under a long-term contract. Horne appeared in numerous films, but her scenes were excised in states that banned movies with black performers. She gained considerable fame for playing Georgia Brown in the all-black musical *Cabin in the Sky* (1943), and for singing the title song in *Stormy Weather* (1943). She was an outspoken civil rights activist. She worked closely with Paul Robeson in the 1930s; and during the war, entertaining the troops, she refused to perform before segregated audiences or those in which black GI's were seated behind German POWs, as was sometimes the case. Her later career, in the 1950s, was blighted by the blacklist that forced her out of Hollywood into clubs and television.

Garson Kanin wrote and directed for the stage and screen. He is best known for *Born Yesterday* (1950). With his wife, actress Ruth Gordon, he wrote two Tracy-Hepburn comedies, *Adam's Rib* (1949) and *Pat and Mike* (1952).

Elia Kazan was a towering figure of the American stage and screen. He was closely associated with "the Method" school of acting, and cofounded the Actors Studio in 1947. He directed its most famous graduate, Marlon Brando, in three films, *A Streetcar Named Desire* (1951), the risible *Viva Zapata!* (1952), and the brilliant *On the Waterfront* (1954), in which the actor gave the greatest performance of his career. Even Kazan's lesser works, like *Panic in the Streets* (1950), *Baby Doll* (1956), *A Face in the Crowd* (1957), and *Wild River* (1960) are compelling. The director also gave Warren Beatty his first starring role in *Splendor in the Grass* (1961). But Kazan was an old lefty from the Group Theatre, and in 1952 he sullied his reputation forever by naming names, that is, throwing his old friends and colleagues to the wolves by testifying against them before the House Committee on Un-American Activities. Many of his associates never forgave him.

Alexander Korda was a Hungarian-born producer and director. After his career floundered in several countries—Hungary, Austria, Germany, and the United States—he relocated to England, where he had immediate success directing Charles Laughton in *The Private Life of Henry VIII* (1933). He went on to direct many more films, including *Four Feathers* (1939) and *The Thief of Bagdad* (1940). He bought into British Lion Films, and entered a coproduction deal with David O. Selznick in 1948. A good friend of Welles's, he hired him for *The Third Man*, released in 1949.

Irving "Swifty" Lazar, one of the first so-called superagents, was reportedly so nicknamed by Humphrey Bogart when he put together three deals for him in one day on a bet. Separated at birth from Mr. Magoo, he was tiny, bald, and wore thick glasses in heavy black frames. But he was an immaculate dresser, and despite his unprepossessing appearance, counted among his clients, at one time or another, Lauren Bacall, Moss Hart, Ernest Hemingway, Cole Porter, and even Madonna. He was known for his abrupt phone manner, called everybody "kiddo," and even the biggest stars killed for invitations to his Oscar parties.

Charles Lederer was the writer, cowriter, or contributor to several classic comedies, including *The Front Page* (1931), *His Girl Friday* (1940), *I Was a Male War Bride* (1949), *Gentlemen Prefer Blondes* (1953), and *Monkey Business* (1952), as well as Richard Widmark's chilling debut film, *Kiss of Death* (1947), and Howard Hawks's sci-fi landmark, *The Thing* (1951). Even more precocious than Welles, Lederer entered college at the age of thirteen, and was entangled with Welles throughout his life. Lederer was raised by Marion Davies, his aunt, who was, of course, Hearst's mistress and one of Welles's ostensible targets in *Kane*. He married Welles's first wife, Virginia Nicholson, at Hearst Castle. Lederer and Welles became great friends. After Rita Hayworth threw Welles out, he lived next door to the Davies estate, where Lederer and Nicholson were living, and dined with them nearly every night. Occasionally, when Davies joined the couple, Welles was barred from the table, and stood outside the window watching them eat. Both he and Lederer were fond of practical jokes.

In 1924, **Louis B. Mayer** became head of the combined Metro Pictures, Goldwyn Pictures, and Mayer Pictures—soon to be Metro-Goldwyn-Mayer. Mayer reported to Nicholas Schenk in New York, whom he disliked and resented, invariably referring to him as "Mr. Skunk," but he ran the lot, located in Los Angeles, like his own fiefdom. Mayer built MGM into the most successful studio in Hollywood, the crown jewel of the golden age of movies, and he is credited, if that's the right word, for inventing the star system. MGM was home to Greta Garbo, Clark Gable, Carole Lombard, Jean Harlow, Judy Garland, John Barrymore, Joan Crawford, and a host of other stars, all of whom the studio held in virtual thralldom. Mayer was extremely conservative and a lifelong Republican.

Louella Parsons and **Hedda Hopper.** Parsons was a preternaturally powerful Hollywood gossip columnist who went to work for William Randolph Hearst in 1923. Before long she was syndicated in more than six hundred papers worldwide, and was read by an estimated 20 million people. Parsons reigned supreme until Hedda Hopper emerged as an equally if not more powerful rival in 1937, writing for competing newspapers. Hopper called her Beverly Hills house "the house that fear built." Long before Bob Dylan mocked Jackie Kennedy's "leopard-skin pill-box hat," Hopper was famous for her flamboyant headgear. An avid supporter of HUAC, Joe McCarthy, and the blacklist, her relentless attacks on Charlie Chaplin for his lefty politics and predilection for young women is at least partially responsible for driving him into exile in Switzerland. She was rumored to have tried to out Cary Grant and Randolph Scott as a couple, and one Valentine's Day she was the recipient of a skunk, courtesy of actress Joan Bennett. Both Parsons and Hopper attacked *Kane*, even before it opened in 1941. Parsons was particularly vituperative, and took an active part in her boss's campaign to block the release of the film, even smuggling one of Hearst's lawyers into a private screening.

David O. Selznick became head of production at RKO in 1931. It was there that he produced *King Kong* (1933). He moved to MGM in 1933. Production head Irving Thalberg's health was failing, and Louis B. Mayer gave Selznick his own production unit. But Selznick, who married Mayer's daughter Irene, had grander ambitions. Two years later he left to start his own company, Selznick International Pictures. He produced *A Star Is Born*, *Nothing Sacred*, and, in conjunction with MGM, *Gone With the Wind*. He brought Alfred Hitchcock from England to America, and produced *Rebecca*, for which he won an Oscar, as well as *Spellbound* and *Duel in the Sun*, among other films.

Erich von Stroheim was regarded as one of the greatest directors of the silent era. When he landed on Ellis Island in 1909, he claimed that his name was Count Erich Oswald Hans Carl Maria von Stroheim und Nordenwall, and that he was descended from Austrian royalty, although in reality he was the son of a hat maker. He did some acting and writing, and directed himself in *Blind Husbands* (1919). Three years later, he clashed with Thalberg over the length of *Foolish Wives*. Von Stroheim will always be mentioned in the same breath as his most notorious film, *Greed* (1924), an eight-hour epic based on Frank Norris's novel *McTeague*. Eventually, he edited it down to six hours, then four, and offered to reduce it further, to three, but Thalberg took it away from him, and it was hacked to pieces, becoming a symbol of studio stupidity, to which Welles could all too strongly relate. Von Stroheim went on to direct *The Merry*

Widow (1925) and *The Wedding March* (1928), and eventually devoted the remainder of his career to acting. Although it was no more than a footnote to a great directing career, he will always be remembered for playing Gloria Swanson's butler in Billy Wilder's *Sunset Boulevard* (1950).

Louis B. Mayer's masterpiece was not a movie but the sickly "boy wonder" **Irving Thalberg**. He was already vice president in charge of production at Mayer Pictures when three companies merged to form MGM. Still under twenty-five, he quickly became a legend in his own right. Thalberg innovated in several areas, introducing story conferences, previews, and reshoots. MGM produced four hundred pictures during his tenure, and he was credited with making the studio the powerhouse it became with pictures such as *Ben Hur* (1925), *Grand Hotel* (1932), *Camille* (1936), *Mutiny on the Bounty* (1935), and *The Good Earth* (1937). He suffered from congenital heart disease and was told as a child that he would die before he was thirty. He in fact died in 1936 at the age of thirty-seven, and was survived by his wife, actress Norma Shearer.

Gregg Toland, a legendary Hollywood cinematographer, was under a long-term contract to Sam Goldwyn, who lent him to Welles for *Citizen Kane*. His name is invariably associated with the deep-focus cinematography for which *Kane* is famous, where objects in the foreground and background are equally sharp.

Darryl Zanuck headed what would become Twentieth Century Fox from 1933 until he left in 1956 to shoot in Europe. In his heyday, he was known for prestige films that tackled social issues, including *The Grapes of Wrath* (1940), *How Green Was My Valley* (1941), and *Gentleman's Agreement* (1947). Once in Europe, his films became vehicles for a succession of girlfriends, including Bella

Darvi, Irina Demick, Geneviève Gilles, and Juliette Gréco. He returned to Fox—sinking fast under the weight of *Cleopatra* (1963)—riding the success of *The Longest Day* (1962). He made his son, Richard, head of production, but was ousted by him, with the help of the board, and left for good in 1971.

Acknowledgments

First and foremost, I would like to thank Henry Jaglom for making his conversations with Orson Welles available to me, and for doing so without any thought of benefitting financially from his close friendship with him. I would also like to acknowledge Eugene Corey, the heroic transcriber, who put in countless hours over many months, transforming what were sometimes no more than barely intelligible grunts recorded in a noisy restaurant into coherent transcripts. My sharp-as-a-tack agent, Kathy Robbins, helped me in more ways than I can count, while my good friend and genius editor Sara Bershtel steadfastly refused to let anything slip by her. Thanks also to transcript wranglers Sharon Lester Kohn and Courtney Kirkpatrick, in Jaglom's office. And finally, to my wife, Elizabeth Hess, for her forbearance while I shut myself away to finish the manuscript, coming out of my office only to bore her with Orson stories that I had already told her.

Notes

Introduction: How Henry Met Orson

2   "Everyone will always owe": Jean-Luc Godard, quoted by Michel Ciment, "Les Enfants Terribles," *American Film*, December 1984, p. 42.

6   "crushing ego": Chris Welles Feder, *In My Father's Shadow: A Daughter Remembers Orson Welles* (New York: Algonquin, 2009), p. 27.

9   "We used to talk": Henry Jaglom, author interview (hereafter AI), July 23, 1993.

10 "He won't do it": Peter Bogdanovich, quoted by Jaglom, AI, March 5, 2012.

11 "You're the arrogant kid": Orson Welles, quoted by Jaglom, AI, March 5, 2012.

13 "Yeah, I'm very moved": Bert Schneider, quoted by Jaglom, AI, March 5, 2012.

13 "Jack was ready": Schneider, AI, February 19, 1995.

14 "I had begun to think": Jaglom, AI, no date.

14 "I've lost my girlish enthusiasm": Jaglom, e-mail, June 26, 2012.

15 "It's not that he didn't": Jaglom, AI, March 5, 2012.

16 "Orson couldn't get a movie done": Jaglom, AI, July 23, 1993.

16 "three weeks later": Jaglom, AI, July 23, 1993.

17 "is a man who has": Welles, quoted by Jaglom in a memo to Jack Nicholson, May 20, 1982.

17 "*The Big Brass Ring* was about": Jaglom, AI, July 23, 1993.

17 "if I got one of six": AI, July 23, 1993.

18 "he needed to bring": Jaglom, e-mail, June 8, 2012.

18 "Then he made me": Jaglom, AI, March 5, 2012.

19 "shower curtain": Patrick Terrail, *A Taste of Hollywood: The Story of Ma Maison* (New York: Lebhar-Friedman, 1999), p. 46.

19 "the fanciest French restaurant": Charles Perry, "Ma Maison, the Sequel," *Los Angeles Times*, October 25, 2001.

19 "The restaurant had become": Terrail, AI, June 2012.

20 "They'll fly you": Terrail, AI, June 2012.

20 "crotch": Terrail, AI, June 2012.

20 "I am flattered": Terrail, AI, June 2012.

20 "HELLO, HOW ARE YOU?!": Jaglom, AI, March 7, 2012.

20 "People would say": Jaglom, AI, March 7, 2012.

20 "You have to do something": Jaglom, AI, March 7, 2012.

20 "was often surreal": Gore Vidal, "Remembering Orson Welles," *The New York Review of Books*, June 1, 1989.

21 "that's the only thing": *My Lunches with Orson*, p. 79.

21 "Underrated": *My Lunches with Orson*, p. 186.

21 "Ruined by all the French chefs": *My Lunches with Orson*, p. 250.

21 "Everyone treated Orson badly": Jaglom, AI, May 10, 1995.

22 "single most destructive enemy": Welles and Bogdanovich, *This Is Orson Welles*, New York, 1998, p. xxi.

22 "Houseman started out": Barbara Leaming, *Orson Welles: A Biography* (New York: Viking, 1989), p. 81.

22 "two dishes of flaming": Simon Callow, *Orson Welles: The Road to Xanadu* (New York: Viking, 1995), p. 477.

23 "Are you OK?": Jaglom, AI, March 7, 2012.

23 "Even Orson was shocked": Jaglom, AI, March 7, 2012.

23 "It just shows me": Barbara Leaming, "Orson Welles: The Unfulfilled Promise," *The New York Times*, July 14, 1985.

25 "Orson is an enigmatic figure": Jaglom, "Who was that masked man?" *Los Angeles Times Book Review*, February 29, 2004, p. 3.

25 "The final scene of *The Lady from Shanghai*": Jaglom, "Who was that masked man?" *Los Angeles Times Book Review*, February 29, 2004, p. 3.

25 "Wait till I die": Jaglom, "Who was that masked man?" Ibid.

26 "I gave him": Jaglom, AI, March 7, 2012.

Part I

119 "Unless we made a 35 millimeter blimp": A blimp is an enclosure that surrounds the camera for the purposes of deadening the sound the camera makes when running.

143 "So a check came": According to a document cited by Simon Callow in the second volume of his biography of Welles, the sum was $5,000. Cf. Simon Callow, *Orson Welles: Hello Americans* (New York: Viking, 2006), p. 8.

Part II

253 **"balling Deanna Durbin":** According to Samantha Barbas, in her book *The First Lady of Hollywood: A Biography of Louella Parsons*, Hopper "falsely" accused Cotton of having an affair with Durbin.

264 **"Susan Smith":** a pseudonym.

272 "But this fellow Carringer found the smoking gun": Nowhere in his memoir, *Unfinished Business*, does Houseman flat-out deny there was a second Welles script, but nowhere does he mention it, either, and gives full writing credit to Mankiewicz. I could not find a reference in Carringer's book to finding a telegram from Houseman to Welles favoring Welles's script over Mankiewicz's, although there is a footnote referring to a telegram Houseman sent to Mankiewicz in which the former wrote that he "liked most of Orson's new scenes" (p. 153).

272 "He has a description of me": I have not been able to find a passage that states that Welles put his arms around Carringer. Carringer himself has not responded to queries.

272 "use of the word *collaborative*": Welles misremembers, slightly. The passage in question appears in Carringer's essay "Orson Welles and Gregg Toland: Their Collaboration on 'Citizen Kane,'" not in his book on *Kane*. It reads: ". . . the very mention of the term collaboration at a wrong moment can be enough to send him into a rage."

283 "this producer *wants* me to say no": It may very well be that the "bad Welles legend" poisoned Mitterand, whom Welles considered his ace in the hole. In a telegram he sent to Kodar on the occasion of Welles's death, he wrote that Welles "may not have been able or may not have wanted to have followed to an end this film." The implication, bizarre at best, is that by *not* financing the film, France was fulfilling Welles's

conscious or unconscious desire. Quoted in Jonathan Rosenbaum, *Discovering Orson Welles* (Berkeley: University of California Press, 2007), p. 86.

287 "terrible wine again": Henry Jaglom, "Orson Welles: Last Take," *Los Angeles Times*, October 14, 1995.

Appendix

292 "It's an essay on Spain": Mary Blume, *International Herald Tribune*, 1983.

292 "Up to now": Mary Blume, Ibid.

294 "You gotta take the sour with the bitter": A. Scott Berg, *Goldwyn: A Biography* (New York: Riverhead, 1998), p. 396.

297 "Mr. Skunk": Edward Baron Turk, *Hollywood Diva: A Biography of Jeanette MacDonald* (Berkeley: University of California Press, 2000), p. 219.

Index

Top Flight 11 passenger Daniel Lewin, probably the first to die on 9/11.

Above The Hanson family, passengers on Flight 175. On the phone to his father, Peter Hanson said: "Don't worry . . . If it happens, it'll be very fast."

Barbara Olson (*left*), known for her appearances on TV, was a passenger on Flight 77 – she managed to phone her husband, the US Solicitor General, to say the plane had been hijacked. Her name and those of sisters Zoe and Dana Falkenberg, aged eight and three respectively, are among those remembered at the Pentagon memorial (*below*). Dana's remains were not found.

Below Flight 93 flight attendant CeeCee Lyles's charred ID card, found after the crash. She had reached her husband to say the passengers were fighting back against the hijackers.

M-CSP-00010424

Office workers at windows of the Trade Center's North Tower. Trapped by fire, many jumped to their deaths.

Of those below the points of impact, most made their way to safety.

After the towers collapsed, New Yorkers ran pell-mell, a dust cloud at their heels. Hundreds have died, and many more are sick, from respiratory disease caused by the dust.

Two days after the attacks, firefighters and other rescue workers retrieve bodies from the rubble of the World Trade Center.

President Bush is told that a second plane has crashed.

In the Emergency Operations Center beneath the White House (*below*), Vice President Cheney speaks by phone with Bush. To the left of him is National Security Adviser Condoleezza Rice. To the left of her, kneeling, is Navy commander Anthony Barnes.

Left The facade of the Pentagon before it collapsed. Skeptics doubted that it could have swallowed a Boeing 757 airliner.

Above Investigators search the Pennsylvania field where Flight 93 crashed. In the foreground is the crater.

Right Wreckage at the Pentagon. Some skeptics suggested that evidence had been planted.

Right Flight 93's Cockpit Voice Recorder – hauntingly, minute by minute, it tracked the progress of the hijacking.

M-CSP-00017681

M-CSP-00004942

Nine months later, draped in the flag, the last steel girder is removed from the ruins of the World Trade Center. It will stand in the memorial at Ground Zero.

TWENTY

HE WAS IN HIS MID-TWENTIES, LEAN, DIMINUTIVE. He had degrees in chemistry and electrical engineering. At college in the United Kingdom, where he had studied, he was thought of as "hard-working, conscientious." A senior FBI official would one day describe him as "poised, articulate, well-educated." He spoke not only English but several other languages.

Ramzi Yousef was more political than he was fanatically religious. The Palestinian blood he claimed, he said, made him "Palestinian by choice," and he believed America's support for Israel gave all Muslims "the right to regard themselves as in a state of war with the U.S. government."

It had been the anti-Soviet war in Afghanistan, however, that first brought Yousef to jihad. In the Afghan training camps, during a break from his studies in Britain, he learned about explosives—learned so well, some said, that he rapidly became an instructor. Fellow trainees dubbed him "the Chemist."

Once America had become the enemy, Yousef's talent made him a deadly adversary. In midsummer 1992, speaking in code on the phone with a like-thinking friend, he referred to his "chocolate training." The friend did not at first understand so he said simply, "Boom!," adding that he was going to work in the United States. The friend got the gist.

In New York two years earlier, Blind Sheikh Rahman had preached the need to "break and destroy the morale of the enemies of Allah." It should be done, he said, by "exploding the structure of their civilized pillars . . . the touristic infrastructure which they are proud of, and their high buildings." He and those around him, an FBI informant recalled, often talked of "targeting American symbols."

The same month Yousef spoke of a mission to America involving explosives, the Blind Sheikh made a phone call to Pakistan. Within weeks, arriving on September 1, the Chemist and an accomplice flew First Class from Karachi to New York's Kennedy Airport.

The mission almost failed before it began, when the accomplice was stopped by Immigration. He was found to be carrying a false Swedish passport, a Saudi passport that had been altered, Jordanian and British passports, instructions on document forgery, rubber stamps for altering the seal on Saudi passports—and what turned out to be bomb-making instructions. Yousef also raised suspicions. In addition to an Iraqi passport, which turned out to be phony, he was carrying ID in the name of his traveling companion.

The companion was detained and would later be jailed. Yousef, who requested asylum on the grounds that he was fleeing persecution in Iraq, was admitted to the country pending a hearing. He headed at once, investigators later came to believe, for the Al Khifa center in Brooklyn, a focal point for Arabs bound for and returning from Afghanistan. A contact there took him, at least once, to see Blind Sheikh Rahman, the man who had called for exploding America's "high buildings."

Over the months that followed, in various apartments

in Jersey City—just across the Hudson River from his target—Yousef the Chemist did the work he had come to do. He and accomplices acquired what he needed: 1,000 pounds of urea, 105 gallons of nitric acid, 60 gallons of sulfuric acid, three tanks of compressed hydrogen. At the apartment where the chemicals were mixed, walls became stained, metal items corroded.

By February 25, 1993, all was ready. Yousef and two accomplices loaded the bomb, packed in four large cardboard boxes, into a rented Econoline van. The cylinders of hydrogen, along with containers of nitroglycerine, blasting caps, and fuses, were laid alongside them.

Just after noon the following day, the bombers parked the van in a garage beneath the North Tower of the World Trade Center. Yousef lit the fuses with a cigarette lighter, closed the doors, and made his escape in a waiting car.

The bomb exploded just before 12:18 P.M. At 1,200 pounds, the FBI would rate it "the largest by weight and by damage of any improvised explosive device that we've seen since the inception of forensic explosive identification"—more than sixty years earlier.

A mile away, people thought there had been an earthquake. Beneath the ground—the Trade Center reached seven stories below the surface—the bomb opened a crater four stories deep. Burning cars hung from ruined parking levels "like Christmas tree ornaments." The explosion devastated an underground train station.

Above the explosion point, the blast rocketed upward, cut power, stopped elevators in mid-journey. One elevator, crammed with schoolchildren, was stranded for five hours. Smoke rose as high as the 82nd floor, and thousands of people rushed for the stairwells. Some crowded around windows as if planning to jump—eerily prefiguring the fatal plunges of almost a decade later.

Miraculously, for all the damage, only six people were killed—even though some hundred thousand people worked in or visited the Trade Center complex on an average weekday. More than a thousand were injured, however, sending more people to the hospital—it is said—than any event on the American mainland since the Civil War. "If they had found the exact architectural Achilles' heel," an FBI explosives specialist said of the tower that was hit, "or if the bomb had been a little bit bigger—not much more, 500 lbs. more—I think it would have brought her down." Yousef would later tell investigators he had wanted to bring the North Tower crashing down on its twin, killing—he hoped—the quarter of a million people he imagined used the complex each day.

He had arranged for a communiqué to be mailed to the press in the name of the "Liberation Army," saying that the attack had been carried out in response to "the American political, economical, and military support to Israel. . . . The American people are responsible for the actions of their government."

When Yousef learned that the bombing had only partially succeeded, he phoned an accomplice to dictate a new ending to the communiqué. It read: "Our calculations were not very accurate this time. However, we promise you that the next time it will be very precise and the World Trade Center will continue to be one [of] our targets."

Yousef apparently phoned in the amendment from a First Class lounge at Kennedy Airport. An hour or so later he was gone, safe aboard an airliner bound for Pakistan.

Thanks to brilliant forensic work, most of the accomplices Yousef left behind were swiftly tracked down and jailed. The bomber himself, though identified, remained at large to plot new mayhem. By January 1995, he was back in the Philippines, with a dual focus. He intended a bombing during the visit to the Pacific region by Pope John Paul II, and—most fiendish and complex of all—a series of bombings of American airliners.

The plot against the Pope proved Yousef's undoing. The plot to bring down U.S. airliners—little understood at the time—was a turning point on the road to 9/11.

ON THE NIGHT of Friday, January 6, 1995, in Manila, smoke was reported billowing out of an apartment building just a block from the papal nunciature, where Pope John Paul would be staying. A patrolman reported that there was nothing to worry about—"Just some Pakistanis," he said, "playing with firecrackers."

Unconvinced, senior police inspector Aida Fariscal decided to take a look for herself. Told that the smoke had come from Suite 603 in the apartment building, and that its two tenants had fled during the initial panic, she asked to see inside. The apartment turned out to be crammed with chemicals in plastic containers, cotton soaked in acrid-smelling fluid, funnels, thermometers, fusing systems, electrical wiring, and explosives instructions in Arabic.

As Fariscal and the officers with her stared at their find, the doorman told them that one of the missing tenants had come back to retrieve something that had been left behind. He spotted the police and started running, but was caught and hauled back to headquarters. The man, who claimed he was "Ahmed Saeed," an innocent tourist, was handed over to agents at a military installation. They were not gentle with him.

According to reporting by two distinguished Filipino reporters, he was tortured over a period of more than two months. "Agents hit him with a chair and a long piece of wood, forced water into his mouth, and crushed lighted cigarettes into his private parts. They dragged him on the floor, from one corner of the interrogation room to the other. . . . They threatened to rape him. . . . His ribs were almost [all] broken."

A partial transcript of one taped session with the prisoner runs as follows:

> INTERROGATOR: What will the bomb be made of ?
> PRISONER: That will be nitroglycerine . . . 5 milliliters of glycerine, 15 of nitrate, and 22.5 of sulphuric acid . . .
> INTERROGATOR: What are your plans?
> PRISONER: We are planning, I'm planning to explode this airplane. I have planning of of—just, I can't breathe, I can't breathe . . .
> INTERROGATOR: What is your plan in America? PRISONER: Killing the people there. Teach them . . .
> INTERROGATOR: What do you do in . . . going to Singapore?
> PRISONER: I'll put the bomb in the United Air . . .

The captive's real name was Abdul Murad, and he was the associate in whom Ramzi Yousef had confided before flying to New York to bomb the Trade Center. Torture notwithstanding, the evidence in Manila linked him firmly to the more recent terrorist activity. Extradited to the United States, in the hands of FBI agents, Murad told a cohesive story.

Yousef had told him the previous year, in Pakistan, of wanting "to blow up unnamed American airliners by placing explosives aboard the aircraft." Training sessions followed, with Murad making notes of formulas and instructions. Then, in December, Yousef had summoned him to the Philippines. They worked on methods of disguise—removal of the obligatory jihadi beard, L'Oréal dye to color the hair, and blue contact lenses—to look "more European."

They bought Casio watches for use as timing devices to trigger the airliner bombs. Yousef ran live experiments, the first time with a small device planted under a seat in a local movie theater. It worked perfectly, without causing serious injury—because the seat was unoccupied at the time. The second test, however, proved lethal.

In early December, posing as an Italian, Yousef boarded a Philippine Air flight bound for Tokyo with 273 passengers. He had with him one of the modified Casio watches, liquid explosive in a contact lens solution bottle, and minute batteries hidden in the heels of his shoes. He assembled the device in flight, concealed it under the seat cushion of Seat 26K, then left the plane at a scheduled stopover.

Two hours later, the bomb went off in mid-flight. Though it killed the unfortunate passenger in 26K and crippled the aircraft's controls, the plane landed safely thanks to the skill of its pilots. The operation had proved to Yousef, however, that his devices could work. He now prepared another bomb, intended for an American airplane.

Murad was to plant the bomb this time. He would avoid suspicion by using two carry-on bags, one to smuggle the liquid on board, the second for components. The detonator was to be concealed inside a Parker pen, the bomb placed in a restroom near the cockpit. Murad would escape by leaving the plane at a stopover, as had Yousef previously. The pair expected to "cause the destruction of the plane and the death of everyone on board."

A date had been picked, a flight chosen—United Airlines Flight 2 from Hong Kong to Los Angeles on January 14. Then on January 6, the plan fell apart—with the telltale smoke emanating from the conspirators' apartment, the police search that followed, and Murad's arrest. It was to retrieve Yousef's laptop computer that

Murad had risked trying to return to the apartment. Now the police had it.

A file on the laptop revealed that the plot called for the bombing of not only United Flight 2 but of *eleven* other American airliners. A number of terrorists, identified on the laptop by pseudonyms, were to transport and plant the devices. Flights targeted included seven operated by United, three by Northwest, and one by Delta. Under the headings "TIMER" and "SETTING," Yousef had meticulously listed at precisely what time one of his Casio watches was to detonate each individual bomb.

The airlines were alerted, flights diverted and grounded, on orders direct from the Clinton White House. In the sort of security scare not to be seen again until after the Millennium, passengers in the Pacific region were searched, all liquids confiscated, for weeks to come.

Catastrophe had been averted thanks only to Inspector Fariscal's insistence on entering the apartment that served as Yousef's bomb factory. Had the plot succeeded, as many as four thousand people could have died—more than the total that were to be lost on 9/11.

The computer file on the plot bore a code name that at first meant nothing to investigators—"BOJINKA." It appears to be a Serbo-Croatian or Croatian word meaning "loud bang," "big bang"—or just "boom." "Boom," the word Yousef had used two and a half years earlier, in plain English, as verbal code for his coming attack on New York's World Trade Center.

Exactly a month after the discoveries in Manila, the bomber was finally betrayed and arrested in Pakistan. Extradited to the United States, thanks to a cooperative Prime Minister Bhutto, he faced trial twice—once for the airliner plot, once for the 1993 Trade Center bombing. Found guilty in both cases, Yousef was sentenced to a theoretical 240 years in jail.

"I am a terrorist and I'm proud of it," he had declared in court. "I support terrorism so long as it is against the United States government and against Israel." In 1995, on the final stage of his return from Pakistan, a helicopter was used to bring Yousef, shackled and blindfolded, to the Correctional Center in Lower Manhattan. As the helicopter approached the Twin Towers, an FBI agent pulled up the blindfold and pointed. "See," he said. "You didn't get them after all." The prisoner responded with a look and a curt "Not yet."

When the towers were finally destroyed, on 9/11, Yousef would prostrate himself in his prison cell and give praise to Allah. He had all along accepted responsibility for the 1993 bombing, but on one point he remained evasive. Was he or was he not the mastermind behind the operation? He would say only that Muslim leaders had inspired his work. Which Muslim leaders? He would not say.

As LATE AS 2004, a former CIA deputy director of intelligence—by then a senior staff member of the 9/11 Commission—would say there was "substantial uncertainty" as to whether Osama bin Laden and his organization had a role in either the Trade Center bombing or the plot to blow up U.S. airliners over the Pacific.

Available information suggests there was in fact a link to bin Laden. Yousef had learned about explosives in bin Laden–funded camps near the Afghan border. In 1991, when he reached the Philippines, he told separatists he was bin Laden's "emissary." The separatist with whom he had most contact was funded by bin Laden, had been close to bin Laden during the anti-Soviet conflict. The accomplice who tried to enter the United States with Yousef—but was refused admission—had carried a bomb manual headed "Al Qaeda," the name for the then-obscure entity headed by bin Laden.

Yousef made a huge number of long-distance calls while preparing to bomb the Trade Center. Checks on the calls after the attack reportedly indicated a link to bin Laden. During Yousef's stays in Peshawar, over several years, he stayed at the Beit Ashuhada [House of the Martyrs], which bin Laden funded. One of the operatives Yousef used in the Philippines was an Afghanistan veteran whom bin Laden has recalled as a "good friend," a man who had "fought from the same trenches" with him.

Bin Laden also connected to the Yousef operation through his own brother-in-law. This was his Saudi friend from university days, Jamal Khalifa, who married bin Laden's sister Shaikha and lived with bin Laden after the wedding. "Imagine how close we are," Khalifa would say after 9/11. "We never disagreed about anything."

By the early 1990s, Khalifa had long been active in the Philippines, fronting as a "missionary" or "philanthropist" and setting up charities to support Muslim causes. In 1992, according to an intelligence report, bin Laden himself visited the Philippines to bestow financial largesse.

Behind the facade, Khalifa spread money around in support of antigovernment rebels. By one report, moreover, he and bin Laden personally introduced one leading Filipino rebel leader to explosives expert Ramzi Yousef. Khalifa remained active in the Philippines until late 1994. Then he abruptly left the country, on the heels of a police report on Muslim groups and terrorism.

Just before Christmas that year, on the U.S. West Coast, Khalifa was arrested by FBI agents—at the very time that, back in the Philippines, Yousef was finalizing his plan to bomb twelve American airliners. In the Saudi's baggage, agents found: a phone book listing a number in

Pakistan that Yousef had called from Manila; a beeper number for one of the accomplices Yousef planned to use to plant his bombs on American planes; the address of Yousef's bomb factory; documents related to explosives and weaponry—and a phone directory entry for Osama bin Laden.

There was more. Khalifa's business card was found both in Manila—at the apartment of one of Yousef's accomplices—and in New York in a suitcase belonging to Blind Sheikh Rahman. One of Khalifa's aliases—he used several—was found on a document belonging to one of Yousef's accomplices. He would eventually be named as an unindicted co-conspirator in the 1993 bombing of the World Trade Center.

Inexplicably, there would not be a single reference to Khalifa in the 9/11 Commission report. Congress's Joint Inquiry report contained just one, characterizing him as the "alleged financier" of the plot to destroy American airliners. Khalifa would never be charged in the United States with any crime.

RAMZI YOUSEF's phone directory, meanwhile, also threw up a lead, a major clue that, successfully pursued, could perhaps have prevented the 9/11 catastrophe. The directory contained the name and contact information in Pakistan for one "Zahid Sheikh Mohammed," brother of a man named "Khalid"—both of them uncles to Yousef.

Zahid's name remains obscure, while Khalid would for years remain a will-o'-the-wisp, a quarry who would not be run to ground until 2003. Today, however, the name of Khalid Sheikh Mohammed sparks instant recognition.

By his own admission, he was the planner and organizer of many attacks—including 9/11. U.S. investigators have long since dubbed him, simply, KSM.

The information on Ramzi Yousef's computer

implicated KSM in the Manila conspiracies and started the hunt for him. Investigators hurried to Zahid's home in Pakistan, to find photographs of bin Laden but no sign of either Mohammed brother. Clues proliferated, however, and much later—in captivity—he would fill in missing parts of the jigsaw.

Some of the many phone calls Yousef had made from New York, while planning the 1993 Trade Center bombing, had been to KSM. They had discussed procedures for mixing explosives on the calls, and the older man helped at least once by wiring his nephew money.

In Manila in 1994, KSM was at very least Yousef's senior accomplice, perhaps the plot's driving force. While Yousef found modest lodgings, KSM took a condominium at Tiffany Mansions, a rather grand address in an affluent part of town. Perhaps as part of their cover, perhaps by inclination, neither man lived the kind of life required of Islamic fundamentalists.

Some of the detail on the Philippines episode comes from the bar girls and dancers with whom uncle and nephew whiled away their nights—and whom they found useful. KSM bribed one of the girls to open a bank account and to purchase a sophisticated mobile phone. The account and the phone were in her name but for his use, ideal for shady financial transactions and unmonitored communication.

To Abdul Murad, the accomplice seized the night police raided the Manila bomb factory, KSM was "Abdul Majid"—one of his thirty-some aliases. Murad had met him once before in Pakistan, when Yousef was recovering from an injury incurred while handling explosives. Then, Yousef had told him "Majid" was a Saudi in the "electronics business." His uncle was in fact Kuwaiti-born and in the terrorism business.

In Manila, as final preparations were made to down

U.S. airliners, KSM came repeatedly to the bomb factory. With chemicals and electronic components scattered in plain sight, Murad was to say that Mohammed "must have known that something was planned." "I was responsible," KSM would one day tell a U.S. military tribunal, "for the planning and surveying needed to execute the Bojinka Operation."

KSM was to tell the CIA that he thought of something else in Manila, a concept radically different from exploding bombs on airliners—the "idea of using planes as missiles." One potential target he and Yousef considered at that time was the CIA headquarters in Virginia. Another was the World Trade Center.

What KSM had to say on that, an indication that flying planes into buildings was under discussion long, long before 9/11, is on its own merely interesting. What sparked lasting controversy, though, is the suggestion that U.S. authorities learned early on what the plotters had in mind—and dropped the ball.

A Philippines police document cites Yousef's accomplice Murad as saying that they discussed a "plan to dive-crash a commercial aircraft at the CIA headquarters in Virginia. . . . What the subject has in his mind is that he will board any American commercial aircraft, pretending to be an ordinary passenger. Then he will hijack said aircraft, control its cockpit and dive it at the CIA headquarters."

No suggestion there that the terrorists discussed targets other than the CIA. One of the Philippines police officers who interrogated Murad, however, has claimed otherwise. Colonel Rodolfo Mendoza told CNN that there was also talk of crashing a plane into the Pentagon. The Philippines presidential spokesman, Rigoberto Tiglao, went much further.

"The targets they listed," he said in 2001, "were CIA

headquarters, the Pentagon, TransAmerica [the TransAmerica Tower, in San Francisco], Sears [the Sears Tower, in Chicago], and the World Trade Center."

Most credible, perhaps, is apparent corroboration from a source who does not cite Murad, whose statements were obtained under torture. Rafael Garcia, the Filipino computer analyst who examined Yousef's computer, recalls having discovered notes of a plan that called for crashing airliners into "selected targets in the United States." These included: "the CIA headquarters in Langley, Virginia; the World Trade Center in New York; the Sears Tower in Chicago; the TransAmerica Tower in San Francisco; and the White House in Washington DC."

The 9/11 Commission Report, which quoted none of these statements verbatim, consigned them to an obscure footnote and referred to them as mere "claims." Its investigation, it stated, found no indication that such information "was written down or disseminated within the U.S. government."

Congress's Joint Inquiry Report, however, said the FBI and the CIA did learn what Murad had said about a plan to crash a plane into CIA headquarters. The FBI, the report stated, later "effectively forgot all about it . . . ignored this early warning sign that terrorists had begun planning to crash aircraft into symbols of American power."

The Philippines National Police intelligence chief, Robert Delfin, said, "We shared that with the FBI. They may have mislooked [sic], and didn't appreciate the info coming from the Philippines police. . . . I believe there was a lapse."

Colonel Mendoza, who said he personally questioned Murad, insisted that he briefed the U.S. embassy on everything Murad told him. Another lead investigator on

FD-302 (Rev. 3-10-82)

3536-B

- 1 -

FEDERAL BUREAU OF INVESTIGATION

Investigation on 4/12-13/95 at Aircraft in Flight   File # 265A-NY-252802 Sub 302-47

SA FRANCIS J. PELLEGRINO, FBI
by SA THOMAS G. DONLON, FBI   Date dictated 4/19/95

This document contains neither recommendations nor conclusions of the FBI. It is the property of the FBI and is loaned to your agency;
it and its contents are not to be distributed outside your agency.

> As for any future terrorist plans, MURAD advised that
> he and RAMZI discussed the possibility of bombing a nuclear
> facility in the United States. They also discussed additional
> attacks on American airline carriers such as United and Northwest
> Airlines. MURAD stated that RAMZI wanted to bomb El-Al Airlines
> but believed that security would be too difficult to penetrate.
> The underlying reason for these attacks would be to make the
> people of the U.S., and their government, "suffer" for their
> support of Israel. MURAD stated that America should remain
> neutral regarding the problems of the Middle East. MURAD advised
> that RAMZI wanted to return to the United States in the future to
> bomb the World Trade Center a second time.

Prisoner Murad said his principal accomplice planned a second attack on the World Trade Center—as early as 1995.

the Manila episode, police Colonel—later General—Avelino Razon, immediately called a press conference when news broke of 9/11. "We told the Americans about the plans to turn planes into flying bombs as far back as 1995," he said. "Why didn't they pay attention?"

Last word to Inspector Fariscal, the officer who discovered Ramzi Yousef's bomb factory. "I still don't understand," she said after 9/11, "how it could have been allowed to happen. . . . The FBI knew all about Yousef's plans. . . . They'd seen the files. . . . The CIA had access to everything, too. . . . This should never have been allowed to happen."

AFTER THE WORLD TRADE CENTER bombing of 1993, well before the Philippines police discovered the Manila bomb factory, the U.S. Defense Department convened a panel to report on how vulnerable the nation might be to terrorism. Presciently, the group discussed the possibility of an airliner being deliberately flown into a public building.

"Coming down the Potomac in Washington," panelist Marvin Cetron recalled saying, "you could make a left turn at the Washington Monument and take out the White House, or you could make a right turn and take out the Pentagon." "Targets such as the World Trade Center," he wrote the following year, "not only provide the requisite casualties but, because of their symbolic nature, provide more bang for the buck. In order to maximize their odds for success, terrorist groups will likely consider mounting multiple, simultaneous operations with the aim of overtaxing a government's ability to respond."

That view did not appear in the published Defense Department report. "It was considered radical thinking," said Douglas Menarchik, the retired Air Force colonel who ran the study, "a little too scary for the times."

Khalid Sheikh Mohammed, who had plotted using planes as missiles to hit targets in the United States, was still at large, still plotting.

TWENTY-ONE

"**Y**OU NEED THE CHARISMATIC DREAMERS LIKE BIN Laden to make a movement successful," a former intelligence analyst was to say. "But you also needed operators like Khalid Sheikh Mohammed who can actually get the job done." KSM's confederates dubbed him "Mukhtar"—an Arabic word to denote a leader, a man respected for his brain. The CIA came to consider him the "manager" of the September 11 plot.

He had been born in the mid-1960s in Kuwait, the son of immigrants from Baluchistan, a fiercely independent frontier region of Pakistan. His father was an imam, his mother a woman who got work preparing women's bodies for burial. The driving force for KSM, though, was the cause of Palestine. Kuwait teemed with Palestinian exiles, and antipathy toward Israel early on became part of KSM's makeup.

At eighteen, in 1983, Khalid traveled to the United States to study engineering at colleges in North Carolina. A fellow student remembered him as "so, so smart," focused on getting his degree—though he took part enthusiastically in amateur theater projects. He also spent a lot of time at his prayers, and tended to reproach contemporaries who strayed from the Muslim diet.

KSM disliked the America he saw. The student body of

one of the colleges he attended was largely black, and life in the South showed him the face of discrimination. He went back to the Middle East with a degree in mechanical engineering and memories of a country that he deemed "racist and debauched."

Then, in 1987, he rallied to the fight to oust the Soviets from Afghanistan. At least one other brother, perhaps two—reports differ—were killed during the conflict. This was a family with a long-term commitment to jihad. At least half a dozen other relatives—KSM's nephew the Trade Center bomber Yousef aside—have been linked to al Qaeda in the years that followed. Most now languish in prison.

In the early 1990s the cause of jihad took KSM across the world, twice to Bosnia, where tens of thousands of Muslims had been slaughtered as the former Yugoslavia collapsed into chaos, to Malaysia, Sudan, China, even Brazil. By late 1994, as he hatched terrorism with Yousef in the Philippines, KSM was nudging thirty. He was short, somewhat overweight, balding, and often—though not always—sported a beard. The beard changed shape from time to time, useful for a man who wanted to confuse pursuers.

Pursuers there were, once Yousef and his would-be bombers had been caught, but KSM made good his escape to the oil-rich Gulf state of Qatar. He found employment there, and powerful support in the shape of Sheikh Abdullah bin Khalid al-Thani, then the minister for religious endowments and Islamic affairs. Sheikh Abdullah had underwritten one of KSM's visits to Bosnia. Now he reportedly saw to it that the fugitive was protected from the long arm of American justice.

Backed up as they were by the authority of a grand jury indictment, U.S. officials hoped Qatar's government would assist in getting KSM to America. An FBI team that flew to the region learned, however, that the quarry was gone. According to the Qatar police chief of the day—himself a member of the royal family—KSM had been tipped off to the danger, given temporary refuge at Sheikh Abdullah's private estate, then assisted in flying out of the country.

There was anger at the FBI and the CIA, and at Bill Clinton's White House, but no effective follow-up. In spite of the offer of a $5 million reward and an "Armed and Dangerous" lookout notice, KSM remained at large.

Half a decade on, the year before 9/11, U.S. analysts received intelligence on an al Qaeda terrorist named "Khalid al-Shaikh al-Balushi," (Khalid al-Shaikh from Baluchistan). The possible connection was noted at the CIA—it was common practice to refer to operatives by land of origin—but not pursued.

Two months before 9/11, KSM felt safe enough to apply for a visa to enter the United States, using an alias but his own photograph. The visa was granted the same day—just weeks after the CIA had received a report that he was currently "recruiting persons to travel to the United States to engage in planning terrorist-related activity."

"Based on our review," the director of Congress's Joint Inquiry concluded that U.S. intelligence had "known about this individual since 1995, but did not recognize his growing importance . . . there was little analytic focus given to him and coordination amongst the intelligence agencies was irregular at best." An executive summary by the CIA inspector general, grudgingly made public only in 2007, conceded there had been multiple errors, including a "failure to produce any [word redacted] coverage of Khalid Sheikh Mohammed from 1997 to 2001."

*

So it was that KSM continued to range free until long after 9/11. His terrorist career would end only in the early hours of March 1, 2003, when a joint team of Pakistani and American agents cornered him at a middle-class home in the Pakistani city of Rawalpindi. A photograph taken at the scene of the arrest showed the prisoner bleary-eyed and unshaven, wearing an under-shirt. "Nothing like James Bond," CIA director George Tenet noted, and saw to it that that was the image fed to the media.

Accounts differ as to how KSM had been tracked down. Suggestions have included betrayal by an al Qaeda comrade—there was by then a $25 million reward—an intercept by the National Security Agency of one of the terrorist's rumored ten mobile phones, or information gleaned from a high-level prisoner.

The capture of KSM was "wonderful," its importance "hard to overstate," said President Bush's press secretary. "This," House Intelligence Committee cochair Porter Goss exalted, "is equal to the liberation of Paris in the Second World War." "No person other than perhaps Osama bin Laden," the CIA's Tenet has said, "was more responsible for the attacks of 9/11 than KSM."

Sources let it be known that U.S. authorities "began an urgent effort to disorient and 'break' Mohammed." For the first two days in captivity, still in Pakistani custody, KSM had reportedly "crouched on the floor in a trance-like state, reciting verses from the Koran." He started talking only later, in the hands of the CIA.

The story the 9/11 Commission gave to the public of how the 9/11 plot evolved depended heavily on the accounts provided by KSM—and some other captives—in response to interrogation. The notes in the Commission Report reference his responses to interrogation 211 times. What readers had no way of knowing, though, is that most if not all of those responses were extracted by using measures the Bush Justice Department defined—in the words of a legal opinion provided to the CIA—as "enhanced interrogation techniques."

Vice President Cheney had hinted right after 9/11 at what was to come. The authorities, he said on *Meet the Press*, intended to work "sort of the dark side . . . It's going to be vital for us to use any means necessary at our disposal . . . we have to make certain that we have not tied the hands, if you will, of our intelligence communities."

A year after 9/11, a senior Justice Department official asserted in a memo to White House counsel Alberto Gonzales that "certain acts may be cruel, inhuman, or degrading, but still not produce pain and suffering of the requisite intensity to fall within Section 2340A's proscription against torture."

The International Committee of the Red Cross, which monitors the Geneva and U.N. Conventions on the treatment of "prisoners of war," long asked in vain for access to KSM and thirteen other detainees. When finally allowed to see them in 2006, the Red Cross reported that the prisoners had indeed been subjected to "torture." Two years later, when its report was leaked, the public learned the details.

Between them, the detainees alleged ill treatment that included "suffocation by water"—better known as waterboarding; prolonged stress standing naked, arms chained above the head for days at a time, often with toilet access denied; beatings and kicking; use of a neck collar to bang the head and body against a wall; confinement in a coffinlike box; enforced nudity for periods up to months; deprivation of sleep by enforcing stress positions, repetitive loud noise or music, or applications of cold water; exposure to cold; threats to harm a detainee's family; restriction of food; and—serious for

SPECIAL REVIEW

TOP SECRET

Enhanced Interrogation Techniques

- The attention grasp consists of grasping the detainee with both hands, with one hand on each side of the collar opening, in a controlled and quick motion. In the same motion as the grasp, the detainee is drawn toward the interrogator.

- During the walling technique, the detainee is pulled forward and then quickly and firmly pushed into a flexible false wall so that his shoulder blades hit the wall. His head and neck are supported with a rolled towel to prevent whiplash.

- The facial hold is used to hold the detainee's head immobile. The interrogator places an open palm on either side of the detainee's face and the interrogator's fingertips are kept well away from the detainee's eyes.

- With the facial or insult slap, the fingers are slightly spread apart. The interrogator's hand makes contact with the area between the tip of the detainee's chin and the bottom of the corresponding earlobe.

- In cramped confinement, the detainee is placed in a confined space, typically a small or large box, which is usually dark. Confinement in the smaller space lasts no more than two hours and in the larger space it can last up to 18 hours.

- Insects placed in a confinement box involve placing a harmless insect in the box with the detainee.

- During wall standing, the detainee may stand about 4 to 5 feet from a wall with his feet spread approximately to his shoulder width. His arms are stretched out in front of him and his fingers rest on the wall to support all of his body weight. The detainee is not allowed to reposition his hands or feet.

- The application of stress positions may include having the detainee sit on the floor with his legs extended straight out in front of him with his arms raised above his head or kneeling on the floor while leaning back at a 45 degree angle.

- Sleep deprivation will not exceed 11 days at a time.

- The application of the waterboard technique involves binding the detainee to a bench with his feet elevated above his head. The detainee's head is immobilized and an interrogator places a cloth over the detainee's mouth and nose while pouring water onto the cloth in a controlled manner. Airflow is restricted for 20 to 40 seconds and the technique produces the sensation of drowning and suffocation.

TOP SECRET

SPECIAL REVIEW

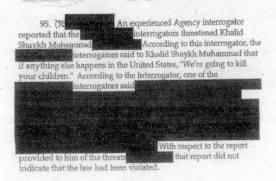

95. (N████████ An experienced Agency interrogator reported that the ███████ interrogators threatened Khalid Shaykh Muhammad ███████ According to this interrogator, the ████ interrogators said to Khalid Shaykh Muhammad that if anything else happens in the United States, "We're going to kill your children." According to the interrogator, one of the ███████ interrogators said ████████████████

████████████████████████████████

████████████████ With respect to the report provided to him of the threats ████████ that report did not indicate that the law had been violated.

Muslim men—forced shaving of the head and beard.

In the event of being taken prisoner, a captured al Qaeda manual showed, operatives had been advised to "complain of mistreatment . . . insist on proving that torture was inflicted." Though alert to false claims, however, the Red Cross was impressed by the consistency of the prisoners' allegations. A then-secret CIA inspector general's review, moreover, had acknowledged—even before the Red Cross reported—that "enhanced interrogation techniques" had indeed been used as described by the prisoners.

KSM told the Red Cross that his ill treatment had ranged right across the U.S. inventory of abuse. During his transfer around the planet, he said, "my eyes were covered with a cloth . . . a suppository was inserted into my rectum. . . . After arrival my clothes were cut off . . . photographs taken of me naked . . . made to stand on tip-toes for about two hours during questioning . . . the head interrogator (a man) and two female interrogators, plus about ten muscle guys wearing masks . . . a tube was inserted into my anus and water poured inside. . . . No toilet access was provided until four hours later."

At some point, physical coercion was compounded by psychological terror. "If anything else happens in the United States," KSM was allegedly told, "we're going to kill your children." KSM had some reason to fear this was true. His sons Yusuf and Abed, aged nine and seven, had been seized months before his own arrest. It has been claimed by another detainee that at some point even they were tormented—supposedly with insects—to scare the children into blabbing clues to their father's whereabouts.

Transported to Poland—KSM thought it was Poland because of a label on a water bottle he saw—three interrogators of non-American extraction told KSM they had approval from Washington to give him "a hard time." He would, they told him, be brought to the "verge of death and back again."

Waterboarding.

"I would be strapped to a special bed, which could be rotated. . . . A cloth would be placed over my face. Cold water from a bottle that had been kept in a fridge was then poured onto the cloth by one of the guards so that I could not breathe. . . . I struggled in the panic of not being able to breathe. . . . The harshest period of the interrogation was just prior to the end of the first month.

. . . The worst day . . . my head was banged against the wall so hard that it started to bleed. . . . Finally I was taken for a session of waterboarding. The torture on that day was finally stopped by the intervention of the doctor."

The average time the CIA expected a subject to endure—before begging for relief and starting to talk—was fourteen seconds. KSM reportedly lasted as long as two to two and a half minutes before providing information. He was submitted to waterboarding 183 times.

THE WATERBOARD has a long history; it was a torture option for the Spanish Inquisition as early as the fifteenth century. In the twentieth century it was used by the British in the 1930s in Palestine, by the Japanese during World War II, by the North Koreans and by the French—in Algeria—in the 1950s, by the Americans in Vietnam in the 1960s, by the Khmer Rouge in Cambodia and the military regimes in Chile and Argentina in the 1970s.

In 1900, an American judge advocate general declared at an Army major's court-martial that waterboarding was "in violation of the rules of civilized war." In the late 1940s, when trying Japanese military personnel who had used waterboarding on American prisoners, the United States deemed them to be war criminals. They were executed.

To the Bush administration in 2006, however, waterboarding had become acceptable. "The United States does not torture," declared President Bush, conceding that the CIA had used an "alternative set of procedures" on detainees. "I cannot describe the specific methods used," he added, but the "separate program" was "vital."

In his 2010 memoir, the former President recalled having been asked by Director Tenet whether he had permission to use waterboarding and other techniques on KSM. "I thought about the 2,973 people stolen from their families by al Qaeda on 9/11," Bush wrote. "And I thought about my duty to protect the country from another act of terror. 'Damn right,' I said."

As Bush recalled it, when told earlier by legal advisers that certain "enhanced" interrogation techniques were legal, he had rejected two that he felt "went too far." Waterboarding, though, "did no lasting harm"—according to medical experts consulted by the CIA.

The "separate" interrogation program was essential, he had said in 2006, because it helped "take potential mass murderers off the streets before they were able to kill." KSM, he said by way of example, had provided information that helped stop a further planned attack on the United States. According to Vice President Cheney, "a great many" attacks had been stopped thanks to information obtained under the program.

Had only conventional interrogation techniques been used on KSM, Director of National Intelligence Mike McConnell said in 2008, he "would not have talked to us in a hundred years." Former CIA director Porter Goss has said the use of "enhanced" techniques produced "provable, extraordinary successes."

Others did not agree. FBI agents involved in the investigation thought ill treatment achieved little or nothing that skilled conventional questioning could not have achieved. Cheney's claim that the program obtained hard intelligence was "intensely disputed." On his first day in office, President Obama banned "alternative procedures."

Coerced admissions, meanwhile, are probably inadmissible in a court of law. "The use of torture," said Professor Mark Danner, who was instrumental in publishing the details of the Red Cross report on the prisoners' treatment, "deprives the society whose laws have been so egregiously violated of the possibility of rendering justice. Torture destroys justice."

THERE IS SOMETHING else, something especially relevant to the information extracted from Khalid Sheikh Mohammed. "Any piece of intelligence which is obtained under duress," said Lieutenant General John Kimmons, the Army's deputy chief of staff for intelligence, "would be of questionable credibility."

Is that the case with KSM, on whose statements much of the 9/11 Commission Report relies? The prisoner positively spewed information, and that is a part of the problem. At a rough count, he confessed to having carried out or plotted some thirty crimes—more than is plausible, surely, even for a top operative.

Transcripts of interrogation sessions with KSM were reportedly transmitted to Washington accompanied by the warning: "Detainee has been known to withhold information or deliberately mislead." In a combined confession and boast, the prisoner himself told the Red Cross: "I gave a lot of false information in order to satisfy what I believed the interrogators wished to hear in order to make the ill-treatment stop. . . . I'm sure that the false information I was forced to invent . . . wasted a lot of their time and led to several false red-alerts being placed in the U.S."

A parallel issue is what torture may have done to KSM's mental condition. His defense attorney at the initial military tribunal proceedings at Guantánamo in 2008, Captain Prescott Prince, thought KSM appeared to have suffered "some level of psychological impairment" as a result of the mistreatment.

When the 9/11 Commission was at work, KSM had yet to admit that he had lied under torture. Nor, at that

INTERNATIONAL COMMITTEE OF THE RED CROSS

REGIONAL DELEGATION FOR
UNITED STATES AND CANADA

ICRC

> During the harshest period of my interrogation I gave a lot of false information in
> order to satisfy what I believed the interrogators wished to hear in order to make the
> ill-treatment stop. I later told the interrogators that their methods were stupid and
> counterproductive. I'm sure that the false information I was forced to invent in order
> to make the ill-treatment stop wasted a lot of their time and led to several false red-
> alerts being placed in the US."

SPECIAL REVIEW

225. (TS.   ) On the other hand, Khalid Shaykh
Muhammad, an accomplished resistor, provided only a few
intelligence reports prior to the use of the waterboard, and analysis of
that information revealed that much of it was outdated, inaccurate, or
incomplete. As a means of less active resistance, at the beginning of
their interrogation, detainees routinely provide information that they
know is already known. Khalid Shaykh Muhammad received 183
applications of the waterboard in March 2003

*The 9/11 commissioners were not told that "enhanced techniques" were used
to interrogate prisoners. The brutal treatment they received taints the
prisoners' admissions.*

time, did the Commission know that he or others had been tortured. "We were not aware, but we guessed," executive director Philip Zelikow has said, "that things like that were going on."

If Zelikow and senior colleagues guessed it, they seem not to have shared their guess with Commission members. "Never, ever did I imagine that American interrogators were subjecting detainees to waterboarding and other forms of physical torture," Commissioner Richard Ben-Veniste has said. "No one raised such a possibility at a Commission meeting. In hindsight we were snookered."

The commissioners asked the CIA to allow its own staff access to detainees, only to meet with a flat refusal. If security was the issue, they then offered, staff could be taken to the prisoners' location wearing blindfolds. Could Commission people at least observe CIA interrogation sessions through a one-way observation window? The CIA blocked all such suggestions.

Commission senior adviser Ernest May thought the CIA's summaries of the results of interrogations "incomplete and poorly written." "We never," he wrote later, "had full confidence in the interrogation reports as historical sources." Former Commission counsel John Farmer warns that, even now, "reliance on KSM's version of events must be considered carefully."

The issue was and remains a huge problem, a blemish on the historical record. As the Report was being assembled, the Commission attempted to resolve the concern by inserting a paragraph or two on a page deep in the text—a health warning to the American public about the product of the CIA interrogations.

"Assessing the truth of statements by these witnesses," it read, "is challenging. . . . We have evaluated their statements carefully and have attempted to corroborate them with documents and statements of others."

*

THERE IS, however, a measure of considerable consolation. Long before they were caught, KSM and a
fellow operative *freely* volunteered much the same
version of events to an Arab television journalist. The
scoop of a lifetime had come to Yosri Fouda, former BBC
journalist and at the time star reporter for the satellite
channel Al Jazeera—the way scoops are supposed to
come, in a mysterious phone call to his London office.

Seven months after the 9/11 attacks, Fouda found himself listening to an anonymous male voice on the
telephone proposing "something special for the first
anniversary . . . exclusive stuff." Then, four days later,
came a fax offering to provide him with "addresses of
people" for a proposed documentary. Then another
phone call, asking him to fly to Pakistan. Fouda did so,
without confiding even in his boss.

After a harrowing process, an internal flight to
Karachi, a change of hotels, a journey by car and rick-
shaw, then—in another car, blindfolded, the final
leg—the reporter was ushered into a fourth floor apartment. The blindfold removed, Fouda found himself
looking into the eyes of the fugitive who was being
hunted more feverishly than anyone in the world except
Osama bin Laden.

KSM and Ramzi Binalshibh, a key accomplice, told
Fouda their story—the story, at any rate, as they wanted
to tell it—over a period of forty-eight hours. "I am the
head of the al Qaeda military committee," KSM said that
first night, "and Ramzi is the coordinator of the Holy
Tuesday operation. And yes, we did it."

After prayers together the following morning, the two
men shared their version of the preparation and
execution of 9/11. Their accounts largely match the
version subsequently extracted from KSM by the CIA.

Binalshibh pulled from an old suitcase dozens of mementos of the operation: information on Boeing airplanes, a navigation map of the American East Coast, illustrations on "How to perform sudden maneuvers"—a page covered in notations made, Binalshibh said, by the hijackers' leader, Mohamed Atta.

The interview over, blindfolded again, reporter Fouda was taken back to the airport. He had—and has—no doubt that the men he had met at the safe house in Karachi were who they said they were, that what they told him was credible. The three-page account of Fouda's work in the London *Sunday Times*, and his TV documentary, *The Road to 11 September*, on the Al Jazeera network, caused a sensation on the first anniversary of the attacks.

Unaccountably, 9/11 Commission staff failed to interview Fouda and mentioned his breakthrough interview only in an obscure footnote. It was included, however, in evidence presented during the military tribunal proceedings at Guantánamo. Two distinguished award-winning reporters, *The Wall Street Journal's* Ron Suskind and CNN contributor Peter Bergen, who both interviewed Yosri Fouda, found his reporting of the Karachi encounter authentic and compelling.

During the reporter's meeting with KSM and Binalshibh, a mysterious visitor had arrived, a man who could not be named. He was, Fouda was told, "a close companion of Sheikh Abu Abdullah, God protect him."

"Abu Abdullah" was one of the several names associates used to refer to Osama bin Laden.

Had al Qaeda been a company in the West, Fouda concluded from what he learned that day, KSM would have been its CEO. The post of chairman belonged to bin Laden.

TWENTY-TWO

AFTER FIRST MEETING TOWARD THE END OF THE ANTI-Soviet conflict in Afghanistan, Bin Laden and KSM had for years followed separate trajectories. Until the mid-1990s, KSM plotted terror with his nephew Yousef, then traveled the world networking with fellow jihadis. Bin Laden stayed most of the time in Sudan, presenting an innocent face to the world.

To *Time* magazine's Scott Macleod, who saw him there, the Saudi seemed "very calm, serene, almost like a holy man. He wanted to show that he was a businessman, and he was a legitimate businessman." Major road-building projects aside, bin Laden's enterprises included a trucks and machinery importing company, a tannery, and more than a million acres of farmland. Rumor had it, too, that bin Laden produced a fabulous sum to capitalize a bank.

Bin Laden the tycoon tended his business empire, but bin Laden the jihadi was never far away. To his guest-house in Khartoum came all manner of men, rich and poor, powerful and humble, all focused on Muslim causes. In 1992, following the collapse of the former Yugoslavia and the beginning of strife between Christians and Muslims, Bosnia became the cause of the moment. The embattled Bosnian regime accepted massive financial support from Saudi Arabia and volunteer fighters, Arab veterans of the war in Afghanistan.

Though bin Laden rarely ventured out of Sudan, he did visit Bosnia. Renate Flottau, of the German magazine *Der Spiegel*, encountered him, "a tall, striking Arab with piercing eyes and a long black beard," while waiting in President Alija Izetbegovic's anteroom. The Arab presented her with his card, but "Osama bin Laden" meant nothing to her then. In passable English, he described eagerly how he was bringing "holy warriors" into the country. The Bosnian president's staff treated him like a dignitary—bin Laden had reportedly been granted honorary citizenship.

Of the Arabs who rallied to the fight in Bosnia, three were to play key roles in the 9/11 operation. Khalid Sheikh Mohammed was in the country twice during the same period. Two others, Saudi fighters, went on to be 9/11 hijackers.

Through bin Laden, massive injections of funds also went to the Muslim separatists in Chechnya. It won him loyalty—there would be dozens of Chechens, it would be reported, among the holdouts who fought on with bin Laden, after 9/11, at Tora Bora.

In Sudan in the early 1990s those who plotted terror found a welcome. There was Ayman al-Zawahiri, the Egyptian doctor turned fundamentalist zealot who had been a close associate in Afghanistan. From Khartoum, he directed bombings and assassinations in his homeland. One attempt came close to killing then-President Hosni Mubarak himself.

There was also a younger man, whose name was never to be as familiar to the public as Zawahiri's. This was Abu Zubaydah, born in Saudi Arabia to a Palestinian father, still in his early twenties but already proving an effective manager of men and facilities. He was to be a key operative in the lead-up to 9/11.

At meetings in Khartoum, bin Laden sounded off regularly about the target he called the snake. "The snake is America, and we have to stop them. We have to cut their head off and stop what they are doing in the Horn of Africa."

In late 1992, in the Yemeni city of Aden, bombs exploded outside two hotels housing U.S. troops on their way to join the United Nations relief mission in Somalia—then, as now, a war-torn country on the east coast of Africa. Though botched—no American soldiers were killed—the attack was later linked to bin Laden.

Bin Laden would later claim that his men, fighting alongside Somalis, a year later played a leading role in the disastrous U.S. raid on a Somali warlord's headquarters. In that bloody fiasco, eighteen American soldiers were killed, seventy-eight wounded, and two Black Hawk helicopters shot down.

For a long time, there were no attacks in bin Laden's homeland, Saudi Arabia. Then, in 1995, a truck bomb exploded outside a National Guard facility in the capital, Riyadh. Seven were killed and sixty injured, and five of the dead were American Army and civilian trainers.

The only link to bin Laden at the time was that the four men accused of the bombing—who were executed—said they had read his writings on jihad. Information developed later, however, indicated that he supplied money to purchase the explosives, that the munitions were stored in a bin Laden warehouse, then moved onward to Saudi Arabia aboard a bin Laden–owned ship.

The attack, bin Laden has said since, was a noble act that "paved the way for the raising of voices of opposition against the American occupation from within the ruling family." He urged Saudis to "adopt every tactic to throw the Americans out of our territory."

Seven months later, a huge bomb exploded outside an American housing complex near Dhahran, in eastern Saudi Arabia. Inside at the time was a large number of troops, many of them personnel serving with the 4404th Fighter Wing at the time patrolling the no-fly zone over Iraq. Nineteen Americans were killed, 372 wounded.

It was the largest terrorist bomb ever to be used against Americans, more powerful than the device used in the 1983 bombing of the Marine barracks in Beirut, or a decade later in the destruction of the Alfred P. Murrah building in Oklahoma City. Who was behind the attack long remained the subject of controversy. A body of evidence indicated that Iran was responsible, but many believe bin Laden was at least complicit.

He had reportedly been in Qatar before the attack, arranging—again—for the purchase and delivery of explosives. In an interview the following year, he said al Qaeda had indeed been involved, that the bombers had been "heroes."

Even before the bombings in Saudi Arabia, bin Laden's life as an exile in Sudan had turned sour. The Saudi royals, and his own family, had tried to persuade him to change course. "They called me several times from the Kingdom," he recalled, "wanting me to return home, to talk about things. I refused. . . . They told me that the King would like me to act as intermediary between the different factions in Afghanistan. King Fahd himself called to try to win me over. . . . They sent my brother to try to convince me, but it didn't work."

The royals persuaded members of bin Laden's family—including his mother, his father's only surviving brother, and the half-brother who now headed the bin Laden company—to visit him in Sudan. "They beseeched him to stop his diatribes against Saudi and the Americans," a family source told the BBC. "Come back and we'll give you a responsible job in the company, one of the top five positions." When that suggestion was rebuffed, the Saudis' patience ran out.

That, at any rate, was the regime's official position. In the spring of 1994, the royal family declared bin Laden's citizenship revoked for "behavior that contradicts the Kingdom's interests." His family followed suit with a statement of "condemnation of all acts that Osama bin Laden may have committed." His share of the family fortune, which had earlier been placed in a trust, was sold off and placed in a frozen account.

Though this sounded draconian, the full picture may have been otherwise. The formal cutoff caused bin Laden only a temporary cash flow problem. Far into the future, he would have huge sums of money at his disposal.

Later, asked whether he had really been disowned, bin Laden would put his hand on his heart. "Blood," he said, "is thicker than water." The DGSE, France's intelligence service, which carefully monitored bin Laden over many years, took the view as late as 2000 that "Osama bin Laden has kept up contact with certain members of the family . . . even though it has officially said the contrary. One of his brothers would appear to be playing a role of intermediary in his professional contacts and the progress of his business."

It would be reported as late as 2006 that bin Laden's half-brother Yeslam had pledged to pay the cost of Osama's legal defense should he be captured. In the years before 9/11, female relatives were used to keep the money coming, perhaps because women in Saudi Arabia are treated as though they are invisible. "Some female members of bin Laden's own family have been sending cash from Saudi Arabia to his 'front' accounts in the Gulf,"

Vincent Cannistraro, former CIA chief of operations and analysis, told a congressional committee after 9/11.

Major funding also came from others. Soon after his funding had officially been cut off, according to the DGSE report, $4.5 million went to bin Laden from "Islamic Non-Governmental Organizations" in the Gulf. Five years later, it was discovered that "at least $3,000,000" believed to be for bin Laden had been funneled through Saudi Arabia's National Commercial Bank. Those behind the payments, the CIA's Cannistraro testified, had been "wealthy Saudis." When the Commercial Bank connection was cut, they switched to "siphoning off funds from their worldwide enterprises in creative and imaginative ways."

The former head of the DGSE's Security Intelligence department, Alain Chouet, who had regular access to secret intelligence, has said that considerable evidence "points to a number of private donors in the Arabian Peninsula, as well as to a number of banks and charities with money pumped in from Saudi or Gulf funds. . . . What was expensive wasn't the terrorist operations themselves but all that's required for recruiting terrorists: financing the mosques, the clubs, the imams, the religious schools, the training camps, the maintenance of 'martyrs' ' families."

Funding for bin Laden's operational needs—weapons, camps, living expenses, operatives' travel—never dried up. As a 9/11 Commission report on terrorist financing noted, al Qaeda's budget in the years before 9/11 amounted to $30 million a year. It was money raised almost entirely from donations, especially from "wealthy Saudi nationals."

The DGSE's Alain Chouet dismissed the revocation of bin Laden's Saudi citizenship as merely a "subterfuge aimed at the gullible—designed to cover a continuing clandestine relationship." For years to come at least—according to Chouet—the Saudi government covertly manipulated bin Laden to act in its strategic interests, as he once had in the Afghan war against the Soviets.

There is information, to be reported later in these pages, that the "wealthy Saudi nationals" who continued to fund bin Laden included members of the ruling royal family.

BY EARLY 1996, when U.S. ambassador to Sudan Timothy Carney sat down for talks with Sudanese foreign minister Ali Taha, the bin Laden problem was on the agenda. Washington, which had recently condemned Sudan for its "sponsorship of terror," claimed that bin Laden was directing and funding a number of terrorist organizations around the world.

Washington wanted Sudan to expel the troublesome exile. But to where? To the United States? What to do with him were he to be flown there? "We couldn't indict him then," President Clinton said after 9/11, "because he hadn't killed anyone in America." To Saudi Arabia? "We asked Saudi Arabia to take him," Clinton recalled. "The Saudis didn't want him back. . . . They were afraid it was too much of a hot potato."

Wherever bin Laden was to go, the Clinton White House believed it would be worthwhile just to get him out of Sudan. "My calculation was, 'It's going to take him a while to reconstitute,'" then–National Security Council counterterrorism director Steven Simon has said, "and that screws him up and buys time."

Following that line of thinking turned out to be a disastrous misjudgment. Not to have acted decisively against bin Laden in 1996, President Clinton would say—in private—after 9/11, was "probably the biggest mistake of my presidency." In Sudan, as former CIA station chief Milton Bearden has said, "perhaps we could have controlled or monitored him more closely, to see what he was doing."

The United States did not do that. It sat idly by when, in May that year, bin Laden returned to the remote, tragically chaotic country that he knew well and where Washington had virtually no leverage—Afghanistan. Allowing that to happen, the CIA's Bearden sardonically remarked, was "probably the best move since the Germans put Lenin in a boxcar and sent him to St. Petersburg in 1917."

"WE WERE WHISKED to a chartered Learjet," his son Omar has recalled. "My father and his party were treated as dignitaries, with no need for the formalities of passports and customs. Besides my father and me, there were only eight other male passengers. Brother Sayf Adel, my father's security chief, and Mohammed Atef, my father's best friend and top commander, were traveling with us."

The plane passed through Saudi airspace without difficulty, refueled in Iran, and landed at the eastern Afghan city of Jalalabad, near the border with Pakistan. Other members of bin Laden's family and entourage followed months later, again aboard a chartered jet.

"Our plane had two configurations: with fifty-six passengers and with seventy-nine," the captain recalled. "They wanted eighty-four. They asked how many extra seats we wanted. They installed the seats overnight. . . . We flew women, children, clothes, rickshaws, old bikes, mattresses, blankets."

After a brief stay in Jalalabad courtesy of a local warlord, bin Laden set up base for a while in the mountains at Tora Bora. Family members thought it a desolate place, but he called it "our new home," was excited to be back at a place he had known while fighting the Soviets.

A major concern, for some time, was how the Taliban—then gaining the upper hand in the civil war—would view his presence. Then their leader, Mullah Omar, sent word that he was welcome. It was by no means religious and ideological compatibility alone that was to ensure bin Laden a lasting welcome. Through him, the 9/11 Commission would calculate, between $10 and $20 million a year was to flow to the Taliban.

Visibly relaxed once he knew he had sanctuary, bin Laden began talking with his son Omar about his "mission in life." "I was put on this earth by God for a specific reason," he said. "My only reason for living is to fight the jihad and to make sure there is justice for the Muslims." He ranted on about America and Israel, and it was evident that there was no limit to what he imagined he could achieve.

"First," he said with the supreme self-confidence that only boundless faith or delusion can bring, "we obliterate America. By that I don't mean militarily. We can destroy America from within by making it economically weak, until its markets collapse. . . . That's what we did with Russia. When that happens, they will have no interest in supplying Israel with arms. . . . We only have to be patient. . . . This is God's plan."

The man who voiced this astounding ambition now lived in a makeshift wooden cabin. There bin Laden spent much of his time, reading deeply into his hundreds of books, most of them religious tomes, never far from his prayer beads, his copy of the Qur'an, and a radio that picked up the BBC's broadcasts from London. At his side, always, was his Kalashnikov assault rifle.

Bin Laden was interested in the techniques of mass communication, the distribution of propaganda by tape cassette and fax machine. He would shortly acquire a state-of-the-art satellite telephone. When the technology became available, his operatives would use the Internet as an everyday tool. Omar noticed that his father now spent much time recording his thoughts on a dictating machine.

The fruit of his latest thinking came in August 1996, with a fax transmission to the office of *al-Quds al-Arabi*— or *The Arab Jerusalem*—an Arabic-language newspaper published in London. It was a twelve-thousand-word message from the mountain, in bin Laden's words from "the summit of the Hindu Kush," one that at the time got little coverage in the West. Across the Middle East, where hundreds of thousands of copies were distributed in cassette form, it had a major impact.

Lengthy, couched in archaic language, replete with religious references, this was bin Laden's "Declaration of Jihad against the Americans occupying the Land of the Two Holy Places."

"Praise be to Allah, we seek his help and ask for his pardon," the declaration began, then launched into a catalogue of the iniquities imposed on Muslims by "the Zionist-Crusaders alliance." The greatest of the aggressions, bin Laden wrote, was the presence of the "American invaders" in Saudi Arabia, followed by U.S. exploitation of Arab oil and the "annexing" of Arab land by Israel.

"After Faith," he went on, "there is no more important duty than pushing the American enemy out of the holy land." Addressing U.S. Defense Secretary William Perry in person, he warned that his recruits to the cause made formidable enemies. "These youths love death as you love life. They inherit dignity, pride, courage, generosity, truthfulness and sacrifice. They are most effective and steadfast in war. . . . They have no intent but to enter Paradise by killing you."

Around the time he issued this proclamation of punishment to come, bin Laden sat down to confer with Khalid Sheikh Mohammed.

WHETHER THE TWO men had seen each other in the recent past remains unclear. According to KSM, he had hoped to meet with bin Laden in Sudan, but settled for seeing his military aide Atef instead. One intelligence lead suggests that he and bin Laden had traveled somewhere together—perhaps on one of the trips they both made to Bosnia. It seems certain, though, that they got together at Tora Bora in mid-1996.

At the meeting, which Atef also attended, KSM came up with a raft of ideas for terrorist attacks, most of them involving airliners. Atef, too, had recently been discussing the idea of attacking aircraft. Terrorist attacks on planes had usually followed a pattern—hijack a plane, have it land in a compliant nation-state, then make demands (often for the release of captured comrades). By the mid-1990s, however, bin Laden operatives had little prospect of finding a "friendly" place to land. For the men meeting at Tora Bora, the focus was simply on destroying planes.

Atef apparently favored finding ways to blow up airliners in midair, as in the 1988 downing of Pan Am 103 over Scotland. He and bin Laden listened, however, as KSM proposed a very different concept—using hijacked planes as weapons.

There are two versions of what he suggested. According to KSM himself, the notion he proposed was ambitious in the extreme. Ten planes would be hijacked, on the same day, to be crashed into target buildings on both coasts of the United States. He himself, as commander, would force a landing at an airport, kill all male passengers, then deliver a speech assailing American support for Israel and "repressive" regimes around the world. This, as the 9/11 Commission put it, would have been "theater, a spectacle of destruction with KSM as the self-cast star—the super-terrorist."

According to another detainee, KSM's proposal was more modest, a suggestion that the World Trade Center should be targeted again—this time not with a bomb but by small planes packed with explosives. This, the detainee said, prompted bin Laden to suggest a grander vision. "Why do you use an ax," he supposedly mused, "when you can use a bulldozer?"

KSM thought it was important to target civilian landmarks. Were only military or government buildings hit, he surmised, ordinary Americans "would not focus on the atrocities that America is committing by supporting Israel against the Palestinian people." The purpose of a further strike on the World Trade Center was to "wake people up."

KSM's proposal may have been premature. He got the impression that bin Laden's priority concern remained the situation in Saudi Arabia. He told KSM he was "not convinced" of the practicality of the planes operation. For now, the discussion went no further.

Nevertheless, a further strike on the World Trade Center apparently remained on the drawing board. Months after the meeting at Tora Bora, a bin Laden operative in Europe traveled to America and shot videotape of various prominent buildings—including the Twin Towers. The footage, seized after 9/11, included shot after shot of the towers, taken from multiple angles.

There were five tapes, with pictures not only of the Trade Center but of the Statue of Liberty, the Brooklyn Bridge, San Francisco's Golden Gate Bridge, Chicago's Sears Tower, and Disneyland.

At his meeting with bin Laden, KSM had suggested

sending operatives "to study in the U.S. flight institutes." Whether or not bin Laden ordered it, it seems that someone in the terrorist milieu was already making such preparations. The FBI had received information that "individuals with terrorist connections had requested and received training in the technical aspects of aviation."

One such individual was a young Saudi who, after a trip to Arizona to learn English, returned home seeming a "different person." He grew a full beard, shunned established friends, and spent most of his spare time reading books on religion and aviation. Then, in 1996, he returned to the Grand Canyon State—to learn to fly. The twenty-four-year-old seemed unsure of himself in the cockpit, even frightened, but he was to return again and again to flight school, even after he got his commercial pilot's license. The Saudi was Hani Hanjour, who in 2001 would fly a hijacked Boeing 757 into the Pentagon.

Mohamed Atta, who was to lead the 9/11 operation, turned twenty-seven the year of the Tora Bora meeting. In Germany, where he was now studying, he struck people—even those familiar with Muslim practices—as religiously obsessed.

IN AFGHANISTAN in 1996 bin Laden had asked the British reporter Robert Fisk to come to see him for a second time—less than three years after their first meeting in Sudan. The Saudi was nearing forty now and visibly aging. His beard was longer and starting to turn gray, the lines around his eyes deeper.

It was night when bin Laden met with the reporter. He talked on and on of how Saudi Arabia had become "an American colony," of how the "evils" of the Middle East were rooted in the policies of the United States. "Resistance against America will spread in many, many places in Muslim countries," he said. "We must drive out the Americans."

In the flickering light of a paraffin lamp, when his interviewee agreed to be photographed, Fisk saw in bin Laden's face the trace of a smile and what looked like vanity. He thought the man "possessed of that quality which leads men to war: total self-conviction. In the years to come I would see others manifest this dangerous characteristic . . . but never the fatal self-resolve of Osama bin Laden."

PART V

PERPETRATORS

TWENTY-THREE

SEVEN THOUSAND MILES AND TWO CONTINENTS AWAY, very few people had yet sensed the real danger in the man.

According to the then-head of the CIA's Counterterrorist Center, Winston Wiley, in a recently released 9/11 Commission interview, President Clinton's administration actually reduced the focus on counterterrorism. Former Clinton officials, and the President himself, have insisted otherwise. One can only report claim and counterclaim, and cite the record.

Two months into the Clinton presidency, in 1993, bin Laden had been characterized in a CIA document as merely an "independent actor who sometimes works with other individuals or governments . . . to promote militant Islamic causes throughout the region." What the Agency told the White House ranged from dismissing bin Laden as "a flake" or—closer to reality—as a "terrorist financier," and the "Ford Foundation" of Sunni Muslim extremism.

In 1995, when the evidence had yet to link bin Laden firmly to any specific attack, a formal Clinton order—aimed at cutting off funding from named terrorist organizations—did not mention him.

In 1995 and 1996, however, the President made nine

speeches mentioning terrorism or calling for tough action. He also issued a Presidential Decision Directive—PDD-39—designed to combat terrorism that targeted the United States. It included, for the first time, a provision for what was to become known as rendition, the forcible removal to the United States of captured terrorist suspects. Policy on the subject was henceforth to be coordinated from the White House.

Anthony Lake, Clinton's first national security adviser, and Richard Clarke—who eventually became national coordinator for counterterrorism—had been badgering the CIA for fuller information on bin Laden. One CIA official recalled having thought that Lake was positively "foaming at the mouth" about him. "It just seemed unlikely to us," Clarke recalled, "that this man who had his hand in so many seemingly unconnected organizations was just a donor, a philanthropist of terror."

CIA Director James Woolsey, who ran the agency until 1995, conceded after 9/11 that there was a period in the 1990s when U.S. intelligence was simply "asleep at the wheel." After the Clinton directive, which called for improving the agencies' performance, the CIA and the FBI responded.

In early 1996, with Lake's approval, a small group of CIA officers and analysts were formed into a unit that focused solely on bin Laden. Only a dozen strong at first, its number would in time grow to forty or fifty people— most of them women—supplemented by a small number of FBI employees. The Bureau staffers were there in the name of liaison, but the relationship was less than happy. The CIA attitude toward the FBI contingent was so hostile, one arriving Bureau supervisor thought, that he felt as though he had "walked into a buzz saw."

That said, the new unit did remarkable work. Working from a base away from CIA headquarters, near a shopping complex, they became passionately committed to the pursuit of bin Laden. They worked inordinate hours, rarely taking a day off, for a zealot of a boss who as often as not turned up for work at four in the morning. This was Michael Scheuer, whose idea the unit had been in the first place. Reflecting the CIA's concept of bin Laden as a mere financier, the bureaucracy initially gave the project the acronym CTC-TFL—for Counter-terrorism Center–Terrorist Financial Links. Scheuer saw the mission as far broader, more operational, and its function gradually shifted from data gathering to locating bin Laden and planning his capture. He changed the unit's moniker to "Alec Station," after one of his children.

Working around the clock, the unit began to get a clearer sense of what confronted them. Bin Laden's August 1996 "Declaration of Jihad" brought Scheuer up short. "My God," he thought as he perused the transcript, "it sounds like Thomas Jefferson. There was no ranting in it. . . . [It] read like our Declaration of Independence—it had that tone. It was a frighteningly reasoned document. These were substantive, tangible issues."

Scheuer concluded there and then that bin Laden was a "truly dangerous, dangerous man," and began saying so as often and as loudly as he could. Though for many months to come there were no new terror attacks, bin Laden's megaphone utterances, in interviews with journalists and in a second formal declaration in February 1998, could not have been clearer.

In the second declaration, presented as a religious ruling and cosigned by Zawahiri and others, he enumer-ated Muslim grievances and declared the killing of Americans—"civilians and military"—a duty for all Muslims. Time after time, with increasing clarity, he emphasized that civilians were vulnerable. "They chose this government and voted for it despite their knowledge of its crimes in Palestine, Lebanon and Iraq and in other places." And: "If they are killing our civilians, occupying our lands . . . and they don't spare any one of us, why spare any one of them?"

IN THE WAKE of Clinton's landmark 1996 Presidential Decision, the heads of relevant U.S. agencies—the Counterterrorism Security Group—had been mulling a possible "snatch" operation to capture bin Laden and bring him to the United States. With satellite surveillance as well as human intelligence, the CIA was to some extent able to track his movements.

Some valuable information came from eavesdropping on the Compact-M satellite phone he had purchased in 1996—number 00-873-682505331. Bin Laden was no longer at Tora Bora, but spending most nights with his family at a training camp near Kandahar.

The CIA developed a plan. A team of Afghans working with the Agency would grab bin Laden while he was sleeping, roll him up in a rug, spirit him to a desert airstrip, and bundle him on board a CIA plane. He would be flown to New York aboard a civilian version of a C-130 airplane within which would be a container, inside which would be a dentist's chair designed for a very tall man.

The chair would be equipped with padded restraints designed to avoid chafing the captive's skin. In the event bin Laden had to be gagged, the tape used would have just the right amount of adhesive to avoid excessive irritation to his face and beard. There would be a doctor on the plane, with sophisticated medical equipment.

The Agency's plan was discussed, modified, and remodified. There were rehearsals. Intelligence agency attorneys conferred solemnly about the provisions for bin

Laden's safety after capture. Then, in May 1998, the operation was scrapped.

CIA director Tenet has said he was responsible for the cancellation. The White House's Richard Clarke has said he thought it "half-assed," that he seconded the decision. In an internal memo, supposedly written at Tenet's direction, Alec Station's Scheuer wrote that the Clinton cabinet had been worried about potential fallout were bin Laden or others to die during the operation.

Scheuer thought the plan had been "perfect," that it should have gone ahead. According to him, it long remained difficult to persuade either the White House, or his superiors at the CIA, or the Defense Department, of the gravity of the bin Laden threat. "They could not believe that this tall Saudi with a beard, squatting around a campfire, could be a threat to the United States of America."

For any who could not see the danger, any last illusion was removed just after 3:30 A.M. Washington time on August 7, 1998. At that moment, a two-thousand-pound truck bomb exploded behind the American embassy in the Kenyan capital of Nairobi. Two hundred ninety-one people were killed, forty-four of them embassy employees. The embassy's city center location compounded the carnage, and some four thousand were injured. The five-story building was damaged beyond repair, an adjacent secretarial school totally destroyed.

Four minutes later at the U.S. embassy in Dar es Salaam, the capital of neighboring Tanzania, a terrorist detonated another truck bomb. Eleven were killed and eighty-five injured—lower casualties than in Nairobi because the building was on the city's outskirts. The explosion left part of the U.S. embassy roofless and damaged the missions of two other countries.

In terms of overall casualty figures, this had been the

worst-ever terrorist attack on Americans. Clues as to who was responsible came fast, and pointed straight to the bin Laden organization. Instead of being blown to pieces, one of two suicide bombers in the Nairobi attack had jumped out and run at the last moment. He had suffered only minor injuries, and was captured within days. It emerged that the bomber was a Saudi, had trained at one of the camps in Afghanistan, and had met with bin Laden several times. He had believed all along that his mission was for bin Laden.

The Saudi gave investigators the number of a telephone outside Kenya that his controllers had told him he could call, and he had called it both the night before and an hour before the bombing. Using his satellite phone, bin Laden had also called the number before and after the attack. The number—967-1-200578—was a crucial lead, one that will become pivotal as this story unfolds.

Of the five men eventually tried and convicted in the United States for the bombings, the reported statement of another man, Saudi-born but of Palestinian origin, said it all. "I did it all for the cause of Islam," Mohamed Odeh told interrogators. Osama bin Laden "is my leader, and I obey his orders."

In Afghanistan on the morning of the bombings, bin Laden had been listening intently to the radio. When the news came through, his son Omar thought his father more "excited and happy" than he had ever seen him. "His euphoria spread quickly to his commanders and throughout the ranks, with everyone laughing and congratulating each other."

A Canadian teenager whose family had joined the jihadis, Abdurahman Khadr, witnessed the jubilation. "The leader of the guesthouse went outside and brought juice for like everybody. Jugs and jugs of juice. He was just giving it out. 'Celebrate, everybody!' And people were even making jokes that we should do this more often. You know, we'd get free juice."

Asked by reporters about the bombings, bin Laden vacillated between obfuscation and claiming credit. "Only God knows the truth," he would say, while praising the bombers as "real men . . . Our job is to instigate and by the grace of God we did that." Nairobi had been picked, he said, because "the greatest CIA center in East Africa is located at this embassy." American "plots" against countries in the region, he said, had been hatched there.

There appeared to be an opportunity for the United States to retaliate—or, with the niceties of international law in mind—"to respond." Bin Laden, the CIA learned, was shortly to attend a gathering of several hundred men at one of the training camps. On the day of his visit, it was decided, U.S. vessels—mostly submarines—would fire salvos of Tomahawk cruise missiles at six sites in Afghanistan. The camps aside, missiles would also strike a bin Laden–financed pharmaceutical factory in Sudan. The CIA believed it was producing the ingredients for nerve gas.

On the appointed day, August 20, the go-ahead was given. Security was exceptionally tight, with one significant exception. Because the missiles were to overfly Pakistan, it was deemed necessary to inform the Pakistani military. To avoid provoking an international incident, though, the Pakistan army was to be told—not consulted—and at the very last minute. The vice chairman of the Joint Chiefs of Staff, General Joseph Ralston, broke the news to a top Pakistani commander over dinner when the missiles were already on their way.

In Washington, Clinton went on television to tell the nation of the action he had taken. "Our target was terror," he said. "Our mission was clear: to strike at the network of radical groups affiliated with and funded by Osama bin Laden."

That was a circumlocution, to avoid mentioning publicly the fact that Clinton had signed memoranda designed to get around the long-standing legal ban on planned assassinations. After Kenya, however, the President was "intently focused," as he later wrote, "on capturing or killing [bin Laden] and with destroying al Qaeda."

In that, the U.S. attack failed miserably. The targets were hit and destroyed, and some people were killed at the camp where bin Laden was supposed to be. The man himself, however, remained very much alive. The factory in Sudan was destroyed, but there never was any proof that it had been more than a legitimate plant producing medicines. The CIA's intelligence had been shaky at best.

The strikes had been expensive in more ways than one. At $750,000 each, just the cost of the sixty-five Tomahawks fired amounted to about $49 million. The embassy bombings in Africa, to which the missiles had responded, are said to have cost around $10,000. Worse by far, the missile strikes and the failure to get bin Laden proved to be a propaganda victory for the intended target. Across the Muslim world, people began sporting Osama bin Laden T-shirts. Bin Laden's life had been spared, his followers were convinced, thanks to the direct intervention of Allah.

The truth was more mundane, as his son Omar revealed in 2009. Shortly before the strikes, he recalled, his father had received "a highly secret communication." "He had been forewarned," former U.S. Defense Secretary William Cohen was to tell 9/11 Commission staff, that "the intelligence [service] in Pakistan had a line in to him." The tight U.S. security had not been tight enough, a failing that one day in the distant future would be remedied—fatally for the target.

If the name Osama bin Laden had been slow to penetrate the American consciousness, it had now become—as it would remain— a fixture. "In 1996 he was on the radar screen," said Sandy Berger, who had succeeded Anthony Lake as national security adviser. "In 1998 he was the radar screen."

Before the embassy bombings, bin Laden had been secretly indicted merely for "conspiracy to attack." After the bombings, a two-hundred-page public indictment charged him with a litany of alleged crimes. A $5 million reward was offered for information leading to his arrest. The figure would rise to $25 million after 9/11, and was later doubled.

At the CIA after the bombings, combating the bin Laden threat was raised to "Tier 0" priority, one of the very highest levels. "We are at war," Director Tenet declared in a memo soon after. "I want no resources or people spared in this effort." President Clinton, for his part, signed a further "lethal force" order designed to ensure it was possible to circumvent the ban on targeted assassination. Nevertheless, and though operations against bin Laden were planned repeatedly during the two years that remained of the Clinton administration, none got the go-ahead.

Since 9/11, there have been bitter recriminations. "Policy makers seemed to want to have things both ways," Tenet wrote. "They wanted to hit bin Laden but without endangering U.S. troops or putting at significant risk our diplomatic relations."

In one year alone, former bin Laden unit head Scheuer wrote in 2008, the CIA presented Clinton with "two chances to capture bin Laden and eight chances to kill him using U.S. military air power." The blame for failing to act on such occasions, according to Scheuer, lay in part with the White House and in part with his own boss.

Quoting Clinton aides, he said, "Tenet consistently denigrated the targeting data on bin Laden, causing the President and his team to lose confidence in the hard-won intelligence . . . it spared him from ever having to explain the awkward fall-out if an attempt to get bin Laden failed."

Scheuer's most savage barb, however, was aimed at the President and aides Berger and Clarke. They, Scheuer would have it, "cared little about protecting Americans and were not manly enough to order such an attack, and their moral cowardice resulted in three thousand deaths on 9/11." The words "moral cowardice," in the context of Clinton and his people, occur no fewer than six times in Scheuer's book.

Richard Clarke, for his part, thought the CIA had proved "pathetically unable to accomplish the mission. . . . I still do not understand why it was impossible for the United States to find a competent group of Afghans, Americans, third-country nationals, or some combination, who could locate bin Laden in Afghanistan and kill him."

Comments by the former President and Berger on the failure to get bin Laden remain in closed Commission files. As recently as 2006, however, Clinton continued to insist that he "authorized the CIA to get groups together to try to kill him . . . I *tried*." The Commission's executive director, Philip Zelikow, agreed that one of the President's secret orders—still withheld today—was indeed a "kill authority." All the same, the Report noted, Clinton and Berger had worried lest "attacks that missed bin Laden could enhance his stature and win him new recruits."

Had the world been able to witness the way bin Laden conducted himself in August 1998, when told of the death and damage the missile attacks had caused, his image would surely not have been enhanced.

"My father," his son Omar recalled, "was struck by the most violent, uncontrollable rage. His face turned red and his eyes flashed as he began rushing about, repeatedly quoting the same verse from the Qur'an, The God kills the ones who attacked! . . . May God kill the ones who attacked! How could anyone attack Muslims? How could anyone attack Muslims? Why would anyone attack Muslims!' "

For a while after the missile attacks, bin Laden went to ground, rarely slept in the same place two nights running. He stopped using his satellite phone, which up to now had been a boon to those tracking him. Within a day of the U.S. onslaught, though, he had his military aide Atef risk a phone call to Abdel Atwan, editor of the London-based newspaper *Al-Quds al-Arabi*.

Having survived the missile strike, Atef said, bin Laden "wished to send this message to U.S. President Bill Clinton: that he would avenge this attack in a spectacular way and would deal a blow to America that would shake it to its very foundations, a blow it had never experienced before."

After the attack on the American embassy in Kenya, the bomber who had run for his life at the last moment—and fallen into U.S. hands—had said something both sinister and significant. A senior accomplice, he told his questioners, had confided that al Qaeda also had targets in America. "But things are not ready yet," the accomplice had added. "We don't have everything prepared yet."

NOT READY YET, but the concept was there. In late 1998 or soon after, Osama bin Laden summoned Khalid Sheikh Mohammed. Two years after rejecting KSM's idea of hijacking planes and crashing them into buildings, he now said he thought it "could work."

KSM, it seems, may have been back in the bin Laden camp for some time. An intelligence report suggests that he may have flown into Kenya, using an alias, before the bombing of the U.S. embassy there. There is a report that, two weeks later, he led a decoy operation designed to conceal bin Laden's whereabouts when America struck the training camps. It had been the East Africa bombings, KSM would say under interrogation, that persuaded him that bin Laden really was committed to attacking the United States.

The idea of flying hijacked airplanes into U.S. targets, bin Laden said at the renewed discussion, had his people's "full support." KSM thought it was probably Mohammed Atef, the military commander, who had led him to change his mind. Asked to run the operation, KSM agreed.

The initial notion was still to seize a number of American airliners and crash them into U.S. targets, so far as possible simultaneously. At a first targeting meeting, bin Laden said his hope was to hit the Pentagon, the White House, and the Capitol in Washington. The World Trade Center, one of KSM's preferences, was apparently raised later. Bin Laden had several operatives in mind for the hijackings and hoped KSM would come up with others.

Early in 1999, the "military committee" met and agreed once and for all that the project should go ahead. KSM thought it would take about two years to plan and execute. Those in the know began speaking of it as the "planes operation."

At some point that year, Omar bin Laden was taken aside by Abu Haadi, an aide of his father to whom he was close. Omar, now eighteen, had over a period become disillusioned, and was yearning for a way to get out of Afghanistan. Now Abu Haadi had a warning for him. "I have heard talk," he said, "that there is something very big in the works. You need to leave."

The something, he suggested, was "gigantic."

AT ABOUT THE TIME bin Laden summoned KSM, in the United States *Forbes* magazine published a thoughtful piece by the writer Peggy Noonan. "History," she wrote,

has handed us one of the easiest rides in all the story of Man. It has handed us a wave of wealth so broad and deep it would be almost disorienting if we thought about it a lot, which we don't. . . . How will the future play out? . . . Something's up. And deep down, where the body meets the soul, we are fearful. . . . Everything's wonderful, but a world is ending and we sense it. . . . What are the odds it will happen? Put it another way: What are the odds it will not? Low. Non-existent, I think.

When you consider who is gifted and crazed with rage . . . when you think of the terrorist places and the terrorist countries . . . who do they hate most? The Great Satan, the United States. What is its most important place? Some would say Washington. I would say the great city of the United States is the great city of the world, the dense 10-mile-long island called Manhattan . . .

If someone does the big, terrible thing to New York or Washington, there will be a lot of chaos. . . . The psychic blow—and that is what it will be as people absorb it, a blow, an insult that reorders and changes—will shift our perspective and priorities, dramatically, and for longer than a while. . . . We must press government officials to face the big, terrible thing. They know it could happen tomorrow.

TWENTY-FOUR

In Afghanistan about this time, Osama bin Laden was seriously injured—horseback riding. "The mighty United States cannot kill me," he quipped as he lay in bed recovering, "while one little horse nearly killed me. Life is very mysterious."

The fall curbed his activities for months, but the 9/11 plot advanced. The first hurdle, a major one, was to find suitable candidates to lead the hijack teams. All the terrorists would need visas to enter the United States, and some would require flying skills.

Bin Laden had four men in mind, two Yemenis and two Saudis. It could be difficult for applicants from Yemen to get U.S. visas, not because of concerns about terrorism but because impoverished Yemenis were thought more likely to be would-be immigrants. Bin Laden's two Yemenis were to apply in vain, leading KSM to suggest dividing the operation into two parts. The Yemenis, he thought, could spearhead a group assigned to U.S. airliners on the Pacific route, not flying planes into targets but exploding them in midair. Bin Laden, however, eventually decided the entire thing was getting too complicated.

For a while, the two Saudis were the only two remaining candidates for the 9/11 operation. Khalid al-Mihdhar, aged about twenty-four, and Nawaf al-Hazmi, a year younger, had grown up in well-to-do families in Mecca, and may have been boyhood friends. Mihdhar, whose family originated in Yemen, was married to a young Yemeni woman whose family was directly involved in terrorism. His wife's family, as things would turn out, was related to another of the future 9/11 conspirators. Once again, just as Yousef the Chemist was related to KSM, terror ran in the family.

Young as they were, Mihdhar and Hazmi could claim to be veteran jihadis. Both had fought in Bosnia. A Saudi friend, "Jihad Ali" Azzam, had been killed the previous year driving the truck used to bomb the U.S. embassy in Kenya. Inspired by his sacrifice, according to KSM, they, too, yearned to die in a martyrdom operation against an American target. It was easy for them—as Saudis—to acquire U.S. visas, and they did so of their own accord even before traveling to Afghanistan.

Mihdhar and Hazmi had sworn *bayat*—the oath of loyalty to bin Laden—on previous visits. KSM, who himself put off taking the oath because he wanted to retain a measure of independence, later described the procedure to CIA interrogators.

Little ceremony was involved. A man pledging loyalty would stand with bin Laden and intone: "I swear allegiance to you, to listen and obey, in good times and bad, and to accept the consequences myself. I swear allegiance to you, for *jihad* and *hijrah* [redemption] . . . I swear allegiance to you and to die in the cause of God." A shake of the hand with bin Laden, and the oath was done. More than as a promise to any mortal, it was seen as a man's commitment to his God.

The Saudi pair notwithstanding, there was still a woeful shortage of suitable recruits for the 9/11 project. One day in 1999, Omar bin Laden has recalled, his father held a meeting to impress on his fighters "the joys of martyrdom, how it was the greatest honor for a Muslim to give his life to the cause of Islam." Osama even called his own sons together to tell them that there was a list on the wall of the mosque "for men who volunteer to be suicide bombers."

When one of the younger brothers ran off to sign the list, Omar dared to speak out in protest. His father's retort was brusque. Omar and the other sons, bin Laden said, held "no more a place in my heart than any other man or boy." "My father," Omar thought, "hated his enemies more than he loved his sons."

Few of the fighters who signed up for martyrdom, however, had the qualifications to enter and operate in enemy territory—the alien land of the United States. Perhaps, bin Laden ventured, KSM would locate such candidates in the area he knew well, the Gulf States. The evidence indicates that KSM traveled even further afield that year, to Italy and—on more than one occasion—to Germany. Not just to Germany but to Hamburg, the second largest city in the country, a port teeming with foreigners—including, we now know, three of the future pilot hijackers and a key accomplice.

THE FIRST OF THOSE four Arabs to arrive in Germany is today a household name—more so, bin Laden aside, than anyone involved in 9/11. His name was Mohamed Mohamed el-Amir Awad el-Sayed Atta. His friends knew him as Amir, but in the public memory he is—indelibly—Mohamed Atta.

Egyptian-born, Atta had come to Europe in 1992 at the age of twenty-three, after studying architecture at Cairo University. His father, a lawyer who long worked for EgyptAir, has said that Atta's mother—from whom he was divorced—"never stopped pampering him," treated him as if he were a girl. The boy would snuggle up on his mother's lap, by one report, even in his teens. As a student, a contemporary remembered, he still had "child feelings, innocent, virgin." He became emotional, according to another, if an insect was killed. Islamic terrorists, Atta said as a young adult, were "brainless, irresponsible."

The Amirs also had daughters, bright, achieving young women—one qualified as a cardiologist, the other as a professor of geology. Their brother did all right at university, but his father nurtured higher aspirations for him. When he learned about two German teachers, visitors in Cairo for an educational exchange program, he arranged a meeting. The couple, Uwe and Doris Michaels, promptly invited young Atta to come to Hamburg and stay in their home. He had a grasp of German—having done a course in the language in Cairo—and accepted. He flew to Germany, and stayed with the Michaelses for about six months.

The couple rapidly discovered that their houseguest was "exceedingly religious . . . never missed his five prayer sessions per day." Atta insisted on preparing his own meals. Impossible to use the family's pots and pans, he said—they had previously been used to cook pork. The young man, they saw, was also a prude. He left the room while showing a video of his own sister's wedding—because it included a belly-dancer wearing a flesh-colored gown. If anything even a little risqué cropped up on television, he covered his eyes. If his middle-aged hostess failed to wear a blouse that covered her arms, the atmosphere became "unpleasant."

The family tolerated all this until the Ramadan day-time fasting period in early 1993, when Atta's obsession with religious observance became too much. After trying to put up with his nocturnal activity—hour after hour of cooking and moving about the house—the Michaelses asked him to leave. To their son, who was living at home, he had become "that person"—someone he didn't want to have anything to do with. Through it all, though, Doris Michaels has recalled, there had been no hint of violence in their student visitor. The problems of the Middle East, he would say, should be resolved peacefully with "words, not weapons."

When he did move to other accommodations, Atta's habits and prejudices again led to clashes. No one, least of all Westerners, could fail to notice his religious zeal and aversion to everything to do with female sexuality. His professor, however, who was familiar with Arab culture, thought Atta merely "a dear human being." He applied himself to his urban engineering and planning course at university, made periodic trips back to the Middle East, and the years slipped by.

In the fall of 1995, another young Arab arrived in Hamburg by ship. He said his name was Ramzi Omar, claimed to be a Sudanese student, spun a tale about having been imprisoned and tortured at home, and asked for political asylum. That was not his real name, and his story was a fabrication. Even so, "Omar" found a way to establish himself in Germany. He finagled phony documentation for himself as a student, then left for his real homeland—Yemen—only to return under his true name, Ramzi Binalshibh.

Though he said he aspired to an economics degree, Binalshibh studied almost not at all. Those who knew him described him as "in love with life . . . charming . . . very funny, made lots of jokes." All the same, he shared Atta's traits. At classes, he objected to the sight of women wearing blouses that showed cleavage. He thought that "disgusting." What distracted Binalshibh during math lessons, a fellow student recalled, was reading the Qur'an under the desk. He was more cheerful about his religion than Atta, to be sure, but faith was at the core of his being.

So it was, too, for a newcomer who was to become Atta's constant companion. Marwan al-Shehhi, just eighteen when he arrived from the United Arab Emirates, was the son of a muezzin—the man who called the faithful to prayer at the mosque in his hometown. In his teen years, before his father's recent death, he had sometimes had the task of switching on the prayer tape for his father.

Friends would remember Shehhi as "a regular guy," like Binalshibh "happy . . . always laughing and telling one joke after another," "dreamy . . . slightly spoiled." Spoiled not least because, after just six months in the military, he had been sent off to study marine engineering in Europe on an army scholarship of $4,000 a month. Happy perhaps, but—an echo of Atta and Binalshibh—he could "explode" with anger on "seeing a male friend looking at a woman." Shehhi never actually spoke to women unless he had to.

Probably thanks to his father the muezzin, Shehhi could recite Islamic texts on cue. Even at his tender age he yearned for the pleasures of Paradise, imagined himself sitting in the shade on the bank of a broad river flowing with honey. Binalshibh, for his part, would exclaim, "What is this life good for? The Paradise is much nicer." To these young men, heaven was no distant concept or possible consolation for the inevitability of death, but a real destination of choice.

The fourth man in the group, who arrived the same month as Shehhi, at first seems not to fit the pattern. Ziad Jarrah, who flew in with his cousin, had grown up in cosmopolitan Lebanon. The son of a well-to-do civil servant and a mother who worked as a French teacher, he had interesting relatives. A great-uncle, it would be reported after 9/11, had been recruited by a department of the former East Germany that handled espionage— and by Libyan intelligence. A cousin, according to *The New York Times* in 2009, confessed to having long spied for Israel—while posing as a supporter of the Palestinian cause.

If such odd details impinge not at all on Jarrah's own story, other factors marked him out. Though his family was Sunni Muslim, he had been sent to the best Christian schools. He had regularly skipped prayers, shown no special interest in religion, and was no stranger to alcohol. "Once," said Salim, the cousin who traveled to Germany with him, "we drank so much beer we couldn't go straight on a bike."

Jarrah enjoyed partying, thought the nightclubs in Europe tame compared to what he was used to in Lebanon—and he liked girls. When he met a strikingly lovely young Turkish woman, within weeks of arriving in Germany, he rapidly won her away from a current boyfriend. He and Aysel Sengün became lovers, beginning an on-off affair that was to endure until his death on 9/11.

For all that, and within months of his arrival, the twenty-two-yearold Jarrah also got religion—and a measure of political fervor he had never evinced before. Perhaps someone got to him during an early trip home to Lebanon, for it was when he got back that cousin Salim first noticed him reading a publication about jihad. Perhaps it was the influence of a young imam in Germany—himself a student—who badgered people he knew to attend the mosque, and pressed anyone who would listen to donate to Palestinian causes. The imam was suspected, the CIA would say later, of having "terrorist connections."

What is clear is that something happened to Jarrah that changed him, changed his directions. Aysel Sengün, herself a Muslim but of moderate bent, was troubled when—as she would tell the police later—he "criticized me for my choice of clothes, which he had not earlier. I was dressing in too revealing a manner for him. . . . He had also started to grow a full beard. . . . He started to ask me more and more frequently whether I would not want to pray with him."

Initially Jarrah had wanted to study dentistry, as did his lover, in the small town of Greifswald. Instead, after just over a year, he switched to an aeronautical engineering course—in Hamburg.

He and Aysel now had to travel to see each other and, when they met, she noticed that he had started talking about jihad. "Someone explained to me," she said after 9/11, that "jihad in the softer form means to write books, tell people about Islam. But Ziad's own jihad was more aggressive, the fighting kind."

Aysel became pregnant at this time, but had an abortion. She felt there were things that were not right about their relationship. She worried about being left with children were her lover to get involved "in a fanatic war." She was increasingly insecure, uncertain what Jarrah was up to, would surreptitiously comb through his papers looking for clues as to what he was doing. What he was doing was spending time in Hamburg with his future 9/11 accomplices. Their religion was inseparable from their politics. Shehhi, who could afford to live comfortably, moved to a shabby apartment with no television. Asked why, he said he was emulating the simple way the Prophet Mohammed had lived.

Given Atta's religious zeal, it may have taken little to add political extremism to the mix. Around 1995, reportedly, he spoke of a "leader" who was having a strong influence on his thinking. In the same time frame, a German student friend would recall, he talked angrily about Israel and America's protection of Israel. He was "always" linking other Muslim issues to "the war going on or the process going on, in Israel and Palestine, which he was very critical of."

In discussion with others, Atta carried on about the Jews' control of the banks and the media. These were not original thoughts, would normally have vanished on the air of heated debate in the mosques, apartments, and eating places in which they were voiced. The flame that was to make them combustible was waiting elsewhere, in Afghanistan. In 1998 or 1999—it is still not clear quite when or by whom—the connection was made.

The umbilical to activism for Atta was probably the Muslim Brotherhood, as once it had been for the young Osama bin Laden. For the Brotherhood, religion is indispensable at every level of existence, in government as in personal life. While the Brotherhood officially abjures violence, it makes exceptions—one of them the struggle in Palestine. The engineering department of Cairo University, where Atta first studied, was one of its known recruiting grounds.

Atta was a member of the engineering club, and he took two German friends there on a trip back to Cairo. The Brotherhood's influence was obvious even to them. In connection with his Hamburg university course, Atta also traveled twice to the Syrian city of Aleppo—where the Brotherhood has deep roots. It may be that he made connections there. Two older men from Aleppo—said to have been members of the Brotherhood and suspected of links to al Qaeda—were to associate with Atta and his little group back in Hamburg.

One of them, Mohammed Zammar, openly enthused about jihad and urged fellow Arabs to support the cause.

The other, Mamoun Darkazanli, was filmed attending a wedding ceremony at a Hamburg mosque with the future hijackers. He has dismissed the connection as "coincidence."

IN THE WAKE OF 9/11, reporters for *Der Spiegel* magazine would discover boxes of books and documents in a room that had been used by an Islamic study group Atta started at college. In one of the books, a volume on jihad, was what amounted to an invitation. "Osama bin Laden," it read, "has said: 'I will pay for the ticket and trip for every Arab and his family who wants to come to jihad.'" Twice in two years, Atta took a trip—to somewhere.

In early 1998, Atta vanished from Hamburg for the best part of three months. When his professor asked where he had been, he claimed he had been in Cairo dealing with a family problem. Pressed, he deflected further questions with, in effect, "Don't ask." Soon afterward, he reported his passport lost and obtained a new one—a trick often pulled by those whose passports contain compromising visa stamps.

The speculation is that Atta, and months later Shehhi and Binalshibh, made trips to Afghanistan that year. Whether they did or not, they would certainly have taken note of the statement bin Laden made in February, calling for war on America. In a list of grievances, U.S. support of Israel, and Israel's occupation of Arab Jerusalem, ranked high. America's wars, he said, "serve the interests of the petty Jewish state, diverting attention from the occupation of Jerusalem."

The 9/11 Commission Report was to duck the issue of what motivated the perpetrators of 9/11. Afterward, in a memoir, Chairman Thomas Kean and Vice Chair Lee Hamilton explained that the commissioners had disagreed on the issue. "This was sensitive ground," they wrote. "Commissioners who argued that al Qaeda was motivated primarily by a religious ideology—and not by opposition to American policies—rejected mentioning the Israeli-Palestinian conflict in the Report. In their view, listing U.S. support for Israel as a root cause of al Qaeda's opposition to the United States indicated that the United States should reassess that policy.

"To Lee, though, it was not a question of altering support for Israel but of merely stating a fact that the Israeli-Palestinian conflict was central to the relations between the Islamic world and the United States—and to bin Laden's ideology and the support he gained throughout the Islamic world for his jihad against America." The commissioners resolved their differences by settling on vague language that circumvented the issue of motive.

All the evidence, however, indicates that Palestine was the factor that united the conspirators—at every level. Bin Laden, who repeatedly alluded to it, would at one point try to get KSM to bring forward the 9/11 attack date to coincide with a visit to the White House by Israeli prime minister Ariel Sharon.

For KSM, concern about Palestine had been a constant ever since his return from college in the United States. He believed a 9/11-style attack would make Americans focus on "the atrocities that America is committing by supporting Israel." Separately, in captivity, he has claimed responsibility for the planning or execution of seven attacks on buildings, planes, and other targets, either in Israel or because they were Israeli or "Jewish."

KSM's nephew Ramzi Yousef, the 1993 Trade Center bomber, said in the only interview he has been allowed that he believed he— and Palestinians—were "entitled to strike U.S. targets because the United States is a partner in the crimes committed in Palestine. . . . It finances these crimes and supports them with weapons."

"If you ask anybody," Yousef's accomplice Abdul Murad told police in the Philippines, "even if you ask children, they will tell you that the U.S. is supporting Israel and Israel is killing our Muslim brothers in Palestine. The United States is acting like a terrorist, but nobody can see that."

Palestine was certainly the principal political grievance—the only clearly expressed grievance—driving the young Arabs in Hamburg. As reported earlier in this chapter, Atta regularly sounded off about the Palestine issue. So did Binalshibh, who would speak of a "world Jewish conspiracy." A woman with whom he had a brief affair recalled how stridently he condemned the United States for its support for Israel. His "great-grandparents, his grandparents, his parents," he said, "hated the Jews and if he should have children, they would hate them too."

Shehhi, though generally a cheery fellow, could on occasion appear saturnine. Asked by an acquaintance why he and Atta seemed rarely to laugh, he responded with a question of his own. "How can you laugh," he wondered, "when people are dying in Palestine?"

Jarrah also felt strongly about the Palestine issue. "He enlightened me," his lover Aysel Sengün would remember, "about the problems Muslims have in the Middle East. He also spoke about the intifada. I wouldn't have known what the intifada meant at that time, because I don't have a political background. When I asked, Ziad explained it was the freedom struggle of the Palestinians against Israel."

In his set-piece statement in 1998, bin Laden had issued a call to arms. "With God's permission," he had said, "we call on everyone who believes in God . . . to kill the Americans and their allies—civilians and military— is an individual duty incumbent on every Muslim in all countries . . . in order to liberate the Al Aqsa Mosque [in Jerusalem] . . . wars are being waged by the Americans for religious and economic purposes, they also serve the interests of the petty Jewish state, diverting attention from its occupation of Jerusalem."

In October 1999, at the mosque for the marriage of a member of their group, Binalshibh made a speech—political in spite of the happy occasion—that echoed bin Laden. "The problem of Jerusalem is the problem of the Muslim nation . . . the problem of every Muslim everywhere. . . . Every Muslim has the aim to free the Islamic soil from the tyrants and oppressors."

By that fall, Binalshibh and Atta and their group had become closer than ever. They met together, prayed together, did jobs to earn money together, and spent much of their time together at the three-room apartment on Marienstrasse in Harburg that Atta had rented late the previous year. They called it Dar al-Ansar—House of the Followers—entered the name in their phone books, even scrawled it on the monthly rent check. It mirrored, almost exactly, the name of the guesthouse bin Laden had established, long ago, to house recruits in Pakistan.

These were young men who had long talked of martyrdom. "It is the highest thing to do, to die for jihad," Binalshibh would say. "The mujahideen die peacefully. They die with a smile on their lips, their dead bodies are soft, while bodies of the killed infidels are stiff." Jarrah, in some ways the odd man out, had declared early on that he was "dissatisfied" with his life, hoped to find some meaning—"not leave Earth in a natural way."

The notion of dying for the faith was parroted at the mosque all the time. These men, however, were eager not merely to talk but to act. Jarrah left behind clear evidence on that score, evidence that shows he had long since been hanging on bin Laden's every word.

Hamburger Mietvertrag für Wohnraum

_____ als Vermieter
Vor- und Zuname

wohnhaft ___Hamburg___
Straße, Hausnummer, Ort

vertreten durch ████████████████████████████████████

| Said Bahaji | 15.07.1975 | Student |
| Mohamed El-Amir | 01.09.1968 | Student |

und Mohamed El-Amir
Vor- und Zuname   geb. am   Beruf

sowie Ramzi Binalshibh   01.05.1972   Student
Vor- und Zuname   geb. am   Beruf

wohnhaft 1.Bunatwiete 6, 2.Harburger Chaussee 115, 3.Etzter Heller 10a, HH als Mieter
Straße, Hausnummer, Ort

schließen, vermittelt durch _____

folgenden Mietvertrag:

(Unter Mieter und Vermieter werden im folgenden die Mietparteien auch dann verstanden, wenn sie aus mehreren Personen bestehen. Alle genannten Personen müssen den Mietvertrag unterschreiben. Soweit einzelne der nachfolgenden Bestimmungen ganz oder teilweise nicht gelten sollen, sind sie jeweils im Einvernehmen der Vertragspartner zu streichen. Gegebenenfalls sind andere bzw. ergänzende Vereinbarungen einzufügen.)

§ 1 Mieträume

1. Zur Benutzung als Wohnung

werden im Hause ___Marienstraße 54 in 21073 Hamburg___
(Straße, Hausnummer, Ort)

vermietet: ___I. OG links___
(Geschoß Mitte/rechts/links)

Three years earlier, in his Declaration of "Jihad" against the Americans, bin Laden had spoken of the brave young Muslims who "love death as you love life," who "have no intent but to enter Paradise by killing you."

In a note dated October 1999, found among his possessions after 9/11, Jarrah used almost the identical phrase: "The morning will come," he wrote. "The victors will come, will come. We swear to beat you. The earth will shake beneath your feet." And then, days later: "I came to you with _men who love the death as you love life_. . . . Oh, the smell of Paradise is rising" (authors' italics).

"Paradise," Atta and Binalshibh would say, "is over-shadowed with swords." A South African–born Muslim convert who hung out with the group, Shahid Nickels, questioned all the talk about fighting for the cause of Palestine. "Muslims," he said, "are too weak to do anything against the U.S.A."

"No, something can be done," replied Atta. "There are ways. The U.S.A. is not omnipotent." The exchange took place in November 1999, and—that month and early the next—Atta, Binalshibh, Shehhi, and Jarrah did do something.

They left for bin Laden's headquarters in Afghanistan.

The future hijackers traveled separately, probably for security reasons, to Karachi in Pakistan and on to Kandahar in Afghanistan. There is no doubt they were there. A former bin Laden bodyguard has recalled meeting Atta, Jarrah, and Shehhi. Another jihadi, a man who had also come from Germany, recalled encountering Binalshibh. A handwritten note on Atta was recovered after 9/11 in the bombed-out ruins of a house military chief Mohammed Atef had used.

Apparent proof that the German contingent went to Afghanistan—a link in the chain that the 9/11 Commission did not have—is a videotape reported to be in the hands of the U.S. government. Almost an hour long, it is said to show Atta and Jarrah at Tarnak Farms near Kandahar—the very camp where the CIA had once hoped to have bin Laden kidnapped and spirited away to the United States.

In still photos reportedly taken from the footage, both men are shown neatly bearded and smiling widely—in Atta's case, an image utterly unlike the grim visage the world was shown after 9/11. Jarrah wears a white robe, apparently over Western clothing, Atta dark trousers and a brown sweater. Atta dons an Afghan-style hat, looks at the camera, takes the hat on and off, then chucks it away. Then he reads to the camera for perhaps ten minutes, to be followed by Jarrah doing likewise.

The video is reportedly silent, but the pair were evidently recording statements to be preserved until after their deaths. The words "al wasiyyah," Arabic for "will," can be clearly seen on a paper that Jarrah holds up for the camera before speaking. As he does so, he and Atta both laugh. Then they turn serious as they read out their statements. Clearly recognizable on the tape, seated on the ground among a crowd of about a hundred, is Ramzi Binalshibh.

A segment of the footage depicts the arrival of a very tall, robed figure, surrounded by bodyguards. Bin Laden, of course. If authentic, the videotape is unique evidence of the future hijackers' presence in Afghanistan.

BOTH KSM and Binalshibh, the sole survivor of the group from Germany, have described the visit to Afghanistan. Except for Shehhi, who left early—he had been suffering from a stomach ailment—they stayed for several weeks, weeks that put them irreversibly on course for 9/11.

For bin Laden, Atef, and KSM, the trio must have seemed, in the true sense of that phrase, sent from God. KSM had only "middling confidence" in Mihdhar and Hazmi, the two remaining pilot hijacker candidates that bin Laden had initially picked. Committed and courageous though they might be, they spoke virtually no English, had no experience of life in the West. The men from Hamburg, by contrast, did have linguistic ability, were far more likely to be able to operate effectively in the United States.

In a series of meetings with bin Laden, Atef, and KSM,

the trio took the oath to bin Laden—"I swear allegiance to you and to die in the cause of God"—before learning the nature of the mission. Bin Laden considered appointing Binalshibh leader, then plumped for Atta instead. He was now the emir—commander—of the operation.

Atta was included in the meeting to select targets. Dozens were discussed, with bin Laden emphasizing that he wanted one target to be military, one political, one economic. It was eventually decided that the team "must hit" the Pentagon, the Capitol—"the perceived source of U.S. policy in support of Israel"—and both towers of the World Trade Center.

Atta was free to choose in addition one other potential target—the White House, the Sears Tower in Chicago, or a foreign embassy in Washington. The name of the embassy has not been released, but it was surely that of Israel. Atta himself suggested a strike on a nuclear power station in Pennsylvania—Three Mile Island?—and bin Laden agreed.

After the talking, the training. There was some fieldwork—Jarrah cheerfully endured long hours on guard duty—but KSM thought the military side of things irrelevant. The new recruits learned the tricks of the terrorist trade—how to remove telltale stamps from passports, the importance of secure communications, of keeping phone calls short. With their very specific mission in mind, they also learned how to read airline schedules.

In a real sense, in counterpoint to its eventual success, the 9/11 operation was amateurish. KSM and bin Laden had thought initially that no special skills were needed to be a pilot, that "learning to fly an airplane was much like learning to drive a car . . . easily accomplished." Totally wrong, as KSM admitted in captivity.

His maxim, though, that "simplicity was the key to

success," was in many ways probably right. He urged team members "to be normal to the maximum extent possible in their dealings, to keep the tone of their letters educational, social, or commercial." Though averse to the unnecessary use of codes, he did develop some. If telephone numbers had to be used in correspondence, KSM directed, they were to be rendered so that the real numeral and the coded one totaled ten. His own number in Pakistan—92-300-922-388—thus became 18-700-188-722.

For Atta, some of the preparation for the mission took the form of what to others counts as fun. He was to be seen "playing video games on a PlayStation—flying a plane." KSM thought Atta "worked hard, and learned quickly." He gave him sufficient authority to be able to make decisions on his own, to press ahead without having to consult too often. One of the Saudis bin Laden had originally chosen, Nawaf al-Hazmi, was to be his deputy.

Each of the five early team members was honored with a *kunyah*, an honorific prefaced by *Abu*—meaning, literally, "father," though the bearer of the name need not have children. In this case, all the *kunyahs* harked back to the days of the Prophet. As Binalshibh remembered them: Atta was "Father of the servant of the Beneficent, the Egyptian," one of the followers to whom the Prophet pledged the certainty of Paradise; Shehhi was *Abu'l'Qaqa'a al-Qatari*, literally "the sound of clashing swords, from Qatar" (though he was in fact a citizen of the United Arab Emirates); and Jarrah was *Abu Tareq al-Lubnani*, literally, "Father of the one who knocks at the door, the Lebanese"—probably after an Arab commander celebrated for his conquests in North Africa and southern Spain.

Bin Laden was keen for all the future hijackers to be on

their way to the United States as soon as possible—including the two Saudis, Nawaf al-Hazmi and Khalid al-Mihdhar. Hazmi was to be *Rab'iah al Makki*, to whom the Prophet promised anything he should ask. Mihdhar was to be *Sinan*, "the Spear." They were to be the trailblazers of the 9/11 operation.

AT THE TURN of the year, on the night of the Millennium, President Clinton had watched a fireworks display and hosted a large dinner at the White House. "It was a wonderful evening," he recalled, "but I was nervous all the time. Our security team had been on high alert for weeks due to numerous intelligence reports that the United States would be hit with several terrorist attacks. . . . I had been focused intently on bin Laden."

The Millennium, a cause for celebration for millions, also seemed just the moment the terrorists might strike. On December 6, in Jordan, a group of terrorists had been caught while preparing to bomb a hotel used by American and Israeli tourists. They had been overheard on a telephone intercept talking with bin Laden's aide Abu Zubaydah.

On December 14, concern about a coming attack on the United States turned to a permanent state of alarm. The driver of a Chrysler sedan, waiting to enter Washington State from a ferry arriving from Canada, caught the attention of an alert Customs officer. There was something about the man. He was fidgeting, sweating profusely, would not look her in the eye. Hidden in the car, officers discovered, were bomb-making materials—RDX and HMTD explosives, chemicals, and Casio watch timing devices.

The man turned out to be Ahmed Ressam, an Algerian who was to admit—much later—that his intended target had been Los Angeles International Airport. The plan, he said, had been to explode the bomb on or about the day of the Millennium. He had learned about explosives in bin Laden's Afghan training camps, and he, too, had had contact with Abu Zubaydah. He had planned the foiled attack himself, Ressam said, but bin Laden had been "aware" of it.

After the Ressam arrest, and with the Millennium looming, everyone thought there was more to come. A round of frenzied activity began. Clinton rang Pakistan's President Musharraf to demand that a way be found to stop bin Laden's operations. National Security Adviser Berger and intelligence chiefs, often with Attorney General Janet Reno present, met almost daily at the White House. A record number of wiretap orders were issued. "Foreign terrorist sleeper cells are present in the U.S.," counterterrorism coordinator Clarke's staff warned, "and attacks in the U.S. are likely."

Berger and Clarke spent the morning of Christmas Day at FBI headquarters and the afternoon at the CIA. Nothing happened. Come the night of the Millennium, thousands of law enforcement agents and military personnel were on duty. FBI director Louis Freeh and Attorney General Reno kept vigil in their offices—Reno would sleep the night on a couch at the Justice Department. In New York's Times Square, local FBI counterterrorism chief John O'Neill waited for the famous ball to fall at midnight.

The ball fell, and no catastrophe came. "I think we dodged the bullet," Berger said when he rang Clarke after midnight. Clarke said he would wait three more hours, until New Year's came in Los Angeles. At 3:00 A.M., when all was still well, he went up to the roof of the White House and "popped open a bottle."

The FBI told Berger after the Millennium, he was to recall, that al Qaeda did not after all have active cells in the U.S. "They said there might be sleepers, but they had that covered. They were saying this was not a big domestic threat."

No one that New Year's spoke publicly about a specific danger, that an attack in the United States might come in the shape of airplane hijackings. Many months earlier, however, bin Laden had spoken of just that. "All Islamic military," he had boasted, "have been mobilized to strike a significant U.S. or Israeli strategic target, to bring down their aircraft and hijack them."

In 1998, indeed, the White House had quietly held an exercise involving a scenario in which terrorists flew an explosives-laden jet into a building in Washington. In December that year, the CIA had told Bill Clinton of intelligence suggesting that "bin Laden and his allies are preparing for attack in the U.S., including an aircraft hijacking."

During 1999, Britain's foreign intelligence service warned its American counterparts that bin Laden was planning attacks in which airliners could be used in "unconventional ways." Two U.S. bodies, moreover, produced prophetic warnings.

"America," the congressionally mandated Commission on National Security forecast in its initial report, "will become increasingly vulnerable to hostile attack on our homeland. . . . Americans will likely die on American soil, possibly in large numbers." The same month, a report by the Library of Congress's Federal Research Division, which had wide circulation within the government, said al Qaeda could be expected to retaliate for the cruise missile attack on bin Laden's camps.

"Suicide bombers belonging to al Qaeda's Martyrdom Battalion," the report went on to say, "could crash-land an aircraft packed with high explosives (C-4 and Semtex) into the Pentagon, the headquarters of the Central Intelligence Agency, or the White House."

IN NOVEMBER 1999, just months after bin Laden had decided on the 9/11 operation, two young Saudi students had boarded as Coach Class passengers on an America West Flight 90 from Phoenix, Arizona, to Washington, D.C. During the flight, one of them—in the words of a flight attendant—"walked into the First Class section and continued walking towards the cockpit door. He tried to open the door. He was very subtle in his actions." A passenger in First Class also saw the Arab man "try to get into the cockpit."

The cockpit door was locked, and the man claimed he had mistaken it for the lavatory. The behavior of the passenger and his traveling companion had made the flight attendants uneasy, though, and they alerted the captain. At a routine stopover in Ohio, the plane had taxied to a remote parking place and the two men had been taken away in handcuffs. After four hours of interrogation and a search of their baggage, they were eventually allowed to continue their journey.

Since 9/11, the suspicion has strengthened that this had been, as one FBI agent put it, a "casing operation." It turned out, according to a Commission memorandum, that both the Saudi passengers were " 'tied' to Islamic extremists." One of those extremist associates, interviewed at home by the FBI before 9/11, had said openly that he thought America a legitimate target. On the wall, in plain sight, was a poster of bin Laden.

Intelligence on the companion of the man who tried the cockpit door indicated that after leaving the United States he received "explosive and car bomb training" in Afghanistan. One of his friends had studied flying in the United States and was arrested after 9/11 along with top bin Laden aide Abu Zubaydah. The traveling companion, moreover, has admitted having met one of the future pilot hijackers.

The America West incident may indeed have been a reconnaissance mission. According to KSM, as many as four bin Laden units made early exploratory trips to the United States.

In 1999, and the previous year, reports reached the FBI that terrorists were planning to send men to learn to fly in the United States. "The purpose of this training was unknown," the 1999 report said, "but the [terrorist] organization leaders viewed the requirement as 'particularly important' and were reported to have approved an open-ended amount of funding to ensure its success."

The FBI's Counterterrorism Division responded to the reports by asking field offices to investigate. Congress's Joint Inquiry, however, found no indication that any investigation was conducted. Paul Kurtz, who at that time was a senior official on the National Security Council, said dealing with the Bureau was "very frustrating," at some levels "totally infuriating." Overall, he said, the FBI was a "freaking black hole."

In November 1999, moreover, when the Bureau's Counterterrorism Division asked the Immigration and Naturalization Service to share data on relevant arrivals in the country, the INS did not respond to the request.

November was the month of the suspicious incident aboard America West Flight 90. It was also the month that, in Afghanistan, KSM and bin Laden assembled the future hijacker pilots and ordered them to head for the United States. As the FBI and the INS dithered, the enemy was at the gate.

TWENTY-FIVE

HAZMI AND MIHDHAR, BIN LADEN'S FIRST CHOICES FOR the "planes operation," had undergone months of preparation in Afghanistan. With other select fighters, they had undergone an intensive course at an old Soviet copper mine used as a training camp. It involved endurance exercises, man-to-man combat, and night operations—most of which KSM deemed, reasonably enough, of little use for the challenge awaiting them.

Once in KSM's hands, the advance guard received tuition in relevant subjects. They perused aviation magazines, were introduced to the mysteries of airline timetables, and viewed flight simulation software. Like Atta, they played computer games involving aviation scenarios. They watched Hollywood movies about hijackings, but with sequences featuring female characters carefully edited out. How instructive that can have been, given the ubiquity of female flight attendants on airliners, remains a question.

Hazmi and Mihdhar, KSM decided, were to stay initially in California. He had yellow and white phone directories, supposedly found in a Karachi market, and tried to teach the men how to use them. The directories would help, KSM thought, in locating apartment rental agencies and language schools—and places to take flying lessons. They also tried to grasp some basic words and phrases in English.

The two young men were coached separately. Mihdhar, who was married to a Yemeni wife, left early. Hazmi trained with the two Yemenis bin Laden had picked but who had been refused U.S. visas. One of them, Walid bin Attash, has recalled talks on choosing the optimal moment to hijack an airplane. They were to take careful note of flight attendants' and pilots' movements, the routine attendants followed when taking meals to the cockpit, the comings and goings to the lavatory of the pilots.

Attash was assigned to do a dry run. He flew first to Kuala Lumpur, the capital of Malaysia, a largely Muslim nation that did not require visas for travelers from certain other Muslim states. Then he flew to Bangkok and onward, aboard an American airliner, to Hong Kong. He took the flight to Hong Kong on December 31, 1999, Millennium Eve, the same day on which U.S. officials were beside themselves with worry about a possible bin Laden attack.

Attash learned a good deal from these rehearsal flights. It was not enough, he realized, just to travel First Class. It was important to reserve a seat with a clear view of the cockpit door. Second, he discovered it was possible to board a plane carrying a box cutter or razor knife. Were the knife to trigger a metal detector, he realized, toiletries that came in metallic tubes or containers—like toothpaste or shaving cream—were probably enough to fool inspectors at security checks. In the event of awkward questions, and to account for the box cutter, Attash also carried art supplies. His bag was opened and he was questioned, but the ploy worked every time.

The reconnaissance completed, Attash, Hazmi, and

Mihdhar—and several other terrorists—spent a few days at a condominium complex on the outskirts of Kuala Lumpur. Then they traveled on to Bangkok, the last stop for Hazmi and Mihdhar before the real start of the 9/11 mission. On January 15, 2000, the pair boarded a United Airlines flight bound for Los Angeles. Armed with the entry visas obtained the previous year, they had no problem at all at Immigration. They were admitted to the U.S. as "tourists."

KSM was to claim "no al Qaeda operative or facilitator" was ready and waiting to help the two future hijackers on arrival. The Commission, however—usually careful not to raise doubt where there was none—did not believe him. With reason.

On the routine form they filled out on arrival, Hazmi and Mihdhar stated they would be staying initially at a Sheraton in Los Angeles. Intensive inquiries after 9/11, however, would produce no trace of them there or at any other hotel or motel. Where did they stay?

A driver who said he did chauffeuring work for the Saudi consulate was to give a detailed account of having chauffeured "two Saudis." Someone else, he indicated, had met them at the airport, then taken them to "an apartment . . . that had been rented for them" on Sepulveda Boulevard. An imam at the King Fahd mosque, near the consulate, had introduced the driver to the new arrivals. The driver gave them a tour, to the beach at Santa Monica and over to Hollywood. Shown a number of photographs of young Arabs, the driver picked out Hazmi and Mihdhar—only to back off and nervously deny having known them.

Knowing that the pair spoke virtually no English and "barely knew how to function in U.S. society," KSM has said, he had "instructed" them—unlike the more sophisticated accomplices who were later to arrive from

Germany—to feel free to ask for assistance at a local mosque or Islamic center. That is what Hazmi and Mihdhar appear to have done, but they likely had more specific guidance than KSM admitted. Another captured terrorist said KSM was in possession of at least one address in the States, perhaps in California.

If there was such a contact, KSM managed to conceal it. The CIA concluded that his principal goal, even under torture, was to protect sleepers—operatives already in the United States. In doing so, he seems to have sought to lay a false trail. On the one hand he claimed under interrogation that he had shown Hazmi and Mihdhar a phone directory that "possibly" covered Long Beach, near Los Angeles, and that they tried to enroll in various language schools in the L.A. area. On the other hand, he referred to definitely having had directories for San Diego and having noted that there were language schools and flight schools in that city. KSM's "idea," he said, was that Hazmi and Mihdhar should base themselves in San Diego.

At any rate, whatever guidance they may have received at the Saudi consulate and mosque in Los Angeles, it was to San Diego that they headed. The man who invited them there and arranged housing for them was to become a major focus of the investigation.

Forty-two-year-old Omar al-Bayoumi was a mystery in his own right. According to a rental application form he filled out, he was a student receiving a monthly income from relatives in India. In fact he was an employee of a subsidiary of a contractor for the Saudi Civil Aviation Authority—paid but, as a colleague put it, a "ghost"—not required to work. He had time on his hands, and spent much of it helping to run a mosque near San Diego.

According to Bayoumi and a companion, they met Hazmi and Mihdhar on February 1, 2000, two weeks after their arrival in the United States. According to the companion, an American Muslim convert named Caysan bin Don, he and Bayoumi drove first to Los Angeles. Bayoumi, he said, met for thirty minutes with a man at the Saudi consulate, then went on to the nearby King Fahd mosque. Bayoumi, for his part, denied that they stopped at the mosque.

Both agreed that they went to eat at the Mediterranean Café, a restaurant that served food suitable for Muslims. As they were waiting to be served, they said, Hazmi and Mihdhar walked in. On hearing them speaking Arabic, Bayoumi invited them to come join them at their table. He did so, according to a *Los Angeles Times* account, after first dropping a newspaper on the floor and bending to retrieve it.

What led Hazmi and Mihdhar to express interest in moving to San Diego, Bayoumi claimed, was his "description of the weather there." They duly showed up in the city, sought him out at the Islamic Center, and—with his assistance—moved for a while into the apartment next door to his own.

The way Bayoumi and bin Don told it, it had been pure chance that they met the two future terrorists. There are factors, though, that suggest it did not happen that way: a witness who quoted Bayoumi as saying before going to Los Angeles that he was on his way "to pick up visitors"; phone records that indicate frequent contact between him and the imam said to have arranged for the "two Saudis'" car tour around Los Angeles; phone records indicating that Hazmi and Mihdhar used Bayoumi's cell phone for several weeks; the fact that Bayoumi appeared to have written jihad-type material; that Bayoumi's salary was approved by the father of a man whose photo was later found in a raid on a terrorist safe house in Afghanistan; and that there was a mark in his passport that investigators associated with possible affiliation to al Qaeda.

"We do not know," the 9/11 Commission Report would conclude, "whether the lunch encounter occurred by chance or design." The staff director of Congress's Joint Inquiry, Eleanor Hill, told the authors she thought Bayoumi's story "very suspicious." An unnamed former senior FBI official who oversaw the Bayoumi investigation was more trenchant. "We firmly believed," he told *Newsweek*, "that he had knowledge . . . and that his meeting with them that day was more than coincidence."

The man most likely to have been a primary contact for Hazmi and Mihdhar was a man who would go on to gain global notoriety—Anwar Aulaqi. American-born Aulaqi, then twenty-nine, was imam at a San Diego mosque familiar to most of the cast of characters mentioned in this chapter. On the day the two terrorists arranged to move in next door to Bayoumi, four phone calls occurred between Bayoumi's telephone and Aulaqi's.

Hazmi and Mihdhar attended the mosque where Aulaqi preached and were seen there in his company. Witnesses told the FBI that the trio had "closed-door meetings." According to a later landlord, Hazmi said he respected Aulaqi and spoke with him on a regular basis.

Aulaqi, for his part, admitted to the FBI after 9/11 that he had met Hazmi several times, enough to be able to assess him as a "very calm and extremely nice person." Congress's Joint Inquiry Report was to characterize Aulaqi as having been the future hijackers' "spiritual adviser."

In the context of holy war, that is to say a good deal. The following year, the year of 9/11, all three men— Aulaqi and, subsequently, the two terrorists—relocated to the East Coast. Hazmi, Mihdhar, and one of the hijacking pilots attended his mosque in Virginia. He claimed that he had no contact with them there.

The Bureau had looked hard at Aulaqi even before the

future hijackers came to California, and also while they were there. One lead investigated was the suggestion that he had been contacted by a "possible procurement agent for bin Laden." There had been nothing, however, to justify prosecuting the imam. The 9/11 Commission described Aulaqi as "potentially significant."

By 2011, Aulaqi would have the world's total attention. At large in Yemen following a brief spell in prison—at the belated request of the United States—the former San Diego imam was suspected of involvement in four serious recent terrorist attacks aimed at the United States. Two had involved attempts to explode bombs on aircraft.

The chairwoman of the House Subcommittee on Intelligence, Jane Harman, has called Aulaqi "Terrorist No. 1."

IN SAN DIEGO in early 2000, Hazmi and Mihdhar appear to have at first sought to pass themselves off as long-stay visitors interested in seeing the sights—as KSM had suggested. Hazmi bought season passes to the San Diego Zoo and SeaWorld. They opened bank accounts, bought a Toyota sedan, obtained driver's licenses and state IDs. When they moved on from Bayoumi's apartment complex, to accommodations elsewhere, Hazmi even allowed his name, address, and telephone number to appear in the Pacific Bell phone directory for San Diego.

```
ALHARK Akram .................. 619 303 7629
    Akram 9716 Osage Sp Vly ........... 619 303 7632
ALHASAN Majed ................. 619 590 0358
AL-HASSAN Hekmat
    1000 S Mollison Av El Caj ......... 619 444 0021
ALHASSOON Omar ................. 619 294 7790
ALHAZMI Nawaf M    Mount Ada Rd . 858 279 5919
ALHMERI Ahmed
    8633 La Mesa Bl La Mesa ......... 619 460 8615
AL-HOSINY Aqel
    1041 N Mollison Av El Caj ......... 619 593 1178
```

Hazmi seems to have been pleasant enough and sociable, and joined a soccer team in San Diego. Mihdhar was a darker, "brooding" character. Early on, told that renting an apartment would involve putting down a deposit, so violently did he fly off the handle that the landlord thought him "psychotic." Not clever for a terrorist living undercover—it was the kind of thing people remembered.

A Muslim acquaintance vividly recalled an exchange he had with Mihdhar. When Mihdhar reproached him for watching "immoral" American television, the acquaintance retorted, "If you're so religious, why don't you have facial hair?" To which Mihdhar replied meaningfully, "You'll know someday, brother."

Had their tradecraft been better, the two men would not have used long-distance communication as much as they did. KSM, concerned about their ability to function in the West, had told them to contact him with urgent questions. Once they had acquired their own cell phones, however, they often used them to call not KSM but relatives in Saudi Arabia and Yemen. They sent emails—both had addresses on Yahoo.com—using their landlord's computer and those provided free at San Diego State University.

Hazmi and Mihdhar failed utterly to live up to bin Laden's early expectations. Though Hazmi enrolled in English classes, he learned hardly anything. Mihdhar apparently did not even start the course. The pair's effort to learn to fly, meanwhile, was tardy, short-lived when it did get started, and hopeless.

More than two months after arriving, the pair attended a one-hour introductory session at a local San Diego flight school. A month later, at another school, they bought equipment and took a few lessons. They said from the start that they wished to fly jets—Boeing airliners—although they had no previous experience. They had no interest in takeoffs or landings. When taken up in a Cessna, one of them began praying loudly.

"They just didn't have the aptitude," instructor Rick Garza would recall. "They had no idea. . . . They were like Dumb and Dumber." He told bin Laden's chosen men that flying was simply not for them. That was the end of that.

On June 9, less than five months after arriving and soon after hearing that his wife had given birth to their first child, Mihdhar dropped out and flew back to the Middle East. By any standard, it was an unforgivable lapse. When KSM said as much, though, he was over-ruled by bin Laden. The operatives' pathetic bumbling, KSM was to tell the CIA, was not really a disaster. His planning was progressive, a step-by-step affair, he said, and the next step had already been taken.

As Mihdhar left the United States, more competent accomplices arrived.

ONCE BACK in Germany from Afghanistan, the Hamburg-based conspirators had changed so much as to be unrecognizable. To outward appearances, they were no longer the obvious fundamentalists they had been before leaving. They shed the clothing and the beards that marked them out as Muslim radicals, no longer attended the mosques known as haunts of extremists.

Atta fired off emails to thirty-one U.S. flight schools. "We are a small group of young men from different Arab countries," he wrote in March 2000. "We would like to start training for the career of professional pilot." The future hijackers declared their passports "lost," received new ones, and applied for visas to enter the United States.

As a Yemeni with no proof of permanent residence,

Ramzi Binalshibh was turned down. His hopes of becoming a pilot hijacker frustrated, he was thenceforth to function as fixer and middle man, liaison to KSM. Binalshibh's three companions, however, encountered no problems.

Marwan al-Shehhi flew into New York first, at the end of May 2000, with Atta following soon after. Beyond the fact that they took rooms in the Bronx and Brooklyn, how they spent the month that followed remains a mystery. Atta bought a cell phone and calling card—the first of more than a hundred cards the team was to use during the operation. Ziad Jarrah, the last to arrive, headed straight for a flight school in Florida. He had signed up while still in Germany, having seen its advertisement in a German aviation magazine.

Florida Flight Training Center, still in business today, sits beside the runway of the airport at Venice, a quiet retirement community on the Gulf Coast near Sarasota. It was a small operation, and Jarrah got on well with the man who ran it. "He was," Arne Kruithof was to remember ruefully, "the kind of guy who wanted to be loved. . . . I remember him bringing me a six-pack of beer at home when I hurt my knee one time." Jarrah himself, Kruithof said, liked an "occasional bottle of Bud."

Jarrah's course was geared to obtaining a Private Pilot License to fly single-engine aircraft. He already had a handle on the theory, having studied aviation mechanics in Germany, and he made quiet, steady progress. A fellow student, Thorsten Bierman, however, found Jarrah self-centered and uncooperative when they flew together. "He wanted to do everything single-handed."

Atta and Shehhi had left New York and traveled first to look at a flight school in Norman, Oklahoma, at which one of bin Laden's personal pilots had once trained to fly. As early as 1998, the FBI's regional office had been

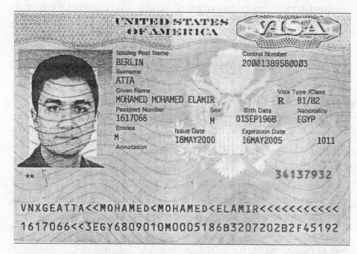

Mohamed Atta's visa, which got him into the United States in spring 2000, was issued without any prior interview. Ziad Jarrah's charred visa (below) was recovered at the site of the crash of United Flight 93.

alerted to the large number of Arabs learning to fly in the area.

After a tour of that school, however, Atta and Shehhi decided not to enroll. They made their way instead to Venice, Florida, and Huffman Aviation, just a block from the school where Jarrah was already at work. No reliable source, however, has spoken of seeing Jarrah with Atta and Shehhi in Venice. Their tradecraft was superior to that of the inept fellows who had arrived earlier in California

Rudi Dekkers, who ran Huffman, would have nothing good to say about Atta. The hijackers' team leader, he said, "had an attitude, like he was standing above everybody . . . very, very arrogant." Shehhi, by contrast, was a "likeable person, he had fun, he was laughing . . . this is a male environment, so we talk about girls, planes. But Atta was never socializing."

Their first flying instructor, Mark Mikarts, was at first just a little nonplussed at the sight of Atta. "When you do flight training," Mikarts said, "you tend to get a little bit dirty—there's oil and fuel. You're sweating. He was always immaculately dressed, with the $200 Gucci shoes, silk shirts, double-hemmed pants. He always overdressed."

Teaching Atta to handle a Cessna 172, meanwhile, turned out to be a nightmare. "Generally," said Mikarts,

the first five to ten hours is where a student learns to fly by visual references. Using outside visual references, we'd keep the horizon at a certain part of the windshield. He had a very difficult time learning that. He would always over-rotate, or he couldn't keep the reference. . . . But he would not listen. . . . It was like he had to do it his way.

Then finally one day he over-rotated the airplane and I thought, "I'm going to let him do whatever he wants to do. Let's see what happens." He pitches the airplane way up. . . . The engine is screaming. The stall horn is blaring. The air speed's bleeding away. We're about to stall and tumble out of the air. I'm saying, "Nose down!" Next time, louder. Third time, I said, "Nose down!" in a rather nasty tone. [Then] I took my hand and shoved the control wheel forward and stamped on the rudder pedal to get it back where it's supposed to be. We pitched down so abruptly that he popped out of his seat from the negative g's—hit his head on the ceiling.

He turned his head towards me and gave me a look like, "You infidel . . ." or something. Like he wanted to kill me. That's it, we turned back and he went and complained to my chief pilot. . . . I said, "If he's going to be that much of a baby about it and not follow instructions, let him go someplace else. Not worth me breaking my neck and you losing an instructor."

Things were no better in September, when Atta and Shehhi tried another flight school. They failed an instrument rating, argued about how things should be done, even tried to wrest control of the airplane from their instructor. They were asked to leave—and got Huffman to take them back again.

Ann Greaves, a student from England, asked the instructor they shared how the two Arabs were getting on. He replied with "a gesture of the hand. Nothing was said. It was sort of, you know, 'So so . . .'" The instructor told her that Atta had connections to Saudi royalty, that Shehhi, who seemed to follow behind, was supposedly his bodyguard. Once, when Greaves reached out to retrieve her seat cushion—Atta, who was short and also needed a cushion, had appropriated it—Shehhi rushed to place himself between them. Royalty and their staff, Greaves thought, ought to have better manners.

What led Shehhi to respond the way he did probably had nothing to do with manners—and everything with the fact that Greaves was a woman. Islam dictates that men and women not married or related to each other may not touch, not even to shake hands. Atta abhorred the idea of proximity to women, even after his death. In his will, written long since at the age of twenty-seven, he had stipulated: "I don't want a pregnant woman or a person who is not clean to come and say goodbye to me ... I don't want women to come to my house to apologize for my death ... I don't want any women to go to my grave at all, during my funeral or on any occasion thereafter."

In Venice, they all remembered Atta's hang-up about women. "We had female dispatchers at the flight school," Mikarts recalled. "He would order them around, tell them this, tell them that. I'd pull him aside and say, 'I don't know how you treat women in your country, but you don't talk to her that way.'" Ivan Chirivella, who taught Atta and Shehhi during their brief stint at another school, remembered that they were both "very rude to the female employees."

The pair were never seen in a woman's company at the Outlook bar, where flight students gathered at the end of the working day. Lizsa Lehman, who worked there, remembered the two of them well. She liked Shehhi, thought him "fun, inquisitive, friendly," while Atta rarely exchanged a word with her. He always stood with his back to the bar, Shehhi explained, because he did not approve of female bartenders.

Atta did break one Muslim taboo. If he did deign to address her, Lehman said, it was to utter the words "Bud Light." There appears to be no truth to allegations made after 9/11 that several of the terrorists, including Atta, drank alcohol to excess. Lehman's clear memory, though, is that Atta and Shehhi were partial to a beer at the end of the day. "Two, maybe, but they never—ever—overindulged."

IN EARLY AUGUST, the diligent Ziad Jarrah was awarded his Private Pilot License. In contrast to Atta, the love of a woman was on his mind. He headed back to Germany in the fall to spend several weeks with his girlfriend, Aysel. They went to Paris together, had themselves photographed up the Eiffel Tower. "I love you . . . don't worry," Jarrah wrote when he got back, then indulged himself a little. He bought a red Mitsubishi Eclipse, spent a weekend in the Bahamas. Over Christmas, he took a week-long trip to Lebanon to see his family.

By late December, and in spite of Atta's obstreperous behavior, both he and Shehhi had qualified to fly not only small private planes but also multi-engine aircraft. Professional, however, the pair were not. The day before Christmas, when their rented plane stalled on the taxiway at Miami Airport, they simply abandoned it and walked away. That fiasco reportedly marked the end of their relationship with Huffman Aviation.

Atta's mind was racing ahead. Even before receiving his certification, he had sent off for flight deck videos for Boeing airliners. In the last week of December, at a training center near Miami, he and Shehhi paid for six hours on a Boeing 727 simulator. "They just wanted to move around in mid-air," said the instructor who supervised the session, "not take off or land. I thought it was really odd. I can see now what I was allowing them to do. It's a terrible thing to live with."

Some have argued that the hijacking pilots did not have the skills required to pull off the maneuvers performed on 9/11. Given that they would not have to face the complexities of takeoff and landing, though, and given the further practice they were to have in the remaining months, their abilities apparently sufficed for their deadly purpose.

On New Year's Eve, at another school, Atta and Shehhi trained on a Boeing 767 simulator. It would be a 767, with Atta at the controls, that eight months later crashed into the North Tower of the World Trade Center.

FAR OFF in Afghanistan, seemingly oblivious to what he was asking of the men he had sent to America, Osama bin Laden had become impatient. In the fall of 2000, when they were still at flight school, he had pressed KSM to launch the operation. It would be enough, he said, simply to bring airliners down, not necessarily to strike specific targets. This was at the time of the second Palestinian intifada, or uprising, that followed then Israeli opposition leader Ariel Sharon's provocative visit to Jerusalem's Temple Mount. Bin Laden, KSM said, wanted to be seen to retaliate against Israel's principal supporter.

As he would time and again, KSM resisted bin Laden's pressure. Lack of readiness aside, there was a cogent new reason not to rush matters. A new pilot hijacker candidate had materialized. Twenty-nine-year-old Hani Hanjour, the son of a well-to-do family in the Saudi city of Ta'if, already had flying qualifications. After years of travel back and forth to American flight schools, he had succeeded in getting his commercial pilot's license. After trying in vain to get work flying for an airline in his own country, however, he had resorted to pretending to his family that he had a job as a pilot in the United Arab Emirates. This was a frustrated young man.

The key to understanding the direction Hanjour now took, though, lies elsewhere. Though described by those who knew him well as "frail," "quiet," "a little mouse," he could show another side. When alcohol was available, this conspirator reportedly went drinking on occasion. Afterward, however, filled with guilt, he would devote an entire day to praying. So moved would he become during prayers that one witness recalled seeing him in tears. Religion figured large for him. Ever since a first trip to Afghanistan at the age of seventeen, he had wanted to make jihad.

In 2000, when Hanjour turned up in one of the Afghan camps and let it be known that he was a qualified pilot, bin Laden's aide Atef sent him to KSM. KSM saw his potential, gave him a basic briefing on how to act in the field, and dispatched him—equipped with a visa obtained in Saudi Arabia—to join Nawaf al-Hazmi in San Diego. They would not stay there long, but would head off to yet another flight school— in Arizona.

Given Hanjour's flying experience, KSM thought his target should be the Pentagon—relatively hard to hit because it is only five stories high. On reaching the States, one of Hanjour's calls would be to a flight school owner he knew from previous visits. He now wanted, he said, to learn how to fly a Boeing 757. The instructor suggested he first get some experience on a smaller business airplane, but Hanjour persisted. "No," he said, "I want to fly the 757." On 9/11, he would be aboard the 757 that hit the Pentagon.

The first name "Hani" means "content." Hanjour liked to say, however, that it meant "warrior," in line with the name that he—like all the hijackers—had been given before setting off for the States. Bin Laden dubbed him "'*Orwah al-Ta'ifi*," after a follower of the Prophet who had died in a shower of arrows in Hanjour's hometown—giving thanks to God for allowing him martyrdom.

In October 2000, as KSM prepared Hanjour for his mission, Atta and Shehhi were well into their course at

Huffman Aviation. They and fellow students had to use a computer provided by the school to prepare for a written test, and people often had to wait their turn. One day, however, as Ann Greaves waited outside for Atta and Shehhi to emerge from the computer room, she realized they were not working on the test at all. She heard hushed voices talking in Arabic, then an outburst of what sounded like delight.

"I went into the room," she recalled, "and they were hugging each other and sort of slapping each other on the back . . . I have no way of knowing what it was that made them so happy." What would certainly have made Atta and Shehhi happy was the news—on the 12th of the month—that came out of Yemen.

At 11:18 a.m. local time that morning, the guided missile destroyer USS *Cole* was about to complete refueling in the port of Aden. Its captain, Commander Kirk Lippold, was preparing to leave harbor. Small craft had been buzzing around, delivering fresh food, clearing the ship's garbage. One such boat, carrying two men in Yemeni dress, approached the destroyer, smiled and waved, then stood as if to attention.

"There was a tremendous explosion," Lippold remembered. "You could feel the entire 8,400 tons of ship violently thrust up and to the right. It seemed to hang in the air for a second before coming back into the water. We rocked from side to side. . . . Then it was dead quiet and there was a wave of smoke and dust that washed over me." Moments later, on deck, the captain looked down at the hull of his vessel.

"The best way to describe it," he said, "would be that it was like someone had taken their fist and literally punched a forty-foot hole all the way in the side of the ship—all the way through, shoving everything out of the way until it came out of the starboard side. . . . The force of an explosion like that does terrible things to a human body."

The men in Arab dress in the small boat had detonated a massive, lethal charge of Semtex explosive and the effect on the Cole was devastating. Seventeen of the sailors on deck or below, waiting for chow in the canteen, were killed. Thirty-nine were injured. The average age of the dead was nineteen.

True to previous form, bin Laden would deny that he was behind the bombing, but praise the perpetrators. Later, during the wedding festivities for one of his sons, he would recite a poem he had written:

> *A destroyer, even the brave might fear . . .*
> *To her doom she progresses slowly, clothed in a huge illusion,*
> *Awaiting her is a dinghy, bobbing in the waves.*

And:

> *The pieces of the bodies of infidels were flying like dust particles,*
> *Had you seen it with your own eyes you would have been very*
> *   pleased,*
> *Your heart would have been filled with joy.*

In a recruitment video that circulated the following year, bin Laden spelled out his grand theory. "With small means and great faith, we can defeat the mightiest military power of modern times. America is much weaker than it seems."

SIX DAYS AFTER the bombing of the *Cole*, President Clinton spoke at a memorial service for the dead. "To those who attacked them we say, you will not find a safe harbor. We will find you. And justice will prevail."

"Let's hope we can gather enough intelligence to

figure out who did the act," said George W. Bush, then in the last weeks of his campaign for the presidency. "There must be a consequence."

A cabinet-level White House meeting after the attack, however, had decided to take no immediate action, to wait for clear evidence as to who was responsible. Michael Sheehan, the State Department representative on the Counterterrorism Security Group, seethed with rage as he talked with Richard Clarke afterward. "What's it gonna take, Dick?" he exploded. "Who the shit do they think attacked the *Cole*, fuckin' Martians?... Does al Qaeda have to attack the Pentagon to get their attention?"

No one doubted bin Laden and his people were behind the bombing. In the final days of the administration, however, and with fresh memories of the failed missile attack following the embassy bombings in Africa, there was going to be no action without clear evidence.

In public and in private, the President had been hot on the issue all year long. Terrorism, Clinton had said in his State of the Union address, would be a "major security threat" far into the future. In February, when sent a memo updating him on efforts to locate bin Laden, he responded with a scrawled note in the margin—"not satisfactory . . . could surely do better."

The Air Force had done better. By September, Clarke and others had sat in amazement as an Air Force drone—an unmanned craft named Predator—beamed back pictures taken from the air over Afghanistan. Not merely pictures but, on two occasions, pictures of a tall man in a white robe—surrounded by what appeared to be bodyguards—at one of bin Laden's camps. The Afghan winter was coming, however, and photography would soon become impossible. Besides, the Predator could not be used to hit bin Laden. It was as yet unarmed.

In late fall, American negotiators were in secret negotiations with the Taliban that reportedly included talk of the possible handover of bin Laden. In December, a U.N. Security Council resolution called for the Saudi's extradition. To no avail.

On December 18, CIA director Tenet warned Clinton that there was increased risk of a new bin Laden attack. The best information indicated it would occur abroad, he said, but the United States itself was also vulnerable. Intelligence had been coming in of terrorist plans similar to what was actually being planned.

A Pakistani recently arrived in the States had told the FBI of having been recruited in England, flown to Pakistan, and given training on how to hijack passenger planes. His instructions, he said, had been to join five or six other men—they included trainee hijacking pilots—already in America. On arrival in New York, however, he had gotten cold feet and turned himself in. Though the man passed FBI lie detector tests, no action was taken. He was simply returned to London.

In Italy in August, a bug planted by Italian police had picked up a chilling conversation between a Yemeni just arrived at Bologna airport and a known terrorist operative. Asked how his trip had been, the Yemeni replied that he had been "studying airplanes." He spoke of a "surprise strike that will come from the other country . . . one of those strikes that will never be forgotten" engineered by "a madman but a genius . . . in the future listen to the news and remember these words. We can fight any power using airplanes."

Such intelligence was routinely shared with other Western intelligence agencies, according to a senior Italian counterterrorism officer interviewed by the authors. How long this fragment of information took to reach American analysts, however, remains unclear.

In September, there was fear of a 9/11-style attack during the Olympic Games in Sydney, Australia. Fighters patrolled overhead, ready to intercept any aircraft that might be used to target the stadium. The principal perceived source of the threat, security chief Paul McKinnon has said, was bin Laden.

The FBI and the Federal Aviation Administration, however, downplayed the notion that an attack was possible within the United States. "FBI investigations," a joint assessment said in December 2000, "do not suggest evidence of plans to target domestic civil aviation." Further investigation of activity at American flight schools, the Bureau's headquarters unit told field offices, was "deemed imprudent."

CIA OFFICIALS had briefed candidate George Bush and his staff on the terrorist threat two months before the election, bluntly warning that "Americans would die in terrorist acts inspired by bin Laden" in the next four years. In late November, after the election but while the result was still being contested, President Clinton authorized the Agency to give Bush the same data he himself was receiving.

The election once settled, Vice President–elect Cheney, Secretary of State–designate Colin Powell, and National Security Adviser–designate Condoleezza Rice received detailed briefings on bin Laden and al Qaeda. "As I briefed Rice," Clarke recalled, "her facial expression gave me the impression she had never heard the term before." Asked about that, Rice said acidly that she found it peculiar that Clarke should have been "sitting there reading my body language." She told the 9/11 Commission that she and colleagues had in fact been quite "cognizant of the group." Clarke, for his part, claimed most senior officials in the incoming administration did not know what al Qaeda was.

Clinton's assistant secretary of defense for special operations, Brian Sheridan, told Rice that al Qaeda was "not an amateur-type deal . . . It's serious stuff, these guys are not going away." Rice listened but asked no questions. "I offered to brief anyone, anytime," Sheridan recalled. No one took him up on the offer.

The Commission on National Security, which had been at work for two and a half years, was about to issue a final report concluding that an attack "on American soil" was likely in the not-too-distant future. "Failure to prevent mass-casualty attacks against the American homeland," the report said, "will jeopardize not only American lives but U.S. foreign policy writ large. It would undermine support for U.S. international leadership and for many of our personal freedoms, as well. . . . In the face of this threat, our nation has no coherent or integrated government structures."

So seriously did Commission members take the threat that they pressed to see Bush and Cheney even before the inauguration. They got no meeting, however, then or later.

Bush, for his part, met with Clinton at the White House. As Clinton was to recall in his 2004 autobiography, he told the incoming president that Osama bin Laden and al Qaeda would be his biggest security problem.

Bush would tell the 9/11 Commission he "did not remember much being said about al Qaeda" during the briefing. In his 2010 memoir, he dealt with the subject by omitting it altogether. According to Clinton, Bush "listened to what I had to say without much comment, then changed the subject."

TWENTY-SIX

"WE ARE NOT THIS STORY'S AUTHOR," GEORGE BUSH told the American people in his inaugural speech on January 20, 2001. God would direct events during his presidency. "An angel," he declared, citing a statesman of Thomas Jefferson's day, "still rides in the whirlwind and directs this storm."

In the months and years since the whirlwind of 9/11, statesmen, intelligence officers, and law enforcement officials have assiduously played the blame game, passed the buck, and—in almost all cases—ducked responsibility. No one, no one at all, would in the end be held to account.

The Clinton administration's approach, Condoleezza Rice has been quoted as saying, had been "empty rhetoric that made us look feckless." The former President, for his part, staunchly defended his handling of the terrorist threat. "They ridiculed me for trying," Clinton said of Bush's people. "They had eight months to try. They did not try."

"What we did in the eight months," Rice riposted, "was at least as aggressive as what the Clinton administration did. . . . The notion [that] somehow for eight months the Bush administration sat there and didn't do that is just flatly false."

Quite early in the presidency, according to Rice, Bush told her: "I'm tired of swatting at flies. . . . I'm tired of playing defense. I want to play offense. I want to take the fight to the terrorists." Counterterrorism coordinator Clarke, who was held over from the Clinton administration, recalled being sent a presidential directive to "just solve this problem."

The record shows, however, that nothing effective was done.

JUST FIVE DAYS after the inauguration, Rice received a memorandum from Clarke headed "Presidential Policy Initiative/Review—the al Qaeda Network." It had two attachments, a "Strategy for Eliminating the Threat" worked up especially for the transition to the new administration, and an older "Political-Military" plan that had the same aim.

Al Qaeda, the memo stressed, was "not some narrow little terrorist issue." It was an "active, organized, major force. . . . We would make a major error if we underestimated the challenge al Qaeda poses." A meeting of "Principals"—cabinet-level members of the government—Clarke wrote, was "*urgently*" required. The italicization and the underlining of the word "urgently" are Clarke's in the original.

Suggestions for action aside, the material said al Qaeda had "multiple, active cells capable of launching military-style, large-scale terrorist operations," that it appeared sleeper agents were active within the United States. It proposed an increased funding level for CIA activity in Afghanistan. It asked, too, when and how the new administration would respond to the attack on the USS *Cole*—the indications, by now, were that al Qaeda had indeed been responsible.

Condoleezza Rice would claim in testimony to the

9/11 Commission that "No al Qaeda plan was turned over to the new administration." Nor, she complained, had there been any recommendation as to what she should do about specific points. The staff director of Congress's earlier Joint Inquiry into 9/11, Eleanor Hill— a former inspector general at the Defense Department —was shocked to hear Rice say that.

30009

NATIONAL SECURITY COUNCIL
WASHINGTON, D.C. 20504

January 25, 2001

INFORMATION

MEMORANDUM FOR CONDOLEEZZA RICE

FROM: RICHARD A. CLARKE

SUBJECT: Presidential Policy Initiative/Review -- The Al-
             Qida Network

Steve asked today that we propose major Presidential policy
reviews or initiatives. We *urgently* need such a Principals
level review on the al Qida network.

Just some Terrorist Group?

As we noted in our briefings for you, al Qida is not some
narrow, little terrorist issue that needs to be included in
broader regional policy. Rather, several of our regional
policies need to address centrally the transnational challenge
to the US and our interests posed by the al Qida network. By
proceeding with separate policy reviews on Central Asia, the
GCC, North Africa, etc. we would deal inadequately with the need
for a comprehensive multi-regional policy on al Qida.

al Qida is the active, organized, major force that is using a
distorted version of Islam as its vehicle to achieve two goals:

    --to drive the US out of the Muslim world, forcing the
withdrawal of our military and economic presence in countries
from Morocco to Indonesia;

Within a week of President Bush's inauguration, counterterrorism coordinator Clarke called for top-level action. By 9/11, eight months later, none had been ordered.

"Having served in government for twenty-some years, I was horrified by that response," Hill said. "She is the national security adviser. She can't just sit there and wait. . . . Her underlings are telling her that she has a problem. It's her job to be a leader and direct them . . . not to sit there complacently waiting for someone to tell her, the leader, what to do."

The Clarke submission had in fact made a series of proposals for action. The pressing request, however, was for the prompt meeting of cabinet-level officials. Far from getting it, Clarke found that he himself was no longer to be a member of the Principals Committee. He was instead to report to a Committee of Deputy Secretaries. There were to be no swift decisions on anything pertinent to dealing with al Qaeda.

Though candidate Bush had declared there should be retaliation for the *Cole* attack, there would be none. Rice and Bush wanted something more effective, the former national security adviser has said, than a "tit-for-tat" response. By the time the Bush team took over, she added, the attack had become "ancient history."

As for the deputy secretaries, they did not meet to discuss terrorism for three full months. When al Qaeda was addressed, at the end of April, Deputy Defense Secretary Paul Wolfowitz was deprecatory about the "little terrorist in Afghanistan." "I just don't understand," he said, "why we are beginning by talking about this one man bin Laden."

It was a tetchy, inconclusive meeting, which agreed only on having more papers written and more meetings held. Not until July would the deputies produce the draft of an overall plan for action.

It was not only Clarke sounding the tom-tom of alarm. The former deputy national security adviser, Lieutenant General Donald Kerrick, who stayed on for a few months in 2001, wrote in a memo, "We are going to be struck again." He received no reply, and would conclude that Bush's people were "gambling nothing would happen." The chairman of the National Commission on Terrorism, Paul Bremer, said in a speech as early as February that the new administration seemed "to be paying no attention to the problem of terrorism. What they will do is stagger along until there's a major incident and then suddenly say, 'Oh, my God, shouldn't we be organized to deal with this?' That's too bad. They've been given a window of opportunity with very little terrorism now, and they're not taking advantage of it."

"The highest priority must invariably be on those things that threaten the lives of Americans or the physical security of the United States," CIA director Tenet told the Senate Intelligence Committee the same month. "Osama bin Laden and his global network of lieutenants and associates remain the most immediate and serious threat."

A scoop article in 2007 in France's newspaper of record, *Le Monde*, made public a large batch of French intelligence documents. Copies of the documents, which the authors have seen, include a January 2001 report stating that bin Laden and others had been planning an airplane hijacking for the past twelve months.

Seven airlines had been considered as potential targets under the plan as initially discussed, the report said, five American, Air France, and Lufthansa. The U.S. airlines mentioned included American and United, the two airlines that were to be hit on 9/11. According to French intelligence sources, the report was passed on to the CIA at the time.

The CIA and the FBI shared at least the gist of perceived threats with the FAA, the body responsible for supervising the safety of the flying public. Bin Laden or ision that, after 9/11, would "improper." Improperly ...rs' leader was back in the preventative action, however, ordered ... to safeguard cockpit security, did not alert the crews ... flew the planes to anything special about the situation.

On most days, at his own request, President Bush met with CIA director Tenet. Every day, too, the President received a CIA briefing known as the PDB—the President's Daily Brief. Between the inauguration and September 10, bin Laden was mentioned in forty PDBs.

THE TERRORIST OPERATION, of course, continued throughout the period. As Bush prepared for the presidency, Atta had made a brief January trip outside the United States, flying to Europe for a secure meeting with Binalshibh. Each of the hijack pilots, he was able to report, had completed their training and awaited further orders.

Marwan al-Shehhi traveled to Morocco for reasons unknown. Ziad Jarrah reentered the United States—this time accompanied by his lover, Aysel. He introduced her around the flight school in Florida and—equipped as he now was with his new pilot's license—flew her to Key West and back. Aysel had had her suspicions about what her lover was up to in the United States, had wondered whether he really was learning to fly. Now she believed him.

Any travel outside the United States was a risk for the terrorists, as there was always the possibility that they would not be allowed back in. Jarrah, with his Lebanese passport and a girlfriend on his arm, encountered no problem and was readmitted as a tourist.

Reentry was not so easy for Atta and Shehhi. Atta, whose visa status was out of order, faced the hurdle of seeing two immigration inspectors. He was allowed in as

a tourist all the same—a de[...]
be ruled as having bee[...]
admitted or not, the hijack[...]
country.

Shehhi, too, almost blew it. When he was referred to a second inspector—because his visa status also looked dubious—he balked at going to the inspection room. "I thought he would bolt," the immigration man was to recall. "I told someone in secondary to watch him. He made me remember him. If he had been smart he wouldn't have done that." Nevertheless, Shehhi was readmitted.

One after another, the systems designed to protect the United States had failed—and would fail again.

In the weeks that followed, Atta and Shehhi turned up in Florida, in Georgia, possibly in Tennessee, and in Virginia. Their movements in those states remain blurred, their purpose unclear. On several occasions, they rented single-engine airplanes. Witnesses who believed they encountered them would say Atta asked probing questions about a chemical plant, about crop duster planes, about a reservoir near a nuclear facility. KSM had left Atta free to consider optional targets.

The fourth of the future hijacking pilots, Hani Hanjour, stayed put in Arizona, devoting himself to learning more about big airliners at a flight training center. Though not deemed a promising student, he received a training center certificate showing that he had completed sixty hours on a Boeing 737–200 simulator. Hazmi, who never succeeded as a pilot at any level, stayed close to Hanjour. On Hanjour's behalf presumably, he sent off for videos from Sporty's Pilot Shop. He received information on Boeing flight systems, and advice on "How an Airline Captain Should Look and Act."

Following a trip to the Grand Canyon, Hazmi and Hanjour headed for the East Coast—and a vital appointment. In early May they were at Washington's Dulles Airport to greet two of the "muscle hijackers," the thirteen additional men trained for the violent, bloody work ahead.

All but one of the new arrivals were Saudis aged between twenty and twenty-eight, from the southwest of their country. None had more than a high school education, an education in which they had been inculcated with authorized government dogma such as "The Hour will not come until Muslims will fight the Jews and Muslims will kill all the Jews."

Saudi officials, on whom American investigators had to rely after 9/11, said only one of the muscle recruits had held a job. He taught physical education. Some were devout—one had acted as imam at his local mosque—but none had been considered zealots. One had suffered from depression, his brother said, until he consulted a religious adviser. Two, according to the Saudis, had been known to drink alcohol. All wound up in a bin Laden training camp, some of them after starting out with plans to join the jihad in Chechnya.

Osama bin Laden himself picked many of these young men for the 9/11 operation, according to KSM. Size and strength were not a primary qualification—most were no more than five foot seven. What was essential was the readiness to die as a martyr—and the ability to obtain a U.S. visa. Before final training, all the Saudis had been sent home to get one.

In Saudi Arabia, with its special relationship to the United States, getting a visa was astonishingly easy— easier by far than the arduous process that had long been the norm for citizens of friendly Western countries. Visa applications were successful even when not properly filled out, let alone when they were literately presented. One future hijacker described his occupation as "teater." Two said they were headed for a city named as "Wasantwn" to join an employer or school identified only as "South City."

Obtaining a visa turned out to be even easier for the last four of the muscle hijackers to apply. Under a new U.S. program named Visa Express, applicants could merely apply through a travel agency, with no need even to appear at the consulate. The in-joke was that "all Saudis had to do was throw their passports over the consulate wall." The then American consul general in Riyadh, Thomas Furey, told the 9/11 Commission he "did not think Saudis were security risks."

Now that the recruits had visas in hand, the final phase of training involved hijacking techniques, advice on how to deal with sky marshals, and lessons in killing. The men bound for America were issued Swiss knives. Then, by way of rehearsal for the slaughter of passengers and aircrew, they used them to butcher sheep and camels.

According to KSM, trainees were also obliged to learn about hijacking trains, carrying out truck bombings, and blowing up buildings. This was "to muddy somewhat the real purpose of their training, in case they were caught while in transit to the U.S." The men were told they were to take part in an airborne suicide operation, KSM said, only when they reached Dubai en route to the United States.

The muscle hijackers arrived during the late spring and early summer, traveling mostly in pairs. Except for one man, who was supposedly on business as "a dealer," the word often used by Saudi applicants to signify "businessman," they masqueraded as tourists. Several had unsatisfactory documentation—one called himself by different names on different forms—yet none had real difficulty getting into the United States. The rickety system was failing still.

By prior arrangement with Atta, some flew into Washington or New York, the others into airports in Florida. Atta looked after logistics in the South, while Hazmi—at this stage viewed as second-in-command—made arrangements in the North. With the newcomers came a fresh supply of money to feed and maintain the terrorists as the countdown to 9/11 began.

As had most of those who preceded them, the thirteen had recorded videotaped martyrdom messages in Afghanistan. "We left our families," one said, "to send a message the color of blood. The message says, 'Oh Allah, take from our blood today until you are satisfied.' The message says: 'The time of humiliation and subjugation is over.' It is time to kill Americans in their homeland, among their sons and near their forces and intelligence."

The hijackers' videotapes would not be released until after 9/11.

WARNINGS THAT something specific was afoot were now reaching the outside world with increasing frequency. Bin Laden's archenemy in Afghanistan, Ahmed Shah Massoud, the most prominent military figure still undefeated by the Taliban, brought a blunt message with him on a visit to Europe in April.

At a press conference at the European Parliament in Strasbourg, Massoud made a wide-ranging appeal for assistance. "If President Bush doesn't help us," he said in response to a reporter's question on al Qaeda, "then these terrorists will damage the United States and Europe very soon, and it will be too late." Though the comment received little if any coverage in the media, the CIA was paying close attention. Two agency officers, sent from

Washington for the express purpose, had a private meeting with Massoud in France. The full detail of what he told them remains classified, but a heavily redacted intelligence document reveals that he had "gained limited knowledge of the intentions of the Saudi millionaire, bin Laden, and his terrorist organization, al Qaeda, to perform a terrorist act against the U.S., on a scale larger than the 1998 bombing of the U.S. embassies in Kenya and Tanzania [two lines deleted]."

CIA director Tenet, for his part, has revealed significantly more about Massoud's warning. He told his Agency visitors that "bin Laden was sending twenty-five operatives to Europe for terrorist activities. The operatives, he said, would be traveling through Iran and Bosnia." The intelligence was not far off target. "Twenty-five" was close to nineteen, the actual number of terrorists dispatched on the 9/11 mission, and some of them did travel through Iran.

Around the time Massoud talked with the CIA officers, ominous information came in from Cairo. Egyptian intelligence, itself ever alert to the threat from the Muslim Brotherhood—and aware that Ayman al-Zawahiri, the long-distance element of that threat, was in Afghanistan at bin Laden's side—had managed to penetrate al Qaeda. "We knew that something was going to happen," President Mubarak would recall, "to the United States, maybe inside the United States, maybe in an airplane, maybe in embassies." Imprecise though it was, the warning was passed to the CIA's station in Egypt.

When he addressed a class at the National War College that month, the CIA's Cofer Black said he believed "something big was coming, and that it would very likely be in the U.S." He also spoke of his foreboding at a meeting with executives at the FBI Academy at Quantico.

The Bureau's director, Louis Freeh, raised the subject of terrorism, that same day, with Attorney General John Ashcroft, to be told, according to one account—which has since been denied by a Justice Department spokesperson—that Ashcroft "didn't want to hear about it." It was not the last time, reportedly, that the attorney general would speak in that vein.

Exactly what warnings CIA director Tenet personally passed to President Bush, what was in the Daily Briefs the President received, and how he responded, we do not know. With one exception, the Bush administration briefs remain classified. Very similar briefing documents, however, went each morning to other very senior officials. Commission staff who read them learned that, in April and May alone, such senior officials received summaries headed "Bin Laden Planning Multiple Operations," "Bin Laden Public Profile May Presage Attack," and "Bin Laden's Networks' Plans Advancing."

That the CIA and other intelligence agencies were getting a stream of intelligence is not surprising. Al Qaeda's security was constantly being breached, notably by Osama bin Laden himself. His "public profile," to use the Agency's wording, reflected in part the fact that the terrorist leader had been making triumphalist speeches to his followers. He was also hopelessly indiscreet.

A young Australian recruit to the cause, David Hicks, got off letter after gushing letter to his mother back home. "They send a lot of spies here," he wrote in May. "One way to get around [the spies] is to send a letter to 'Abu Muslim Australia'. . . . By the way, I have met Osama bin Laden about twenty times, he is a lovely brother. . . . I will get to meet him again. There is a group of us going."

A follower who served bin Laden as bodyguard, Shadi Abdalla, would recall his leader boasting of plans to kill thousands of people in the United States. "All the people [in the camp] knew that bin Laden said that there would be something done against America ... America was going to be hit."

Even one of the future hijackers was blabbing. Khalid al-Mihdhar, still in the Middle East following his impetuous return home to see his wife and newborn baby, chattered to a cousin in Saudi Arabia. Five attacks were in the works, he said—close to the eventual total of four—and due by summer's end. He quoted bin Laden as having said, "I will make it happen even if I do it by myself."

Bin Laden himself went even further, asking a crowd in one of the camps to pray for "the success of an attack involving twenty martyrs." Had Ramzi Binalshibh not been refused a visa, and had it not proved impossible to replace him, there would have been twenty hijackers on 9/11.

"It's time to penetrate America and Israel and hit them where it hurts," said bin Laden. "Penetrate."

The Taliban regime, worried in part about the potential consequences, asked bin Laden to moderate his outbursts. Their guest got around that by calling in an MBC—Middle East Broadcasting Corporation—TV reporter and telling him—off camera and off mic—that there would soon be "some news." Then he sat back as an aide, Atef, said: "In the next few weeks we will carry out a big surprise, and we will strike or attack American and Israeli interests." Others told the reporter that the "coffin business will increase in the United States." Asked to confirm the nature of the "news"—again off camera— bin Laden just smiled.

Behind the scenes with KSM, he had again become impatient. He was a man with a penchant that many in his culture shared, for auguries and superstition. At one point that spring, with no more justification than that the number 7 was by tradition auspicious, bin Laden urged KSM to bring forward the hijackings and strike on May 12. That date, he pointed out, would be exactly seven months after the successful attack on the *Cole*. KSM told him the team was not yet ready.

In mid-June, following reports in the media that Israel's prime minister Ariel Sharon was within days due to visit President Bush at the White House, bin Laden bombarded KSM with requests for the operation to be activated at once. The MBC television team had been told during their recent visit that the coming strike would be "a big gift for the intifada."

A strike coinciding with the Sharon trip—not least when Palestinian leader Yasser Arafat had pointedly received no invitation from the White House—must have seemed highly desirable. KSM, however, again persuaded bin Laden that precipitate action would be ill-advised.

All this was terrible tradecraft, amateurish folly that could have doomed the 9/11 plan to failure.

IN WASHINGTON, meanwhile, Richard Clarke still pressed in vain for expeditious action. Fearing that he was becoming "like Captain Ahab with bin Laden as the White Whale," he had long since thought he should consider finding other work. Yet he was still there at the end of May, still worrying.

A recently released Commission staff note, written following a review of National Security Council files, observes that it was clear that "Clarke was driving process in the new Bush Administration, not Condi Rice or Steve Hadley. Not much was going on at their level against AQ. Highest levels of government were not engaged, were not driving the process."

"When these attacks occur, as they likely will," Clarke wrote Rice on May 29, "we will wonder what more we could have done to stop them."

The following day, Rice asked George Tenet and CIA colleagues to assess the gravity of the danger. On a scale of one to ten, she was told, it rated a seven.

Two weeks later, a report reached the CIA that KSM was "recruiting people to travel to the United States to meet with colleagues already there." On June 21, with the wave of threat information continuing, the intelligence agencies—and the military in the Middle East—went on high alert. As the month ended, with the July 4 holiday approaching, the National Security Agency intercepted terrorist traffic indicating that something "very, very, very, very big" was imminent. Clarke duly advised Rice.

The holiday passed without incident, but the anxiety remained. On July 10, according to Tenet, his counterterrorism chief, Cofer Black, delivered a threat assessment that made his hair stand on end. With Black and the head of the bin Laden unit at his side, the director rushed immediately to see Rice at the White House. There followed a deeply unsatisfactory encounter—one the 9/11 Commission Report failed to mention.

The CIA chiefs told Rice flatly: "There will be a significant terrorist attack in the coming weeks or months." The bin Laden unit head went through the bald facts of the intelligence. His colleagues described CIA ploys that might disrupt and delay the attack. Then they urged immediate decisions on measures that would tackle the overall problem. The slow, plodding deliberations of the deputy secretaries were taking too long.

Rice asked Richard Clarke, who was also present, whether he agreed. Clarke, according to Tenet, "put his elbows on his knees and his head fell into his hands and he gave an exasperated yes." "The President," Tenet told Rice, "needed to align his policy with the new reality." Rice assured them that Bush would do that.

She did not convince the deputation from the CIA. According to the *Washington Post*'s Bob Woodward, writing in 2006, they "felt they were not getting through to Rice. She was polite, but they felt the brush-off. . . . Rice had seemed focused on other administration priorities, especially the ballistic missile defense system that Bush had campaigned on. She was in a different place. . . . No immediate action meant great risk."

In Cofer Black's view, Woodward wrote, "The decision to just keep planning was a sustained policy failure. Rice and the Bush team had been in hibernation too long." "Adults," Black said, "should not have a system like this."

Black had been sure for months that catastrophe was coming. Sure, too, that as counterterrorist head he would take the flak for it, he had long had his resignation signed and ready in his desk. The bin Laden unit head—his name is still officially withheld—and Michael Scheuer, his predecessor, were also now talking of resigning.

The same day the CIA chiefs tried to get action from the White House, an FBI agent in Arizona sent a memo to a number of headquarters officials, including four members of the Bureau's own bin Laden unit. Agent Kenneth Williams reported: "The purpose of this communication is to advise the Bureau and New York of the possibility of a coordinated effort by Osama bin Laden to send students to the United States to attend civil aviation universities and colleges. Phoenix has observed an inordinate number of individuals of investigative interest who are attending or who have attended. . . . These individuals will be in a position in the future to conduct terror activity against civil aviation targets."

Over eight pages, Williams laid out the reasons for his concern. One man he named was a known contact of bin Laden's senior accomplice Abu Zubaydah. Another connected to the two Saudis who two years earlier had come under suspicion for their behavior during an America West flight. Investigators were later to conclude that the same man's associates had included Hani Hanjour—the 9/11 hijacking pilot who had trained in Arizona.

Agent Williams recommended checking on flight schools around the nation. Yet he got no response, and his prescient message received minimal circulation. FBI officials worried that the checks he proposed would risk accusations of "racial profiling."

Only a week earlier, all FBI regions had been alerted to the terrorist threat and urged to "exercise extreme vigilance." "I had asked to know if a sparrow fell from a tree," counterterrorism coordinator Clarke would write long after 9/11. "Somewhere in FBI there was information that strange things had been going on at flight schools. . . . Red lights and bells should have been going off."

Had the FBI recipients of Williams's memo been aware of the attitude of the man who headed the Bush Justice Department, their torpor might have been more understandable. Acting Director Thomas Pickard has said that, following Director Freeh's resignation that June, he tried repeatedly to get Attorney General Ashcroft to give the terrorist threat his attention. When he approached the subject for the second time, on July 12, Ashcroft abruptly cut him off—as he reportedly had Freeh back in the spring.

"I don't want to hear about that anymore," snapped the attorney general, according to Pickard. "There's nothing I can do about that." Pickard remonstrated, saying he thought Ashcroft should speak directly with his CIA counterpart, but the attorney general made himself even clearer. "I don't want you to ever talk to me about al Qaeda, about these threats. I don't want to hear about al Qaeda anymore."

"Fishing rod in hand," CBS News noted two weeks later, "Attorney General John Ashcroft left on a weekend trip to Missouri aboard a chartered government jet." Asked why he was not using a commercial airline, the Justice Department cited a "threat assessment," saying he would fly only by private jet for the remainder of his term. Asked whether he knew the nature of the threat, Ashcroft himself responded, "Frankly, I don't."

Late on July 20, when President Bush arrived in Italy to attend a G8 summit, antiaircraft guns lined the airport perimeter. He and other leaders slept not on land but on ships at sea. Next day, Bush had an audience with the Pope not at the Vatican but at the papal residence outside Rome. Wherever he went, the airspace was closed and fighters flew cover overhead. Egypt's President Mubarak had reportedly warned of a possible bin Laden attack using "an airplane stuffed with explosives."

TWENTY-SEVEN

I N THE UNITED STATES, MEANWHILE, THE TERRORISTS
had continued to move toward their goal. On July 4, as
Americans celebrated the holiday and security officials
fretted, Khalid al-Mihdhar had flown back into JFK
Airport—unchallenged. It should not have been that way.

The CIA had identified Mihdhar as a prime suspect
eighteen months earlier—it was to emerge after 9/11—
when the Saudi flew to join fellow terrorists in Kuala
Lumpur. While he was on his way there, during a
stopover in Dubai, the local intelligence service broke
into his hotel room at the request of the CIA. His passport, which was copied, had given the Agency two superb
leads. It now knew not only Mihdhar's full identity but
also the fact that he had a valid entry visa for the United
States.

Even so, and although the CIA firmly believed he and
his companions in Kuala Lumpur were terrorists, it had
not placed Mihdhar on the TIPOFF list of known and
suspected terrorists. And it had withheld what it knew
from the FBI. The CIA's handling of its intelligence on
Mihdhar—and the almost identical information on the
companion with whom he arrived in the States,
Nawaf al-Hazmi—had allowed the first of the 9/11
operatives to enter the States under their own names and

live openly in California in the months that followed.

The CIA's action—or failure to take appropriate action—had also allowed Mihdhar to depart freely in mid-2000, when he returned to the Middle East for an extended period. Then in summer 2001, and because the CIA continued to withhold what it knew about him from U.S. Immigration, he had easily obtained yet another entry visa to get back into the country.

So it was, on July 4, that Mihdhar was able to breeze back into America and join his accomplices as they made final preparations for the 9/11 operation. His return brought the hijackers' numbers up to nineteen, the full complement of those who were to attack on 9/11. Had the CIA's performance been merely an appalling blunder, as it would later claim? Or, as another theory holds it, does the Agency's explanation hide an even more disquieting intelligence truth? That possibility will be considered later.

The team was now divided into two groups, north and south. Mihdhar made the short trip to Paterson, New Jersey, where Hazmi, Hanjour, and three of the muscle hijackers were already based. Six of them lived there, crammed into a one-bedroom apartment, during this phase of the operation. The other operatives settled in Florida, mostly around Fort Lauderdale. There are clues to how some of them spent their private time.

Hazmi had earlier been trawling the Internet for a bride. Some Muslims hold that marriage is obligatory under Islam—being married is seen as a central statement of one's faith. Even Atta, who behaved as though he loathed everything about women, had told his first German hosts that it was difficult for him to be unmarried at the age of twenty-four. Then, he had said he expected to return to Egypt and marry and have children there. When he stayed on in Germany, however, and a fellow student looked for a suitable wife for him, Atta turned out not to be interested.

None of this means that he was not heterosexual. Sexual self-denial can be a feature of the committed jihadi life. One al Qaeda operative, it was recently reported, recommended that his comrades take injections to promote impotence—as he did himself—to avoid being distracted by the female sex.

Marriage had continued to be a goal for Hazmi, though, even when he was in the United States and launched on a mission in which he knew he was going to die. KSM encouraged the aspiration, promising a $700-a-month stipend should he succeed. The hijacker-to-be even advertised for a wife on muslimmarriage.com, letting it be known that he was open to taking a Mexican bride—apparently hoping that a Hispanic woman would at least somewhat fit the bill.

Hazmi apparently lost interest, however, when only one person responded to the post, an Egyptian woman he apparently deemed unsuitable. A morsel of documentary evidence suggests that he fell back on more leisurely pursuits in spring 2001. He went to Walmart and bought fishing equipment.

Over the final months, others—Muslim zealots though they might be, they shared the lusts of ordinary mortals—sampled the offerings of the American sex industry. A witness at Wacko's strip club in Jacksonville said she recognized Jarrah—from photographs—as having been a customer. On a trip to Nevada, Shehhi reportedly watched lap dancing at the Olympic Garden Topless Cabaret. He also turned up at a video store in Florida, accompanied by one of the muscle hijackers who was to fly with him, and bought $400 worth of porno-graphic movies and sex toys. In Maryland, where two of the team spent a few days, another of the terrorists returned repeatedly to the Adult Lingerie Center. He purchased nothing, just flipped through the smut on offer, looked "uncomfortable," and left.

Ziad Jarrah, the only pilot hijacker known to have had a long-term relationship with a woman, went back and forth between the United States and Germany to see his lover, Aysel Sengün. When in the States, he took a series of lessons in one-on-one combat. His trainer was Bert Rodriguez, of the US-1 Fitness Center in Dania, Florida, who had previously taught a Saudi prince's bodyguard.

Jarrah "was very humble, very quiet . . . in good shape," Rodriguez remembered. "Ziad was like Luke Skywalker. You know when Luke walks the invisible path? You have to believe it's there. And if you do believe, it *is* there. Ziad believed it." In four months, he gave Jarrah more than ninety lessons. They discussed fighting with knives. "It's always good policy to bleed your opponent," Rodriguez advised. "Try to cut him so that he sees where he's cut. If you have a choice, cut under the arm."

Over the months, the evidence would show, several of the hijackers attended fitness classes. Some would buy knives—or utility tools, like box cutters, that would serve their deadly purpose just as well as knives.

Jarrah, who also worked at his flying, went up to Hortman Aviation near Philadelphia hoping to rent a light aircraft. He flew well enough, but proved inept at landing the plane and using the radio. Accompanying him was a man he said was his "uncle," an older Arab whose identity has never been established. Hortman's owner would recall that Jarrah wanted to fly the Hudson River Corridor—a congested route known to pilots as a "hallway"—which passed several New York landmarks, including the World Trade Center.

Hani Hanjour, apparently still striving to become a competent pilot, did manage to fly the Hudson Corridor with an instructor. Presumably because he made errors, he was turned down when he asked to fly the route again. Later, however, he had a practice flight that took him near Washington, D.C.—where weeks later he would pilot the 757 that struck the Pentagon.

Four of the hijacker pilots, and one of the muscle men, took time to familiarize themselves with the routine on transcontinental flights within the United States. Shehhi first, then Jarrah, followed by Atta—twice, in his case— muscle hijacker Waleed al-Shehri, Hazmi, and Hanjour all made trips to Las Vegas. All flew First Class aboard Boeing 757s and 767s, the aircraft types that would be downed on 9/11.

THERE WERE GLITCHES. On July 7, an apparently frantic Atta dialed a German cell phone seventy-four times. It had been decided earlier that he and intermediary Binalshibh, who had been in Afghanistan taking instructions from bin Laden, needed to talk at this critical point—and in person—to avoid the risk of a communications intercept. Then, after Atta made contact to say he could not make it to Southeast Asia, they settled on a rendezvous in Europe—though not in Germany. Too many people knew them there, and they feared being seen together.

Last-minute problems disentangled, they arranged to get together in Spain. During a stopover in Zurich Atta bought two knives, perhaps to check that he could get away with taking them on board on the onward leg to Madrid. He and Binalshibh conferred for days when they finally met up.

Binalshibh arrived with the now familiar message. Bin Laden wanted the attacks to go forward as rapidly as possible, and this time not merely because he was impatient. With so many operatives now in holding positions in the United States, he had become understandably anxious about security. Binalshibh also came with a reaffirmation of the preferred targets. All were to be "symbols of America," the World Trade Center, the Pentagon, the Capitol, and hopefully the White House. Given the option, bin Laden "preferred the White House over the Capitol."

Atta thought the White House might be too tough a target—he was waiting for an assessment from Hani Hanjour. Were he and Shehhi not able to hit the World Trade Center, he said, they would crash the planes they had hijacked into the streets of Manhattan. Final decisions on targeting, KSM has said since, were left "in the hands of the pilots."

At Atta's request, Binalshibh had brought necklaces and bracelets from Southeast Asia. Atta hoped that by wearing them on the day, the hijackers would pass as wealthy Saudis and avoid notice. Binalshibh returned to Germany once their business was done. Once there, as agreed, he organized himself for the communications that would be necessary in the weeks to come.

He obtained two new phones, one for contacts with Atta and the second for liaison with KSM. The evidence would suggest they had agreed on using simple codes for security purposes.

Atta, meanwhile, flew back to the United States, to be admitted yet again without difficulty—in spite of the fact that, given his travel record, he should have faced probing questions.

He returned to what appeared to him to be a crisis in the making. There had been growing tension between himself, the single-minded authoritarian, and Ziad Jarrah. Atta found his fellow pilot's repeated trips out of the country disquieting. Was a key member of the team about to drop out?

Jarrah may indeed have been wavering between devotion to the cause and the love of a woman. He telephoned Aysel Sengün more than fifty times during the early part of July, then decided to take off for Germany to see her again—without making a return reservation.

Binalshibh, whom Atta had told of his concern during the meeting in Spain, had in turn mentioned it to KSM. KSM responded with alarm. A "divorce," he said, apparently referring to the difficulties between Atta and Jarrah, would "cost a lot of money." As though keeping a close eye on him, Atta went to the airport to see Jarrah off when he left for Europe. Binalshibh met him on arrival at Düsseldorf.

During an "emotional" exchange, Binalshibh urged Jarrah not to abandon the mission. Jarrah's priority, however, appeared to be to get to Aysel as rapidly as possible. The lovers, she would remember, spent almost two weeks with each other. "We spent the entire time together," she recalled. "I did not study, but spent all the time alone with him."

In the end, Jarrah's commitment to the mission proved more potent than the pull of Aysel's love for him. On August 5, he flew back to Florida and the apartment that he was renting all summer. Outside the house, on a quiet street in Fort Lauderdale, hung a wind chime with the message "This House Is Full of Love."

Jarrah made an out-of-the-blue call to his former landlady in Germany that month, and surprised her by saying that he was in America learning to fly "big planes." So he was. Purchases he made included a GPS system, cockpit instrument diagrams for a Boeing 757, and a poster of a 757 cockpit.

In an ideal world, had the law enforcement and intelligence system functioned to perfection, the 9/11 operation might by now have run into problems—for the most mundane of reasons. Mohamed Atta and his second-in-command, Nawaf al-Hazmi, had been noticed, or should have been noticed, or had actually been stopped by the police, many times that year.

It had been routine, when Atta was pulled over for speeding in Florida in July, for the officer who stopped him to run a check on his name. The check should have told him that there was a bench warrant out for Atta's arrest—he had failed to appear in court in connection with a previous violation. Hazmi, for his part, had been stopped for speeding in April, had possessed the gall to report that he had been attacked by a mugger in May, and had rear-ended a car on the George Washington Bridge in June. His driving, moreover, had also caught the attention of a traffic policeman in New Jersey.

Because the CIA had long since identified Hazmi as a suspected terrorist, because the Agency knew he was likely in the United States, there should long since have been an alert out for him. As there should have been for his comrade Mihdhar, when he slithered back into the country on July 4.

"Every cop on the beat needs to know what we know," CIA director Tenet was to say. But that would be after the fact of 9/11—when all was lost. The Agency had shared what it knew with no one in law enforcement.

At their meeting in Spain, when Binalshibh told Atta that bin Laden wanted the operation to go forward rapidly, the hijackers' leader had responded that he was not yet quite ready. He would come up with a date for the attacks, he said, in "five or six weeks." As the first week of August ended, three of those weeks had passed.

Atta had recently tapped out a message to several associates in Germany. It read: "Salaam! Hasn't the time come to fear God's word? Allah. I love you all."

*

IN WASHINGTON, warnings of impending attack had been coming in all summer. From France's intelligence service, the DGSE; from Russian counterintelligence, the FSB; and—again—from Egypt. Citing an operative inside Afghanistan, the Egyptian report indicated that "20 al Qaeda members had slipped into the U.S. and four of them had received flight training."

The most ominous warning, had it been heeded, reached the State Department from a source uniquely well placed to get wind of what bin Laden was hatching. The Taliban foreign minister, Wakil Muttawakil, had sent an emissary across the border into Pakistan to seek out a U.S. official to whom he could pass information.

Muttawakil, according to the emissary, had learned from the leader of one of the fundamentalist groups working with bin Laden of a coming "huge" attack on the United States. Already worried about the activities of Arab fighters in Afghanistan, the foreign minister now feared they were about to bring disaster down on his country in the shape of American retaliation. "The guests," as he put it, "are going to destroy the guesthouse."

So it was, in the third week of July, that the Taliban emissary met at a safe house with David Katz, principal officer of the U.S. consulate in the border town of Peshawar. Also present, reportedly, was a second, unnamed American. The emissary did not reveal exactly who in the Taliban regime had dispatched him on the mission. Muttawakil was taking a great risk in sending the message at all.

The bin Laden attack, the emissary said, "would take place on American soil and it was imminent. . . . Osama hoped to kill thousands of Americans. . . . I told Mr. Katz they should launch a new Desert Storm, like the campaign to drive Iraq out of Kuwait, but this time they should call it Mountain Storm and they should drive the foreigners out of Afghanistan."

According to diplomatic sources quoted in 2002, principal officer Katz—an experienced diplomat—did not pass on the warning to the State Department. "We were hearing a lot of that kind of stuff," one of the sources said. "When people keep saying the sky's going to fall in and it doesn't, a kind of warning fatigue sets in."

The CIA and counterterrorism coordinator Clarke, fielding incoming intelligence in July, reported up the line that bin Laden's plans seemed to have been temporarily postponed. One CIA brief for senior officials read: "Bin Laden Plans Delayed but Not Abandoned," another: "One Bin Laden Operation Delayed. Others Ongoing." Intelligence on a "near-term" attack had eased, Clarke said in an email to Rice, but it "will still happen."

New York Times reporter Judith Miller, busy working on a series of articles about al Qaeda, had been finding her Washington contacts unusually open about their worries. officials, she was to recall, had recently been "very spun-up . . . I got the sense that part of the reason I was being told of what was going on was that the people in counterterrorism were trying to get word to the President or the senior officials through the press, because they were not able to get listened to themselves."

The desperately slow progress of the Deputy Secretaries Committee, charged with deciding on a course of action against bin Laden, had been frustrating Clarke all year. In July, however, the deputies had finally decided on what to recommend to cabinet-level officials. "But the Principals' calendar was full," Clarke would recall, "and then they went away on vacation, many of them in August, so we couldn't meet in August."

*

PRESIDENT BUSH and Vice President Cheney were among those on vacation. Both, it was reported, planned to spend a good deal of time fishing. Bush was expected to spend the full month on his 1,583-acre ranch in Texas, not returning until Labor Day. "I'm sure," said his press secretary, "he'll have friends and family over to the ranch. He'll do a little policy. He'll keep up with events." This would tie with the longest presidential vacation on record in modern times, enjoyed by Richard Nixon, and 55 percent of respondents to a CNN/*USA Today*/Gallup poll thought that "too much."

For a president, however, there is no getting away from the CIA's daily intelligence brief—the PDB. The one Bush received on August 6 was to haunt him for years to come. CBS News would be first to hint at what it contained, in a story almost a year after 9/11. Apparently thanks to a leak, national security correspondent David Martin was to reveal that Bush had been warned that month that "bin Laden's terrorist network might hijack U.S. passenger planes."

Bombarded with questions the following day, White House press secretary Ari Fleischer would say the August 6 PDB had been a "very generalized" summary brought to the President in response to an earlier request. In a follow-up, he told reporters the PDB's heading had read: "Bin Laden Determined to Strike U.S." Condoleezza Rice, in her own separate briefing, made no reference to the title of the document. She went out of her way, however, to say the PDB had been "not a warning" but "an analytic report that talked about bin Laden's methods of operation, talked about what he had done historically." She characterized the document repeatedly as having been "historical," that day and in the future.

Rice said there had indeed been two references to hijacking in the PDB, but only to "hijacking in the traditional sense . . . very vague." No one, she thought, "could have predicted that these people would take an airplane and slam it into the World Trade Center, take another one and slam it into the Pentagon—that they would try to use an airplane as a missile."

In spite of efforts to slough it off, though, the August 6 PDB became the story that would not go away, the center of a two-year struggle between the Bush administration and panels investigating 9/11. The White House line was that, as the "the most highly sensitized classified document in the government," the daily briefs had to remain secret. The CIA, for its part, refused even to provide information on the way in which a PDB is prepared.

The nature of the daily briefs was in fact no mystery, for several of those delivered to earlier presidents had been released after they left office. A PDB consists of a series of short articles, enclosed in a leather binder, delivered to the President by his ubiquitous CIA briefer. It has been described as a "top-secret newspaper reporting on current developments around the world" and "a news digest for the very privileged." A PDB may contain truly secret information, but can as often be less than sensational, even dull.

Congress's Joint Inquiry was to press in vain for access to all relevant PDBs delivered to both Presidents Bush and Clinton. The 9/11 Commission would return to the fray—not least so as to be seen to have resolved the celebrated question that had once been asked about President Nixon during Watergate: "What did the President know and when did he first know it?" The more the Bush White House stonewalled, however, the more the commissioners pressed their case. "We had to use the equivalent of a blowtorch and pliers," Commissioner Richard Ben-Veniste recalled.

They did get to the PDBs in the end. The section of the August 6 brief on 9/11, just one and a half pages long, was finally released in April 2004 with redactions only of sources of information. This established a number of things that earlier White House flamming had obscured.

The heading of the August 6 PDB had not read, as Bush's press secretary had rendered it: "Bin Laden Determined to Strike U.S." Not quite. Inadvertently or otherwise, the secretary had omitted a single significant two-letter word. The actual title had been "Bin Laden Determined to Strike in U.S." The headline had itself been a clarion message to President Bush that bin Laden intended to attack on the U.S. mainland.

The very first sentence of the PDB, moreover, had told the President—in italicized type—that secret reports, friendly governments, and media coverage had indicated for the past four years that bin Laden wanted to attack within the United States. He had even said, according to an intelligence source—identity redacted—that he wanted to attack "in Washington."

In another paragraph, the PDB told the President that al Qaeda had personnel in the United States and "apparently maintains a support structure that could aid attacks." FBI information, the PDB said, "indicates patterns of suspicious activity in this country consistent with preparations for hijackings or other types of attacks, including recent surveillance of federal buildings in New York."

The day after the release of the PDB, President Bush told reporters that the document had "said nothing about an attack on America. It talked about intentions, about somebody who hated America. Well, we knew that . . . and as the President, I wanted to know if there was any-thing, any actionable intelligence. And I looked at the August 6th briefing. I was satisfied that some of the

have foreseen terrorists using planes as weapons? How to credit that, in light of the warnings in summer 2001 that the G8 summit in Genoa might be attacked by airborne kamikazes? Had Bush known about the Combat Air Patrol enforced over cities he visited in Italy? Had he known about the Egyptian president's warning? No, Bush said, he had known nothing about it.

If there had been a "serious concern" in the weeks before 9/11, Bush volunteered, he would have known about it. Ben-Veniste restrained himself from pointing out that the CIA brief of August 6 had been headed "Bin Laden Determined to Strike in U.S." Had the President not rated that as "serious"?

Ben-Veniste asked Bush whether, after receiving the PDB, he had asked National Security Adviser Rice to follow up with the FBI. Had she done so? The President "could not recall." Nor could he remember whether he or Rice had discussed the PDB with Attorney General Ashcroft.

There is another, bizarre and unresolved, anomaly. Rice—and Bush—have said the national security adviser was not present during the August 6 briefing at the President's ranch. She was in Washington, she said, more than a thousand miles away. CIA director Tenet, however, told the Commission in a formal letter that Rice was present that day.

Finally, and for a number of reasons, there is doubt as to whether the Agency produced the relevant section of the August 6 PDB because—as Rice indicated and Bush flatly claimed—he had himself "asked for it."

Had he really requested the briefing? It is reliably reported that, having received it, Bush responded merely with a dismissive "All right. You've covered your ass now." Ben-Veniste has made the reasonable point that if the President himself had called for the briefing, his response would hardly have been so flippant.

The President had indeed asked over the weeks whether available intelligence pointed to an internal threat, Director Tenet was to advise the Commission in a formal letter. But: "There was no formal tasking."

According to Ben-Veniste's account, the two analysts who drafted the PDB told him that "none of their superiors had mentioned any request from the President as providing the genesis for the PDB. Rather, said Barbara S. and Dwayne D., they had jumped at the chance to get the President thinking about the possibility that al Qaeda's anticipated spectacular attack might be directed at the homeland."

The threat, they thought, had been "current and serious." CIA officials, sources later told *The New York Times*'s Philip Shenon, had called for the August 6 brief to get the White House to "pay more attention" to it.

The Agency analysts, Ben-Veniste reflected, "had written a report for the President's eyes to alert him to the possibility that bin Laden's words and actions, together with recent investigative clues, pointed to an attack by al Qaeda on the American homeland. Yet the President had done absolutely nothing to follow up."

WHAT THEN of the time between August 6 and September 11, the precious thirty-six-day window during which the terrorists could conceivably perhaps have been thwarted? There were two major developments in that time, both of which—with adroit handling, hard work, and good luck—might have averted catastrophe.

The first potential break came on August 15, when a manager at the Pan Am International Flight Academy in Minneapolis phoned the local FBI about an odd new student named Zacarias Moussaoui. Thirty-three-year-old Moussaoui, born in France to Moroccan parents, had

applied for a course at the school two months earlier, saying in his initial email that his "goal, his dream" was to
pilot "one of these Big Bird." That he as yet had no
license to fly even light aircraft appeared to discourage
Moussaoui not at all. "I am sure that you can do something," he had written, "after all we are in AMERICA,
and everything is possible."

It happened on occasion that some dilettante applied to
buy training time on Pan Am's Boeing 747 simulator.
Moussaoui himself was to say that the experience would be
"a joy ride," "an ego boosting thing." The school did not
necessarily turn away such aspirants. Moussaoui arrived,
paid the balance of the fee—$6,800 in cash he pulled out of
a satchel—saying that he wanted to fly a simulated flight
from London to New York's JFK Airport. At his first
session he asked a string of questions, about the fuel
capacity of a 747, about how to maneuver the plane in
flight, about the cockpit control panel—and what damage
the airliner would cause were it to collide with something.

Sensing that this student was no mere oddball, that he
might have evil intent, the school's instructors agreed
that the FBI should be contacted. The reaction at the
Minneapolis field office was prompt and effective.
Moussaoui was detained on the ground that his visa had
expired, and agents began questioning him and a
companion—a Yemeni traveling on a Saudi passport.
They learned rapidly that Moussaoui was a Muslim, a
fact he had denied to his flight instructor.

The companion, moreover, revealed that the suspect
had fundamentalist beliefs, had expressed approval of
"martyrs," and was "preparing himself to fight." Within
the week, French intelligence responded to a request for
assistance with "unambiguous" information that
Moussaoui had undergone training at an al Qaeda camp
in Afghanistan.

One of the Minneapolis agents, a former intelligence officer, felt from early on "convinced . . . a hundred percent that Moussaoui was a bad actor, was probably a professional mujahideen" involved in a plot. Though he and his colleagues had no way of knowing it at the time, their suspicions were well founded. KSM would one day tell his interrogators that Moussaoui had been slated to lead a second wave of 9/11-type attacks on the United States. In a post-9/11 climate, KSM had assumed, the authorities would be especially leery of those with Middle Eastern identity papers. In those circumstances, and though Moussaoui was a "problematic personality," his French passport might prove a real advantage. Osama bin Laden, moreover, favored finding a role for him.

Before flying into the States, the evidence would eventually indicate, Moussaoui had met in London with Ramzi Binalshibh. Binalshibh had subsequently wired him a total of $14,000. Binalshibh's telephone number was listed in one of Moussaoui's notebooks and on other pieces of paper, and he had called it repeatedly from pay phones in the United States.

In August 2001, however, the agents worrying about Moussaoui knew nothing of the Binalshibh connection, were not free to search the suspect's possessions. In spite of a series of appeals that grew ever more frantic as the days ticked by—the lead agent wound up sending Washington no fewer than seventy messages—headquarters blocked the Minneapolis request to approve a search warrant.

In late August, in response to a tart comment from headquarters that he was just trying to get people "spun up," the Minneapolis supervisor agreed that was exactly his intention. He was persisting, he said with unconscious prescience, because he hoped to ensure that Moussaoui did not "take control of a plane and fly it into the World Trade Center."

work-
les on
000—
CIA
ek by
about
tates.
plice
-four
tling

o happen," a headquarters official
have enough to show that he is a

OPMENT, of enormous potential
anwhile been evolving—and abort-
oast. The episode centered on the
between the FBI and the CIA, a blot
ent since anyone could remember.
he two agencies liaised on counter-

terrorism, in practice they coexisted at best awkwardly.
From early in 2001, according to the sequence of events
published in the 9/11 Commission Report, some in the
CIA's bin Laden unit had been looking again at the case
of Khalid al-Mihdhar.

New information indicated that Mihdhar, whom the
Agency had identified as a terrorist the previous year,
who it had known had a visa to enter the United States—
yet had failed to share the information with the FBI or
Immigration—was linked to bin Laden through his
trusted operative Walid bin Attash. Yet still the FBI was
kept in the dark about Mihdhar.

In the spring of 2001, a CIA deputy chief working
liaison with the Bureau's terrorism unit in New York—
now known to have been Tom Wilshire—reportedly
reconsidered the overall picture on Mihdhar. The
suspect with a U.S. visa was an associate of Nawaf
al-Hazmi, who—the CIA knew—definitely had entered
the United States many months earlier. With growing
indications that an attack was coming, it is said to have
occurred to Wilshire that "Something bad was definitely
up." When he asked a CIA superior for permission to
share what he knew with the FBI, however, he got no
reply.

In late July, apparently on his own initiative, Wilshire

suggested to Margarette Gillespie, an FBI analyst ing with the CIA's bin Laden unit, that she review f the terrorist meeting in Malaysia back in January 2 the meeting that had first brought Mihdhar to attention. Gillespie did so, and—piece by piece, we week—began putting together the alarming facts Mihdhar, his visa, and his plan to visit the United S

On August 21, she found out about his accon Hazmi's arrival in the United States. Within twenty hours, when she consulted the INS, she made a star discovery. Not only that Hazmi was probably *still* in the country, but that Mihdhar had very recently been readmitted. "It all clicked for me," Gillespie was to recall.

The final days of August were a combination of rational action and bureaucratic confusion. On the 22nd, at Gillespie's request, the CIA drafted a message asking the FBI, INS, the State Department, and Customs to "watch-list" Mihdhar and Hazmi. The watchlisting, though, applied only to international travel, not to journeys within the United States—and the FAA was not informed at all.

Gillespie's colleague Dina Corsi, meanwhile, sent an email to the FBI's I-49 unit—which handled counter-terrorism—requesting an investigation to find out whether Mihdhar was in the United States.

At that point the process became tied up in much the same red tape as the push in Minnesota to find out what Moussaoui was up to. Mihdhar could not be pursued as a criminal case, Corsi stipulated, only as an intelligence lead. This was a misinterpretation of the rules, but—even though only one intelligence agent was available—Corsi and a CIA official insisted on the condition. One I-49 agent was angered by their insistence. "If this guy is in the country," Steve Bongardt said acidly during a call to colleagues on August 28, "it's not because he's going to fucking Disneyland!"

Within twenty-four hours, Bongardt's frustration surfaced again. "Someday," he wrote in an email, "someone will die . . . the public will not understand why we were not more effective and throwing every resource we had at certain 'problems.'"

The job of finding Mihdhar, nevertheless, went to an intelligence agent, Robert Fuller, working on his own. Corsi marked the assignment "Routine" because—she would later tell investigators—she "assigned no particular urgency to the matter." The designation "Routine" gave Fuller thirty days to get under way. It was August 29.

LIKE PRESIDENT BUSH, CIA director Tenet had spent part of August on vacation—again like the President, fishing. By his own account, however, he kept very much abreast of developments. That month, he wrote in 2007, he had directed his counterterrorism unit to review old files—and thus took part of the credit for the "discovery" that Mihdhar and Hazmi might be in the United States.

Tenet, too, had been briefed on the detention of the suspect flight student in Minneapolis. The FBI early on sent fulsome information on Moussaoui to the Agency, and the details went to Tenet on August 23 in the form of a document headed "Islamic Extremist Learns to Fly." The director's staff took the matter very seriously, urging that the Bureau give it real attention. "If this guy is let go," one CIA officer wrote on the 30th to a colleague liaising with the Bureau, "two years from now he will be talking to a control tower while aiming a 747 at the White House."

Did Tenet share the developments on Mihdhar and Hazmi, and the alert over Moussaoui, with the President? It would seem surprising had he not done so—especially in the month Bush had received a Daily

Brief entitled "Bin Laden Determined to Strike in U.S." When the President was asked the question, Commissioner Ben-Veniste recalled, his "brow furrowed." Bush said he recalled no mention of Moussaoui, that "no one ever told him there was a domestic problem."

Tenet, for his part, stumbled badly in an appearance before the Commission. He claimed in sworn testimony that he had not seen Bush in August. "I didn't see the President," he said. "I was not in briefings with him during this time. . . . He's in Texas and I'm either here [in Washington] or on leave [in New Jersey]." "You never get on the phone or in any kind of conference with him to talk," asked commissioner Tim Roemer, "through the whole month of August?" "In this time period," replied Tenet, "I'm not talking to him, no."

It seemed astonishing, and for good reason: it was not true. Hours after Tenet had testified, CIA spokesman Bill Harlow told reporters that the director had in fact briefed the President in person twice in August, at the Texas ranch on August 17 and in Washington on August 31.

Could Tenet possibly have forgotten his one trip to see Bush in August, the very first time he had visited the ranch, in the sweltering heat of Texas? Roemer thought it possible that Tenet had lied.

Writing in 2007, Tenet made no mention of the lapse. Instead, he said he had indeed traveled to Texas, "to make sure the President stayed current on events." According to the known record, the director would not have known of the Moussaoui and Mihdhar-Hazmi developments on the 17th. Both were well under way, however, by the time he saw the President on the 31st. Would they not have fit within the frame of keeping the President "current on events"? In a private interview, Tenet told the

Commission that he did "not recall any discussions with the President of the domestic threat during this period."

"THE QUESTION," Michael Hirsh and Michael Isikoff wrote in *Newsweek*, is in the end "not so much what the President knew and when he knew it. The question is whether the administration was really paying much attention."

In her testimony to the Commission, Rice rejected any notion that the administration let things slide. "I do not believe there was a lack of high-level attention," she said. "The President was paying attention to this. How much higher level can you get?"

Lawrence Wilkerson, a trusted aide to Secretary of State Colin Powell, worked with a colleague on the preparation of Rice's testimony. The job, he said, had been "an appalling enterprise. We would cherry-pick things to make it look like the President had been actually concerned about al Qaeda. . . . They didn't give a shit about al Qaeda. They had priorities. The priorities were lower taxes, ballistic missiles, and the defense thereof."

Commissioner Ben-Veniste, for his part, came away from his work on the Commission drawing the gravest possible conclusion. "There was no question in my mind," he has written, "that had the President and his National Security Advisor been aggressively attentive to the potential for a domestic terrorist attack, some of the information already in the possession of our intelligence and law enforcement agencies might have been utilized to disrupt the plot."

TWENTY-EIGHT

HELLO JENNY,
Wie geht's dir? Mir geht's gut . . .
Wie ich Dir letze mal gesagt habe die Erstsemester
wird in drei wochen beginn kein
Aendrugen!!!!!! . . .

The start of a coded email message written in broken
German that Atta sent to Binalshibh in the third week of
August. It is phrased as though it were a letter to his girl-
friend Jenny. Translated, the entire message reads:

DEAR JENNY,
How are you? I'm fine . . .
As I told you in my last letter, the first semester
starts in three weeks. No changes!!!!!! Everything's
going well. There's high hope and very strong
thoughts for success!!! Two high schools and two
universities . . . Everything is going according plan.
This summer is for sure going to be hot. I want to
talk to you about some details. Nineteen
certificates for specialized studies and 4 exams. . . .
Regards to your professors . . .
Until then . . .

The key part of the message is the reference to "high schools" and "universities." In an earlier discussion of targeting—Atta and Binalshibh had still been discussing the option of striking the White House—they had used "architecture" to refer to the World Trade Center, "arts" to mean the Pentagon, "law" the Capitol, and "politics" to denote the White House.

The true meaning of the message, Binalshibh would explain in the interview he gave before he was captured, was:

Zero hour is going to be in three weeks' time.
There are no changes. All is well. The brothers
have been seeing encouraging visions and dreams.
The Twin Towers, the Pentagon and Capitol Hill.
Everything is going according to plan. This
summer is for sure going to be hot. I want to talk
to you about some details. Nineteen hijackers
and four targets. Regards to Khalid [KSM]/
Osama.
Until we speak.

In the early hours of August 29, in Germany, Binalshibh was woken by the telephone. The caller was Atta, his Egyptian-accented voice instantly recognizable.

Atta had a riddle for Binalshibh, a joke as he put it: "'Two sticks, a dash, and a cake with a stick down' . . . What is it?" Binalshibh, half asleep, was stumped for a moment. Then—presumably he was expecting such a call—he figured out the answer. The puzzle, he told Atta, was "sweet."

"Two sticks" signified "11." The "dash" was a dash. A "cake with a stick down" was a "9."

11–9—the way most of the world renders the days of the calendar. Or, as Americans render them:

9/11
The date was set.

BINALSHIBH PASSED on the date to KSM, and the hijackers' operation entered its final phase. Everything now depended on Atta's organizing ability and success in maintaining security. An effort to bring the total number of terrorists up to twenty—four five-man teams, one for each target—had recently risked wrecking the entire endeavor.

In early August, at Orlando, Florida, a U.S. immigration inspector had had his doubts about a newly arrived young Saudi. Standing instructions were to take it easy on Saudis—they were a boost to tourism—but this man had no return ticket and had not filled out customs and immigration forms. The inspector sent the man on for a "secondary," a grilling that was to last two hours.

The would-be "tourist," twenty-five-year-old Mohamed el-Kahtani, said that, though he would be staying only a few days, he did not know where he would be going next. He first said that someone due to arrive from abroad would be paying for his onward travel, then that another "someone" was waiting for him in Arrivals. Secondary inspector José Meléndez-Pérez noted, too, that the subject was belligerent.

"He started pointing his finger . . . Whatever he was saying was in a loud voice—like 'I am in charge—you're not going to do anything to me. I am from Saudi Arabia.' People from Saudi think they are untouchable . . . He had a deep staring look . . . [like] 'If I could grip your heart I would eat it' . . . This man intimidated me with his look and his behavior."

The inspector felt in his gut that Kahtani had evil intent—he thought he might be a hit man—and recommended that he be sent back to Saudi Arabia. This was the one occasion, after a series of inefficiencies involving the terrorists, that an alert INS official had really done his job. KSM was to admit under interrogation that the suspect had indeed been sent to the States to join the terrorist team—to "round out the number of hijackers."

It is rational to think that, but for the inspector's acumen, there would have been five rather than four hijackers aboard United Flight 93. With Kahtani's additional muscle—Meléndez-Pérez remembered him as having looked trim, "like a soldier"—they might have been better able to resist the passengers' attempt to retake the cockpit. Instead of plunging to the ground in Pennsylvania, Flight 93 might have stayed on course and struck its target in Washington.

There had indeed been a "someone" waiting to meet Kahtani at Orlando. Evidence gathered after 9/11 established to a virtual certainty that Mohamed Atta had been at the airport that day. He did not leave, parking records showed, until it was clear that the new recruit was not going to emerge from Immigration. Had those handling Kahtani taken the investigation of him one step further, had they thought the suspect might be engaged in terrorism, the leader of the operation might himself have come under the microscope. Atta might have been unmasked.

As it was, Atta remained free, putting thousands of miles on rental cars, flying hither and thither, coordinating communications, the whirl of logistics involved in getting nineteen men—most of them with minimal familiarity with the West or the English language—in place and ready for the appointed day.

Most of the time in August, the terrorists stayed in their apartments and motels. They did what in other men would have been everyday activities: in Florida, exercising, two of them, at a Y2 Fitness Center; going shopping—for jewelry at a store called the Piercing Pagoda, for a dress shirt at Surreys Menswear; getting clothes cleaned at a Fort Dixie Laundry.

There were some signs of movement. The men crowded into the apartment in Paterson, New Jersey, moved out, leaving behind a few items of clothing, glasses in the bathroom—and flight manuals. Crowded they remained, though. By late that month five of them were squeezed into one room at the Valencia Motel, a cheap joint in Laurel, Maryland. They seemed rarely to leave the room, opening the door to the maid only to take in fresh towels. Guests who used a next-door room "thought they were gay."

Mostly, the men avoided attracting attention. An exception was the day at the end of August in Delray Beach, Florida, when a woman named Maria Simpson was startled by two men tugging unceremoniously at the door of her condominium. To her relief it turned out that, without asking permission, they were merely trying to retrieve a towel that had fallen from their balcony on the floor above. Simpson was to recognize them later, when she looked at FBI mug shots, as two of the muscle hijackers who took down United Flight 93. Their faces looked harder in the photographs, she thought, than she remembered them.

There was little about the hijackers—with the exception on occasion of Atta—that struck people as sinister. Richard Surma, who ran the Panther Motel in Fort Lauderdale, rented rooms to groups of them twice in the final weeks. "They looked young," he recalled, "like they're trying to make it, like students."

Brad Warrick, the boss of a rental car company at Pompano Beach, supplied cars several times to Shehhi and Atta. Warrick prided himself on his "gut check," the eye he ran over new customers to see if they gave him a bad feeling. "Didn't have it with those guys," he would remember. "They were just great customers. . . . They both spoke very well, of course with an accent. . . . Atta was a very normal, nice guy. Nothing weird about him. Never had an eerie feeling."

Ziad Jarrah, however, whose resolve had seemed to Atta to be wavering, may have been getting edgy. A man who resembled him, along with a companion, asked to use the Internet at the Longshore Motel in Hollywood, Florida, but left in a huff within hours. Manager Paul Dragomir asked the pair to use the line in his office—he was worried about the bill they might run up—and they had angrily objected. "You don't understand," the man he later thought had been Jarrah exclaimed. "We're on a mission."

The manager put the "mission" remark out of his mind until after 9/11. Jarrah, if it was Jarrah, may just have been overtired, having trouble with his English. In other ways, though, the operation was less than secure.

Hijacker Nawaf al-Hazmi, the terrorist who spent the longest time in the States, may have been seriously indiscreet—or shared news of what was coming with a loose-lipped associate, not himself one of the hijackers. Investigators came to suspect that in late August, as final preparations for the attacks were being made, Hazmi phoned a Yemeni student friend in San Diego named Mohdar Abdullah.

Abdullah had known Hazmi and Mihdhar early on, had helped them apply for driving lessons and flying lessons. Evidence found later on a computer, moreover, suggested that he in turn was in contact with an activist fervently opposed to U.S. support for Israel. His circle of friends also included another man, himself linked to Hazmi, who had Osama bin Laden propaganda.

When he was detained after the attacks, Abdullah's belongings were found to include a spiral notebook with references to "planes falling from the sky, mass killings and hijacking." In late August 2001, about the time of the supposed call from Hazmi, Abdullah reportedly stayed away from work and school, began "acting very strange," appeared "nervous, paranoid, and anxious."

In the weeks before the strikes, Atta had his men working on their personal documentation. Some of the terrorists had only passports, and young men with Arab passports might have prompted closer scrutiny at airport security. With the help of individuals prepared to vouch for them—in return for a bribe—several now obtained state IDs.

Even before Atta passed the date of the planned strikes up the line, the terrorists had already begun making airline reservations and purchasing tickets for September 11. Over the phone or using the Internet, sometimes from computers at small-town libraries, on different days and in different places, all would acquire their tickets before the end of the first week of September.

Atta and Mihdhar, perhaps keen to appear to be ordinary travelers, set up frequent flier accounts. The Shehri brothers made reservations, then changed their seat assignments—so as to sit on the side of the First Class aisle that afforded the best view of the cockpit door. Hamzi and his brother Salem ordered special meals suitable for the Muslim diet, meals they knew they would never eat. Perhaps to avoid appearing to be in a group, seven terrorists booked to travel on beyond the destinations of their targeted flights—by which time they would be long dead.

All the flights booked, of course, were for transcontinental flights scheduled to depart in the morning. Transcontinental, in part because they would take off heavily laden with fuel. The more fuel in an airplane's tanks, the greater the explosive force on impact. In the morning, at a time, Atta thought, when most people in the target buildings would have arrived in their offices.

Key operatives, meanwhile, had shopped around for weapons. Using a Visa card at a Sports Authority store, Shehhi purchased two short black knives, a Cliphanger Viper and an Imperial Tradesman Dual Edge model. Each of the knives had a four-inch-long blade, the maximum length permitted aboard planes under FAA regulations. Fayez Banihammad and Hamza al-Ghamdi, who were to fly with Shehhi, bought a Stanley two-piece snap knife and a Leatherman Wave multi-tool. Nawaf al-Hazmi also picked Leatherman knives.

Atta, who two weeks earlier had purchased two knives in Europe, had been at a Dollar House, looking for box cutters with Hazmi and Jarrah. Days later, at a Lowe's Home Improvement Warehouse, he, too, picked up a Leatherman. Atta also had a large folding knife, but that would not be carried on board on 9/11.

For the men who had practiced slaughter techniques on sheep and camels, there would be a sufficiency of knives.

ON SEPTEMBER 4, as the hijackers completed their ticketing arrangements, Bush cabinet-level officials—the Principals—convened at the White House for the long-delayed, very first meeting to discuss the bin Laden problem. They had in front of them the draft National Security Presidential Directive the deputies had agreed on before the August vacation. It outlined measures—long-term measures—designed to destroy the terrorists in their Afghan sanctuary.

The State Department had already told the Taliban regime that the United States would hold it responsible, as the host government, for any new bin Laden attack. That line of approach was to be stepped up, along with forging closer links to forces still resisting the Taliban. There was some talk of one day perhaps using U.S. forces on the ground, but nothing decisive.

There was debate at the meeting, but no decision, about use of the Predator, the unmanned drone that had long since proven capable of stunningly clear air-to-ground photography. Prolonged experiment—a model of a house bin Laden was known to frequent was used for target practice—had established that the Predator could be transformed into a pinpoint-accurate, missile-bearing weapon. Were the drone to get bin Laden in its sights, as it had as long ago as fall 2000, there was every likelihood he could be killed almost instantly.

At the September 4 meeting, though, Chairman of the Joint Chiefs General Myers and CIA director Tenet merely dueled over whether handling the Predator should be the mission of the military or of the CIA. "I just couldn't believe it," counterterrorism coordinator Clarke remembered. "This is the Chairman of the Joint Chiefs and the Director of the CIA sitting there, both passing the football because neither one of them wanted to go kill bin Laden." Their argument, apparently, was primarily about which agency was to foot the bill for operating the Predators. All that was resolved was that the CIA should consider using the Predator again for reconnaissance purposes.

As for the directive as a whole, Clarke came away from the meeting as frustrated as ever. All the things he had recommended back in January 2001, he was to tell the Commission, were to get done—after 9/11. "I didn't really understand," he said, "why they couldn't have been done in February."

Clarke had been trying in vain, his aide Paul Kurtz

recalled, to get Bush officials to "grasp the enormity of this new, transnational, networked foe ... people thought he was hyping it up." "It sounds terrible," Clarke's then-deputy Roger Cressey recalled, "but we used to say to each other that some people didn't get it— it was going to take body bags."

Hours before the September 4 meeting, Clarke had sent National Security Adviser Rice a strongly worded note, with several passages underlined. The real question before the participants that day, he wrote, was: "Are we serious about dealing with the al Qaeda threat? ... Is al Qaeda a big deal? ... <u>Decision makers should imagine themselves on a future day when the CSG</u> [Counterterrorism Security Group] <u>has not succeeded in stopping al Qaeda attacks and hundreds of Americans lay dead in several countries, including the U.S. ...</u> What would those decision makers wish that they had done earlier? That future day could happen at any time ... <u>You are left waiting for the big attack</u>, with lots of casualties."

September 4 ended with the Presidential Directive approved subject to just a few final adjustments by the Deputies Committee. It would be ready for the president's signature—soon.

A THOUSAND MILES to the south, Atta found time for a matter of financial integrity. He told Binalshibh on September 5 that he and his men had money left over. Since they would soon have no further need of it, it should be reimbursed. For the hijackers, FBI investigators were to conclude, not to have returned remaining funds would have been to die as thieves.

In dribs and drabs over the next few days, by Western Union, bank transfer, and express mail, the terrorist team arranged for some $36,000 to be sent to the accomplice in Dubai who had been handling funds. The entire 9/11 operation, the Commission was to calculate, cost al Qaeda and Osama bin Laden less than $500,000.

Across the world, accomplices and men with guilty knowledge were by now running for safety. The "brothers," as Binalshibh put it later, "were dispersed." He himself flew from Germany to Spain, was met by a Saudi who furnished him with a phony passport, then took off on an airborne marathon that took him via Greece, the United Arab Emirates, and Egypt to Pakistan.

Soon after he arrived, Binalshibh would tell his interrogators, a messenger set off overland with a status report for the leadership in Afghanistan. "The message was great news for Sheikh Abu Abdallah," Binalshibh said, using one of the many names followers used for bin Laden. "May Allah protect him."

ACCORDING TO a British government source, communications intercepts at this time picked up messages between bin Laden and senior comrades. One of them, probably a contact with KSM in Pakistan, "referred to an incident that would take place in America on or around September 11"—and the repercussions that might follow.

Egyptian intelligence, with its penetration agent inside al Qaeda, received and passed on "information about some people planning an operation in the United States." "It was one week before," recalled President Mubarak. "The wheels were going."

On September 6, oblivious to such specifics, former senator Gary Hart attended a meeting at the White House. Having tried in vain in January to get the Bush administration to pay real attention to the warnings of the Commission on National Security he had cochaired, he had begun to think there was movement at last.

President Bush had said in the spring that he was establishing a new office, supervised by Vice President

Cheney and devoted to "preparedness" for all forms of terrorist strikes on American soil. He himself, the President said, would periodically chair meetings to review the office's work. That had not happened, but now here was Hart at the White House in early September, offering his commission's expertise to help with the project. Rice, he was to recall, merely "said she would pass on the message."

Their vacations over, President Bush and CIA director Tenet met six times in the first eight days of September. It is not known what they discussed.

AT AN FBI OFFICE in New York, meanwhile, the lone FBI agent charged with looking for Hazmi and Mihdhar was just getting started. Agent Robert Fuller had not been instructed that the matter was especially urgent, nor that the two men posed a serious threat. On a request form he sent to another agency about Mihdhar, he did not even tick the box to indicate that the subject was wanted in connection with "security/terrorism."

He did put out some tentative feelers. Mihdhar had written on his most recent immigration form that he planned to stay at a Marriott hotel in New York City. Unsurprisingly, checks showed that no one with his name had registered at any of the six local Marriotts.

Mihdhar and Hazmi had both used their own names while in the States, and several commonly used databases might well have thrown up information on them. By his own account, Fuller did check the National Crime Information Center, the NCIC, credit and motor vehicle records, and—with a colleague's help—the ChoicePoint service. Whether he in fact trawled all those sources, though, has been questioned.

While Mihdhar had been out of the country for much of the past year, Hazmi had for months been on the East

Coast. Had the hunt for him been treated seriously—had his case been given the priority of, say, the search for a wanted bank robber—tracking him would not have been a hopeless quest. Three days before Agent Fuller received his assignment, Hazmi had come to the notice of a traffic policeman while driving a rental car in Totowa, New Jersey. The patrolman had reportedly taken down the license plate and entered it as a matter of routine in the NCIC.

As reported earlier in these pages, moreover, Hazmi had also featured in three other traffic episodes: another recent "query" by police in Hackensack, New Jersey, a collision outside New York City, and a speeding ticket in Oklahoma. He had even filed a police report in Washington, D.C, using his own name, complaining of having been mugged. One or more of this total of five incidents ought to have made it to the NCIC.

All that aside, Hazmi and Mihdhar had for more than eighteen months lived in the United States—in plain sight—leaving a trail of credit card, bank account, telephone, and accommodations records behind them. Yet Agent Fuller turned up nothing on them. Having made a start on September 5, it appears that he then let the matter drop—until the day before the attacks.

WITH U.S. INTELLIGENCE and law enforcement in a state of paralysis, the terrorists were moving into position. On September 6, if a later FBI analysis is correct, those in Florida held some sort of get-together. According to the manager and bartender at Shuckums, a sports bar in Hollywood, Atta, Shehhi, and a companion spent three hours there relaxing.

There may be truth to the story. Atta and Shehhi were in the state that day, had long been close, and may have chosen to have a last evening together. It may even be true that the man thought to have been Atta, faced with a sizable bill, declared arrogantly that he was an airline pilot and could well afford to pay.

What is less likely is that, as the press first reported, the trio all got drunk on vodka and rum—contrary to the dictates of Islam. Shehhi, known to have enjoyed a beer and knowing that he was not long for this world, may perhaps have downed spirits. For Atta to have gotten inebriated, though, would have been out of character. In a later version of the story, he merely drank cranberry juice and nibbled on chicken wings.

The following day, Friday the 7th, Atta sold his car, a 1989 Pontiac Grand Prix, for $800. Ziad Jarrah sold his, a 1990 Mitsubishi with 97,000 miles on the clock, for $700. They both then headed north, to Baltimore and Newark, respectively. Omari and Suqami, Saudis in their twenties who were to fly with Atta aboard American 11, had arrived earlier at a hotel in Boston. They seized a last opportunity to dally with earthly pleasures.

According to an FBI report, the Sweet Temptations escort agency supplied the two young men with prostitutes that night. Two days later, according to the person who drove her, a woman from another Boston escort service—it advertised escorts for "the most important occasion"—visited one of the terrorists twice in a single day. Four of the men reportedly wanted to indulge, but decided the price for the service—$100 apiece—was too high. One man made do with a pornographic video piped into his hotel room. Another, in New Jersey, paid a dancer $20 to dance for him in a go-go bar.

By early on the 9th, all but one of the terrorists were in hotels in or near Boston, Washington, and New York. Only Marwan al-Shehhi, who had probably helped manage the movement north, remained at the Panther

Motel near Fort Lauderdale. Then he in turn flew up to Boston, where two of the hijack crews were gathered. The Panther was a mom-and-pop operation, and owners Richard and Diane Surma themselves cleared up the room Shehhi and his comrades had used.

In the drawer of a dresser, they found a box cutter. In the garbage, there was a tote bag from a flight school containing a German-English dictionary, three martial arts books, Boeing 757 manuals, an eight-inch-thick stack of aeronautical charts, and a protractor. There was also a syringe with an extraordinarily long needle. The Surmas puzzled over these items, then put them aside.

The previous night, on I-95 in Maryland, a state trooper had stopped a man driving at ninety miles per hour. It was Ziad Jarrah in a rental car heading toward Newark, New Jersey, where his hijack crew was billeted. The officer noted that he seemed calm and cooperative, gave him a speeding ticket, and let him go.

Jarrah had his family on his mind, as well as his lover, Aysel Sengün. In the past week alone, he had called his family in Lebanon nine times and Aysel three. There were family matters to discuss with his father. Money his father had recently sent him, $2,000 "for his aeronautical studies," had arrived safely. Having failed to get back to Lebanon for the recent wedding of one of his sisters, he said, he intended to be home for another family wedding in just two weeks' time. He would definitely be there, he promised, with Aysel at his side. He had even bought a new suit for the occasion.

Soon after, Jarrah prepared a package for Aysel. He enclosed his FAA Private Pilot License, his pilot logbook, a piece of paper with his own name written over and over, a postcard of a beach—and a four-page handwritten letter. Written in German interspersed with Arabic and Turkish, it read in part:

000281

بسم الله الرحمن الرحيم

Salamualyokum Ganim Ayrelim

Aller erstens ich will, daß Du ganz fest glaubst, und ganz

sicher gehst, daß ich Dich vom ganzen Herzen liebe.

Du darfst keinen Zweifel daran haben. Ich liebe Dich

und ich werde Dich Immer lieben bis zur Ewigkeit;

Habibi, Hayatim, Askim, Ganim, Albi; inte Habibi?

ich will nicht, daß Du traurig wirst, ich lebe noch

Ich bin deinen Prinz und Ich werde Dich

Abholen

Auf wiedersehen !!

Deinen mann für Immer

Ziad Jarrah

10-9-2001

Hijacker Jarrah's farewell letter to his lover—he misaddressed it.

Salamualyakum, Canim, Ayselim, [Peace be upon you, my soul, my Aysel]

First, I want you really to believe and be very sure that I love you with all my heart . . . I love you and I will love you for all eternity; my love, my life, my love, my soul, my heart—are you my heart? I do not want you to be sad. I am still alive somewhere else where you cannot see and hear me, but I will see you . . . I will wait for you until you come to me. There comes a time for everyone to make a move. I am to blame for giving you so many hopes about marriage, wedding, children, family . . . I did not flee from you, but did what I was supposed to do. You ought to be very proud of it, because it is an honor and you will see the outcome and everybody will be glad . . . Until we meet again, and then we'll have a beautiful eternal life, where there are no problems and no sorrow, in palaces of gold and silver . . . I thank you and apologize for the wonderful, hard five years that you have spent with me.

Your patience will be rewarded in Paradise, God willing. I am your prince and I will come for you.

Goodbye!

Your husband for ever,

Ziad Jarrah

The letter did not reach Aysel but was returned through the mail, for Jarrah had misaddressed this last sad letter of his short life. It wound up in the hands of the FBI, and she would be told of it only months later. For a while she would hope against hope that Ziad might still be alive, had not after all died on 9/11 and would turn up at her door as he had in the past—with gifts and an apologetic grin.

A packet Khalid al-Mihdhar had hoped would reach his wife, Hoda, in Yemen had also ended up with the FBI. A letter in it, sent with a bank card for an account containing some $10,000, expressed his love for her and their daughter and his desire for her to have the money.

Atta had told the hijackers not to contact their families. He himself, though, apparently placed a call to his father in Cairo on September 9.

In Afghanistan, Osama bin Laden and KSM were taking precautions. KSM crossed over into Pakistan. Bin Laden ordered some followers to disperse, others to stay on high alert. His son Omar had left Afghanistan for good months earlier, disillusioned and following a further warning by the jihadi he trusted that the "big plan" was ongoing, that it was time for him to be "far, far away." Omar had urged his mother, Najwa, the wife who had borne bin Laden eleven children, to leave as well. "My mother," he had urged her, "come back to real life."

Najwa asked her husband for permission to leave, and he agreed on one condition. She was to leave behind several of their sons and daughters, the youngest aged only eight and eleven. On the morning she left, she gave her husband a ring as a remembrance of their long life together. Then, with her two youngest children and a twenty-three-year-old son who was mildly retarded, she climbed into a vehicle to be driven to the border and safety.

Najwa and Osama had been together for almost thirty years, since they were children. Then, he had been the "soft-spoken, serious boy" not yet in his teens. Now, at forty-four, he was the most wanted man in the world, accused of multiple mass murders.

On her way out of Afghanistan, Najwa has said, she prayed for peace.

PART VI

TWENTY-FOUR HOURS

TWENTY-NINE

SEPTEMBER 10, LESS THAN TWENTY-FOUR HOURS BEFORE the onslaught.

In New York, after five days of inaction on the case, the FBI began again the leisurely search for Hazmi and Mihdhar. Having failed to find Mihdhar at any Marriott hotel in Manhattan, Agent Fuller now hoped to find a trace of them in Los Angeles. Both men, immigration records showed, had said when they first arrived eighteen months earlier that they planned to stay at a "Sheraton hotel" in the city. Checking records in Los Angeles was a job for the local field office, so Agent Fuller wrote up a routine request.

The request was not sent, merely drafted, to be transmitted only the following day—September 11. Had anyone looked, and looked in a timely fashion, Hazmi and Mihdhar had left tracks all over the place in California. There was Hazmi's name, address, and phone number of the day, bold as brass in the 2000–2001 Pacific Bell White Pages directory for San Diego. Better yet, there were their names on bank records, driver's license and car registration records, which could have enabled investigators to leapfrog onto traffic police records in New Jersey and elsewhere—even to the purchase of tickets for the flight they were soon to hijack.

But these are "what ifs." The hunt for the two terrorists, if it can be described as a hunt, was all too little too late. So it went, too, with the great lead the FBI had been handed almost a month before in Minneapolis, with the detention of Zacarias Moussaoui, a flight student who—the information they learned led them to believe—might be planning to hijack a Boeing jumbo jet. By September 10, local case agents had been begging headquarters, again and again over a period of three weeks, for clearance to search the prisoner's belongings. Only to be blocked by headquarters, time and time again, with legal quibbles.

By mid-afternoon on the 10th, in deep despond, the Minneapolis agent running the case in Minneapolis, Harry Samit, shared his feelings about the deadlock with a headquarters official who had shown herself to be sympathetic to his appeals for action. It could even become necessary, he wrote in an email, to set Moussaoui free. The official, Catherine Kiser, emailed back:

> HARRY,
> Thanks for the update. Very sorry that this matter
> was handled the way it was, but you fought the
> good fight. God Help us all if the next terrorist
> incident involves the same type of plane.
> take care, Cathy

Permission to search Moussaoui's possessions was to be granted only the following day, after the attacks.

It happened that on the 10th, as the Moussaoui probe ran into the ground, Attorney General Ashcroft formally turned down an FBI request for additional funding and agents to fight terrorism—even though the number of agents working on counterterrorism had not increased since 1996. The Bureau of 2001, a new FBI director was to admit months later, was a "very docile, don't-take-any-risks agency."

Warnings had meanwhile continued to reach the United States from friendly countries. Just days before the attacks, according to CNN—some weeks earlier in another account—Jordanian intelligence reported having intercepted a terrorist communication that referred to an operation code-named "al Urous al Kabir": "The Big Wedding." This was apparently code for a major attack on U.S. territory in which "aircraft would be used." France had also reportedly passed threat intelligence to the CIA.

Those in the United States still trying to get the attention of the White House included U.S. senator Dianne Feinstein, who served on two committees that dealt with terrorist issues and had gone public with her worries two months earlier. "One of the things that has begun to concern me very much," she told Wolf Blitzer on CNN, "is as to whether we really have our house in order. Intelligence staff have told me that there is a major probability of a terrorist incident within the next three months."

So concerned had Feinstein been in July that she contacted Vice President Cheney's office to urge action on restructuring the counterterrorism effort. On September 10, she tried again. "Despite repeated efforts by myself and staff," she recalled, "the White House did not address my request. I followed this up . . . and was told by Scooter Libby [then Cheney's chief of staff] that it might be another six months before he would be able to review the material. I did not believe we had six months to wait."

Just overnight, savage news had come out of Afghanistan. The most formidable Afghan military foe of the Taliban—and of Osama bin Laden—Ahmed Shah

Massoud, had been assassinated. The killers had posed as Arab television journalists, then detonated a bomb in the camera as the interview began. The "journalists'" request to see Massoud, it would later be established, had been written on a computer bin Laden's people used.

No one doubts that bin Laden ordered the Massoud hit—the widow of one of the assassins was later told as much. Doing away with Massoud, bin Laden well knew, was more than a favor to the Taliban. Were the imminent attack in the United States to succeed, the murder of Massoud would deprive America of its most effective military ally in any attempt to retaliate.

Massoud dead. Massoud, who just months ago had warned CIA agents in private that something was afoot, who had publicly declared, "If President Bush doesn't help us, then these terrorists will damage the United States and Europe very soon, and it will be too late."

People with specialist knowledge in America saw the turn things were taking. The legendary counterterrorism chief at the FBI's New York office, John O'Neill, had warned publicly long ago that religious extremists' capacity and will to strike on American soil was growing. In mid-August, frustrated and exhausted after heading the probe into the bombing of the USS *Cole*, he had resigned from the Bureau after thirty years' service—to become head of security at the World Trade Center.

On the night of September 10, having just moved into his new office in the North Tower, O'Neill told a colleague, "We're due for something big. I don't like the way things are lining up in Afghanistan." He was to die the following morning, assisting in the evacuation of the South Tower.

In Russia, President Vladimir Putin was jolted by the news of Massoud's murder. "I am very worried," he told President Bush in a personal phone call on the 10th. "It makes me think something big is going to happen. They're getting ready to act."

The chief of the CIA's bin Laden unit had learned of the assassination within hours in a call from one of Massoud's aides. CIA officials discussed the development with Bush on the morning of the 10th during his daily briefing, and analyzed the implications. In his 2010 memoir, however, the former President refers neither to the Putin call, nor to the Agency briefing, nor to how he himself reacted to Massoud's murder at the time.

That day at the White House, at long last, the Deputies Committee tinkered with the Presidential Directive one last time and finalized the plan to eliminate bin Laden and his terrorists over the next three years. The directive, White House chief of staff Andy Card was to say, was "literally headed for the President's desk. I think, on the 10th or 11th of September." Condoleezza Rice was to tell Bob Woodward she thought the timing "a little eerie."

For Bush, September 10 was a day filled largely by meetings with the prime minister of Australia. Then, in early afternoon, he boarded a helicopter at the Pentagon to head for Air Force One and the journey to Florida to publicize his campaign for child literacy. By early evening he was settling in at the Colony Beach and Tennis Resort on Longboat Key, near Sarasota—the ocean to one side, a perfectly groomed golf course to the other. Bush enjoyed a relaxed evening, dined Tex-Mex, on chili con queso, with his brother Jeb and other Republican officials, and went to bed at 10:00.

The President's public appearance the next morning—reading with second graders at Emma E. Booker Elementary—was, in White House schedulers' parlance, to be a "soft event."

At the National Security Agency outside Washington

that evening—as yet untranslated—were the texts of two messages intercepted in recent hours between pay phones in Afghanistan and individuals in Saudi Arabia.

The intercepts would not be translated until the following day. Analysts would realize then that a part of the first of the intercepts translated as: "Tomorrow is zero hour."

The second contained the statement: "The match begins tomorrow."

To SOME INTIMATES of the terrorists, the event that was coming was no secret. On the morning of the 10th in California—around noon East Coast time—a group of Arabs gathered at the San Diego gas station where Nawaf al-Hazmi had worked for a while the previous year. It was rare for them to get together in the morning, but six did that day. One, according to a witness interviewed by the FBI, was Mohdar Abdullah, the friend who had helped Hazmi settle in the previous year. The mood was "somewhat celebratory," and the men gave each other high fives. "It is," the witness remembered Abdullah saying, "finally going to happen."

Just outside Washington that afternoon, Hazmi and Mihdhar and the other members of their unit checked into a hotel near Dulles Airport. In and around Boston and Newark, most of their accomplices were in position at their various hotels. In the afternoon, however, the remaining two terrorists—Atta and Abdul Aziz al-Omari—took a car journey north.

They drove from Boston to Portland, Maine, a distance of more than a hundred miles, then checked into a Comfort Inn near the airport. Security camera tapes retrieved later would show that they withdrew a little money from ATMs, and stopped at a gas station and a

Walmart—a witness recalled having seen Atta looking at shirts in the men's department. They had bought a take-out dinner at a Pizza Hut—the pizza boxes, removed from their room the next morning by a maid, would be found in the Dumpster behind the hotel.

Phone records established that Atta made and received a number of telephone calls while in Portland. He called Shehhi's mobile phone from a pay phone at the Pizza Hut, and ten minutes later called Jarrah at his hotel. The terrorists' emir was apparently busy organizing to the last, checking that everyone was in place.

Why, though, did Atta go to Portland at all? Neither the 9/11 Commission nor anyone else has ever located evidence that would explain that last-minute journey. Of various hypotheses, two in particular got the authors' attention. Former Commission staff member Miles Kara, who has continued over the years to study the hijackers' plan of attack, suggests Atta may have seen the diversion to Portland as his Plan B. Were other hijackers due to leave from Boston stopped for some reason, he and Omari—arriving seemingly independently from Portland—might still succeed alone.

An alternative speculation—made by Mike Rolince, a former FBI assistant director who specialized in counter-terrorism—is that Atta went to Portland to meet with someone. But with whom? What could possibly have made the time-consuming diversion necessary on the very eve of the 9/11 operation?

Whatever the reason for the Portland trip, it was a risky expedition. The flight Atta and Omari were to take in the morning, to get back to Boston's Logan Airport in time for the American Airlines flight they were to hijack, involved a tight connection. Had their plane been just a little late, the leader of the 9/11 gang—the man from whom the others all took their lead—would have blown the plan at the last moment. Portland must have been important.

In Boston, meanwhile, solemn ritual had been under way behind the door of Room 241 of the Days Inn on Soldiers Field Road. It was the ritual called for in the hijackers' "spiritual manual," copies of which were to be recovered in Atta's baggage, Hamzi's car, and—a partial copy—in the wreckage in Pennsylvania.

A maid admitted to clean the room "noticed large amounts of water and body hair on the floor . . . all body lotion provided for the room had been used. . . . Room occupants [had] slept on top of the bed sheets and placed light silk cloth over the pillows." In the final hours, there was also a great deal of praying to be done.

Pray, remain awake, renew "the mutual pledge to die," think about God's blessing—"especially for the martyrs." Spit on the suitcase, the clothing—the knife. Then, moving through the phases as instructed, prayers on the way to the airport, avoiding any sign of confusion at the airport. Prayers and more prayers.

"Smile in the face of death, young man, for you will soon enter the eternal abode." Ramzi Binalshibh was to say that, shortly before the end, Atta told him with assurance that their next meeting would be, "God willing, in Paradise." Binalshibh responded with a request to Atta. "I asked him [that] if he was to see the Prophet Mohammed, peace be upon Him, and reach the highest place in Heaven, he should convey our *salaam* to Him."

Atta promised he would do so, then shared something his comrade Marwan al-Shehhi had told him:

"Marwan had a beautiful dream, that he was flying high in the sky surrounded by green birds not from our world, that he was crashing into things, and that he felt so happy."

Green birds. In a passage in the Qur'an, it is said that

in Paradise people "will wear green garments of fine silk." Green is said to have been the Prophet Mohammed's favorite color. During the Crusades, to distinguish themselves from the Christians, Arab soldiers wore green into battle.

SEPTEMBER 11,

the way Ramzi Binalshibh would remember that morning:
When the news started and we heard the news of the collision of the first aircraft, as it was wrecking the World Trade Center, guided by our brother Mohamed Atta—may Allah have mercy on his soul—the brothers shouted "Takbir!"—"Allah is Greatest!" . . . And they prostrated themselves to Allah in gratitude and they wept.

The brothers thought that this was the one and only part of the operation, so we said to them, "Patience, patience!" And suddenly our brother Marwan was wrecking the southern tower of the World Trade Center in a very fierce manner. I mean, in an unimaginable way we were witnessing live on air. We were saying, "Oh, Allah, show us the right way, show the right way" . . . So the brothers prostrated themselves in thanks to Allah . . . and they sometimes wept for joy and at other times from sadness for their brothers. . . .

They thought it was over. We said to them, "Follow the news. The matter is not over yet. Make prayers for your brothers. Pray for them . . ." Imagine! Within forty-five minutes, in the space of this record time, the [third] aircraft was wrecking the Pentagon building, the building of the American Defense Ministry. The aircraft was guided by our brother Hani Hanjour. . . . The joy was tremendous. . . .

Then came the news of the aircraft which was flown by our brother Ziad Jarrah, which was downed in the suburbs of the capital, Washington. At this the brothers shouted "Allah is Greatest!" and they prostrated themselves and embraced. . . .

It was a sign from Allah for the whole world to see. . . . Allah the Almighty says: "Did they not travel through the earth and see the end of those before them who did evil. Allah brought utter destruction on them, and similar fates await those who reject Allah." [Qur'an, Surah 47, Verse 10]. The divine intervention was without a doubt very clear and palpable. . . . Praise and gratitude be to Allah!

The blessed day of Tuesday, 11 September in Washington and New York was one of the glorious days of the Muslims . . . it represents a calamitous defeat for the greatest power on earth, America . . . a fatal blow in her heart, which is filled with animosity and hatred for Islam. . . . Allah the Almighty has decided to inflict upon her a punishment—to be executed by the hands of this group of believing mujahideen, whom Allah has chosen and ordained for this mighty task. Praise and glory be to Him!

PART VII

UNANSWERED
QUESTIONS

THIRTY

THE STORY OF SEPTEMBER 11, 2001—THAT OF THE victims and of the terrorists—is told. The identity of the perpetrators is not in doubt. As told in these pages, the essential elements are as described in the conclusions of the two official inquiries.

There are two areas, though, on which the 9/11 Commission fudged or dodged the issue: the full truth about U.S. and Western intelligence before the attacks; and whether the terrorist operation ten years ago had the support of other nation-states or of powerful individuals within those nation-states. There remain multiple and serious questions and yawning gaps in our knowledge of which the public knows little or nothing.

A case in point, one that we include because it is not covered at all in the Commission Report—and because our interviews indicate that there may possibly be some substance to it—is a report that surfaced seven weeks after the attacks in the leading French newspaper *Le Figaro*. It was carried by major news agencies and newspapers, denied by the CIA, then forgotten. If the *Le Figaro* story was correct, U.S. intelligence officials had had a face-to-face meeting with Osama bin Laden in early July 2001, sitting down with a deadly foe, a man wanted for the mass murder of Americans.

According to the report, bin Laden that month traveled secretly from Pakistan to Dubai in the United Arab Emirates, a destination that until 9/11 remained relatively friendly territory for him. He spent several days there reportedly, in private accommodations at the prestigious American Hospital. The ostensible reason for the visit was to undergo medical tests related to his kidney function, long said to have caused him problems. Such tests may have been conducted, but the claim is that he also agreed to meet with a locally based CIA agent and—reportedly—a second official sent in from Washington.

The reporter who originated the story, Alexandra Richard, told the authors that she happened on the story during a visit to the Gulf weeks before 9/11. Checks she made in Dubai, with a senior administrator at the American Hospital, with an airport operative at the point of origin of bin Laden's alleged journey—Quetta in Pakistan—and with a diplomatic contact she consulted, convinced her that the episode did occur.

The then–head of urology at the hospital, Dr. Terry Callaway, declined to respond to reporter Richard's questions. Hospital director Bernard Koval was reported as having flatly denied the story.

The authors, however, spoke with Richard's original source, who said he spoke from firsthand knowledge. The source said he had been present when the local CIA officer involved in the meeting—who, the witnesses interviewed have said, went by the name Larry Mitchell—spoke of the bin Laden visit while out for a social evening with friends. That a professional could have been so loose-lipped seems extraordinary, if not entirely unlikely. It remains conceivable, though, that the bin Laden visit to Dubai did occur. A second kidney specialist, an official source told the authors, described the visit independently, in detail, and at the time. The specialist was able to do so because he, too, was flown to Dubai to contribute to bin Laden's treatment.

Seeming corroboration of the CIA–bin Laden meeting, meanwhile, came to the authors in a 2009 interview with the official who headed the Security Intelligence department of France's DGSE, Alain Chouet, who is cited elsewhere in this book.

Did Chouet credit the account of the contact in Dubai? He replied, "Yes."

Did the DGSE have knowledge at the time that CIA officers met with bin Laden? "Yes," Chouet said. "Before 9/11," Chouet observed. "It was not a scoop for us—we weren't surprised [to learn of it]. We did not consider it something abnormal or outrageous. When someone is threatening you, you try to negotiate. Our own service does it all the time. It is the sort of thing we are paid to do."

The Dubai episode, Chouet noted, would have occurred "at the time of the Berlin negotiations— through interested parties—between the U.S. and the Taliban. The U.S. was trying to send messages to the Taliban. We didn't know whether [the meeting with bin Laden] was to threaten or to make a deal."

There were contacts with the Taliban through intermediaries that July, the latest stage in a long series of approaches. At initial meetings in Europe organized by the United Nations, American emissaries—not speaking officially for the U.S. government—had suggested the possibility of improved relations, cooperation on a strategically important oil pipeline project, and long-term assistance. They had also urged the Taliban to hand over bin Laden.

According to the *Le Figaro* report, the Dubai contact between bin Laden and U.S. intelligence occurred between July 4 and 14. The final contact, DGSE's

Chouet believes, was on the 13th. According to Chouet, the United States had a twofold approach. At the discussions in Germany, negotiators would both attempt to cool down relations between Washington and the Taliban and ask for the handover of bin Laden. The contact in Dubai, Chouet surmises, was arranged through Saudi Arabia's intelligence chief, Prince Turki—whose agency had handled bin Laden during the anti-Soviet war in the 1980s.

The hope, Chouet said, was to persuade bin Laden "not to oppose the negotiations in Berlin, and above all to leave Afghanistan and return to Saudi Arabia with a royal pardon—under Turki's guarantee and control. In exchange, the U.S. would drop efforts to bring him to justice for the attacks in Nairobi and Dar es Salaam and elsewhere in Arabia."

Chouet believes the overtures to bin Laden were bluntly rebuffed. At the forthcoming U.N.-sponsored meetings in Berlin, between July 17 and 21, former U.S. diplomat Tom Simons pressed even harder for the handover of bin Laden. Should he not be handed over, and should solid evidence establish that the terrorist leader had indeed been behind the attack on the USS *Cole*, he indicated, the United States could be expected to take military action.

If that was the threat, nothing came of it. After the 9/11 attacks in early fall, of course, there would be no more serious discussion. The Taliban did not give up bin Laden, and were rapidly ousted.

There is nothing in the 9/11 Commission Report about a July meeting with bin Laden in Dubai, but there is what may conceivably be a small clue. At a May 29 meeting with CIA officials, the report notes, National Security Adviser Rice had asked "whether any approach could be made to influence bin Laden."

The genesis of these straws in the historical wind about a purported meeting between CIA officers and bin Laden in summer 2001 may have been disinformation spread for some political purpose. The 9/11 Commission, though, should have investigated the matter and been seen to have done so.

OTHER PUZZLES remain, some of them with serious implications, as to what Western intelligence services knew about the hijackers before 9/11.

Very soon after 9/11, major newspapers on both sides of the Atlantic ran stories stating that Western intelligence had known about Mohamed Atta for some time. The *Chicago Tribune* reported as early as September 16 that Atta had been "on a government watchlist of suspected terrorists." Kate Connolly, a reporter for the British newspaper *The Guardian*, vividly recalls being told by German officials that operatives "had been trailing Atta for some time, and keeping an eye on the house he lived in on Marienstrasse."

No evidence was to emerge of Atta having been on a watchlist. It is evident, though, that both German intelligence and the CIA had long been interested not merely in Islamic extremists in Germany but—at one stage—in the men on Marienstrasse. Congress's Joint Inquiry Report aired a little of this, but the Commission Report virtually ignored the subject.

So far as can be reconstructed, the sequence of events was as follows. Well before the future terrorists rented the Marienstrasse apartment, German intelligence took an interest in two men in particular. The first was Mohammed Zammar, who seemed to be facilitating jihadi travel to Afghanistan. The name of a second man, a Hamburg businessman named Mamoun Darkazanli, came up repeatedly—especially when a card bearing his address was found in the possession of a suspect in the 1998 East Africa embassy bombings. There was intermittent physical surveillance of both men, and Zammar's telephone was tapped.

It was an incoming call, picked up by the Zammar tap in January 1999, that first drew attention to the apartment on Marienstrasse. A German intelligence report of the call, a copy of which is in the authors' possession, shows that the name of the person calling Zammar was "Marwan." The conversation was unexciting, an exchange about Marwan's studies and a trip Zammar had made. In a second call, a caller looking for Zammar was given the number of the Marienstrasse apartment—76 75 18 30—and the name of one of its tenants, "Mohamed Amir." On a third call, in September, Zammar sent "Mohamed Amir" his greetings.

Amir, of course, was the last name most used—prior to his departure for the United States—by the man who was to become known to the world as Mohamed Atta.

Those tapped calls are of greatest interest today in the context of the CIA's performance. The Germans reportedly thought the "Marwan" lead "particularly valuable," and passed the information about it to the CIA. The caller named "Marwan," they noted, had been speaking on a mobile phone registered in the United Arab Emirates. According to George Tenet, testifying in 2004 to the Senate Intelligence Committee, the CIA "didn't sit around" on receipt of this information, but "did some things to go find out some things."

According to security officials in the UAE, the number could have been identified in a matter of minutes. The "Marwan" on the call is believed to have been UAE citizen Marwan al-Shehhi, who in 2001 was to fly United 175 into the World Trade Center's South Tower. Was Shehhi's mobile phone ever monitored by the CIA?

Queried on the subject in 2004, U.S. intelligence officials said they were "uncertain."

The CIA on the ground in Germany did evince major interest in the Hamburg coterie of Islamic extremists. In late 1999, an American official who went by the name of Thomas Volz turned up at the office of the Hamburg state intelligence service—the Landesamt für Verfassungsschutz—with a pressing request.

Though he used the cover of a diplomatic post, Volz was a CIA agent. The Agency believed that Mamoun Darkazanli "had knowledge of an unspecified terrorist plot." Volz's hope, he explained, was that the suspect could be "turned," persuaded to become an informant and pass on information about al Qaeda activities.

The Germans doubted that Darkazanli could be induced to do any such thing. They tried all the same, and failed. Volz, however, repeatedly insisted they try again. So persistent was he, reportedly, that the CIA's man eventually tried approaching Darkazanli on his own initiative. To German intelligence officials, this was an outrageous intrusion, a violation of Germany's sovereignty.

All this at the very time, and soon after, that Atta and his comrades—whom Darkazanli knew well—had traveled to Afghanistan, sworn allegiance to bin Laden, and committed to the 9/11 operation. What really came of Volz's efforts remains unknown.

The 9/11 Commission Report did not mention the Volz episode. The public remains uninformed, moreover, as to what U.S. intelligence may have learned of the hijackers before they left Germany and became operational in the United States.

THE LEAD on Shehhi arising from the Hamburg phone tap aside, there is information suggesting there was early

U.S. interest in his accomplice Ziad Jarrah. In late January 2000, on his way back from the future hijackers' pivotal visit to Afghanistan, Jarrah was stopped for questioning while in transit at Dubai airport.

"It was at the request of the Americans," a UAE security official was to say after 9/11, "and it was specifically because of Jarrah's links with Islamic extremists, his contacts with terrorist organizations." The reason the terrorist was pulled over, reportedly, was "because his name was on a watchlist" provided by the United States.

During his interrogation, astonishingly, Jarrah coolly told his questioners that he had been in Afghanistan and now planned to go to the United States to learn to fly—and to spread the word about Islam.

While the airport interview was still under way, according to the UAE record, the Dubai officials made contact with U.S. representatives. "What happened," a UAE official elaborated in 2003, "was we called the Americans. We said, 'We have this guy. What should we do with him?' . . . their answer was, 'Let him go, we'll track him.' . . . They told us to let him go."

At the relevant date in FBI task force documents on Jarrah, and next to another entry about the terrorist's UAE stopover, an item has been redacted. The symbol beside the redaction stands for: "Foreign Government Information."

Was there also interest in Mohamed Atta before *his* arrival in the United States? Several former members of a secret operation run by the DIA, the U.S. military's Defense Intelligence Agency, went public four years after 9/11 with a disquieting claim. The names of four of the hijackers-to-be, Atta, Shehhi, Hazmi, and Mihdhar, they claimed, had appeared on the DIA's radar in early 2000, even before they arrived in the United States.

According to the lieutenant colonel who first made the

claim, Anthony Shaffer, the names came up in the course of a highly classified DIA operation code-named Able Danger. He and his staff had carried out "data mining," under a round-the-clock counterterrorist program Shaffer described as the "use of high-powered software to bore into just about everything: any data that was available—and I mean anything. Open-source Internet data, e-mails believed to be terrorist-related, non-secret government data, commercial records, information on foreign companies, logs of visitors to mosques."

According to Shaffer, such data also drew on U.S. visa records. If so, and given the reference to information obtained from mosques, it would seem that Able Danger perhaps could have picked up information on the named terrorists—even before they arrived in the United States.

Atta had applied for a U.S. green card in late 1999. Shehhi had gotten his U.S. entry visa by January 2000. Hazmi and Mihdhar had arrived that same month, having applied for and obtained their visas in the summer of 1999. All these documents were in the record.

All the documentary evidence involved, however, was destroyed well before 9/11 because of privacy concerns by Defense Department attorneys. Absent a future discovery of surviving documentary evidence, the Able Danger claims depend entirely on the memories—sometimes rusty memories—of those involved in the operation.

IN GERMANY, and as an outgrowth of surveilling the extremists in Hamburg, a border watch—or Grenzfahndung—was ordered on at least two of the men who frequented the Marienstrasse apartment. The routine was not to arrest listed individuals, but discreetly to note and report their passage across the frontier. It is hard to understand why, if the names of two of the

Marienstrasse group were on the list, those of Atta and Shehhi would not have been. If they were under border watch, their departure for the United States ought to have been noted.

German federal officials were unhelpful when approached by the authors for interviews on the subject of either monitoring the terrorists or on the relationship with U.S. agencies before 9/11. "Sadly," said an official from Germany's foreign intelligence service, the Bundesnachrichtendienst, "due to considerations of principle, your request cannot be granted. We ask for your understanding."

The official who was in 2001 and still is deputy chief of Hamburg domestic intelligence, Dr. Manfred Murck, was in general far more cooperative. He had no comment, however, on the subject of collaboration with U.S. intelligence.

The Islamic affairs specialist with the domestic intelligence service in Stuttgart, Dr. Herbert Müller, for his part, offered a small insight into where the Germans' monitoring of the men at Marienstrasse had led them. "Atta," he said, "was going through the focus of our colleagues. . . . He came to their notice."

Did the Germans share with the United States every-thing they learned about the future hijackers? "Some countries," a 9/11 Commission staff statement was to state tartly, "did not support U.S. efforts to collect intelligence information on terrorist cells in their countries. . . . This was especially true of some of the European services." Information gathered by Congress's Joint Inquiry, and what we have of a CIA review, make it clear that there was intermittent friction between the U.S. and German services.

A former senior American diplomat, on the other hand, cast no aspersions on the Germans. "My impression the entire time," former deputy head of mission in Berlin Michael Polt told the 9/11 Commission, "[was] that our level of interaction with counterterrorism and cooperation with the Germans was extremely high and well coordinated. . . . And the reason the Germans would want to share those concerns with us [was] because they were expecting from us some information that they could use to go ahead and go after these people."

For all that, German officials the authors contacted remained either evasive or diplomatic to a fault. Were they concealing the failures of their own intelligence apparatus, or courteously avoiding placing the blame on the ally across the Atlantic?

"They lied to my face for four years, the German secret service," said Dirk Laabs, a Hamburg author who has reported on the 9/11 story for the *Los Angeles Times* and the *Frankfurter Allgemeine Zeitung*. "Then I found information that they passed on everything to the CIA. . . . We only know a little bit of the true story, what really went on."

The release to the authors in 2011 of a single previously redacted sentence on a 9/11 Commission staff document makes crystal clear what was left fuzzy in the Commission Report. The document summarized the coded conversation between KSM and Binalshibh not long before the attacks—described in an earlier chapter—as to whether lovelorn Ziad Jarrah would stay the course.

The sentence that heads the document's summary of the exchange, now made public for the first time, reads:

On July 20, 2001, there was a call between
KSM and Binalshibh. They used the codewords
Teresa and Sally.

The only way the authorities could have known of such a phone call, on a known date and in great detail, was thanks to a telephone intercept. The call was intercepted and recorded while it was in progress.

That certainty leads to a string of further questions.

Which intelligence service tapped the call? The only probable candidates are those of the United States or of Germany. If the intercept was American, which service was responsible?

If KSM was in Afghanistan for the call, it may be that U.S. intelligence did not make the intercept. Ludicrous wrangling had been going on, first between the CIA and the FBI, and then—until just before 9/11—between different components within the CIA. The former British minister responsible for security matters, David Davis, claimed in 2012 that the opportunity to eavesdrop on calls was missed until the very eve of 9/11.

What though of the NSA—the National Security Agency? It is the NSA's mission to spy on international communications, yet its pre-9/11 performance is only minimally reported in the Commission Report.

If the intercept cited above was made in Germany by the Germans, was the take passed to the Americans at the time—or only after 9/11?

The questions do not end there. What other conversations between key 9/11 players were tapped into during the run-up to the attacks? If other conversations were captured, were they all in code that was incomprehensible at the time? Did such intercepts result in any action being taken?

A breakthrough answer on the German intelligence issue came to the authors from a very senior member of the U.S. Congress, a public figure with long experience of intelligence matters, who has held high security clearances, speaking not for attribution.

"We were told by the German intelligence," the member of Congress said of a visit to Berlin following 9/11, "that they had provided U.S. intelligence agencies with information about persons of interest to them who had been living in Hamburg and who they knew were in, or attempting to get into, the United States. The impression German intelligence gave me was that they felt the action of the U.S. intelligence agencies to their information was dismissive."

Sour grapes, or an accurate account of the American response to pertinent intelligence?

THIRTY-ONE

THE CIA CERTAINLY HAD KNOWN EARLY ON ABOUT TWO of the 9/11 terrorists.

The way it gained that intelligence speaks to the Agency's operational efficiency, in a brilliant operation a full twenty months before the attacks. Its subsequent performance, however, reflects disastrous inefficiency, perhaps the greatest fiasco in CIA history. Depending on how the evidence is interpreted, it points to something even more culpable.

This is a scenario that began to unravel for the CIA on 9/11 itself, just four hours after the strikes. Soon after 1:00 P.M. that day, at Agency headquarters, an aide hurried to Director Tenet with a handful of papers—the passenger manifests for the four downed airliners. "Two names," he said, placing a page on the table where the director could see it. "These two we know."

Tenet looked, then breathed, "There it is. Confirmation. Oh, Jesus . . ."

A long silence followed. There on the Flight 77 manifest, allocated to Seats 5E and 5F in First Class, were the names of Nawaf al-Hazmi and his brother Salem. Also on the list, near the front of the Coach section at 12B, was Khalid al-Mihdhar's name.

The names Hazmi and Mihdhar were instantly

familiar, Tenet has claimed, because his people had learned only weeks earlier that both men might be in the United States. According to his version of events, the CIA had known of Mihdhar since as early as 1999, had identified him firmly as a terrorist suspect by December that year, had had him followed, discovered he had a valid multiple-entry visa to allow him into the States, and had placed him and comrades—including Hazmi—under surveillance for a few days. Later, in the spring of 2000, the Agency had learned that Hazmi had arrived in California.

Yet, the director had claimed in the wake of 9/11, the CIA had done absolutely nothing about Mihdhar or Hazmi. It had not asked the State Department to watchlist the two terrorists at border points, had not asked the FBI to track them down if they were in the country, until nineteen days before 9/11.

Tenet blamed these omissions solely on calamitous error.

"CIA," he wrote in 2007, "had multiple opportunities to notice the significant information in our holdings and watchlist al-Hazmi and al-Mihdhar. Unfortunately, until August, we missed them all . . .

"Yes, people made mistakes; every human interaction was far from where it needed to be. We, the entire government, owed the families of 9/11 better than they got."

But was it just that CIA "people made mistakes"? Historical mysteries are as often explained by screwups as by darker truths. Nevertheless, senior Commission staff became less than convinced—and not just on the matter of Mihdhar and Hazmi—that Tenet was leveling with them.

When the director was interviewed, in January 2004, on oath, he kept saying "I don't remember" or "I don't recall." Those with courtroom experience among the commissioners reflected that he was "like a grand jury witness who had been too well prepared by a defense lawyer. The witness's memory was good when it was convenient, bad when it was convenient."

Executive Director Philip Zelikow was to say later of Tenet, "We just didn't believe him anymore." Tenet, for his part, declared himself outraged by the remark, and insisted that he had told the truth about everything.

What is known of the evidence on Hazmi and Mihdhar, however, makes it very hard for anyone to swallow the screwup excuse. Not least because, the CIA version of events suggests, its officials blew the chance to grab the two future hijackers not once, not twice, but time and time again.

This is a puzzle that has confounded official investigators, and reporters and authors, for a full decade now. It will not be solved in these pages, but readers may perhaps see its stark outline, its striking anomalies, its alarming possible implications, more clearly than in the past. To trace the chapter of supposed accidents we must start with a pivotal development that occurred as long as five years before 9/11.

SOMETIME IN 1996, the National Security Agency— which intercepts electronic communications worldwide —had identified a number in Yemen that Osama bin Laden called often from his satellite telephone in Afghanistan. The number, 967-1-200-578, rang at a house in the capital, Sana'a, used by a man he had first known in the days of the anti-Soviet war in Afghanistan. The man's name was Ahmed al-Hada, and—a great benefit for bin Laden, who in Afghanistan had no access to ordinary communications systems—his house had long served as an al Qaeda "hub," a link to the wider world.

The NSA did not immediately share this information either with the CIA or with other agencies—a symptom of the interagency disconnect that long plagued U.S. intelligence. The CIA did learn of the intercepts, however, and eventually obtained summaries of intercepted conversations. It was the start of a period of frustratingly sporadic, incomplete access granted by the NSA to material harvested from the hub.

Hada's telephone also came to loom large for the FBI. One of the Kenya bombers called the number before and after the 1998 attack on Nairobi, and—once agents learned that the number also took calls from bin Laden's sat-phone on the day of the bombing and the following day—they had a vital evidentiary link between the East Africa attacks and al Qaeda.

The intercepts of Hada's phone conversations were a priceless resource, and in 1999 yielded the first factual pointer to the preparations for 9/11. Hada's daughter, U.S. intelligence learned at some stage, was married to a young man named "Khalid"—full name, as we now know, Khalid al-Mihdhar. In December 1999, crucially, the NSA reported to both the CIA and the FBI that it had intercepted an especially interesting call on the Hada telephone, one that mentioned an upcoming trip by "Khalid" and "Nawaf " to Malaysia.

From the start, CIA officers guessed that this was no innocent excursion. Its purpose, one staffer suspected, was "something more nefarious." The travel, one cable stated, "may be in support of a terrorist mission." The men were referred to early on as members of an "operational cadre" or as "terrorist operatives."

The episode that was eventually to bring the Agency lasting shame began as textbook undercover work. As foreshadowed in an earlier chapter, Mihdhar's Saudi passport was photographed during the stopover in

Dubai—leading to the startling revelation that the terrorist had a visa valid for travel to the United States.

As veteran FBI counterterrorism specialist Jack Cloonan was to say, "This is as good as it gets. . . . How often do you get into someone's suitcase and find multiple-entry visas? How often do you know there's going to be an organizational meeting of al Qaeda any-place in the world? . . . This is what you would dream about."

Intelligence bounty continued to rain down on the CIA following the look inside Mihdhar's passport. The suspect was tracked as he traveled on to the Malaysian capital, Kuala Lumpur. He was watched, start-ing on January 5, as he met and talked with fellow suspects—including his associate Nawaf al-Hazmi. Courtesy of Malaysia's Special Branch, the men were covertly photographed, observed going out to pay phones, surveilled when they went to an Internet café to use the computers. The computers' hard drives were reportedly examined afterward.

The whirl of suspicious activity was of interest not merely to CIA agents in the field, nor only to CIA head-quarters at Langley. For it all occurred in the very first days of January 2000, the post-Millennium moment when Washington was more than usually on the alert— at the highest level—for any clue that might herald a terrorist attack. Regular situation reports went day by day not only to the directors of the CIA and the FBI but also to National Security Adviser Sandy Berger and his staff, who included Richard Clarke, at the White House.

Three days later, on January 8, Mihdhar and two of his comrades—one of them later to be identified as having been Hazmi and the other as senior bin Laden henchman Tawfiq bin Attash—took the brief two-hour flight from Kuala Lumpur to the Thai capital Bangkok. There, according to the CIA, and though communication with a Bangkok hotel was logged on one of the pay phones used by the suspects in Kuala Lumpur, the trail was lost.

Nothing would be known of the operatives' whereabouts, the available record indicates, until two months later. Only then, according to the known record, did Thai authorities respond to a January CIA request to watch for the suspects' departure. At last, however, in early March, two Agency stations abroad reported a fresh development. Their message said that Hazmi and an unnamed comrade—only later to be named as Mihdhar—had flown out of Bangkok as long ago as January 15, bound for Los Angeles. The men, the cables noted, were "UBL [bin Laden] associates."

This was stunning information, information that should have triggered an immediate response. Yet, we are asked by the CIA to believe, no one reacted. No one did anything at all. The first cable to arrive with the news was marked "Action Required: None."

This in spite of the fact that, just before the Millennium, Director Tenet had told all CIA personnel overseas, "The threat could not be more real. . . . The American people are counting on you and me to take every appropriate step to protect them."

Tenet's Counterterrorist Center had circulated an unambiguous instruction just a month before the al Qaeda meeting in Kuala Lumpur. "It is important," the document had warned, "to flag terrorist personality information in DO [Directorate of Operations] reporting for the [State Department watchlist program] so that potential terrorists may be watchlisted."

Yet in March 2000, although it had learned that Hazmi, a bin Laden operative, had entered the country, the CIA did not alert the State Department. Nor, back in January, had it alerted State to the fact that Mihdhar had a U.S. entry visa. The Agency was not to request that either man be watchlisted until late August 2001.

While the Kuala Lumpur meeting was still under way, a 9/11 Commission document notes, top FBI officials had been told that the CIA "promised to let FBI know if an FBI angle to the case developed." The CIA is prohibited from undertaking operations in the United States, and the FBI has responsibility for domestic intelligence and law enforcement.

Even so, with the revelation that Mihdhar had a U.S. visa—very much an FBI angle—the CIA left the Bureau in the dark just as it did the State Department. It certainly should have alerted the FBI the moment it learned that Hazmi had entered the United States. Information that, if shared, may have led to an earlier hunt for Hazmi and Mihdhar.

After 9/11, when its horrendous failure to do any of these things came out, the CIA would attempt to claim that it had not been quite like that. Later investigations by Congress's Joint Inquiry and the Department of Justice's inspector general were to produce vestigial portions of emails and cables written right after the discovery that Mihdhar had a U.S. entry visa. The picture that emerged is not immediately clear.

The very day the CIA learned that Mihdhar had a U.S. visa, a CIA bin Laden unit desk officer—identified for security reasons only as "Michelle"—informed colleagues flatly that his travel documents, including the visa, had been copied and passed "to the FBI for further investigation."

In an email to CIA colleagues the following day, an Agency officer assigned to FBI headquarters—identified as "James"—wrote of having told two senior FBI agents what had been learned of Mihdhar's activity in Malaysia. He had advised one of them: "as soon as something concrete is developed leading us to the criminal area or to known FBI cases, we will immediately bring FBI into the loop."

Were one to know only that about the CIA record, it might seem that the FBI *was* given the crucial visa information. Serious doubt sets in, though, on looking at the wider picture. In an email to CIA colleagues, the Justice Department inspector general discovered, "James" had "stated that he was detailing 'exactly what [he] briefed [the FBI] on' *in the event the FBI later complained* that they were not provided with all of the information about al-Mihdhar. This information did not discuss al-Mihdhar's passport or U.S. visa [authors' italics]."

"James," the inspector general noted, refused to be interviewed.

The inspector general was given access to "Michelle," the desk officer who had written flatly that Mihdhar's passport and visa had been passed to the FBI. She prevaricated, however, saying she could not remember how she knew that fact. Her boss, Tom Wilshire, the deputy chief of the CIA's bin Laden unit, said that for his part he had no knowledge of the "Michelle" cable. He "did not know whether the information had been passed to the FBI."

Other documents indicate that the opposite was the case, that Wilshire had deliberately ensured that the information would *not* reach the FBI. This emerged with the inspector general's discovery of a draft cable—one prepared but never sent—by an FBI agent on attachment to the CIA's bin Laden unit.

Having had sight of a CIA cable noting that Mihdhar possessed a U.S. visa, Agent Doug Miller had responded swiftly by drafting a Central Intelligence Report, or CIR, addressed to the Bureau's bin Laden unit and its New

York field office. Had the CIR then been sent, the FBI would have learned promptly of Mihdhar's entry visa.

As regulations required, Agent Miller first submitted the draft to CIA colleagues for clearance. Hours later, though, he received a note from "Michelle" stating: "pls hold off on CIR for now per [Wilshire]."

Perplexed and angry, Miller consulted with Mark Rossini, a fellow FBI agent who was also on attachment to the CIA unit. "Doug came to me and said, 'What the fuck?,'" Rossini recalled. "So the next day I went to [Wilshire's deputy, identity uncertain] and said, 'What's with Doug's cable? You've got to tell the Bureau about this.' She put her hand on her hip and said, 'Look, the next attack is going to happen in South East Asia—it's not the FBI's jurisdiction. When we want the FBI to know about it, we'll let them know.'"

After eight days, when clearance to send the message still had not come, Agent Miller submitted the draft again directly to CIA deputy unit chief Wilshire along with a note asking: "Is this a no go or should I remake it in some way?" According to the CIA, it was "unable to locate any response to this e-mail."

Neither Miller nor Rossini was interviewed by 9/11 Commission staff. Wilshire was questioned, the authors established, but the report of his interview is redacted in its entirety.

In July 2001, by which time he had been seconded to the FBI's bin Laden unit, Wilshire proposed to CIA colleagues that the fact that Mihdhar had a U.S. entry visa should be shared with the FBI. It never happened.

Following a subsequent series of nods and winks from Wilshire, the FBI at last discovered for itself first the fact that Mihdhar had had a U.S. entry visa in 2000, then the fact that he had just very recently returned to the country. Only after that, in late August, did the FBI begin to search for Mihdhar and Hazmi—a search that was to prove inept, lethargic, and ultimately ineffectual.

An eight-member 9/11 Commission team was to reach a damning conclusion about the cable from CIA officer "Michelle" stating that Mihdhar's travel documents had been passed to the FBI. "The weight of the evidence," they wrote, "does not support that latter assertion." The Justice Department inspector general also found, after exhaustive investigation, that the CIA had failed to share with the FBI two vital facts—"that Mihdhar had a U.S. visa and that Hazmi had travelled to Los Angeles."

In 2007, Congress forced the release of a nineteen-page summary of the CIA's own long-secret probe of its performance. This, too, acknowledged that Agency staff neither shared what they knew about Mihdhar and Hazmi nor saw to it that they were promptly watchlisted. An accountability board, the summary recommended, should review the work of named officers. George Tenet's successor as CIA director, Porter Goss, however, declined to hold such a review. There was no question of misconduct, he said. The officers named were "amongst the finest" the Agency had.

The excuse for such monstrous failures? According to the CIA's internal report, the bin Laden unit had had an "excessive workload." Director Tenet claimed in sworn testimony, not once but three times, that he knew "nobody read" the cable that reported Hazmi's actual arrival in Los Angeles. Wilshire, the officer repeatedly involved, summed up for Congress's Joint Inquiry: "All the processes that had been put in place," he said, "all the safeguards, everything else, they failed at every possible opportunity. Nothing went right."

There are those who think such excuses may be the best the CIA can offer to explain a more compromising

OIG Report on CIA Accountability
With Respect to the 9/11 Attacks

(S) Separately, in March 2000, two CIA field locations sent to a number of addressees cables reporting that al-Hazmi and another al-Qa'ida associate had traveled to the United States. They were clearly identified in the cables as "UBL associates." The Team has found no evidence, and heard no claim from any party, that this information was shared in any manner with the FBI or that anyone in UBL Station took other appropriate operational action at that time.

(S) In the months following the Malaysia operation, the CIA missed several additional opportunities to nominate al-Hazmi and al-Mihdhar for watchlisting; to inform the FBI about their intended or actual travel to the United States; and to take appropriate operational action. These included a few occasions identified by the Joint Inquiry as well as several others.

(S) The consequences of the failures to share information and perform proper operational followthrough on these terrorists were potentially significant. Earlier watchlisting of al-Mihdhar could have prevented his re-entry into the United States in July 2001. Informing the FBI and good operational followthrough by CIA and FBI might have resulted in surveillance of both al-Mihdhar and al-Hazmi. Surveillance, in turn, would have had the potential to yield information on flight training, financing, and links to others who were complicit in the 9/11 attacks.

The CIA kept to itself the fact that it knew long before 9/11 that two of the future hijackers—known to be terrorists—had U.S. visas, and that one had definitely entered the United States.

truth. "It is clear," wrote the author Kevin Fenton, an independent researcher who completed a five-year study of the subject in 2011, "that this information was not withheld through a series of bizarre accidents, but intentionally. . . . Withholding the information about Mihdhar and Hazmi from the FBI makes sense only if the CIA was monitoring the two men in the U.S. itself."

That notion is not fantasy. The CIA's own in-house review noted that—had the FBI been told that the two future hijackers were or might be in the country—"good operational follow-through by CIA and FBI might have resulted in surveillance of both Mihdhar and Hazmi. Surveillance, in turn, would have had the potential to yield information on flight training, financing and links to others who were complicit in the 9/11 attacks."

If the FBI had known, then—New York Assistant Special Agent in Charge Kenneth Maxwell has said, "We would have been on them like white on snow: physical surveillance, electronic surveillance, a special unit devoted to them." After 9/11, and when the CIA's omissions became known, some of Maxwell's colleagues at the FBI reacted with rage and dark suspicion.

"They purposely hid from the FBI," one official fulminated, "purposely refused to tell the FBI that they were following a man in Malaysia who had a visa to come to America. . . . And that's why September 11 happened. . . . They have blood on their hands. They have three thousand deaths on their hands."

Could it be that the CIA concealed what it knew about Mihdhar and Hazmi because officials feared that precipitate action by the FBI would blow a unique lead? Did the Agency want to arrange to monitor the pair's activity? The CIA's mandate does not allow it to run operations in the United States, but the prohibition had been broken in the past.

The CIA had on at least one occasion previously aspired to leave an Islamic suspect at large in order to surveil him. When 1993 Trade Center bomber Ramzi Yousef was located in Pakistan two years later, investigative reporter Robert Friedman wrote, the Agency "wanted to continue tracking him." It "fought with the FBI," tried to postpone his arrest. On that occasion, the FBI had its way, seized Yousef, and brought him back for trial.

With that rebuff fresh in the institutional memory, did the CIA decide to keep the sensational discovery of Mihdhar's entry visa to itself? Or did it, as some Bureau agents came to think possible, even hope to recruit the two terrorists as informants?

The speculation is not idle. A heavily redacted congressional document shows that, only weeks before Mihdhar's visa came to light, top CIA officials had debated the lamentable fact that the Agency had as yet not penetrated al Qaeda: "Without penetrations of OBL organization ... [redacted lines] ... we need to also recruit sources inside OBL's organization. Realize that recruiting terrorist sources is difficult ... but we must make an attempt."

The following day, CIA officers went to the White House for a meeting with a select group of top-level National Security Council members. Attendees discussed both the lack of inside information and how essential it was to achieve "penetrations." "Many "unilateral avenues" and "creative attempts" were subsequently to be tried. Material on those attempts in the document has been entirely redacted.

President Clinton himself aside, the senior White House official to whom the CIA reported at that time was National Security Adviser Sandy Berger. After 9/11, while preparing to testify before official inquiries into the attacks, Berger was to commit a crime that destroyed his shining reputation, a folly so bizarre—for a man of his stature—as to be unbelievable were it not true.

On four occasions in 2002 and 2003, Berger would make his way to the National Archives in Washington, the repository of the nation's most venerated documents—including the Declaration of Independence, the Constitution, and the Bill of Rights. This trusted official, alumnus of Cornell and Harvard, former lawyer and aide to public officials, a former deputy director of policy planning at State, had crowned his career by becoming national security adviser during President Clinton's second term.

It was at Clinton's request, and in his capacity as one of the very few people allowed access to the former administration's most secret documents, that Berger went to the Archives to review selected files. Given his seniority, he was received with special courtesy and under rather less than the usual stringent security conditions. All the more astounding then that on his third visit a staff member "saw Mr. Berger bent down, fiddling with something that could have been paper, around his ankle."

Under cover of asking for privacy to make phone calls, or in the course of uncommonly frequent visits to the lavatory, the former national security adviser was purloining top secret documents, smuggling them out of the building hidden in his clothing, and taking them home. He was caught doing so, publicly exposed, forced to resign from his senior post with the 2004 Democratic campaign for the presidency, charged with taking classified documents, and—a year later—fined $50,000 and sentenced to one hundred hours of community service.

What had possessed Berger? What seemed so compromising to himself or to the Clinton administration—or so essential to be hidden from 9/11 investigators— as to drive him to risk national disgrace?

What is known is that Berger took no fewer than five copies of the Millennium After Action Review, or MAAR, a thirteen-page set of recommendations that had been written in early 2000, focused mostly on countering al Qaeda activity inside the United States. While the MAAR is still classified, it seems somewhat unlikely that it is the item that Berger deemed potential dynamite. It may have been handwritten notes on the copies that he thought potentially explosive, former 9/11 Commission senior counsel John Farmer has surmised. That would account for the former official's apparently frantic search for additional copies.

The National Archives inspector general and others worried about what other documents Berger may have removed from the Archives. Short of a further admission on his part, the director of the Archives' presidential documents staff conceded, we shall never know. Whatever he took, Farmer pointed out, it made him appear "desperate to prevent the public from seeing certain papers."

"What information could be so embarrassing," House Speaker Dennis Hastert asked, "that a man with decades of experience in handling classified documents would risk being caught pilfering our nation's most sensitive secrets? . . . Was this a bungled attempt to rewrite history and keep critical information from the 9/11 Commission?"

The question is all the more relevant when one notes that, so far as one can tell, Berger's focus was on the period right after the CIA's resolve to "penetrate" bin Laden's terrorist apparatus, or "recruit" inside it, an aspiration followed in rapid order by the discovery of Khalid al-Mihdhar's U.S. entry visa—and the highly suspect failure to share that information with the State Department and the FBI.

*

THOUGH FRAGMENTARY, there are pointers suggesting that the CIA did not promptly drop its coverage of Mihdhar. On January 5, 2000—the day of the discovery of Mihdhar's visa, and in the same cable that claimed the FBI had been notified—desk officer "Michelle" noted that "we need to continue the effort to identify these travelers and their activities." As late as February, more- over, a CIA message noted that the Agency was still engaged in an investigation "to determine what the subject is up to."

Mihdhar was to tell KSM, according to the CIA account of KSM's interrogation, that he and Hazmi "believed they were surveilled from Thailand to the U.S." KSM seems to have taken this possibility seriously—sufficiently so, the CIA summary continues, that he "began having doubts whether the two would be able to fulfil their mission." Later, in 2001, two other members of the hijack team sent word that they thought they, too, had been tailed on a journey within the United States.

The hijackers may have imagined they were being followed. Given their mission, it would have been a natural enough fear. There is another relevant lead, though, that has more substance.

In the early afternoon of September 11, the senior aide to Defense Secretary Rumsfeld penned a very curious handwritten note. Written by Deputy Under Secretary Stephen Cambone at 2:40 P.M., following a phone call between Rumsfeld and Tenet, it appears in a record of the day's events that was obtained in 2006 under the Freedom of Information Act.

The note reads:

AA 77—3 indiv have been followed since Millennium &
Cole

1 guy is assoc of Cole bomber
3 entered US in early July
(2 of 3 pulled aside and interrogated?)

Though somewhat garbled, probably due to the rush of events in those hectic hours, the details more or less fit. Mihdhar, Hazmi, and Hazmi's brother were hijackers aboard American Flight 77, the airliner that was flown into the Pentagon. Mihdhar had been an associate of USS *Cole* planner Attash, the most significant of the fellow terrorists with whom he met in Kuala Lumpur. Mihdhar, certainly, had entered the United States—for the second time, after months back in the Middle East—in "early July," on July 4.

Cambone's note on three individuals having "been"

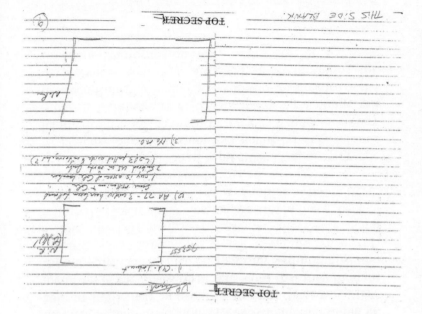

followed" could be interpreted in two ways. Had Tenet meant during his conversation with Secretary Rumsfeld merely to convey the fact that three of the terrorists had at an earlier point *come to the notice* of the intelligence community? Or had he—conceivably—meant what the note says he said, that the terrorists' movements had indeed been monitored?

Was it Tenet's knowledge of some intelligence operation that had targeted Mihdhar and Hazmi—whether in the shape of monitoring them or attempting to recruit them—that led to the director's flash of recognition and his "Oh, Jesus" exclamation on seeing their names on the Flight 77 manifest?

If an operation had been attempted, contrary to the rules that govern CIA activities, to whom was it entrusted? To try to answer that question is to fumble in the dark. There are pointers, though, in the evidence as to whether any foreign nation-state—other than Afghanistan, where the Taliban played host to bin Laden—had responsibility at any level for the 9/11 attacks.

THIRTY-TWO

A QUESTION THE 9/11 COMMISSION SOUGHT TO answer, its chairmen Thomas Kean and Lee Hamilton recalled, was "Had the hijackers received any support from foreign governments?"

"The terrorists do not function in a vacuum," Defense Secretary Donald Rumsfeld had told reporters the week after 9/11. They "live and work and function and are fostered and financed and encouraged, if not just tolerated, by a series of countries. . . . I know a lot, and what I have said, as clearly as I know how, is that states are supporting these people." Pressed to elaborate, Rumsfeld was silent for a long moment. Then, saying it was "a sensitive matter," he changed the subject.

Three years later, the 9/11 Commission would consider whether any of three foreign countries in particular might have had a role in 9/11. Two were self-avowed foes of the United States—Iran and Iraq. The third was the country long since billed—by both sides—as a close friend of the United States, Saudi Arabia.

The Commission stated that it had seen "no evidence that Iraq cooperated with al Qaeda in developing or carrying out any attacks against the Unites States."

Iran, the Commission found, had long had contacts with al Qaeda and had allowed its operatives—including a number of the future hijackers—to travel freely through its airports. The Comission Report, however, said there was no evidence that Iran "was aware of the planning for what later became the 9/11 attack." The commissioners urged the government to investigate further.

There is nothing to indicate that federal agencies have probed further. In 2011, however, it was reported that a suit filed by lawyers for bereaved U.S. family members would include revealing testimony from three Iranian defectors. Former senior Commission counsel Dietrich Snell was quoted as saying in an affidavit that there was now "convincing evidence the government of Iran pro-vided material support to al Qaeda in the planning and execution of the 9/11 attack."

In December 2011, in a significant development, a fed-eral judge ruled that the plaintiffs had "provided direct support to al Qaeda for the 9/11 attacks." The case was continuing as this edition went to press.

Also significantly, there was no finding in the 9/11 Commission Report that categorically exonerated America's "friend" Saudi Arabia—or individuals in Saudi Arabia—from any involvement in the 9/11 plot. The decision as to what to say about Saudi Arabia in the Report had been made amid discord and tension.

Investigators who had probed the Saudi angle believed their work demonstrated a close link between hijackers Mihdhar and Hazmi and the Saudi government. Their written findings reflected that.

Then, late one night, as last-minute changes to the Report were being made, the investigators received alarming news. Senior counsel Snell, their team leader, was at the office, closeted with executive director Zelikow, making major changes to their material and removing key elements.

The lead investigators, Michael Jacobson and Rajesh De, hurried to the office to confront Snell. With lawyerly caution, he said he thought there was insufficient substance to their case against the Saudis. They considered the possibility of resigning, then settled for a compromise. Much of the telling information they had collected was to survive in the Report—but only in tiny print, hidden in the endnotes.

Prince Bandar, then still Saudi ambassador to Washington, expressed delight when the Commission Report was published. "The clear statements by this independent, bipartisan commission," he declared, "have debunked the myths that have cast fear and doubt over Saudi Arabia." Quotations from the Report favorable to Saudi Arabia were posted on the embassy's website and remained there still in early 2012.

Foremost among the quotes Prince Bandar liked was a Commission finding that it had located "no evidence that the Saudi government as an institution or senior Saudi officials individually funded" al Qaeda. The full quote, which was not cited, was less satisfying.

"Saudi Arabia," the same paragraph said, "has long been considered the primary source of al Qaeda funding," and—the Report noted—its conclusion "does not exclude the likelihood that charities with significant Saudi government sponsorship diverted funds to al Qaeda . . . al Qaeda found fertile fund-raising ground in Saudi Arabia."

Another major passage did not appear on the embassy site. "Saudi Arabia," it read, "has been a problematic ally in combating Islamic extremism. At the level of high policy, Saudi Arabia's leaders cooperated with American diplomatic initiatives . . . before 9/11. At the same time, Saudi Arabia's society was a place where al Qaeda raised money directly from individuals and through charities

… the Ministry of Islamic Affairs … uses *zakat* [charitable giving, a central tenet of Islam] and government funds to spread Wahhabi beliefs throughout the world…. Some Wahhabi-funded organizations have been exploited by extremists to further their goal of violent jihad against non-Muslims."

The long official friendship between the United States and Saudi Arabia, the Report said, could not be unconditional. The relationship had to be about more than oil, had to include—this in bold type—"a commitment to fight the violent extremists who foment hatred."

For a very long time, there had been no such clear commitment on the part of the Saudis. More than seven years before 9/11, the first secretary at the Saudi mission to the United Nations, Mohammed al-Khilewi, had defected to the United States—bringing with him thousands of pages of documents that, he said, showed the regime's support for terrorism, corruption, and abuse of human rights. At the same time, he addressed a letter to Crown Prince Abdullah, calling for "a move towards democracy." The Saudi royals, Khilewi said, responded by threatening his life. The U.S. government, however, offered little protection. FBI officials, moreover, declined to accept the documents the defecting diplomat had brought with him.

In support of his claim that Saudi Arabia supported terrorism, Khilewi spoke of an episode relevant to the earliest attempt to bring down the Trade Center's Twin Towers. "A Saudi citizen carrying a Saudi diplomatic passport," he said, "gave money to Ramzi Yousef, the mastermind behind the [1993] World Trade Center bombing" when he was in the Philippines. The Saudi relationship with Ramzi Yousef, the defector claimed, "is secret and goes through Saudi intelligence."

The reference to a Saudi citizen having funded Yousef

closely fit the part played by Osama bin Laden's brother-in-law, Jamal Khalifa. He was active in the Philippines, fronted as a charity organizer at the relevant time, and founded a charity that funded Yousef and KSM during the initial plotting to destroy U.S. airliners. There was telephone traffic between Khalifa's cell phone and an apartment the conspirators used.

When Khalifa eventually returned to Saudi Arabia in 1995—following detention in the United States and subsequent acquittal on terrorism charges in Jordan—he was, according to CIA bin Laden unit chief Michael Scheuer, met with a limousine and a welcome home from a "high-ranking official." A Philippines newspaper would report that it had been Prince Sultan bin Abdul Aziz, then a deputy prime minister and minister of defense and aviation, until his recent death the heir to the Saudi throne, who "allegedly welcomed" Khalifa.

Information obtained by U.S. intelligence in that period, veteran investigative reporter Seymour Hersh has written, had been the very opposite of the 9/11 Commission's verdict of "no evidence" that senior Saudi officials funded al Qaeda.

"Since 1994 or earlier," Hersh noted, "the National Security Agency has been collecting electronic intercepts of conversations between members of the Saudi Arabian royal family. . . . The intercepts depict a regime increasingly corrupt, alienated from the country's religious rank and file, and so weakened and frightened that it has brokered its future by channeling hundreds of millions of dollars in what amounts to protection money to fundamentalist groups that wish to overthrow it. The intercepts had demonstrated to analysts that by 1996 Saudi money was supporting Osama bin Laden's al Qaeda. . . .

"'96 is the key year," Hersh quoted an intelligence

official as saying, "Bin Laden hooked up to all the bad guys—it's like the Grand Alliance—and had a capability for conducting large-scale operations." The Saudi regime, the official said, had "gone to the dark side."

Going to the dark side, by more than one account, began with a deal. In June 1996, while in Paris for the biennial international weapons bazaar, a group of Saudi royals and financiers is said to have gathered at the Royal Monceau hotel near the Saudi embassy. The subject was bin Laden, and what to do about him. After two recent bombings of American targets in Saudi Arabia, one of them just that month, the fear was that the Saudi elite itself would soon be targeted.

At the meeting at the Monceau, French domestic intelligence reportedly learned, it was decided that bin Laden was to be kept at bay by payment of huge sums in protection money. To the tune, one account had it, of hundreds of millions of dollars. The *Los Angeles Times* was in 2004 to quote 9/11 Commission member Senator Bob Kerrey as saying that officials on the Commission believed Saudi officials had received assurances of safety in return for their generosity, even if there was no hard specific evidence.

In years to come, senior Saudi princes would deride reports of payoffs or simply write them out of the script of history. "It's a lovely story," Prince Bandar would say, "but that's not true." GID's Turki, for his part, recalled exchanges with the Taliban about bin Laden in 1996 during which he asked them to "make sure he does not operate against the Kingdom or say anything against the Kingdom." In 1998—and at the request of the United States—according to Turki, he made two unsuccessful secret visits to try to persuade the Taliban to hand over bin Laden.

Others say Turki actually traveled to Afghanistan in

both 1996 and 1998. In sworn statements after 9/11, former Taliban intelligence chief Mohammed Khaksar said that in 1998 the prince sealed a deal under which bin Laden undertook not to attack Saudi targets. In return, Saudi Arabia would provide funds and material assistance to the Taliban, not demand bin Laden's extradition, and not bring pressure to close down al Qaeda training camps. Saudi businesses, meanwhile, would ensure that money also flowed directly to bin Laden.

Turki would deny after 9/11 that any such deal was done with bin Laden. One account has it, however, that he himself met with bin Laden—his old protégé from the days of the anti-Soviet jihad—during the exchanges that led to the deal. Citing a U.S. intelligence source, the author Simon Reeve reported as much in 1999—well before it became an issue after 9/11.

Whatever the truth about Turki's role, other Saudi royals may have been involved in a payoff. A former Clinton administration official has claimed—and U.S. intelligence sources concurred—that at least two Saudi princes had been paying, on behalf of the Kingdom, what amounted to protection money since 1995. "The deal was," the former official said, "they would turn a blind eye to what he was doing elsewhere.' You don't conduct operations here, and we won't disrupt them elsewhere.' "

American and British official sources, speaking later with Simon Henderson—Baker fellow at the Washington Institute for Near East Policy—named the two princes in question. They were, Henderson told the authors, Interior Minister Naif and the minister of defense and aviation, Prince Sultan bin Abdul Aziz. The money involved in the alleged payments, according to Henderson's sources, had amounted to "hundreds of millions of dollars." It had been "Saudi official money"—not their own."

Unlike other surviving monarchies, the Saudi royal family comprises a vast number of princes—modest estimates put their number at some seven thousand. All are hugely wealthy, though only a much smaller number have real clout. There were Saudi royals, some came to believe, whose relations with bin Laden extended to active friendship.

Four-star General Wayne Downing, who headed the task force that investigated the 1996 bombing in Saudi Arabia, said he learned of princes who went to Afghanistan and fraternized with bin Laden. "They would go out and see Osama, spend some time with him, talk with him—you know—live out in the tents, eat the simple food, engage in falconry . . . ride horses. And then be able to have the insider secret knowledge that, 'Yes, we saw Osama, and we talked to him.' "

At the State Department, the director of the Office of the Coordinator for Counterterrorism concluded that the relationship with some royals went way beyond recreational pursuits. "We've got information about who's backing bin Laden," Dick Gannon was saying by 1998, "and in a lot of cases it goes back to the royal family. There are certain factions of the royal family who just don't like us."

In the years and months before 9/11, American officials visiting Riyadh usually discovered that it was futile to ask the Saudis for help in fighting terrorism. George Tenet, who had become CIA director during Bill Clinton's second term, has vividly recalled an audience he was granted by the crown prince's brother Prince Naif. Naif, who as interior minister oversaw domestic intelligence, began the exchange with "an interminable soliloquy recounting the history of the U.S.–Saudi 'special' relationship, including how the Saudis would never, ever keep security-related information from their U.S. allies."

There came a moment when Tenet had had enough. Breaching royal etiquette, he placed his hand on the prince's knee, and said, "Your Royal Highness, what do you think it will look like if someday I have to tell the *Washington Post* that you held out data that might have helped us track down al Qaeda murderers?" Naif's reaction, Tenet thought, was what looked like "a prolonged state of shock."

Vice President Al Gore, who saw Crown Prince Abdullah soon afterward, renewed an existing request for access to a captured al Qaeda terrorist, a man known to have information on al Qaeda funding. "The United States," the 9/11 Commission was to note dourly, "never obtained this access."

So it went, year after year. Robert Baer, a celebrated former CIA field officer in the Middle East, recalled that Prince Naif "never lifted a finger" to get to the bottom of the 1996 bomb that killed and injured U.S. servicemen in Saudi Arabia. Baer pointed out, too, that it was Naif—in 1999—who released from prison two Saudi clerics long associated with bin Laden's cause.

Congress's Joint Inquiry was to note that it had been told "the Saudi government would not cooperate with the United States on matters relating to Osama bin Laden [name and information censored]." Words, perhaps, out of the mouth of Michael Scheuer, former chief of the CIA's bin Laden unit.

"As one of the unit's first actions," Scheuer recalled in 2008, "we requested that the Saudis provide the CIA with basic information about bin Laden. That request remained unfulfilled." The U.S. government, he bitterly recalled, "publicly supported a brutal, medieval Arab tyranny . . . and took no action against a government that helped ensure that bin Laden and al Qaeda remained beyond the reach of the United States." To Scheuer, looking back, America's supposed ally had in reality been simply a "foreign enemy."

On a flight home from Saudi Arabia in the late 1990s, FBI director Louis Freeh told counterterrorism chief John O'Neill that he thought the Saudi officials they had met during the trip had been helpful. "You've got to be kidding," retorted O'Neill, a New Jersey native who never minced his words. "They didn't give us anything. They were just shining sunshine up your ass."

Several years later, in two long conversations with an investigator for a French intelligence agency, O'Neill was still venting his frustration. "All the answers, all the clues that could enable us to dismantle Osama bin Laden's organization," he said, "are in Saudi Arabia."

The answers and the clues, however, remained out of reach. In part, O'Neill told the Frenchman, because U.S. dependence on Saudi oil meant that Saudi Arabia had "much more leverage on us than we have on the Kingdom." And, he added, because "high-ranking personalities and families in the Saudi Kingdom" had close ties to bin Laden.

The conversations took place in June and late July of 2001.

A YEAR AFTER 9/11, former Saudi intelligence chief Prince Turki—the longtime head of GID—expounded at length on his service's relationship with the CIA.

From around 1996, he said, "At the instruction of the senior Saudi leadership, I shared all the intelligence we had collected on bin Laden and al Qaeda with the CIA. And in 1997 the Saudi Minister of Defense, Prince Sultan bin Abdul Aziz, established a joint intelligence committee with the United States to share information on terrorism in general and on bin Laden and al Qaeda in particular."

That the GID and U.S. services had a long if uneasy understanding on sharing intelligence is not at issue. A year after his initial comments, though, by which time he had become ambassador to London, Turki spoke out specifically about 9/11 hijackers Mihdhar and Hazmi.

In late 1999 and early 2000, he said—when Mihdhar and Hazmi were headed for the terrorist meeting in Malaysia—GID had told the CIA that both men were terrorists. "What we told them," he said, "was these people were on our watchlist from previous activities of al Qaeda, in both the [East Africa] embassy bombings and attempts to smuggle arms into the Kingdom in 1997."

The Saudi ambassador to the United States, Prince Bandar, had hinted right after 9/11 that the intelligence services had known more about the hijackers in advance than they were publicly admitting. Then, his remarks had gone virtually unnoticed.

In 2007, however, by which time he had risen to become national security adviser to former crown prince—now King—Abdullah, Bandar produced a bombshell. He went much further than had Prince Turki on what—he claimed—GID had passed to the CIA. "Saudi security," Bandar said, had been "actively following the movements of most of the terrorists with precision. . . . If U.S. security authorities had engaged their Saudi counterparts in a serious and credible manner, in my opinion, we would have avoided what happened."

The same week, speaking not of 9/11 but of the 2005 London Underground train bombings that killed more than fifty people and injured some eight hundred, King Abdullah made astonishing remarks. "We have sent information before the terrorist attacks on Britain," the king said, "but unfortunately no action was taken . . . it may have been able to avert the tragedy."

Such claims might be rejected out of hand, were it not that they came from Saudis at the very top of the power structure. A British government spokesman publicly denied King Abdullah's remarks, saying that information received from the Saudis had been "not relevant" to the London bombings and could not have been used to prevent the attacks. The comments about Mihdhar and Hazmi led to a mix of denial, rage—and in one case, a curious silence.

"There is not a shred of evidence," the CIA's Bill Harlow said of Turki's 2003 claim, "that Saudi intelligence provided CIA any information about Mihdhar and Hazmi prior to September 11 as they have described." Harlow said information on the two hijackers-to-be had been passed on only a month *after* the attacks.

Prince Turki stood by what he had said, while eventually acknowledging that it had not been he himself who had given the information to the Americans. The prince's former chief analyst, Saeed Badeeb, said it was he who briefed U.S. officials—at one of their regular liaison meetings—warning that Mihdhar and Hazmi were members of al Qaeda.

There was no official reaction to the most stunning allegation of all, Prince Bandar's claim that the GID had followed most of the future hijackers, that 9/11 could have been averted had U.S. intelligence responded adequately. The following year, the CIA's earlier bin Laden unit chief Michael Scheuer dismissed the claim—in a book—as a "fabrication." By failing to respond to it publicly, he wrote, U.S. officialdom had condoned the claim.

Though senior 9/11 Commission staff interviewed Prince Bandar, they did so well before he came out with his claim about the Saudis having followed most of the hijackers "with precision." The record of what the prince told the Commission—even at that early stage—

remains classified on grounds of "national security."

As interesting, of course, would be to know what former Saudi intelligence chief Prince Turki told the Commission—if indeed he was interviewed. On finding no reference to any Turki contact in listings of Commission documents—even if only referred to as withheld—the authors sent an inquiry to the National Archives. The response was remarkable, one that the experienced archivist with whom we dealt said she had never had to send before.

"'I can neither confirm nor deny the existence of a Prince Turki Memorandum for the Record,' the archivist wrote in early 2011. 'I'm not allowed to be any clearer. . . . I can't tell you, or I'm revealing more than I'm allowed to. . . . If we have an MFR for Prince Turki, it would also be withheld in full.'

Legal advice to the authors is that the umbrella nature of the withholding—under which the public is not allowed to know whether a document on a subject even *exists*—is rare. Information about the GID, and what really went on between the Saudi and U.S. intelligence services before 9/11, apparently remains highly sensitive.

WITH THE U.S. authorities blocking access to inform-ation, one can but sift the fragments of information that have surfaced. Did the GID "follow" Mihdhar and Hazmi, or indeed any of the terrorists?

A former head of operations and analysis at the CIA Counterterrorist Center, Vincent Cannistraro, has said that—as one might expect—Saudi intelligence had in the past "penetrated al Qaeda several times." A censored paragraph on Hazmi in Congress's Joint Inquiry states that the future hijacker returned to Saudi Arabia in early 1999, where [words withheld], he disclosed information about the East Africa bombings.

Al Mihdhar's first trip to the Afghanistan training camps was in early 1996. [three lines withheld] In 1998, al Mihdhar traveled to Afghanistan and swore allegiance to Bin Laden.

Hazmi "disclosed information"? To whom—to the GID? That possibility aside, there is a clue in a 9/11 Commission staff report. Mihdhar and Hazmi and Hazmi's brother "presented with their visa applications passports that contained an indicator of possible terrorist affiliation."

Depending how one reads a footnote in the Commission Report, all fifteen Saudi hijackers were vulnerable due to the fact or likelihood that their passports "had been manipulated in a fraudulent manner" by al Qaeda. According to the author James Bamford, however, Mihdhar's two passports "contained a secret coded indicator, *placed there by the Saudi government* [authors' emphasis], warning of a possible terrorist affiliation."

What then of the claims by Princes Turki and Bandar that the Saudis shared information on Mihdhar and Hazmi with the CIA? Two years after the attacks, the authors Joseph and Susan Trento suggested a mind-boggling possible answer to that question. They claimed that a former CIA officer, once based in Saudi Arabia, had told them, "We had been unable to penetrate al Qaeda. The Saudis claimed they had done it successfully. Both Hazmi and Mihdhar were Saudi agents."

Citing not only that officer but other CIA and GID sources, the Trentos have written that Mihdhar and Hazmi—assumed at the time to be friendly double agents—went to the January meeting of terrorists in

Kuala Lumpur "to spy on a meeting of top associates of al Qaeda associates. . . . The CIA/Saudi hope was that the Saudis would learn details of bin Laden's future plans."

As noted earlier, the CIA knew even before Mihdhar reached Kuala Lumpur that he had a multiple-entry visa for the United States—a fact it said it discovered when his passport was photographed en route to Malaysia.

The reason the CIA did not ask the State Department to watchlist Mihdhar and Hazmi, according to the Trento account, was that the men "were perceived as working for a friendly intelligence service"—the GID. In any case, the Trentos quote one of their sources as saying that CIA operations staff allowed names to go forward to the watchlist only with reluctance. "Many terrorists act as assets for our case officers," the source said. "We do deal with bad guys and, like cops protect snitches, we protect ours . . . none of those guys is going to show up on the no-fly list."

The reason the FBI was not told anything about Mihdhar and Hazmi, the Trentos quote a source as telling them, was "because they were Saudi assets operating with CIA knowledge in the United States."

Then the kicker. According to the Trentos, Mihdhar and Hazmi had not been thoroughly vetted by either the CIA or the GID. "In fact they were triple agents—loyal to Osama bin Laden." And so it was, months later, that catastrophe followed.

Is this mere disinformation? Early on in his career, Joe Trento worked for the columnist Jack Anderson, famous in his day for breaking big stories, often without naming his sources. He has also worked for CNN. The Trentos have long written on intelligence, and have repeated their claim about the handling of Mihdhar and Hazmi in another book, in a 2010 article, and in a conversation with the authors.

The scenario they paint, though, bumps up against known events and evidence. It seems likely that the Trentos' intelligence sources fed them morsels of fact mixed in with deliberate disinformation—a common enough ploy. Their account, though, does prompt a much closer look at the interplay between the CIA and the Saudi GID.

The CIA's own inspector general, reporting in 2005, found that its bin Laden station and "[name redacted] were hostile to each other and working at cross purposes for a number of years before 9/11." In context, it is clear that the redacted name refers to the GID. Pulitzer-winning *New York Times* reporter James Risen, who, writing later, revealed that—as early as 1997—Alec Station, the CIA unit that specifically targeted bin Laden, had seen its GID counterparts as a "hostile service."

The signs were, Risen reported, that intelligence given to the GID about al Qaeda was often passed on to al Qaeda. Once CIA staff shared intercepts with the GID, they found, al Qaeda operatives would abruptly stop using the lines that had been monitored. Congress's Joint Inquiry Report hinted at the true picture. "On some occasions," one passage read—followed by several redacted lines—"individuals in some [foreign] liaison services are believed to have cooperated with terrorist groups."

The legal defense fund of Blind Sheikh Omar Abdel Rahman, on trial in the mid-1990s for plotting to bomb New York landmarks, had been supported with GID money. Osama bin Laden himself, who had made his name under GID direction during the anti-Soviet war in Afghanistan, remained a hero for many.

A number of Saudi officials, a friendly intelligence service told the CIA well before 9/11, used bin Laden's picture as the screen saver on their office computers.

Little was to change. Even three years after the attacks—following the shock of serious al Qaeda attacks inside Saudi Arabia, and severe reprisals by the regime—one senior Arab source would still be telling the London *Times* that Saudi intelligence was "80% sympathetic to al Qaeda."

In 2001, sympathy for al Qaeda and bin Laden was widespread across the spectrum of Saudi society. It extended, even, to approval of the strikes on America.

THIRTY-THREE

AT FIRST ON SEPTEMBER 11, EARLY ESTIMATES HAD BEEN that as many as tens of thousands might have died in the New York attacks alone. There was a universal sense of catastrophe across the Western world. In Saudi Arabia, as in a number of countries across the region, many expressed delight.

Drivers honked their horns. In Internet cafés, many young men adopted shots of the blazing Twin Towers as screen savers—and restored the photographs if proprietors removed them. Students in class seemed "quite proud." Some people killed sheep or camels and invited friends to a feast.

Satisfaction over the blow to the United States was not confined to the street. The hostess at a lunch for society women was shocked to hear many of her guests evince the sentiment that, at last, "somebody did something." There was a tangible feeling abroad that the attacks had been a good thing, that "someone had stood up to America." At King Fahd National Guard Hospital in Riyadh, one foreign doctor had a unique insight into the reaction of ordinary patients and medical professionals alike.

Dr. Qanta Ahmed, a British-born Muslim of Pakistani origin, had trained in Britain and the United States. Like millions of others, she had spent the hours after the attacks watching satellite television news in horror, phoning friends in New York to ask if they were safe. On arriving at the hospital next morning, though, what she sensed was an atmosphere of "muted exaltation . . . relish in the face of destruction."

On the general medical and surgical wards, nurses told her, Saudi patients had clapped and cheered as TV pictures showed the Twin Towers crumbling. What had outraged one fellow foreigner most, though, was when two Saudi obstetricians sent out to the Diplomat Bakery for cakes—the sort of cakes customarily used at moments of *mabrouk*, when congratulation or celebration is due. When the cakes arrived, they passed out slices to their colleagues and to the patients who had clapped.

"So, they lost thousands of Americans," a New York–trained Pakistani doctor said. "They are guessing three thousand right now. Do you have any idea how many people die in Palestine every day, Qanta? The loss of these lives is hardly equal to the daily losses of lives in the Muslim world in past years."

The mood was pervasive and lasting. Later that week, at the grocery in the hospital complex, the man at the checkout was eager as usual to chat. "This news in New York has been very good, Doctora!" he said. And then: "The Americans deserved it."

A month later, a survey of educated Saudi professionals found that 95 percent of respondents favored bin Laden's cause. Asked to comment, Crown Prince Abdullah's half-brother, Prince Nawwaf bin Abdul Aziz, opined that this reflected the "feelings of the people against the United States . . . because of its unflinching support for Israel against the Palestinians."

Several years later, conducting interviews in Saudi Arabia, 9/11 Commission staff interviewed several dozen young to middle-age men said to be "moderates."

"Almost unanimously," Commission chairmen Kean and Hamilton noted, the men were "harshly critical of the United States. . . . They did not defend crashing planes into buildings, but they believed strongly that the United States was unfair in its approach to the Middle East, particularly in its support for Israel.

"These feelings were not surprising, but hearing them firsthand from so-called moderates drove home the enormous gap between how we see ourselves and our actions in the Middle East, and how others perceive us."

AT HIS RESIDENCE outside Washington on the morning of 9/11, Saudi ambassador Prince Bandar had been in his bedroom when the planes hit the Trade Center. He became aware of the first of the crashes, he recalled, when—as he glanced up at one of his ten television screens—he saw flames erupting from the North Tower. Then, when a second plane struck the South Tower, he realized that America was being attacked. He said he had hoped "they were not Arabs."

"My God," he said he thought later, on seeing pictures that showed Palestinians apparently celebrating in the street. "The whole impression this nation is going to have of us, the whole world, will be formed in the next two days."

Each for their own complex mix of reasons, the Saudis and the Bush administration were suddenly struggling to keep the fabled U.S.–Saudi "friendship" from falling apart. Bandar rushed out a statement of condolence. The kingdom, an embassy statement said, "condemned the regrettable and inhuman bombings and attacks which took place today. . . . Saudi Arabia strongly condemns such acts, which contravene all religious values and

Behind the political scenery, and on the festering subject of Israel, relations between Riyadh and Washington had very recently become unprecedentedly shaky. Crown Prince Abdullah had long fumed about America's apparent complacency over the plight of the Palestinians. In the spring, he had pointedly declined an invitation to the White House. Three weeks before 9/11, enraged by television footage of an Israeli soldier putting his boot on the head of a Palestinian woman, he had snapped. His nephew Bandar had been told to deliver an uncompromising message to President Bush.

"'I reject this extraordinary, un-American bias whereby the blood of an Israeli child is more expensive and holy than the blood of a Palestinian child. . . . A time comes when peoples and nations part. . . . Starting today, you go your way and we will go our way. From now on, we will protect our national interests, regardless of where America's interests lie in the region." There was more, much more, and it rocked the Bush administration. The President responded with a placatory letter that seemed to go so far toward the Saudi position of endorsing the creation of a viable Palestinian state. As of September 7, it looked as though the situation had stabilized. Then came the shattering events of Tuesday the 11th.

In Riyadh, and within twenty-four hours, Abdullah pulled the lever that gave his nation its only real power, the economic sword it could draw or sheathe at will. He ordered that nine million barrels of oil be dispatched to the United States over the next two weeks. The certainty of supply had the effect, it is said, of averting what had otherwise been a possibility at that time—an oil shortage that would have pushed prices through the roof and

human civilized concepts; and extends sincere condolences."

caused—on top of the real economic effects of the 9/11 calamity—a major financial crisis.

On the night of Wednesday the 12th, though, a CIA official phoned Ambassador Bandar with the news that fifteen of the hijackers had been Saudis. As Bandar recalled it, he felt the world collapsing around him. "That was a disaster," Crown Prince Abdullah's foreign affairs adviser Adel al-Jubeir has said, "because bin Laden, at that moment, had made in the minds of Americans Saudi Arabia into an enemy."

All over the country, royal and rich Saudis scrambled to get out of the United States and home. These were people used to being able to travel at will, if not aboard their own jet, then by chartered airplane. This was no normal time, however, and U.S. airspace was closed. Seventy-five royals and their entourage, ensconced at that wholly un-Islamic venue, Caesars Palace hotel and casino in Las Vegas, had decamped within hours of the attacks to the Four Seasons. They felt "extremely concerned for their personal safety," they explained to the local FBI field office, and bodyguards apparently deemed the Four Seasons more secure.

On the other side of the country, Saudis who wished to leave included members of the bin Laden family. One of Osama's brothers, never named publicly, had hastily called the embassy wanting to know where he could best go to be safe. He was installed in a room at the Watergate Hotel and told to stay there until advised that transportation was available. Across the country, more than twenty bin Laden family members and staff were getting ready to leave.

In Lexington, Kentucky, the thoroughbred racing mecca of America, Prince Ahmed bin Salman—a nephew of King Fahd—had been attending the annual yearling sales. After the attacks, Ahmed began quickly to round up members of his family for a return to Saudi Arabia. He ordered his nephew Prince Sultan bin Fahd and a couple of friends, who were in Florida, to charter a plane and get themselves to Lexington to connect with the plane he was taking home.

Prince Sultan was at first unable to charter a plane, because U.S. airspace was closed. On September 13, however, he and his group did succeed in getting to Kentucky. They managed it, one of them told the security man hired for the flight, because "his father or his uncle was good friends with George Bush Sr."

In spite of the fact that it was known that fifteen of those implicated in the attacks had been Saudis, President George W. Bush did not hold the official representative of Saudi Arabia at arm's length. He kept a scheduled appointment to receive Saudi ambassador Prince Bandar at the White House. The two men, who had known each other for years, reportedly greeted each other with a friendly embrace. They smoked cigars together on the Truman Balcony and conversed, looking relaxed, with Cheney and Rice.

Later that night, Bandar's assistant rang the FBI's assistant director for counterterrorism, Dale Watson. He needed help, the assistant said, in getting bin Laden "family members" on a flight out of the country. Watson said Saudi officials should call the White House or the State Department. The request found its way to counter-terrorism coordinator Richard Clarke.

The confluence of events—the White House meeting and the subsequent calls—would set off a firestorm of criticism when it became known. A photograph of Bush's September 13 meeting on the balcony with Prince Bandar was published in a 2006 book by Bob Woodward. When the authors asked for a copy of the photograph before publication of this book, however, the George W.

Bush presidential library responded that the former President's office was "not inclined to release the image from the balcony at this time."

Had Ambassador Bandar used his influence and connections to whisk Saudi citizens—some of whom had links to Osama bin Laden himself—out of the country? There was speculation, too, that some Saudis were allowed to fly before U.S. airspace reopened, perhaps on the authority of President Bush. Had they, others asked, all been properly investigated before departure? Richard Clarke, who has acknowledged that he gave the go-ahead for the flights, said he had "no recollection" of having first cleared it with anyone more senior in the administration.

One flight especially queried—on the grounds that it had supposedly occurred before U.S. airspace opened—was the charter flight from Tampa, Florida, to Lexington, Kentucky, on the afternoon of September 13. Contrary to previous reporting, however, FAA and other records show that U.S. airspace had by the time of the plane's takeoff opened not only to commercial flights but also to charters.

Prince Ahmed and his party would stay on in Kentucky until the weekend, when they left the country aboard a 727 so luxurious that it could accommodate only twenty-six passengers. By then, with the press in full cry over the news that most of the 9/11 hijackers had been Saudi nationals, all or most of the frightened Saudi elite were on their way home.

It may be that none of the flights carrying Saudis occurred contrary to the emergency closure of U.S. air-space. The FBI's checks on those who boarded the charter flights, though, were less than thorough. The 9/11 Commission found no evidence, for example, that the names of any of some 144 people who departed on charters within days of the airspace reopening had been checked against the State Department's watchlist. Nor were most of those leaving questioned by the FBI before departure.

The Bureau did speak—albeit, it seems, briefly—with almost all of the bin Laden relatives involved in the exodus, including one of Osama's nephews, Omar Awadh bin Laden.

Omar had once shared an address in Falls Church, Virginia, with his brother Abdullah bin Laden. The Bureau had briefly investigated Abdullah in the late 1990s because of his role in running a suspect Saudi organization known to preach extreme Islamism. The investigation had been closed after he produced a Saudi diplomatic passport. Questioned after 9/11, his brother Omar said he had had no contact with his uncle Osama and knew none of the Arabs suspected of involvement in the attacks, and he was allowed to go on his way.

An FBI memo written two years after the exodus appears to acknowledge that some of the departing Saudis may have had information pertinent to the investigation. "Although the FBI took all possible steps to prevent any individuals who were involved in or had knowledge of the 9/11/01 attacks from leaving the U.S. before they could be interviewed," the memo reads, "it is not possible to state conclusively that no such individuals left the U.S. without FBI knowledge."

It is a point on which the Bureau and the Saudi government seem to agree. Asked on CNN the same year whether he could say unequivocally that no one on the evacuation flights had been involved in 9/11, Saudi embassy information officer Nail al-Jubeir responded by saying he was sure of only two things, that "there is the existence of God, and then we will die at the end of the world. Everything else, we don't know."

This was not an answer likely to satisfy anyone in the United States.

EVEN AS THE Saudi aristocracy fled homeward, the embassy was mounting a propaganda campaign to counter the perception that Saudi Arabia was in any way responsible for 9/11. Millions of dollars—more than $50 million over the next three years—were to flow to public relations firms to restore the country's image as friend, ally, and Middle East peacemaker. Another firm was paid to get the Saudi message to members of Congress. Ambassador Bandar got the Saudi line over on *Larry King Live*. "We feel what happened to the United States—the tragedy and the cowardly attack on the United States—was not against the United States at all. It's really against all civilized people in the world. . . . Our role is to stand shoulder-to-shoulder with our friends."

It had soon become evident that, far from confronting the Saudis, the Bush administration wanted rapproche-ment. The President invited Crown Prince Abdullah to visit the United States, pressed him to come when he hesitated, and—when he accepted—welcomed him to his Texas ranch in early 2002. Vice President Cheney was there, as were Secretary of State Powell, National Security Adviser Rice, and First Lady Laura Bush. The Saudi foreign minister and Ambassador Bandar, with his wife, Princess Haifa, accompanied the crown prince.

9/11, it seems, barely came up during the discussions. The principal topic was the Saudi concern over Palestine, which had led to such tension the previous summer. Speaking with the press afterward, the President cut off one reporter when he started to raise the subject of the fifteen Saudi hijackers. "Yes, I—the Crown Prince has been very strong in condemning those who committed the murder of U.S. citizens," Bush said. "We're constantly working with him and his government on intelligence-sharing and cutting off money ... the government has been acting, and I appreciate that very much."

The President was being economical with the facts. Saudi spokesmen had from early on waxed equivocal as to whether any of the hijackers had even been Saudi nationals. Two days after Ambassador Bandar had been told of the CIA's estimate that some fifteen of the hijackers were Saudi, his spokesman said the terrorists had probably used stolen identities.

In Saudi Arabia, historian Hatoon al-Fassi has said, "most people were in denial" over the American claim that their compatriots had been responsible. "They thought that, 'Here's Americans and the CIA trying to fabricate ...'" Senior officials encouraged that notion.

"There is no proof or evidence," claimed Sheikh Saleh al-Sheikh, minister of Islamic affairs, "that Saudis carried out these attacks." Defense Minister Prince Sultan bin Abdul Aziz doubted whether only bin Laden and his followers were responsible, and hinted that "another power with advanced technical expertise" must have been behind 9/11. As of December 2001, Interior Minister Naif—a half-brother to the crown prince—was saying he still did not believe fifteen hijackers had been Saudis.

Not until February 2002 was Naif to acknowledge the truth. "The names we have got confirmed [it]," he then conceded. "Their families have been notified. I believe they were taken advantage of in the name of religion, and regarding certain issues pertaining to the Arab nation, especially the issue of Palestine."

Sultan and Naif were still not done, however. They began pointing to a familiar enemy. "It is enough to see a number of [U.S.] congressmen wearing Jewish yarmulkes," Sultan said, "to explain the allegations

against us." In late 2002, Naif blamed the "Zionists," saying "we put big question marks and ask who committed
the events of September 11 and who benefited from
them. . . . I think they [the Zionists] are behind these
events."

As for cooperation over the investigation of 9/11, the
Saudis had been less than helpful. "We're getting zero
cooperation," former CIA counterterrorism chief
Cannistraro said a month after the attacks. Requests for
name checks and personal information on the hijackers
and other suspects were turned down. "They knew that
once we started asking for a few traces the list would
grow," a U.S. source said. "It's better to shut it down
right away." American investigators were not allowed
access to the suspects' families.

Three months after 9/11, a senior Bush administration
official was saying that the Saudis were prepared only to
"dribble out a morsel of insignificant information one
day at a time." Contrary to what the President would
imply after his meeting with the crown prince, moreover,
the Saudis reportedly delayed or blocked attempts to
track the sources of terrorist funding in their country. "It
doesn't look like they're doing much," former FBI
assistant director Robert Kallstrom said in spring 2002,
"and frankly it's nothing new."

As for the attacks themselves, Saudi Arabia would long
remain a black hole for U.S. investigators. Also confronting them, obstruction and obfuscation aside, was the
vast cultural gulf and the language gap; pathetically few
staff in any agency had fluent Arabic. What they did
begin to accumulate, as they looked for a possible
umbilical linking the largely Saudi hijacking team to
forces in Saudi Arabia, were some fragmentary clues and
some suspects.

The suspects were the men believed to have met with or helped Mihdhar and Hazmi when they first arrived in California—as outlined in an earlier chapter. The blur of witness accounts permits the following scenario:

The imam named Fahad al-Thumairy, an accredited diplomat appointed by the Saudi Ministry of Islamic Affairs to liaise with the huge nearby mosque, served at the time at the Saudi consulate in Los Angeles. According to one witness, Thumairy had at the relevant time arranged for two men—whom the witness at first identified from photographs as having been the two future terrorists—to be given a tour of the area by car. A fellow Saudi, a San Diego resident named Omar al-Bayoumi, who was said to have had frequent contact with Thumairy, stated—according to a person interviewed by the FBI—that he was going to Los Angeles "to pick up visitors."

Bayoumi did make the trip north, accompanied by an American Muslim named Caysan bin Don. On the way there, Bayoumi mentioned that he was accustomed to going to the consulate to obtain religious materials. They did stop at the consulate, where—according to bin Don—a man "in a Western business suit, with a full beard—'two fists length'"—greeted Bayoumi and took him off to talk in an office for a while. Bayoumi emerged some time later, carrying a box of Qur'ans. Bayoumi described the encounter differently, said he was "uncertain" whom he met with and "didn't really know people in Islamic Affairs."

After that, the two men have said, they went to a restaurant and—this is the crucial moment in their story—met and talked with the two new arrivals, future hijackers Mihdhar and Hazmi. Was the encounter really, as Bayoumi and bin Don were to tell the FBI, merely a chance encounter? That reported detail, that Bayoumi dropped a newspaper on the floor, bent to retrieve it, and then approached the two terrorists, may—with a bow to espionage cliché—indicate otherwise.

The rest requires no lengthy retelling. Bayoumi urged Mihdhar and Hazmi to come south to San Diego, assisted them in finding accommodations, and stayed in touch. On the day they moved into the apartment they first used, an apartment next door to Bayoumi, there were four calls between his phone and that of Anwar Aulaqi—the local imam, who was later to travel to Yemen, there to plot attack after attack on America.

There is another factor in this tangled tale, one that involves money flow—and yet another local Saudi. Bayoumi's income, paid by a Saudi company—though he did no known work—reportedly increased hugely following the future hijackers' arrival. Also on the money front, enter another Saudi named Osama Basnan. A three-page section of Congress's Joint Inquiry Report, containing more lines withheld than released, tells us only that he was a close associate of Bayoumi in San Diego, who at one point lived across the street from Mihdhar and Hazmi.

According to former U.S. senator Bob Graham, cochair of the joint investigation, and to press reports, regular checks paid to Basnan's wife at some point began flowing from the Basnans to Bayoumi's wife. The payments, ostensibly made to assist in paying for medical treatment, originated with the Saudi embassy in Washington.

Thumairy, Bayoumi, and Basnan all have suspect backgrounds. Thumairy, who had a reputation as a fundamentalist, was to be refused reentry to the United States—well after 9/11—on the grounds that he "might be connected with terrorist activity." Bayoumi had first attracted the interest of the FBI years earlier, and the

Bureau later learned he had "connections to terrorist elements." Bayoumi left the country two months before the attacks.

As for Basnan, his name had come up in a counter-terrorism inquiry a decade earlier. He had reportedly hosted a party for Blind Sheikh Omar Abdel Rahman when he visited the United States, and had once claimed he did more for Islam than Bayoumi ever did. He is said to have celebrated 9/11 as a "wonderful, glorious day." A partially censored Commission document suggests that—after Mihdhar and Hazmi and the hijacker pilots arrived in the United States to learn to fly—a Basnan associate was in email and phone contact with accused key conspirator Ramzi Binalshibh. A year after 9/11, Basnan was arrested for visa fraud and deported.

Available information suggests two of the trio were employed by or had links to the Saudi regime—Thumairy through his accreditation to the Ministry of Islamic Affairs and Bayoumi through his employment by a company connected to the Saudi Civil Aviation Authority. Several people characterized Bayoumi as a Saudi government agent or spy. The CIA, former senator Graham has said, thought Basnan was also an agent. The senator cited an Agency memo referring to "incontrovertible evidence" of support for the terrorists within the Saudi government.

IN 2003 AND 2004, but only following a high-level request from the White House, 9/11 Commission staff were able to make two visits to Saudi Arabia to interview Thumairy, Bayoumi, and Basnan. All interviews were conducted in the presence of officials from Prince Naif's internal security service.

The U.S. questioners, a recently released Commission memo notes, believed Thumairy was "deceptive during both interviews. . . . His answers were either inconsistent or at times in direct conflict with information we have from other sources." "Most significantly, he denied knowing Bayoumi, let alone Mihdhar and Hazmi. Shown a photograph of Bayoumi, he did not budge. He knew no one of that name, he said. Then, prompted by a whispered interjection from one of the Saudi officials present, he said he had heard of Bayoumi—but only from 9/11 news coverage.

At a second interview, told by Comimission staff that witnesses had spoken of seeing him with Bayoumi, Thumairy said perhaps he had been mistaken for some-one else. Perhaps, too, there were people who might "say bad things about him out of jealousy." Finally told that telephone records showed numerous calls between his phones and Bayoumi's phones, just before the arrival of Mihdhar and Hazmi in the United States to boot, Thumairy was stumped.

Perhaps, he ventured, his phone number had been allotted to somebody else after he had it? Perhaps the calls had been made by someone else using Bayoumi's phone? He flailed around in vain for an explanation. Everything Thumairy came up with, his Commission questioners noted, was "implausible."

Bayoumi, who was interviewed earlier—though not by staff with firsthand experience of the California episode—had made a more favorable impression. He stuck to his story about having met Mihdhar and Hazmi by chance. He said he had rarely seen Mihdhar and Hazmi after they came to San Diego, that they had been his neighbors for only a few days. Bayoumi said he had then decided he did not want to have much to do with them. Commission executive director Zelikow, who was present during the interview, did not think Bayoumi had been a Saudi agent.

The Commission Report, however, was to note that Bayoumi's passport contained a distinguishing mark that may be acquired by "especially devout Muslims"—or be associated with "adherence to al Qaeda." Investigators had also turned up something else, something disquieting. Bayoumi's salary had been approved by a Saudi official whose son's photograph was later found on a computer disk in Pakistan—a disk that also contained some of the hijackers' photographs.

The son, Saud al-Rashid, was also produced for interview in Saudi Arabia. He admitted having been in Afghanistan—and to having "cleansed" his passport of the evidence that he had traveled there. He said, though, that he had known nothing of the 9/11 plot. Commission staff who questioned him thought Rashid had been "deceptive." They noted that he had had "enough time to develop a coherent story . . . even may have been coached."

Finally, there was Basnan. The Commission's interview with him, senior commission counsel Dietrich Snell wrote afterward, established only "the witness' utter lack of credibility on virtually every material subject." This assessment was based on "a combination of confrontation, evasiveness, and speechmaking . . . his repudiation of statements made by him on prior occasions," and the "inherent incredibility of many of his assertions when viewed in light of the totality of the available evidence."

Two men did not face Commission questioning in Saudi Arabia. One of them, a Saudi religious official named Saleh al-Hussayen, certainly should have, although his name does not appear in the Commission Report. Hussayen, who was involved in the administration of the Holy Mosques in Mecca and Medina, had been in the States for some three weeks before 9/11. For four days before the attacks, he had stayed at a hotel in Virginia.

Then on September 10, the very eve of the attacks, he had made an unexplained move. With his wife, he had checked into the Marriott Residence Inn in Herndon, Virginia—the very hotel at which Mihdhar and Hazmi were spending their last night alive.

Commission memos, one of them heavily censored, state that FBI agents arrived at Hussayen's room at the Marriott after midnight on the 11th. As questioning began, however, he began "muttering and drooping his head," sweating and drooling. Then he fell out of his chair and appeared to lose consciousness for a few moments. Paramedics summoned to the room, and doctors who examined Hussayen at a local hospital, found nothing wrong. An FBI agent said later that the interview had been cut short because—the agent suggested—Hussayen "feigned a seizure."

Asked by one of the Bureau agents why they had moved to the Marriott, Hussayen's wife said it was because they had wanted a room with a kitchenette. There was no sign, however, that the kitchenette in the room had been used, and the fridge was empty. Asked whether she thought her husband could have been involved in the 9/11 attacks in any way, the wife replied—oddly, the agents thought—"I don't know."

Agents never did obtain an adequate interview with Saleh al-Hussayen. Instead of continuing with his tour of the United States, he flew back to Saudi Arabia—and went on to head the administration of the two Holy Mosques. It remains unknown whether he had contact with Mihdhar and Hazmi on the eve of 9/11, or whether his presence at the Marriott—that night of all nights—was, as Bayoumi claimed of his meeting with the two terrorists, just a matter of chance.

As Hussayen left Virginia for home, other FBI agents in the state were interviewing the imam Anwar Aulaqi. As reported earlier, he did not deny having had contact with Mihdhar and Hazmi in California and later—with Hazmi—in Virginia. He could not deny that his own move from San Diego to the East Coast had paralleled theirs. Yet he made nothing of it—and U.S. authorities apparently pursued the matter no further at that time.

Aulaqi, almost uniquely for a suspect in this story, is American-born, the son of a former minister in the government of Yemen. Hard to credit though it is in light of what we now know of him, he had reportedly preached in the precincts of the U.S. Capitol shortly before 9/11. Not long afterward, moreover, he had lunched at the Pentagon—in an area undamaged by the strike in which his acquaintances Mihdhar and Hazmi had played such a leading role. The reason for the lunch? An outreach effort to ease tensions between Muslim Americans and non-Muslims.

Aulaqi remained in the United States for more than a year before departing, first for Britain and eventually for Yemen. He had been allowed to move about unimpeded, even though the phone number of his Virginia mosque had turned up in Germany in the apartment of 9/11 conspirator Ramzi Binalshibh. Only seven years later, starting in 2009, did he at last begin to become known around the world.

Aulaqi's name was associated with: the multiple shootings by a U.S. army major at Fort Hood, an almost successful attempt to explode a bomb on an airliner en route to Detroit, a major car bomb scare in Times Square, and a last-minute discovery of concealed explosives on cargo planes destined for the United States. When Aulaqi's name began to feature large in the Western press, Yemen's foreign minister cautioned that—pending real evidence—he should be considered not as a terrorist but as a preacher. Briefed on the intelligence about him, President Obama took a different view. In early 2010, he authorized the CIA and the U.S. military to seek out, capture, or kill the Yemeni—assigning Aulaqi essentially the same status as that assigned at the time to Osama bin Laden.

Commission staff had never had the opportunity to interview Aulaqi. Executive Director Zelikow, however, had long thought he merited more attention. Aulaqi would remain, as Zelikow memorably noted when his name finally hit the headlines, "a 9/11 loose end."

In the fall of 2011, the authors came upon another loose end—one the FBI has claimed it investigated but discounted—and contrary to its public assertions—appears not to have shared with either of the official investigations. It raises the possibility that—as in California—the 9/11 terrorists may have had a Saudi point of contact in Florida.

A month after the attacks, the senior administrator of a gated community in Sarasota—close to Venice, where Mohamed Atta and two other pilot hijackers had learned to fly—felt it his duty to call the Sheriff's Department. The administrator, Larry Berberich, reported what he felt had been a suspicious event. Patrick Gallagher, a resident who shared his concern, had emailed the FBI right after 9/11. They and others had noted the seemingly abrupt departure, shortly before the attacks, of a wealthy Saudi couple who had lived in the community since the mid-nineties.

The Saudis, Abdulaziz al-Hijji, his wife Anoud and their young children, who had occupied a luxury home at 4224 Escondito Circle since about 1995, had decamped in August 2001 in what appeared to be great haste. When their empty house was eventually investigated, a counterterrorist officer told us on condition of anonymity, there was "mail on the table, dirty diapers in one of the bathrooms . . . the toiletries still in place . . . clothes hanging in the closet . . . TVs . . . opulent furniture, equal or greater in value than the house . . . the pool running."

Three vehicles sat abandoned in the driveway and garage. Florida Department of Law Enforcement documents we obtained, moreover, state that, as recently as mid-August, the al-Hijjis had "purchased a new vehicle and renewed the registration on several other vehicles . . ." It made no sense to the officer who initially investigated. In the words of one of the FDLE reports, the "manner and timing" of the family's departure was "suspicious."

It became more than suspicious, the counterterrorist officer—and Berberich—told us, as the investigation proceeded. The license plates of cars entering the community in which the al-Hijjis lived, it emerged, had been routinely photographed by CCTV. Often, especially at night, the gate guards asked to see ID and kept notes of the documents that drivers or passengers produced.

"The registration numbers of the vehicles that had passed through the North Gate in the months before 9/11," the counterterrorist source said, "coupled with the identification documents shown by incoming drivers on request, showed that Mohamed Atta and several of his fellow hijackers, and another Saudi suspect still at large, had visited 4224 Escondito Circle."

The visitors, the source said, had included Marwan al-Shehhi—who would be at the controls of the second plane to crash into the World Trade Center—and Ziad Jarrah, who was to commandeer the cockpit of the fourth plane seized. Also in one of the cars bound for the al-Hijji

Osama bin Laden and his "holy war" against the United States, acclaimed by crowds in Pakistan after 9/11.

Khalid Sheikh Mohammed (*centre right*) claimed credit for the plot. Ramzi Binalshibh (*upper left*) acted as a go-between for the hijackers. Abu Zubaydah (*right*), a key al Qaeda logistics man, was gravely wounded during his arrest.

How reliable are their confessions, obtained under "enhanced" interrogation?

Mohamed Atta, the hijackers' leader, and Flight 93 hijacker Ziad Jarrah in Afghanistan (*below left*) preparing to videotape martyrdom statements. The beards came off on their return to Europe. Atta as a youngster, (*below right*) with his sisters.

Saudi "friend" whom al-Hijji brought to a soccer game, he said, was Shukrijumah, the suspected Atta associate still at large today.

According to Hammoud, "Osama bin Laden was a hero of al-Hijji." Al-Hijji showed him a "website containing information about bin Laden," spoke of "going to Afghanistan and becoming a freedom fighter . . ." He also discussed "taking flight training in Venice," the town just nineteen miles from Sarasota where Atta and two accomplices learned to fly. He said he believed "al-Hijji had known some of the terrorists from the September 11, 2001 attacks."

Asked about al-Hijji in 2012, Hammoud repeated what he had told the FBI. His wife and sister-in-law said they too had known al-Hijji and his wife and were familiar with elements of Hammoud's account.

We followed up, meanwhile, on the al-Hijjis' movements after leaving the United States on the eve of 9/11 and—as law enforcement checks revealed—heading for Saudi Arabia. A lead in an FDLE report indicated that, two years later, they traveled to England. Checks there showed that they stayed briefly in rented accommodation in the southern town of Southampton, then moved on without leaving a forwarding address.

Al-Hijji had told his Southampton landlord that he had a job with Aramco, the Saudi state oil company. It turned out that, as of early 2012, he was indeed working at Aramco's London office—he apparently held the post of "career counsellor"—and living in an apartment in central London. He was asked, in an impromptu, rapidly terminated interview, about the suggestion that Atta and his terrorist comrades had visited his house in Florida. Al-Hijji replied, "Never, never, never . . ." He said news of the allegation, first published in the *Miami Herald*, had come as "a shock, I mean really, for all of us. It was a shock to hear these things."

Later, when al-Hijji agreed to respond to questions by email, he strongly denied having had any involvement with the 9/11 terrorists or having had anything to do with the 9/11 conspiracy. "I have neither relation nor association with any of those bad people and the awful crime they did," he wrote, "I feel very saddened and oppressed by these false allegations . . . We were a young couple living in an association full of seniors and retirees, so possibly you can imagine the gossip." The reason he had abandoned his Florida home, he said, had been merely that, "We were trying to secure the Aramco job." The family had left Sarasota, he said, "like any normal people would do."

Al-Hijji said he had not been questioned by the FBI about the Sarasota matter, although he had made a return visit to the United States in 2005. His wife and mother-in-law, however, were interviewed when they went back to Sarasota to sort out outstanding matters in connection with the house at Escondito Circle. Al-Hijji had "no idea," he wrote in an email, why his relatives had been interviewed. Asked about parties alleged to have taken place at his house, attended by Saudis, he responded, "No, not true. My friends were very limited and normally I don't hold parties in the house because I have two little kids . . . I was not a frequent [sic] to any bars." He acknowledged that Wissam Hammoud and his wife had been friends, and that he had attended a gym with Hammoud. He did not respond, however, to a further emailed question asking why Hammoud would have claimed that bin Laden had been al-Hijji's "hero" and that al-Hijji had wanted to go to Afghanistan and become a "freedom fighter."

The FBI has said interviews with family members cleared up the case to its satisfaction. As late as 2003, however, a Florida attorney involved in settling issues over the property has said that the FBI asked him to try to convince al-Hijji's Saudi father-in-law Esam Ghazzawi —as a co-owner of the house—to return to America to sign documents. Instead, Ghazzawi signed at the American consulate in Beirut.

Esam Ghazzawi had for years been an adviser to Prince Fahd bin Salman, a nephew of Saudi Arabia's late King Fahd. (As reported on another page, Fahd's son Prince Sultan bin Fahd was in Florida, not far from Sarasota, at the time of the 9/11 attacks. With his uncle, Prince Ahmed bin Salman, and other Saudis, he left for Saudi Arabia days later.)

Ghazzawi—and Abdulaziz al-Hijji—according to one of the FDLE reports—had been "on the FBI watch list" prior to 9/11.

The entire episode, former Senator Graham has said, "is the most important thing about 9/11 to surface in the last seven or eight years. It is very important for the White House to take control of the situation."

For now, and absent FBI release of documents on its investigation into the al-Hijji matter—either publicly or to the appropriate body—the matter remains an item of unfinished business in the search for the full truth about 9/11.

Congress's Joint Inquiry, its co-chair Graham told the authors, found evidence "that the Saudis were facilitating, assisting, some of the hijackers. And my suspicion is that they were providing some assistance to most if not all of the hijackers. . . . It's my opinion that 9/11 could not have occurred but for the existence of an infrastructure of support within the United States. By 'the Saudis,' I mean the Saudi government and individual Saudis who are for some purposes dependent on the government—

which includes all of the elite in the country."

Those involved, in Graham's view, "included the royal family" and "some groups that were close to the royal family." Was it credible that members of the Saudi royal family would knowingly have facilitated the 9/11 operation? "I think," the former senator said, "that they did in fact take actions that were complicit with the hijackers."

9/11 Commission executive director Zelikow has limited his comments on the issue of possible Saudi involvement. In a passage on whether al Qaeda received support from foreign governments, or whether there was a "support network" for the 9/11 terrorists within the United States, published in the Afterword to a 2011 edition of the Commission Report, he did not name Saudi Arabia once.

In response to questions from *The New York Times'* Philip Shenon, Zelikow said the Commission "did not find evidence to make the case" that Mihdhar and Hazmi linked up in California with "Saudi government agents." On the other hand, Zelikow believed there was "persuasive evidence of a possible support network."

The Saudi world is alien territory, where hard information is scarce and proof—for outsiders—a mirage.

At page 396 of the congressional Joint Inquiry's report, the final section of the body of the Report, a yawning gap appears. All twenty-eight pages of Part Four, entitled "Finding, Discussion and Narrative Regarding Certain Sensitive National Security Matters," have been redacted. The pages are there but—with the rare exception of an occasional surviving word or fragmentary, meaningless clause—they are entirely blank. While many words or paragraphs were withheld

REPORT

OF THE

U.S. SENATE SELECT COMMITTEE ON INTELLIGENCE

AND

U.S. HOUSE PERMANENT SELECT COMMITTEE ON INTELLIGENCE

~~~~~~~~~~~~~~~~~~~~~~~~~~~~~~~~~

PART FOUR—FINDING, DISCUSSION AND NARRATIVE REGARDING
CERTAIN SENSITIVE NATIONAL SECURITY MATTERS

20. Finding: [Through its investigation, the Joint Inquiry developed information
suggesting specific sources of foreign support for some of the September 11 hijackers while
they were in the United States. The Joint Inquiry's review confirmed that the Intelligence
Community also has information, much of which has yet to be independently verified,
concerning these potential sources of support. In their testimony, neither CIA nor FBI

~~~~~~~~~~~~~~~~~~~~~~~~~~~~~~~~~

[Given the serious national security implications of this information, however, the
leadership of the Joint Inquiry is referring the Joint Inquiry Staff's compilation of relevant
information to both the FBI and the CIA for investigative review and appropriate investigative
and intelligence action].

[————————————————————————————
——————————————————————————].

[————————————————————————————
————————————————————————————
————————————————————————————
————————————————————————————
————————————————————————————
————————————————————————————
————————————————————————————
————————————————————————————
————————————————————————————]:

• [————————————————————————————
————————————————————————————
————————————————————————————
————————————————————————————
————————————————————————————
————————————————————————————
————————————————————————————
————————————————————————————
————————————————————————————

396

*The start of the final section of the Joint Inquiry's Report. Its focus is
reportedly the matter of support for the hijackers from Saudi Arabia. The
material was withheld from the public on the orders of President Bush.*

elsewhere in the Report, the decision to censor that entire section caused a furor in 2003.

Inquiries established that, while withholdings were technically the responsibility of the CIA, the Agency would not have obstructed release of most of the twenty-eight pages. The order that they must remain secret had come from President Bush himself.

The Democratic and Republican chairmen of the Joint Committee, Senators Graham and Richard Shelby, felt strongly that the bulk of the withheld material could and should have been made public. So did Representative Nancy Pelosi, the ranking Democrat for the House. "I went back and read every one of those pages thoroughly," Shelby said. "My judgment is that 95% of that inform-ation could be declassified, become uncensored, so the American people would know."

Know what? "I can't tell you what's in those pages," the Joint Committee's staff director, Eleanor Hill, was to say. "I can tell you that the chapter deals with information that our Committee found in the CIA and FBI files that was very disturbing. It had to do with sources of foreign support for the hijackers." The focus of the material, leaks to the press soon established, had been Saudi Arabia.

There were, sources said, additional details about Bayoumi, who had helped Mihdhar and Hazmi in California, and about his associate Basnan. The censored portion of the Report had stated—even then, years before he came to haunt the West as a perennial threat—that Anwar Aulaqi, the imam, had been a "central figure" in a support network for the future hijackers.

There had been, an official let it be known, "very direct, very specific links" with Saudi officials, links that "cannot be passed off as rogue, isolated or coincidental." The *New York Times*' Philip Shenon has written that

Senator Graham and his investigators became "convinced that a number of sympathetic Saudi officials, possibly within the Islamic Affairs Ministry, had known that al Qaeda terrorists were entering the United States beginning in 2000 in preparation for some sort of attack. Graham believed the Saudi officials had directed spies operating in the United States to assist them."

Most serious of all, the information uncovered by the investigation had reportedly drawn "apparent connections between high-level Saudi princes and associates of the hijackers." Absent release of the censored pages, one can only surmise as to what the connections may have been.

One clue is the first corroboration—in an interview with a former CIA officer for this book—of an allegation relating to the capture in Pakistan, while the Joint Inquiry was at work, of senior bin Laden aide Abu Zubaydah. Many months of interrogation followed, including, from about June or July 2002, no less than eighty-three sessions of waterboarding. Zubaydah was the first al Qaeda prisoner on whom that controversial "enhanced technique" was used.

John Kiriakou, then a CIA operative serving in Pakistan, had played a leading part in the operation that led to Zubaydah's capture—gravely wounded—in late March. In early fall back in Washington, he informed the authors, he was told by colleagues that cables on the interrogation reported that Zubaydah had come up with the names of several Saudi princes. He "raised their names in sort of a mocking fashion, [indicating] he had the support of the Saudi government." The CIA followed up by running name traces, Kiriakou said.

Zubaydah had named three princes, but by late July they had all died—within a week of one another. First was Prince Ahmed bin Salman bin Abdul Aziz, the leading figure in the international horseracing community whose name came up earlier in the authors' account of Saudis hurrying to get out of the United States after 9/11. In what may have been a serious omission, the prince had not been interviewed by the FBI before departure. Ahmed, a nephew of both then-King Fahd and defense and aviation minister Prince Sultan bin Abdul Aziz, died of a heart attack at the age of forty-three, following abdominal surgery, according to the Saudis. Prince Sultan bin Faisal bin Turki bin Abdullah al Saud, also a nephew of the then-king and his defense minister though not a top-rank prince, reportedly died in a car accident. A third prince, Fahd bin Turki bin Saud al-Kabir, a more distant family member whose father was a cousin of Fahd and Sultan, was said to have died "of thirst."

In his interview for this book, former CIA officer Kiriakou said his colleagues told him they believed that what Zubaydah told them about the princes was true. "We had known for years," he told the authors, "that Saudi royals—I should say elements of the royal family— were funding al Qaeda."

In 2003, during the brouhaha about the redacted chapter in the Joint Inquiry Report, Crown Prince Abdullah's spokesman, Adel al-Jubeir, made a cryptic comment that has never been further explained. The regime's own probe, he said, had uncovered "wrongdoing by some." He noted, though, that the royal family had thousands of members, and insisted that the regime itself had no connection to the 9/11 plot.

Joint Inquiry cochair Bob Graham did not share that view. What Zubaydah is reported to have said about the princes, he told the authors, is credible. Graham has said publicly, meanwhile, that the hijackers "received assistance from a foreign government which further facilitated their ability to be so lethal." The assistance, a very senior Committee source told the authors, "went to major names in the Saudi hierarchy."

In all, more than forty U.S. senators clamored for the release of the censored pages. Committee cochairs Graham and Shelby aside, they included John Kerry, Joe Lieberman, Charles Schumer, Sam Brownback, Olympia Snowe, and Pat Roberts.

Nothing happened.

Graham, with his long experience in the field as member and cochair not only of the 9/11 probe but of the Intelligence Committee, has continued to voice his anger over the censorship even in retirement. President Bush, he wrote in 2004, had "engaged in a cover-up . . . to protect not only the agencies that failed but also America's relationship with the Kingdom of Saudi Arabia. . . . He has done so by misclassifying information on national security data. While the information may be embarrassing or politically damaging, its revelation would not damage national security."

Graham's Republican counterpart on Congress's probe, Senator Shelby, concluded independently that virtually all the censored pages were "being kept secret for reasons other than national security."

"It was," Graham thought, "as if the President's loyalty lay more with Saudi Arabia than with America's safety." In Graham's view, Bush's role in suppressing important information about 9/11, along with other transgressions, should have led to his impeachment and removal from office.

Within weeks of his inauguration in 2009, Bush's successor, Barack Obama, made a point of receiving bereaved relatives of 9/11. The widow of one of those who died at the World Trade Center, Kristen Breitweiser, has said that she brought the new President's attention to the infamous censored section of the Joint Inquiry Report. Obama told her, she said afterward, that he was willing to get the suppressed material released. As of this writing, two years later, the chapter remains classified.

"If the twenty-eight pages were to be made public," said one of the officials who was privy to them before President Bush ordered their removal, "I have no question that the entire relationship with Saudi Arabia would change overnight."

THIRTY-FOUR

THE 9/11 COMMISSION REPORT BLURRED THE TRUTH about the Saudi role. By the time it was published in July 2004, more than a year had passed since the invasion of Iraq, a country that—the report said—had nothing to do with 9/11.

In the eighteen months before the invasion, however, the Bush administration had persistently seeded the notion that—Saddam Hussein's other sins aside—there was an Iraqi connection to 9/11. While never alleging a direct Iraqi role, President Bush had linked Hussein's name to that of bin Laden. Vice President Cheney had gone further, suggesting repeatedly that there had been Iraqi involvement in the attacks.

Polls suggest that the publicity about Iraq's supposed involvement affected the degree to which the U.S. public came to view Iraq as an enemy deserving retribution. Before the invasion, a Pew Research poll found that 57 percent of those polled believed Hussein had helped the 9/11 terrorists. Forty-four percent of respondents to a Knight-Ridder poll had gained the impression that "most" or "some" of the hijackers had been Iraqi. In fact, none were. In the wake of the invasion, a *Washington Post* poll found that 69 percent of Americans believed it likely that Saddam Hussein had been personally involved in 9/11.

Of the many reports and rumors circulated alleging an Iraqi role, two dominated. One, which got by far the most exposure, had it that Mohamed Atta had met in spring 2001 in Prague with a named Iraqi intelligence officer. The Iraqi officer later denied it, a fact that on its own might carry no weight. The best evidence, meanwhile, is that Atta was in the United States at the time.

A second allegation, persistently propagated before and after 9/11 by Laurie Mylroie, a scholar associated with the conservative think tank American Enterprise Institute, proposed that Ramzi Yousef—the terrorist responsible for the 1993 World Trade Center bombing—had been an Iraqi agent using a stolen identity. Investigation by others, including the FBI, indicated that the speculation is unsupported by hard evidence.

Mylroie, meanwhile, appeared to believe that Saddam Hussein had been behind multiple terrorist attacks over a ten-year period, from the East Africa embassy bombings to Oklahoma City and 9/11. "My view," said Vincent Cannistraro, a former head of the CIA's Counterterrorist Center, "is that Laurie has an obsession with Iraq." Mylroie's claim about Yousef nevertheless proved durable.

None of the speculative leads suggesting an Iraqi link to the attacks proved out. "We went back ten years," said former CIA bin Laden unit chief Michael Scheuer, who looked into the matter at the request of Director Tenet. "We examined about 20,000 documents, probably something along the line of 75,000 pages of information, and there was no connection between [al Qaeda] and Saddam."

A CIA report entitled "Iraqi Support for Terrorism," completed in January 2003, was the last in-depth analysis the Agency produced prior to the invasion of Iraq in March. "The Intelligence Community," it concluded, "has no credible information that Baghdad had foreknowledge of the 11 September attacks or any other al Qaeda strike."

After exhaustive trawls of the record, official probes have concluded that senior Bush administration officials applied inordinate pressure to try to establish that there was an Iraqi connection to 9/11, and that American torture of al Qaeda prisoners was a result of such pressure. CIA analysts noted that "questions regarding al Qaeda's ties to the Iraqi regime were among the first presented to senior operational planner Khalid Sheikh Mohammed following his capture." KSM was one of those most persistently subjected to torture.

The CIA's Charles Duelfer, who was in charge of interrogations of Iraqi officials after the invasion, recalled being "asked if enhanced measures, such as waterboarding, should be used" on a detainee who had handled contacts with terrorist groups and might have knowledge of links between the Hussein regime and al Qaeda.

The notion was turned down. Duelfer noted, however, that it had come from "some in Washington at very senior levels (not in the CIA)" who thought the detainee's interrogation had been "too gentle." Two U.S. intelligence officers, meanwhile, have said flatly that the suggestion came from Vice President Cheney's office.

"There were two reasons why these interrogations were so persistent and why extreme methods were used," a former senior intelligence official said in 2009. "The main one is that everyone was worried about some kind of follow-up attack [after 9/11]. But for most of 2002 and into 2003, Cheney and Rumsfeld, especially, were also demanding proof of the links between al Qaeda and Iraq that [former Iraqi exile leader Ahmed] Chalabi and others had told them were there."

A former U.S. Army psychiatrist, Major Paul Burney, told military investigators that interrogators at the

Guantánamo Bay detention center were under "pressure" to produce evidence of ties between al Qaeda and Iraq. "We were not successful," Burney said in interviews for the Army's inspector general, but "there was more and more pressure to resort to measures that might produce more immediate results."

In the absence of evidence, according to the author and Pulitzer winner Ron Suskind, it was in one instance fabricated. Suskind has reported that in fall 2003—when the U.S. administration was still struggling to justify the invasion of Iraq—the White House asked the CIA to collaborate in the forgery of a document stating that hijacker leader Atta had spent time training in Iraq.

The forgery took the form of a purported memo to Saddam Hussein from the former head of the Iraqi intelligence service. The memo was dated two months before 9/11—the actual former intelligence chief was prevailed upon to put his signature to it long after its supposed writing—and it stated that Atta had just spent time training in Iraq "to lead the team which will be responsible for attacking the targets that we have agreed to destroy."

The story of this fakery raised a brief media storm and a spate of denials. Rebuttals included a carefully phrased statement from Suskind's primary source, a former head of the CIA's Near East Division named Rob Richer—to which Suskind responded by publishing a transcript of one of his interviews with Richer.

Another former CIA officer, Philip Giraldi, meanwhile, placed responsibility for the fabrication on the Pentagon's Office of Special Plans, at the instigation of Vice President Cheney. According to Giraldi, the Pentagon, unlike the CIA, had "no restrictions on it regarding the production of false information to mislead the public" and had "its own false documents center."

If it happened, the forgery was the most flagrant attempt, in a long line of such maneuvering, to blame 9/11 on Iraq—and it has never been officially investigated.

A former deputy director of the CIA's Counterterrorist Center, Paul Pillar, has called the case against Iraq "a manufactured issue."

In 2008, by a bipartisan majority of ten to five, the Senate Intelligence Committee produced its "Report on Whether Public Statements Regarding Iraq by U.S. Government officials Were Substantiated by Intelligence Information." "Unfortunately," said its chairman, John D. Rockefeller,

> our Committee has concluded that the administration made significant claims that were not supported by the intelligence. In making the case for war, the administration repeatedly presented intelligence as fact when in reality it was unsubstantiated, contradicted, or even non-existent.
>
> It's my belief that the Bush administration was fixated on Iraq and used the 9/11 attacks by al Qaeda as justification for overthrowing Saddam Hussein. To accomplish this, top administration officials made repeated statements that falsely linked Iraq and al Qaeda as a single threat and insinuated that Iraq played a role in 9/11. Sadly, the Bush administration led the nation into war under false pretenses.

IN THE SEVEN YEARS since the invasion of Iraq, reputable estimates indicate, more than 4,000 American soldiers have died and 32,000 have suffered serious injury as a result of the invasion and the violence that followed. Some 9,000 Iraqi men in uniform were killed, and 55,000 insurgents. Figures suggest that more than

100,000 civilians died during and following the invasion.

A total of some 168,000 people, then, have died—and tens of thousands have been injured—as the result of an attack on a nation that many Americans had been falsely led to believe bore some if not all of the responsibility for the attacks of September 11.

The 3,000 who died in New York, Washington, and the field in Pennsylvania, the many hundreds who have died since from exposure to the toxins they breathed in at Ground Zero, and all their grieving relatives, deserved better than to have had their tragedy manipulated in such a way.

THIRTY-FIVE

IN THE YEARS THAT THE CONFLICT IN IRAQ HAD THE world's attention, the real evidence that linked other nations to Osama bin Laden and 9/11 faded from the public consciousness. This was in part the fault of the 9/11 Commission, which blurred the facts rather than highlighting them. It was, ironically, a former deputy homeland security adviser to President Bush, Richard Falkenrath, who loudly expressed that uncomfortable truth.

The Commission's Report, Falkenrath wrote, had produced only superficial coverage of the fact that al Qaeda was "led and financed largely by Saudis, with extensive support from Pakistani intelligence." Saudi Arabia's murky role has been covered in these pages. The part played by Pakistan—not least given the stunning news that was to break upon the world in spring 2011—deserves equally close scrutiny.

Pakistan has a strong Islamic fundamentalist movement—it was, with Saudi Arabia and the United Arab Emirates, one of only three nations that recognized the Taliban. Bin Laden had operated there as early as 1979, with the blessing of Saudi intelligence, in the first phase of the struggle to oust the Soviets from neighboring Afghanistan. The contacts he made were durable.

"Pakistani military intelligence," the Commission Report did note, "probably had advance knowledge of his coming, and its officers may have facilitated his travel" when he returned to Afghanistan in 1996. Pakistan "held the key," the Report said, to bin Laden's ability to use Afghanistan as a base from which to mount his war against America.

Time was to show, moreover, that Pakistan itself was central not only to the terrorist chief's overall activity but also to the 9/11 operation itself. Al Qaeda communications, always vulnerable and often impractical in Afghanistan, for years functioned relatively safely and certainly more efficiently in Pakistan. Pakistan, with its teeming cities and extensive banking system, also offered the facilities the terrorists needed for financial transactions and logistical needs.

As reported in this book, World Trade Center bomber Ramzi Yousef had family roots in Pakistan. He traveled from Pakistan to carry out the 1993 attack, and it was to Pakistan that he ran after the bombing. Yousef would eventually be caught in the capital, Islamabad, in 1995. His bomb-making accomplice Abdul Murad, though seized in the Philippines, had lived in Pakistan.

It was through Pakistan that the future pilot hijackers from Europe made their way to the Afghan training camps, and to their audiences with bin Laden. The first two Saudi operatives inserted into the United States, Mihdhar and Hazmi—and later the muscle hijackers—were briefed for the mission in the anonymity of Karachi, Pakistan's largest city.

The family of the man who briefed the hijackers and who was to claim he ran the entire operation, Khalid Sheikh Mohammed, hailed from Baluchistan, Pakistan's largest province. Though high on the international "most wanted" list, he operated with impunity largely from Pakistan over the several years devoted to the planning of 9/11. KSM, though in Afghanistan when the date for the attacks was set, then left for Pakistan. He remained there, plotting new terrorist acts, until his capture in 2003—in Rawalpindi, headquarters of the Pakistan military command.

Ramzi Binalshibh, who had functioned in Germany as the cutout between KSM and lead hijacker Atta, ran to Pakistan on the eve of the attacks. In the spring of 2002, at a safe house in Karachi, he and KSM had the effrontery to give a press interview boasting of their part in 9/11. It was in the city's upmarket Defense Society quarter that he was finally caught later that year. Abu Zubaydah, the first of the big fish to be caught after 9/11, had been seized in Faisalabad a few months earlier.

What bin Laden himself had said about Pakistan two years before 9/11 seemed to speak volumes. "Pakistani people have great love for Islam," he observed after the U.S. missile attack on his camps in the late summer of 1998, in which seven Pakistanis were killed. "And they always have offered sacrifices for the cause of religion." Later, in another interview, he explained how he himself had managed to avoid the attack. "We found a sympathetic and generous people in Pakistan . . . receive[d] information from our beloved ones and helpers of jihad."

Then again, speaking with *Time* magazine in January 1999: "As for Pakistan, there are some governmental departments which by the grace of God respond to the Islamic sentiments of the masses. This is reflected in sympathy and cooperation." The next month, in yet another interview, he praised Pakistan's military and called on the faithful to support its generals.

"Some governmental departments." "The generals." Few doubt that these were allusions to bin Laden's support from within the Inter-Services Intelligence

Directorate, or ISI, Pakistan's equivalent to the CIA. The links went back to the eighties and probably—some believe certainly—continue to join al Qaeda to elements of the organization today.

PAKISTAN, CHAIRMAN OF the U.S. Joint Chiefs of Staff Mike Mullen reflected in a recent interview, is "the most complicated country in the world." The bin Laden/ISI connection had been made during the Afghan war against the Soviets, when the CIA—working with the ISI and Saudi intelligence—spent billions arming and training the disparate groups of fighters. Once the short-term goal of rolling back the Soviets had been achieved, the United States had walked away from Afghanistan. Pakistan had not.

It saw and still sees Afghanistan as strategically crucial, not least on account of an issue of which many members of the public in the West have minimal knowledge or none at all. Pakistan and India have fought three wars in the past half-century over Kashmir, a large disputed territory over which each nation has claims and that each partially controls, and where there is also a homegrown insurgency. Having leverage over Afghanistan, given its geographical position, enabled Pakistan to recruit Afghan and Arab volunteers to join the Kashmir insurgency —and tie down a large part of the Indian army.

The insurgents inserted into Kashmir have by and large been mujahideen, committed to a cause they see as holy. As reported earlier, the man who headed the ISI in 1989, Lieutenant General Hamid Gul, himself saw the conflict as jihad. Osama bin Laden made common cause with Gul and—in the years that followed—with like-minded figures in the ISI. ISI recruits for the flght in Kashmir were trained in bin Laden camps. Bin Laden would still be saying, as late as 2000, "Whatever information regarding 9/11 had been passed both to Congress' Joint Inquiry and to the Commission. Research, however, fails to support that assertion. Checks at the National Archives, which holds copies of records handed over by the FBI, drew a blank. High-level members of both the Inquiry and the Commission do not recall having been advised of the Florida episode.

Notably, meanwhile, the FBI has declined to comment on the claim that the al-Hijji house was linked to the terrorists by car registration numbers recorded at the gated community's entrance.

Bob Graham, the former co-chair of Congress' inquiry, who as a two-time Florida Governor had a special interest, has pursued this matter with vigor. As a result, and following meetings at the FBI and at the Obama White House, he was given sight of documents bearing a "Secret" classification. One, according to Graham, showed that an FBI agent filed a report "not consistent with the public statements of the FBI that there was no connection between the 9/11 hijackers and the Saudis at the Sarasota home." The material he saw, Graham added, indicated too "that the investigation was not the robust inquiry claimed by the FBI."

Documents released by the FDLE, meanwhile, refer to a 2004 jail interview with an Arab of Lebanese origin named Wissam Hammoud. Hammoud, who is classified as an International Terrorist Associate, talked about al-Hijji with an FBI agent and a Sarasota County Sheriff's Office detective.

Having met al-Hijji through relatives, he said, the two men had worked out together at a Sarasota gym and played soccer at the local Islamic Society. He had stayed away, however, Hammond told the FBI, when al-Hijji entertained "Saudis" at "parties" at his home because— he said—he himself "did not drink or smoke cannabis." A house, he said, was Walid al-Shehri, a muscle hijacker who was to fly with Atta. The Saudi terrorist suspect still at large said to have visited al-Hijji was Adnan Shukrijumah who—according to other testimony—associated with Atta in spring 2001. As of this writing, Shukrijumah is still on the FBI's Most Wanted list.

According to the source, the gate records indicated that the terrorists visited the house on Escondito Circle on multiple occasions. Analysis of incoming and outgoing calls made on the landline at the al-Hijji house, moreover, "lined up with the known suspects."

Information connecting the terrorists to the house also came in from an unexpected source. Following an appeal to the public for information after 9/11, two female employees at a local pub called the Gingerbread Man told the FBI that they had been at after-hours parties at Escondito Circle. One, who said she attended at least five parties, identified Atta, al-Shehri and Jarrah as having been present. She admitted to having had sexual intercourse with Jarrah.

The second woman said three other 9/11 terrorists, Walid and Wail al-Shehri, Satam al-Suqami—and Shukrijumah—had been at the house when she was there. She acknowledged having had sex with a number of the men.

FBI agents, the counterterrorist officer said, were informed of the original lead, supplied with the gate records said to have documented the terrorists' visits to the al-Hijji house, and had interviewed the women who came forward. Inquiries to the FBI by the authors and others, however, have met with a series of denials.

In its most recent statement, while admitting that it had followed up on the information about the al-Hijjis, the Bureau claimed that "there was no connection found to the 9/11 plot." The statement asserted that all

Waleed M. Alsheri

Mohammed Atta

Wail M. Alshehri

Abdulaziz Alomari

Satam M. A. al-Suqami

Ahmed Alnami

Ahmed Ibrahim A. al Haznawi

Ziad Samir al-Jarrah

Saeed Alghamdi

Khalid Almihdar

Majed Moqed

Nawaf Alhazmi

Salem Alhazmi

Hani Hanjour

Marwan Alshehhi

Ahmed Alghamdi

Mohand Alshehri

Hamza Alghamdi

Fayez Rashid
Ahmed Hassan
al-Qadi Banihammad

The nineteen hijackers, sixteen of whom were Saudis. To some, they were heroes. A poster (*right*), produced two years after the attacks, glorified the terrorists.

The men believed to have been at the controls of three of the hijacked airliners: Marwan al-Shehhi (*above left*), Hani Hanjour (*above centre*), and Ziad Jarrah, with his lover Aysel Sengün (*above right*), and in the cockpit of a light aircraft – he had recently completed pilot training.

Below right Anwar Aulaqi, an American-born imam, at a mosque after 9/11. He is characterized as having been "spiritual adviser" to two future hijackers. Now in Yemen, he is considered a possible successor to bin Laden.

Above Saleh al-Hussayen, a Saudi religious official. On the eve of 9/11, he stayed at the same hotel as two lead hijackers.

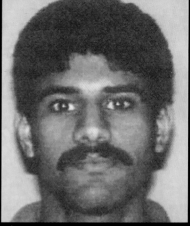

Khalid al-Mihdhar (*above left*) and Nawaf al-Hazmi (*above right*) were the first future hijackers to arrive in the United States.

Omar al-Bayoumi, a Saudi living in California (*below left*), and American-born Caysan bin Don (*below centre*), said they met future hijackers Mihdhar and Hazmi in a restaurant by chance. Did Mohdar Abdullah (*below right*), who also befriended the terrorists, get advance information that an attack was coming?

CIA Director George Tenet (*centre*), had a standing arrangement that ensured effective liaison with his counterpart in Saudi Arabia, GID chief Prince Turki (*left*) – in theory. Saudi Interior Minister Prince Naif (*right*), who dealt with domestic security, was to say he did not believe most hijackers had been Saudis. It has been alleged that Naif paid protection money to bin Laden.

Saudi Prince Bandar (*rear left*) meeting at the White House with President Bush, Vice President Cheney, and National Security Adviser Rice, two nights after the attacks.

Seven months after 9/11, Bush invited Saudi Crown Prince Abdullah to his Texas ranch (*left*). He again welcomed Abdullah, soon to become King, in 2005 (*above*).

Left The joint chairmen of Congress's probe, Senators Bob Graham (*centre*) and Richard Shelby (*right*), with their Report in 2003. They pointed out that many pages had been suppressed, on President Bush's orders. The pages are still withheld today.

Below 9/11 Commission members and staff watching video of the Twin Towers burning, at a hearing in 2004.

Left Some of the bereaved who pressed for the Commission's creation and closely followed its progress rejected its findings.

Left Osama bin Laden, apparently pictured here in hiding in Pakistan, was shot dead by US commandos in May 2011.

Americans celebrated the feared terrorist's death, yet faced an uncertain future.

Pakistan does in the matter of Kashmir, we support it."

Such action and talk paid off in ways large and small. The ISI at one time even reportedly installed the security system that protected bin Laden in one of the houses he used in Afghanistan.

The tracks of the ISI and al Qaeda converged in other ways. Months after the Taliban had begun hosting bin Laden in 1996, they had been, as *Time* magazine put it, "shoehorned into power" by the ISI—thus ensuring Pakistan's influence over most of Afghanistan. The need to keep things that way, and to fend off rebellion on its own border, a Pakistani official told the State Department in 2000, meant that his government would "always" support the Taliban.

So powerful was the ISI in Afghanistan, former U.S. special envoy Peter Tomsen told the 9/11 Commission, that the Taliban "actually were the junior partners in an unholy alliance"—ISI, al Qaeda, and the Taliban. As it grew in influence, the ISI liaised closely with Saudi intelligence—and the Saudis reportedly lined the pockets of senior Pakistani officers with additional cash.

The ISI over the years achieved not only military muscle but massive political influence within Pakistan itself—so much so that some came to characterize it as "the most influential body in Pakistan," a "shadow government."

The United States, caught between the constraints of regional power politics and the growing need to deal with bin Laden and al Qaeda, long remained impotent.

By the late nineties, former U.S. ambassador to Pakistan Thomas Simons has recalled, American efforts to bring pressure on the Pakistanis and the Taliban over bin Laden resulted only in "a sense of helplessness." Concern about the tensions between India and Pakistan loomed larger at the State Department than Islamic extremism—not least after both those nations tested nuclear weapons.

In 1999, then–Pakistani prime minister Nawaz Sharif held out the possibility of working with the CIA to mount a commando operation to capture or kill bin Laden. Nothing came of it, the National Security Agency reported, because the plan was compromised by the ISI. In early 2000, though, after General Pervez Musharraf seized power, Washington made a serious effort to ratchet up the pressure.

President Clinton insisted on making a visit to Islamabad, the first by an American head of state in more than thirty years. He did so in spite of CIA and Secret Service warnings that a trip to Pakistan would endanger his life. Air Force One arrived without him, as a decoy, while he flew in aboard an unmarked jet. At a private meeting with Musharraf, Clinton recalled, he offered the Pakistani leader "the moon . . . in terms of better relations with the United States, if he'd help us get bin Laden." Nothing significant came of it. Clinton had avoided pushing too hard about bin Laden at an earlier meeting—because ISI members were in the room.

The following month, when then–ISI director General Mahmoud Ahmed was in Washington, Under Secretary of State Thomas Pickering warned that "people who support those people [bin Laden and al Qaeda] will be treated as our enemies." Later, at Pakistan's interior ministry, Pickering confronted a senior Taliban official with evidence of bin Laden's role in the embassy bombings in East Africa. The official said the evidence was "not persuasive."

About this same time, Assistant Secretary of State Michael Sheehan suggested giving Pakistan an ultimatum: Work with the United States to capture bin Laden or face a cutoff of vital financial aid. Fears of the possible consequences—that Pakistan might opt out of talks to ensure that it did not share its nuclear know-how with rogue nations—loomed larger than concerns about terrorism. Sheehan's idea went nowhere.

Come early 2001, the start of the Bush presidency, and his warning memo to Condoleezza Rice about al Qaeda, counterterrorism coordinator Richard Clarke stressed how important it was to have Pakistan's cooperation. He noted, though, that General Musharraf had spoken of "influential radical elements that would oppose significant Pakistani measures against al Qaeda." Musharraf had cautioned, too, that the United States should not violate Pakistani airspace when launching strikes within Afghanistan.

Nothing effective was achieved by the Bush administration. At the CIA, director Tenet sensed a "loss of urgency." It had been obvious for years, he wrote later, that "it would be almost impossible to root out al Qaeda" without Pakistan's help. The Pakistanis, moreover, "always knew more than they were telling us, and they had been singularly uncooperative." "We never did the Full Monty with them," another former senior CIA official has said. "We don't trust them. . . . There is always this little dance with them."

On September 11, however, the dancing and the diplomatic dithering stopped. While no hard evidence would emerge that Pakistan had any foreknowledge of the attacks—let alone an actual role in the plot—Washington now issued a blunt warning. It was then—according to ISI director Ahmed, who was visiting Washington at the time—that U.S. deputy secretary of state Richard Armitage said the United States would bomb Pakistan "back to the Stone Age" should it now fail to go along with seven specific American demands for assistance.

Musharraf weighed up the likely consequences of failure to comply, not the least of them the fact that the U.S. military could pulverize his forces. With a couple of reservations—he says he could not accept the U.S. demands for blanket rights to overfly Pakistan and have the use of all its air bases and port facilities—he cooperated as required. "We have done more than any other country," the former president has said, "to capture and kill members of al Qaeda, and to destroy its infrastructure in our cities and mountains." Musharraf's administration indeed cracked down on extremism, at a terrible cost in human life that persists to this day. In one year alone, 2009, 3,021 Pakistanis died in retaliatory terrorist attacks—approximately the same number as the American dead of 9/11. Musharraf 's army thrust into the tribal badlands near the Afghan border, and some 700 purported al Qaeda operatives were rounded up across Pakistan. As of 2006, according to Musharraf, 369 of them had been handed over to the United States—for millions of dollars in bounty money paid by the CIA.

The former CIA station chief in Islamabad, Robert Grenier, recently confirmed that Pakistani cooperation against al Qaeda did improve vastly after 9/11. The arrests of the three best-known top al Qaeda operatives—Abu Zubaydah, Ramzi Binalshibh, and Khalid Sheikh Mohammed—were, it seems, made by Pakistani intelligence agents and police, in some if not all cases working in collaboration with the Agency.

Former CIA officer John Kiriakou, who was involved in operations on the ground in Pakistan during the relevant period, told the authors that this statement by Musharraf was "generally accurate." He said, however: "The truth is, we allowed the Pakistanis to believe they were taking the lead. Certainly they were the first through the door, but on those high-profile captures we never told them who the target was. We were afraid they would leak the information to al Qaeda and the target would escape. The information leading to the captures was a hundred percent CIA information. The Pakistanis had no role in the intelligence."

The biggest name of all, of course, long eluded pursuit. Last on the list of Washington's post-9/11 demands, as Musharraf recalled it, had been to help "destroy bin Laden." "We have done everything possible to track down Osama bin Laden," Musharraf wrote in 2006, "but he has evaded us."

No one, according to Musharraf, had been more anxious than the Pakistanis to resolve the mystery of bin Laden's whereabouts. As the months and years passed, however, there were those who believed otherwise.

FROM THE TIME America routed al Qaeda after 9/11, information indicated that the ISI continued to remain in touch with bin Laden or aware of his location. ISI officials, former special envoy Tomsen told the 9/11 Commission, were "still visiting OBL [bin Laden] as late as December 2001"—and continued to know his location thereafter. In 2007 Kathleen McFarland, a former senior Defense Department official, spoke of bin Laden's presence in Pakistan as a fact. "I'm convinced," military historian Stephen Tanner told CNN in 2010, "that he is protected by the ISI. I just think it's impossible after all this time to not know where he is."

Why would the ISI have allowed bin Laden to enjoy safe haven in Pakistan? The ISI, Tanner thought, would see him as a trump card—leverage over the United States in the power play involved in Pakistan's ongoing dispute with India.

It went deeper, and further back than that. "You in the

West," the veteran London *Sunday Times* reporter Christina Lamb has recalled former ISI head General Gul telling her twenty years ago, "think you can use these fundamentalists and abandon them, but it will come back to haunt you." It was clear to Lamb that "For Gul and his ilk, support for the fundamentalist Afghan groups, and later the Taliban, was not just policy but also ideology." In spite of the vast sums in U.S. aid doled out to Pakistan, a 2010 poll suggested that a majority of Pakistanis viewed the United States as an enemy.

There was special suspicion of the S Section of the ISI, which is made up of personnel who are officially retired but front for certain ISI operations. S Section, *The New York Times* has quoted former CIA officials as saying, has been "seen as particularly close to militants."

In Washington, trust in the Pakistanis had long since plummeted. "They were very hot on the ISI," said a member of a Pakistani delegation that visited the White House toward the end of the Bush presidency. "When we asked them for more information, Bush laughed and said, 'When we share information with you guys, the bad guys always run away.' "

The lack of trust notwithstanding, policy on Pakistan did not appear to change. Better to do nothing and have some cooperation, the thinking in the new Obama administration seemed to be, than come down hard and get none. In early 2011, on Fox News, former government officials called on the administration to take a tougher line with Pakistan.

Obama had vowed during his campaign for the presidency, "We will kill bin Laden. ... That has to be our biggest national security priority." In office, he made no such public statements. The hunt for bin Laden, meanwhile, seemed to be getting nowhere—and not to be a high priority. In retrospect, though, there was a trickle of fresh information that suggested otherwise.

General David Petraeus, commander of U.S. and NATO forces in Afghanistan, was asked on *Meet the Press* in 2010 whether it was now less necessary to capture bin Laden. "I think," he replied, "capturing or killing bin Laden is still a very, very important task for all of those who are engaged in counterterrorism around the world."

For those who doubted that bin Laden was still alive, late fall 2010 brought two new bin Laden audio messages. There had been intercepts of al Qaeda communications, CIA officials told *The New York Times*, indicating that he still shaped strategy. Then, within weeks, CNN was quoting a "senior NATO official" as saying that bin Laden and his deputy Zawahiri were believed to be hiding not far from each other in northwest Pakistan, and not "in a cave." The same day, the New York *Daily News* quoted a source with "access to all reporting on bin Laden" as having spoken of two "sightings considered credible" in recent years—and even of "a grainy photo of bin Laden inside a truck." The sources were vague, though, as to where bin Laden might have been. Defense Secretary Robert Gates, for his part, was at pains in an ABC interview to suggest that it had been "years" since any hard intelligence had been received on bin Laden's likely location.

In late March 2011, out of Hong Kong, came a story suggesting that the CIA had "launched a series of secret operations in the high mountains of the Hindu Kush . . . consistent reports have established that Osama bin Laden has been on the move through the region in recent weeks."

It is a fair guess that much if not all of this was disinformation, planted to suggest to the quarry that U.S.

intelligence had lost the scent, had no strong lead as to where precisely bin Laden might be, and had no plan for an imminent strike against him.

At 10:24 p.m. on the night of Sunday, May 1, 2011— an improbably late hour—this bulletin came over the wires:

> Breaking News Alert: White House says Obama to make late-night statement on an undisclosed topic.

Soon after, there was this from *The Washington Post*:

> Osama bin Laden has been killed in a CIA operation in Pakistan, President Obama will announce from the White House, according to multiple sources.

At 11:35 P.M., the President appeared on television screens across the globe to say:

> Tonight I can report to the American people and to the world that the United States has conducted an operation that killed Osama bin Laden, the leader of al Qaeda and a terrorist who's responsible for the murder of thousands of innocent men, women and children. . . .
>
> The images of 9/11 are seared into our national memory. . . . And yet we know that the worst images are those that were unseen to the world. The empty seat at the dinner table. Children who were forced to grow up without their mother or their father. Parents who would never know the feeling of their child's embrace. Nearly three thousand citizens taken from us. . . .
>
> Osama bin Laden avoided capture and escaped across the border into Pakistan. . . . Shortly after taking office I directed Leon Panetta, the director of the CIA, to make the killing or capture of bin Laden the top priority of the

war against al Qaeda. . . . Then, last August, after years of painstaking work by our intelligence community, I was briefed on a possible lead to bin Laden. . . . I met repeatedly with my security team as we developed more information about the possibility that we had located bin Laden hiding within a compound deep inside of Pakistan. And finally, last week, I determined that we had enough intelligence to take action. . . .

Today, at my direction, the United States launched a targeted operation. . . . A small team of Americans carried out the operation with extraordinary courage. . . . No Americans were harmed. . . . After a firefight, they killed Osama bin Laden and took custody of his body.

It was a total suprise—and a momentous victory. Jubilant Americans thronged in front of the White House, in Times Square, and at Ground Zero. For many days, there was wall-to-wall coverage in newspapers, television, and radio. The Internet has hummed with information, misinformation and rumor ever since.

A long article, published in the *New Yorker* in August 2011, was seen as the first informed independent account of the operation that did for bin Laden. It told how two years of painstaking intelligence work led to the tentative belief that bin Laden was alive, holed up in a compound in the Pakistani town of Abbottabad, a hundred and twenty miles from the Afghan border. U.S. Navy Seal commandos began training on a replica of the compound in the eastern United States. The concept was that they would fly to Abbottabad by helicopter and attack under cover of darkness. President Obama gave the go-ahead.

So it was that in the moonless night of May 1, twenty-three commandos aboard two U.S. helicopters—

with others as back-up—crossed from Afghanistan into Pakistan and headed for the target. The operation began badly when one of the helicopters crash-landed on the perimeter wall of the compound. Uninjured though, the commandos emerged from the aircraft, blasted their way through metal barriers, shot dead three men and a woman they encountered, and reached a staircase leading to an upper floor. Each of the men were reportedly armed and one—a son of bin Laden—is said to have opened fire before being killed.

The raiders' first view of their quarry, according to the *New Yorker* account, was of a "tall, rangy man with a fist-length beard peeking out from behind a bedroom door." As the Americans entered the bedroom their way was blocked by two of bin Laden's wives, who "placed themselves in front of him." One of the women was shot in the leg and both were pushed aside. A commando then killed bin Laden with two shots, one to the chest, one to the head.

In the White House, some seven thousand miles away, Obama and his senior advisers were monitoring night vision images—transmitted by an unmanned drone flying over the compound—and radio traffic. According to U.S. sources, they listened now as the commando who had shot bin Laden reported: "For God and Country— Geronimo, Geronimo, Geronimo . . . E.K.I.A." Geronimo was the night's code word for bin Laden. E.K.I.A. meant: "Enemy killed in action."

Operation completed, the American raiders departed the way they had come, by helicopter, taking bin Laden's corpse with them. It was photographed—samples of DNA had been taken at the scene—flown to a U.S. aircraft carrier, and buried at sea.

There are a few variants to this account of the killing of the world's most wanted man. A retired Pakistani army brigadier, Shaukat Qadir, who examined the compound and interviewed relevant officers, concluded that—contrary to U.S. claims—none of the men killed at the scene had been armed. He suspected that some of those harboring bin Laden may have betrayed him—and been shot not in combat but to ensure their silence. As this edition went to press, Pakistan's official commission of inquiry had yet to issue its findings.

Pakistan was severely compromised by the fact that bin Laden had been hiding—by all accounts for years, and comfortably housed—in not just any Pakistani city but Abbottabad. The town is not only home to many serving and retired military officers, but within shouting distance of the nation's most prestigious military academy—the equivalent of America's West Point. The ISI also had a presence there.

Officials in Washington did not mince their words when these facts became public. The Pakistanis, CIA director Panetta said, had been either "involved or incompetent." The President's counterterrorism advisor, John Brennan, thought it "inconceivable" that bin Laden had not had a "support system" in Abbottabad. On CBS's *60 Minutes*, Obama himself speculated "whether there might have been some people inside of government, people outside of government, [supporting bin Laden] . . . that's something we have to investigate, and more importantly the Pakistani government has to investigate."

Bin Laden, Pakistan's President Zardari said helplessly, "was not anywhere we had anticipated he would be." The ISI, long the principal object of U.S. suspicion, denied that it had shielded the terrorist or had known where he was. Former ISI chief Hamid Gul, the veteran supporter of jihad, declared it "a bit amazing" that bin Laden could have been living in Abbottabad incognito.

According to U.S. sources, bin Laden had been tracked to Abbottabad thanks to satellite surveillance of one of the men who was killed with him. This was Abu Ahmed al-Kuwaiti, said to have chosen his leader's last refuge and to have hand-carried his messages to associates. Behind that assertion, however, may lie a more complex truth.

As early as 2005, five years before the U.S. caught up with bin Laden, Pakistani investigators had captured and transferred to U.S. custody another very senior bin Laden aide, Abu Faraj al-Libi. In the course of pursuing him, as Pakistan's former president Musharraf revealed publicly soon afterwards, the investigators learned that he had used no fewer than three safe houses—in Abbottabad. Far from being a place where one would not expect a top terrorist to be hiding, the town had a known track record for being exactly that.

Retired Pakistani brigadier Qadir, moreover, has claimed that in 2010—almost a year before bin Laden was killed—Pakistan's intelligence agency ISI had become suspicious of Ahmed al-Kuwaiti and "made a request to the CIA for satellite surveillance"—of the very building where he (and as it was to turn out) bin Laden were living. Did Pakistan deserve at least some of the credit for pinpointing bin Laden's hideout?

According to Leon Panetta, who was CIA Director at the time, U.S. authorities gave the Pakistanis no advance notice of the strike that killed bin Laden—although the operation involved a highly sensitive incursion, an over-flight of Pakistan's airspace, and action on the ground deep inside Pakistani territory. "It was decided," Panetta told *Time* magazine, "that any effort to work with the Pakistanis could jeopardize the mission. They might alert the targets."

Both U.S. and Pakistani officials, however, initially

suggested that Pakistan may have been informed—"a few minutes" in advance. Some sources in the Pakistani capital claimed even then that they had been cooperating with the United States, and had been keeping the building in Abbottabad under surveillance.

There is yet another wrinkle, one that may conceivably one day illuminate the truth about the attitude of those in authority in Pakistan—whatever knowledge some Pakistani element may have had of bin Laden's presence in the town. Ten days after the strike against bin Laden, it was reported that a decade ago—after 9/11—President Bush struck a deal with then–Pakistan president Musharraf. Under the deal, should bin Laden be located inside Pakistan's borders, the U.S. would be permitted unilaterally to conduct a raid.

"There was an agreement," a former senior U.S. official was quoted as saying, "that if we knew where Osama was, we were going to come and get him. The Pakistanis would put up a hue and cry, but they wouldn't stop us." Musharraf has denied that the reported deal was made. A Pakistani official, however, reportedly offered corroboration for the story. "As far as our American friends are concerned," he said, "they have just implemented the agreement."

Pakistan did, sure enough, protest the violation of its sovereignty after bin Laden was killed. Should anything similar occur in the future, Prime Minister Yousaf Gilani said sternly, his country would be within its rights "to retaliate with full force." That, though, according to the U.S. source of the story, was merely the "public face" of the arrangement. Gilani himself had reportedly long since said of similar possible American action: "I don't care if they do it, so long as they get the right people. We'll protest in the National Assembly and then ignore it."

How much of what has been alleged by sources in both

countries, Pakistan and the United States alike, is spin? Credible accounts of the hunt for Osama bin Laden and of his bloody end are emerging, but an unvarnished telling—shorn of any nation's propaganda—is likely to remain elusive.

IN THE ALMOST ELEVEN YEARS SINCE 9/11, WORLD-shaking events have grown out of the catastrophe—and resolution of very little.

"We are sure of our victory against the Americans and Jews, as promised by the Prophet," bin Laden had said three years before 9/11. In 2009, in a letter to the military judges at Guantánamo, Khalid Sheikh Mohammed said the attack had been "the noblest victory known to history over the forces of oppression and tyranny."

Victory? Amid all his flowery verbiage, the essential elements of what bin Laden demanded are clear. He called for: the "complete liberation of Palestine"; an end to the American "Crusaders' occupation of Saudi Arabia"; an end to the U.S. "theft" of Arab oil at "paltry prices"; and the removal of [Arab] governments that "have surrendered to the Jews."

A great upheaval is underway across the Middle East. Dictatorships have been toppled, others rocked to one degree or another by rebellion or protest. It seems improbable, though, that the outcome of the convulsion will be the sort of Middle East bin Laden would have wanted. "Rage against geriatric autocrats is only one part of it," the experienced observer Robin Wright has written. "Most of the region is also actively rebelling against radical ideologies. Muslim societies are now moving beyond jihadism . . ."

Oil, which bin Laden had variously said should retail at $144 a barrel and "$100 a barrel at least," at one point since 2001 peaked at $146. In spring 2012, it stood at $103.

As for the presence of U.S. forces in Saudi Arabia, all were gone by fall 2003. Only conditional upon a subsequent pullout, reportedly, had Crown Prince Abdullah permitted the use of Saudi bases for the invasion of Iraq. The Palestine issue, though—a constant in bin Laden's rhetoric from the start and so far as one can tell the primary motivation for KSM and the principal operatives involved in the 9/11 attacks—festers on.

How much the activity of bin Laden and al Qaeda had to do with what has changed is another matter. Though rumors swirl, there is no good evidence that Islamist extremism is playing an important role in the latest turmoil across the region. The price of oil vacillates not so much according to doctrine as according to the law of supply and demand. On the other hand, the threat of more terrorist attacks—in both America and Saudi Arabia—was surely a factor in the decision to remove the U.S. military from Saudi territory.

The decade has seen some American pressure applied to Israel over its persistent occupation of Palestinian territory and its overall treatment of the Palestinians. It has been ineffectual pressure, though, and the United States' commitment to Israel seems undiminished. Few people, it seems, are even aware that the Palestine issue was a primary motivation for the perpetrators of 9/11.

The true effect of the 2001 onslaught is less what it achieved than what it triggered. Bin Laden and some of those closest to him had fervently hoped to goad the

United States into retaliating. "We wanted the United States to attack," his military chief Mohammed Atef said after an earlier attack. ". . . They are going to invade Afghanistan . . . and then we will start holy war against the Americans, exactly like the Soviets." The notion was that the United States could be bled into defeat, literally and financially, as the Soviets had been in Afghanistan, and bin Laden shared it.

Then there was Iraq. "I am rejoicing," he said in 2003, "that America has become embroiled in the quagmires of the Tigris and Euphrates. Bush thought that Iraq and its oil would be easy prey, and now here he is, stuck in dire straits."

More than a decade after 9/11, with bin Laden dead and gone, we cannot know the end of the story. The invasion of Afghanistan that some al Qaeda leaders had desired brought disruption and death to both the organization and the country that hosted it. The United States and its allies did become bogged down in Afghanistan and Iraq but—as of the situation in early 2012—not as fatally as bin Laden had hoped.

When U.S. troops pulled out of Iraq in late 2011, however, they left behind them a country that was still dangerously volatile. An American force 99,000 strong, along with some 31,000 troops from allied countries, remained in Afghanistan as of the spring of 2012. With withdrawals either underway or scheduled, however, it was evident that the Taliban and their allies remained not only undefeated but resurgent.

Human casualties aside, the dollar cost of the "war on terrorism"—Afghanistan, Iraq, and other post-9/11 operations—was estimated in 2010 to have been $1.5 trillion. That, a Congressional Research Service report indicated, made the conflict second only to the cost of World War II—even with adjustments for inflation. A

2011 report from Brown University's Institute for International Studies put the cost as high as $2.3 to $2.7 trillion.

With the killing of bin Laden, some believe al Qaeda is defeated, a spent force. Even before he was killed, a Pew Research survey had indicated that its support had faded in the Muslim countries studied. The handful of terrorist attacks aimed at U.S. targets since 9/11 have not succeeded. Anwar Aulaqi, the preacher with dual American-Yemeni citizenship who acted as "spiritual adviser" to two key 9/11 terrorists and then resurfaced as an al Qaeda leader in Yemen, was killed by a U.S. drone strike in fall 2011. Over the months, other terrorists and terrorist suspects have reportedly met the same fate.

In early May 2012, after long years of indecision as to how and even whether they could be put on trial, five alleged key planners and accomplices in the 9/11 conspiracy were arraigned before a military court at Guantánamo. The five, Khalid Sheikh Mohammed, Ramzi Binalshibh, Walid bin Attash, Ammar al-Baluchi, and Mustafa al-Hawsawi, face a possible death sentence if convicted.

Ayman al Zawahiri, bin Laden's longtime deputy—who may have been al Qaeda's effective leader since soon after 9/11—remained at large as this edition went to press. On formally taking over in 2011, he had promised a "jihadist renaissance" and a new "black Tuesday," an attack on the United States along the lines of 9/11. He said bin Laden, who had "terrified America in life," would "continue to terrify it after death."

IN THE UNITED States in 2011, there was crass posturing and prolonged squabbling, with predictably tragic results.

In Florida, after months of threatening to do so—and

after many appeals that he desist, including one by President Obama—the pastor of a fringe church he called the Dove World Outreach Center burned a copy of the Qur'an. He had earlier held a mockery of a "trial" at which the Muslims' holy book was found guilty of "crimes against humanity." A "jury" convened by the pastor, Terry Jones, had chosen burning over three other ways of destroying the sacred text: shredding, drowning, or firing squad.

In Afghanistan, when news of the burning of the Qur'an spread, thousands of protesters took to the streets. Seven United Nations employees were killed, two of them by beheading, when a mob overran one of the organization's compounds. Violence over three days resulted in further deaths and dozens of injuries. Back in Florida, Jones said that he did not feel responsible, and that the time had come "to hold Islam accountable."

In New York City by the spring of 2012, a new tower—officially One World Trade Center, more familiarly Freedom Tower—had risen almost to its zenith. Completed, its spire will be 1,776 feet from the ground, a homage to the year of America's Declaration of Independence.

At ground level, there had been protracted discord over numerous issues. Argument swirled around plans to build a new Muslim community center and mosque on a spot only two blocks from the site of the 9/11 attacks. Its sponsors said it would be a symbol "that will give voice to the silent majority of Muslims who suffer at the hands of extremists." Opponents said the center would be "sacrilege on sacred ground," a "gross insult to the memory of those that were killed." It had opened, as of fall 2011, in a temporary building.

More melancholy disagreements centered on what really is and always will be hallowed ground—the memorial at Ground Zero, with which we opened this book. Seventy feet below ground, in what will be the September 11 Museum, the steel bases of the Twin Towers stand exposed at the point of bedrock, preserved by order of the federal government. Nearby, sheathed in a climate-controlled covering, stands the last steel column removed from the debris of the World Trade Center, a column that in the aftermath of 9/11 served as a memorial in and of itself.

The plan, as of this writing, is that the museum will hold something else, the collection of some 9,000 fragments of humanity, the remains of the 1,119 people whose body parts cannot be identified. They would repose, hidden from the public eye yet hauntingly present. The plan's proponents maintained that the presence of the remains would enhance the sanctity of the memorial, making it a place where generations would come to pay their respects and reflect. Its opponents objected to what is left of their loved ones being turned into what they saw as a lure for tourists. Placement in the museum space, relatives thought, was tantamount to creating "a freak show" put on for "gawkers."

Two thousand miles away, in Phoenix, Arizona, state senators were voting to remove wording on the city's 9/11 memorial that they deemed objectionable. A memorial, one senator said, should display only "patriotic, pro-American words." The inscribed words he and others found upsetting included "VIOLENT ACTS LEADING US TO WAR"; "MIDDLE EAST VIOLENCE MOTIVATES ATTACKS IN US"; "YOU DON'T WIN BATTLES OF TERRORISM WITH MORE BATTLES"; "FEELING OF INVINCIBILITY LOST"; "MUST BOMB BACK"; "FOREIGN-BORN AMERICANS AFRAID"; and "FEAR OF FOREIGNERS."

The fury that flamed across America after 9/11 was shot through with fear, fear of a foe few citizens could even begin to understand, fear of the unknown, fear that more was coming. Wisdom still holds, as that three-term President told the nation almost eighty years ago, that the only thing to be feared is fear itself. Yet fear, unspoken, remains pervasive, in airports and train stations, in the places where great issues are debated, in the living rooms of families across the nation.

In its fury and its fear, some say, America lost its way. Perhaps it did. On the other hand, the extreme measures its terrorist enemies espouse will lead not to utopia for anyone, only to further horrors. Crammed together on a small planet beset with desperate problems, the more than three hundred million non-Muslim Americans, the world's 1.65 billion Muslims, and the billions of others of differing religions and none must find other ways to resolve what divides them.

In New York, there was quibbling over even the quotation from Virgil's *Aeneid* chosen for the wall at the Ground Zero memorial behind which the unknown dead would lie. Should the quotation survive the debate, it at least will—however unintentionally—remain valid for both the murdered victims of 9/11 and their murderers. It reads:

"No day shall erase you from the memory of Time."

ACKNOWLEDGMENTS

This is the eighth heavily researched book project we have undertaken. All involved difficult challenges or required us to tackle intractable questions. Sometimes we have managed to answer the questions. Often, we hope, we have managed to clear up historical muddle or confusion. Nothing, however, quite prepared us for the tangle of fact, fallacy, and fantasy that enmesh this dark history.

We were reminded at every step of the way that the story on which we were embarked was freighted with human suffering: that of those who died on September 11 itself, of those killed in earlier and subsequent attacks, and of the more than 100,000 people who have died and continue to die in the ensuing conflicts—and those left grieving across the world.

In this Acknowledgments section of our book, then, we honor first and foremost those who will never be able to read it.

Writing *The Eleventh Day* has been a task for which we needed more than usual guides to people and places, nations and cultures, that do not readily reveal themselves. Our personal thanks, then, to those we can name: Hugh Bermingham, who has lived and worked in Saudi Arabia for almost thirty years; the author Jean Sasson, who also lived there and who has the trust of the first wife and the fourth son of Osama bin Laden; Flagg Miller, associate professor of religious studies at the University of California at Davis, who has analyzed bin Laden's writing in unique depth; editor and author Abdel Atwan, who interviewed bin Laden and reads the galloping pulse of history in the Middle East with rare expertise; and Alain Chouet, former head of security intelligence with the DGSE—France's foreign intelligence service—and an accomplished Arabist in his own right.

Others with a variety of backgrounds shared experience or special knowledge: Captain Anthony Barnes, who on 9/11 was deputy director of presidential contingency planning in the White House Military Office; Jean-Charles Brisard, lead investigator for lawyers representing families bereaved on 9/11, who opened up his vast archive of documents to us; Dan Christensen, veteran Florida investigative reporter, founder of *Broward Bulldog*, and a colleague and friend of many years, worked with us with flair and determination on research into possible support for the hijackers in Florida; John Farmer, former senior counsel to the 9/11 Commission, now dean of Rutgers University Law School, who was an eminently informative source on the military response to the attacks; former U.S. senator and Florida governor Bob Graham, onetime chairman of the Senate Committee on Intelligence and cochair of the House-Senate Joint Inquiry into intelligence activities before and after September 11, 2001, who gave us time in Florida, Massachusetts, and London, and who champions truth-telling in a milieu where truth is so often a stranger; Simon Henderson, who heads the Gulf and Energy Policy Program at the Washington Institute for Near East Policy; Eleanor Hill, a former Defense Department inspector general and the Joint Committee's

relentless staff director; former FBI intelligence analyst
Mike Jacobson, who served with both the Joint
Committee and the 9/11 Commission and surfaced facts
that others preferred suppressed; Miles Kara, a former
career intelligence officer with the U.S. Army, who also
served on both official probes—with a special focus on
the FAA and NORAD while on the Commission team—
and who was endlessly patient and responsive to our
queries; Ryan Mackey, research scientist at NASA's Jet
Propulsion Laboratory and author of a paper on conspiracy theories about 9/11, who applied a "baloney
detection kit" to great effect; Sarandis Papadopoulos of
the Naval Historical Center, who conducted research
and interviews and coauthored the report on the
Pentagon attack for the Office of the Secretary of
Defense; Mete Sozen, professor of structural engineering
at Purdue University in Indiana, who explained in a way
we could understand—and believe—how it appeared that
American Flight 77 was swallowed up by the Pentagon;
teacher and literacy coach Dwana Washington, who
vividly described for us the September 11 visit by
President Bush to the Emma E. Booker Elementary
School in Sarasota, Florida.

Like so much of history, work on this project has been
a paper chase. We owe sincere thanks to the National
Archives, where the hugely able Kristen Wilhelm
handled document applications and dealt with difficult
questions with skill and evident integrity—wondrously
refreshing for authors inured over the years to sustained
obstruction to the public's right to know. In 2010 and
2011, as we labored on far from Washington, and as tens
of thousands of 9/11 Commission documents became
available for the first time, we enjoyed the generous
collegiate help of Erik Larson. The National Security
Archive at George Washington University, which

collects and publishes material obtained through the Freedom of Information Act, was often useful.

In Europe, too, we learned much. In Germany, Dr. Manfred Murck, who before 9/11 and since has been deputy chief of Hamburg's domestic intelligence service, put up with persistent quizzing for longer than we could have expected and, when obliged to limit what he could tell us, was frank about doing so; from Stuttgart, Dr. Herbert Müller, Islamic affairs specialist at the parallel organization in that city, gave ready assistance; Hamburg attorney Udo Jacob helped document the story of the young Islamists who gathered in the cause of jihad before 9/11—and who included several of the 9/11 perpetrators. Without his help we could not have gained admission to Fuhlsbüttel prison to visit Mounir Motassadeq, who is serving fifteen years for his supposed role as accessory to the murders of those aboard the four hijacked airliners on 9/11. Motassadeq, for his part, put up with our questions over a period of hours. It is not clear to us that he is guilty as charged, and should we not return to his case ourselves, we hope other investigators will. Also in Germany, Hans Kippenberg, professor of comparative religious studies at Bremen's Jacobs University, and Dr. Tilman Seidensticker, professor of Arab and Islamic studies at Jena's Friedrich Schiller University, helped with interpretation and translation of the hijackers' "manual" and of Ziad Jarrah's farewell letter to his Turkish lover.

In Milan, Italy, deputy chief prosecutor and counterterrorism coordinator Armando Spataro gave us a first glimpse of the brutal injustices meted out in the name of the War on Terror; Bruno Megale, deputy head of counterterrorism, described police surveillance operations in northern Italy before 9/11. While we failed to get to Spain, our friend Charles Cardiff's reading of the Spanish dossier—accumulated by Judge Baltasar

Garzón—persuaded us of al Qaeda's pre-9/11 reach in that country.

The fellow journalists who helped us are too numerous to name. Of their number, we thank especially Thomas Joscelyn, Gerald Posner, Jeffrey Steinberg, and Joseph Trento in the United States; Guillaume Dasquié, Richard Labévière, and Alexandra Richard in France; and Josef Hufelschulte in Germany. Also in Germany, we much appreciated the hard-earned knowledge and professionalism of Dirk Laabs, an all-around reporter and practitioner of the time-honored school of shoe-leather journalism.

Yosri Fouda, the brave reporter who interviewed Khalid Sheikh Mohammed, was helpful to us from Cairo—as was his colleague Nick Fielding, who subsequently worked with him on a book about the experience.

We have on our shelves more than three hundred books that relate one way or another to 9/11, al Qaeda, and the roots from which al Qaeda sprang. Those of Peter Bergen, Steve Coll, Jim Dwyer and Kevin Flynn, former 9/11 Commission senior counsel John Farmer, Yosri Fouda and Nick Fielding, William Langewiesche, Jere Longman, Terry McDermott, Philip Shenon, and Lawrence Wright are essential reading. No one who wishes to explore the intelligence angles should miss the works of J. M. Berger, Peter Lance, and former senior CIA officer Michael Scheuer; Kevin Fenton's deconstruction of the roles of the CIA, the FBI, and the 9/11 Commission, kindly made available to us by the author before publication, was valuable and provocative. Paul Thompson's encyclopedic *The Terror Timeline* and, above all, his "Complete 9/11 Timeline," updated regularly on the Net, were indispensable. The author Peter Dale Scott has taken his scalpel to the jugular of the story of President Bush and the aides who surrounded him.

On the "skeptical" front, we thank author Daniel Hopsicker, investigator of the hijackers' activities in Florida. He introduced us to Venice, shared his time unstintingly, and trusted us down the months—long after it became clear that where he saw conspiracy we saw coincidence or happenstance. There was something to be learned, as in the past, from John Judge, a veteran of alternative history in Washington, D.C.

These days more than ever, nonfiction authors must head down the long research trail on shrunken budgets. It has been all the more rewarding, then, to have the loyalty and commitment of a new colleague. Hannah Cleaver, a Berlin-based journalist with prior expertise and knowledge of the case, made it clear that the story itself and the comradeship were as important to her as professional gain. The inquiring mind of intern Stefani Jackson produced useful research.

The efficient Sinéad Sweeney, in Ireland, has long been far more valuable to us than a mere assistant. Moss McCarthy of LED Technology rescued us from more than one computer crisis. Martina Coonan helped out on the last lap, when every hour was precious. Pauline Lombard and Ann Dalton put up with our demands yet again. We thank, too, Ger Killalea, who keeps the office functioning, and Jason Cairns, who cheerfully turns his hand to anything under the sun.

The Eleventh Day would not exist without the initial interest and backing of our publishers at Random House. Group president Gina Centrello and Ballantine publisher Libby McGuire in New York, and Transworld's Bill Scott-Kerr in London, kept us going along a bumpy trail.

Our editors, Mark Tavani and Simon Thorogood, were there for us in the final months with skill and good judgment. Where they saw clutter, they pointed the way to clarity. Our agent, Jonathan Lloyd, also reads everything we write with a keen editorial eye—a bonus for us—for he is himself a former publisher. He has steadied us, once again, with his combination of common sense and uncommon good humor.

We thank our good friends and neighbors, who have been endlessly supportive. Our neglected children heroically put up with the neglect—though one has asked, "When are we going to be a family again?"

The Eleventh Day is dedicated to our steadfast friends Chris and Gaye Humphreys—who know why—and to Angela Amicone, who turns ninety-six this year. Angela has been teaching children to read since 1940, and has no intention of giving up now.

Anthony Summers and Robbyn Swan
Ireland, 2012

NOTES AND SOURCES

ABBREVIATIONS USED IN NOTES AND SOURCES

AP	Associated Press
BG	*Boston Globe*
CF	Files of the National Commission on Terrorist Attacks upon the United States, held at the National Archives, Record Group 148. Cited documents are listed here, as they are at the Archives, by folder name, box [B] and team [T] numbers. Many documents were supplied to the authors by an independent researcher, and others obtained on line via www.scribd.com or directly from the Archives.
CO	Website of the National Commission on Terrorist Attacks upon the United States, archived at http://govinfo.library.unt.edu/911/about.html
conv.	conversation
corr.	Authors' correspondence
CR	Final Report of the National Commission on Terrorist Attacks upon the United States, NY: W. W. Norton, 2004
FBI IG	Review of the FBI's Handling of Intelligence Information Related to the September 11 Attacks, Office of the Inspector General, U.S. Department of Justice, November 2004
FEMA	Federal Emergency Management Agency, U.S. Department of Homeland Security

int.	interview (by authors unless otherwise noted)
INTELWIRE	FBI documents sourced in the notes of the 9/11 Commission Report, obtained by Intelwire under FOIA (Freedom of Information Act) and available on its website, www.intelwire.com
JI	Joint Inquiry into Intelligence Community Activities Before and After the Terrorist Attacks of September 11, 2001, House Permanent Select Committee on Intelligence and Senate Select Committee on Intelligence, 107th Congress, 2nd Session
KSM SUBST	Substitution for the Testimony of Khalid Sheikh Mohammed, Defense Exhibit 941, *U.S. v. Zacarias Moussaoui*, Cr. No. 01-455-1, U.S. District Court for the Eastern District of Virginia
LAT	*Los Angeles Times*
MFR	Memorandum for the Record of 9/11 Commission staff interviews, available on National Archives website, http://www.archives.gov/legislative/research/9-11/commission-memoranda.html
NARA	National Archives and Records Administration
NIST	National Institute of Standards and Technology, U.S. Department of Commerce
NTSB	National Transportation Safety Board
NYT	*New York Times*
OBL	Osama bin Laden
TF	Oral histories of 503 first responders conducted by the Fire Department, City of New York, archived by *The New York Times* at http:// graphics8.nytimes.com/packages/html/nyregion/20050812_WTC_GRAPHIC/met_WTC_histories_full_01.html
WP	*Washington Post*
WSJ	*Wall Street Journal*

PREFACE

17–18 **memorial:** *NY Daily News,* 8/20/01, *NYT,* 6/10/09, www.wtcsitememorial.org, www.national911memorial.org/ site, int. Michael Frazier for National September 11 Memorial and Museum; **disease:** AP, 6/24/09.

18 **tens of thousands:** Documenting the number of dead in any conflict is difficult, fraught as such figures are with political ramifications. Americans in particular, given the lingering specter of the Vietnam War, are sensitive to rising casualty counts among servicemen and women. Nor does any military readily accept responsibility for civilian casualties. The issue is further complicated by determining which deaths qualify as having been the result of war—does one, for example, include deaths due to disease or starvation—conditions brought about by conflict? In citing the figure of many tens of thousands of dead, the authors have relied on casualty counts from the U.N. Assistance Missions in Afghanistan and Iraq, and the websites icasualties.org and iraqbodycount.org.

18 **graves/remains:** AP, 4/1/09, www.911research.wtc7.net, *Israel National News,* 2/1/08, *NYT,* 2/23/08, MFR 03009720; **Riches:** *NYT,* 11/5/02, 4/21/08, www.NY1.com, 4/17/08, *NY Post,* 4/13/02; **McIntyre:** AP, 5/19/06, *Independent on Sunday* (U.K.), 10/7/07; **Dillard:** Arlington historian Thomas Sherlock to authors, 9/11/09, *WP,* 5/26/07, *NY Observer,* 6/20/04; **Breitweiser:** Kristen Breitweiser, *Wake-up Call,* NY: Warner, 2006, Preface, 110, 240.

19 **Martin:** *WP,* 11/2/06, *Newsweek,* 12/25/06, transcript, 9/12/01, FBI 265D-NY-280350, report, 9/12/01, FBI 265D-NY-280350-CE, courtesy of INTELWIRE. Though Martin suffered serious injuries early in the first hijacking, it is probable that a First Class passenger—Daniel Lewin—was the first to die. See Ch. 1, p. 15.

19–23 **safe to breathe:** "EPA's Response to the World Trade Center Collapse," Office of the Inspector General, U.S. Environmental Protection Agency, 8/21/03, 4; **Riches ill:** www.NY1.com, 4/17/08, www.sohoblues.com, citing *Time*; **"dead or alive":** CNN, 9/17/01; **backtrack:** press release, 3/13/02, www.whitehouse.gov; **Obama:** *NY Post,* 2/7/09; **Zubaydah:** *NY Daily News,* 9/10/06, & see later refs.; **Dillard questions:** CNN, 3/28/04, ACLU statement, 12/12/08; **Breitweiser testimony/questions:** testimony, 9/18/02, JI, Breitweiser, 100–, int. Kristen Breitweiser, *St. Petersburg*

Times, 8/12/05; **CIA/two hijackers:** see later refs.; **kept secret:** Bob Graham with Jeff Nussbaum, *Intelligence Matters*, NY: Random House, 2004, 228, 231; **Breitweiser/Obama:** *NYT*, 6/24/09; **Commission Final Report received:** Philip Shenon, *The Commission*, NY: Twelve, 2008, 415–; **Kean/Hamilton:** *NYT*, 12/8/07 & 1/2/08, www.rawstory.com, 12/24/07, *International Herald Tribune*, 12/8/07; **Kerrey:** *Newsweek*, 3/23/09, Air America radio, 3/2/08; **Cleland:** *Salon*, 11/21/03, *NYT*, 10/26/03; **"first draft":** CBC transcript, 8/21/06; **CBS poll:** www.angus-reid.com/polls, www.alternet.com, 9/16/06; **Scripps poll:** Scripps Howard News Service, 11/23/07; **Zogby poll:** Zogby International, Aug. 2007; **sixteen thousand:** Reuters, 9/10/08, www.alternet.com, 9/16/08; **Iraq/attacks:** *NYT*/CBS News polls cited at www.angus-reid.com; **Angus Reid poll:** released 3/17/10, www.angus-reid.com; **criticism: (senators)** Lincoln Chaffee, Mark Dayton, Mike Gravel, Patrick Leahy, Charles Schumer; **(representatives)** Dennis Kucinich, Cynthia McKinney, Ron Paul, Curt Weldon; **(governor)** Jesse Ventura; **(deputy attorneys general)** Roy Andes, Philip Berg, Donald Bustion; **(state legislators)** Peter Allen, Peter Espiefs, Karen Johnson, Barbara Richardson, Charles Weed, Suzi Wizowaty; **(public officials/ diplomats/engineers/officers)** see https://patriotsquestion911. com; **Texas candidates:** "Texas GOP Gubernatorial Candidate Questions Government Involvement in 9/11," Fox News, 2/12/10, "Shami Questions US Involvement in 9/11 Attack," KTBS TV, 2/14/10; **CIA/FBI:** e.g., letter to Congress regarding the 9/11 Commission Report signed by twenty-five military, intelligence, and law enforcement veterans, 9/13/04, National Security Whistleblowers Coalition; **Freeh:** *WSJ*, 11/17/05, CNN, 11/30/05; **Mondale:** int. Minnesota, "We Are C.H.A.N.G.E.," 2/3/08, www.youtube.com; **Clark:** *This Week with George Stephanopoulos*, ABC News, 3/5/06; **Graham:** ints. Bob Graham, *Salon*, 9/9/04, Graham with Nussbaum.

23 **300,000 pages:** corr. Kristen Wilhelm, 2011. Only some 35 percent of the Commission documents held by the National Archives had been reviewed for release as of April 2012. Of the documents reviewed, 15 percent remain classified, largely under national security and privacy restrictions. The remaining 20 percent, some 300,000 documents, are available to researchers.

Part I: **ATTACK**

CHAPTER 1

27–8   **recognized:** Martin Gilbert, *Israel*, London: Black Swan, 1999, 189; **day in 1938:** Robert Lacey, *The Kingdom*, NY: Avon, 1983, 262; **40,000 planes:** Jane Garvey testimony, 1/27/04, CO; **Rosenzweig/Mladenik/Gordenstein/Theodoridis/Iskandar/Filipov:** "DOJ Documents Requests #35–13," B13, T7, CF, "AAL Misc. Folder—AA11 and AA77," B18, T7, CF; **Cuccinello:** eds. *Der Spiegel* magazine, *Inside 9–11*, NY: St. Martin's, 2001, 37; **Gay:** AP, 9/25/01, Raytheon press release, 9/10/07; **Morabito:** *Post-Standard* (Syracuse, NY), 10/20/07; **Berenson:** Richard Bernstein, *Out of the Blue*, NY: Times Books, 2002, 171; **Angell:** *People*, 5/17/04; **Lewin:** *BG*, 9/12/01.

28   **five young men:** *BG*, 9/13/01. Some have raised questions about the identities of the hijackers. The issue will be covered in Ch. 14 and its related notes.

28   **Ogonowski:** Bernstein, 110–, James Ogonowski remarks at Safety Awards Banquet, 9/11/02, "Ogonowski Legacy," Public Radio International, 9/13/02.

28–31   **5:00 A.M.:** Unless otherwise indicated, all times in this book are rendered as the times in use by civilians on the U.S. East Coast on the day in question (i.e., EDT)—as opposed to the times used by the military or the aviation industry, or in other time zones; **McGuinness:** website of Cheryl McGuinness (widow), www.beautybeyondtheashes.com; **"turn-around":** MFR 04016228, 2/10/04; **take off due:** CR, 2; **cleaners/fuelers:** "FBI 302s of Interest Flight 11," B17, T7, CF, "FBI 302s Arestegui," B10, T7, CF; **flight attendants:** "FBI 302s Homer Folder re Kathleen Nicosia," B10, T7, CF; **"organized":** *NYT*, 12/9/01; **backup:** "FBI 302s Arestegui," B10, T7, CF; **joked:** *Cape Cod Times*, 9/14/01; **sick/standby:** "FBI 302s Arestegui," B10, T7, CF; **odd incident:** Staff Report, "The Four Flights and Civil Aviation Security," note 22, CF, MFR 04020636, 2/2/04, MFR 03007050, 8/15/03, *Miami Herald*, 9/22/01; **Filipov/"suspicious":** "DOJ Documents Requests 35–13," B13, T7, CF; **Howland:** "FBI 302s Cockpit and American and Hijacker," B11, T7, CF; **profiling system:** CR 4, MFR 04018154, 11/24/03, Staff Report, "The Four Flights and Civil Aviation Security," 2, 77, CF, John Raidt comments, 1/27/04, CO; **crutch:** *BG*, 11/10/01;

"sweating bullets": *World Net Daily*, 9/21/01; **last to board:** MFR 04020636, 2/2/04; **greeted by Martin/final checks:** "FBI 302s Arestegui," B10, T7, CF; **seating:** CR, 2, *BG*, 9/13/01; **Sweeney call:** *NY Observer*, 2/15/04, FBI 302 Michael Sweeney, 9/21/01, INTELWIRE; **switch off phones:** "FBI 302s Arestegui," B10, T7, CF; **pushed back/takeoff:** Joseph Gregor, "Air Traffic Control Recording," NTSB, 12/21/01, CR, 2, 4; **"severe clear":** Lynn Spencer, *Touching History*, NY: Free Press, 2008, 3; **air-to-ground exchanges:** Gregor, 2–, & see FAA Memo, Full Transcript: Aircraft Accident AA11, New York, NY, 9/11/01, "Boston Center, Shirley Kula," B3, T8, CF; **"a brief unknown sound":** "Summary of Air Traffic Hijack Events, Sept. 11, 2001, FAA," Report on Investigation of 9/11 Commission Staff Referral, Dept. of Transportation, Office of Inspector General, Appendix 3; **Ong to Reservations:** quotes attributed to Ong & nature of her call come from FBI 302 of Vanessa Minter, 9/12/01, FBI 302 of Craig Marquis, 9/16/01, & "Charlotte to Director," FBI 265D-NY-280350-CE, 9/13/01, "Flight Call Notes," & Transcript of 9/11 Telephone Calls, "AA Phone Calls," B13, T7, CF, FBI 302 of Nydia Gonzalez, 9/12/01, "FBI 302s—Knife and American Flight 11," B11, T7, CF, FBI 302 of Winston Sadler, 9/13/01, INTELWIRE, Nydia Gonzalez testimony, 1/27/04, CO.

32–3   **"sterile cockpit":** The interjection appears on the transcript but is only partially audible on the tape version as heard by the authors; **Lewin dead?:** Lewin was an American-Israeli citizen who as "Daniel Levin" had served in the Israel Defense Forces as a member of Sayeret Matkal—in its Unit 269, which specializes in counterterrorism (FBI 302 of Anne Lewin, 9/21/01, "Flight Calls Notes," B13, T7, CF, UPI, 3/6/02, ints. Tom Leighton, Marco Greenberg, *Ha'aretz*, 9/15/06).

33   **man in 10B:** Ong also identified the passengers in Seats 2A and 2B as hijackers, while her colleague Sweeney—whose call was not recorded—is variously reported as identifying hijackers in 9B, 9C, 9D, 9E, 9G, 10B, and 10C. 2A, 2B, and 10B were indeed the assigned seats of three of the five Arab passengers traveling. (Ong re 2A/2B: Transcripts of 9/11 Telephone Calls, "AA Phone Transcripts," & Charlotte to Director, FBI 265D-NY-280350-CE, 9/13/01, "Flight Call Notes," B13, T7, CF; Sweeney re Seats: FBI 302 of Michael Woodward, 9/14/01, & of James Sayer, 9/13/01, "FBI 302s—

Olsen," B10, T7, CF); **Sweeney/Woodward call:** Quotes
attributed to Sweeney & nature of her call come from CR,
453n32, FBI 302 of Michael Woodward, 9/14/01, & of James
Sayer, 9/13/01, "FBI 302s—Olsen," B10, T7, CF, Staff
Report, "The Four Flights and Civil Aviation Security," 14,
CF.

33 **borrowed card:** The calling card was provided to Sweeney by
another flight attendant, Sara Low—who also passed information on the hijackers' seat location to colleagues (*NY
Observer,* 6/20/04, AP 3/5/09, ABC News, 7/18/02).

33–4 **keys:** CR, 5, 453n26, FBI 302 of Michael Sweeney, 9/21/01,
INTELWIRE, John Farmer, *The Ground Truth,* NY:
Riverhead, 2009, 109; **"no warning":** *NY Observer,* 6/20/04;
"refrain": Staff Report, "The Four Flights and Civil Aviation
Security," 81, CF; **not panicky/"static":** ABC News,
7/18/02.

CHAPTER 2

35 **data processor:** (Chuck Allen), eds. *Der Spiegel, Inside 9–11,*
46–; **steelworker:** (Joe Libretti), Wayne Barrett and Dan
Collins, *Grand Illusion,* NY: Harper, 2006, 245; **construction
workers/composer:** (Juan Suarez & "Artie" & composer Jim
Farmer) Bernstein, 199; **student:** *9/11: Dust & Deceit at the
World Trade Center,* documentary, www.dust.org.

36 **8:46 A.M.:** 8:46 A.M. is the generally accepted time of the impact
on the North Tower. Scientists measuring seismic data at the
Lamont-Doherty Earth Observatory at the New Jersey
Palisades, twenty-one miles from New York City, initially—in
2001—calculated the impact time as 8:46:26. In 2005, they
adjusted the estimate to 8:46:29. The 9/11 Commission,
meanwhile, relied on the flight path study for Flight 11 provided by the NTSB, reckoning the impact time as 8:46:40.
(Similar discrepancies appear in times given for the subsequent crash into the South Tower.) While too complex to
detail here, several plausible explanations have been offered
for this anomaly. Though minimal, the discrepancies have
been used by critics of the conventional account to bolster the
notion that—in addition to the planes—explosives were used
in the attacks on the Twin Towers. The differing timings
supplied by the seismic station, the critics claim, reflect
explosions in the towers *before* the impact of the airplanes.
That theory does not hold, however, because the seismic data

reflect only a single event. Had there been first an explosion, then an impact, the seismic instruments would have registered *two* events. They did not ("Seismic Waves Generated by Aircraft Impacts and Building Collapses at World Trade Center," by Won-Young Kim et al., www.ldeo.columbia.edu, "Federal Building and Fire Safety Investigation of the WTC Disaster," NCSTAR1–5A, NIST, 22–, CR, 7, 454n39, "Seismic Proof—9/11 Was an Inside Job," by Craig T. Furlong & Gordon Ross, www.journalof911studies.com, "On *Debunking 9/11 Debunking*," by Ryan Mackey, 5/24/08, 79–, authors' corr. Dr. Won-Young Kim & NTSB's Ted Lopatkiewicz, 2009).

36–41 **Rubenfien:** Leo Rubenfien, *Wounded Cities*, Göttingen, Germany: Steidl, 2008, 32–; **Naudet:** David Friend, *Watching the World Change*, NY: Farrar, Straus & Giroux, 2006, 185–; **Naudet image:** *9/11*, documentary film, Jules & Gedeon Naudet et al., CBS Television, 2002; **Allen:** eds. *Der Spiegel*, 48, Chuck Allen profile on LinkedIn.com; **Gartenberg:** WABC (NY), 9/11/01, videotape on www.youtube.com, eds. *Der Spiegel*, 89; **93rd and 99th floors:** CR, 285; **10,000 gallons:** "Visual Evidence, Damage Estimates, and Timeline Analysis, Federal Building and Fire Safety Investigation of the World Trade Center Disaster," NIST, released April 2005, liii; **Fireballs:** CR, 285, 292; **"The windows"/"I just didn't":** Friend, 188, Naudet documentary, Jim Dwyer & Kevin Flynn, *102 Minutes*, NY: Times Books, 2005, 280; **milling around:** Brian Jenkins and Frances Edward-Winslow, "Saving City Lifelines: Lessons Learned in the 9/11 Terrorist Attacks," Mineta Transportation Institute report, 9/03, 11; **1,344 souls:** *NYT*, 1/15/04; **stairways blocked:** CR, 285; **Meehan:** Dwyer & Flynn, 36, *NYT*, 9/25/01, www.damianmeehan.org (family website); **San Pio Resta:** Bernstein, 177; **Richards:** *The Independent* (U.K.), 9/24/01, *Village Voice*, 6/6/02, *Art News*, 11/01; **Fred Alger:** *NY Sun*, 9/11/06; **Marsh:** *Insurance Journal*, 9/6/04; **"Oh, my God!":** Dwyer & Flynn, 14; **remains:** ibid., 20; **658 people:** www.cantor.com/public/charities; **Wittenstein:** eds. *Der Spiegel*, 51; **Rosenblum:** Bernstein, 212; **van Auken:** CNN, 9/13/01; **dead staffer:** William Langewiesche, *American Ground*, NY: North Point, 2002, 134; **Windows:** ibid., 56–; **meetings:** Dwyer & Flynn, 11; **Risk Waters:** ibid., 12, Bernstein, 175; **Kane:** Dwyer & Flynn, 14;

calls/Olender/Heeran: ibid., 38–, 138, 127, 277, James Bamford, *A Pretext for War*, NY: Doubleday, 2004, 21–, Bernstein, 205–, *Times Union* (Albany), 8/20/06; **Wortley:** Dwyer & Flynn, 130; **two helicopters:** CR, 291–; **blocked:** Thomas Kean & Lee Hamilton, *Without Precedent*, NY: Alfred A. Knopf, 2006, 220, "Crisis Management," Staff Statement 14, CO, Dwyer & Flynn, 126–41–; **cut:** MFR 03003644, 7/21/03, CF; **"Be advised":** Dwyer & Flynn, 58; **"We got jumpers"/too shocking:** Friend, 188, 128–, *Esquire*, 9/03.

41–2 **Reiss:** Dwyer & Flynn, 18 & cf. 136–; **Naudet:** *9/11*, documentary; **clutching briefcase/skirt:** *Economist*, 5/6/06; **burning shirt:** Dwyer & Flynn, 32; **groups/paratroopers:** Friend, 134, int. of Jason Charles, TF, 1/23/02, *New Yorker*, 9/24/01; **Smiouskas:** Dwyer & Flynn, 137; **"As the debris":** int. Kevin McCabe, TF, 12/13/01; **"looked like":** int. Derek Brogan, TF, 12/28/01; **"We started":** Bernstein, 5.

42 **"Christ!":** "Why No Rooftop Rescues on September 11?," ABC News, 11/8/01.

CHAPTER 3

43 **"We have *some planes*":** ATCR-AA11, 7–.

43 **Zalewski/colleagues:** MFR 04016801, 9/22/03, CR, 6. On the second transmission, at 8:24 A.M., the hijacker said: "Nobody move. Everything will be okay. If you try to make any moves you'll endanger yourself and the airplane. Just stay quiet." There would also be a third transmission. At 8:33, the hijacker said: "Nobody move, please. We are going back to the airport. Don't try to make any stupid moves." Contrary to the notion that this was an inadvertent blunder by the American 11 hijacker, Commission staff member Miles Kara ventures the thought that the transmission was deliberate—a way of letting his accomplice aboard United 175, who could listen in to radio traffic on cabin channel 9, know that the operation had begun. (MFR 04016801, 9/22/03, corr. Miles Kara, 2011.)

44–8 **Horrocks:** www.michaelroberthorrocks.com; **Saracini:** *NYT*, 12/31/01; **attendants:** CR, 454n41, www.afanet.org, www.airlineride.org; **usual mix:** FBI 302, 10/01/01, "FBI 302s, Arestegui," B10, T7, CF, Bernstein, 180, INN.com, 2/1/08, *The Sun* (Ireland), 9/11/06, *Northeastern University Voice*, 12/11/01; **Arabs First or Business:** UA175 manifests, "Flight 175 Misc. Manifest—Check in—Boarding," B17, T7,

CF & Exhibit P200018, *U.S. v. Zacarias Moussaoui*, Cr. No. 01-455-A, U.S. District Court for the Eastern District of VA; **boarding card:** FBI 302 re int. of [name redacted], 9/12/01, "Flight 175 Info.," B16, T7, CF; **buy ticket:** FBI 302 re Gail Jawahir, 9/21/01, INTELWIRE; **in line:** FBI 302 re Mike Castro, 9/15/01, "302s of Interest Flight 175," B17, T7, CF; **Flight 175 course/We figured/suspicious:** "Flight Path Study—UA Flight 175," NTSB, 2/19/02, MFR 04016823, 10/1/03. As noted above, none of the hijacker transmissions from Flight 11 heard by ground control included these precise words; **Channel 9:** *Time,* 9/14/01, *PRWeek,* 3/10/08 & see Farmer, 124, 143; **Allentown:** MFR 04016828, 10/1/03; **Policastro:** MFR 04017221, 11/21/03, MFR 04017218, 11/21/03; **Hanson:** FBI 302 re Lee Hanson, 9/11/01, "FBI 302—Mace and Flight," B11, T7, CF, Bernstein, 7; **"We might":** MFR 04016823, 10/1/03, MFR 04016828, 10/1/03, "Flight Path Study—UA Flight 175," NTSB, 2/19/02, map; **8:58:** FBI 302 re [name redacted], 9/28/01, INTELWIRE, *NY Daily News,* 3/9/04, but see CR, 8; **Sweeney:** *Hyannis News,* 9/13/01, *Metrowest Daily News,* 9/18/01, *WP,* 9/14/01; **Peter Hanson 2nd call:** FBI 302 of Lee Hanson, 9/11/01, "FBI 302—Mace and Flight," B11, T7, CF; **"planes, as in plural":** Position 15, Parts 2 & 3, "ATCSCC Tape Transcript," B1, T8, CF, CR, 23, 460n131; **"He's going in":** *WP,* 9/17/01; **Statue of Liberty:** Peter Lance, *1000 Years for Revenge,* NY: Regan, 2003, 12; **rocked:** Bamford, *Pretext,* 28.

48   **Mosiello:** int. Steven Mosiello, TF, 10/23/01. Mosiello was one of 503 firefighters, paramedics, and emergency medical technicians who contributed oral history interviews after 9/11. The interviews were released by city authorities—and transcripts were published by *The New York Times* as "World Trade Center Task Force" interviews—in 2005. They will be cited frequently—sourced as "TF"—in the chapters that follow (*NYT,* 8/12/08).

48–9 **O'Clery:** Conor O'Clery, *May You Live in Interesting Times,* Dublin: Poolbeg, 2009, 4; **Praimnath:** *NYT,* 5/26/02, Staff Statement 13, CO, Dwyer & Flynn, 92; **Clark:** "A Survivor's Story," transcript, PBS *Nova,* Bernstein, 222, CR, 293, CTV News (Canada), 9/6/02, CNN, 9/9/02; **Many others:** "Final Report on the Collapse of the World Trade Center," NCSTAR 1, NIST, 23,41.

CHAPTER 4

50–1   **CNN break:** transcript, 09/11/01, www.transcripts.cnn.com, Bamford, *Pretext*, 16; **Sawyer/Gibson:** transcript, "ABC News Special Report: Planes Crash into World Trade Center," 09/11/01, & tape on www.youtube.com; **"stupidity":** "Five Years Later: Media Recollections of 9/11," 9/11/06, citing Dorian Benkoil, www.mediabistro.com; **pilot drunk:** Dwyer & Flynn, 86; **Hayden:** James Bamford, *The Shadow Factory*, NY: Doubleday, 2008, 86.

51   **Tenet:** Bob Woodward, *Bush at War*, NY: Simon & Schuster, 2002, 3–. Tenet reversed the sequence of the attacks in his book, inaccurately indicating that the first plane crashed into the South Tower of the Trade Center, the second into the North Tower. What he meant, though, becomes clear as one reads on. (George Tenet with Bill Harlow, *At the Center of the Storm*, NY: HarperCollins, 2007, 161–).

51   **Rumsfeld:** int., Larry King show, CNN, 12/6/01, & testimony, 5/23/04, www.defenselink.mil, notes of int. Rumsfeld, B7, T2, CF; **Clarke:** Richard Clarke, *Against All Enemies*, NY: Free Press, 2004, 1; **Cheney:** ibid., 2, *Meet the Press*, NBC, 9/16/01, *WSJ*, 8/15/07; **Rice:** *Newsweek*, 12/31/01.

51   **Bush in Sarasota:** *Sarasota Magazine*, 11/01. In the early hours of the morning of September 11, a police report shows, a Sudanese man had contacted Sarasota police to say he feared an associate and two companions then visiting Sarasota might pose a threat to the President—who was staying at the Colony resort hotel on nearby Longboat Key. The associate, it was later reported, had links to the Sudanese People's Liberation Army. Officers and Secret Service agents went to an address on 32nd Street in Sarasota, a law enforcement source told the authors, and found eleven Arab men up and about— "apparently at morning prayer." One of the men had a card for a resort not far from the President's—the Longboat Key Club. The men were questioned, held until the President had left, then released. There was nothing to indicate they were linked to the 9/11 plotters, the source told the authors. There appears to be no substance to other reports of threats to the President at Longboat Key (Incident Report, Sarasota Police Dept., 4:07 A.M., 9/11/01, obtained by authors, conv. Monica Yadav, ABC 7 [affiliate], int. Sheriff's Dept. source, ints. Carroll Mooneyhan, Murf Klauber, Katy Moulton).

51   **Draper:** *Albuquerque Tribune*, 9/10/02; **Morell:** Tenet, 165–.

52   **President first learned:** At 9:17 that morning, in a conversation live with presenter Peter Jennings, reporter John Cochran stated from Sarasota that as Bush "got out of his hotel suite this morning, was about to leave, reporters saw the White House chief of staff, Andy Card, whisper into his ear. The reporter said to the President, 'Do you know what's going on in New York?' He said he did, and he said he will have something about it later. His first event is [in] about half an hour at an elementary school in Sarasota." This report has been taken to indicate that President Bush was already aware of the first impact on the Trade Center as he left his hotel. This would be impossible, however, as the President reportedly left his hotel at 8:35, some eleven minutes *before* the crash of American Flight 11. Bush did tell a reporter he would "talk about it later," but at a later stage, well into his visit to Booker Elementary, after the second airplane had hit and just before 9:17 when Cochran spoke to Peter Jennings. The authors conclude that, in the rush of unfolding events, Cochran conflated disparate events—perhaps not reporting all of them firsthand (Cochran: "ABC News Special Report: Planes Crash into World Trade Center," transcript, 9/11/01 & tape on www.youtube.com; 8:35 at hotel: *WP*, 1/27/02; "talk . . . later": ABC News, 6/22/04).

52   **Loewer:** AP, 11/26/01; **Card:** Rep. Adam Putnam in *GW Hatchet*, 4/8/02; **"The first report":** *Washington Times*, 10/7/02; **"I thought":** CBS, 9/10/03; **"We're going":** AP, 8/19/02.

52–5   **three alarms:** Dwyer & Flynn, 47–; **first responders:** Staff Statement 13, 14, CO; **"twenty-four hours":** int. Richard, World Trade Center Task Force, 10/10/01; **Instructions not heard:** Staff Statement 13, co; **"no need":** Dwyer & Flynn, 72; **9:02:** CR, 289; **4,000 people:** *USA Today*, 12/20/01; **On Channel 5:** *NYT*, 8/27/10; **"One plane's":** Bamford, *Pretext*, 92, 89; **Rumsfeld:** Torie Clarke, *Lipstick on a Pig*, NY: Free Press, 2006, 217–, int. Torie Clarke on WBZ (Boston), 9/16/01, int. Donald Rumsfeld by Alfred Goldberg and Rebecca Cameron, 12/23/02, "Rumsfeld on Intel," B7, T2, CF; **"With all hell":** Tenet, 162; **Clarke:** Richard Clarke, 1–; **"Get ready":** footage of Bush's visit to Booker Elementary is viewable on www.youtube.com; **phonics-based:** *New Yorker*, 7/26/04.

55   **picked up readers:** The President held his book the correct
      way up, contrary to persistent claims that he held it upside
      down. A photograph purporting to show him holding a book
      upside down—on another occasion—was doctored. In the
      original AP photograph of that occasion, Bush was clearly
      holding the book the correct way up (claims: e.g., refs. to the
      "Pet Goat" story on Google, Jude Cowell blog, 11/19/08,
      www.judecowell.wordpress.com, *Asia Times*, 10/30/04;
      doctored: "Dubya, Willya Turn the Book Over?" 11/16/02,
      www.wired.com).

55   **news coverage:** Televisions were available at the school.
      President Bush would be excoriated, later, for appearing to
      claim—in Florida in December 2001 and subsequently—that
      he had seen TV coverage of the *first* plane hitting the Trade
      Center. What he said in December was: "And I was *sitting out-
      side the classroom waiting to go in* [authors' italics], and I saw an
      airplane hit the tower—the television was obviously on, and I
      used to fly myself, and I said, 'There's one terrible pilot.'"
      Bush was in error in saying that he saw one of the strikes on
      TV before entering the classroom. There was no live footage
      of the first strike on the Trade Center. The footage of Flight
      11's impact, shot by documentary filmmaker Jules Naudet,
      was on video and not shown until much later. Bush, moreover,
      would be in the classroom with the schoolchildren—not
      watching television—when the TV showed live pictures of the
      second plane flying into the Trade Center. The footage of the
      second strike, however, was shown again and again in the
      minutes and hours that followed. What Bush recalled having
      seen on TV at the school was surely one of the reruns, trans-
      mitted *after* he had left the classroom. A photograph taken at
      the school features Bush standing near a TV screen—one that
      appears to show smoke billowing from the Trade Center.
      Given the tumultuous events that followed on September 11
      and later, and given the President's infamous propensity to
      muddle his utterances, there is no reason to attach signifi-
      cance to his error in saying he saw one of the strikes on
      television before entering the classroom (there were TVs:
      Summers tour of school, int. Dwana Washington; "And I was
      sitting": interview George Bush, 12/04/01, www.whitehouse.
      gov; much later: Paul Thompson, *The Terror Timeline*, NY:
      Regan, 2004, 388, & see Friend, 187; photo: AP).

55   **Marine:** *Sarasota Herald-Tribune*, 9/10/02.

55   **"It took me"/"Captain Loewer says":** AP, 11/26/01.

55   **"A second plane":** CR, 38. To calculate the timing of the classroom session and when Bush was informed of the second strike, the authors studied the footage of the session available on YouTube and in the relevant section of Michael Moore's *Fahrenheit 9/11*, which includes specific time points. The authors' calculation as to the delay before Bush was told of the second strike—"ninety seconds"—would mean that Card interrupted him somewhat after 9:04—a little earlier than the 9:05 timing cited in the Commission Report. The delay was in any case minimal (*Fahrenheit 9/11*, Sony Pictures, 2004, CR, 38).

56   **Brian Clark:** Bernstein, 224–; **emergency calls:** *NY Daily News*, 9/30/01.

56–7   **Compton:** ABC News, 9/11/02; **Daniels:** *St. Petersburg Times*, 9/8/02; **Jones-Pinkney/Radkey:** AP, 9/11/06; **"Can you get":** *St. Petersburg Times*, 7/4/04; **"The Pet Goat":** eds. Siegfried Engelmann & Elaine Bruner, *Reading Mastery 2, Storybook 1*, NY: McGraw-Hill, 1995; **"DON'T SAY":** *Washington Times*, 10/7/02.

57   **Gartenberg/Puma:** WABC (NY), 9/11/01, eds. *Der Spiegel*, 85–, 212–.

58–60   **Flight 77:** Farmer, 160–, 186, "Air Traffic Control Recording," NTSB, 12/21/01, CR, 8–, 24–; **"Whose plane":** MFR 04017175, 11/20/03, CF; **Ballinger/Boston warned:** Staff Report, "The Four Flights and Civil Aviation Security," 8/26/04, CF, CR, 455n67; **Command Center failed:** ibid.; **Boston advised/NY issued:** CR, 23, "Staff Report"; **"Beware":** CR, 11. One such message went to Flight 175, which, still unknown to Ballinger, had already crashed; **4,546:** Pamela Freni, *Ground Stop*, NY: iUniverse, 2003, 59.

60   **May call:** Las Vegas to Dallas, 9/12/01, Dallas to Las Vegas, 9/11/01, Dallas to Dallas, 9/11/01, "Misc. Comms from 4 Flights," B13, T7, CF; **mother got through:** "Through My Eyes," by Toni Knisley, submission for National September 11 Memorial & Museum, http://ns11makehistory. appspot.com, MFR 04017206, 11/19/03; **some wondered:** Farmer, 162; **videoconference:** CR, 36; **"I need":** Stephen Hayes, *Cheney*, NY: HarperCollins, 2007, 331–; **"The Cabinet":** Barton Gellman, *Angler*, London: Allen Lane, 114.

61   **"very aware":** *Newsweek*, 12/3/01; **Cheney/Rice:** CR, 39, 463n204, *St. Petersburg Times*, 9/8/02.

CHAPTER 5

62–3   **Olson calls:** FBI 302 of Lori Keyton, 9/14/01, "Flight Call Notes and 302s," B13, T7, CF, FBI 302 of Ted Olson, 9/11/01, INTELWIRE, int. Ted Olson on *Larry King Weekend*, CNN, 1/6/02, Farmer, 163; **undetected:** Staff Monograph, "The Four Flights and Civil Aviation Security," 8/26/04, CF; **speeding east/notified Reagan/Secret Service:** Flight 77 map and timeline, "Timelines 9-11, 1 of 2," B20, T7, CF.

63–4   **Ladies and gentlemen:** AP, 9/11/01; **"We're under":** *Clear the Skies*, BBC documentary, 9/1/02.

64   **"We've got":** Alfred Goldberg et al., *Pentagon 9/11*, Washington, D.C.: Office of the Secretary of Defense, 2007, 13; **agents acted:** CR, 39–, 464n209, Gellman, 114–, int. of Dick Cheney on *Meet the Press*, NBC, 9/16/01. Questions have been raised about the timing of Cheney's move from his office to the underground shelter—to be reported in Ch. 13.

65–6   **P-56/O'Brien:** Spencer, 145–; **horrified controllers:** ibid., 158, *USA Today*, 8/11/02; **fire engine crew:** "Arlington County After-Action Report," www.co.arlington. va.us/fire/edu/about/pdf/after_report.pdf, Annex A, A-4; **policeman:** Goldberg et al., 13; **priest:** Penny Schoner, "Analysis of Eyewitness Statements on 9/11, American Airlines Flight 77 Crash into the Pentagon," www.ratical.org, pt. 8; **Anderson/Benedetto/Riskus:** ibid., pts. 13, 18, 3; **"I looked out":** "Personal Experience at the Pentagon on September 11, 2001," by Penny Elgas, Smithsonian Institution.

66–7   **Jester:** Goldberg et al., 151–; **Boger:** ibid., 27, 64–; **Others heard:** ibid., 137, 134; **fuel/mph/had struck:** ibid., 16–; **"simply melt":** statement of Penny Elgas, http:// americanhistory.si.edu.

67   **"I saw":** The source of this quote is blogger Rebecca Gordon, a resident of Virginia, writing as "Skarlet" on www.punkprincess.com (corr. Rebecca Gordon, 2009, column at Gordon's blog www.meanlouise.com).

67–8   **"I expected":** Christopher Hilton, *The Women's War*, Stroud, U.K.: History Press, 2003; **impact:** Goldberg et al., 17; **dead/injured:** ibid., 23–, 49, 117–, 123; **Morrison/Cruz/ Kurtz/Moody/Gallop:** ibid., 28–; **Marines:** ibid., 53–; **firefighters:** ibid., 64–, 78–, 93–.

69   **CIA briefer/room shaken:** interview of Donald Rumsfeld by

Alfred Goldberg & Rebecca Cameron, "Rumsfeld on Intel," B7, T2, CF; **left office/"it was dark":** Andrew Cockburn, *Rumsfeld*, NY: Scribner, 2007, 1–; **"hundreds":** int. of Rumsfeld; **"people lying":** transcript of Rumsfeld int. for *Parade* magazine, 10/12/01, www.defenselink.mil & see Donald Rumsfeld, *Known and Unknown*, NY: Sentinel, 2011, 336–; **examined/gurney:** Cockburn, 2; **photographed:** Goldberg et al., photo section 82–; **"suit jacket":** Torie Clarke, 221. Victoria "Torie" Clarke, whose timing of 10:15 we have used, took notes of events that day. Rumsfeld himself believed he was back inside the Pentagon from the crash site "shortly before or after 10:00," and then used the phone before proceeding to the Executive Support Center (took notes: int. of Rumsfeld; "shortly before or after": testimony of Donald Rumsfeld, 3/23/04, CO).

69–70   **news reached/escort to advise:** CR, 39, 463n206; **President hurried:** Bamford, *Pretext*, 62; **"Sounds like":** CR, 39; **"They were taxiing":** int. law enforcement officer, now member of Joint Terrorism Task Force, who asked not to be identified; **"like a rocket":** CBS News, 9/10/03; **north-east/west:** corr. Miles Kara, 2011, Stephen Hayes, 341, *St. Petersburg Times*, 7/4/04; **Instead of returning:** CR, 39, 325.

CHAPTER 6

71   **Melodie/Leroy Homer:** int. of Melodie Homer on *American Morning*, CNN, 9/11/06, CR, 11, 456n70, FBI 302 of Tara Campbell, "FBI 302s ACARS," B11, T7, CF; **Dahl nonplussed:** CR, 11, 456n70.

71–2   **"Mayday!"/"Ladies and gentlemen":** "Air Traffic Control Recording," NTSB, 12/21/01. The hijackers' transmission is rendered with minor variations—though essentially the same—in the 9/11 Commission Report, the NTSB's "Air Traffic Control Recording," and the transcript of the Cockpit Voice Recorder prepared for the trial of Zacarias Moussaoui in 2006. We have used the latter (CR, 12, "Air Traffic Control Recording," Government Exhibit P200056T 01-455-A [ID], "Transcript of the Flight Voice Recorder for UA Flight 93, Commission Copy," B17, T7, CF).

72   **panting:** Jere Longman, *Among the Heroes*, NY: Perennial, 2003, 70, 83; **Some investigators:** CR, 12.

72   **Recorder survived:** Every commercial aircraft is required to carry two black boxes that record data about each flight—a

Cockpit Voice Recorder (CVR) and a Flight Data Recorder (FDR). Skeptics have raised questions as to the whereabouts of the recorders that were aboard the four flights that crashed on 9/11. Both of Flight 93's recorders were recovered in readable condition. The CVR for Flight 93 ran on a loop, constantly recording over itself, represented by the thirty-one surviving minutes of sound that we have from inside the cockpit.

The recorders from Flight 77 were found, but only the FDR contained usable data—its CVR was too badly burned to be decipherable.

Both the NTSB and the FBI have said that none of the four recorders from Flights 11 and 175 was located during the cleanup at Ground Zero. A 2003 book reported a claim by former firefighter Nicholas DeMasi to have found three of the four black boxes at Ground Zero during the recovery operation. His account of having found the boxes was corroborated by Mike Bellone, who also worked on the recovery operation. Something that NTSB spokesman Ted Lopatkiewicz told the authors may explain the DeMasi claim. The agency sent several dummy black boxes to Ground Zero, he recalled, specimens to help nonexpert volunteers in the hunt for the real ones. It may be the dummy boxes that DeMasi described (boxes general/re four flights: "Cockpit Voice Recorders & Flight Data Recorders," www.ntsb.gov, CR, 456n76, corr. Ted Lopatkiewicz, 2009; DeMasi: Gail Swanson, *Behind the Scenes at Ground Zero*, NY: TRAC Team, 2003, 108–; Bellone: *CounterPunch*, 12/19/05, *NYDN*, 9/28/05, *NY Post*, 4/5/04, "Black Box Cover-Up," 12/12/04, www.AmericanFreePress.net; FBI/NTSB denied: *CounterPunch*, 12/19/05).

72   **partial record:** The authors have drawn on the transcript as released in 2009; **Welsh:** CR, 455n62, *NYT*, 3/27/02, www.unitedheroes.com; **Green:** CR, 455n62.

73   **cockpit key/coded knock:** Longman, 6. Accounts vary as to whether United attendants carried keys. The FBI was told that "some flight attendants used to carry the cockpit key on their security badge neck chains." Jere Longman, a *New York Times* reporter who has written an excellent book on the Flight 93 hijacking, suggests that attendants did not carry keys (FBI 302 of [name redacted], 12/19/01, "FBI 302s Arestegui," B10, T7, CF, Longman, 6).

73   **forty-nine/tough, etc.:** ibid., 25–, www.flightattendants.org,

Post-Gazette (Pittsburgh), 10/28/01; **Green doubled:** ibid.; **Basmala:** "An Exegesis of the Basmala," http://muslimmatters.org, "Bismillah," defined at http://wahiduddin.net.

74   **voice not heard again:** The 9/11 Commission concluded that the voice recorder data indicated that a flight attendant was "killed or otherwise silenced." United Airlines officials would later tell Deborah Welsh's husband, Patrick, that an attendant was stabbed early in the hijacking, implying that the victim was his wife (CR, 12, *NYT,* 3/27/02).

74   **"We are going back":** As before, the terrorist's words were heard not as intended by the passengers but by ground control and by other aircraft.

74   **Bradshaw/Starfix:** MFR re Richard Belme, 11/21/03, "DOJ Doc. Request 35," B12, T7, CF, MFR 04020029, 5/13/04, MFR 04017218, 11/21/03, "Ref. Lead Control No. SFA62," FBI int. of [name redacted], 9/11/01, INTELWIRE, FBI 302s of Richard Belme, Ray Kime, & Andrew Lubkemann, 9/11/01, "Key 302s," B19, T7, CF. Starfix was the same United facility that had earlier taken a call from an attendant on hijacked Flight 175—see p. 46.

74   **"knives were":** Timeline compiled by Joe Vickers, "Timelines 9-11, 2 of 2," B20, T7, CF.

74   **"lying on the floor":** This information derives from accounts of the phone call made from the plane by passenger Todd Beamer, who from 9:43 used a seatback phone to hold a long conversation with Verizon supervisor Lisa Jefferson. Jefferson said afterward that Beamer was being passed information by a flight attendant whose voice sounded "African-American." Of the two African-American flight attendants on Flight 93, Wanda Green and CeeCee Lyles, the attendant who spoke to Beamer is more likely to have been Lyles—who worked to the rear of the plane (MFR 04020031, 5/11/04, FBI 302 of [name redacted], 9/22/01, INTELWIRE, Lisa Jefferson and Felicia Middlebrooks, *Called,* Chicago: Northfield, 2006, 36, recording of conversation, 5/10/04, "Flight #93 Calls—Todd Beamer," B12, T7, CF).

75   **Sliney first day:** *USA Today,* 8/12/02; **Delta flight:** Spencer, 167, MFR 04017314m, 10/2/03, CR, 10, 455n68, 28; **bomb/"ground stop":** CR, 25, 28.

75   **"Order everyone":** *USA Today,* 8/12/02. There has been controversy over the origin of this order. Secretary of

Transportation Norman Mineta, testifying later to a congressional committee, said *he* "immediately called the FAA, told them to bring all the planes down. . . . [It] was the right thing to do." Bob Woodward and Dan Balz, writing in *The Washington Post*, attributed the decision to land all planes to Mineta. The book *Out of the Blue*, by *The New York Times*'s Richard Bernstein, states that the order was issued by FAA administrator Jane Garvey. Joshua Green, for *Slate*, reported that the decision was in fact taken by the FAA's acting deputy administrator, Monte Belger. The 9/11 Commission credited Sliney, citing the Command Center traffic transcript. In an interview with the authors, FAA spokeswoman Laura Brown emphasized that the decision was collaborative—taken not only by Ben Sliney but also by facility manager Linda Schuessler and other senior staff at the Command Center. Schuessler said as much in a 2001 interview (testimony of Norman Mineta, 5/23/03, CO, *WP*, 1/27/02, Bernstein, 188, *Slate*, 4/1/02, CR, 29, 461n165, int. Laura Brown, *Aviation Week & Space Technology*, 12/17/01, see also Freni, 65, testimony of Monte Belger and Ben Sliney, 6/17/04, CO, MFR 04018154, 4/20/04, MFR 04017327, 7/22/03).

75   **4,540:** Freni, 59; **By 12:16:** *WSJ*, 3/22/04.

76–7   **Clarke's videoconference:** The Commission Report states that the White House teleconference began around 9:25. Information the authors have learned, however, suggests that it started with some—but not all—officials on line at about 9:37. At the Pentagon, a "significant event" conference call—already under way for some minutes—was upgraded to an "air threat" conference call at around the same time. The FAA, for its part, had begun its own teleconference at about 9:20. The White House teleconference, and Clarke's desire to have the most senior representative of each agency participating, had the effect of "decapitating" the agencies at various points. Taking part in the White House conference call meant that individual agency heads were away from the very people from whom they could receive the most accurate incoming information, and to whom they needed to give moment-by-moment instructions (CR, 36–, corr. Miles Kara, 2011); **Defense:** Farmer, 184–, Tenet, 163; **first matter:** Tenet, 163; **contingency/Hastert:** Bamford, *Pretext*, 70–, 80–, transcript, *9/11*, ABC News, 9/11/02, *WP*, 3/2/02; **Byrd:** corr. Jesse Jacobs, 2010; **people pouring:** int. Eleanor Hill; **White**

House evacuation: testimony of Norman Mineta, 5/23/02, CO, Richard Clarke, 8, CNN, 9/11/01, *Newsweek*, 9/24/01; **"CNN says"/"Does it":** Richard Clarke, 9; **humor:** Dwyer & Flynn, 175.

77   **golf club/computers:** Dwyer & Flynn, 175–; **"There's another":** int. Edward Chacia, TF, 12/6/01; **"They hit":** int. James Canham, TF, 12/18/01; **"What happened?":** Dwyer & Flynn, 178.

77–8 **locked doors:** CR, 294. Any faint possibility of going up had vanished at 9:30, when security officers tried and failed to activate a lock release programmed to open all doors—including doors leading to the roof—as explained on p. 22; **Beyea:** Dwyer & Flynn, 178, 243; **Lillo:** int. Manuel Delgado, 10/21/01, TF, *NY Post*, 9/21/01; **"The Chief said"/Suhr:** int. Paul Conlon, TF, 1/26/02, *NY Daily News*, 11/1/01.

78   **"We didn't have":** Staff Statement 13, CO. The World Trade Center did have such a radio repeater system, but most chiefs were unable to use it on the day—either because it was malfunctioning or because they failed to use it properly. To bridge the communications gap, chiefs attempted to use shorter range equipment available—sometimes even their own cell phones—with little success. This left the chiefs in the lobby or outside the towers largely in the dark about the progress of the units moving up and around the building ("FDNY Fire Operations Response on September 11," www.nyc.gov, CR, 188).

78–9 **"People watching"/men struggled:** Staff Statement 13, CO.

79   **towers' casualties/survivors:** "Federal Investigators Classify WTC Victims' Locations," 7/20/04, NIST, Staff Statement 13, CO, Dwyer & Flynn, 252, 312. Estimates vary as to the number of people in the Twin Towers at the time of the attacks. We have here drawn on numbers cited in *102 Minutes*, by Jim Dwyer and Kevin Flynn—which take into account not only the 2005 Final Report of the National Institute of Standards and Technology, but also of figures supplied by the Port Authority of New York (Dwyer & Flynn, 280, "Final Report on the Collapse of the World Trade Center Towers," Washington, D.C.: National Institute of Standards and Technology, Sept. 2005, 19, 34, 37–, 48).

79–80 **Clark/Praimnath:** Bernstein, 225– ; **Rooney:** Banford, *Pretext*, 32–58; **70th floor:** Staff Statement 13, CO; **Palmer:**

Dwyer & Flynn, 206; **PEOPLE TRAPPED:** *NY Daily News,* 9/30/01; **overwhelmed:** Staff Statement 13, CO; **"Some of them":** int. Roberto Abril, TF, 1/17/02.

81   **Turi wondered:** int. Albert Turi, TF, 10/23/01, CR, 302, 549n134—the chief is not identified in line with the 9/11 Commission's agreement with the city of New York, corr. Kristen Wilhelm, 2010.

81–2   **He shared:** int. Peter Hayden, TF, 10/23/01, & see Staff Statement 13, CO; **"The potential"/"I think":** int. Peter Hayden, TF, 10/23/01, Dennis Smith, *Report from Ground Zero,* NY: Viking, 2002, 33; **"Everything above":** *New Yorker,* 2/11/02; **"Tommy":** int. Richard Carletti, TF, 1/2/02; **"I believe":** Dwyer & Flynn, 149–, De Martini's comments were made in an interview for the History Channel, *NYT,* 8/29/03; **707/"low on fuel":** *Seattle Times,* 2/27/93, *MedServ,* 9/11/01, "Painful Losses Mount in the Construction Family," 10/1/01, www.construction.com, "WTC Building Performance Study," FEMA, 5/02, Ch.1.17; **drooping/molten metal:** "World Trade Center Investigation Status," 12/03, & "Investigation of the Sept. 11 World Trade Center Disaster—FAQs," 8/30/06, NIST, "World Trade Center Building Performance Study," Ch. 2., Pt. 2.2.3, FEMA, May 2002; **"large pieces":** CR, 304, 321, 549n148; **9:37 call:** *NY Daily News,* 9/30/01, "Increasing FDNY Preparedness," FDNY report, 8/19/02, 46–.

CHAPTER 7

83   **over Ohio/Flight 93:** "Flight Path Study—United Flight 93," 2/19/02, NTSB, ed. James Boyd, *After September 11,* Saddle River, NJ: Prentice Hall, 2003, 88; **managed to telephone:** MFR 04020029, 5/13/04—detailed study of phone records, used throughout chapter, Moschella to Marcus (& attachments), 4/26/04, "Flight 11 Calls—DOJ Response," B13, T7, CF. In addition to the passengers named in the text, several others succeeded in making or attempted to make calls to the ground. Three who did get through were Linda Gronlund, Lauren Grandcolas, and Joseph DeLuca. Two others, Andrew Garcia and Waleska Martinez, got through only momentarily (several others: MFR 04020029, 5/13/04, Longman, 190).

83   **Bingham:** This is what Bingham said to his aunt by marriage, the first family member to get to the phone. Some, who

question the authenticity of the calls from the air on 9/11, have made much of the fact that—when afterward his mother came on the line—he reportedly said, "Hello, Mom, this is Mark *Bingham* [authors' italics] . . ." No one, the skeptics suggest, would address his own mother with such formality. There is no tape or transcript of the call so far as the authors know—the earliest version of the quote is in an FBI report. Bingham's mother, Alice Hoglan, however, herself remembered her son greeting her that way. To her, she said, it merely showed that he was a "little rattled" and fell back on the way that—as a young businessman—he regularly introduced himself on the phone. One cannot hang any significant doubt on the reported formality—least of all the idea, as some suggest, that the Bingham call itself is part of some complex fabrication. The call, like the other calls from Flight 93, is included in a list of air and cell phone calls compiled with the help of GTE engineers and released in 2009. For further discussion of the "fake calls" issue, see Ch. 11 ("This is Mark"/"*Bingham*": FBI 302 of ints. Alice Hoglan, Carol Phipps, & Kathy Hoglan, 9/11/01, "Flight 93 Calls," B12, T7, CF, FBI 302s of [names redacted], 9/19/01 & 9/23/01, INTELWIRE; doubt: David Ray Griffin, *Debunking 9/11 Debunking*, Northampton, MA: Olive Branch, 2007, 89–, James Fetzer cited in "Osama Tape Appears Fake," PR Web, 5/30/06; "little rattled"/repeatedly: transcript of int. Hoglan, *Newsnight*, 2001, www.bbc.co.uk, int.of Hoglan, *The Flight That Fought Back*, Brook Lapping Productions for Discovery Channel, 2005).

83 **Burnett:** FBI 302 of int. Deena Burnett, 9/11/01, INTEL-WIRE, Longman, 107, MFR 04020024, 4/26/04.

83 **knife point/bomb:** Burnett also told his wife that he thought one of the hijackers had a gun. His wife believed this, because her husband was familiar with guns. Fellow passenger Jeremy Glick, however, specifically told his wife that he saw no guns on the hijackers, only knives. Janet Riffe, an FAA security inspector assigned to American Airlines on 9/11, told the 9/11 Commission that she was told by an American employee that day of a flight attendant's report that Flight 11 passenger Daniel Lewin had been shot. Riffe said she was later told she had been wrongly informed. A partly redacted FBI summary states that passenger Peter Hanson, who phoned his father from Flight 175, said he had seen a flight attendant shot.

Available reports of what Hanson said include no such reference. The presence of guns aboard any of the hijacked flights would of course indicate a grave security lapse. The 9/11 Commission concluded that the reports of guns were mistaken, that the weight of the evidence indicated that knives were the only weapons the hijackers brought on board (Burnett told: MFR 04020024, 4/26/04, Longman, 108; very familiar: *The Times* [London], 8/11/02, bio at www.tomburnettfoundation.org; Glick: *Reader's Digest* [U.K.], 9/06, MFR 04020025, 4/22/04, "FBI Documents—Inc. Joanne Makely Call Transcript," B13, T7, CF; Riffe: MFR 03007067, 9/11/03, "Flight 11 Gun Story," B16, T7, CF; Hanson: Chicago to Director, 9/12/01, FBI 265D-NY-280350-CG, INTELWIRE; Commission: CR 13, 452n25, 457n82).

84–5   **Glick:** *Reader's Digest* (U.K.), 9/06, FBI 302 of Lyzbeth Glick, 9/12/01, INTELWIRE, Longman, 146; **told him/"My God"/"A group":** FBI 302 of int. Deena Burnett, 9/11/01, INTELWIRE, Longman, 110–; **"I'm going":** *Reader's Digest* (U.K.), 9/06; **equipped:** Longman, 19, 108–, 114, 27–,137–, 132–; **Beamer:** ibid., 17–, 200, 202; **Jefferson account:** Jefferson & Middlebrooks, 29–; **"Shit!":** "Recording of Conversation," 9/15/01, "Flight 93 Calls," B12, T7, CF; **"Oh, my God":** Jefferson & Middlebrooks, 44–; **Flight Data Recorder:** "Study of Autopilot, Navigational Equipment, and Fuel Consumption Activity Based on UA Flight 93 and AA Flight 77 Digital Flight Recorder Data," 2/13/02, www.ntsb.gov; **23rd Psalm:** Longman, 200; **"We just lost":** Joseph Gregor, "Air Traffic Control Recording," NTSB, 12/21/01, int. John Werth.

85   **executive jet:** transcript of audiotape, FAA Cleveland Air Traffic Control Center—Lorain position, 9/11/01, int. John Werth, CR, 30. There had not yet been time to comply with the nationwide grounding order. The FAA transcript indicates that the plane that sighted Flight 93 was Executive Jet 956. The authors' reading of relevant sources, including a transcript of the Cleveland Air Traffic Control recording, suggests the Jet 956 sighting occurred soon after 9:41. The 9/11 Commission Report, meanwhile, refers to a sighting of Flight 93 by an aircraft at about 9:53. The sources cited in the Report do not make entirely clear whether this reference is to a sighting by Executive 956 or by another airplane (CR, 29–,

461n167, Full Transcription, "Air Traffic Control System Command Center, National Traffic Management Officer, East Position, 9/11/01," B1, NY Office files, CF, int. John Werth).

86   **navigational aid:** CR, 457n85.

86–7   **Britton:** Interviewed by the FBI after the attacks, Britton's friend Frank Fiumano said he "assumed she had borrowed a cell phone from another passenger" to make her call because Britton's own cell phone was not working. Records released in 2009 make clear, however, that Britton used a seatback phone (Britton's friend: FBI 302 of [name redacted], 9/20/01, & Pittsburgh to Pittsburgh, 9/22/01, INTELWIRE, Longman, 162; 2009 records: United Airlines Flight 93, Telephone Calls, "Flight 11 Calls—Response to DOJ Documents Requests," B13, T7, CF); **plane turning:** "Flight Path Study—United Flight 93," 2/19/02, NTSB; **"I know":** *Reader's Digest* (U.K.), 9/06; **"to jump":** Jefferson & Middlebrook, 52–; **"the impression":** MFR 04020031, 5/11/04; **Greene:** Chicago to Counterterrorism Baltimore et al., 10/4/01, "Flights 175 and 93 Load Patterns," B20, T7, CF, Longman, 182–. Another passenger on Flight 93, Andrew Garcia, had served in the California Air National Guard and trained as an air traffic controller. Even with his limited knowledge of aviation, he might have been of some help in the cockpit. As to the possibility that Greene could conceivably have landed the plane, the authors consulted Gerry Humphries, a working pilot with thirty-five years' experience who regularly flies a plane similar to a King Air (Garcia: *Post-Gazette* [Pittsburgh], 10/28/01, Humphries: int. Gerry Humphries); **Boeing:** "757–200 Technical Characteristics," www.boeing.com; **flying erratically:** "Flight Path Study—United Flight 93," 2/19/02, NTSB; **"commotion":** Longman, 204; **"Are you guys":** MFR 04020031, 5/11/04, FBI 302 of Lisa Jefferson, 9/11/01, INTELWIRE, Longman, 202; **"OK":** *Reader's Digest* (U.K.), 9/06; **Wainio:** www.elizabethwainio.com, Longman, 168, 171–, FBI 302 of [name redacted], 9/12/01, INTELWIRE; **Bradshaw:** MFR of Philip Bradshaw, 6/15/04, "Flight 93 Calls," B12, T7, CF, FBI 302 of int. Philip Bradshaw, 9/11/01 & 9/12/01, INTELWIRE.

87   **Lyles:** Longman, 180. Lyles had phoned her police officer husband earlier. He had been asleep, after coming home from a night shift, and she had left a message on the answering

machine (FBI 302 of int. Lorne Lyles, 9/17/01, "FBI 302s Homer," B10, T7, CF).

87–91   **"I think":** FBI 302 of [name redacted], 9/12/01, INTEL-WIRE; **Burnett's wife recognized:** MFR 04020024, 4/26/04; **rolling:** "Flight Path Study—United Flight 93," 2/19/02, NTSB; **"The wings started":** pilot Bill Wright cited at Longman, 192–, *Flight 93's Last Moments*, WTAE TV, 9/19/01, & see CR, 30; **Glick's father-in-law/"roller coaster":** *Reader's Digest* (U.K.), 9/06; **"wind sounds":** FBI 302 of int. [name redacted], 9/12/01, INTELWIRE.

91   **scrapyard:** *St. Petersburg Times*, 9/12/01; **"nosediving":** *WP*, 9/16/01; **"sort of whistling":** *St. Petersburg Times*, 9/12/01; **"barely fifty":** *The Mirror* (U.K.), 9/12/02.

91   **It was 10:03:** For the time Flight 93 crashed, the authors have relied—as did the 9/11 Commission—on the impact time established by the combination of the Cockpit Voice Recorder, the Flight Data Recorder, and Air Traffic Control and radar data. In 2002, geologists at the Lamont-Doherty Earth Observatory produced a report—based on seismic data—that put the impact time of Flight 93 as some three minutes later, at 10:06. In the years since, the scientists themselves have stressed that the seismic signals cited in respect to Flight 93 were too weak and speculative to be relied upon. It should be noted, too, that the NTSB does not characteristically rely on seismic data to establish crash time. Commission staff considered the Lamont-Doherty time of 10:06 to be a significant anomaly and therefore asked for the time according to satellite infrared imaging—as a "tiebreaker." This further established the 10:03 time for the crash of UA 93. The timing discrepancy has been seized on by those who suggest the U.S. military shot down Flight 93, an issue that will be addressed in Ch. 12 (CR, 30, 461n168, Won-Young Kim & Gerald Baum, "Seismic Observations During September 11, 2001 Terrorist Attack," Spring 2002, corr. Won-Young Kim, Ted Lopatkiewicz, 2009, & see Terry Wallace cited in "Cockpit Voice Recording Ends Before Flight 93's Official Time of Impact," 9/16/02, www.phillynews.com, corr. Terry Wallace, 2010, Miles Kara, 2011).

91–2   **strip mine/"Where's the plane":** "Flight 93 Crash Site Left Most of the Horror to the Imagination," KDKA radio, 2006; **crater burning/couple of feet:** *Post-Gazette* (Pittsburgh),

9/12/01; **recorder buried:** *WP,* 9/15/01; **clothing:** *Post-Gazette* (Pittsburgh), 9/12/01. All sorts of identifiable bits and pieces would eventually be collected at the crash site. Douglass personal effects administrators would circulate a list and photographs of many personal items that had belonged to those aboard Flight 93—pieces of jewelry, snapshots, clothing, and shoes. Jeremy Glick's widow, Lyz, recognized a picture of a pair of black briefs as her husband's. An American Express personal organizer was returned to her, with notes in Glick's still legible handwriting (*Reader's Digest* [U.K.], 9/06).

92 **"shiny stuff":** *WP,* 9/14/01; **Lisa Beamer:** Longman, 220–; **Lyz Glick/father:** Moschella to Marcus (& attachments), 4/26/04, & see *Reader's Digest* (U.K.), 9/06.

CHAPTER 8

93 **Peruggia/instructions:** int. John Peruggia, TF, 10/25/01. The Office of Emergency Management was in the building known as World Trade Center 7, which would itself collapse later in the day. Mayor Rudolph Giuliani apparently never made it to the OEM that morning, because the building was being evacuated. He set up a temporary base elsewhere (CR, 283–, 293, 301–, 305, 311, Rudolph Giuliani with Ken Kurson, *Leadership,* NY: Hyperion, 2002, 5–, but see also Barrett & Collins, 5–); **engineer/Peruggia/Zarrillo:** int. Peruggia, int. Richard Zarrillo, TF, 10/25/01, Dwyer & Flynn, 203–; **command and control:** CR, 301–.

94 **"We stared"/"You know":** *A Survivor's Story,* www.pbs.org/wgbh/nova/wtc/above.html.

94 **Cosgrove/911:** *Newsday,* 4/10/06, Dwyer & Flynn, 207; **Rooney:** *Chicago Tribune,* 10/31/01.

95 **"Listen":** int. Zarrillo, int. Steven Mosiello, TF, 10/23/01.

95 **"started to lean":** int. Richard Carletti, TF, 1/21/02; **"bulge out"/"snapping sounds":** *NY Daily News,* 9/11/01; **"real loud"/"groaning":** e.g., entry for 9:59 a.m., September 11, 2001, "Some Witnesses Hear Explosions," www.cooperativeresearch.org, Jim Marrs, *The Terror Conspiracy,* NY: The Disinformation Co., 2006, 47. Critics of official accounts of 9/11 have used such references to "explosions" to suggest that the Twin Towers collapsed at least partially as the result of explosive devices planted in the buildings. Those claims will be covered in Chapter 11.

96 **"The entire":** *The Independent* (U.K.), 9/12/01.

96 **Jennings/Dahler:** transcript & video on YouTube, "ABC News Special Report: Planes Crash into World Trade Center," 9/11/01, *9/11*, ABC News, 9/11/02; **9:59:** CR, 305—more precisely, 9:58:59. The 9/11 Commission Report used the figure of ten seconds. For the collapse time of some twenty seconds, the authors have relied on explanations by the National Institute of Standards and by scientist Ryan Mackey, who estimated that it took fifteen to twenty seconds for the tower's roof to hit the ground (CR, 305–,"NIST's Investigation of the Sept. 11 World Trade Center Disaster—FAQ," 8/30/06, http://wtc.nist.gov, Ryan Mackey, "On *Debunking 9/11 Debunking*," 5/24/08, www.jod911.com); **"From a structure":** int. James Cannon, TF, 12/18/01.

97–8 **garages:** int. Pedro Carrasquillo, TF, 10/16/01; **"I took":** int. Zarrillo; **"I grabbed":** int. Peruggia; **"Everybody's like":** int. Jody Bell, TF, 12/15/01; **"smoked"/"Everything started":** int. Timothy Brown, TF, 1/15/02; **16 firefighters:** CR, 308; **Marriott sliced:** "The 9/11 Hotel, pt. 3 of 5" documentary on www.youtube.com; **"stared in awe":** "A Survivor's Story"; **"huge tidal":** *The Independent* (U.K.), 9/12/01; **"all the walking":** *NY Daily News*, 9/11/01.

99–100 **few aware:** Staff Statement 13, CO, int. Joseph Pfeifer, TF, 10/23/01; **"We felt it":** int. Michael Brodbeck, TF, 12/10/01; **"You just":** int. Derek Brogan, TF, 12/28/01; **"It didn't register":** int. James Canham, TF, 12/18/01; **"To think that":** Staff Statement 13, CO; **burst of energy:** Dwyer & Flynn, 242; **pitch black:** int. Peter Hayden, TF, 10/23/01; **fatally for some:** Smith, 30–; **Judge:** *USA Today*, 2/19/03, Bernstein, 231; **Pfeifer:** int. Pfeifer, int. Joseph Callan, TF, 11/2/01, Smith, 42–; **evacuation:** Staff Statement 13, CO.

100 **"get the fuck":** The 9/11 Commission credited Picciotto both with the "Get the fuck out!" initiative and with the radioed instructions. He himself said words to that effect on a CBS television show days after 9/11. His autobiographical accounts of events later in the day, however, have been rebutted by colleagues ("Get!"/radioed: CR, 307, 550n165; CBS show: transcript of int., *Montel Williams Show*, 9/17/01; autobiography: Richard Picciotto with Daniel Paisner, *Last Man Down*, NY: Berkley, 2002; rebutted: *NY Daily News*, 11/26/02, *New York*, 9/11/03).

100 **"knew that he had men":** int. Mosiello; **"We're not fucking":** CR, 310, 552n183; **McGinnis:** Dwyer & Flynn, 237.

101   **"What we didn't"**: "Emergency Preparedness & Response," Staff Statement 13, CO; **blind:** int. Callan, Staff Statement 13, CO.

101   **"There was gas"**: int. Derek Brogan, TF, 12/28/01. The Twin Towers were sheathed in aluminium (e.g., see "Cladding Fragment," exhibit description, Division of Work & Industry, National Museum of American History).

101   **"littering"**: int. Robert Byrne, TF, 12/7/01; **Pilots:** ibid., NYPD Call Routing & Message Dispatch Report, 7/23/02, "NYPD folder," B9, NY Office files, CF, CR, 309, 551n176.

101–2   **10:28:** CR, 311; **"do a little rock"**: int. Carletti; **"explosions"/"pop"/"thunderous"**: int. Craig Carlsen, TF, 1/25/02, int. Pfeifer; **"the entire"**: int. Dean Beltrami, TF, 12/17/01; **"looking like"**: int. Bell; **"I opened up"**: int. James Basile, TF, 10/17/01; **"This beautiful"**: Staff Statement 13, CO; **twenty seconds:** see note at source entry for "9:59," above.

102–3   **alarms:** Lance, 419; **343:** CR, 311; **firefighters killed:** Smith, 193; **Ganci:** int. Mosiello, Bernstein, 149, 231; **brother Kevin:** http://americanhistory.si.edu/September11, www .septembereleven.net; **families:** Smith, 33, 53, 15, 44, 349, Damon DiMarco, *Tower Stories*, NY: Revolution, 2004, 189, Langewiesche, 70, 131–, 145–; **Port Authority/NYPD dead:** CR, 311; **Morrone:** Port Authority press release, 8/13/02, www.PANYNJ.gov; **5 dead PAPD:** William Keegan with David Bart, *Closure*, NY: Touchstone, 2006, 67; **policewoman:** Smith, 67, *NY Daily News*, 3/24/02, www.irishtribute.com entry for Moira Smith.

103   **"The number"**: transcript of press conference, CNN, 9/11/01; **7,000:** John Ashcroft cited in MFR 04020543, 12/17/03, & see Knight Ridder report, 10/11/01.

103   **2,763:** The authors' rendering of the total number of 9/11 deaths in New York City includes the ten hijackers of the two planes that hit the Trade Center. The figure used in the 9/11 Commission Report did not include the hijackers, nor did it include three victims injured that day whose deaths were registered later outside New York. The total used here does not include those deemed to have died of illnesses contracted as a result of 9/11, an issue that will be covered elsewhere (CR, 311, 552n188, "World Trade Center Operational Statistics," Office of the Chief Medical Examiner, 1/30/09, *NYT*, 7/22/04, ed. Robyn Gershon, *High Rise Building*

Evacuation, Chicago: Univ. of Chicago Press, 2006, 19, CR, 552n188); **other countries:** *NYT,* 4/19/02; **immigrants:** *Hoy,* cited by *AM New York,* 9/7/06.

104 **Ground Zero:** The term "Ground Zero" appears to have been used for the first time on the evening of 9/11, by CBS reporter Jim Axelrod (CBS News, 9/11/01, video at www.archive.org); **"All that remained"/final throes:** Langewiesche, 6, 4, www.national911memorial.org; **lesser giants:** frontispiece, ibid., "World Trade Center Building Performance Study," Washington, D.C.: FEMA, May 2002, 3–.

105–6 **WTC 7:** "Final Report on the Collapse of World Trade Center Building 7," Federal Building and Fire Safety Investigation of the World Trade Center Disaster, Washington, D.C.: NIST, 11/08, NCSTAR 1A, 4.2. There has been a long-running controversy about the collapse of WTC 7—the thrust of it being the suggestion that the building collapsed not solely because of fire and damage but, skeptics suggest, because explosives were used. The controversy will be covered in Ch. 11; **Verizon:** MFR 04018174, 2/25/04, DiMarco, 302–, Smith, 198–; **NY Stock Exchange:** MFR 03013078, 12/11/03, MFR 04016224, 1/21/04; **American Stock Exchange:** MFR 04014516, 1/14/04; **"visiting":** MFR 04017265, 12/18/03; **NASDAQ:** MFR 04014517, 1/14/04; **Federal Reserve NY:** MFR 04016224, 1/21/04; **Greenspan:** MFR 04014512, 1/9/04, MFR 04018180, 1/20/04, MFR 04016224, 1/21/04; **liquidity/ATMs:** MFR 04014512, 1/9/04, MFR 04016224, 1/21/04, MFR 04018180, 1/20/04; **$83/95 billion:** *Real Estate Weekly,* 9/11/02.

CHAPTER 9

107 **"Ambulances going":** int. Michael Cahill, TF, 10/17/01; **Melisi:** "America Rebuilds," transcript of int. Melisi, www.pbs.org.

108 **Two civilians:** They were Tom Canavan, who had worked at First Union Bank on the 47th floor of the North Tower, and a second, unknown man who escaped with him (*USA Today,* 9/5/02).

108–9 **Jonas & rescued group:** "A Day in September," www.recordonline.com, "World Trade Center Survivors," http://911research.wtc7.net, Picciotto with Paisner, 128–,

New York, 11/26/02; **Buzzelli:** *USA Today*, 9/5/02, Langewiesche, 103–; **McLoughlin/Jimeno/Marines:** *Slate*, 9/10/02, *NY Post*, 8/7/06, *Times Herald-Record*, 1/18/02. The two former Marines were David Karnes, at the time an accountant with Deloitte Touche, and Jason Thomas, who on 9/11 was attending the John Jay College of Criminal Justice in New York City.

110 **fellow overboard:** Langewiesche, 62.

110–11 **"onslaught":** MFR 04018541, 4/15/04; **personnel/ surgeons:** int. Dr. Glenn Asaeda, TF, 10/11/01; **by midnight:** "DOD Medical Support to the Federal Response Plan," Washington, D.C.: Office of the Inspector General, Dept. of Defense, 5/10/02, 7; **"A person's torso":** int. Benjamin Badillo, TF, 1/24/02; **"I-beams":** int. Charles Blaich, TF, 10/23/01; **"A woman's":** DiMarco, 270; **"The body":** eds. *Der Spiegel*, 243; **"You couldn't":** Barrett & Collins, 248; **21,744:** *New York*, 1/7/10; **medical examiner:** *NYT*, 7/14/02, & see "World Trade Center Operational Statistics," Office of the Chief Medical Examiner, NYC, 9/9/03; **2009:** update, "DNA Testing of Remains," 2/1/09, Office of the Chief Medical Examiner, www.nyc.gov; **Deutsche Bank:** "Deutsche Bank Building—FAQ," Lower Manhattan Development Corporation, www.renewny.com; **manholes/road:** AP, 4/8/08.

111 **Fresh Kills:** *NYT*, 3/24/07. According to a sworn affidavit by Eric Beck, a supervisor for Taylor Recycling, the process at Fresh Kills involved creating a mixture used to pave city streets and fill potholes. Troubled by the implication that fragments of their loved ones may have become part of this mixture, relatives of the dead went to federal court in 2007 to plead that the sifted debris be removed from the site and reburied in a more appropriate setting on a site nearby. In 2009, a judge dismissed the families' suit, citing in part the city's intention of redeveloping the now closed Fresh Kills landfill into a park and nature reserve that would include a memorial to the 9/11 victims (*NYT*, 3/24/07, *Staten Island Advance*, 7/7/08, *NY Post*, 7/8/08); **also sent:** *WP*, 2/28/12; **1,229:** *NYT*, 7/14/02; **404:** authors' calculation based on figures in *NYT*, 7/14/02, 5/12/11, ABC News, 5/13/11, *Las Vegas Review Journal*, 2/10/12, and press release, Office of the Chief Medical Examiner, 2/12/12.

112–16 **"I see this":** int. Jason Charles, TF, 1/23/02; **"The** ambulances": int. Michael Cahill, TF, 10/17/01; **"People were"**: int. Richard Broderick, TF, 10/25/01; **"Nobody could"**: int. David Blacksberg, TF, 10/23/01; **"Everybody's coughing"**: int. Jody Bell, TF, 12/15/01; **"Our face-pieces"**: int. Paul Bessler, TF, 1/21/02; **"My lungs were"**: int. Paul Adams, TF, 11/1/01; **"The sergeant asked"**: int. Jason Charles, TF, 1/23/02; **9:59/FC:** *NY Daily News*, 9/30/01; **asbestos, etc., in dust:** "EPA's Response to the World Trade Center Collapse," Washington, D.C., Office of the Inspector General, Environmental Protection Agency, 8/21/03, Cate Jenkins [EPA] to Monona Rossol, 11/15/01, www.whitelung.org, *NYT,* 9/14/01, *Newsweek,* 10/5/01, *Der Spiegel,* 12/20/06, DiMarco, 130, Gail Sheehy, *Middletown, America,* NY: Random House, 2003, 41; **seven blocks:** *Village Voice,* 7/31/07; **"We lost"/Torcivia:** DiMarco, 191–, *St. Petersburg Times,* 2/3/02; **2007 study:** UPI, 5/9/07; **2,000 firefighters:** *Guardian* (U.K.), 1/28/08; **"The World Trade Center dust"**: Voice of America, 4/8/10; **young attorney:** (Felicia Dunn-Jones) "NYC Links First Death to Toxic Dust," www.msnbc.com, 5/23/07; **"sick and under"**: Fact Sheet, http://stws.org, *Sacramento Bee,* 1/6/11; **479 people:** *NY Post,* 9/6/09; **One by one:** e.g., *WSJ,* 12/9/10, *Dallas Morning News,* 11/29/10, *New York Post,* 1/10/11, *NY Daily News,* 3/30/11; **risen to 664:** *NY Post,* 9/12/10; **James Zadroga Act/ \$4.2 billion/"We will never"**: *USA Today,* 2/2/11, H.R. 847 James Zadroga 9/11 Health & Compensation Act 2010, http://thomas.loc.gov; **cancer:** *WSJ,* 2/17/12, *Downtown Express,* 4/11/12, Fox News, 3/5/12, NY1.com, 2/13/12, *Brooklyn Daily Eagle,* 2/13/12, *NYT,* 6/8/12; **"very reassuring"**: "EPA's Response to the WTC Collapse"; **"safe to go"**: ibid., *NYT,* 9/18/01.

116   **"safe to breathe"**: "EPA's Response to the WTC Collapse." John Henshaw has since explained that a decision not to enforce safety regulations was made because of the delay that would have caused: "We had to deploy a strategy that achieved compliance as soon as the hazard was recognized so corrective action was immediate." Christine Todd Whitman, for her part, told a congressional committee that allegations that she misled New Yorkers about air quality in lower Manhattan were "outright falsehoods." She said that reassurances that air quality was safe applied to lower Manhattan, not to Ground Zero itself (*EHS Today,* 6/27/07).

116   **"I want":** Richard Clarke, 24. The President also discussed
the closure of the markets with his assistant for economic
policy, Larry Lindsey, urging a "return to normal as soon as
possible." Lindsey discussed with the EPA's Christine Todd
Whitman "the need to get the financial markets open
quickly." Whitman has denied that Lindsey pressured her.
The EPA's own inspector general, meanwhile, has said that the
Agency's press releases were "influenced" by the White House
Council on Environmental Quality. According to the EPA's
Tina Kreischer, there was "extreme pressure from the White
House" (Lindsey: MFR 04018180, 1/20/04; Whitman denied:
CR, 555n13; "influenced"/"extreme pressure": "EPA's
Response to the WTC Collapse," 7, 16–, CR, 555n13).

116–17 **9:55:** CR, 325; **"The President":** *9/11*, transcript, ABC
News, 9/11/02; **Card:** White House transcripts of ints. of
Andy Card for ABC, 8/12/02, CNN, 8/12/02, NBC, 8/15/02,
CBS, 8/16/02; **Bush said:** CR, 40, 464n212; **"inexcusable":**
60 Minutes, transcript, CBS News, 9/11/02; **"could not
remain":** Kean & Hamilton, 265; **"The military":** *60
Minutes*, 9/11/02; **flickering TV:** *9/11*, ABC News;
"credible" threat/Armed guards: CR, 325, 554n1, *60
Minutes*, Bill Sammon, *Fighting Back*, Washington, D.C.:
Regnery, 2008, 128; **cell phones:** *Salon*, 9/12/01; **saluted:**
Spencer, 255–.

118   **baseless scare:** The Secret Service tracked down the source
of the "threat" within hours, and concluded that the flap had
arisen because of a watch officer's misunderstanding. Even so,
press secretary Fleischer would still be talking of the threat at
a press briefing the next day—and describing it as having been
"real and credible" (CR, 554n1).

118–20 **"The American people":** *60 Minutes*; **"faceless coward":**
CNN, 9/12/01; **running backward:** int. Dan Alcorn, *Salon*,
9/12/01; **"We're at war":** *60 Minutes*, 9/11/02; **"very much
in control":** *World-Herald* (Omaha), 2/27/02; **took part:**
Sammon, 122; **"I'm not going":** *Telegraph* (U.K.), 12/16/01;
"tin-horn terrorist": *60 Minutes*, 9/11/02; **"increasingly
difficult":** *Telegraph* (U.K.), 12/16/01; **"The mightiest":**
9/11, ABC News; **"We will stand":** CNN, 9/12/01, Graham
with Nussbaum, 100; **Bush address:** *60 Minutes*, 9/11/02,
BBC News, 9/12/01; **key officials:** CR, 330; **al
Qaeda/Taliban:** *WP*, 1/27/02.

120   **"You know":** The authors have here cited Clarke's interview

with *Vanity Fair* in 2009, in which he stated that Rumsfeld made these remarks on the night of September 11. In his 2004 memoir, however, Clarke appeared to indicate that the remarks were made at a meeting the following day (*Vanity Fair*, 2/09, Richard Clarke, 31).

120–1 **bed early:** *Telegraph* (U.K.), 1/15/08; **He balked, etc.:** *Newsweek*, 12/3/01, Sammon, 133–; **"Incoming plane!":** Spencer, 282, 279; **Ground Zero:** DiMarco, 269–.

121 **one more survivor:** This was Genelle Guzman, who had worked for the Port Authority in the North Tower and was found in the same area as was Pasquale Buzzelli earlier. She suffered serious leg injuries, but recovered in the hospital (*Time*, 9/1/02, Langewiesche, 107).

121 **"heaved":** Langewiesche, 72; **flames:** Barrett & Collins, 247; **would burn:** ABC News, 12/19/01.

Part II: DISTRUST AND DECEIT

CHAPTER 10

125–6 **"not a fringe":** *Time*, 9/3/06; **"no dependable":** Matt Taibbi, *The Great Derangement*, NY: Spiegel & Grau, 2009, 189; **"tend to be"/poll:** *San Diego Union Tribune*, 12/4/06; **18 to 29:** "Questions with Kathryn Olmsted," 4/13/09, http://theaggie.org; **Arab Americans/Arabs worldwide:** *NY Post*, 5/23/07, "Muslim Public Opinion on US Policy, Attacks on Civilians and al Qaeda, 2007" & "No Public Consensus on Who Was Behind 9/11, 2008," www.worldpublicopinion.org; **"well-educated, pious":** Taibbi, 171; **"conspiracy theories dominate":** Najwa bin Laden, Omar bin Laden, and Jean Sasson, *Growing Up bin Laden*, NY: St. Martins, 2009, 290; **"unfounded":** "The Top September 11 Conspiracy Theories," 5/5/09, www.america.gov.

127 **MIHOP/LIHOP:** BBC News, 7/4/08, *Vanity Fair*, 8/06; **As late as 2011:** *Conspiracy vs. Science*, National Geographic Channel, & see re first aired *NY Post*, 9/2/09.

127–32 **Rostcheck/"Is it just":** corr. David Rostcheck, 2010, Rostcheck message on USAttacked@topica.net, 9/11/01, 3:12 p.m., cited on www.serendipity.li, Rostcheck profile, www.linkedin.com, Rostcheck to Ira Glasser, ACLU, 7/4/01, www.keepand beararms.com; **million Web pages:** *NY Post*, 9/12/06; **"I don't believe"/"conspiracy":** "Who We Are," &

"Criminal Negligence or Treason," www.emperors-clothes.com; **"for thinking people":** See the "About" page on Meyer's website, www.serendipity.li; **doubt expressed:** "Reply to Popular Mechanics," www.serendipity.li; **Valentine:** Valentine articles, "Operation 911: No Suicide Pilots," 10/6/01, www.public-action.com, "Internet Censorship and Jewish Destiny," http://library.flawlesslogic.com, "Waco Holocaust Electronic Museum: Fire," www.public-action.com, & "Waco Suits for Waco Suckers," www.web-ak.com;**Vialls/"electronically hijacked":** "Flight 93 Saddest Flight of All," and various Vialls articles at www.vialls.homestead.com, "Home Run, Electronically Hijacking the WTC Attack Aircraft," 10/01, www.geocities.com; **"very strange":** "Reality Check," No. 82, 10/12/01, www.ratical.org; **Dewdney:** "Ghost Riders in the Sky," 1/22/02, www.ilaam.net; **"ordered to land":** "Operation Pearl," 8/03, www.seren dipity.li; **Dewdney professor:** Dewdney bio. on University of W. Ontario website, www .csd.uwo.ca; **North Ph.D:** www.garynorth.com; **"aeronautical engineer":** www.vialls.homestead.com; **Valentine:** "About" page on www.comeandhear.com; **Meyer degrees:** "Interzine" int. of Meyer at www.deoxy.org; **Christian/"attempt to apply":** see masthead of North's periodical *Remnant Review* & see Gary North & Gary DeMar, *Christian Reconstructionism: What It Is, What It Isn't,* Tyler, TX: Institute for Christian Economics, 1984; **Cuba "soon":** "China Backs Iran Against the Great Satan," 12/22/04, www.web.archive.org, "Why the March 8.7 Quake Did Not Cause a Tsunami," www.whale.to; **Waco Museum/shot:** "Waco Holocaust Electronic Museum: Catalogue of Evidence," www.public-action.com, "Internet Censorship & Jewish Destiny," 11/8/98, http://library.flawlesslogic.com; **Meyer indulged/"Timewave Zero":** "Interview of TWZ Programmer Peter Meyer," *Interzine*, issue 2, http://deoxy.org, "DMT & Hyperspace," & "Interpretations of the Experience" by Peter Meyer, *Psychedelic Monographs & Essays*, no. 6, www.lycaeum.org.

132–4   *The Big Lie:* Thierry Meyssan, *9/11: The Big Lie*, NY: Carnot, 2002, esp. 24, 28, 39, 56, 60, 139, www.effroyable-imposture.net, eds. David Dunbar & Brad Reagan, *Debunking 9/11 Myths*, NY: Hearst, 2006, 60. The book was first published in France as *L'Effroyable Imposture*, which translates as

The Appalling Deception; **Griffin bio/"dean" of opposition:** e.g., Griffin as "high priest of the 'truther' movement," *The News Statesman* (U.K.), 9/24/09; **"show that the attacks":** Griffin speech, University of Wisconsin, 4/18/05, *BookTV*, C-SPAN2; *Loose Change:* viewable on www.youtube.com in various editions—the authors have primarily viewed *Loose Change—The Final Cut* (Louder Than Words, 2007) and *Loose Change 9/11—An American Coup* (Collective Minds Media, 2009); **125 million:** "Fact Sheet," www.loosechange911.com; **"This is our":** *Vanity Fair,* 8/06; **$2,000/$1 million:** "Fact Sheet"; **Avery:** "Bios," www.loosechange911.com; **"to get the":** Barrie Zwicker, *Towers of Deception,* Gabriola Island, B.C.: New Society, 2006, 303.

135   **Falk/foreword:** to U.S. edition of David Ray Griffin, *The New Pearl Harbor,* Northampton, MA: Interlink, 2004, foreword also posted at www.transnational.org, & see *Jerusalem Post,* 1/27 & 1/31/11; Falk has praised the professor's work as "objective and compelling" as recently as 2008—and his comments on 9/11 were still causing controversy in early 2011. He referred then to "the apparent cover up" (Richard Falk, "9/11: More than Meets the Eye," 11/9/08, www.journal-online.co.uk, Sky News, 1/29/11, "Interrogating the Arizona Killings from a Safe Distance, 1/11/11," http://richardfalk.wordpress.com).

135   **Internet groups:** David Ray Griffin, *The Mysterious Collapse of World Trade Center 7,* Northampton, MA: Olive Branch, 2010, 5; **skeptics:** e.g., "Reply to Scientific American's Attempted Debunking of 9/11 Skeptics," www.serendipity.li.

135   **Fetzer/Jones:** Fetzer bio, www.d.umn.edu; Jones CV, www.physics.byu.edu, *Deseret News* (Salt Lake City), 10/22/06. Fetzer's group retains the name Scholars for 9/11 Truth, while Jones' group took the name Scholars for 9/11 Truth and Justice. The appellation "Scholars" is loose—the membership ranges from people with Ph.D.'s in anything from physics to classics to French, medical doctors and dentists, attorneys, college students, and a yoga instructor. In a public statement in 2005, Jones's department and college administrators at Brigham Young University said they were "not convinced that his analyses and hypotheses [on 9/11] have been submitted to relevant scientific venues that would ensure rigorous technical peer review." Jones took early retirement in 2007 (membership ranges: "Full Member List,"

www.911scholars.org, "Members," http://stj911.org; Jones: "BYU Discredits Prof. Jones for 9/11 WTC Paper!," by Greg Szymanski, 11/29/05, www.rense.com, Jones CV, *Deseret News* [Salt Lake City], 10/22/06).

135–8 **members "believe"/"established"/"high-tech":** "Scholars for 9/11 Truth—Who Are We?" & "Scholars: On Its First Anniversary," www.9/11scholars.org; **"discretion"/ "Scientific":** "What Is the Goal of the 9/11 Truth Community?," by Steven Jones, http://stj911.org; **"inside job":** *Guardian* (U.K.), 9/5/06; **MacDonald:** cited at www .patriotsquestion911.com; **Reynolds:** "Bush Insider Says WTC Collapse Bogus," by Greg Szymanski, undated 2005, www.americanfreepress.net; **Roberts:** "What We Don't Know About 9/11," by Paul Roberts, 8/16/06, www.informationclearinghouse.info; **CIA veterans:** "Seven CIA Veterans Challenge 9/11 Commission Report," 9/23/07, www.opednews.com; **Christison:** "Stop Belittling the Theories About September 11," 8/14/06, www.dissidentvoice.org; **Charlie Sheen:** int. on *Alex Jones Show*, 3/20/06; **Cotillard:** "Plus Fort Que Thierry Meyssan," 2/29/08, www.marianne2.fr; **Lynch:** int. on *Wereldgasten*, VPRO (Dutch TV), 12/3/06; **O'Donnell:** *The View*, ABC News, 3/29/07; **Nelson:** int. on *Alex Jones Show*, 2/4/08; **Ventura:** "9/11," *Conspiracy Theory with Jesse Ventura*, 12/9/09, www.trutv.com, int. on *Alex Jones Show*, 4/2/08; Jesse Ventura with Dick Russell, *American Conspiracies*, NY: Skyhorse, 2010; **Hirschhorn:** "Painful 9/11 Truth," by Joel Hirschhorn, www.blogcritics.org, bio on http://word.world-citizenship.org; **Deets:** profile on www.ae911truth.org—the adjective "pyroclastic" is used to refer to material formed by volcanic or igneous action; **Erickson:** profile on www.ae911truth.org; **Griscom:** Griscom blog, www.impactglassman.blogspot.com; **Waser:** profile on www.ae911truth.org; **thousand architects & engineers:** Examples of others who have made their views known on the collapses, or joined their names to petitions, include: *In the United States:*

Dr. Robert Bowman, formerly an Air Force lieutenant colonel who served as director of Advanced Space Programs Development, questioned the towers' collapses and called for a new investigation (bio on www.thepatriots.us)

Major Jon Fox, former Marine Corps fighter pilot and pilot

for Continental Airlines, thought research "proved" the use of explosives (statement to http://patriots question911.com)

Former Navy commander Dennis Henry, who worked as a civil engineer for thirty-four years, doubted the simple collapse account (profile on www.ae911truth.org)

Commander Ralph Kolstad, former fighter pilot and commercial airline captain, said the collapse story did not "make any sense" (statement to http://patriotsquestion911-.com)

Joel Skousen, a fighter and commercial airplane pilot, thought there was "significant evidence that the airplane impacts did not cause the collapse" ("Debunking the Debunkers," by Joel Skousen, 2/14/06, www.rense.com)

Roy Andes, a former assistant attorney general of the state of Montana, signed a petition on the collapses (petition at www.ae911truth.org)

Barbara Honegger, a senior military affairs journalist at the Naval Postgraduate School, suggested that "the U.S. military, not al Qaeda, had the sustained access weeks before 9/11 to also plant controlled demolition charges throughout the superstructures of WTC 1 and WTC 2, and in WTC 7, which brought down all three buildings" ("The Pentagon Attack Papers," by Barbara Honegger, www.physics911.net)

Karen Johnson, a member of the Arizona state legislature, expressed doubt about the collapses and joined her name to a call for a new investigation (*Arizona Republic*, 5/3/08, petition at www.ae911truth.org)

William Nugent, former assistant director of research for Technology Services at the Library of Congress, thought "controlled demolition the only scientifically plausible explanation" of the collapses (statement at www.ae911truth. org)

Lon Waters, a former staff member of a Defense Department–funded computing and research facility in Hawaii, signed the architects and engineers' petition on the collapses (petition at www.ae911truth.org)

Outside the United States:

In Denmark: Commander Jens Claus Hansen, of the Danish Defense Academy, thought "bombs must have been placed inside the Trade Center towers" (http://patriots question911.com)

In Finland: Heikki Kurtila, a veteran in the investigation of pressure-vessel explosion accidents, said the "great speed of the [Building 7] collapse and the resistance factor strongly suggest controlled demolition" ("Collapse Examination of WTC7," by Heikki Kurtila, 11/18/05, www.syyskuun11.ja)

In Japan: Yukihisa Fujita, a member of the upper house of the Diet, included doubt about the collapses in a forty-minute presentation to the Committee on Foreign Affairs in 2008 (http://patriotsquestion911.com)

In Malaysia: Former prime minister Tun Mahathir bin Mohammad expressed doubts about the collapses and said he "could believe" the U.S. government would organize the strikes to have an excuse for war in Iraq ("No Place for War Criminals," 10/6/07, www.globalresearch.ca)

In Norway: Lieutenant Commander Rolf Hustad, a navy weapons specialist, said the statistical likelihood of the "only three steel-framed buildings ever to collapse [due to fire] . . . is just too remote to grasp" (profile at www.ae911truth.org)

In Switzerland: Lieutenant Colonel Albert Stahel, senior lecturer in strategic studies at the Federal Institute of Technology, has raised questions about the collapses, and especially about Building 7 ("Je Mehr Wir Forschen, Desto Mehr Zweifeln Wir," 9/15/06, www.blick.ch)

Celebrities:

Actors Ed Asner, Juliette Binoche, Janeane Garofalo, and Woody Harrelson have expressed doubts in a more general sense (*Post Gazette* [Pittsburgh], 11/27/06, Asner letter, 4/26/04, www.septembereleventh.org, *Telegraph* [U.K.], 9/1/07, http://patriots question911.com)

138   **Nelson:** "Aircraft parts and the Precautionary Principle," www.physics911.net, bio. at www.patriotsquestion911.com.

138–9 **Latas:** bio. at www.latasgroup.com, int. of Jeff Latas for Pilots for 9/11 Truth, audio on www.youtube.com; the Flight Data Recorder from Flight 77 was recovered from the ruined section of the Pentagon, in decipherable condition. The voice recorder, though also recovered, was reportedly so badly damaged as to be of no use (corr. NTSB's Ted Lopatkiewicz, 2010, "Specialist's Factual Report of Investigation Digital Flight Data Recorder, NTSB no. DCA01MA064," 1/31/02, www.ntsb.gov); **Davis:** www.patriotsquestion911.com; **Kwiatkowski:** eds. David Ray Griffin & Peter Dale Scott, *9/11 and American Empire*, Northampton, MA: Olive Branch, 2007, 28–; **Citizen Investigation Team:** www.citizeninvestigationteam.com.

CHAPTER 11

140–3 **200, etc.:** FAQ, 8/30/06, http://wtc.nist.gov; **NIST/FEMA conclusions/"no corroborating":** Executive Summary, "World Trade Center Building Performance Study," FEMA, Washington, D.C., 2002, & Executive Summary, "Final Report on the Collapse of the World Trade Center Towers," NIST, Washington, D.C., 9/05; **"pancaked"/bowing:** FAQ, 8/30/06; **Mackey:** "On *Debunking 9/11 Debunking*: Examining Dr. David Ray Griffin's Latest Criticism of the NIST World Trade Center Investigation," 5/08, corr. Ryan Mackey, 2009, 2010; **"baloney"/"violates":** cited in Mackey, 137–,147; **"are so numerous":** ibid., 2; **"breaking":** David Ray Griffin, *Debunking*, 157, Mackey, 25; **"would be very":** Griffin, *Debunking*, 248–, 181–; **no good evidence/ "particularly"/"high-temperature":** Mackey, 82–, 86; **Jones's four samples:** Niels H. Harrit, Jeffrey Farrer, Steven E. Jones, et al., "Active Thermitic Material Discovered in Dust from 9/11 World Trade Center Catastrophe," *Open Chemical Physics Journal*, Vol. 2 (April 3, 2009): 7–31, www.bentham.org; **fellow scientists:** corr. Ryan Mackey, 2010, "Active Thermitic Material Claimed in Ground Zero Dust May Not Be Thermitic at All," 4/13/09,http://undisettembre. blogspot.com, "Steven Jones," article at www.ae911truth.info; **university website:** Steven Jones, "Why Indeed Did the WTC Buildings Collapse?," http://web.archive.org; *Journal:* Steven Jones, "Why Indeed Did the WTC Buildings Completely Collapse?," www.journalof911studies.com; **coeditor/"peer-reviewed":** "Home" page, http://www.journalof911studies.com; **"masquerade":** Mackey, 13, 40, Mackey corr. 2010, but see Dr. Jones's riposte to such criticism in "An Open Letter to Dr. Steven Jones by James Bennett, with Replies by Steven Jones," www.journalof911studies.com. When Jones's and his colleagues' most recent take on thermite was published in 2009, in *The Open Chemical Physics Journal*, the person whose name appeared on the masthead as "editor" promptly disassociated herself from the publication. The article, said Marie-Paule Pileni, a highly distinguished French scientist, had been printed without her knowledge. She characterized the periodical itself as "sheer nonsense . . . I do not want my name associated with this kind of stuff" ("sheer nonsense": "Chefredaktór skrider efter kontroversiel artikel om 9/11," videnskab.dk, 4/28/09, excerpts translated from the Danish by Marianne Gurnee, 2010, corr. Marie-Paul Pileni, 2010).

144   **"heard":** *WSJ*, 4/8/02; **"individual floors":** Bussey cited in Cathy Trost & Alicia Shepard, *Running Toward Danger*, Lanham, MD: Rowman & Littlefield, 2002, 87; **"It just descended":** Judyth Sylvester & Suzanne Hoffman, *Women Journalists at Ground Zero*, Lanham, MD: Rowman & Littlefield, 2002, 19—in his article "Explosive Testimony," www.911truth.org, Griffin rendered the text's word "*im*plosion" as "*ex*plosion."

144–5   **Romero:** *Albuquerque Journal*, 9/11/01, 9/21/01. Undeterred, skeptics resorted to innuendo. One coupled Romero's retraction to a "rumor" that he had "since found preferment from the federal government." Griffin has written that Romero had been "a very successful lobbyist for Pentagon contracts." "Saying that the government got to me," Romero has said, "is the farthest thing from the truth." In his initial comment, he would insist, he had "only said that that's what it looked like" ("rumor": Webster Griffin Tarpley, *9/11: Synthetic Terror*, Joshua Tree, CA: Progressive, 2005, 225; "very successful": Griffin, *Debunking*, 255; "Saying that"/"looked": eds. Dunbar & Reagan, 49); **"Then we":** int. John Sudnik, TF, 11/7/01; **"First I":** int. Timothy Julian, TF, 12/26/01; **"There was":** int. Frank Cruthers, TF, 10/31/01; **"The lowest":** int. Brian Dixon, TF, 10/25/01.

145   **Griffin seized:** Griffin, "Explosive Testimony." In his quote of *Journal* reporter Bussey, Griffin omitted the reporter's description of the initial sounds he heard as having been "metallic." He also left out a sentence in which the reporter, amending what he had at first assumed about the use of planted explosives, added, "In fact, the building was imploding down." Griffin attributed the quote starting "individual floors . . ." to "another *Wall Street Journal* reporter"—as distinct from Bussey. In fact, the source makes clear, Bussey is the source of both quotes used (Griffin, "Explosive Testimony" & see source for "individual floors," above).

145   **formal interviews:** published online by the *NYT* at http://graphics8.nytimes.com. Griffin cited Professor Graeme MacQueen, who did study all 503 Fire Department statements, as finding that 118 of them—some 23 percent of the group—"appear to have perceived, or thought they perceived, explosions that brought down the towers." Our

reading of the actual study suggests it is flawed. For example, MacQueen acknowledged having excluded from his analysis "a host of similes and metaphors referring to freight trains, jet planes and the like." Significantly, he has glossed over the fact that—even under his own criteria—the majority of the 503 witnesses do *not* claim to have heard explosions. The authors note, too, that MacQueen's analysis wrongly suggests—and he makes a point of this—that "fire chiefs on the scene thought the collapse of the towers was impossible." As the authors have noted, the possibility of partial collapse was discussed by fire chiefs early on, see Ch. 6 (Griffin, *Debunking*, 76, Graeme MacQueen, "118 Witnesses: The Firefighters' Testimony to Explosions in the Twin Towers," 8/21/06, www .journalof911studies.com).

145–6   **bangs:** e.g., int. Julio Marrero, TF, 10/25/01; **thunder:** e.g., int. Mark Stone, TF, 10/12/01, int. Eric Hansen, TF, 10/10/01, int. Jody Bell, TF, 12/15/01; **rumbling:** e.g., int. Patricia Ondrovic, TF, 10/11/01, int. Scott Holowach, TF, 10/18/01, int. John Delendick, TF, 12/6/01, int. John Picarello, TF, 12/6/01, int. Anthony DeMaio, TF, 1/28/02; **trainlike:** e.g., int. Louis Giaconelli, TF, 12/6/01, int. Paul Curran, TF, 12/18/01, int. Mark Ruppert, TF, 12/4/01, int. Joseph Fortis, TF, 11/9/01, int. Dominick Muschello, TF, 12/6/01; **"You heard":** int. Salvatore Torcivia cited in DiMarco, 188; **"relaying":** Mackey, 75; **Griffin on Kingdome:** Griffin, *Debunking*, 188, & see *U.S. News & World Report*, 6/22/03, www.controlleddemolition.com/ seattle-kingdome; **"produced no":** Mackey, 94; **"for alternative":** Executive Summary, NIST, xxxviii.

147   **"Achilles' Heel"/ "smoking gun":** Griffin, *Mysterious*, xi; see pp. 97–99; **first known/"a mystery":** *NYT*, 11/29/01.

147   **"fire-induced":** "Final Report on the Collapse of World Trade Center Building 7," Federal Building & Fire Safety Investigation of the World Trade Center Disaster, National Institute of Standards and Technology, Washington, D.C., 11/08, ES-3, xxxvi. Author Griffin wrote off that finding as "scientific fraud," claiming that the institute's experts ignored numerous items of physical evidence, fabricated and falsified evidence, and ignored a recommendation that their documentation should be peer-reviewed. Evidence ignored, the professor asserted, included in particular the evidence in dust of thermitic material—Griffin thought the "most likely

explanation" was that WTC 7, like the Twin Towers, was brought down by explosives ("scientific fraud," etc.: Griffin, *Mysterious*, 245–; "most likely": ibid., xii).

147   **"When it fell"**: int. Frank Fellini, TF, 12/3/01; **Hayden:** *Firehouse*, 4/02, Smith, 31–, 159–, int. Ray Goldback, TF, 10/24/01, int. Richard Banaciski, TF, 12/6/01, int. Robert Sohmer, TF, 1/17/02, int. Frank Cruthers, TF, 10/31/01.

148   **Nigro:** int. Daniel Nigro, TF, 10/24/01, "Chief of Department FDNY (ret.) Daniel Nigro Addresses Conspiracy Theories," http://guide.googlepages.com/danielnigro. Brent Blanchard, a senior writer on *ImplosionWorld*, an online magazine for the demolition industry, has written, "Any detonation of explosives within WTC 7 would likely have been detected by seismographs monitoring ground vibration.... To our knowledge, no such telltale 'spike' or vibratory anomaly was recorded.... Several demolition teams had reached Ground Zero by 3:00 p.m. on 9/11, and these individuals witnessed the collapse of WTC 7 from within a few hundred feet.... We have spoken with several who possess extensive experience in explosive demolition, and all reported hearing or seeing nothing to indicate an explosive detonation precipitating the collapse." Readers who wish to delve deeper could consult Blanchard's paper; Ryan Mackey's paper, at p. 112–; the BBC documentary film *The Conspiracy Files: 9/11—The Third Tower*, July 6, 2008; and of course Dr. Griffin's book *The Mysterious Collapse of World Trade Center 7*. (Brent Blanchard, "A Critical Analysis of the Collapse of WTC Towers 1, 2 and 7 from an Explosives and Conventional Demolition Industry Viewpoint," www.implosionworld.com).

148   **photos:** credited to Corporal Jason Ingersoll, USMC; Goldberg et al., 159, 245n30, & see photo section, photos also at http://911research.wtc7.net; **18 feet/"How could"**: David Ray Griffin, *The 9/11 Commission Report: Omissions and Distortions*, Gloucestershire, U.K.: Arris, 2005, 34; **wingspan/tail:** Goldberg et al., 17fn; **"fits"**: Griffin, *Omissions*, 38.

148   **Eyewitnesses:** e.g., see p. 44. Many more such witnesses are on record.

148–51 **evidence/opinions:** Paul Mlakar et al., "The Pentagon Building Performance Report," Reston, VA: American Society of Civil Engineers, 1/03, 1–; **removed/FBI warehouse:** ibid., 24, *Libération*, 3/30/02, "Arlington County

After-Action Report," www.co.arlington.va.us/fire/edu/
about/pdf/after_report.pdf, Annex C, 53–; **report concluded:**
Mlakar et al., 58; **"hogwash"/"To look":** corr. Mete Sozen,
2010; **Empire State:** "B-25 Empire State Building Collision,"
www.aerospaceweb.org, "Ask the Pilot," *Salon*, 5/19/06;
photos: Goldberg et al., photo section; **"planted":** Griffin,
Debunking, 265.

151   **"Don't be taken in":** "New Study from Pilots for 9/11 Truth:
No Boeing Hit the Pentagon, *Global Research*, 6/24/07. Fetzer
was impressed by the suggestion from James Hanson, a
retired attorney, who claimed that he had traced the debris
that was found at the Pentagon to an American Airlines 757
that crashed in Colombia in 1995! (ibid. & *Idaho Observer*,
2/8/05); **aircraft remains:** "Photos of Flt 77 Wreckage Inside
the Pentagon," by Sarah Roberts, www.rense.com (referred to
the authors by Sarandis Papadopoulos, an editor of *Pentagon
9/11*, whom Roberts consulted), "Pentagon & Boeing 757
Engine Investigation," www.aerospace.org, "Airplane
Fragment in Patriotic Box," exhibit description, http://
americanhistory.si.edu, *Libération*, 3/30/02.

152   **Carter:** address at Coalition on Political Assassinations conference, 2002. The ashes given to May's fiancé are interred in
Maryland.

152   **Flight 77 crew remains:** Submission by Toni Knisley,
American Airlines flight service administration manager,
National September 11 Memorial & Museum,
http://ns11make history.appspot.com, Burlingame bio. at
www.arlingtoncemetery.net. Forensic work on the Pentagon
victims was done by the Armed Forces Institute of Pathology
at Dover, Delaware. Remains of five individuals also found at
the crash scene, and believed to be those of the hijackers, were
eventually handed over to the FBI (Goldberg et al., 183, 178).

152–3   **remains identified:** Goldberg et al., 177–, 183, 204, "Attack
on the Pentagon," www.arlingtoncemetery.net; **photos:**
Exhibits P200042, P200045, P200047, P200048, *U.S. v.
Zacarias Moussaoui*, www.vaed.uscourts.gov; **"A stillness":**
Goldberg et al., 195; **"the bodies"/"For all we know":**
Griffin, *Debunking*, 268–.

153   **"cell phone calls":** "Operation Pearl," 8/03, www.
serendipity.li. Wireless and cell phone industry sources have
said cell phone calls from planes were possible—even from
high altitudes—at the time of 9/11, though connections were

sporadic (e.g., *NYT*, 9/14/01, "Final Contact," 11/1/01, www.connectedplanet.com, eds. Dunbar & Reagan, 83–, David Aaronovitch, *Voodoo Histories*, London: Jonathan Cape, 2009, 224).

154   **seatback not cell phone:** In May's case, the skeptics' claims grew out of early news reports that the attendant used her cell phone to call home—the record shows she did not. Solicitor General Theodore Olson, for his part, made it clear in a Fox News interview after 9/11 that he simply did not know what sort of phone his wife had used to call. The records now available show that *only* seatback phone calls, or attempted calls, were made from Flight 77.

The skeptics have claimed flatly that American Airlines 757s "were not equipped with seatback phones." Though the airline had apparently decided to discontinue seatback phone service prior to 9/11, analysis indicates that such phones were still in use on some flights as late as March 2002. That they were still in use on 9/11 is evident from the phone records alone.

The skeptics have also claimed that the reports of passengers' calls from Flight 93—see Ch. 7—are suspect. Griffin even suggests that Todd Beamer's long call to operator Lisa Jefferson did not occur. Beamer's call, however, is listed in the telephone company records now available. As in the case of Flight 77, early reports of "cell phone calls" made from Flight 93 sowed confusion. Deena Burnett, widow of Flight 93 passenger Tom Burnett, told the FBI that her husband made a series of three to five calls home on his cell phone. The records show that Burnett made three calls on a seatback phone. There is no way of knowing whether Mrs. Burnett simply misremembered the exact number of calls she got from her husband, or whether he did use his cell phone to make some of the calls. The records show that many Flight 93 calls, initially described as being by cell phone, in fact originated from seatback phones (early news: *Las Vegas Review Journal*, 9/13/01; made it clear: Olson, Fox News, 9/14/01; *only* seatback phone: DOJ "Briefing on Cell and Phone Calls from AA77," 5/20/04, in "Flight 93 Calls" folder [inc. details on other flights], B12, T7, CF, & Moschella to Marcus [& attachments], 4/26/04, in "Flight 11 Calls folder—Calls from AA11, AA77, UA175, & UA93, ATT Wireless & GTE Airphones," B13, T7, CF; "were not equipped": Griffin, *Debunking*, 266–;

discontinue/analysis: "Airline Grounds In-Flight Phone Service," 2/6/02, www.news.cnet.com, *Business Week*, 9/30/02, AA spokesman John Hotard cited at "American Airlines Flight 77 Calls," www.911myths.com; suspect: e.g., Griffin, *Debunking*, 86–, 292–; Griffin re. Beamer: "The Ultimate 9/11 Truth Showdown," 10/6/08, www.alternet.org; Burnett: FBI 302 of int. Deena Burnett, 9/11/01, INTELWIRE, Moschella to Marcus [& attachments], 4/26/04, records show: MFR 04020029, 5/13/04, CF, FBI 302 of int. Mark Rugg, 7/1/02, "Key 302s," B19, T7, CF).

154   **"have had a little":** "Comments on the Pentagon Strike," www.cassiopaea.org; **"transformers"/"morphing":** Griffin, *Debunking*, 89, 86; **"Either Ted"/"is based on":** "The Ultimate 9/11 Truth Showdown, www.alternet.org; **scattered in three:** Exhibit P200318, *U.S. v. Zacarias Moussaoui*.

154   **"It took":** transcript, *Larry King Weekend*, CNN, 1/6/02; Mrs. Olson is indeed interred in Door County, at Ellison Bay Cemetery. Had Dr. Griffin cared to check, he could have established this long before he made his most recent suggestion, in 2008, that she might be alive. (Ellison Bay Cemetery: int. Mayor's Office, Liberty Grove, WI, Barbara K. Olson listing, www.findagrave.com).

155   **"cannot ignore":** Griffin, *Debunking*, 266, & see Griffin, *New Pearl Harbor: Disturbing Questions About the Bush Administration and 9/11*, Moreton-in-March, U.K.: Arris, 2009, 28; **"overwhelming"/"an inside":** Griffin, *Debunking*, 1, 309, & see Griffin & Scott, *Empire*, 12; **"a prima facie":** Griffin, *New Pearl Harbor*, 2009, 131.

155   **Project:** "Rebuilding America's Defenses," Washington, D.C.: Project for the New American Century, Sept. 2000, 10, 4, 51, "Statement of Principles," www.newamerican century.org.

155   **"the Pearl Harbor":** *WP*, 1/27/02; This part of the passage echoed almost word for word testimony before the Senate Armed Services Committee in 1999. The then–executive director of the Center for Strategic and Budgetary Assessments, Andrew Krepinevich, spoke of the difficulties in transforming the U.S. military, "in the absence of a strong external shock to the United States—a latter-day 'Pearl Harbor' of sorts" (testimony of Andrew Krepinevich, 3/5/99).

155–6   **in public:** Sammon, 205, 316; **"Who benefits?":** Griffin & Scott, *Empire*, 103; **precedents:** e.g., Zwicker, multiple refs.

to false flag ops., & Griffin in ed. Ian Woods, *9/11*, Vol. 2, Ontario: Global Outlook, 2006, 15; **Roosevelt:** Zwicker, 273, & see "FDR Knew Pearl Harbor Was Coming," *New York Press*, 6/14/01.

156   **false flag/pounced:** "11 September 2001—Another Operation Northwoods?," 9/17/01, www.blythe.org, & see "Operation 911: No Suicide Pilots," 10/6/01, www.public-action.com. The reference was to Operation Northwoods, which was revealed in the book *Body of Secrets* by the author James Bamford (NY: Doubleday, 2001—see 82–, 300–).

157–8   **"We must":** "11 September 2001—Another Operation Northwoods?"; **Corn objected:** *LAT*, 7/3/02, "Van Jones & the 9/11 Conspiracy," http://motherjones.com; **"I won't":** "When 9/11 Conspiracy Theories Go Bad," by David Corn, 3/1/02, www.zcommunications.org; **howl of rage:** *Nation*, 5/31/02.

159   **thousands of pages:** see refs in sourcing for Chs. 1–9; Some skeptics suggest that the absence of formal NTSB investigations on Flights 11 and 175—as well as the other two hijacked flights—is suspicious. From the outset, however, these crashes were deemed to have been "criminal acts," which meant jurisdiction fell not to the NTSB but to the FBI. Within two days of the attacks, though, the FBI requested technical assistance from the NTSB. According to the NTSB's chairman, some sixty NTSB experts worked "around the clock in Virginia, Pennsylvania, New York, and at our headquarters in Washington, D.C., assisting with aircraft parts identification, searching for and analyzing flight recorders." Some of the research done by NTSB experts has emerged in recent years, especially with the 2009 opening of 9/11 Commission files and absence of reports: e.g., notation on NTSB DCA01MA060 [Flight 11], www.ntsb.gov; (suspicious: e.g., "A Little Known Fact About the 9/11 Planes," http://sabbah.biz, "Flight 77 Black Boxes," http://911review.org; "criminal acts"/FBI requested: NTSB Advisory, 9/13/01, www.ntsb.gov; "around the clock": Testimony of NTSB Chairman Marion C. Blakey, 6/25/01, Committee on Commerce, Science & Transportaion, U.S. Senate, www.ntsb.gov, corr. NTSB's Ted Lopatkiewicz, 2009).

159   **300,000:** corr. NARA's Kristen Wilhelm, 2011; **"distracts people":** *Nation*, 7/12/02.

CHAPTER 12

160–3 **memo/"How," etc.:** Philip to Tom & Lee, 9/6/04, "Farmer Memo re False Statements," B4, Dana Hyde files, CF; **chairman/vice chairman:** Kean & Hamilton, 25; **Roemer/"false":** int. Roemer on *American Morning*, CNN, 8/2/06; **shocked:** *WP*, 8/2/06; **"deception":** Farmer, 4; **Farmer questioned:** Farmer, 4–, 227–; **Meyers confused/had launched:** Testimony of General Richard Myers, Hearings, U.S. Senate Armed Services Committee, 107th Cong., 1st Ses., 9/13/01; **"We responded awfully":** transcript, OnLine NewsHour, 9/14/01, www.pbs.org; **Weaver timeline/"There was no":** *Dallas Morning News*, 9/15/01, *Seattle Times*, 9/16/01; **Cheney/"toughest decision":** transcript, *Meet the Press*, 9/16/01, www.msnbc.msn.com; **"Did we shoot":** cited by Bob Woodward and Dan Balz in "10 Days in September," a series of articles based on interviews with Bush, Cheney, and other official sources, *WP*, 1/27/02; **"It's my understanding":** CR, 43, 465n233; **"Oh, my God":** Testimony of Norman Mineta, 5/23/03, CO; **never missiles:** Spencer, 277; **report incorrect:** *Cape Cod Times*, 8/21/02.

163 **Rumors circulating:** A retired Army colonel, Donn de Grand-Pre, claimed in 2004 that Flight 93 was shot down by a pilot flying for the North Dakota National Guard. He named the pilot supposedly responsible and said he had sent a report on the matter to a named general. Flight records reportedly show that the alleged pilot was on other duties at the relevant time—and the general denied even knowing de Grand-Pre. A contributor to a 2008 blog, posted by a person identifying himself only as a former Langley Air Force Base mechanic, quotes a colleague at second hand as having said, "They shot one down . . . One of those 16s came back with one less missile than it left with." The claim has no value as information—it is anonymous, and the supposed veteran did not himself speak with the original source of the quote. Conspiracy theorists, meanwhile, seized on the alleged content of a 911 call made from Flight 93 by passenger Edward Felt shortly before the airliner crashed. According to a staffer at the emergency center that took the call, Felt mentioned that there been an explosion on board, and "white smoke." The dispatcher who actually took the call, however, denied that Felt said anything about an explosion. The call was recorded, and there is no such reference in the transcript.

David Griffin refers in his books to "considerable evidence"
that 93 was shot down—yet cites none of substance (De
Grand-Pre: eds. Dunbar & Reagan, 77–; blog: "The US Air
Force Shot Down Flight 93," 4/11/08, http://georgewashington.
blogspot.com; Felt: FBI 302 of [name redacted], 9/19/01,
Pittsburgh to Counterterrorism, New York, 9/17/01, & FBI
302 of [name redacted], 9/11/01, INTELWIRE, transcript of
call 9/11/01, "Flight 93 Calls," B12, T8, CF; Griffin: e.g.,
Debunking, 70, & David Griffin, *The New Pearl Harbor
Revisited*, Northampton, MA: Olive Branch Press, 2008,
127–).

163–5 **Commission "required":** Public Law 107–306, 11/27/02,
www.archives.gov; **delays/obstruction/tapes withheld/
recalcitrant:** Kean & Hamilton, 83–, 258–, Shenon, 203–;
"incomplete": corr. Miles Kara, 2011; **Scott time-
line/"9:24"/"awful decision"/In one breath, etc.:**
Testimonies of Larry Arnold & Alan Scott, 5/23/03, CO,
Farmer, 262–; **leery/proof/subpoena:** Shenon, 203–, Kean &
Hamilton, 88, 260; **"Whiskey tango foxtrot":** Farmer, 265.

165–8 **NORAD/more than 100 squadrons/14 "alert"/intercepts:**
CR, 16–, Spencer, 286–; **planes as weapons:** Staff
Monograph "The Four Flights and Civil Aviation Security,"
55–, CF, Farmer, 98–; **hijacking protocol:** CR, 17–, Farmer,
117; **multiple Centers:** e.g., Miles Kara, "Archive of the
'Transponders and Ghosts' Category," www .oredigger61.org
—Centers involved were Boston, New York, D.C.,
Indianapolis, and Cleveland; **"primary target":** MFR
04016798, 9/22/03, "Aeronautical Information Manual,"
2/11/10, www.faa.gov; **"coast mode"/coastline:** *Avionics*,
6/1/05, Farmer, 135, 9/11 NEADS Tape Transcription,
"NEADS-CONR-NORAD, NEADS Transcripts Channel
4," B3, NYC files, CF, MFR 04016774, 10/27/03; **not know
NORAD:** MFR 04017316, 10/2/03; **units different
training:** MFR 04020720, 3/11/04; **unable to
communicate/frequencies/none worked:** MFR
040176171, 10/2/03; **Transcripts/In that book, etc.:**
Farmer, 215–; **"Washington [Center] has no clue":** 9/11
NEADS Tape Transcription, "NEADS-CONR-NORAD
Transcripts, NEADS Transcripts Channel 7," B3, NYC files,
CF; **"It's chaos"/"The challenge"/Kara:** Miles Kara,
"Chaos Theory and 9–11, Some Preliminary Thoughts,"
6/12/09, www.oredigger61.org, & see Archives, 911

Revisited, www.oredigger61.org, Kara Career Summary, 12/12/02, "Commission Meeting 4/10/03, Tab 7," B1, Front Office files, CF.

168 **evidence of tapes and logs:** In writing this account of the FAA/military response to the attacks, the authors relied—as did the 9/11 Commission—on the tapes and transcripts of conversations between the various FAA and NORAD sites. As the Commission's Miles Kara wrote in 2009, the "complete set of information needed to attempt any analysis of the events [of that morning] includes the radar files and the software to run them, time-stamped tapes, and any transcripts that were made" (Commission account: Miles Kara, "Archive for the NEADS files category," www.oredigger61.org; NORAD audio files are available at the National Archives, B82 & B110, GSA Files, CF, but—for ready availability—at http://911depository.info).

168 **nerve center:** *Vanity Fair,* 9/06, Spencer, 2.

168 **Marr/hijacking/Vigilant Guardian:** *Vanity Fair,* 9/06, CR, 458n116. The military exercise scheduled for September 11, and several others that took place earlier in the year, have been the source of speculation. Some thought aspects of the exercises indicated U.S. government foreknowledge of the manner and timing of the 9/11 attacks. Others suggested that September's Vigilant Guardian exercise had a negative effect on NORAD's ability to react to the attacks. The 9/11 Commission found that the timing of the drill may have had a positive impact, because more personnel were on duty that day. The tapes and transcripts, though, reflect temporary confusion within NORAD as to whether the attacks were part of the war game or were real-world (Miles Kara, "9–11 Training, Exercises, and War Games, Some Collected Thoughts," 9/11 Revisited, www.oredigger61.org, "Exclusive Report: Did Military Exercises Facilitate the 9/11 Pentagon Attack?," by Mathew Everett, 7/06, www.911truth.org, *Aviation Weeks & Space Technology,* 6/3/02, "NORAD Exercises Summary," Team 8 files, posted on www.scribd.com, CR, 458n116).

169 **"on the shitter":** NEADS audiotape, DRM1, CH2, www.oredigger61.org; **Arnold in FL:** MFR 04016749, 2/3/04; **Dooley et al.:** 9/11 NEADS Tape Transcription, "NEADS-CONR-NORAD Transcripts, NEADS Channel 4," B3, NYC files, CF; **"Real World Unknown":** Memorandum for CC et al. from NEADS Sector/CVX,

8/23/01, "RDOD 03013146, Entire Contents, Vigilant Guardian," B116, GSA files, CF.

169 **Cooper call:** MFR 04016791 & 04016790, 9/22/03, CR, 20. Disregarding the official FAA/military protocol, Boston Center had made two earlier attempts to contact the military on a "freelance" basis. The first such call, which went to the New Jersey Air National Guard's 177th Fighter Wing at Atlantic City, got nowhere because the wing was not on alert status. Boston's second early attempt to reach the military—through the FAA's Cape Cod facility—did eventually lead to an alert being passed to NEADS, but only after the call made by the FAA's Cooper. These calls were made at the initiative of Boston Center's traffic management supervisor, Dan Bueno. Bueno—who was aware of the protocols in place—told the Commission that his actions were based on the "urgency of the situation." Cooper's use of "F-16" was a misspeak for "F-15" (CR, 20, Position 15, pts. 2 & 3, "ATCSCC Tape Transcription," B1, T8, CF, *Bergen Record* [N.J.], 12/5/03, MFR 04016791, 9/22/03, MFR 04016790, 9/22/03, MFR 03012969, 9/30/03, CF, Spencer, 22–).

169–70 **"Cool"/all business/Boston could say:** 9/11 NEADS Tape Transcription, "NEADS-CONR-NORAD Transcripts, NEADS Channel 4," B3, NYC files, CF, *Vanity Fair*, 9/06; **8:41 battle stations:** CR, 20, Farmer, 123; **conferred Arnold/ordered:** "Conversation with Maj. Gen. Larry Arnold," www.codeonemagazine.com, 1/02, CR, 20; **without direction/assigned:** CR, 20; **"Oh, God":** 9/11 NEADS Tape Transcription, "NEADS-CONR-NORAD Transcripts, NEADS Channel 4," B3, NYC files, CF; **Mulligan:** Full Transcript: Command Center; NOM Operational Position, Sept. 11, 2001, 10/14/03, "NOM Operation Position (5)," B1, NYC files, CF, CR 22.

170 **Air Force knew nothing:** Some skeptics have seized on an early NORAD chronology that appeared to suggest that the FAA notified the military of the hijacking of Flight 175 at 8:43 A.M., claiming that this was evidence that U.S. forces failed to react promptly—even "stood down"—as the attacks unfolded. The contention is spurious—the 8:43 notification time in the NORAD chronology was simply incorrect. Although 8:43 A.M. does approximate the time the plane was hijacked, that fact was not at the time known to the FAA (critics: Griffin, *The New Pearl Harbor Revisited*, 8–; 8:43 notification: Chronology

of the September 11 Attacks & Subsequent Events Through
Oct. 24, 2001, "Timelines, 1 of 2," B20, T7, CF, "FAA
Believed Second 9/11 Plane Heading Towards New York for
Emergency Landing," & linked FAA document 4, 9/5/05;
time incorrect: www.gwu.edu, Miles Kara, "Chaos Theory &
9/11," 9/11 Revisited, www.oredigger61.org, corr. Miles
Kara, 2010).

170   **Otis pilots holding:** *Cape Cod News*, 8/21/02, *BG*, 9/11/05,
Vanity Fair, 9/06. The speed at which the fighters traveled and
their exact route to New York has been the subject of some
debate. Available tapes, and Commission interviews with the
pilots and the mission commander, make clear that when they
were first launched the flights headed for military-controlled
airspace where they stayed in a holding pattern until after
NEADS learned the second tower had been hit. The fighters
then proceeded to New York, where they established a
Combat Air Patrol (CAP) over the city at 9:25. The F-15
fighter, when new and stripped of its armament, is capable of
doing a speed of Mach 2.5—some 1,650 miles per hour. Pilot
Nash told the Commission that he and Duffy never exceeded
Mach 1.1 (727 mph) as they flew toward New York. Duffy
estimated that the fighters had reached between Mach 1.1 and
1.3, but said the pair "throttled back" on learning of the
second strike—to conserve fuel. While it is possible that the
Otis fighters went supersonic on the final leg of the journey to
New York, radar data showed that the pair averaged a less-
than-supersonic speed of Mach.86 (debate: see refs,
"Complete 9/11 Timeline," www.historycommons.org;
record scanty: CR, 459n120; available tapes/interviews:
transcripts from Voice Recorder, 11/9/01 1227Z-1417Z,
Channel 24, "Trip 2 of 3, NEADS Transcript Color Coded,"
B20, T8, CF, 9/11 ATCSCC Tape Transcription, "NEADS-
CONR-NORAD Transcripts, NEADS Channel 5," B3, NYC
files, CF, MFR 04016778, 1/22 & 1/23/04, MFR 03012972,
10/14/03, MFR 04016756, CF, CR, 21–, 23–, corr. Kris
Wilhelm, Miles Kara, 2010).

170–1   **Long Island:** Full Transcript: Command Center; NOM
Operational Position, Sept. 11, 2001, 10/14/03, "NOM
Operation Position (5)," B1, NYC files, CF, CR 22; **Five
minutes after:** CR, 23–; **"I thought":** *Cape Cod Times*,
8/21/02; **"We don't know"/"We need"/urged/Marr at
first:** 9/11 NEADS Tape Transcription, "NEADS-CONR-

NORAD Transcripts, NEADS Channel 2," B3, NYC files, CF & re Boston, authors' check of audiotape, CR, 460n137; **"Listen"**: Position 15, Parts 2 & 3, "ATCSCC Tape Transcript, Position 15," B1, T8, CF.

171–2 **9:21 call/Scoggins/checked D.C./"First I heard"/ Scoggins insisted:** MFR 04016798, 9/22/03, 9/11 NEADS Tape Transcription, "NEADS-CONR-NORAD Transcripts, NEADS Channel 7," B3, NYC files, CF. Scoggins has said he is "99% certain the person who made that call on the Telcon [about Flight 11 still being airborne] was Dave Cannoles." The FAA's Cannoles told 9/11 Commission staff that he did not recall doubt as to whether Flight 11 had crashed into the Trade Center. Another staff member, Doug Davis, thought the chief of staff for the director of air traffic at FAA head-quarters, Mary Ellen Kraus, said Flight 11 was still airborne. Kraus denied it ("Losing Flight 77," www.911myths.com, handwritten notes of Dave Canoles interview, 3/25/04, "Dave Canoles, FAA WOC," B2, Dana Hyde files, CF, MFR of int. Mary Ellen Kraus, 4/27/04, "FAA HQ—Mary Ellen Kraus," B6, T8, CF).

172 **new "track":** Miles Kara, "Archive for the 'Transponder & Ghosts' Category," 9/11 Revisited, www.oredigger61.org, Traffic Situation Display (TSD) Demo, 4/13/04, "FAA HQ Floor Position Maps—Herndon," B19, T8, CF; **"listening on a Telcon":** int. of Colin Scoggins at www.911myths.com; **"Shit!":** 9/11 NEADS Tape Transcription, "NEADS-CONR-NORAD Transcripts, NEADS Channel 2," B3, NYC files, CF, CR, 461n149.

173 **9:30 fighters into air:** CR, 27. Two planes on alert duty were ready and loaded with live missiles, while the third—the "spare"—had only its 20mm gun. The pilots were Major Lou Derrig, Captain Dean Eckmann, and—piloting the spare— Captain Craig Borgstrom (Spencer, 115–, 142–).

173 **Nasypany figured:** MFR 04016778, 1/22 & 23/04, MFR 04016771, 10/27/03.

173 **NEADS ordered/tower sent:** "Staff Statement 17," CO, MFR 04016771, 10/27/03. The Commission Report offers three explanations for the change of course. One, that the scramble order had given no distance to the target, nor where it was. Two, that the pilots followed a "generic" flight plan designed to get them out of local airspace. Three, that the lead pilot and the local FAA controller assumed that the

Langley tower's instruction superseded the order received from NEADS. According to author Lynn Spencer, who interviewed members of the unit involved, Captain Dean Eckmann assumed the fighters were "being vectored eastward in order to fly around the traffic in their way. He doesn't second-guess the instructions. . . . The jet's targets are customarily out over the ocean." There is, however, no mention of traffic on the Air Traffic Control tapes (CR, 27, Spencer, 143–; corr. Miles Kara, 2011).

173–4 **NEADS finally learned:** American Airlines executive vice president Gerard Arpey had been told at 9:00 A.M. that communications with American 77 had been lost. As reported in Ch. 4, the FAA controller at Indianapolis Center had his last routine contact with Flight 77 as early as 8:54 (CR, 8–); **"Let me tell":** 9/11 ATCSCC Tape Transcription, "NEADS-CONR-NORAD Transcripts, NEADS Channel 5," B3, NYC files, CF; **"Latest report"/"not sure"/"rumor":** 9/11 NEADS Tape Transcription, "NEADS-CONR-NORAD Transcripts, NEADS Channel 7," B3, NYC files, CF; **"Get your fighters":** "Transcripts from Voice Recorder, Channel 14," B20, T8, "NEADS Transcripts color-coded," CF; **asked where fighters/"I don't care":** 9/11 NEADS Tape Transcription, "NEADS-CONR-NORAD Transcripts, NEADS Channel 2," B3, NYC files, CF; **Scoggins back/"Delta 1989"/"And is this one?":** Chronology of Events at Mission Coodinator Position, 9/24/03, "Boston Center—Colin Scoggins," B3, T8, CF, 9/11 NEADS Tape Transcription, "NEADS-CONR-NORAD Transcripts, NEADS Channel 7," B3, NYC files, CF. Based on a Commission staff timeline, the authors have taken 9:39 as the time Scoggins warned NEADS about Delta 1989—even though the Commission Report uses a time of 9:41. ("Timeline of the Events of the Day," www .scribd.com, & see MCC log, "Miles Kara trips," B19, T8, CF, Farmer, 193– v. CR, 28).

174 **Boston speculated:** Miles Kara, "Archive for the Delta 1989 category," 9/11 Revisited, www.oredigger61.org, & see Position 15, Parts 2 & 3, "ATCSCC Tape Transcription," B1, T8, CF. In a chronology he gave the Commission of the day's events, Scoggins noted that an "Open Telcon reports that DAL1889 [*sic*] is NORDO [no radio]" and described his own subsequent action as "call NEADS to advise" suggesting that

his concern about 1989 was piqued only after hearing of it from others. In an interview much later, Scoggins said he thought Delta 1989 might have become suspect because it "missed a frequency transfer" or "didn't make a transmission back" when given a frequency change ("Open Telcon": Chronology of Events at Mission Coordinator Position, 9/24/03, "Boston Center—Colin Scoggins," B3, T8, CF, & see Position 15, Parts 2 & 3, "ATCSCC Tape Transcription," B1, T8, CF; later interview: "Q & A with 9/11 Boston Air Traffic Controller," http://sites.google.com).

174   **NEADS tracked:** MFR 04016777, 10/28/03, Miles Kara, "Archive to the 'Transponders & Ghosts' Category, 9/11 Revisited," www.oredigger61.org, Kara to Brinkley, 1/26/04, "Misc. Loose Documents re. Delta 1989," B5, T8, CF, UA93 & Andrews Timeline, "Andrews AFB Logs—Timelines, UA93 & Andrews," B4, Dana Hyde files, CF.

174–5   **only plane able to tail:** NEADS had also been able briefly to pinpoint and track Flight 77, even though the FAA alerted it to the problem with the airliner only at 9:34, only some three minutes before it struck the Pentagon (Miles Kara, "Archive for the 'Transponders & Ghosts' Category, 9/11 Revisited, www.oredigger61.com); **"land immediately"/"Confirm"/ "unreliable"/Cleveland panic/pilots feared/"you're a** *trip*"/assured/"bomb area"/"bad movie": Dave Dunlap (copilot) memoir, "September 11, 2001,"www.3dlanguage. net, DAL 1989 Order of Events, "FAA Subpoena Compendium, Delta 1989 Timeline," B15, T8, CF, int. John Werth, MFR 04017313, 10/2/03; **Scoggins, "might not be":** 9/11 NEADS Tape Transcription, "NEADS-CONR-NORAD Transcripts, NEADS Channel 7," B3, NYC files, CF, Summary [slugged as Timeline of Events of the Day], "Boston Center—Colin Scoggins," B3, T8, CF, Farmer, 211.

175   **trying to get fighters:** MFR 04016778, 1/22 & 23/04, MFR 04016771, 10/27/03, 9/11 NEADS Tape Transcription, "NEADS-CONR-NORAD Transcripts, NEADS Channel 2," & ATCSCC Tape Transcription, "Channel 5," B3, NYC files, CF, Staff Report, "The Four Flights and Civil Aviation Security," 8/26/04, CF, 101n391. NEADS asked two additional bases to provide fighters—Selfridge, in Michigan, and Toledo, in Ohio. Contrary to reports at the time, it appears that they were unable to help during the Delta episode. The Selfridge Air National Guard fighters were in

the air, but had expended all their ammunition on a training exercise. They did not land until 10:29. Two Toledo F-16s were to take off, but—according to Colonel Marr—only after the Delta 1989 episode was over and after United 93 had been shot down ("The Unthinkable Had Happened," 2007, www.candgnews. com, *The Wolverine*, Fall 2006, Spencer, 178–, *Toledo Blade*, 12/9/01, MFR 03012970, 10/27/03).

176–7 **I believe:** ATCSCC Tape Transcription, "Channel 5"; **NEADS told nothing:** ibid., 9/11 NEADS Tape Transcription, "NEADS-CONR-NORAD Transcripts, NEADS Channel 2," B3, NYC files, CF, MCC Log, "Miles Kara Trips," B19, T8, CF, CR, 30; **controller heard/reported promptly:** int. John Werth, CR, 28, FAA Memo, "Full Transcription: Air Traffic Control System Command Center, National Traffic Management Officer, East Position, 9/11/01," B1, NYC files, CF; **Uh, do we want to think?/FAA staffer reported/"does not believe":** ibid., MFR 04018154, 11/24/03, CR, 461n167.

177 **NEADS knew nothing:** MCC/T Log, "Miles Kara Trips— MCC Log," B19, T8, CF. Ironically, this was the one time during the morning that U.S. forces might have been in a position to intercept one of the hijacked flights. In the words of Commission staffer Kara, "it was only because of a pro-active error by Boston air traffic controller Colin Scoggins [suggesting that Flight 11 might still be aloft] . . . that the nation's air defenders had any real chance to defend against Flight 93." The flap over the nonexistent Flight 11 got fighters from Langley in the air, where they established a Combat Air Patrol over Washington by 10:00. It was a patrol at that stage, however—an impotent patrol. It had no rules of engagement, no knowledge of the real flight that was missing, United 93 ("Archive for the Andrews Fighters Category," www.oredigger61.org); **"we were always":** int. of Colin Scoggins (under his Internet name of Cheap Shot), "Q&A with Boston Center Air Traffic Controller," http://sites.google.com.

177 **"We believe":** Spencer, 286; **"watching United":** "Conversation with Maj. Gen. Larry Arnold," www.codeonemagazine.com, 1/02.

178 **magical feat/no one reported:** The FAA's call alerting the military to United 93's situation was at 10:07, and the airliner had crashed at 10:03. Seven minutes later, NEADS was told

that the plane was down. (9/11 ATCSCC Tape Transcription, "NEADS-CONR-NORAD Transcripts, NEADS Transcripts Channel 5," B3, NYC files, CF, MCC Tech logbook, "Miles Kara FAA HQ 3 of 3," B19, T8, CF).

178   **Arnold concedes:** Testimony of Larry Arnold, 6/17/04, CO, MFR 04016749, 2/3/04, *Vanity Fair,* 9/06 & see re officers conceding same MFR 04016769, 1/23/04.

178   **conflated Delta 1989:** Miles Kara, "Archive for Delta 1989 Category," 9/11 Revisited, www.oredigger.com—with which the authors concur, int. John Werth, & see MFRs 04016769, 1/23/04, 04016749, 2/3/04. Colonel Marr, the NEADS battle commander, also offered inaccurate information about NEADS and Flight 93. The Air Force's official 9/11 history, published as *Air War over America* in January 2003, quoted him as saying he and colleagues called in fighters from the airbase at Selfridge "so they could head 93 off at the pass . . . get in there, close on him, and convince him to turn." The request to Selfridge was made, however, at about 9:43, before NORAD knew anything about Flight 93. The request was made, rather, in connection with Delta 1989, which—as discussed in the text—had not in fact been hijacked ("so they could": Staff Monograph, "The Four Flights and Civil Aviation Security," 8/26/04, CF, 100n391; Selfridge request: 1989: 9/11 NEADS Tape Transcription, "NEADS-CONR-NORAD Transcripts, NEADS Transcripts Channel 2," B3, NYC files, CF, Staff Monograph, "The Four Flights and Civil Aviation Security," 8/26/04, CF, 101n391).

178   **Sudoku/shoddy work:** Miles Kara, "NORAD's Sudoko Puzzle, a Failure to Tell the Truth" & "Archive of the 'May 23, 2003 Hearing' Category," 9/11 Revisited, www. oredigger61.org.

178–9   **Marcus pointed:** Marcus to Schmitz & Mead plus attachments, 7/29/04, "Referral of False Statements by Government Officials to FAA & DOD Inspectors General," CF; Kara, for his part, told the authors that in his view the press release in question had been a "rush to judgment" by NORAD, that NORAD had simply wanted to "get out in front of FAA before the upcoming White House meeting to sort things out"; the tape malfuntion referred to, Kara said, did indeed occur (corr. Miles Kara, 2011); **"didn't get together":** Testimony of Ralph Eberhart, 6/17/04, CO; **"NORAD's public chronology"/"whoever at FAA":** "Sen. Dayton's

'NORAD Lied' Transcript," www.scoop.co.nz; **"At some"**: Farmer, 4–.

CHAPTER 13

180–1 **Wolfowitz:** Online NewsHour, 9/14/01, www.pbs.org; **"horrendous decision":** *Meet the Press*, NBC, 9/16/01; **"I recommended":** Office of the Vice President Internal Transcript, Telephone Interview of the Vice President by *Newsweek*, "Farmer—Misc.," B9, NYC files, CF; **"You bet":** *WP*, 1/27/02; **"emphasized":** CR, 40, 464n214; **2010 memoir:** Bush, 129–.

181 **"The operational chain":** Dept. of Defense Directive 5100.1, 9/25/87. The authors have here referred to the directive effectuating the Goldwater-Nichols Department of Defense Reorganization Act of 1986, the relevant law on 9/11. Other Defense Department regulations in force in 2001 stated—on the matter of military cooperation with civilian authorities (like the FAA)—that the defense secretary had to approve "any request for potentially lethal support," and that "only the President" could request the use of the military to respond to domestic terrorism. It was "understood" in 2001, the 9/11 Commission stated, that a shoot-down order would have to come from the National Command Authority—"a phrase used to describe the President and the Secretary of Defense." Dr. David Griffin, the prominent skeptic, has suggested that the military did not in fact require authorization—that they could act at once in cases requiring "immediate responses." The authors' reading of the regulation Griffin cites is that in certain circumstances and "where time does not permit" prior approval, the military could indeed take "necessary action." The sort of action it could take, however, is very specifically described and does *not* include the use of force ("understood": CR 17, 43; Griffin: *New Pearl Harbor Revisited*, 265n12; regulation: DOD Directives, "Military Assistance to Civil Authorities," 3025.1, 1/15/93, 3025.15, 2/18/97, Joint Chiefs of Staff Instructions, "Aircraft Piracy [Hijacking] and Destruction of Derelict Airborne Objects," 3610.01, 7/31/97, 3610.01A, 6/1/01).

182 **generals understood/exercise:** Testimony of Larry Arnold & Craig McKinley, 5/23/03, CO, CR 457n98; **"derelict balloon"/Only President:** MFR 04016749, 2/3/04, Testimony of Larry Arnold, 5/23/02, CO, CR 457n98;

Cheney furious: Shenon, 267, 411–, but see Kean & Hamilton, 261; **clear hint:** CR, 40–, 464n213–216; **"We just didn't":** Shenon, 265; **"The official version":** Farmer, 255.

183–4 **"My recommendation":** 9/11 NEADS Tape Transcription, "NEADS-CONR-NORAD Transcripts, NEADS Channel 2, B3, NYC files, CF; **Nasypany began asking:** *Vanity Fair,* 9/06; **"I don't know":** 9/11 NEADS Tape Transcription, "NEADS-CONR-NORAD Transcripts, NEADS Channel 4," B3, NYC files, CF, FAA Memo, Full Transcript, Aircraft Accident: UAL175; New York, NY, 9/11/01, "AAL 11, UAL 175: FAA Produced documents, Transcripts used in interviews," B2, NYC files, CF; **Rumsfeld movements from 9:37:** see Ch. 5; **NMCC looked:** CR, 37–; **"outrageous":** Cockburn, 3–; **"one or more calls":** Testimony of Donald Rumsfeld, 3/23/04, CO; **"tried without success":** Goldberg et al., 131; **"Are you okay?":** ibid., 131, 240n6. The assistant was Major Joseph Wassel, who set up the call. Wassel was interviewed for the Defense Department's "Pentagon 9/11" report, but not by the staff of the 9/11 Commission. Wassel described an initial attempt to call the President through the White House Situation Room—a call he came to believe did not go through. Sometime later—Wassel could not pinpoint the time, but placed it as being when Rumsfeld was back in his Pentagon office, having returned from the crash site—the President called the defense secretary from Air Force One (Goldberg et al., 131, 240n6, *AF News,* 3/8/01, Fenner to Campagna & attachments, 12/21/03, "DOD Documents Produced," B22, T2, CF, int. of Joseph Wassel by Alfred Goldberg, 4/9/03, B115, GSA files, CF).

184 **"brief call"/"just gaining"/10:35/There's been;** CR, 43–, 465n234, Farmer, 230, "Dana Hyde Notes of Air Threat Conference Call," released to authors under Mandatory Declassification Review 2011. The text of this conversation is taken from the Defense Department transcript of the "Air Threat" teleconference that began at 9:37 a.m., a key document in the context of establishing the time of the actions and knowledge of senior officials. The Defense Department and Commission staff held that the transcript had a three-minute margin of error. The authors obtained the release of Commission staffer Dana Hyde's detailed notes on the Air Threat call, which support the timeline in the Commission's Report. The transcript of the teleconference remains classi-

fied as of this writing (CR, 37, 462n194, Levin to Zelikow, 8/22/03, "Air Threat Call," B1, Daniel Marcus Files, CF, "Dana Hyde Notes of ATC Call," CF, corr. Kristen Wilhelm, 2010).

184–5 **"had come"/"Technically"/testimony/withheld:** "Interview with Donald Rumsfeld, 12/23/02," B7, T2, CF, Goldberg et al., 131, testimony of Donald Rumsfeld, 3/23/04, CO, corr. NARA's Kristen Wilhelm, 2010. The defense secretary's full testimony on the point was: "In the National Military Command Center (NMCC), I joined the Air Threat Conference call in progress. One of my first conversations during the Conference Call was with the Vice President. He informed me of the President's authorization to shoot down hostile aircraft coming toward Washington, D.C." In the 2011 memoir, Rumsfeld said Cheney told him there had been "at least three instances" of reports of planes approaching Washington—"a couple were confirmed hijack. And, pursuant to the President's instructions, I gave authorization for them to be taken out" (Rumsfeld, 339).

185–7 **"Very little"/"To a person":** Hyde to Front Office, 3/2/04, "Daniel Marcus," B8, T8, CF; **White House keeps track:** Shenon, 265; **notes by individuals:** CR, 464n216; **sought to limit/record unreliable:** Hyde to Front Office, 3/2/04, "Daniel Marcus," B8, T8, CF; **teleconferences/"In my mind"/cell phones:** CR, 36–, 463n190, int. Anthony Barnes, int. Joseph Wassel by Alfred Goldberg, 4/9/03, B115, GSA files, CF, *Sunday Times* (U.K.), 9/5/10.

187 **logged in 9:58:** Hyde to Front Office, 3/2/04, Dan Marcus Files, CF. Much-publicized recollections, particularly those of former transportation secretary Norman Mineta, appear to suggest that Cheney was moved to the PEOC before 9:30 A.M. According to the authors' analysis, they are in error. Mineta himself, moreover, was not logged into the PEOC until 10:07.

187 **disputed call:** CR, 40. Cheney had also called Bush minutes earlier, from a wall phone in a tunnel on the way to the bunker. In that call, he said, they discussed principally the matter of whether the President should return to Washington. Cheney's aide, Scooter Libby, who arrived in the tunnel during the call, thought the gist of it was "basically conveying what was happening." Neither he nor Mrs. Cheney, who was also there, heard any discussion of the shoot-down issue. It is evident from a Defense Department

transcript that a White House official requested a Combat Air Patrol over the capital at about that time, but made no mention of a shoot-down order. Counterterrorism co-ordinator Clarke, moreover, was still talking of "asking the President for authority to shoot down aircraft."

Neither Libby's notes, however, nor Mrs. Cheney's, reflect contact with Bush at the time mentioned by Cheney. National Security Adviser Condoleezza Rice did tell the Commission she heard Cheney's end of a conversation with the President at that time. While she recalled a reference to a Combat Air Patrol, however, she did not hear Cheney recommend the shoot-down of hijacked airliners. A separate statement by Rice, moreover, mightily diminishes her credibility. She told ABC News that shoot-down authority was "requested through channels, by Secretary Rumsfeld, Vice President passed the request, the President said, 'Yes.' " Far from requesting shoot-down authority, Rumsfeld—as reported in the text—learned of the shoot-down order only after the fact, from Cheney (Cheney called: CR 40, 464n211/213, Interview of Scooter Libby by *Newsweek*, 11/16/01, & Interview of Mrs. Cheney by *Newsweek*, 11/9/01, "Farmer Misc.," B10, NYC files, CF; transcript: CR 38, 463n201; "asking": CR 36, 463n191, MFR 04018415, 12/16/03, CF; Libby/Cheney notes/Rice: CR 40–, 43; "requested": "9/11," ABC News, 9/11/02, transcript at http://s3.amazonaws.com, Farmer, 259).

187   **staff received/Kurtz:** CR, 36, MFR 04018415, 12/16/03, CF.

187   **suspect aircraft:** The reports of inbound aircraft originated, as Mrs. Cheney's notes suggest, as information from the Secret Service's Joint Operations Center (JOC), which was in turn getting its information directly from the FAA. The incoming aircraft was likely United 93, which the Secret Service and its FAA contact were tracking on a screen that showed its *projected* path. Both were unaware that, as of 10:03, the flight that appeared on the screen to be approaching the capital had in fact already crashed. Within a minute or so of the confusing reports about Flight 93, the fighters out of Langley—just arriving over Washington—were also briefly mistaken as a threat (CR, 40–, Staff Statement 17, CO, Miles Kara, "9-11: Rules of Engagement," www.oredigger61.org).

188   **Mrs. Cheney noted:** notes, "Office of the VP Notes," B1, Dana Hyde files, CF. The content of Mrs. Cheney's notes

come from a handwritten digest done by Commission staff, which was released in 2009. Mrs. Cheney's original notes, like those of Scooter Libby, have not been released at the time of writing, nor has the Commission staff's record of its interview of Josh Bolten. Bolten has disputed the way he was reported in the Commission Report. According to Cheney biographer Stephen Hayes, he said "he suggested Cheney call Bush not because the Vice President had overstepped his authority, but as a reminder that they should notify the President." In his November interview with *Newsweek*, Libby would say, "I wouldn't be surprised that there were—that there had already been discussion with the President about getting CAP [Combat Air Patrol] up. . . . I'm almost certain that they had already had discussions . . . as I say, I was not on those phone calls." (Mrs. Cheney's notes: "OVP Notes," B1, Dana Hyde files, CF; Cheney/Libby/Bolten notes: corr. NARA's Kristen Wilhelm, 2010; Bolten disputed: Hayes, 546n20; "I wouldn't": int. Libby by *Newsweek*, 11/16/01).

188   **"I'm talking":** int. Anthony Barnes. According to Barnes, it was not he who warned Cheney of an approaching aircraft. That information reached the Vice President from someone else. The Commission Report identifies the source of the "aircraft 80 miles out" report only as a "military aide." The aide could perhaps have been the Vice President's military aide, Douglas Cochrane, who was also in the PEOC at some point (CR, 40–).

188–9 **Libby/"Yes":** int. Libby by *Newsweek*, 11/16/01; **lt. col. "confirmed":** CR 42, 465n227; **"pin-drop":** MFR 04020719, 4/29/04; **Libby note:** CR, 465n220; **"wanted to make sure":** CR, 41.

189–90 **Fleischer kept record:** Ari Fleischer, *Taking Heat*, NY: William Morrow, 2005, 141, transcript *60 Minutes*, CBS, 9/11/02. The note Fleischer made on 9/11, which firmly timed the President's comment as having been made at 10:20, remains classified. The press secretary's memoir—published after the Commission's Report came out—refers to the timing of the authorization only vaguely, as "shortly after we took off" (classified: corr. Kristen Wilhem, 2010, "shortly": Fleischer, 141); **"he had authorized":** CR, 41, 465n221; **not "alert":** Cherie Gott, "Brief Look at the Effect of Considering Prior Years' More Robust Alert Facility Architecture on Events of 11 Sep 2001," www.scribd.com;

"Capital Guardians": "Andrews AFB Guide," www. dcmilitary.com.

190 **SS/FAA contact early on:** CR, 464n208. Secret Service agent Nelson Garabito had first discussed how to react with his usual FAA liaison, Terry Van Steenbergen, who said what was needed was "fighters airborne." Van Steenbergen initiated contacts with the National Guard at Andrews. Told by a colleague at the base of the approach, Major Daniel Caine in turn called another Secret Service agent, Ken Beauchamp, asking whether he could be of assistance. Though Beauchamp initially made no request, he phoned back later—after the Pentagon was hit at 9:37. (Garabito/Van Steenbergen: MFR of int. Terry Van Steenbergen, 3/30/04, "FAA HQ," B6, T8, CF, MFR 04017326, 7/28/03, CR, 464n208, USSS Statements & Interview Reports, 7/28/03, "Secret Service Requests," B5, Dana Hyde files, CF; Caine/Beauchamp: MFR 04020717, 3/8/04, Spencer, 124).

190 **Pentagon/Wherely at run:** MFR 03005418, 8/28/03, *WP,* 4/8/02.

190 **"Get anything":** Wherley Interview, "Andrews AFB Logs-Timelines," B4, Dana Hyde files, CF. This wording fits closely with a "Memo for Record" written on September 16 by Andrews's Aircraft Generation Squadron Commander, Lieutenant Colonel Charles Denman. "At 10:10," he noted, "we received word to 'Get something up.' " "10:10" may or may not be a correct timing—a time Denham gave for a later event in the Andrews sequence seems inconsistent with other information (Memo for Record, 9/16/01, "Andrews AFB Timelines," B4, Dana Hyde files, CF).

191 **"someone a little higher"/"It's coming"/Ediger:** "Andrews AFB Timelines," BH, Dana Hyde files, CF, MFR 03005418, 8/28/03; **asked to speak/"wasn't going"/made do/"unidentified male":** MFR of int. David Wherley, 2/27/04, "General Wherley," B1, Dana Hyde, CF; **"put aircraft"/"any force"/"understandable":** MFR 03005418, 8/28/03; **After the crash:** Prewitt (USSS) to Monaghan re FOIA 20080330 & 20080331 & attachments, 4/23/10, "USSS Memos & Timelines," www.scrib.doc re [Barnes] USSS Interview notes, 7/28/03, "USSS Requests & Notes," B5, Dana Hyde files, CF, int. Anthony Barnes, MFR 03005418, 8/28/03, National Society of Black Engineers press release, "Igniting the Torch," 2008.

192   **Barnes cannot pin down:** A further document, a Commission memo on the Secret Service records, suggests the contacts with Barnes took place at about the time Cheney was arriving at the PEOC—linking it to efforts to protect the White House. "All air traffic," the document indicates, "would be halted and forced to land" (memo, 7/28/03, "USSS Requests & Notes," B5, T8, CF); **10:04:** Relevant Andrews Transmissions, 2/17–18/04, "Andrews AFB Logs," B4, Dana Hyde files, CF, corr. Miles Kara, 2011.

192   **Cheney would deny/"aware that":** CR, 44; **"acted on its own"/"the agents' ":** *WSJ*, 3/22/04.

192   **On own initative?:** While there is no documentary evidence of a call between Bush and Cheney in which Bush authorized a shoot-down, Commission notes released to the authors in 2011 do indicate that the Vice President felt the need to get Bush's authorization at a later point. At 10:44, while speaking with Defense Secretary Rumsfeld about raising the military's alert status to Defcon 3, Cheney told Rumsfeld, "I'll have to run that by him [Bush] and let him make the call." It is arguable that Cheney would have felt the same need for authority to engage hijacked airliners ("Dana Hyde Notes of Air Threat Conference Call," CF, corr. Miles Kara).

192   **sec. def. out of touch/intermittent contact:** As reported earlier, the President recalled that it repeatedly proved difficult to get through to Cheney on 9/11. Richard Clarke described Cheney, in the PEOC, complaining, "The comms [communications] in this place are terrible." Presidential press secretary Ari Fleischer recalled the President saying, "The communications equipment was good, not great, as he often had to wait to get people on the phone. After September 11, Air Force's One's communications equipment received a major modernization." (Bush recalled: see Ch. 9; "The comms": Richard Clarke, 19; "The communications": Fleischer, 141).

193   **Wherley no immediate way:** Miles Kara, "The Andrews Fighters": An Expeditionary Force, Not an Air Defense," 9/11 Revisited, www.oredigger61.org, CR, 44, Charles J. Gross, Memo for the Record, 9/19/01, "Andrews AFB Logs-Timelines," B4, Dana Hyde files, CF.

193   **less than certain/"check out":** MFR 03005418, 8/28/03, MFR of int. David Wherley, 2/27/04, "General Wherley," B1, Dana Hyde files, CF. This first fighter to go up from

Andrews carried no missiles, and its gun was loaded only with training rounds. Its pilot, Major Billy Hutchison, would later claim that the general told him to "intercept [an] aircraft coming toward D.C. and prevent it from reaching D.C." Another officer at the base, however, Major David McNulty, said Hutchison was tasked to do nothing more than identify an aircraft approaching along the Potomac. (That plane, it later turned out, had been just a helicopter.) Senior Commission counsel John Farmer in 2009 roundly rejected an account that suggested Hutchison located United 93 on his radar and considered ramming it—Hutchison did not even take off until 10:38, more than half an hour after Flight 93 had crashed ("intercept": Hutchison [typed notes of int.] & MFR of Hutchinson, "Billy Hutchinson Andrews AFB," B3, Dana Hyde files, CF; McNulty: MFR 04020718, 3/11/04; Farmer rejected: Farmer, 375, & see Miles Kara, "The Scott Trilogy: Cutting to the Chase," 9/11 Revisited, www.orediger61.org; considered ramming: Spencer, 219–; 10:38: Relevant Andrews Timelines, "Miles Kara Docs 3," B8, T8, CF).

193 **Four more fighters:** ibid., MFR 04020720, 3/11/04, Charles Gross, Memo for the Record, UA 93 and Andrews Timeline, & transcript ints. Igor Rasmussen & Leslie Filson, 9/18/03, "Andrews AFB Logs-Timelines," B4, Dana Hyde files, CF.

193 **"weapons free"/"uncomfortable":** MFR of int. David Wherley, 2/27/04, "General Wherley," B1, Dana Hyde files, CF, Staff Statement 17, CO, transcript ints. McNutz/Thompson/Sasseville, & ints. Thompson & Penney, undated, "Andrews AFB Logs-Timelines," B4, Dana Hyde files, CF, & see Kara to Hyde & Azzarello, 5/25/04. The general may have had reason to feel uncomfortable. According to NORAD commanding general Eberhart, Wherley "did not have the authority to give a 'weapons-free' order." Wherley said later that he "didn't feel comfortable until he heard Vice President Cheney's interview with Tim Russert [on September 16, on *Meet the Press*]" (Eberhart: MFR 04018141, 3/1/04; "didn't feel": MFR of int. David Wherley, 2/27/04, "General Wherley, Zelikow Notes & MFRs," B1, Dana Hyde files, CF; "had not been aware": CR, 44).

193–4 **formal rules:** MFR of int. David Wherley, 2/27/04, "General Wherley," B1, Dana Hyde files, CF, CR, 465n234; **made its way/10:31/You need to read:** 9/11 NEADS Tape

Transcription, "NEADS-CONR-NORAD Transcripts, NEADS Channel 2," B3, NYC files, CF, & Channel 2 audio at B82 & B110, GSA files, CF, Spencer, 240–, Shootdown references, "Miles Kara and Dana Hyde Work Papers," B8, T8, CF, CR, 4; **Marr/Nasypany unsure:** CR, 43; **"hostile act":** MFR 0401841, 3/1/04.

194   **Any track:** Kara to Hyde et al., 5/24/04. It is not clear whether the voice on the tape is that of Nasypany or that of his weapons officer, Major James Fox (CF, DH, B5, "Langley Pilots Interviews Fdr.—email thread re Flight 93—NEADS Tapes," B5, Dana Hyde files, CF).

194–5   **Wolfowitz/FAA & military versions:** see earlier refs in Chapters 12 & 13; Farmer, 245, 251, 255, CR, 31–.

195   **referred to inspectors general:** The inspectors general of both the Defense Department and the Department of Transportation delivered their reports in 2006. Neither conceded that there was evidence that either department's officials connived to reconstruct the story on events on 9/11. The Commission's John Farmer—as a former attorney general of New Jersey a man well used to weighing evidence—challenged that finding. "There is no question," he has written, "that the official version . . . served the interest of every institution involved. . . . It is impossible to conclude honestly, from the two Inspector General reports, that the official version of the events of 9/11 was the result of mere administrative incompetence; too many questions remained unanswered." The full body of evidence is extremely complex, too complex to be dealt with in this book. The authors suggest that interested readers consult Commission general counsel Marcus's referral letter to the inspectors general, the resulting IG reports, and Farmer's 2009 book, *Ground Truth* (referral: Marcus to Schmitz and Mead & attachments, 7/29/04; IG reports: "Memorandum for Under Secretary of Defense of Intelligence," 9/12/06, "Results of OIG Investigation of 9/11 Commission Staff Referral," Todd Zinser to Acting Secretary, FAA, 8/31/06; "There is no question": Farmer, 287–).

195   **"in my opinion":** Testimony of Monte Belger, 6/17/04, CO; **"In my opinion":** Testimony of Richard Myers, 6/17/04, CO; **"were talking mainly"/"leadership was irrelevant"/was not simply wrong:** Farmer, 186–, 290, 277, 288–.

Part III: **AMERICA RESPONDS**

CHAPTER 14

199–200 **garbage can/"Allah will be":** Chicago to Director, 9/12/01, FBI 265D-NY-280350-CG, INTELWIRE; **kept an eye/"Mission failed":** FBI 302 of int. Grant Besley, 9/16/01, B11, T7, CF, Chronology ADA-30, Operations Center, Terrorist Attacks NYC-DC 9/11/01, "FAA 3 of 3 Chronology ADA Ops Center," B19, T8, CF; **Picciotto/The guy:** Picciotto, 75–.

200 **5,000/"remained in custody":** "The September 11 Detainees: A Review of the Treatment of Aliens Held on Immigration Charges in Connection with the Investigation of the September 11 Attacks," Washington, D.C.: U.S. Dept. of Justice, Office of the Inspector General, 6/03. The figure of 5,000 is taken from the study by Professors David Cole and Jules Lobel, which is in turn derived from official U.S. government reports. *The Washington Post* reported that 1,182 "potential terror suspects" had been detained by November 2001. In addition, some 4,000 were detained under two post-9/11 INS initiatives, the Special Registration and Alien Absconder programs. "The vast majority" of the 5,000, Professor Cole told the authors, were detained "on immigration charges, ranging from overstaying a visa to working without a permit or even to failing to file a notice of change of address" (corr. David Cole, 2010, *LAT,* 11/18/07, *WP,* 11/6/01, 6/16/04, Anjana Malhotra, "Overlooking Innocence," www.aclu.org, & see "The September 11 Detainees," Office of the Inspector General, U.S. Department of Justice, 4/03, 2–, CR, 327–, 556n17, Philip Heymann, "Muslims in America after 9/11: The Legal Situation," conference paper, 12/15/06, www.ces.fas.harvard.edu).

201 **conditions included/abuse:** The abuse occurred especially at the Federal Bureau of Prisons' Metropolitan Detention Center in Brooklyn ("The September 11 Detainees," 4–).

201 **only one convicted:** As of 2009 the only post-9/11 detainee convicted was Ali al-Marri, who had been arrested in December 2001. Marri was sentenced to eight years for plotting with and materially supporting al Qaeda. Zacarias Moussaoui, who is serving life without the possibility of parole for conspiracy to commit acts of terrorism and air

piracy, had been arrested before 9/11 (Marri: corr. David Cole, 2010, AP, 10/30/09, *LAT*, 5/1/09; Moussaoui: AP, 9/25/09, BBC News, 5/4/06, AFP, 1/4/10, CR, 247); **Ziglar/"a moment":** MFR 04016455, 11/14/03; **anti-Arab hostility/Sikh shot:** *New Republic*, 9/24/01, *Queens Tribune*, 9/18/01; **Egyptian pilot:** DiMarco, 314–.

201   **Flight 23/"four young Arab":** Spencer, 102–, MFR 04020009, 4/14/04, CBS News, 9/14/01. The account of the Flight 23 incident is drawn principally from notes of a Commission interview with Ed Ballinger, the United dispatcher in charge of the airline's transcontinental flights that day, and from Lynn Spencer's book *Touching History*. Ballinger cited what he had been told by United's chief pilot, and Spencer apparently interviewed Flight 23 crew members. There were other, less well documented reports of possible threats to planes on 9/11. Flight attendants told the Commission of Arab passengers having behaved in a way they thought suspicious aboard United Flight 962 from Los Angeles to Washington, D.C. A passenger who flew aboard yet another United plane, Flight 915 from Paris to Washington, D.C., told the Commission there had been a major security alert at Charles de Gaulle Airport before take-off—and before the attacks began in the United States—and that guards removed a suspect from the terminal. In the States, the FBI reportedly searched for passengers who had been aboard another grounded airliner, American Flight 43. In Canada, authorities detained a Yemeni arrested aboard a U.S.-bound plane that had been diverted to Toronto. He was reportedly carrying several different passports, had papers with Arabic writing sewn into his clothing, and his baggage contained Lufthansa crew uniforms. A U.S. Justice Department spokesman said box cutters, similar to those used as weapons on the hijacked planes, were later found on other aircraft. Though the authors surmise that few if any of these accounts relate to real threats, the incident involving United 23 may indeed have been serious (Ballinger/Spencer: MFR 04020009, 4/14/04, Spencer, 102–; UA962: FBI 302, ints. Elizabeth Anderson & Elizabeth Henley, 9/20/01, "FBI 302s—ACARS," B11, T7, CF, MFR 03007051, undated, 8/03; AA43: BBC News, 9/18/01; Yemeni: CBS News, 9/14/01, *Hamilton Spectator* [Canada], 9/26/01; box cutters: CNN, 9/24/01, & see MFR 04017172, 9/29/03, MFR

04019897, 7/29/03, FBI 302, 9/15/01, *Chicago Tribune*, 9/23/01, *Guardian* [U.K.], 10/13/01).

202   **Mihdhar:** Bamford, *Shadow Factory*, 64; **"We think we had":** *Globe and Mail* (Toronto), 6/13/02.

202–5   **"Who do you think":** Ronald Kessler, *The Terrorist Watch*, NY: Crown, 2007, 8–; **some Arabs celebrate:** Fox News, 9/12/01, "Bulls-Eye Say Egyptians as They Celebrate Anti-US Attacks," AFP, 9/11/01, *NYT,* 9/13/01, 9/26/01, 10/27/01; **"should feel":** CNN, 9/18/01; **Palestinians/rifles/candy:** Fox News, 9/12/01, *New Yorker,* 9/24/01, BBC News, 9/14/01, *The Times* (London), 9/11/01, Reuters, 9/12/01; **caller/DFLP:** BBC News, 9/12/01, "Sept. 11 One Year On," www.rte.ie, 9/11/02, CNN, 9/11/01; **Osama poster:** AP, 9/14/01; **"Congratulations":** The dissident was Saad al-Fagih, of the Movement for Islamic Reform in Arabia, transcript, *Frontline:* "Saudi Time Bomb," 9/15/01, www.pbs.org, & see Corbin, 250; **"This action":** *New Yorker,* 6/2/08; **CRS report:** Kenneth Katzman, "Terrorism: Near Eastern Groups and State Sponsors, 2001," Washington, D.C.: Congressional Research Service, 9/10/01; **17th:** an approximation. Osama's father reportedly had some twenty-two wives over the years, and at least four other sons were born during the year of Osama's birth. It is safe to say, though, that he fell between sons number seventeen and twenty-one (Steve Coll, *The Bin Ladens*, London: Allen Lane, 2008, 72–); **$300 million:** For a more detailed analysis of bin Laden's fortune, see Chapter 22; **"for some time":** CBS News, 9:12–9:54 A.M., 9/11/01, www.archive.org; **"We've hit":** *Newsweek*, 9/13/01, Bamford, *Pretext*, 54, notes of Stephen Cambone, 9/11/01, released under FOIA to Thad Anderson, www.outragedmoderates.com; **"Although in our":** Tenet, 167; **"beyond a doubt":** Tenet, xix.

205   **"We could then":** *60 Minutes*, CBS News, 9/11/02. The flight manifests were not released by any government source at the time. The airlines involved, however, quickly released lists of those they described as "victims" or passengers whose next of kin had been identified—but did not include the names of those believed to have been hijackers. That omission, especially, led to speculation that there had not really been any Arabs on the flights, that some hijackers might have used stolen identities, or that some of those being named in the press as hijackers might still be alive. The authors have

analyzed the available material—including passenger lists for the four flights as released by the FBI to author Terry McDermott, lists submitted as exhibits during the trial of Zacarias Moussaoui, and lists for Flights 175 and 93 that appear in released 9/11 Commission files. The names on the above match the list of those believed to have been hijackers released by the FBI on September 14, 2001. The names, moreover, occur consistently in the documented evidence of the hijackers' activity in the months and weeks before 9/11. Finally, photographs—apparently mostly from visa forms— were "verified by family members of thirteen of the hijackers—including presumed hijacking pilots Marwan al-Shehhi (175) and Hani Hanjour (77). That Ziad Jarrah had been aboard United 93 was established by comparison of DNA material from the home of his girlfriend Aysel Sengün in Germany and from one of four sets of unidentified human remains recovered at the crash site of Flight 93 ("victims"/next of kin: United Airlines press release, 9/12/01, American Airlines press release, 9/12/01; questions: e.g., see "Hijack 'Suspects' Alive and Well," www.bbc.co.uk, 9/23/01, *Telegraph* [U.K.], 9/23/01, *Newsday*, 10/22/01, "Passenger Lists," www.911research.wtc7.net, Gerard Holmgren, "Media Published Fake Passenger Lists for AA Flight 11," 5/14/04, www.archive.indymedia.be; manifests: McDermott, manifests reproduced in photo section, "Flight 93 Manifest," & "Flight 175 Misc. Manifest," B17, T7, CF, corr. Kristen Wilhelm, 2010, *U.S. v. Zacarias Moussaoui*, Exhibits P200018; FBI list: "FBI Announces List of 19 Hijackers," 9/14/01, www.fbi .gov—Flight 175 hijacker Fayez Ahmed Banihammad is identified on the FBI list only as Fayez Ahmed—the portion of his name that appears on the manifest, and misspells Flight 93 hijacker Ziad Jarrah's last name—correctly rendered on the available manifest—as "Jarrahi"; documented evidence: e.g., "Hijacker's True Name Usage," *U.S. v. Zacarias Moussaoui*, Exhibit OG00013, Dulles Airport Command Post, Intelligence Log, FBI 265D-NY-280350, "Aliases & Id," B62, T5, CF, & see Jeremy Hammond, "9/11 Hijackers Not on Manifests," www.foreignpolicyjournal.com, 4/5/10, "No Hijacker Names on Passenger Manifests," www.911myths. com, "Panoply of the Absurd," www.spiegel.de, 9/8/03; photographs: Legat Riyadh to Counterterrorism, 11/20/01, "Aliases & Ids," B62, T5, CF; Jarrah DNA: PENTTBOM,

Misc. Req. 42, "Aliases & Ids," B62, T5, CF).

205–8 **flight attendants/Suqami/Shehris/Atta:** FBI 302 of int. Kip Hamilton, 9/11/01 & re Lead Control Numbers DL267 and CE66, 9/13/01, "DOJ Documents Requests #35-13," B13, T7, CF, *New York Observer,* 2/15/04, entry for 10:59 a.m., Chicago to Director, 9/12/01, INTELWIRE, entries for 10:51 a.m. & 11:26 a.m., TSA Incident Log, 9/11/01, "DOJ Documents Request," B20, T7, CF, MFR 03007067, 9/11/03; **Graney/"clenched":** FBI 302 of int. Diane Graney, 9/22/01, "FBI 302s—Ground Security Coordinator," B1, T7, CF, MFR 04020036, 4/15/04, MFR 04020016, 5/27/04; **camera recorded/calls:** "Chronology of Events for Hijackers, 8/16/01," *U.S. v. Zacarias Moussaoui,* Exhibits OG00020.2, FO07011, FO07021, FO07022, FO07023, FO07024, "265D-NY-280350, TWINBOM-PENTTBOM, Biographical Report," 11/26/01, National Drug Intelligence Center for the FBI, authors' collection, FBI press release, 10/14/01, entries for 9/10/01 & 9/11/01, "Hijackers Timeline [redacted]," 11/14/03, INTELWIRE, FBI 302 of [name redacted], 10/15/01, "FBI 302s of Interest," B17, T7, CF, FBI Timeline of 9-11 Hijacker Activity & Movements, "Timelines 9-11, 2 of 2," B20, T7, CF; **Nissan:** ibid., *WP,* 10/6/01; **Hyundai/Banihammad/Milner/ticket:** MFR 04020636, 2/2/04, "American Airlines Flight 11, PENTTBOM, 265A-NY-280350," 4/19/02; **Mitsubishi found:** "American Airlines Flight 11, PENTTBOM, 265A-NY-280350," 4/19/02, Staff Report, "The Four Flights & Civil Aviation Security," CF, exhibits list, "Breeder Documents," B8, T5, CF, MFR 04020636, 2/2/04, MFR 03007050, 8/15/03; **Park Inn:** "American Airlines Flight 11, PENTTBOM, 265A-NY-280350," 4/19/02; **Ghamdis/Charles Hotel/taxi:** MFR 04020636, 2/2/04; **draped towels:** *WP,* 9/16/01; **novels/*Penthouse*/condoms:** Warrant Issued on Vehicle ID JT2AE92E9J3137546, 9/13/01, "FBI 302s of Interest," B17, T7, CF, "Ziad Jarrah," FBI summary, 4/19/02, www.scribd.com; **prostitutes:** *BG,* 10/10/01, MFR 04020636, 2/2/04; **phone records:** MFR 04020636, 2/2/04.

208 **money trail:** ibid., Evidence Inspected at FBI HQ 5/14/04, "Breeder Documents," B8, T5, CF, Staff Report, "Monograph on Terrorist Financing, CO, *Newsweek,* 11/11/01. The two key financial facilitators in the UAE were Ali Abdul Aziz Ali and Mustafa al-Hawsawi. Both men,

arrested in Pakistan in 2003, became part of the group known as "High-Value Detainees" held at Guantánamo Bay. As of spring 2012, they were still there (Staff Report, "Monograph on Terrorist Financing," CO, *NYT*, 6/30/10, "The Guantánamo Docket," www.nyt.com); **"A maid"**: Counterterrorism to All Field Offices, 9/22/01, FBI 265A-NY-280350, released under FOIA to Mike Williams, www.911myths.com, "Hijackers Timeline [redacted]," 11/4/03, INTELWIRE.

208–9 **ominous indications/"sleepers"**: Of these three leads, the authors found no indication that the first—relating to the man who answered the door at the Park Inn—was ever resolved. The two names were found at Dulles Airport in a car registered to Nawaf al-Hazmi, one of the Flight 77 hijackers. One was that of Osama Awadallah, a Yemeni living in San Diego who turned out to have known two of the hijackers and had material about bin Laden. Though suspected of having had prior knowledge of the attacks, he was not charged in that connection. The name written in highlighter related to Mohamed Abdi, a naturalized U.S. citizen working as a Burns security guard. Like Awadallah, he was not charged with any terrorism offense (Awadallah: MFR 04017544, 11/18/03, CR, 220, 250, 532n175, *San Diego Union-Tribune*, 9/14/02, *NYT*, 11/18/06; Abdi: *U.S. v. Mohamed Abdi*, Case No. 01–1053-M, U.S. District Court for the Eastern District of Virginia, www.findlaw.com, MFR 04016253, 10/16/03, *WP*, 9/27/01, 1/12/02, *Human Events*, 10/15/01).

209 **Dulles/Security camera/pass:** The available evidence, however, is less than consistent. An FBI document states that the video evidence "indicates that two of the hijackers . . . passed through the security checkpoints and baggage claim areas" on September 10. This appears to have occurred at 4:51 p.m. on the eve of the attacks. Checkpoint supervisor Eric Safraz Gill, however, spoke of having challenged an "Arab-looking" man equipped with a swipe pass, and two with apparently adequate identification at about 8:15 P.M. They had attempted to get two other men—who had no such ID—through a secure door. All the men left, following an altercation with Gill ("indicates": Counterterrorism to Field Offices, 9/22/01, FBI 265A-NY-280350, & see entry for 9/10/01, "Hijackers Timeline [redacted]," 11/14/03, INTELWIRE, MFR 04020030, 4/6/04, MFR 04016235, 2/10/04; Gill: Susan B.

Trento & Joseph J. Trento, *Unsafe at Any Altitude*, Hanover, NH: Steerforth, 2007, 1–, 43–).

209–10 **Corolla/personal belongings/investigative treasure/ involvement in aviation:** "Nawaf al-Hazmi," FBI summary, 4/19/02, www.scribd.com, Warrant Issued on Vehicle IDJT2AE92E9J3137546, 9/13/01, "FBI 302s of Interest," B17, T7, CF, Criminal Complaint, *U.S. v. Mohamed Abdi*, Case No. 01–1053-M, U.S. District Court for the Eastern District of Virginia, 9/23/01, MFR 04016253, 10/16/03, San Diego to Ottawa et al., 4/11/02, Leads from Hijackers' Cars, INTELWIRE, "Ali Ahmad Mesdaq," 1/28/02, FBI Document re PENTTBOM, INTELWIRE. Also recovered, at Newark Airport, was a red Mitsubishi Galant rented by Ziad Jarrah. Jarrah, a Lebanese citizen, is believed to have led the hijack team on United Flight 93. Though the car contained far less evidence than did Hazmi's, agents did recover a speeding ticket Jarrah had incurred in the early hours of September 10. In a trash can at Newark's Days Inn, meanwhile, the FBI found the used Spirit Airlines ticketing that had brought Jarrah and Saudis Saeed al-Ghamdi, Ahmed al-Nami, and Ahmad al-Haznawi from Fort Lauderdale to Newark on September 7. Other evidence aside, the joint travel before 9/11 indicated that the four men shared a common purpose (Ziad Jarrah summary, Prepared by UA93 Investigative Team, FBI, 4/19/02, www.scribd.com, Evidence Inspected at FBI HQ 5/14/04, "Breeder Documents," B8, T7, CF, Longman, 101).

210–11 **duffel bags:** MFR 04017509, 11/5/03, "Hijackers Timeline [redacted]," 11/14/03, INTELWIRE, *San Diego Union-Tribune*, 9/3/02; **Portland car:** Evidence Inspected at FBI HQ, 5/14/04, "Breeder Documents," B8, T5, CF; **manuals:** "Ziad Jarrah," FBI summary, www.scribd.com; **"Everybody was gathered":** int. Mark Mikarts; **"It was the sort"/"His bearing":** *Birmingham Post* (U.K.), 9/25/01, Jane Corbin, *The Base*, London: Pocket, 2003, 162; **Dekkers:** transcript of interview of Rudi Dekkers, ibid., *News-Press* (Fort Myers, FL), 9/13/01.

211 **Atta luggage:** Review of Investigation Conducted by the FBI of Atta's Suitcases at Boston, 2/10/04, "Detainee Reports," B53, T5, CF, FBI 302 of [redacted] DePasquale, 9/17/01, "Atta Luggage," B18, T7, CF, Recovered Identification Documents, "Breeder Documents," B8, T5, CF. Also in Atta's

bag were a folding knife and some First Defense pepper spray. Omari's bag contained an Arabic-to-English dictionary, English grammar books, his Saudi passport, and a bank checkbook (Recovered Identification Documents, "Breeder Docs.—Entire Contents," B8, T5, CF, MFR of Review of Investigation by the FBI of Atta's suitcases at Boston, 2/10/04, "Detainee Reports," B53, T5, CF).

212   **document in luggage/at Dulles/at 93 site:** "Synopsis of Captioned Investigation as of 11/4/01," PENTTBOM, Major Case 182, 11/5/01, authors' collection. The document has been variously referred to as having five, four, and three pages. The first report, by Bob Woodward in *The Washington Post*, had it as five. A 2006 study, by Professor Hans Kippenberg and Professor Tilman Seidensticker, suggests that a fifth page was recovered but not published. CBS News, which reported on a copy of the Dulles Airport document, said it was "similar but not identical to the document found in Atta's luggage, and parts of a document found in the Pennsylvania wreckage" (Woodward: *WP*, 9/28/01; four: eds. Hans Kippenberg & Tilman Seidensticker, *The 9/11 Handbook*, London: Equinox, 2006, 1–, *Observer* [London], 9/30/01; three: "PENTTBOM, Major case 182, Summary of Captioned Investigation as of 11/4/01," FBI document, 11/5/01; CBS News: "Translated Text: Hijackers' How-To," www.cbsnews.com, 10/1/01).

212   **Commission not mention:** Congress's Joint Inquiry report on the attacks did cite a statement by FBI director Mueller including the fact that a "three-page letter handwritten in Arabic" had been found, and stating that it contained "instructions on how to prepare for a mission applicable, but not specific, to the September 11 operation" (JI, Report, 142–, Statement of Robert Mueller, 9/25/02, www.fas.org).

212   **"Spiritual Manual"/"Handbook"/"mutual pledge":** all from the translation in eds. Kippenberg & Seidensticker, 11–. There have been several translations and commentaries of the document the FBI released. The authors of this book have relied primarily on the 2006 book *The 9/11 Handbook*, by Hans Kippenberg, professor of Comparative Religious Studies at Jacobs University in Bremen, Germany, and Tilman Seidensticker, professor of Arab and Islamic Studies at the Friedrich Schiller University in Jena. There have been other commentaries of note—by Professor Kanan Makiya of Brandeis University and Hassan Mneimneh, a senior fellow at

the Hudson Institute, Professor Juan Cole of the University of Michigan, and David Cook, an associate professor at Rice University. In their book *Masterminds of Terror,* Al Jazeera's Yosri Fouda and *The Sunday Times*'s Nick Fielding reported Fouda's 2002 interview of self-confessed 9/11 conspirator Ramzi Binalshibh—which offered confirmation that the "Spiritual Manual" is authentic. All the sources mentioned treat the document as having been written for the 9/11 hijackers. The translators of the version used by CBS News in 2001, however, stated in a note that the document did "not in any way sound like instructions to a hijacker or a terrorist." In the context of its content and circumstances of discovery, however, the document can only be pertinent to 9/11 (Kanan Makiya & Hassan Mneimneh, "Manual for a Raid," *NY Review of Books,* 1/17/02, Yosri Fouda & Nick Fielding, *Masterminds of Terror,* Edinburgh: Mainstream, 2003, 141–, Juan Cole, "Al Qaeda's Doomsday Document and Psychological Manipulation," 4/9/03, www.juancole.com, David Cook, *Understanding Jihad,* Berkeley: Univ. of Calif. Press, 2005, 195–, "Translated Text: Hijackers How-To," 10/1/01, www.cbsnews.com).

212–16 **manual:** FBI press release, 9/28/01, www.fbi.gov; **re "q"/Qiblah:** Fouda & Fielding, 147; **"To those who":** corr. Hans Kippenberg, 2010. Some, pointing to anomalies in the document, have raised the possibility that the hijackers' manual might be a forgery. Professor Kippenberg, however, who has conducted the most in-depth analysis, cites a skein of persuasive evidence to the contrary (anomalies: e.g., Robert Fisk, *The Great War for Civilization,* London: Fourth Estate, 2005, 1039–; **evidence:** Kippenberg, 4–).

217–18 **"We believe":** *Telegraph* (U.K.), 9/13/01, int. of Jamal Ismael for Palladin InVision, 2006, supplied to author, *WP,* 12/9/01, Peter L. Bergen, *The Osama bin Laden I Know,* New York: Free Press, 2006, 312; **"I would like"/Taliban accepted:** CNN, 9/17/01; **"As a Muslim":** *Daily Ummat* (Karachi), 9/28/01, www.justresponse.net; **"Whenever we kill"/"As concerns":** ed. Bruce Lawrence, *Messages to the World,* London: Verso, 2005, 106–.

218–19 **On the eve:** The night before the attacks, according to a CBS News report citing Pakistani intelligence sources, bin Laden entered a military hospital in Rawalpindi, Pakistan, for kidney dialysis. This report appears to have been unfounded. There was an oft-repeated story that he required dialysis, but the best evidence is that he did not. Al Qaeda operatives' accounts, moreover, place bin Laden at a camp in Afghanistan the following morning, September 11 (CBS news, 1/28/02, and see notes for Ch. 30, pp. 548–49); **call to mother/"In two days"/"I would never"**: *NYT*, 10/2/01, MSNBC, 10/1/01, *Mail on Sunday* (U.K.), 12/23/01.

219   **"I asked Osama"**: Mir quoted in Georgie Anne Geyer, "Reporting on Terrorist Can Be Deadly," http://sentinelsource.com, 6/28/09, but see Bergen, *OBL I Know,* 319, corr. Peter Bergen, 2010. The only other post-9/11 interview bin Laden gave was for television, with Taysir Alluni of Al Jazeera. Alluni was later arrested in his home country, Spain, on charges of supporting al Qaeda, and not released until 2005.

     Only in 2007, on an audiotape that a U.S. official judged authentic at the time would bin Laden clearly admit responsibility for 9/11. The voice believed to be his on the tape said, "The events of Manhattan were retaliation against the American-Israeli alliance's aggression against our people in Palestine and Lebanon, and I am the only one responsible for it. The Afghan people and government knew nothing about it. America knows that" (Alluni: ed. Lawrence, 106–, 139–; 2007 tape: msnbc.com, 11/29/07).

CHAPTER 15
This is a transitional chapter, and the majority of episodes described in it will be more fully covered and sourced in later chapters. For that reason, there is reference in the sources below only to points that will not be covered elsewhere.

220   **"Without conspiracy"/"Official answers"**: *Nation*, 5/31/02, 7/12/02.

220   **"No one has taken"**: Richard Falkenrath, "The 9/11 Commission Report: a Review Essay," *International Security*, Vol. 29, No. 3, Winter 04/05, Shenon, 392, 438n, & see *CounterPunch*, 2/23/08, *WP*, 7/13/08. The rather larger death toll figure of 2,973, used by the authors in the Prologue, was the official figure as of 2012.

221–2   **"Why did"**: int. of Patrick Leahy by Amy Goodman, www.democracynow.org, 9/29/06; **"As each day"**: *NYT*, 10/26/03; **"officials from FAA"**: Statement of Bogdan Dzakovic, 5/22/03, CO; **half summaries/"encouraged"/no** drive: Farmer, 98–, Staff Statement 3, CO; **"bad feeling"**: *Chicago*, 3/11; **"I've been with"**: *New York Observer*, 6/20/04.

223   **"September the 11th"**: ABC News, 12/19/02. The fellow agent was John Vincent, the assistant U.S. attorney Mark Flessner. The 9/11 Commission did not interview any of the three.

223–5 **"more than"**: Phoenix, Squad 16 to Counterterrorism, 7/10/01, www.justice.gov; **"well-managed"**: *WP*, 8/21/07; **"no examination"**: Executive Summary, "Report on CIA Accountability with Respect to the 9/11 Attacks," Office of the Inspector General, Central Intelligence Agency, 6/05; **"points"/"Both the CIA"**: Graham with Nussbaum, xv; **irritated**: Tenet, 169.

226   **Mossad**: The Mossad—more formally the Institute for Intelligence and Special Operations—can and does operate all over the world, emboldened by the knowledge that the United States is Israel's staunch ally and protector. Mossad's audacity was exemplified as recently as 2010, when its operatives were caught using the forged passports of several other nations in the course of a hit on a Hamas leader in Dubai.

The full extent of Israeli and U.S. liaison on intelligence, however, is a foggy area. Days after 9/11, the *Telegraph* newspaper in the U.K., citing a "senior Israeli security official," reported that "two senior experts" with Mossad had been sent to Washington in August to warn that a large terrorist cell was "preparing a big operation." The *Los Angeles Times* picked up the story, only to amend it within days and publish a CIA denial that there had been such a warning.

The authors looked at specific episodes that have been taken to suggest Israeli intelligence activity within the United States at the time. One occurred on the morning of 9/11, when a woman in a New Jersey apartment across the river from Manhattan telephoned the police. She had seen below her a group of men, on the roof of a van, shooting video footage of the burning Trade Center and—she thought—celebrating. Film taken from the men's camera, sources said later, did appear to show them "smiling and clowning around." The onlooker who called the police reported the van's registration number, noting that it was marked "Urban Moving Systems."

Arrested that afternoon, the men with the van turned out to

be five young Israelis. They were held for more than two months, questioned repeatedly, and eventually deported back to Israel. Their boss, Dominic Suter, also an Israeli, abruptly left the United States soon after the attacks. Two of the men, it was later reported, had been Mossad operatives and one— Paul Kurtzberg—said he had previously worked for Israeli intelligence in another country.

Former CIA counterterrorism chief Vincent Cannistraro told ABC News that—though the men "probably" did not have advance knowledge of 9/11—there was speculation in U.S. intelligence that Urban Moving was a front for spying on "radical Islamics in the area." Available information indicates that the Israelis had been living and working in New Jersey within a few miles of locations where Hazmi, Mihdhar, and four other members of the hijacking team had spent from spring to midsummer.

Some 400 pages of investigative materials on the van episode, recently released by the FBI, deserve further in-depth study.

A study by lawyer Gerald Shea, submitted to the 9/11 Commission and the Senate and House Intelligence Committees, drew attention to the odd activities in 2000 and 2001 of more than a hundred Israelis—working in groups of eight to ten across the United States, who had represented themselves as art students peddling artwork. Because the "students" were repeatedly noticed at Drug Enforcement Administration offices, DEA Security investigated—and came to suspect the "students" might be involved in organized crime.

Lawyer Shea, though, noted that those identified had primarily operated in Florida—close to the main southern staging area for the hijackers. He suggested in his study that the Israelis' purpose had included "keeping Arab groups in our country under surveillance, including the future hijackers." There is good reason to doubt Shea's theory, however, for the Israeli students also operated in states where the hijackers had not been located.

The puzzling incident of the New Jersey Israelis, however, did deserve serious public examination. Yet the possible role of Israeli intelligence in the 9/11 case—at any level—has been investigated by no official body (Dubai: *NYT,* 2/18/10; "senior Israeli": *Telegraph* [U.K.], 9/16/01, *LAT,* 9/20/01, 9/21/01;

men on van: *20/20*, ABC News, 6/21/02—transcript available at www.911myths.com, *Forward*, 2/3/03, *CounterPunch*, 3/07/07; "art students": Gerald Shea, "Israeli Surveillance of the Future Hijackers and FBI Suspects in the Sept. 11 Attacks," Memorandum to the National Commission on Terrorist Attacks Upon the United States et al., 9/15/04. Also, see Justin Raimondo, *The Terror Enigma*, NY: iUniverse, 2003).

227   **"hostile service":** James Risen, *State of War*, NY: Free Press, 2006, 181.

CHAPTER 16

228–30 **"BUSH CALLS"/memorial service, etc./"After all":** int. Ari Fleischer by Scott Pelley, 8/6/02, & by Terry Moran, 8/9/02, "EOP Press Interviews," B1, T3, CF, *NYT*, 9/15/01, "With the President: A Reporter's Story of 9/11," www.rochester.edu; **"hunt down":** CNN, 9/12/01; **"We're gonna":** Sammon, 113; **McWilliams/flag:** "Raising the Flag at the WTC," www.famouspictures.org, "About the Photo," www.groundzerospirit.org, DiMarco, 181fn; **memorial service/"Battle Hymn":** ABC News video at www.youtube.com, int. Condoleezza Rice by Bob Woodward, 10/24/01, "Farmer Misc.," B9, NYC files, CF; **"monumental":** "Remarks by the President," 9/12/01, www.avalon.law.yale.edu. See Note re death toll in sourcing for Preface. Accounts differ on the authorship of the President's speech and the way it developed. Gerson aside, aides involved Bush's counselor Karen Hughes, and speechwriters Matthew Scully and David Frum (*WP*, 1/27/02, "Present at the Creation," *Atlantic*, 9/07, "The President's Story," 9/11/02, www.cbsnews.com, *Nation*, 2/13/03, David Frum, *The Right Man*, NY: Random House, 2003, 142, Michael Gerson, *Heroic Conservatism*, NY: HarperOne, 2007, 69); **war council:** CR, 330; **Muttawakil:** "Defending Bin Laden," www.newsweek.com, 9/11/01; **Taliban propose:** *Foreign Policy Journal*, 8/12/09; **"We're not only":** int. Ari Fleischer by Scott Pelley; **never considered:** int. Condoleezza Rice by Bob Woodward; **ultimatum:** "Bush Delivers Ultimatum," www.unwire.org, 9/21/01; **rejected:** *LAT*, 9/22/01.

230   **Musharraf:** Pervez Musharraf, *In the Line of Fire*, NY: Free Press, 2006, 201–. According to the 9/11 Commission Report, and the 2006 biography of Colin Powell, Musharraf complied

with all the U.S. demands. In a memoir the same year, Musharraf said he balked at permitting the U.S. military "blanket overflight and landing rights" and "use of Pakistan's naval ports, air bases and strategic locations on borders." Instead, he wrote, he offered "only a narrow flight corridor" and "only two bases . . . for logistics and aircraft recovery." Deputy Secretary of State Richard Armitage, who delivered the American demands, for his part denied that he had threatened to bomb Pakistan. There was clearly massive pressure, however. In the words of CIA director Tenet, Armitage "dropped the hammer on them" (CR, 331–, Karen DeYoung, *Soldier*, NY: Alfred A. Knopf, 2006, 349, Tenet, 179).

231 **"Need to move":** Notes of Stephen Cambone, 9/11/01, released under FOIA to Thad Anderson, www.outragedmoderates.com; **"I know":** DOD press conference, 9/18/01, www.defenselink.mil; **"urged the President":** CR, 330, 558n34; **OBL/hijackers Saudis:** Staff Report, "Monograph on Terrorist Travel," CO.

231–2 **"do Iraq":** CR, 335, Bob Woodward, *Plan of Attack*, NY: Simon & Schuster, 2004, 26. The need to "do Iraq" is referred to in Ch. 9, p. 120. As noted there, it is not clear whether Rumsfeld spoke of "doing" Iraq on the night of 9/11 or at a meeting the following day. **"Look":** Richard Clarke, 32–, CR, 334 & see Ben-Veniste, 302; **Pressure to act:** CR, 334–, MFR of int. Colin Powell, 1/21/04, CF; **formal order:** Woodward, *Plan of Attack*, 26; **contingency plan:** CR, 335, Testimony of Condoleezza Rice, 4/8/04, CO, & see MFR 04021460, 4/9/04. The most vocal proponent of hitting Iraq was Deputy Defense Secretary Wolfowitz. To Secretary of State Powell, it seemed that "some of his colleagues were trying to use the events of 9/11 to promote their own policy obsessions and settle old scores" (MFR of Colin Powell, 1/21/04, CF, DeYoung, 348–, CR, 335–).

232–4 **Camp David/prayer:** DeYoung, 350–; **"patience":** DOD press conference, 1/9/02, www.defenselink.mil; **Black briefed:** Tenet, 177; **Shelton:** DeYoung, 351–; **"When we're through":** Ron Suskind, *The Price of Loyalty*, NY: Simon & Schuster, 2004, 185; **"comfort food"/"Amazing Grace"/ O'Neill:** ibid., 189–; **CIA proposing/Memorandum:** *New Yorker*, 8/17/07, 8/4/03, *NYT*, 9/10/06, 12/15/02, Joseph Margulies, *Guantánamo and the Abuse of Presidential Power*, NY:

Simon & Schuster, 2006, 189, CR, 333, "Who Authorized the Torture of Abu Zubaydah," www.huffingtonpost.com, 4/28/09; **"war on terrorism"**: *NY Daily News*, 9/17/01, BBC News, 9/16/01; **"war on terror"**: Bush address, CNN, 9/20/01.

234   **joint session:** The joint session was on September 30. On the 14th, the Congress had passed a resolution authorizing the use of "all necessary and appropriate force against those nations, organizations, or persons he [the President] determines planned, authorized, committed, or aided" the 9/11 attacks "or harbored such organizations or persons." The resolution passed in the Senate by 98 votes to 0, in the House by 420 votes to 1 (Richard Grimmett, "Authorization for Use of Military Force in Response to the 9/11 Attacks," Congressional Research Service); **"I want"**: CNN, 9/17/01, int. Dan Bartlett by Scott Pelley, 8/12/02, "Press Interviews of Staff," B1, T3, CF; **"platter"**: *Meet the Press*, www.cbsnews.com, 9/16/01; **"Gentlemen"**: Gary C. Schroen, *First In*, NY: Ballantine, 2005, 40; **"The mission"**: Ron Suskind, *The One Percent Doctrine*, NY: Simon & Schuster, 2006, 21.

235   **British commandos:** The British contingent was from the Special Boat Service, or SBS, similar to the better known SAS—Special Air Service—but drawn largely from the ranks of the Royal Marines. Though specializing in amphibious operations, the unit also operates overland. British and American special units have long collaborated. As for the overall number of operatives initially sent into Afghanistan, the authors have used the figure given by the commander of the Delta Force unit on the ground. Perhaps referring to a total at a somewhat later stage of the operation, Bob Woodward referred in his book *Bush at War* to a larger figure: "about 110 CIA officers and 316 Special Forces personnel" (SBS: "The Special Boat Service," www.hmforces.co.uk, "British Special Forces Member Killed in Afghanistan," *Guardian* [U.K.], 7/2/10, Alastair Finlan, "The [Arrested] Development of UK Special Forces and the Global War on Terror," *Review of International Studies*, Vol. 35, 2009; overall number: Dalton Fury, *Kill bin Laden*, NY: St. Martin's, 2008, xix, Woodward, *Bush at War*, 314).

235   **"This is why"**: Schroen, 33; **"Tell them"**: Gary Berntsen & Ralph Pezzullo, *Jawbreaker*, NY: Three Rivers, 2005, 289.

235–9 **Dalton Fury:** "Dalton Fury" is the pen name the major used as author of a 2008 book on the operation against bin Laden. While protecting his identity, the media have accepted his authenticity (Fury, 200; major media: e.g., *60 Minutes*, CBS, 10/5/08); **"A cloudy":** Fury, xx; **$100 bills/"Money":** Schroen, 29,38, 88, 93–; **duffel bags:** Fury, 105; **defeat:** Tommy Franks with Malcolm McConnell, *American Soldier*, NY: Regan, 2004, 322; **"God has":** ed. Lawrence, 104; **"great, long-term":** Bergen, *OBL I Know*, 316; **"safe and sound":** ibid., 322; **poor intelligence:** Berntsen & Pezzullo, 156, 108; **Atef:** Hamid Mir, "How Osama Has Survived," www.rediff.com, 9/11/07, bin Ladens & Sasson, 271; **OBL Jalalabad:** *Christian Science Monitor*, 3/4/02, Berntsen & Pezzullo, 239, *Sunday Times* (London), 1/15/09, John Miller & Michael Stone with Chris Mitchell, *The Cell*, NY: Hyperion, 2002, 319, Corbin, 262–; **"Black Widow":** *Newsweek*, 12/10/01, BBC News, 9/27/08; **Towr Ghar:** Fury, 107, "The Caves & Graves of Tora Bora," www.legionmagazine.com, 9/1/03; **"purpose-built":** *The Independent* (U.K.), 11/27/01 & see "The Lair of Bin Laden," www.edwardjepstein.com; **no electricity/water:** bin Ladens & Sasson, 185–; **schoolhouse:** Berntsen & Pezzullo, 253, Fury, 108; **Afghan generals:** e.g., Berntsen & Pezzullo, 272, 275, 280–, Fury, 114–, 124, 129–, 257; **negotiating:** Berntsen & Pezzullo, 289–, *NYT*, 9/11/05, Fury, 216–, 234, 244; **OBL largesse/sons:** Fury, 209, 108; **"flawed":** Fury, 99, Berntsen & Pezzullo, 213–; **reluctance:** Berntsen & Pezzullo, 277–, 290, 295, 305–, 309, 314, "In the Footsteps of Bin Laden," CNN, 8/23/06; **airpower:** e.g., Berntsen & Pezzullo, 270, 274–, Fury, 170–, 192; **Marine:** Berntsen & Pezzullo, 34–, 283–; **"tall":** ibid., 291; **6´4˝:** "Most Wanted Terrorists," www.fbi.gov; **BLU-82:** description at www.globalsecurity.org, Berntsen & Pezzullo, 291, Fury, 127; **Used on plains:** Berntsen & Pezzullo, 137–; **delivered:** ibid., 295–, Fury, 149–; **BLU-82:** described at www.fas.org, Michael O'Hanlon, "A Flawed Masterpiece," *Foreign Affairs*, 3/02; **"too hot"/"hideous":** "Tora Bora Revisited: How We Failed to Get Bin Laden and Why It Matters Today," Report, U.S. Senate Committee on Foreign Relations, Washington, D.C.: U.S. Government Printing Office, 2009, 7; **movement orders:** Fury, 230.

239   **"victory or death"/"Father":** According to Delta Force leader Fury, bin Laden was overheard saying in desperation,

"arm your women and children against the infidel!" His lead bodyguard Abu Jandal has recalled that "all bin Laden's wives knew how to handle weapons. They had taken a military course while al Qaeda was in the Sudan." It seems unlikely, though, that the terrorist leader would have expected young children to take part in the battle (Fury, 233, Nasser al-Bahri [Abu Jandal] with Georges Malbrunot, *Dans l'Ombre de Ben Laden,* Neuilly-sur-Seine, France: Michel Lafon, 2010, 199).

239   **Dec. 13/listened to a voice:** The CIA's Gary Berntsen dated this last intercept as having occurred not on December 13 but the 15th. Fury suggested that bin Laden was overheard once more, a day or so later. What he said, Fury wrote, came over as "more of a sermon than issuing orders" (Fury, 233–, 236–, Berntsen & Pezzullo, 307).

240–1   **devastation:** Fury, 270, 272, Berntsen & Pezzullo, 296; **not a trace/"punched"/rubble/Exhumations:** Fury, 286, 282, *Newsweek,* 10/31/08; **"real war":** Fury, 293; **"We need":** Berntsen & Pezzullo, 290; **Dailey:** Berntsen & Pezzullo, e.g., 307, 276; **"We have not said":** DOD press conference, 11/8/01, www.defense.gov, & see Franks with McConnell, 388; **skirted discussion:** ibid.

241   **As recently as 2009:** In testimony to the Senate Armed Services Committee, and on the PBS program *Frontline,* Franks suggested that the drive to "get into Tora Bora" came from the Afghan commanders. A decision was made, he said, to support the Afghan operation and to "work with the Pakistanis along the Pakistani border." He declared himself "satisfied with the decision process." CIA's Gary Berntsen has responded by writing that Franks was "either badly misinformed or blinded by the fog of war." Berntsen had made it clear in his reports, he said, that the Afghans were less than keen to attack Tora Bora. General Franks, meanwhile, has also said he had concerns as to the amount of time it would have taken to get U.S. troops into the mountains. He has pointed out, too, most recently in 2009, that relying principally on Afghan ground forces in the field had worked in overthrowing the Taliban ("get into"/"work with": int. Tommy Franks for *Frontline,* www.pbs.org; "satisfied": Testimony of Tommy Franks, U.S. Senate Armed Services Committee, 7/31/02, www.access.gpo.gov; Berntsen: Berntsen & Pezzullo, 290–; concerns: *New Republic,* 12/22/09).

241 **"conflicting"**: *New Republic*, 12/22/09 & see *NYT*, 10/19/04, MFR 04021460, 4/9/04. General Michael DeLong, who had been Franks's deputy at CentCom, wrote in his September 2004 memoir that bin Laden "was definitely there when we hit the caves." Then, after Franks had expressed doubt in an October 19 article, he abruptly reversed himself. "Most people fail to realize," DeLong wrote in a November 1 article in *The Wall Street Journal*, "that it is quite possible that bin Laden was never in Tora Bora to begin with." There was a report the same month—citing what Taliban sources had purportedly said at the time—that bin Laden had been "nowhere near Tora Bora" but had sent a decoy there to deceive U.S. intelligence. If the Taliban did make such a claim, there is no good reason to credit it. If bin Laden was indeed at Tora Bora, the claim was as likely disinformation designed to take pressure off. (For what it is worth, bin Laden himself in a 2003 audiotape spoke of the Tora Bora battle as though he was present.) The intelligence cited by Berntsen and Fury as to bin Laden having been at Tora Bora, on the other hand—information from human sources coupled with voice recognition of intercepted radio conversations—remains persuasive ("was definitely": U.S. Senate, *Tora Bora Revisited*, 8; "Most people": *WSJ*, 11/1/04 & see MFR 04021460 4/9/04, CF; "nowhere near": *CounterPunch*, 11/1/04—citing Kabir Mohabbat; bin Laden: ed. Lawrence, 18-).

241 **"The generals"**: Fury, xxiii-.

241–2 **"never took"**: *NYT*, 10/19/04. During his 2004 campaign against Bush for the presidency, Senator John Kerry claimed the President "took his eye off the ball, off of Osama bin Laden" (second Bush-Kerry debate, 4/10/08, cbsnews.com); **"get" bin Laden**: Woodward, *Bush at War*, 254, 224, 311, *The Times* (London), 10/14/01; **"going to lose"**: Suskind, *One Percent*, 58-; **"asking"**: Fury, 148; **"obsessed"**: Suskind, *One Percent*, 96, Woodward, *Bush at War*, 338; **"Terror's bigger"**: Bush press conference, http://archives.cnn.com, 3/13/02.

242–3 **taken Rumsfeld**: Woodward, *Plan of Attack*, 1-; **"Goddamn!"**: ibid., 8 & see Franks, 315; **general pestered**: Woodward, *Plan of Attack*, 31, 36-, 42- & see Michael Gordon & Bernard Trainor, *Cobra II*, NY: Pantheon, 2006, 25-.

243 **"a natural"**: *al-Wafd* (Egypt), 12/26/01, citing Pakistan *Observer*, www.opednews.com, Fox News, 12/26/01;

escape/wound: *Newsweek*, 10/31/08, Fury, 286, *New Republic*, 10/22/07, *NYT*, 9/23/02, Bergen, *OBL I Know*, 334–, U.S. Senate, *Tora Bora Revisited*, 2; **2011 reports/tribes:** *Guardian* (U.K.), 4/26/11, Michael Scheuer, *Osama bin Laden*, NY: Oxford University Press, 2011, 131.

244 **Good evidence/02/03/04:** Not included here as an indication of bin Laden's survival is a videotaped statement shown by Al Jazeera on December 26, 2001. Though that transmission postdated the Tora Bora battle, all one knows for sure—because of a reference in the statement to the bombing "some days ago" of a mosque at Khost—is that it was recorded shortly after November 16. Thus not necessarily after the Tora Bora conflict ended—on December 17 (ed. Lawrence, 151–, U.S. Senate, *Tora Bora Revisited*, 14).

244 **"We agreed":** Though not all the hijacked flights took off on time on 9/11, they had been scheduled to take off within the same twenty-five-minute period. The authors have in these paragraphs cited letters and tapes attributed to bin Laden, edited by Professor Bruce Lawrence, humanities professor of religion at Duke University, translated by James Howarth, and published in book form.

"Although the question of authenticity inevitably arises whenever a message is released in bin Laden's name," Howarth wrote, the statements in the book had all "been accepted as genuine by a majority of the experts and officials who have examined them." Lawrence and others have cast doubt on the authenticity of other taped statements attributed to bin Laden, allowing for the possibility of forgery for propaganda purposes.

It is not a ridiculous notion, for the CIA is on record as having fabricated film footage. In the late 1950s it arranged for the making of a film purportedly showing President Sukarno of Indonesia in bed with a woman in the Soviet Union. As late as 2003, before the invasion of Iraq, there was discussion about making a video showing Saddam Hussein having sex with a teenage boy. According to a *Washington Post* report, the CIA actually did make a video "purporting to show Osama bin Laden and his cronies sitting around a campfire swigging bottles of liquor and savoring their conquests with boys."

Doubts have been expressed about a videotape released in December 2001, supposedly following its seizure by U.S. troops in Afghanistan. It purports to show bin Laden in conversation the previous month with a visiting sheikh, openly acknowledging his foreknowledge of the 9/11 attack. While there may be other good reasons to doubt the tape's authenticity, the authors suggest that a couple of points made in support of the forgery theory have no validity.

Skeptics noted that the bin Laden figure wears a ring in the video—supposedly out of character for him, perhaps even contrary to religious law. As noted in another chapter, his wife Najwa had given him a ring as a token of her affection just before leaving Afghanistan on the eve of 9/11. He is, moreover, shown wearing a ring in another video accepted as authentic. Bin Laden's son Omar, meanwhile, has scotched the argument that a shot of his father writing with his right hand is a giveaway—as the real Osama was supposedly left-handed. "My father," Omar wrote in 2009, "is right-handed."

That is not to say that the "confession" videotape is necessarily authentic. Professor Lawrence did not use the transcript of it in his published collection on bin Laden, and has reportedly expressed the view that the tape is indeed a fake. No quotations from it have been used in this book (scheduled: CR, 10; ed. Lawrence, 158–244 & see BBC News, 4/15/04, "The Osama bin Laden Tapes," Special Report, undated, www.guardian.co.uk; Sukarno: Interim Report, "Alleged Assassination Plots Involving Foreign Leaders," U.S. Senate Select Committee to Study Govt. Ops with Respect to Intelligence Activities, 94th Cong., 1st Sess., Washington, D.C.: U.S. Govt. Printing Office, 11/20/55, 74n4, Anthony Summers, *Goddess*, NY: Macmillan, 1985, 182; Hussein sex/"purporting": *WP*, 5/25/10; video 12/01: transcript by Defense Dept. cited www.defenselink.mil, *NYT*, 12/14/01; not ring: e.g., Griffin, *The New Pearl Harbor Revisited*, 209, "Farce: Control of the Village Through Terror," 2/6/07, www.opednews.com; had ring: bin Ladens & Sasson, 282 & see "Confession Video," www.911myths.com; left-handed: David Ray Griffin, *Osama bin Laden*, Gloucestershire, U.K.: Arris, 2009, 30, Bergen, *OBL I Know*, 335; "right-handed": bin Ladens & Sasson, 159–; reportedly expressed: Griffin, *OBL*, 36).

244   **"I knew":** Fury, 286; **"This was where":** *National Geographic*, 12/04.

Part IV: **PLOTTERS**

CHAPTER 17

249 **phenomenon:** Staff Statement 13, CO, Lawrence Wright, *The Looming Tower*, NY: Alfred A. Knopf, 2006, 176–, CR, 278; **target:** James F. Pastor, *Security Law & Methods*, NY: Butterworth-Heinemann, 2006, 522, 539, Barrett & Collins, 107.

249 **OBL visit to U.S.:** bin Ladens & Sasson, 25–, 302, & see (1981 visit) *New Yorker*, 12/14/08. Though the best, firsthand source, Najwa is not the first to refer to an early bin Laden visit to America. Kahled Batarfi, a boyhood friend, has spoken of the episode, offering details that to some extent conform with Najwa's account. Bin Laden's sometime supervisor at the family construction firm, Walid al-Khatib, said bin Laden made "trips" to America. Allowing for confusion over the date, Khatib's and Najwa's recollections may be corroborated by the account of wealthy Saudi businessman Yassin Kadi. Kadi said he met bin Laden in Chicago in 1981, when the future terrorist leader was recruiting engineers for the family business. Khaled Bahaziq, a boyhood friend of bin Laden who knew Azzam, has recalled that Azzam was "lecturing in America in the 1970s." He certainly visited repeatedly in the 1980s (Batarfi: Bergen, *OBL I Know*, 22, Coll, *Bin Ladens* 209–; Khatib: Coll, *Bin Ladens*, 209–, but see *New Yorker*, 6/30/09, citing Khatib as referring to visiting "once"; Kadi: *NYT*, 12/13/08, Bahaziq: Robert Lacey, *Inside the Kingdom*, London: Hutchinson, 2009, 114–).

250–1 **lectured/led prayers:** Andrew McGregor, "Jihad and the Rifle Alone," *Journal of Conflict Studies* (Univ. of New Brunswick), Fall 2003, Gilles Kepel, *Jihad*, Cambridge, MA: Belknap, 2002, 314, Abdel Bari Atwan, *The Secret History of Al Qaeda*, Berkeley: Univ. of Calif. Press, 2006, 42, Wright, 95; **third-year:** bin Ladens & Sasson, 25; **"cleric":** Gerald Posner, *Secrets of the Kingdom*, NY: Random House, 2005, 36, Bergen, *OBL I Know*, 92; **"scholar":** e.g., Bergen, *OBL I Know*, int. Jamal Ismael, courtesy Paladin InVision, 2006, "Jihad and the Rifle"; **village overrun:** bin Ladens & Sasson, 29, Bamford, *Pretext*, 98; **"Emir":** e.g., Anouar Boukhars, "At the Crossroads, Saudi Arabia's Dilemma," *Journal of Conflict Studies* (Univ. of New Brunswick), Summer 2006; **jihad:** John Esposito, *Islam*, NY: Oxford Univ. Press, 1998, 20–; **liberate:**

Atwan, 73–; **imposing/speaker:** Wright, 95; **Sadat:** Gerald
Posner, *Why America Slept*, NY: Ballantine, 2003, 30;
Mohammed/Sayid Qutb: "Jihad & the Rifle"; Jason Burke,
Al Qaeda, London: Penguin, 2004, 47, Kepel, 314, ed.
Lawrence, xii, Ian Hamel, *L'Énigme Oussama Ben Laden*, Paris:
Payot, 2009, 64; **Qutb re Jews:** Sayyid Qutb, *In the Shade of
the Qu'ran*, Falls Church, VA: WAMY International, 1995,
WP, 8/10/10; **read Qutb:** Bergen, *OBL I Know*, 19; **OBL at
lectures:** Hamel, 64, Wright, 79–; **Azzam travel:** Lacey,
Inside the Kingdom, 115, Rohan Gunaratna, *Inside Al Qaeda*,
NY: Columbia Univ. Press, 2002, 101, Terry McDermott,
Perfect Soldiers, NY: HarperCollins, 2005, 96–; **Azzam useful:**
corr. Barnett Rubin, 2010, 9/10. *New Yorker*, 3/27/95;
McDermott, 96–, eds. *Der Spiegel*, 169, Samuel Katz, *Relentless
Pursuit*, NY: Forge, 2002, 38–. Pulitzer Prize–winning author
Steve Coll wrote in 2004 that Prince Turki al-Faisal and the
GID "became important supporters" of Azzam. In a letter to
Coll the following year, however, Turki would claim that
"Azzam was never supported by me or the GID." Support for
the mujahideen, Turki wrote, was "measured by the ISI
[Pakistani intelligence] and then evaluated by both the CIA
and G.I.D." ("became": Coll, *Ghost Wars*, 156; "Azzam was":
Coll, *Bin Ladens*, 295, 612n21).

251 **GID/CIA liaison:** int. Prince Turki al-Faisal in *Arab News*,
9/18/02, Anthony Cordesman, "Saudi Security & the War on
Terror," paper for Center for Strategic & International
Studies, 4/22/02, Posner, *Secrets*, 80–, int. Joseph Trento,
Joseph Trento, *Prelude to Terror*, NY: Carroll & Graf, 2005,
xiii, 100–, Coll, *Ghost Wars*, 79–, press briefing, U.S. Dept. of
State, 11/2/07; **Azzam & OBL:** *Arab News*, 11/7/01;
Encyclopedia: *Time*, 10/21/01, Burke, 3; **"To our much":**
Burke, 294n5.

251 **"a man worth":** The authors have here used the translation
provided by the Arab satellite TV channel Al Jazeera, but
"worthy of a nation" might be more apt. The Arabic word bin
Laden used was *"umma"*—which Professor Bruce Lawrence
interprets as meaning "the global Islamic community, or
Islamic supernation" (Transcript, "Usamah Bin-Ladin, the
Destruction of the Base," Al Jazeera, 6/10/99 & see ed.
Lawrence, 4fn4, 77).

251 **found al Qaeda:** Wright, 129–; **economics:** bin Ladens &
Sasson, 29.

251   **"God Almighty":** transcript, "Usamah bin-Ladin, The Destruction of the Base," Al Jazeera, 6/10/99.

252   **1377 hegira:** Year 1 hegira relates to the year the Prophet Mohammed moved from Mecca to the city of Medina in—Western style—a.d. 622. The February 15 birth date is taken from the 2009 book by bin Laden's first wife, Najwa, and her son Omar. Bin Laden himself said he thought he was born in the Islamic month that corresponds to January 1958. Other birth dates offered have included March 10, June 30, and July 30, 1957. The author who studied the family in greatest depth, Steve Coll, notes that most Saudis did not note birth dates. The Saudi government was not keeping records at the time bin Laden was born (hegira: ed. Lawrence, x; Feb. 15: bin Ladens & Sasson, 301; himself: Coll, *Bin Ladens*, 74; other birth dates: AP, 3/11/07, Jean-Charles Brisard & Guillaume Dasquié, *Forbidden Truth*, NY: Thunder's Mouth, 2002, 226, German Nachrichtendienst note seen by authors).

252   **full name/al-Qatani:** bin Ladens & Sasson, 301; **"Lion":** e.g. entry, Muslim Internet Dictionary.

252   **"I was named":** transcript, int. of OBL, ABC News, 1/2/99, & see "Usama's Expedition," www.al-islam.org. According to Bin Laden's son Omar, "Ossama Binladen" is the more correct rendering. U.S. officialese, meanwhile, frequently renders the first name as "Usama." The authors use "Osama bin Laden" because that is the version most commonly used in Western publications. Variations arise as a result of transliteration from the Arabic (bin Ladens & Sasson, 291 & re "Usama" e.g., "Most Wanted List," www.fbi.gov).

252   **"My father":** transcript, "Usmah bin-Laden, Destruction of the Base." The exact year of Mohamed bin Laden's birth remains unknown, but he was apparently born in the first decade of the twentieth century. Family biographer Steve Coll writes that he was fourteen or fifteen when he arrived in Saudi Arabia, while author Lawrence Wright reckoned he was twenty-three (Coll, *Bin Ladens*, 26, 583n11, Wright, 62, & see bin Ladens & Sasson, 292).

253   **Mohamed legend/rise, etc.:** For the historical background of the bin Ladens' early lives, the authors have, except where indicated, drawn on Steve Coll's definitive study, *The Bin Ladens*, and on Lawrence Wright's authoritative *The Looming Tower*.

253–4   **memory:** Wright, 65; **Mohamed/Saudi royals/loan:** Wright, Simon Reeve, *The New Jackals*, London: André

Deutsch, 1999, 158–, Atwan, 40–; **"Religion":** Coll, *Bin Ladens*, 201; **Religion/royalty/banning/Wahhabism:** Stephen Schwartz, *The Two Faces of Islam*, NY: Doubleday, 2002, 69–, 261, Posner, *Secrets*, 18–, Lacey, *Inside the Kingdom*, 10–, Yaroslav Trofimov, *The Siege of Mecca*, NY: Doubleday, 2007, 13–, 16, Wright, 63; **"fascism":** Schwartz, 105; **beheading/crucifixion:** Amnesty International, "Reported Death Sentences and Executions 2009," 3/10, John R. Bradley, *Saudi Arabia Exposed*, NY: Palgrave Macmillan, 2006, 144, Reuters, 2/22/09, Mark Hollingsworth with Sandy Mitchell, *Saudi Babylon*, Edinburgh: Mainstream, 2006, 62, 228, UPI, 11/4/09, Amnesty International, "Man Beheaded & Crucified," 6/1/09, AP, 8/19/10; **Human rights:** *Economist*, 7/25/09, AFP, 7/23/09; **Women:** Lacey, *Inside the Kingdom*, 277, Qanta A. Ahmed, *In the Land of Invisible Women*, Naperville, IL: Source Books, 2008, refs.; **Mohamed devout/"Your highness":** transcript, int. OBL by Hamid Mir, 3/19/97, translated by FBIS, bin Ladens & Sasson, 17, Craig Unger, *House of Bush, House of Saud*, London: Gibson Square, 2007, 91.

254   **Osama product:** Osama told an interviewer he was one of twenty-five sons fathered by Mohamed bin Laden. Author Coll refers to twenty-five sons and twenty-nine daughters. Osama's son Omar believes Osama was the eighteenth of twenty-two sons. The total number of Mohamed's offspring must remain approximate (int. of OBL by Hamid Mir, 3/18/97, translation by FBIS, Coll, *Bin Ladens*, 126–, bin Ladens & Sasson, 292).

254–6   **short marriage/Allia:** bin Ladens & Sasson, 291–, Atwan, 41–, Wright, 72; **"a shocking":** bin Ladens & Sasson, 169; **remarried/loved "more":** Wright, 73, Atwan, 41, bin Ladens & Sasson, 166; **"In my whole"/"when he met":** bin Ladens & Sasson, 190, 168–, 40, Bergen, *OBL I Know*, 17; **"Most of us":** *Evening Standard* (U.K.), 5/26/06; **"very anti-Israel":** Bergen, *OBL I Know*, 7–, Unger, *House of Bush, House of Saud*, 91, *Der Spiegel*, 6/6/05; **bellicose noises/tanks:** John Ciorciari, "Saudi-US Alignment After the Six-Day War," *Middle East Review of International Affairs*, Vol. 9, No. 2, 6/05, David Holden & Richard Johns, *The House of Saud*, NY: Holt, Rinehart & Winston, 1981, 251–. This according to the Pakistani editor Hamid Mir, citing one of his interviews with Osama bin Laden (Bergen, *OBL I Know*, 7–); **father/10,000:**

Coll, *Bin Ladens*, 128, Gunaratna, 17; **"right arm"**: transcript, int. OBL by Hamid Mir, 3/19/97; **$1 billion:** as calculated at www.measuringworth.com; **present/cars:** bin Ladens & Sasson, 20, 169–; **"shy . . . aloof,"** etc.: Atwan, 41, Coll, *Bin Ladens*, 138–, Bergen, *OBL I Know*, 8, *In the Footsteps of Bin Laden*, CNN, 8/23/06; **Quaker school Beirut/Saudi school:** Coll, *Bin Ladens*, 140–, Wright, 75. Published reports have suggested that later, as a teenager, bin Laden indulged in Beirut's fabled nightlife. That seems out of character, and family biographer Coll concludes that such stories are mere rumor. They may reflect confusion with one of Osama's siblings (reports: e.g., see Rex Hudson, *The Sociology & Psychology of Terrorism*, Washington: Federal Research Division, Library of Congress, 1999, 117, Reeve, 159–, rumor: Coll, *Bin Ladens*, 141); **"extraordinarily"/"not very"/mediocre:** Bergen, *OBL I Know*, 8–; **"normal":** Wright, 75; **"No calculator":** bin Ladens & Sasson, 42; **"top fifty":** Bergen, *OBL I Know*, 8; **taller:** Bergen, *OBL I Know*, 8, 214, Wright, 83; **soccer/movies/bully:** *In the Footsteps of Bin Laden*, CNN, 8/23/06. Coll, *Bin Ladens*, 141, Lacey, *Inside the Kingdom*, 57, Bergen, *OBL I Know*, 13–.

257–60 **Syria/camping/"soft-spoken"/"unanticipated"/wedding/ "so conservative"/married life/11 children:** bin Ladens & Sasson, 8–, 12–, 17, 19–, 22, 25, 270, Bergen, *OBL I Know*, 17; **arduous work:** Scheuer, *Osama bin Laden*, 35; **shaking hands, etc./rules:** Bergen, *OBL I Know*, 20–, 14–, bin Ladens & Sasson, 19–, 41, Carmen bin Ladin, *The Veiled Kingdom*, London: Virago, 2004, 76, 91, *Le Monde*, 10/13/02, Wright, 75–; **"Around 18 or 19":** "Dateline," NBC, 7/10/04; **"His family":** Carmen bin Ladin, 77; **"following the example":** Bergen, *OBL I Know*, 22; **economics:** transcript, int. OBL by Hamid Mir, 3/18/97, Bergen, *OBL I Know*, 16, bin Ladens & Sasson, 29; **"I was almost":** Bergen, *OBL I Know*, 16; **Osama no longer:** ibid., 16, 21, Wright, 77, bin Ladens & Sasson, 187; **"impassioned":** bin Ladens & Sasson, 22; **Syrian teacher/Muslim Brotherhood/Qur'an:** Coll, *Bin Ladens*, 144–, Lacey, *Inside the Kingdom*, 59–, Wright, 78; **wept re Palestine:** Wright, 75–; **"religious chants":** Bergen, *OBL I Know*, 15; **'73 war/embargo:** Hollingsworth with Mitchell, 93–, 98, Dore Gold, *Hatred's Kingdom*, Washington, D.C.: Regnery, 2003, 84–; **new century:** Peter L. Bergen, *Holy War Inc.*, NY: Free Press, 2001, 48.

260 **toppling monarchy Iran:** Iran, of course, ascribes over-
whelmingly not to the Sunni but the Shia branch of Islam.
The former predominates in Saudi Arabia; **"For forty years":**
int. OBL by Hamid Mir, 3/18/97.

260–1 **Mahdi/Grand Mosque seizure:** Trofimov, refs. & see esp.
46–, 66–, 69–, 160–. During the siege, according to Jamal
Khashoggi, Osama and his half-brother Mahrouz were
arrested on suspicion of involvement, but released. Osama's
friend Batarfi said Osama had thought it crazy to "seize the
holiest place in Islam, then bring in weapons and kill people."
An Afghan journalist, on the other hand, has quoted him as
saying that the men who seized the mosque were "innocent of
any crime . . . true Muslims" (arrested: Trofimov, 247,
Wright, 94; Batarfi: Lacey, *Inside the Kingdom*, 59; Afghan
journalist: Burke, *Al-Qaeda*, 57, 41).

261 **40,000/100,000:** "The 1978 Revolution & the Soviet
Invasion," www.globalsecurity.org; **terrible conflict:** Coll,
Ghost Wars, 49–.

262 **"My father":** Bergen, *Holy War Inc.*, 52; **"I was put":** bin
Ladens & Sasson, 176; **"the nightmare":** *Mail on Sunday*
(U.K.), 12/23/01.

CHAPTER 18

264 **Badeeb:** Coll, *Bin Ladens*, 248–; **"decent":** ibid., 249, citing
Badeeb int. Orbit TV, 2001; **Turki:** profile at www.
saudiembassy.net; **GID/CIA liaise:** Coll, *Ghost Wars*, 79–,
Wright, 99; **shuttling/ISI/worked together:** ibid., 82–.

265 **"When the invasion":** *The Independent* (U.K.), 12/6/03,
Scheuer, *Osama Bin Laden*, 49. Some historians doubt that bin
Laden involved himself in the Afghan episode as promptly as
he claimed, but there is no special reason to question his
account. One can speculate that his early visit or visits, to
Pakistan rather than Afghanistan itself, were made at bin
Laden's initiative—and triggered GID's decision to use him.

265 **"To confront":** *France-Soir*, 8/27/98, citing int. of 1995;
Turki admitted: *Arab News*, 11/7/01, & see int. Turki al-
Faisal, "Inside the Kingdom," www.pbs.org; **"had a strong":**
Coll, *Bin Ladens*, 295–, citing Badeeb int. Orbit, TV, 2001;
"He was our": Coll, *Ghost Wars*, 87; **"to provide":** Ahmed
Rashid, *Taliban*, New Haven: Yale Univ. Press, 2000, 131, int.
of Robert Fisk, 3/5/07, www.democracynow.org; **spread/
cultivate:** Coll, *Bin Ladens*, 250–; **"will not end":** Bergen,

Holy War, 53; **Saudi support/Azzam's request:** Coll, *Bin Ladens*, 254, 282, bin Ladens & Sasson, 51.

266   **Beit al-Ansar:** Rashid, *Taliban*, 13, Bergen, *OBL I Know*, 29, Wright, 103–, Coll, *Bin Ladens*, 256. While the building in Pakistan was "Beit" [Place of] al-Ansar, the apartment used in Germany by Mohamed Atta and his comrades was known by them as "Dar" [House of] al-Ansar. Translations vary—e.g. House of the Supporters v. House of the Followers (CR, 164, 495n82, Fouda & Fielding, 108).

266   **Azzam toured:** Bergen, *OBL I Know*, 33, John Cooley, *Unholy Wars*, London: Pluto, 2002, 69–; **Azzam "enlisted":** corr. Barnett Rubin, 2010, *New York*, 3/27/95.

266–7 **CIA ratcheted/deniability/Pakistan control/ ISI:** Cooley, xvii, 41–, 64–, 69, 87–, Bergen, *Holy War*, 63–, 54, Rashid, *Taliban*, 129–, 184, 248. Veteran intelligence officer Vincent Cannistraro, who was involved in Afghan policy at the time, has said that only half a dozen CIA officers—"administrators"—served in Pakistan at any one time. Milton Bearden, who was station chief in the Pakistani capital, said the agency "did not recruit Arabs." More obliquely, Bearden has said he "stayed pretty much away from the crowd of Gulf Arabs who were doing the fund-raising. . . . They were not a major part of the war." He also said, "We knew who bin Laden was back then." (Cannistraro: Bergen, *Holy War Inc.*, 65; Bearden: Coll, *Ghost Wars*, 155, *BG*, 9/23/01).

267   **officers trained/Special Forces:** Cooley, 13, 21, 64, 67–, 70, 75–. *Jane's Defence Weekly* reported that Pakistani ISI operatives received instruction from "Green Beret commandos and Navy Seals in various U.S. training establishments." (*Jane's Defence Weekly*, 9/14/01; **cash went/collaborate OBL:** Bergen, *Holy War Inc.*, 68–, Cooley, 47, Rashid, *Taliban*, 132–; **Springmann:** transcript of int. Michael Springmann, 7/3/02, www.bt internet.com, "Newsnight," 11/6/01, http://news.bbc.co.uk, Michael Springmann, "The Hand that Rules the Visa Machine Rocks the World," *Covert Action Quarterly*, Winter 01.

267–8 **"former CIA"/"U.S. emissaries":** Reeve, 167, 176n33. Another allegation linking bin Laden to the CIA, however, is certainly unreliable. The author Jim Marrs reported a claim that bin Laden, under the name "Tim Osman," was brought to America in 1986 to meet government agents. According to Marrs, the meeting was "confirmed" by one of those present, a former FBI agent named Ted Gunderson. Gunderson, however, has made other entirely bizarre assertions (Marrs, 103,415n103, www.tedgunderson.net); **OBL "was a product"**: *Guardian* (U.K.), 7/8/05; **"I created"**: *France-Soir,* 8/27/98, citing int. of 1995; **"Personally"**: *The Independent* (U.K.), 12/6/96.

268–72 **"The Saudi government"**: transcript of int. OBL of 10/21/01, CNN, 2/5/02; **Najwa overheard/ helicopter/"stop thinking"**: bin Ladens & Sasson, 32–; **Jaji/running**: Bergen, *OBL I Know,* 55, *In the Footsteps of Bin Laden,* CNN, 8/23/06; **Lion's Den**: Scheuer, *Osama bin Laden,* 61; **bravery**: int. Huthaifa Azzam, 2006, courtesy Paladin InVision; **crying**: Bergen, *Holy War Inc.,* 12; **"thirst"**: Wright, 106; **"martyrdom"**: ibid., *The Independent* (U.K.), 12/6/93; **"requires"**: Coll, *Bin Ladens,* 255–; **"As Muslims"**: *The Independent* (U.K.), 12/6/93; **Russian pullout/new phase**: Wright, 137, Coll, *Bin Ladens,* 334, Coll, *Ghost Wars,* 184–; **Jalalabad/"took charge"**: Bergen, *OBL I Know,* 87–, Coll, *Bin Ladens,* 340; **disagreements**: Bergen, *OBL I Know,* 62–, 68, Coll, *Bin Ladens,* 304, Wright, 112; **Azzam death**: bin Ladens & Sasson, 78, Bergen, *OBL I Know,* 92–; **hero/Abdullah/feted/talks**: Posner, *Why America Slept,* 44, Lacey, *Inside the Kingdom,* 123, Posner, *Why America Slept,* 45, bin Ladens & Sasson, 73; **back to work**: "The Sociology & Psychology of Terrorism," Federal Research Division, Library of Congress, 9/99, 117–, Rashid, *Taliban,* 133; **wives/"his aim"**: bin Ladens & Sasson, 49–; **jokes**: Bergen, *OBL I Know,* 47, *Telegraph* (U.K.), 7/23/07; **"I have"**: ibid.; **children/divorce/annulment, etc.**: bin Ladens & Sasson, 301–; **"I never"**: Bergen, *OBL I Know,* 26; **"a good"/ "corrupted"/forbade/milk/"We were"/"live just"/asthma/ "From the time"**: bin Ladens & Sasson, 42–, 54, 60–; **"how to be"**: Bergen, *OBL I Know,* 26; **Abdullah war zone**: bin Ladens & Sasson, 77, 305; **"like a"**: Coll, *Ghost Wars,* 153 & see Miller & Stone, 185, int. of Fouad Ajami, 2006, courtesy of Paladin InVision; **"still, silent"**: *Canada Free Press,* 9/14/06, www.mail-archive.com.

272 **CIA thought:** Coll, *Ghost Wars,* 182–.

272–3 **"tactical alliance"/"In our struggle":** *France-Soir,* 8/27/98, citing int. of 1995. During the anti-Soviet conflict, bin Laden appeared grateful for the American contribution—in private. "In the mid-eighties," Saudi Arabia's Prince Bandar, who was his country's ambassador to the United States, told CNN's Larry King, "he came to thank me for my efforts to bring the Americans, our friends, to help us against the atheists" (*Larry King Live*, CNN, 10/1/01).

273   **"Every Muslim":** ed. Lawrence, 87.

273–4 **Rohrabacher:** speech, 5/5/04, *USA Today*, 9/18/01. Rohrabacher, a Republican who was elected to Congress in 1989, is a controversial figure. Given the corroborative accounts that follow, however, this story about bin Laden is credible (controversial: e.g., "Rogue Statesman," www.ocweekly.com, 9/5/02, *Telegraph* (U.K.), 9/13/08); **Girardet:** *National Geographic*, 12/1/01, *In the Footsteps of Bin Laden*, CNN, 8/23/06; **Simpson:** John Simpson, *Simpson's World*, NY: Miramax, 2003, 82–, *Telegraph* (U.K.), 9/16/01, Bergen, *Holy War Inc.*, 65.

275   **"vanguard"/"al qaeda":** Bergen, *OBL I Know*, 75, Gunaratna, 3–; **discussed plans:** "TAREEKHOSAMA/50/Tareekh Osama," minutes of meeting 8/11/88, INTELWIRE, Coll, *Bin Ladens*, 336–, Bergen, *OBL I Know*, 74–, Wright, 131–, Burke, 1–, ed. Lawrence, 108.

275   **never heard/first used:** Flagg Miller, "*Al-Qaeda* as a 'Pragmatic Base,' " *Language & Communications*, Vol. 28, 2008, "On 'The Summit of the Hindu Kush': Osama bin Laden's 1996 Declaration of War Reconsidered," speech by Flagg Miller, supplied to authors, int. Huthaifa Azzam, 2006, courtesy Paladin InVision. Only in 1996 did a CIA report refer to "al-Qaeda." The word was first used by the State Department in 1998 (ed. Lawrence, 108fn); **"He rang":** Lacey, *Inside the Kingdom*, 148; **"playing":** Rashid, *Taliban*, 129; **"In our common zeal":** Benazir Bhutto, *Daughter of the East*, London: Simon & Schuster, 2008, 410. Bhutto said she first heard of bin Laden in 1989, when told he had bribed members of parliament to vote against her in a no-confidence motion. In 2008, after Bhutto's assassination, a newspaper editor in Pakistan claimed to have been present when bin Laden tried to bribe then–Pakistan Muslim League party leader—later prime minister—Nawaz Sharif to see that the no-confidence motion was tabled. The newspaper editor had reportedly himself been prosecuted on a separate matter, and the authors have seen no corroboration of this allegation (Bhutto, 405–, Bergen, *Holy War Inc.*, 61, Coll, *Ghost Wars*, 212, *Daily Frontier Post* [Pakistan], 7/1/01, & see Reeve, 171, 179).

276–7 **Zawahiri:** Wright, 128, 139–, Bergen, *OBL I Know*, 203, 319–, int. Huthaifa Azzam, 2006, courtesy PaladinInVision; **Rahman:** bin Ladens & Sasson, 130–, Wright 138, Bergen, *OBL I Know*, 68; **Mohammed:** McDermott, 121, *Financial Times*, 2/15/03, Bergen, *OBL I Know*,300; **Yousef:** Reeve, 120, Miller & Stone, 78, *Newsday*, 4/16/95, Bergen, *Holy War Inc.*, 138; **Atta:** McDermott, 15–, CR, 160; **Hanjour/ Jarrah/Shehhi:** eds. *Der Spiegel*, 253–, McDermott, 50, *The Independent* (U.K.), 9/16/01; **"concerned, sad":** Wright, 75–.

277 **"to reclaim":** Bergen, Scheuer, *OBL I Know*, 15, *Osama bin Laden*, 77. Suggestions that Palestine was not an issue for bin Laden do not appear well founded. It appears true, however, that he neither directed terrorist attacks on Israeli targets nor supplied funds to Palestinian groups. The Palestinian author and journalist Abdel Bari Atwan, who interviewed him in 1996, said Palestine "wasn't actually No. 1 on his agenda . . . he wasn't really that informed about Palestine. He didn't like Yasser Arafat . . . maybe because he was involved with the Soviets . . . used to be considered an unbeliever." For obvious reasons, organizations like Hamas and Islamic Jihad have been careful not to associate their groups with bin Laden (not a genuine: e.g., Gold, 10; Atwan: int., 2007; Hamas, etc.: Burke, 12).

277 **boycott:** bin Ladens & Sasson, 61, 110, ed. Lawrence, 115; **not drink:** bin Ladens & Sasson, 60, Bergen, *OBL I Know*, 39.

277 **"The Americans":** ed. Lawrence, 115. Recalling this speech in an interview after 9/11, bin Laden said it occurred in 1986. Author Lawrence Wright, in his book *The Looming Tower*, cites a speech with almost identical wording that he made in 1990. That speech did not mention Palestine (ed. Lawrence, 115, Wright, 151, 405n); **time and again:** e.g., ed. Lawrence, 9, 36, McDermott, 253–, CBS News, 5/16/08.

277–8 **"America allowed"/"The idea":** Lawrence, 239. Then–U.S. secretary of state Alexander Haig was to insist that the United States was not a party to the Israeli invasion. Others, including the military correspondent for Israel's *Ha'aretz* newspaper, have said Washington gave Israel "the green light" (Haig: *Business Week*, 2/20/10; others: *Foreign Policy*, Spring 1983, Fisk, *The Great War*, 1037); **"The events":** MSNBC, 11/29/07.

CHAPTER 19

279–83 **stocked up/despised Saddam/"will attack":** bin Ladens & Sasson, 79–, Coll, *Bin Ladens*, 373, Bergen, *OBL I Know*, 179; **"The defense":** David Ottoway, "The U.S. and Saudi Arabia Since the 1930s," *Foreign Policy Research Institute*, 8/09; **"If you ask":** William Simpson, *The Prince*, NY: Regan, 2006, 205; **delegation:** ibid., 209–, Richard Clarke, 57–; **"flooding":** H. Norman Schwarzkopf with Peter Petre, *It Doesn't Take a Hero*, NY: Bantam, 1992, 353; **"This is something":** int. Prince Amr ibn Mohammad al-Faisal, *Frontline:* "House of Saud," www.pbs.org; **religious study/"the last":** excerpts, *Frontline:* "Saudi Time Bomb," www.pbs.org; **Committee raids:** Felice Gaer et al., "Report on Saudi Arabia," U.S. Commission on International Religious Freedom, Washington, D.C., 5/2/03; **Censors:** bin Ladin, 63; **hall/phone recordings:** *New Yorker*, 1/5/05; **Bible:** *WSJ*, 5/20/05; **"The unbelievers":** ed. Nina Shea, "Saudi Publications on Hate Ideology Invade American Mosques," Center for Religious Freedom, Washington, D.C., 1/28/05; **debate/Abdullah urged:** Rachel Bronson, *Thicker than Oil*, NY: Oxford Univ. Press, 2006, 194, Posner, *Secrets*, 135–; **"Okay":** William Simpson, 209; **female soldiers/ entertainers/carols/Sabbath/Bibles/Ramadan:** Schwarzkopf, 386–, 430, 461–, William Simpson, 225–; **"Pollution":** bin Ladens & Sasson, 84; **OBL meetings/Sultan/"kept asking":** MFR 04019365, 2/24/04, Snell et al. to Zelikow, "Summary of Interviews Conducted in Saudi Arabia," 2/25/04, CF, *Arab News*, 11/7/01, bin Ladens & Sasson, 82–, ed. Lawrence, 257; Prince Sultan bin Abdul Aziz, who died in 2011, was the father of long-time Saudi ambassador to the U.S. Prince Bandar (William Simpson, 12); **"didn't care":** MFR 04019365, 2/24/04; **"Don't call":** transcript, *Frontline:* "House of Saud," 11/23/04, www.pbs.org; **OBL outraged/ "colony":** bin Ladens & Sasson, 83–; **5,000 remained/bases:** Alfred Prados, "Saudi Arabia, Current Issues and U.S. Relations," Foreign Affairs, Defense & Trade Division, Congressional Research Service, Washington, D.C., 9/15/03, "Desert Stronghold," *Air Force Magazine*, 2/99, BBC News, 4/29/03.

283   **groundswell:** *NYT*, 3/7/04, Gold, 161, **Yemen:** int. of Abdul Bari Atwan for PaladinInVision, 2006, Miller & Stone, 158–, Lacey, *Inside the Kingdom*, 155; **passport/movements:** Lacey,

Inside the Kingdom, Atwan, 161; **cleared:** CR, 57; **"One day"/business:** bin Ladens & Sasson, 85; **conference:** Coll, *Ghost Wars,* 231–; **"We didn't say":** int. Prince Bandar bin Sultan, *Frontline:* "Looking for Answers," www.pbs.org.

284   **"the U.S. government":** Coll, *Ghost Wars,* 231. Bin Laden himself would reportedly claim that, far from the Saudis having asked to protect him, the regime asked the intelligence services in Pakistan—his first stop on leaving his homeland—to kill him. (*NYT,* 1/14/01); **"using the":** Scheuer, *Osama bin Laden,* 83, 218n27.

284   **"pledge":** Wright, 161. The PBS *Frontline* program, meanwhile, obtained a document stating that an unnamed bin Laden brother persuaded Naif's younger brother, Deputy Interior Minister Prince Ahmed bin Abdul Aziz, to lift the travel ban while Naif was out of the country (Prince Ahmed: Documents supplied to *Frontline* by an associate of OBL, "Hunting bin Laden," www.pbs.org).

284   **"with help":** CR, 57. On the purported help from a "dissident" royal family member, the sources the Commission cited were self-confessed 9/11 planner Khalid Sheikh Mohammed and fellow terrorist Tawfiq bin Attash—under interrogation after their capture—and bin Laden associate Jamal al-Fadl, who defected in 1996. (CR, 57, 467n33).

285–7   **"Go to Sudan":** Reeve, 172; **property:** Bergen, *Holy War Inc.,* 78; **wives/motorcade/guest:** bin Ladens & Sasson, 94, Burke, 143–; **Khartoum houses/no pictures/austerity:** bin Ladens & Sasson, 94–, 107–, 111–, Bergen, *OBL I Know,* 123; **"You know":** int. Jamal Khashoggi for Paladin InVision, 2006; **no air conditioning:** bin Ladens & Sasson, 115, *Los Angeles Times,* 12/19/09; **no education for girls:** bin Ladens & Sasson, 109–; **more time:** ibid., 96; **"wooden cane":** ibid., 116; **apoplectic/"Why do":** ibid., 164; **"My husband":** bin Ladens & Sasson, 97; **"agriculturalist":** *The Independent* (U.K.), 12/6/93; **training/plotting:** MFR 04013804, 12/4/04, Staff Statement 15, CO; **"Jihad":** Burke, 73–; **"every place":** ed. Lawrence, 49.

287–8   **Yousef Philippines:** Fouda & Fielding, 94, Maria N. Ressa, *Seeds of Terror,* NY: Free Press, 2003, 26; **Yousef names:** statement by Michael McCurry, U.S. Dept. of State, 7/23/93, Reeve, 112.

288   **"emissary":** Zachary Abuzza, "Belik Terrorism: The Return of the Abu Sayyaf," Strategic Studies Institute, U.S. Army

War College, 9/05. The source of the "emissary from bin Laden" quote was Edwin Angeles, a Philippines government agent who penetrated the separatist group. Angeles is variously described as having been an "undercover agent for the Defense Intelligence Group in the Philippines' Defense Department"—penetrating the Abu Sayyaf group—or a defector. The Abu Sayyaf group launched some seventy attacks between 1991 and 1995, killed about 136 people and injured hundreds ("Balik-Terrorism: The Return of the Abu Sayyaf," *WP*, 6/5/95, Marites Dañguilan Vitug & Glenda M. Gloria, *Under the Crescent Moon*, Quezon City, Philippines: Ateneo Center for Social Policy, 2000, 198–, 205).

288 **on behalf of Rahman:** *WP*, 6/5/95; **OBL would claim:** ed. Lawrence, 53.

CHAPTER 20

289 **twenties/lean/degrees/"hard-working":** Lance, *1000 Years*, 9, 460n19, *The Times* (London), 10/18/97; **"poised"/ languages:** Statement of Thomas Pickard, 4/13/04, CO; **political/"Palestinian"/"the right":** *The Times* (London), 10/18/97, Reeve, 125, 127, Bergen, *OBL I Know*, 145; **explosives/"Chemist":** Bergen, *OBL I Know*, Abuzza, "Belik Terrorism"; **phone call:** *U.S. v. Omar Ahmad Ali Abdel Rahman et al.*

289 **"Boom!":** McDermott, 130. The friend, Abdul Murad, was later to become deeply involved in Yousef's plotting and later—once captured—talked at length. The "chocolate" story is from the record of an FBI interview (FBI 302 of int. Abdul Hakim Ali Murad, 5/11/95, "Various Interrogation Reports," B24, T1, CF).

290 **"break"/"exploding":** *U.S. v. Omar Ahmad Ali Abdel Rahman et al.*, U.S. Court of Appeals for the 2nd District, 189 F.3d 88, 8/16/99, "The Muslim Interfaith Charade," 5/6/08, www.militantislammonitor.org, Daniel Benjamin & Steven Simon, *The Age of Sacred Terror*, NY: Random House, 2003, 6–. Heavy with implication as they are, one cannot read too much into the Blind Sheikh's remarks. In captivity, Yousef would insist that the 1993 World Trade Center bombing was his idea and his alone. His contact Abdul Murad, for his part, would reportedly claim he proposed the bombing—after Yousef asked him to suggest a suitable "Jewish" target (McDermott, 130, Lance, *1000 Years*, 199, Peter Lance, *Triple*

Cross, NY: Regan, 2006, 121); **"targeting":** *Village Voice*, 3/30/93.

290   **flew NY/passports/suspicions/asylum:** Staff Report, "Monograph on Terrorist Travel, CO, *The Times* (London), 10/18/97, MFR 04020564, 3/22/04. The accomplice was Ahmad Ajaj. He would remain incarcerated until Yousef's attempt to bring down the Twin Towers in February 1993, was later tried as an accomplice, and is serving a life sentence (Staff Report, "Monograph on Terrorist Travel," CO).

290   **Al Khifa contact:** The contact at the Al Khifa center was Mahmoud Abouhalima, an Egyptian-born veteran Yousef had reportedly known in Afghanistan. Yousef's principal accomplices in the weeks that followed were Mohammad Salameh, a Palestinian whose grandfather and uncle had served time in Israeli prisons, Nidal Ayyad, a chemical engineer—like Yousef born in Kuwait—and a Jordanian named Eyad Ismoil. There was no hard evidence to implicate Blind Sheikh Omar Abdel Rahman, but he was charged in the summer of 1993 with conspiring with others to commit bombings of other New York landmarks (Reeve, 143, 114, 62, *Village Voice*, 3/30/93, *U.S. v. Omar Ahmad Ali Abdel Rahman et al.*, S5 93 Cr. 181, 1/17/96).

291–2   **Yousef acquired/loaded/rented/escape:** Reeve, 6–, 24–, 36–, Burke, 101; **"largest":** Reeve, 154; **earthquake/"like Christmas tree"/devastation/elevators/dead:** ibid., 10–, 13–, 15; **"Achilles' heel":** *New Yorker*, 3/30/93; **bring down Tower:** *NYT*, 6/9/02, Wright, 178; **"Liberation"/"The American"/"Our calculations"/phoned in:** Lance, *Triple Cross*, 116, Burke, 111, *WP*, 9/13/01.

292   **tracked down/identified:** Reeve, 39–, 42–, 56, *U.S. v. Ramzi Ahmed Yousef et al.*, U.S. Court of Appeals for the 2nd Circuit, 8/01, CR, 72–.

292   **plot new mayhem:** In July 1993, five months after attacking the World Trade Center, Yousef tried to bomb the home of Pakistan's Benazir Bhutto, then a candidate for prime minister. He suffered a serious eye injury when the detonator exploded, and spent months recovering. By early 1994 he was in Thailand and again preparing a bomb attack—on the Israeli embassy. That attack also failed at the last moment, when an accomplice crashed the van carrying the bomb to the target. Yousef mulled attacking President Bill Clinton, either with explosives or a rocket, when he visited Manila in November 1994. The following month, with Pope John Paul due to

arrive in the city, he prepared a number of pipe bombs. He and accomplice Abdul Murad had already purchased priest's clothing, Bibles, and crucifixes—as cover for those carrying the bombs to the target—when police raided their bomb factory (see text) (Bhutto: Reeve, 50–, 69, Vitug & Gloria, 231; Thailand: Reeve, 63–; Clinton: Reeve, 76–, CNN, 8/25/98; John Paul: Ressa, 31–, Reeve, 78, 85–).

293   **Pope/"Just some"/"Saeed" arrest:** *WP,* 12/30/01.

293   **tortured/"Agents hit":** Vitug & Gloria, 223, McDermott, 153. The reporters were Marites Dañguilan Vitug, who has reported for *Newsweek* and *The Christian Science Monitor,* and Glenda Gloria, who holds a master's degree in political sociology from the London School of Economics. The reporting cited here is from the award-winning book on the Muslim rebellion in Mindanao, in the eastern Philippines. (Vitug & Gloria, 222–).

294–6   **transcript:** Murad Interrogation, 1/7/95, posted at www.thesmokinggun.com, & see *NY Daily News,* 7/24/96, Ressa, 39–; **Murad/"to blowup"/summoned/disguises/watches:** FBI 302 of int. Abdul Hakim Ali Murad, 5/11/95, "Various Interrogation Reports," B24, T1, CF, Lance, *1000 Years,* 259; **device in theater:** Reeve, 77, Benjamin & Simon, 493, Lance, *1000 Years,* 236–; **Italian/bomb:** Lance, *1000 Years,* 237–, Reeve, 78–; **Murad bomb/Parker pen/"cause":** FBI 302 of int. Abdul Hakim Ali Murad; **United Flight 2:** Philippine National Police (PNP) "After Debriefing Report," 1/17/95; **11 airliners/terrorists:** Reeve, 90–, 94–; **"TIMER":** *WP,* 12/20/01; **airlines alerted/grounded:** Richard Clarke, 93–, MFR 04017178, 11/21/03, Lance, *Triple Cross,* 441; **4,000 could have died:** Reeve, 90.

296   **"BOJINKA":** Khalid Sheikh Mohammed reportedly told CIA interrogators after 9/11 that *bojinka* was not a Serbo-Croatian word for "big bang," as reported—just "a nonsense word he adopted after hearing it on the front lines in Afghanistan." The authors have been unable to pin down a meaning for the word in Serbo-Croat, but there is a Croatian word *bo˘cnica,* meaning "boom" (explosion: *Time,* 1/1/95; loud bang: *WP,* 5/19/02; big bang: www.FrontPageMagazine.com, 5/20/02; boom: www.eudict.com; "a nonsense": CR, 488n7).

296   **Yousef arrested:** Katz, 162–, 186–, Reeve, 101; **cooperative Bhutto:** John Esposito, *Political Islam,* Boulder: Lynne

Rienner, 1997, 150; **face trial:** Reeve, 237; **Found guilty/
"I am":** ibid., 242, CNN, 9/5/96, 11/12/97; **240 years:** *NYT,*
4/5/03.

297 **helicopter/"See":** Coll, *Ghost Wars,* 272. This exchange has
been described several times, with varying details. They are
summarized by author Peter Lance in his book *1000 Years for
Revenge,* 298, 482n13; **prostrate:** Lance, *1000 Years,* 9–;
mastermind: Coll, *Ghost Wars,* 273, *NYT,* 4/12/95—citing *Al
Hayat;* **leaders inspired:** Coll, *Ghost Wars,* 272.

297–8 **"substantial":** Staff Statement 15, CO, Peter Lance, *Cover-
Up,* NY: Regan, 2004, 209—the staff member was Douglas
MacEachin; **camp:** Corbin, 46–, Reeve, 120, Benjamin &
Simon, 8, 503n14, *Los Angeles Times,* 9/11/02 & see Evan
Kohlmann, "Expert Report I: U.S. v. Oussama Kassir," 3/09;
"emissary": Abuza, "Balik Terrorism"; **separatist:** *Time,*
6/17/02, Reeve, 136, 156–; **manual:** *NYT,* 1/14/01, 6/9/02,
Lance, *1000 Years,* 110; **calls:** Reeve, 47–, Lance, *1000 Years,*
234; **Beit Ashuhada:** "Summary of Captioned Investigation
as of 11/4/01," PENTTBOM, 11/5/01, authors' collection,
Cooley, 102, "State Dept. Fact Sheet on Bin Laden," 8/14/96
reprinted in Brisard & Dasquié, 169.

298 **"good friend"/"trenches":** transcript int. of OBL for ABC
News, *Frontline:* "Hunting bin Laden," www.pbs.org, Miller
& Stone, 138–, 189. The separatist leader with whom Yousef
had early contact in the Philippines was Abdurajak Janjalani,
the founder of the extremist Abu Sayyaf group. As identified
in a previous note, the companion refused admission was
Ahmad Ajaj. The Yousef accomplice who had fought with bin
Laden was Wali Kahn Amin Shah (Reeve, 136, 156–, CR, 59).

298–9 **Shaikha/"Imagine":** CNN, 11/24/04, 9/24/06, Bergen, *OBL
I Know,* 46–, Wright, 97–; **"missionary":** "Mohammad
Khalifa's Network in the Philippines," in ed. J. M. Berger,
Mohammed Jamal Khalifa, Vol. 1, INTELWIRE, 2007;
"philanthropist": *The Inquirer* (Philippines), 1/22/07, Vitug
& Gloria, 208, 213, 235–; **OBL Philippines:** Ressa, 16;
spreading money: ibid., 27, 73, 107, 227n22, *Christian Science
Monitor,* 2/1/02; **introduced Yousef:** Ressa, 108; **left
country/police report:** Ressa, 10–, 16; **arrested:**
"Memorandum of Points and Authorities in Support for
Motion re Return of Property," *Mohammad Jamal Khalifa v.
U.S.,* U.S. District Court for the Northern District of
California, Cr 95–, in ed. Berger; **phone book:** *U.S. v.*

Benevolence International Foundation, Inc. et al., U.S. District Court for the Northern District of Illinois, 02 CR 0414, 4/29/02, in ed. Berger; **bomb factory:** J. M. Berger, "Mohammad Jamal Khalifa: Life and Death Secrets," 1/31/07, INTELWIRE; **explosives/weaponry:** "In the Matter of Mohammad J. Khalifah, Respondent," U.S. Dept. of Justice, Immigration and Naturalization Service, A29–457–661, 3/10/95, in ed. Berger; *Khalifa*, **entry for OBL:** *U.S. v. Benevolence International Foundation, Inc., et al.*; **card in suitcase/Khalifa alias:** *U.S. v. Benevolence International Foundation Inc., et al.*; **co-conspirator:** ed. Berger, *Khalifa*, iii.

299   **"alleged financier":** JI, Report, 128. The "alleged financier" reference also appears in a post-9/11 FBI report. A CIA investigation, the BBC was reportedly told by an agency interviewee in 1998, indicated that bin Laden was "Yousef's principal financial backer." The overall story of the way Khalifa was handled by U.S. authorities in 1995 remains complex and unsatisfactorily explained. His U.S. visa had been withdrawn on the ground that he had "engaged in terrorist activity," not in the United States but in Jordan, where he had been convicted in absentia in connection with a bombing campaign. Khalifa was subsequently deported to Jordan, retried, and acquitted—though he admitted that he had known the bombers and sent them funds. Khalifa was then allowed to leave for Saudi Arabia. He claimed in interviews after 9/11, in the face of all evidence to the contrary, that he and bin Laden had been estranged since the war against the Soviets in Afghanistan. Khalifa was killed by unknown assailants in Madagascar in 2007—days after Interpol had forwarded a bulletin on him to U.S. agencies. Relevant Interpol documents are heavily redacted. ("alleged financier": "Summary of Captioned Investigation as of 11/4/01," PENT-TBOM, 11/5/01, authors' collection; "Yousef's principal": Vitug & Gloria, 234; "engaged": *Mohammad Jamal Khalifah v. U.S.*, Memorandum of Points and Authorities in Support of Motion for Return of Property, U.S. District Court for the Northern District of California, CR 95–, 3/6/95; in absentia/retried/acquitted: ed. Berger, *Khalifa*, ii–; admitted: *John Doe v. Al Baraka Investment & Development Corporation et al.*, Complaint, U.S. District Court for the District of Columbia; estranged: e.g. CNN, 9/2/07, Wright, 113; killed/Interpol: J.

M. Berger, "U.S., Interpol Tracking Khalifa in Days Before Madagascar Murder," 2/16/07, INTELWIRE).

299   **never charged:** ed. Berger, i.

299   **clues/"Zahid":** Miller & Stone, 137, McDermott, 162.

299   **Zahid uncle:** Reeve, 48. Khalid Sheikh Mohammed has long been described as Ramzi Yousef's uncle. The most informative account, by journalist Terry McDermott and colleagues at the *Los Angeles Times,* concludes that he is the brother of Yousef's mother, Hameda. Author Steve Coll writes that the CIA concluded that Mohammed is not only Yousef's uncle, but that the two men's wives are sisters. Absent documentation, the exact nature of their relationship remains elusive—Arabs sometimes use the word "uncle" loosely. Both men were apparently born in Kuwait to immigrant families from the Baluchistan region of southwest Pakistan. "I am Palestinian on my mother's side," Yousef told an Arab newspaper in 1995. "My grandmother is Palestinian" (uncle: e.g. Corbin, 47, Reeve, 91, *Time,* 6/17/02; informative: McDermott, 107–, 128, & see Fouda & Fielding, 88–; wives: Coll, *Ghost Wars,* 326; "I am Palestinian": int. Yousef by Raghida Dergham, *Al Hayat,* 4/12/95 & see *NYT,* 4/12/95).

300   **photos of OBL:** *Financial Times,* 2/15/03.

300   **no sign of either brother:** KSM's brother Zahid spent much of the 1990s in the United Arab Emirates, until being deported in 1998 for involvement with the Muslim Brotherhood. He was working as a business executive in Bahrain as of 2010 (*New Yorker,* 9/13/10).

300–1   **Yousef many calls:** Miller & Stone, 137, NBC News, 10/18/00; **call to KSM:** CR, 147, 488n6; **Tiffany Mansions:** McDermott, 144; **bar girls/phone:** Ressa, 18–; **"Abdul Majid"/met in Pakistan/electronics business/"must have":** FBI 302 of int. Abdul Hakim Ali Murad, 5/11/95, "Various Interrogation Reports," B24, T1, CF, CR, 147; **"I was":** "Verbatim Transcript ISN 10024"; **"idea":** "Substitution for the Testimony of Khalid Sheikh Mohammed," *U.S. v. Zacarias Moussaoui;* **target CIA/WTC:** CR, 153, 491n33.

301   **"plan":** Philippines National Police, "After Debriefing Report," 1/20/95. A 1995 FBI memo refers to Murad's statement about attacking CIA HQ, but cites him as saying he would fly a plane filled with explosives into the building" (*WP,* 6/6/02, Coll, *Ghost Wars,* 278–, Lance, *Triple Cross,* 188, Appendix XI).

301   **Mendoza:** CNN, 9/18/01. Former CIA official and deputy

director of the State Department's Office of Counterterrorism, Larry Johnson, has characterized Mendoza's assertions as "bullshit." Contemporary Philippines police reports on the Murad interrogation, Johnson asserted in 2006—publishing copies of some of them—do not reflect questioning of Murad by Mendoza. Nor, he said, do they contain any reference to talk of flying airliners into buildings other than the CIA. Johnson wrote that author Peter Lance, who gave credence to Mendoza's account in his books on 9/11, had been "sold a bill of goods." Johnson, however, is himself a controversial character, said to have been instrumental in spreading a smear story about President Obama's wife, Michelle. He has been mocked for having written a *New York Times* piece stating that "terrorism is not the biggest security challenge confronting the United States"—two months before 9/11 (Larry Johnson, "Peter Lance's Flawed *Triple Cross*,"12/6/06, www.huffingtonpost.com, David Weigel, "Larry Johnson's Strange Trip," 6/24/08, www.prospect.org, Larry Johnson, "Whitey Tapes," 10/21/08, www.noquarterusa.net, *Time*, 6/12/08).

301   **"The targets":** "Investigating Terror," CNN, 10/20/01, Ressa, 32—citing 9/16/01 int. of Tiglao.

302   **Garcia/"selected targets":** *Village Voice*, 9/25/01, Rafael Garcia, "Decoding Bojinka," *Newsbreak* (Philippines), 11/15/01, Fouda & Fielding, 99, Lance, *Triple Cross*, 185 & see "Authorities Told of Hijack Risks," AP, 3/5/02. In other versions of his account, Garcia recalled that the computer file also named the Pentagon as a proposed target. "Murad," Garcia wrote, "was to fly the plane that would be crashed into the CIA headquarters." The subject of the computer, and other evidence on it, came up at Yousef's trial in 1996. Defense attorneys sought unsuccessfully to challenge the evidence on the computer, alleging tampering ("Murad": Rafael Garcia, "Decoding Bojinka," *Newsbreak* [Philippines], 11/15/01, *Village Voice*, 9/25/01, Fouda & Fielding, 99; tampering?: *NYT*, 7/18/96, *WP*, 12/6/01).

302–3   **"claims":** CR, 491n33; **FBI "effectively":** JI, Report, 9, 101–, 210; **"We shared"/"I believe":** *Portsmouth Herald*, 3/5/02, CNN, 3/14/02; **Mendoza insisted:** Lance, *1000 Years*, 282; **"We told"/"I still":** *WP*, 12/30/01.

304   **Defense Dept. panel/"Coming"/"It was":** *WP*, 10/2/01 & see re not in published version "Terror 2000," www.dod.gov.

CHAPTER 21

305–6 **"You need":** *NYT,* 11/14/09—agent was Daniel Byman; **"manager":** "Khalid Shaykh Muhammad: Preeminent Source on Al Qa'ida," CIA, 7/13/04, released 2009; **"Khalid"/born Kuwait:** JI, Report, 30, *New Yorker,* 9/13/10; **imam/washed bodies:** Fox News, 3/14/07; **Palestinians:** McDermott, 109; **"so smart"/theater:** *Financial Times,* 2/15/03, *New Yorker,* 9/13/10. KSM studied first at Chowan College, in Murfreesboro, then at North Carolina Agricultural and Technical State University in Greensboro. Also attending the latter college was Ramzi Yousef's brother (New York to Counterterrorism, Charlotte, 6/10/02, FBI 265A-NY-252802, INTELWIRE, CR, 146); **Palestine/ prayers/reproach:** New York to Counterterrorism, Charlotte, 6/10/02, FBI 265A-NY-252802, INTELWIRE, CR, 146, McDermott, 115–; **"racist":** KSM, "Preeminent Source," McDermott, 114–; **1987/Afghan conflict:** CR, 146. During the war, KSM became aide to Abdul Rasool Sayyaf, a former Kabul theology professor and an adherent to a form of Islam similar to the creed practiced in Saudi Arabia. Sayyaf, who lived for some time in Saudi Arabia, had links to bin Laden (Fouda & Fielding, 91); **one brother/two killed:** CR, 488n5, *Financial Times,* 2/15/03; **KSM relatives:** e.g. "KSM: Preeminent Source," Staff Report, "9/11 and Terrorist Travel," CO, *Time,* 5/1/03, Reu-ters, 2/1/08, *WP,* 4/13/07, **across world/Bosnia:** CR, 488n5, Fouda & Fielding, 97, Al Jazeera, 5/5/03, McDermott, 175; **short/balding:** Fouda & Fielding, 88, *Los Angeles Times,* 9/1/02, "Khaled Shaikh Mohammad," information sheet for Rewards for Justice program, Bureau of Diplomatic Security, U.S. Dept. of State; **employment:** NY to National Security, Bangkok et al., FBI 265A-NY-252802, 7/8/99, INTELWIRE; **Thani:** CR, 147–, 488n5; **indictment:** ibid., 73.

307 **tipped off/assisted flying out:** The circumstances in which KSM was allowed to escape have been told in some detail by former CIA case officer Robert Baer, drawing on information given him in 1997 by former police chief Sheikh Hamad bin Jassem bin Hamad al-Thani, then in exile in Syria. The Qatari fiasco has also been described by Richard Clarke, and—more circumspectly—by former FBI director Louis Freeh (Baer: Robert Baer, *Sleeping with the Devil,* NY: Three Rivers, 2003, 18, 190–, Robert Baer, *See No Evil,* NY: Three Rivers, 2002,

270; Freeh: Statement & Testimony of Louis Freeh, 4/13/04, CO & see CR, 147, 488n5, Staff Statement 5, CO, Bamford, *Pretext*, 164, Coll, *Ghost Wars*, 326–, 631n35).

307   **anger:** Richard Clarke, 152–; **$5 million/"Armed"/lookout:** "Mohammad," information sheet, FBI, INS Lookout Notice, 2/13/96, "KSM, FBI-INS Misc. Info.," B11, T5, CF.

307   **"al-Balushi":** CR, 276–. e.g., KSM's nephew Ammar al-Baluchi (also of Baluchi nationality and otherwise known as Ali Abdul Aziz Ali) was allegedly involved in transferring al Qaeda funds to the 9/11 hijackers; another example is senior al Qaeda military commander Abu Faraj al-Libi (the Libyan Mustafa al-'Uzayti). Both were among the group of U.S. captives known as High Value Detainees ("Detainee Biographies," www.defense.gov); **visa/alias:** Staff Report, "Monograph on Terrorist Travel," CO; **"recruiting":** CR, 255; **"Based on":** Statement of Eleanor Hill, 9/18/02, JI.

307   **"failure":** Executive Summary, "CIA Accountability with Respect to the 9/11 Attacks," Office of the Inspector General, CIA, 6/05. Though a summary was made public after congressional pressure, the full inspector general's 2005 "Report on CIA Accountability with Respect to the 9/11 Attacks" has not been released. ("Executive Summary," Central Intelligence Agency, Office of the Inspector General, 06/05, www.cia.gov, *NYT,* 10/5/05, AP, 5/18/07).

308–9   **KSM capture:** Fouda & Fielding, 181–, Tenet, 251–. Questions were raised as to the circumstances and timing of the arrest. The family of one of the men detained with KSM denied that the fugitive had been in the house. Some reports suggested he had been captured by Pakistani forces acting alone, others that it had been a joint U.S.-Pakistani operation. There were differing claims, too, as to who had custody of the suspect in the immediate aftermath. Red Cross staff and KSM's own defense team, however, who interviewed the prisoner, have not apparently raised questions as to the timing and circumstances of the arrest. The most reliable account of the hunt for and capture of KSM is almost certainly the 2012 book *The Hunt for KSM: Inside the Pursuit and Takedown of the Real 9/11 Mastermind,* by Terry McDermott & Josh Meyer, which reached the authors as this edition went to press—too late for detailed analysis (NY: Little, Brown, 2012). (questions: e.g. *Sunday Times* [London], 3/9/03, *NYT,* 3/3/03, *The Guardian* [U.K.], 3/3/03, ABC News, 3/11/03, Fouda &

Fielding, 181– & see Paul Thompson, "Is There More to the Capture of Khalid Shaikh Mohammed than Meets the Eye?," 3/4/03, www.historycommons.org; Red Cross/defense team: Red Cross Report, 5, 20, 33–, "Verbatim Transcript of Combatant Status Review Tribunal Hearing for ISN 10024," www.defense.gov); **"Nothing like"**: Tenet, 252; **leads/$25 million**: *LAT*, 3/2/03, Suskind, *One Percent*, 204–, *Guardian* (U.K.), 3/11/03, Tenet, 253; **"wonderful"/"hard"**: *LAT*, 3/2/03; **"This is equal"**: Fox News, 3/3/03; **"No person"**: Tenet, 250; **"disorient"/"break"**: *LAT*, 3/2/03; **"crouched"**: *Der Spiegel*, 10/27/03, *New Yorker*, 8/13/07; **Commission Report/211**: authors' analysis based on Robert Windrem, "Cheney's Role Deepens," 5/13/09, www.thedailybeast.com; **"enhanced"**: Special Review, "Counterterrorism Detention and Interrogation Activities," Office of Inspector General, CIA, 5/7/04, www.cia.gov; **"dark side"**: transcript, int. of Richard Cheney, *Meet the Press*, NBC, 9/16/01; **"certain acts"**: "Memorandum for Alberto Gonzales from Asst. A.G. Jay Bybee," 8/1/02.

309   **Red Cross monitors/asked in vain/"torture"/leaked/ "suffocation," etc.**: FAQ, www.icrc.org, Mark Danner, "The Red Cross Torture Report: What It Means," *NY Review of Books*, 4/30/09, "Report on the Treatment of Fourteen 'High Value' Detainees," International Committee of the Red Cross, 2/07, www.nyrb.com. Measures defined as "torture" or "cruel, inhuman or degrading treatment" of prisoners of war are illegal under the Third Geneva Convention (1949) and the U.N. Convention Against Torture (1984). To circumvent the treaties, and after advice from the Justice Department, President Bush formally determined in early 2002 that the 1949 Geneva Convention did not apply to the conflict with al Qaeda, and that the group's detainees therefore did not qualify as "prisoners of war."

The Red Cross determined that—in addition to KSM— thirteen other prisoners, suspected of having been in al Qaeda's "inner circle," suffered mistreatment constituting torture. The authors here confine themselves to U.S. treatment of prisoners relevant to the 9/11 story, but the mistreatment extended to captives elsewhere—as at Abu Ghraib prison after the invasion of Iraq. As well as pertinent documents referred to below, there has been groundbreaking reporting by Seymour Hersh, Jane Mayer, and Mark Danner ("inner circle": Summary of High Value Detainee Program, Office of the Director of National Intelligence, 9/06, www. c-span.org; torture: Red Cross Report; pertinent documents: e.g. as excerpted in eds. John Ehrenberg et al., *The Iraq Papers*, NY: Oxford Univ. Press, 2010, 403–. In addition to the previously cited Red Cross Report, see also "The Treatment by the Coalition Forces of Prisoners of War and Other Protected Persons by the Geneva Conventions in Iraq During Arrest, Internment & Interrogation," Report, International Committee of the Red Cross, 2/04).

311   **"complain":** "Lesson 18," al Qaeda Manual, www.justice.gov. The "manual" was among items confiscated in May 2000 from the home of a suspected al Qaeda member, Anas al-Liby, following a search by the Manchester (U.K.) police. The document was supplied to the United States, translated, and used by the prosecution in the 2001 embassy bombings trial (transcript, *U.S. v. Usama bin Laden et al.*, U.S. District Court for the Southern District of NY, S [7] 98-CR-1023, 3/26/01, "Inquiry into the Treatment of Detainees in U.S. Custody," Committee on Armed Services, U.S. Senate, 110th Cong, 2nd Sess., Washington, D.C., U.S. Govt. Printing Office, 11/20/08, Executive Summary, xii).

311   **review acknowledged:** Special Review, "Counterterrorism," & see "Memorandum for John Rizzo, CIA from Asst. A.G. Jay Bybee, 8/1/02, & see *LAT*, 12/22/02, *Telegraph* (U.K.), 3/9/03; **"my eyes":** Red Cross Report.

312   **"If anything":** Special Review, "Counterterrorism." The reference to a threat to kill KSM's children appears in the CIA's 2004 "Special Review" of counterterrorism detention and interrogation activities. According to the 2007 statement of another detainee's father, KSM's children were at one point "denied food and water," at another "mentally tortured by having ants or other creatures put on their legs to scare them and get them to say where their father was hiding." A Justice Department memo released in 2009 shows that approval was given to use insects to frighten an adult detainee into talking, while another document reports that the CIA never used the technique. According to a cousin, one of KSM's sons is mentally disabled and the other epileptic. As of this writing both boys were reportedly with their mother in Iran (threat: Special Review, Office of the Inspector General, CIA, 5/7/04, www.cia.gov; statement: "Verbatim Transcript of Combatant

Status Review Tribunal Hearing for ISN 10020," www.defense.gov—the statement was made by Ali Kahn, father of Majid Kahn; memos: Memorandum for John Rizzo, CIA from Jay Bybee, Asst. A.G., 8/1/02, Memorandum for John Rizzo, CIA from Stephen Bradbury, Principal Asst. Deputy A.G., 5/10/05, www.aclu.org; disabled/epileptic: *New Yorker*, 9/13/10; with mother: ibid., *WP*, 11/14/09).

312   **Poland/"verge"/"I would":** Red Cross Report; **14 seconds/2? minutes:** ABC News, 11/18/05; **183 times:** Special Review, "Counterterrorism."

313–14 **long history:** "Waterboarding: A Tortured History," NPR, 11/3/07, *NYT*, 3/9/08, *WP*, 11/5/06, Margulies, 73–; **"in violation":** ibid., 74; **executed Japanese:** "History Supports McCain's Stance on Waterboarding," 11/29/07, www. politifact.com; **"The United States"/"alternative"/ "separate program"/"I thought"/"take potential":** "President Bush Discusses Creation of Military Commissions to Try Suspect Terrorists," 9/6/06, http://georgewbush-whitehouse.archives. gov, George Bush, *Decision Points*, London: Virgin, 2010, 169; **"a great many":** *NY Review of Books*, 4/30/09; **"would not":** *New Yorker*, 1/21/08; **"provable":** *Toronto Star*, 11/20/10; **agents:** *NYT*, 6/22/08, 4/23/09; **"intensely disputed":** *NY Review of Books*, 4/30/09; **Obama banned:** ibid.; **"The use":** Mark Danner, "US Torture: Voices from the Black Sites," *NY Review of Books*, 4/9/09.

315   **"Any piece":** *NY Review of Books*, 4/30/09.

315   **spewed information:** KSM's most recent known admissions, to the military tribunal in Guantánamo, included the "A to Z" of 9/11, the 1993 attack on the Trade Center, the beheading of *Wall Street Journal* reporter Daniel Pearl, the failed attack on a plane by shoe bomber Richard Reid, and the murder of U.S. soldiers in Kuwait. He said he planned more than twenty other crimes, including a "Second Wave" of attacks on American landmarks to follow 9/11, attacks on nuclear power plants, on London's Heathrow Airport, on Gibraltar, on the Panama Canal, on NATO headquarters in Brussels, on four Israeli targets, and on targets in Thailand and South Korea. Whatever the truth about most of this string of claims, there may now be less doubt than previously as to his claim to have killed reporter Pearl. A 2011 study by Georgetown University and the International Consortium of Investigative Journalists, however, indicated that KSM had—as he claimed—been the

killer. A man named Ahmed Omar Saeed Sheikh was sentenced to death in connection with Pearl's murder in 2002 and is currently imprisoned in Karachi awaiting an appeal ("Verbatim Transcript of Combatant Status Review Tribunal Hearing for ISN 10024," www.defense.gov, AP, 3/18/07, *New Yorker*, 1/21/08, *Irish Times*, 1/21/11, JTA, 1/20/11, *Times of Oman*, 3/28/11, Musharraf, 228).

315–17 **"Detainee has":** *New Yorker*, 8/13/07; **"I gave":** Red Cross Report; **"some level":** *Times-Dispatch* (Richmond, VA), 7/6/08; **"We were not":** "Cheney's Role Deepens," 5/13/09, www.thedailybeast.com; **"Never, ever":** Richard Ben-Veniste, *The Emperor's New Clothes*, NY: Thomas Dunne, 2009, 248; **Commission not told/turned down/blocked:** MFR of int. George Tenet, 12/23/03, Kean & Hamilton, 119–; **"incomplete":** Shenon, 391; **"We never":** *New Republic*, 5/23/05; **"reliance":** Farmer, 362; **"Assessing":** CR, 146. Of 1,744 footnotes in the report, it has been estimated that more than a quarter refer to information extracted from captives during questioning that employed the interrogation techniques authorized after 9/11 (*Newsweek*, 3/14/09).

318–19 **Fouda scoop:** Fouda & Fielding, 23–, 38, 105, 114–, 148–, 156–, & see int. Yosri Fouda for Paladin InVision, 2006, conv. Nick Fielding, corr. Yosri Fouda, 2011. Fouda's book on the case, written with Nick Fielding of the *Sunday Times* (London), was published as *Masterminds of Terror* in 2003; **Binalshibh:** Ramzi Binalshibh, a Yemeni, was an associate of the three 9/11 hijackers based in Germany until 2000, when they left for the United States. He had himself wished to take part in the operation but, unable to obtain a U.S. visa, functioned as go-between. Like KSM, Binalshibh was by 2002 a fugitive (Staff Report, "9/11 and Terrorist Travel," CO, 5, 11–, 36); **footnote:** CR, 492n40; **evidence:** "Summary of Evidence for Combatant Status Review Tribunal," 2/8/07, http://projects.nytimes.com & see int. Udo Jacob—Motassadeq attorney; **Suskind:** Suskind, *One Percent*, 102–, 133–, 156; **Bergen:** Bergen, *OBL I Know*, 301–.

319   **authentic:** Others, notably Paul Thompson and Chaim Kupferberg, have raised doubts about Fouda's account. Both noted that Fouda did not tell the truth about the date of the interview with KSM and Binalshibh, raising the possibility that his overall reporting of the interviews may be inaccurate. It is true that the reported date of the interview changed after

the story broke in September 2002. While Fouda initially claimed the interviews were conducted in Karachi in June of that year, he later revealed that the interviews had taken place two months earlier, in the third week of April. Questioned about the discrepancy in late 2002, Fouda said, "I lied because I needed to lie . . . if something went wrong and I needed to get in touch with them . . . they [KSM and Binalshibh] would be the only ones who would know that I had met them one month earlier than I had let on, and so I'd know I was talking to the right people" (doubts: Paul Thompson, "Is There More to the Capture of Khalid Shaikh Mohammed Than Meets the Eye?," 3/03, www.historycommons.org, Chaim Kupferberg, "Khalid Sheikh Mohammed: The Official Legend of 9/11 Is a Fabricated Setup," 3/15/07, www.globalresearch.ca; changed dates: *Sunday Times* (London), 9/8/02, *Guardian* (U.K.), 3/4/03, Fouda & Fielding, 23, 29, 148; "I lied": int. Fouda by Abdallah Schleifer, Fall/Winter 2002, www.tbsjournal.com.

319 **"a close":** Fouda & Fielding, 113; **chairman:** ibid., 117.

CHAPTER 22

320–1 **first meeting:** CR, 488n1; **"very calm":** *In the Footsteps of Bin Laden*, CNN, 8/23/06; **projects:** MFR 04013804, 12/4/03, Wright, 168–; **all manner:** Bergen, *OBL I Know*, 133; **rich and poor:** bin Ladens & Sasson, 111, 115; **financial support S.A.:** *Time*, 9/15/03, Peter Dale Scott, *The Road to 9/11*, Berkeley: Univ. of Calif. Press, 2007, 149–; **veterans:** Bergen, *Holy War Inc.*, 86, Richard Clarke, 137; **OBL to Bosnia/citizenship:** *Ottawa Citizen*, 12/15/01, *WSJ*, 11/1/01; **Flottau:** John Schindler, *Unholy Terror*, Minneapolis: Zenith, 2007, 123– & see "British Journalist Eye-Witnessed Osama Bin Laden Entering Alija Izetbegovic's Office," 2/3/06. www.slobodan-milosevic.org, *The Times* (London), 9/28/07; **KSM twice:** CR, 147, 488n5; **funds Chechnya:** Benjamin & Simon, 113, Loretta Napoleoni, *Terror Incorporated*, NY: Seven Stories, 2005, 95; **holdouts:** *Newsweek*, 8/19/02.

321–3 **Two hijackers:** JI, Report, 131, Testimony of George Tenet, 6/18/02, JI. The future 9/11 hijackers who fought in Bosnia were Khalid al-Mihdhar and Nawaf al-Hazmi. Zacarias Moussaoui, who was arrested before 9/11, reportedly served as a recruiter for the Chechen mujahideen (Mihdhar/Hazmi: Staff Statement 16, CO; Moussaoui: Legat, Paris to

Minneapolis, FBI 199M-MP-60130, 8/22/01, Defense
Exhibit 346, *U.S. v. Zacarias Moussaoui*, Tenet, 202); **Zawahiri
in Sudan/directed/Mubarak:** Wright, 185–, 213, 215–, bin
Ladens & Sasson, 129–; **Zubaydah/manager:** CR, 59, 169,
175, Thomas Jocelyn, "The Zubaydah Dossier," 8/17/09,
www.weeklystandard.com; **"The snake":** Testimony of Jamal
al-Fadl, *U.S. v. Usama Bin Laden et al.*, U.S. District Court for
the Southern District of NY, S(7) 98-CR-1023, 2/6/01, CR,
59; **Yemen attacks:** Staff Statement 15, CO, Atwan, 166.
There were no American fatalities in the bombings, but an
Australian tourist was killed (Staff Statement 15, CO);
Somalia/Black Hawks: transcript int. of OBL by Hamid Mir,
3/18/97, www.fas.org, Staff Statement 15, CO, int. Abdel Bari
Atwan, Atwan, 36; **Riyadh attack:** CR, 60, Staff Statement
15, CO, Wright, 211–, Burke, 154–; **"paved":** ed. Lawrence,
36–; **"adopt":** int. OBL by Hamid Mir; **Dhahran:** Staff
Statement 15, CO, CR, 60, Bamford, *Pretext*, 163, Benjamin
& Simon, 224, William Simpson, 275; **Iran responsible?:**
CR, 60; **traveled Qatar/purchase:** Christopher Blanchard,
"Qatar: Background & U.S. Relations," Congressional
Research Service, Washington, D.C., 1/24/08, Stephen
Hayes, "Case Closed," 11/24/03, www.weeklystandard.com,
Gareth Porter, "Investigating the Khobar Tower Bombing,"
6/24/09, *CounterPunch*.

323–4 **"heroes":** ed. Lawrence, 52. The debate over responsibility
for the Dhahran attack was prolonged and bitter. Vital reading on the subject includes the relevant part of a memoir by
the FBI director of the day, Louis Freeh, and—for a very
different view—a series of 2009 articles by reporter Gareth
Porter (Louis Freeh, *My FBI*, NY: St. Martin's, 2005, 1–,
Gareth Porter, *CounterPunch*, 6/24/09); **interview:** int. Abdel
bari Atwan, Atwan, 36; **"They called":** *France-Soir*, 8/27/98,
citing int. of 1995 & see bin Ladens & Sasson, 127; **royals
persuaded/"They beseeched":** bin Ladens & Sasson, 104,
Corbin, 57, MFR 04013955, 12/3/03, AP, 6/15/08, Bergen,
OBL I Know, 150; **"behavior":** "State Dept. Issues Fact Sheet
on Bin Laden," 8/14/96 cited at Brisard & Dasquié, 169;
share sold off: Staff Report, "Monograph on Terrorist
Financing, CO, Lacey, *Inside the Kingdom*, 177–, AP, 6/15/08.

324 **formal cutoff/future:** Bergen, *Holy War Inc.*, 102, CR, 62, bin
Ladens & Sasson, 128. Men who worked for bin Laden in
Sudan have recalled him saying that money was short. One

man, Jamal al-Fadl, defected following a clash over funding and became a useful informant for the United States. Bin Laden's son Omar remembered a time in the Sudan when funds were limited after his father "lost access to his huge bank accounts in the Kingdom" (money short/Fadl: Testimony of L'Hossaine Kerchtou, 2/22/01, & Jamal al-Fadl, 2/7/01, *U.S. v. Usama bin Laden et al.*, U.S. District Court for the Southern District of NY, S[7]98-CR-1023, CR, 62; "lost": bin Ladens & Sasson, 12).

324   **"Blood is":** int. of Rahimullah Yusufzai for Paladin InVision, 2006, Bergen, *OBL I Know*, 203 but see FBI 302s of int. bin Laden family members, "Saudi Flights," B70, T5, CF; **"OBL has kept":** Note de Synthèse, 7/24/00 in "Oussama Bin Laden," leaked DGSE report, 9/13/01, seen by authors; **Yeslam:** Scheuer, *Osama bin Laden*, 28; **"Some female":** Statement of Vincent Cannistraro, Hearings, Committee on International Realations, U.S. House of Reps, 107th Cong., 1st Sess., 10/3/01.

325   **funding cut off:** Whether or not bin Laden was really "disowned" by his family, there were over the years many suggestions that he had a personal fortune of some $300 million—from which he funded operations. According to the 9/11 Commission, this is merely "urban legend." A commission analysis suggests he received approximately $1 million a year from the family coffers between 1970 and 1993—the year in which his share of the family business was sold and OBL's portion "frozen." The author Peter Bergen, writing in 2001, cited a source close to the family as saying bin Laden's inheritance from his father was $35 million. In his 2008 biography of the bin Laden clan, Steve Coll stated that the value placed on OBL's share of the family business at the time he was reportedly stripped of it was a surprisingly low $9.9 million. Even taken together, these sums total far less than the rumored $300 million figure.

The approximately $30 million consumed annually by al Qaeda operations prior to 9/11 apparently came from a core of "financial facilitators" and "fundraisers" in the Gulf—particularly in Saudi Arabia. The 9/11 operation itself cost only $400,000–$500,000. Khalid Sheikh Mohammed told his interrogators that bin Laden provided 85–90 percent of that. Investigators believe, however, that this money came not from personal funds, but rather from monies he controlled (official estimates: MFR 03010990, 11/4/03, CF, FBI memo, "Ali Ahmad Mesdaq, International Terrorism, Usama bin Laden," 1/28/02, INTELWIRE, *WP*, 8/28/98; popular reports: e.g. *WP*, 8/28/98, "Tracing bin Laden's Money," 9/21/01, www.ict.org; "myth"/$1 million: Staff Report, "Monograph on Terrorist Financing," CO; $35 million: Bergen, *Holy War Inc.*, 101–; $9.9 million: Coll, *Bin Ladens*, 405–, 485–; $30 million/"fundraisers"/KSM: Staff Report, "Monograph on Terrorist Financing," CO).

325 **$4.5 million:** Note de Synthèse; **"$3,000,000"/"wealthy Saudis"/"siphoning":** Statement of Vincent Cannistraro, *Boston Herald*, 10/14/01; **considerable:** Chouet int. for *Le Monde*, 3/29/07, http://alain.chouet.free.fr, *Politique Étrangère*, March/April 03, int. Alain Chouet; **$30 million/donations/"wealthy":** Staff Report, "Monograph on Terrorist Financing," CO; **"subterfuge"/manipulate:** Chouet int. for *Le Monde*, 3/29/07, http://alain.chouet.free.fr, int. Alain Chouet.

326–7 **"sponsorship"/OBL funding:** MFR 04013804, 12/4/03, MFR 04013803, 12/30/03, *WP*, 10/3/01; **"We couldn't"/"We asked"/"hot potato":** *USA Today*, 11/12/01, Bill Clinton, *My Life*, NY: Alfred A. Knopf, 2004, 797–; **"My calculation":** *WP*, 10/3/01; **"probably the biggest":** *Sunday Times* (London), 1/5/02; **"perhaps"/"probably the best":** *Frontline:* "Hunting bin Laden," www.pbs.org, *New Yorker*, 1/24/00.

327–9 **"whisked"/refueled:** bin Ladens & Sasson, 139–, 142, 309. Other accounts have suggested that the plane was allowed to refuel in Qatar. The authors have deferred to what Omar bin Laden—who was there—said. According to him, the plane stopped to refuel at Shiraz, in Iran (Coll, *Ghost Wars*, 325); **"Our plane":** bin Ladens & Sasson, 180–, *Asia Times*, 11/28/01; **Jalalabad:** bin Ladens & Sasson, 149–, CR, 65; **desolate/"new home"/"I was put":** bin Ladens & Sasson, 150–, 156, 161, 174–, 176–; **cabin:** Atwan, 28, Bergen, *Holy War Inc.*, 93; **Kalashnikov:** bin Ladens & Sasson, 165; **tapes/fax:** int. Dr. Flagg Miller, Univ. of Calif.; **satellite phone:** Bamford, *Shadow Factory*, 8, Guna-ratna, 141; **dictating:** bin Ladens & Sasson, 165; **fax transmission:** int. Abdel Bari Atwan, Atwan, 53; **"summit"/hundreds of thousands:** Flagg Miller, "On 'The Summit of the Hindu Kush': Osama bin Laden's 1996 Declaration of War

Reconsidered," unpub. ms. courtesy of Miller.

329–30 **"Declaration":** full text, "Ladenese Epistle: Declaration of War," Pts. I, II, III, www.washingtonpost.com [web only], 9/21/01. Though often described as a fatwa, the declaration seems not to fit the usual meaning of that word—"a ruling on a point of Islamic law given by a recognized authority" (worldnetweb.princeton.edu/perl/webwn); **KSM-Atef meeting:** CR, 148.

330 **traveled together:** The authors suggest that the travel together may have been to Bosnia, because—as noted earlier in this chapter—bin Laden and KSM are both known to have made visits there during that period (JI, Report, 313).

330–1 **KSM proposal/"theater"/"Why do you":** KSM SUBST, CR, 148–, 153–, 489n11–14, Tenet, 251. The source of this second version of the proposal, citing bin Laden's supposed retort, was reportedly Abu Zubaydah—another senior aide to bin Laden (CR 491n35, JI, Report, 130); **"would not focus":** KSM SUBST; **OBL priority:** Tenet, 248.

331 **"not convinced":** KSM SUBST. Bin Laden did, however, invite KSM to join al Qaeda, he told the CIA. He demurred, he said, because he wanted to retain the ability to approach other terrorist groups (CR 154).

331 **video of Twin Towers, etc.:** "The Fifth Estate: War Without Borders," www.cbc.ca, AP, 7/17/02, CR, 530n145, AP, 7/17/02. The filming in the United States was done in 1997 by a Syrian living in Spain named Ghasoub al-Abrash Ghalyoun, who was arrested after 9/11. According to the Spanish Interior Ministry, "the style and duration of the recordings far exceed tourist curiosity." Spanish investigators believed that an al Qaeda courier delivered copies of the tapes to Afghanistan (AP, 7/17/02, CR, 530n145, "The Fifth Estate: War Without Borders," www.cbc.ca).

332 **"to study":** KSM SUBST.

332 **"individuals":** Statement of Eleanor Hill, 2/17/02, JI. The 9/11 Commission noted that there had been significant radical Islamic activity in Arizona prior to 9/11. The Islamic Center of Tucson was a branch of the Office of Services, long since established by bin Laden and Abdullah Azzam in Pakistan. It had begun distributing its journal throughout the United States as early as 1986. Two former FBI informants claimed after 9/11 that they had alerted the FBI to the presence of suspicious Arabs at Arizona flight schools in 1996

(Commission: CR, 226–, 520–; Center: Steven Emerson, *American Jihad*, NY: Free Press, 2002, 129–, *Frontline:* "The Man Who Knew," www.pbs.org, *NYT*, 6/7/02; claim: *WP*, 9/23/01, 5/24/02, *NYT*, 5/24/02, FBI IG, Aukai Collins, *My Jihad*, Guilford, CT: Lyons, 2002, 213–).

332   **"different person"/beard, etc.:** "Hijackers Timeline [redacted]," FBI, 2/1/07, INTELWIRE, Report, JI, 135, Testimony of George Tenet, 6/18/02, JI, Graham with Nussbaum, 40–; **Atta/27:** Staff Statement 16, *WSJ*, 10/16/01, McDermott, 2–, 31 but see re Mecca twice 57; **"colony"/ "Resistance":** Fisk, *The Great War*, 21–.

Part V: PERPETRATORS

CHAPTER 23

337–42 **Wiley:** MFR 04017164, 11/25/03; **"independent":** JI, Report, Appendix, 5; **"flake":** Benjamin & Simon, 243; **"terrorist financier":** Richard Clarke, 96, Tenet, xi; **"Ford Foundation":** Benjamin & Simon, 242; **not named:** Executive Order 12947, 1/23/95, *Federal Register*, Vol. 60, No. 16, Staff Report, "Monograph on Terrorist Financing," CO; **9 speeches:** Richard Clarke, 129–, e.g., "American Security in a Changing World," speech, 8/5/96, U.S. Department of State, Dispatch, Vol. 7, No. 32, & see "Presidential Speech Archive," www.millercenter.org; **PDD39/rendition/ coordinated:** "Memorandum for the Vice President et al. from William J. Clinton," 6/21/95 [PDD-39], www .fas.org, Benjamin & Simon, 230, CR, 101; **badgered:** Richard Clarke, 135; **"foaming":** Benjamin & Simon, 243; **"It just seemed":** Clarke, 135; **"asleep":** Hollingsworth with Mitchell, 101; **approval of Lake:** Bamford, *Pretext*, 205, int. Michael Scheuer for Paladin InVision; **dozen/40:** CR, 479n2; **FBI liaison/"buzz saw":** Statement of George Tenet, 10/17/02, JI, FBI IG; **focus/women/shopping complex/ committed/zealot:** Shenon, 188–, MFR 04020389, 6/21/04, CR, 109; **CTC-TFL:** Staff Report, "Monograph on Terrorist Financing," CO; **more operational:** MFR 04017164, 11/25/03; **changed name:** Tenet, 100; **"My God"/"truly dangerous":** Shenon, 189; **"civilians and military":** int. of OBL for ABC News, transcript available at *Frontline:* "Hunting bin Laden," www.pbs.org; **"They chose":** int. of

OBL for CNN, 3/97, www.cnn.com; **"If they":** Bergen, *OBL I Know*, 242; **"snatch":** Richard Clarke, 149; **surveillance/human intelligence:** Farmer, 29; **eavesdropping/phone:** Bamford, *Pretext*, 162–, Gunaratna, 12, *WP*, 4/24/01; **training camp:** CR, 111; **CIA plan/"half-assed"/"perfect":** Tenet, 112–, Wright, 265–, Michael Scheuer, *Marching Toward Hell*, New York: Free Press, 2008, 272n3, CR, 111–, Richard Clarke, 149; **memo:** Scheuer, *Marching*, 271; **"They could not":** Shenon, 190; **Nairobi bomb/casualties:** Report of Accountability Review Boards, Bombings of the US Embassies in Nairobi, Kenya and Dar es Salaam, Tanzania on Aug. 7, 1998, U.S. Dept. of State, www.fas.org, Wright, 270, Corbin, 73; **Dar es Salaam:** Report of Accountability Review Boards, *The Independent* (U.K.), 8/8/98; **worst:** Unger, *House of Bush, House of Saud*, 183, Robert Johnston, "Worst Terrorist Attacks—Worldwide," www.johnstonarchive.net; **bomber/met OBL/for OBL:** Testimony of Stephen Gaudin, *U.S. v. Usama Bin Laden et al.*, U.S. District Court for the Southern District of NY, S(7) 98-CR-1023, 1/8/01, Bergen, *Holy War Inc.*, 107, Corbin, 71, Criminal Complaint Against Mohamed Rashed Al-'Owhali, U.S. Federal Court for the Southern District of NY, 8/26/98, http://avalon.law.yale.edu, Reeve, 198–; **bomber/OBL calls:** Gaudin testimony, JI, Report, 129–, Wright, 276–.

342   **"I did"/Odeh/"my leader":** Bergen, *Holy War Inc.*, 53, 113, Reeve, 201. The four men convicted for their roles in the Kenya and Tanzania bombings were Mohamed al-'Owhali, Mohamed Odeh—the two terrorists referred to in the text—Khalfan Mohamed, and bin Laden's former secretary Wadih al-Hage. They were convicted in May 2001. A fifth man, Ahmed Ghailani, who had been charged on a total of 285 counts, was in 2010 acquitted of multiple murder and attempted murder charges. Though found guilty only of conspiracy to damage U.S. property, he was handed a life sentence (4 men: AP, 11/24/08; Ghailani: BBC, 1/25/2011).

342–3   **"excited and happy":** bin Ladens & Sasson, 237; **"juice":** int. of Abdulrahman Khadr, *Frontline:* "Son of al Qaeda," www.pbs.org, "Al Qaeda Family: The Black Sheep," 3/3/04, www.cbc.ca; **"Only God"/"real men"/"Our job":** int. of OBL for ABC News, 12/23/98 available at http://pws.prserv.net, *Time*, 1/11/99; **"the greatest":** int. of OBL for Al Jazeera, 12/98, http://wasarch.ucr.edu;

"respond": MFR 04021459, 1/29/04; opportunity/attack: Tenet, 115–, Miller & Stone, 210–, Clinton, 803–, Burke, 52; Security tight: MFR 04021469, 12/19/03, Richard Clarke, 187; told Pakistan/Ralston: Clinton, 799, Richard Clarke, 186–; "Our target": text of President Clinton's address, CBS News, 8/20/98.

344   circumlocution: CR, 113–, 126–, 484n101, Executive Order 12333, United States Intelligence Activities, 12/4/81. National Security Adviser Sandy Berger, who had succeeded Lake, would tell the 9/11 Commission that the intention of the missile strikes had been "to be bouncing bin Laden into the rubble." Under Secretary for Political Affairs Thomas Pickering told commission staff the primary objective had been "to kill bin Laden and other senior leaders he was meeting with" (Berger: testimony of Sandy Berger, 3/34/04, CO; Pickering: MFR 04013744, 12/22/03, CF).

344   "intently focused": Clinton, 798.

344   some fatalities: CR, 117, bin Ladens & Sasson, 240–, Bergen, *Holy War Inc.*, 121–, int. of OBL for ABC News, 12/23/98. National Security Adviser Berger told the 9/11 Commission that "20–30 people in the camps" were killed. Interviewed in late 1998, bin Laden acknowledged that seven "brothers" were killed and "20-something Afghans." In addition, according to Bruce Lawrence, editor of bin Laden's public statements, seven Pakistanis also died (CR, 117, 482n46, int. of OBL by Rahimullah Yusufzai, 12/23/98, ABC News online, www.cryptome.org, ed. Lawrence, 83fn); factory destroyed/intelligence shaky: Reeve, 202, Tenet, 117, CR, 118, Stephen Hayes, "The Connection," 6/7/04, www.weeklystandard.com; $750,000: Bamford, *Pretext*, 209; $10,000: CR, 498n127; propaganda victory/T-shirts: Hamel, 216, *WP*, 10/3/01; "a highly": bin Ladens & Sasson, 238.

344   "He had been": MFR 03013620, 12/12/03, CR, 117. Bin Laden himself appeared to confirm as much a month later when he told Al Jazeera: "I was hundreds of kilometers away from there. As for the information that was supposed to have reached us, we found a sympathetic and generous people in Pakistan who exceeded all our expectations, and we received information from our beloved ones and helpers of jihad for the sake of God against the Americans." Omar bin Laden's recent account seems more worthy of credence than the story

told by one of his father's former bodyguards, Abu Jandal. According to Jandal, only a whimsical change of mind led bin Laden to change his plans and head for Kabul instead of the targeted camp ("I was hundreds": ed. Lawrence, 7; whimsical: Nasser al-Bahri with Georges Malbrunot, *Dans l'ombre de Ben Laden*, Neuilly-sur-Seine, France: Michel Lafon, 2010, 149–, transcript, *CNN Presents: In the Footsteps of bin Laden*, 8/23/06).

345   **"In 1996":** JI, Report, 217; **"conspiracy":** ibid., 129, Statement of Mary Jo White, 10/2/02, JI, Report; **200-page/$5 million:** Indictment, *U.S. v. Usama bin Laden et al.*, U.S. District Court for the Southern District of NY, 98 CR, 11/4/1998, *WP*, 11/5/98; **$25 million/double:** Kenneth Katzman, "Terrorism: Near Eastern Groups and State Sponsors, 2002," Congressional Research Service, Washington, D.C., 2/13/02, BBC News, 7/13/07 **"Tier 0":** JI, Report, 40; **"We are":** CR, 357, JI, Report, 124.

345   **"lethal force":** CR, 131–, 485n123, Shenon, 357. Clinton, Berger, and others told the 9/11 Commission that the president's intent was clear—he wanted bin Laden dead. According to Tenet, however: "Almost all the 'authorities' [presidential authorizations] provided to us with regard to bin Laden were predicated on the planning of a capture operation." Other senior officials agreed with this interpretation. Attorney General Janet Reno, Tenet wrote later, "made it clear . . . that she would view an attempt simply to kill bin Laden as illegal" (intent: CR, 133; Tenet: Tenet, 111–, "Director's Statement on the Release of the 9/11 IG Report Executive Summary," 8/21/07, www.cia.gov; Reno: CR, 132–).

345   **operations against:** Executive Summary, "Report on CIA Accountability with Respect to the 9/11 Attacks," 6/05, CR, 132–, 142; **"Policy makers":** Tenet, 123.

345   **"two chances":** Scheuer, *Marching Toward Hell*, 61. The Scheuer reference relates to the period between May 1998 and May 1999. A 9/11 Commission staff report noted only three occasions in that time frame on which strikes were considered. In December 1998, when there was intelligence indicating that bin Laden was at a location near Kandahar, an operation was called off—according to Tenet—because of doubt as to whether the information was good and the risk of killing people in a nearby mosque. In February 1999, bin Laden was firmly believed to be at a location in the desert in

Helmand province. U.S. officials vacillated, however, because members of the government of the United Arab Emirates were hunting nearby. The opportunity passed. Another strike was considered in May 1999, but scrubbed because some doubted the reliability of the source. In July that year, President Clinton authorized the CIA to work with Pakistani and Uzbek operatives to capture bin Laden. It is not clear what stage that project reached (Staff Statement 6, CO, CR, 130–, 485n116–488n194, & see Scheuer, *Marching Toward Hell*, 284n8, 285n15).

346   **"Tenet consistently":** *WP*, 4/29/07.

346   **"cared little"/"moral cowardice":** Scheuer, *Marching Toward Hell*, 48, 75, 82, 84, 85, 290. Scheuer was closely informed on everything to do with the pursuit of bin Laden until some point in 1999. Sometime after the aborted strike in February 1999 (see previous note), however, he was removed as head of Alec Station—after a clash with an FBI manager assigned to the unit. Much of Scheuer's 2008 book comes over as a furious venting of his feelings (Wright, 291–, Shenon, 188, Scheuer, *Marching Toward Hell*, refs.).

346–7   **"pathetically":** Clarke, 204; **"authorized":** int. of Bill Clinton by Fox News, 9/24/06; **"kill authority":** Shenon, 357–; **"attacks":** CR, 120; **"My father":** bin Ladens & Sasson, 239; **went to ground:** ibid.; **stopped using phone:** *Mail on Sunday* (U.K.), 12/23/01, Kessler, 84–, Corbin, 88, JI, Report, 69; **"wished to send":** Atwan, 55–.

347   **"But things":** Gaudin testimony. The bomber arrested after running away was Mohamed al-'Owhali (see above). The accomplice he named was Abdullah Ahmed Abdullah (aka Saleh), who is still at large. FBI agent Stephen Gaudin, who questioned him in Nairobi, cited the passage quoted in federal court (Testimony of Stephen Gaudin, *U.S. v. Usama Bin Laden et al.*, U.S. District Court for the Southern District of NY, S[7] 98-CR-1023, 1/8/01).

347–8   **summoned/"could work":** KSM SUBST, Terry McDermott & Josh Meyer, *The Hunt for KSM*, NY: Little, Brown, 2012, 137. KSM provided "inconsistent information" as to whether bin Laden approved the operation in late 1998 or in early 1999, according to CIA accounts of his various interrogation sessions (CR, 492n38); **Kenya/alias:** JI, Report, 313.

348   **decoy:** *Financial Times*, 2/14/03. Another report, however, has it that—as of that same month—KSM was working as an

"escort" for his longtime mentor Sheikh Abdul Sayyaf, leader of Ittehad-e-Islami, the Islamic Union Party (NY to Bangkok et al., FBI265A-NY-253802, 7/8/09, INTELWIRE, CR, 146–); **persuaded:** CR, 149, 490n16.

348   **"full support"/Atef:** KSM SUBST, CR, 154. Al Qaeda suspects questioned in Jordan were to allege that Atef seized on the concept following the 1999 EgyptAir crash off the coast of Massachusetts, which was never satisfactorily explained. The NTSB found that the crash probably occurred "as a result of the relief first officer's flight control inputs. The reason for the relief first officer's actions was not determined." The first officer's exclamation was initially interpreted as "I place my fate in the hands of God," and later revised to "I rely on God." EgyptAir and Egypt's Civil Aviation Authority advised that the statement was "very often used by the Egyptian layman in day to day activities to ask God's assistance for the task at hand." The officer uttered the exclamation nine times while alone, twice more after the captain returned to the cockpit. Two hundred and seventeen people died in the crash (Aircraft Accident Brief, EgyptAir 990, NTSB, 3/13/02, www.ntsb.gov).

348   **change his mind:** *WP,* 9/11/02.

348–9   **targeting/operatives:** KSM SUBST, CR, 154. The plan was adjusted according to the number of suitable operatives available. It would turn out early on that only two of four men originally selected to be pilot hijackers were able to obtain U.S. visas. The two who had no visas, it was then hoped, would explode planes in midair over Asia at the same time their accomplices were hitting targets in the United States. Thinking it too difficult to synchronize the operation, bin Laden would later cancel the Asia part of the operation (KSM SUBST); **"military committee":** Fouda & Fielding, 158; **two years:** KSM SUBST; **"planes operation":** CR, 154; **Omar disillusioned:** bin Ladens & Sasson, 201, 212–, 218–, 248–; **"I have heard":** ibid., 254; **"gigantic":** ibid., 277.

349   **Noonan/"History":** *Forbes,* 11/30/98.

CHAPTER 24

350–2   **"The mighty"/curbed:** bin Ladens & Sasson, 244, Bergen, *OBL I Know,* 321, 455n20; **candidates/two parts/too complicated:** KSM SUBST; **Yemenis' visas/in vain:** Staff Report, "9/11 and Terrorist Travel," CO, 13–. The Yemenis were Walid bin Attash—also known as Khallad—who had lost a leg on the Afghan battlefield, and Abu Bara al-Tai'zi, on whom there appears to be scant information. Bin Laden had known Attash in Saudi Arabia. He was to play a role at later points in the story (KSM SUBST, CR 155–) **two Saudis/ aged 24/23:** National Drug Intelligence Center for the FBI, "265D-NY-280350, TWINBOM-PENTTBOM, Biographical Report," 11/26/01, authors' collection, Blair Oakley to Janice Kephart, 3/23/04, "Hijacker Primary Documents—AA77," B50, T5, CF; **friends:** Testimony of George Tenet, 6/18/02, JI, Bamford, *Shadow Factory*, 9; **well-to-do/married Yemeni/veterans:** ibid., 9, Staff Statement 16, CO, Report, JI, 131, Wright, 309–. Mihdhar's relations by marriage were the Hada family in Yemen's capital, Sana'a— their connection to terrorism will be reported later. The future 9/11 conspirator to whom Mihdhar was linked by marriage was Ramzi Binalshibh, one of the Germany-based accomplices (marriage: Bamford, *Shadow Factory*, 7–; McDermott, 183 & see AP, 12/23/07; Binalshibh: *WP*, 9/11/02); **"Jihad Ali"/Inspired:** KSM SUBST, Testimony of Stephen Gaudin, *U.S. v. Usama Bin Laden et al.*; **Saudi visas easy:** Staff Report, "9/11 and Terrorist Travel," CO, 14–, 116–; **had sworn:** JI, Report, 131–, Testimony of George Tenet, JI, 6/18/02; **"I swear"/"*hijrah*":** KSM SUBST. In its literal sense, the word *hijrah* or *hegira* refers to the Prophet's move from Mecca to what is now Medina in A.D. 622—the first year of the Muslim era. It has thus come to be synonymous with migration. In the context used here it appears to denote a spiritual "migration" or transformation of the self (corr. Hans Kippenberg, 2010); **"the joys"/"My father":** bin Ladens & Sasson, 262–; **candidates in Gulf:** KSM SUBST; **Italy:** McDermott, 209, 299n65. The source cited on the reported KSM visit to Italy is a senior Italian investigator; **Germany:** Leading U.S. news sources have cited "intelligence reports" indicating that KSM visited Hamburg in 1999. "We have indications from various sources," Walter Wellinghausen, a senior official of the Hamburg Interior Ministry, told *The New York Times*, "that [KSM] was in Hamburg for a period, but we have not been able to definitively verify this" (*Newsweek*, 9/9/02, *NYT*, 11/4/02, *WP*, 9/11/02).

352–3 **Atta:** Texas Service Center, 911 Terrorist Review, "Hijacker

Primary Documents—AA11," B51, T5, CF, McDermott, 10; **friends:** int. Mounir Motassadeq; **1992/architecture/Cairo:** McDermott, 18–; **father divorced:** Timeline Pertaining to Hijackers in Florida, "Timelines 9/11, 2 of 2," B20, T7, CF; **"never stopped":** *NYT*, 10/10/01; **mother's lap:** *Sunday Times* (London), 1/6/02; **"child feelings":** *Frontline:* "Inside the Terror Network," 1/17/02, www.pbs.org; **insect/ "brainless":** *Time*, 9/30/01; **cardiologist/professor:** McDermott, 14; **did all right/arranged meeting:** ibid., 19.

353 **flew to Germany:** Atta had done a course in German at Cairo's Goethe Institute. In Germany, he was at some stage sponsored by the Carl Duisberg Gesellschaft, which assists young professionals from many foreign countries (Goethe: Uwe Michaels statement to Bundeskriminalamt, Hamburg, 10/2/01, authors' collection; Duisberg: *Tagespiel* [Germany], 10/16/01).

353–8 **"exceedingly":** Uwe Michaels Statement to Bundeskriminalamt, Hamburg, 10/2/01, authors' collection; **own meals/pots/video/risqué:** *Chicago Tribune*, 3/7/03; **blouse:** *Sunday Times* (London), 1/26/02, *LAT*, 1/27/02; **"that person":** int. of Michaels Jr. by Hannah Cleaver; **"words":** *Chicago Tribune*, 1/27/02; **clashes:** McDermott, 25–; **"a dear human":** *Newsweek*, 10/1/01 **applied self/trips:** transcript, int. Dittmar Machule, 10/18/01, *Four Corners: A Mission to Die For*, 10/18/01, www.abc.net.au; **Omar arrive/phony/ returned:** MFR 04016498, 1/13/04, *LAT*, 9/1/02, CR, 161; **aspired:** CR, 161, Fouda & Fielding, 74; **"in love":** McDermott, 48; **"very funny":** int. Mounir Motassadeq; **"disgusting"/read Qur'an:** eds. *Der Spiegel*, 197; **new-comer/father muezzin:** McDermott, 55; **prayer tape:** Corbin, 134; **"regular guy":** CR, 162; **"happy":** int. Mounir Motassadeq; **jokes:** Miller & Stone, 263; **"dreamy":** McDermott, 54; **military:** CR, 162; **marine engineering:** McDermott, 53–; **$4,000:** Corbin, 136; **"explode":** *Sun Sentinel* (Fort Lauderdale), 9/23/01; **never spoke:** McDermott, 54; **recite/imagined:** ibid., 54, 87; **"What is":** ibid., 48; **Jarrah flew in/grew up:** Corbin, 137, *LAT*, 10/23/01, CR, 163, "The Fifth Estate: The Story of Ziad Jarrah," www.cbc.ca, 10/10/01; **civil servant/teacher:** Fisk, *The Great War*, 1052, Aysel Sengün statement to Bundeskriminalamt, 9/15/01, authors' collection; **great-uncle:** *Der Spiegel*, 9/17/08, conv. Gunther Latsch, Fouda &

Fielding, 85; **cousin:** *NYT,* 2/19/09; **Sunni/Christian schools/skipped prayers:** Aysel Sengün statement to Bundeskriminalamt, 9/15/01, authors' collection, Fisk, *The Great War,* 1051–; **alcohol/"Once":** Corbin, 137, eds. *Der Spiegel,* 190; **nightclubs:** *The Independent* (U.K.), 9/16/01, *LAT,* 10/23/01; **girls:** eds. *Der Spiegel,* 246; **Sengün:** Aysel Sengün statement to Bundeskriminalamt, 9/15/01, authors' collection, Corbin, 137, McDermott, 51, 80; **got religion:** McDermott, 51; CR, 163, *Newsday,* 8/15/07; **imam/ "terrorist":** Tenet identified the imam as Abdulrahman al-Makhadi (Testimony of George Tenet, JI, 6/18/02, & see National Drug Intelligence Center for the FBI, "265D-NY-280350, TWINBOM-PENTTBOM, Biographical Report," 11/26/01, authors' collection); **"criticized":** Aysel Sengün statement to Bundeskriminalamt, 9/15/01, authors' collection; **dentistry/switched:** CR, 163; **"Someone explained"/pregnant:** *LAT,* 1/27/03; **Shehhi moved/ emulating:** CR, 162–; **Atta/"leader":** transcript, int. Dittmar Machule; **talked angrily:** *MSNBC Investigates: The Making of the Death Pilots,* MSNBC, 4/7/02 & see *Chicago Tribune,* 9/11/04.

358 **"always"/"the war":** *Four Corners: A Mission to Die For,* 10/18/01, www.abc.net.au. The student was Ralph Bodenstein. One account of Bodenstein's recollections states that Atta was angered by Israel's treatment of Palestinians but that—as an Egyptian—he was "most vehement about matters in his own country." He often raised the Palestine issue at religious classes he gave to younger Muslims. In his youth, Atta may have been influenced on the Palestine issue by his father. Australian reporter Liz Jackson has recalled that after 9/11, when she approached Atta Sr. for an interview, he "said he'd only talk if we paid US $25,000 to the Palestinian intifada. Without that, if we continued filming, he'd break the camera" (one account: Miller & Stone, 251; raised: *Chicago Tribune,* 9/11/04, McDermott, 36; Atta Sr.: *Four Corners: A Mission to Die For,* 10/18/01, www.abc.net.au).

358 **Brotherhood abjures violence:** see "History of the Muslim Brotherhood," www.ikhan web.com; **exceptions:** Benjamin & Simon, 86; **recruiting grounds/engineering club:** *WP,* 9/22/01; **men from Allepo:** transcript, int. Dittmar Machule, McDermott, 29.

358–9 **Zammar/Darkazanli:** CR, 164, 167, McDermott, 72–.

Zammar has languished in a jail in Syria since his arrest the month after 9/11. A Syrian court convicted him of membership of the Muslim Brotherhood, which is banned in Syria. Because he was allegedly tortured in prison, Amnesty International has issued an appeal on his behalf. Darkazanli has not been accused of any crime in Germany. Spanish prosecutors sought his extradition, however, in 2004, citing alleged contacts with al Qaeda operatives there. Darkazanli was in Spain in summer 2001 at approximately the same time as Atta and Binalshibh (Zammar: "Unfair Trial & Sentencing of Muhammad Haydar Zammar," Appeal Case, 3rd Update, 3/22/07, www.amnestyusa.org, *Der Spiegel*, 11/21/05; Darkazanli: "Germany's Imam Mamoun Darkazanli," www.jamestown.org, 8/27/10, JI, Report, 183–).

359 **"coincidence":** *Chicago Tribune*, 11/16/02, Derek Flood, "Germany's Imam Mamoun Darkazanli," Vol. 1, No. 8, www.jamestown.org.

359 **boxes/books/"I will pay":** *WP*, 9/11/02; **Atta vanished/"Don't ask":** CR, 168, Fouda & Fielding, 123, transcript, int. Dittmar Machule, *LAT*, 9/1/02, but see Corbin, 139—which suggests he disappeared for more than a year. Tenet so speculated, even though KSM apparently denied to interrogators that Atta went to Afghanistan prior to late 1999 (Testimony of George Tenet, JI, 6/18/02, KSM SUBST).

359–63 **passport lost/new one:** Testimony of George Tenet, JI, 6/18/02, McDermott, 57; **speculation:** ibid., Testimony of George Tenet, MFR 04019351, 12/10/03; **"serve the interests":** ed. Lawrence, 60–; **"This was sensitive":** Kean & Hamilton, 284–; **bring attack forward:** KSM SUBST; **KSM concern:** McDermott, 117–; **"the atrocities":** KSM SUBST; **KSM claims:** "Verbatim Transcription of Combatant Status Review Tribunal hearing for ISN 10024," 3/10/07, www.defense.gov; **"entitled":** int. Yousef by Raghida Dergham, *Al Hayat*, 4/12/95; **"If you ask":** McDermott, 13; **"world Jewish conspiracy":** CR, 161; **"great-grandparents":** *LAT*, 10/17/04; **"How can you":** CR, 162; **"He enlightened":** McDermott, 80; **"With God's":** ed. Lawrence, 61; **"The problem":** McDermott, 82; **met/prayed, etc.:** ibid., 58–; **apartment:** "Hamburger Mietvertrag für Wohnraum," Marienstrasse 54, 10/31/98, authors' collection; **Dar al-Ansar:** McDermott, 63, CR, 164,

495n82. See Notes for Ch. 18, p. 501; **"the highest":** McDermott, 62; **"dissatisfied":** ibid., 51–, 275n15; **dying for faith:** ibid., 49; **"love death":** "Ladenese Epistle: Declaration of War," pts. I, II, III, www.washingtonpost.com.

363–4 **"The morning"/"the smell":** McDermott, 88, 280n43. Jarrah's notes, found with his Hamburg college papers, are in German police files. The 1996 bin Laden declaration—reported in Ch. 22, p. 253—not only includes the "death as you love life" reference but also multiple references to Paradise. Bin Laden was to use almost exactly the same phrase in a letter in Arabic posted on the Internet in October 2002 (notes: McDermott, 89, 280n43; OBL letter: ed. Lawrence, 172); **"Paradise":** McDermott, 85; **"Muslims are":** *WP*, 9/11/02, CR, 496n88. *Washington Post* reporter Peter Finn dated the Atta-Nickels exchange as having occurred in November 1999. The commission dates it merely to the year 1999 (*WP*, 9/11/02, CR, 496n88).

364 **traveled Afghanistan:** "Hijackers Timeline [redacted], FBI, 2/1/07, INTELWIRE, Report, JI, 134–, MFR 04019351, 12/10/03. Binalshibh, the sole survivor of the group from Germany, would tell interrogators that they had initially planned to fight in Chechnya. The decision to go instead to Afghanistan, he claimed, was the outcome of an encounter with a man he and two others of the Hamburg group met by chance on a train. This claim may or may not be true. According to Binalshibh, the man on the train—whom he identified as Khalid al-Masri—advised them to talk with a second man named Mohamed Slahi. Slahi, when they went to see him, allegedly said it was difficult to get to Chechnya and suggested they travel instead to Afghanistan via Pakistan. Khalid al-Masri, if he ever existed, has yet to be identified. (He is not the man of the same name who after 9/11 was seized in Macedonia by a U.S. "snatch team," reportedly tortured, and—when CIA officials concluded he had been wrongfully detained—released by being dumped at the roadside in Albania.) Slahi was arrested soon after 9/11 and eventually transferred to Guantánamo. A Senate inquiry found that he was subjected to serious ill treatment. Though Slahi admitted having met Binalshibh and his two comrades, he denied having suggested they go to Afghanistan. At the time of writing he remains in Guantánamo but has not been charged. A federal judge ruled in March 2010 that a prosecution of

Slahi was impossible because his file was "so tainted by coercion and mistreatment." In November 2010, a U.S. appeals court ordered the judge to review the case. Mohammed Zammar, meanwhile—who had also reportedly been tortured, not in U.S. custody but in a Syrian jail—told visiting German investigators that *he* "helped" Binalshibh and the others get to Afghanistan (encounter/Masri/advised: CR, 165, 496n90, German translation of interrogation of Binalshibh provided to prosecution in Motassadeq case, *Vereinigte Staaten Von Amerika gegen Zacarias Moussaoui*, 4/28/05, authors' collection; snatched/dumped Albania: *WP*, 12/4/05, *The Independent* [U.K.], 5/1907; Slahi: Report, "Inquiry into the Treatment of Detainees in U.S. Custody," U.S. Senate, Committee on Armed Services, 110th Cong. 2nd Sess., 11/20/08, http:/-/armed-services.senate.gov, 138–, *Miami Herald*, 11/5/10, *WP*, 3/24/10; Zammar: *Der Spiegel*, 11/21/05).

364 **bodyguard recalled:** The bodyguard was Nasser al-Bahri. Fahd al-Quso, a Yemeni interrogated after 9/11, said he, too, had seen Shehhi in Kandahar, when he became sick (Bahri: *Newsweek*, 9/3/07, Wright, 366 & see *Sunday Times* [London], 10/1/06; Quso: *New Yorker*, 7/10 & 17/06); **Another jihadi:** Bergen, *OBL I Know*, 262; **handwritten note:** FBI translation,12/21/01, "Misc. Requests for Documents, FBI-03013592, Packet 2," CF.

365 **videotape/"will":** The footage was described in a story by Yosri Fouda in the London *Sunday Times* on October 1, 2006. The same day, NBC News showed still photos from the videotape. According to the *Times* article, the videotape was "obtained through a previously tested channel." The article also said that sources from both al Qaeda and the United States had confirmed the authenticity of the tape, "on condition of anonymity." Date marks on the footage show that bin Laden was filmed on January 8 and the future hijackers on January 18, 2000. Atta, Jarrah, and Binalshibh apparently were in Afghanistan on both those days. The different date marks seem to indicate that bin Laden was not present when Atta and Jarrah recorded their martyrdom statements. NBC's story reported, however, that "U.S. government analysis . . . identifies hijackers Atta and Jarrah in the large crowd at bin Laden's feet" (*Sunday Times* [London] & NBC News, 10/1/06).

365–7 **KSM/Binalshibh described:** KSM SUBST, CR, 166–,

Fouda & Fielding, 123–, 126, Staff Statement 16, CO; **Shehhi left/ailment:** ibid., CR, 166, *New Yorker,* 7/10/06, "PENT-TBOM, Summary of Captioned Investigation," 11/5/01, authors' collection; **"middling":** KSM SUBST; **oath:** Staff Statement 16, CO, CR, 166–. Shehhi had apparently taken the oath before leaving (CR 166–); **OBL considered/select targets:** KSM SUBST; **Jarrah endured:** Fouda & Fielding, 128; **tricks of trade:** KSM SUBST; **airline schedules:** Staff Statement 16, CO **"learning"/"be normal":** KSM SUBST; **phone code:** *New Yorker,* 9/13/10; **"PlayStation":** *Daily Mail* (U.K.), 4/17/10; **"worked hard"/Hazmi deputy:** KSM SUBST; *kunyahs*: These *kunyahs,* and all the honorifics assigned to what became a nineteen-man hijack team, appear in *Masterminds of Terror,* by Yosri Fouda and Nick Fielding, 110, 121n15.

368–9 **"wonderful evening":** Clinton, 881; **Jordan/Zubaydah:** *NYT,* 1/15/01, Tenet, 125; **Ressam caught/plan:** Counterterrorism to All Field Stations, FBI 265A-SE-83340, etc., 12/29/1999, INTELWIRE, CR, 176–, Staff Statement 15, CO, Richard Clarke, 211, Bergen, *Holy War Inc.,* 140–, *NYT,* 12/15/01, Burke, 198–, 208–; **"aware":** Burke, 209, Report, JI, Appendix, 44, CR, 261; **Clinton rang:** Coll, *Ghost Wars,* 487; **Berger met:** Shenon, 234, 261; **wiretap orders:** Farmer, 39; **"Foreign":** CR, 179; **Berger/Clarke Christmas:** Richard Clarke, 213, MFR 04021455, 2/13/04; **thousands on duty/vigil:** Richard Clarke, Testimony of Louis Freeh, 4/13/04, CO; **O'Neill:** Miller & Stone, 222–.

369 **"I think"/"popped":** Richard Clarke, 214. U.S. intelligence worried not only about December 31 as the date of a possible attack, but also about January 3 and 6. The 3rd is considered a night of destiny in Islam, while January 6, 2000, coincided with the end of Ramadan. As discovered later, an attack was indeed planned for the 3rd—a bombing of the U.S. destroyer *Sullivans,* which was visiting the Yemeni port of Aden. The explosives-loaded boat, however, sank in the surf before the operation could be carried out. This botched effort preceded by nine months the successful attack on the USS *Cole,* also in Aden, which is covered in Ch. 25. Walid bin Attash, one of the Yemenis bin Laden initially selected for the 9/11 operation, reportedly played a role in planning both bombings (Jan. 3/6: FBI IG; *Sullivans*/Attash: Staff Statement 2, CO).

370   **"They said":** Benjamin & Simon, 313.

370   **"All Islamic":** Staff Report, "Monograph on the Four Flights and Civil Aviation Security," 8/26/04, CF; **1998 exercise:** Kean & Hamilton, 109, CR, 345; **"bin Laden and his":** CR, 128; **"unconventional":** *Sunday Times* (London), 6/9/02; **"America":** "New World Coming: American Security in the 21st Century," Commission on National Security, 9/15/99, www.fas.org. The commission was chaired by former U.S. senators Gary Hart and Warren Rudman; **Library of Congress report:** Rex Hudson, "The Sociology & Psychology of Terrorism: Who Becomes a Terrorist and Why?," Federal Research Division, Library of Congress, Washington, D.C., 9/99, 7, *NYT,* 5/18/02.

371   **America West/"walked into"/door locked/alerted/hand-cuffs/interrogation:** Judgment, *Muhammad Al-Qudhai'een et al. v. America West Airlines et al.,* Case No. C-2-00-1380, US District Court for the Southern District of Ohio, Eastern Division, 4/30/03 Manager, Chicago Civil Aviation Security Office to Director, undated FAA Memo, "Other Flights 9/11, FAA Memo re America West 90," B7, T7, CF, Report, JI, 6; **"casing":** MFR 04017521, 1/7/04, MFR 04019354, 7/22/03; **"tied":** MFR 04019354, 7/22/03; **poster:** Statement of Eleanor Hill, 9/24/02 (as supplemented 10/17/02), JI; **"explosive":** ibid.

371–2   **arrested with Zubaydah:** CR, 521n60. The man who tried the cockpit door was Muhammad al-Qudhai'een and his companion Hamdan al-Shalawi. Both insisted that Qudhai'een had merely wished to find the airplane lavatory. They subsequently sued America West, alleging racial stereotyping, but the suit was dismissed. Qudhai'een, interviewed in Saudi Arabia by 9/11 Commission staff, said he thought the perpetrators of 9/11 were "ignorant" people. In his interview, Shalawi said he recalled having encountered future pilot hijacker Hani Hanjour before the incident on the airplane. He acknowledged having done "charity work" in Afghanistan back in 1987, but denied ever having been there since. Three officers of the Mabahith, Saudi Arabia's internal security service, were present during the Commission's interviews of both Shalawi and Qudhai'een. The associate with a bin Laden poster on his wall was Zacaria Soubra, then a student at Embry-Riddle Aeronautical University in Prescott, Arizona (Qudhai'een, Shalawi sued: Judgment, *Muhammad Al-*

Qudhai'een et al. v. America West Airlines et al., No. C-2–00–1380, US District Court for the Southern District of Ohio, 4/30/03; "ignorant"/"charity work"/Mabahith: MFR int. Muhammad al-Qudhai'een, 10/26/03 & MFR int. Hamdan bin al-Shalawi, 10/23/03, "Staff Delegation International Trip," T1A, CF; Soubra: Statement of Eleanor Hill, 9/24/02 [as supplemented 10/17/02], JI, FBI IG).

372   **exploratory trips:** Fouda & Fielding, 158, Bergen, *OBL I Know*, 302; **1999 reports:** Report, JI, 334, Statements of Eleanor Hill, 9/18/02, 9/24/02 (as supplemented 10/17/02), JI, FBI IG; **"The purpose"/found no indication/INS:** ibid., Statement of Eleanor Hill, 9/24/02, (as supplemented 10/17/02), JI; **"very frustrating";** MFR 04018415, 12/16/03, CF.

CHAPTER 25

373–4   **training camp/combat/magazines/games/movies:** CR, 157, 493n50, 54; **phone directories/English/two Yemenis:** KSM SUBST, CR, 157–.

374   **Mihdhar left early:** Detainees' accounts varied as to whether Mihdhar completed the physical training course. KSM said Mihdhar was not present for the familiarization-with-U.S.-life sessions that Hazmi attended—he had supposedly had similar instruction earlier (CR, 493n50 & 53); **on choosing optimal:** ibid., 158, 493n54; **Attash dry run/no visas/he learned:** ibid., 158–, KSM SUBST; **box cutter/knife:** CR, 159, "Charge Sheet, Khalid Sheikh Mohammed," 4/15/08, www.findlaw.com; **toothpaste/art supplies:** CR, 493n59; **ploy worked:** ibid., 159.

375   **condominium in K.L.:** ibid. It remains unclear who exactly may have been with the trio at the condominium, which belonged to a former Malaysian army captain named Yazid Sufaat. Their comrade from the training period, Abu Bara al Tai'zi (see notes for Ch. 24), was there. So, too, reportedly, was Riduan Isamuddin, an Indonesian terrorist leader known as "Hambali." In his insightful book *The Looming Tower*, Lawrence Wright wrote that a dozen terrorist associates came and went from the condominium. There have also been unconfirmed reports that KSM and Ramzi Binalshibh joined the group. The claim that KSM was present is unsupported by any available evidence. A senior German police official has referred to evidence, apparently credit card receipts,

indicating that Binalshibh was there (Tai'zi/Sufaat: CR, 156–; Isamuddin: *New Straits Times* [Malaysia] 2/10/02, *Time Asia*, 4/1/02 CR, 158; dozen: Wright, 311; KSM: e.g. *Newsweek*, 7/9/03; Binalshibh: *LAT*, 9/1/02, *NYT*, 8/24/020).

375 **boarded UA flight/"tourists":** Staff Report, 9/11 and Terrorist Travel," CO, 13–, Timeline, "Hijackers Primary Docs, AA77, 2 of 2," & FBI 302 of Special Agent [redacted], 9/12/01, "Hijackers Primary Docs, AA77, 1 of 2," B50, T5, CF. After 9/11 it would emerge that U.S. intelligence had been aware, even before it began, that suspected terrorists were to meet in Kuala Lumpur. The men were surveilled while they were there and an attempt was made to follow them afterward, when they left for Thailand. Most stunning of all, the CIA knew even before Mihdhar reached Kuala Lumpur that he had a current visa to enter the United States. Within months, moreover, it learned the equally alarming fact that Hazmi had entered the United States. Agency spokesmen have claimed that, even so, the CIA took no action until just before 9/11. Why not? The issue is of enormous significance and will be covered in Ch. 31 (e.g., Staff Statement 2, CO, CR, 353–, FBI IG).

375 **no "facilitator":** KSM SUBST; **Commission not believe:** CR, 215; **no trace:** CR, 514n8, Staff Statement 16, CO, MFR 040204580, 6/23–24/04, CF.

375 **chauffeur/"two Saudis"/"an apartment"/tour:** int. of Qualid Benomrane, FBI 302, 265A-LA-228901, 4/6/02, INTELWIRE. The statements of the driver, a Tunisian named Qualid Benomrane, contain unresolved issues. He did not, for example, have an official taxi driver's license until several months after Hazmi and Mihdhar's arrival. Benomrane said it was Fahad al-Thumairy, an imam at the King Fahd mosque, who asked him to drive the two Saudis around—at the request, in turn, of someone at the Saudi consulate. At one point, however, he said the "two Saudis" were sons of a sick father seeking treatment in Los Angeles—which would not fit Hamzi and Mihdhar. Thumairy, for his part, denied knowing Benomrane but said he did know a "son and sick father." Commission staff who interviewed Thumairy in Saudi Arabia, however, judged him "deceptive."

9/11 Commission senior counsel Dieter Snell asserted in a 2004 memo that Benomrane's information appeared to be of "uniquely significant value" to understanding the facts behind the 9/11 attacks. Benomrane had by then been deported from the United States, however, and the Commission never did interview him. Journalist Judith Miller reported in 2007 that Los Angeles Police Department detectives were convinced that "Benomrane and al-Thumairy were militants in the al Qaeda support network and that Benomrane's passengers were, in fact, the two hijackers" (license: e.g. MFR 04018787, 4/19/04, MFR 04018782, 4/21/04; Thumairy: CR, 515n14, Line of Inquiry: Qualid Moncef Benomrane, B36, T1A, CF; sons of sick father: int. Qualid Benomrane, FBI 302, 265A-LA-228901, 4/6/02; Thumairy denied: MFR 04019362, 2/23/04; "deceptive": Dieter Snell et al. to Philip Zelikow, 2/25/04, Summary of Interview Conducted in Saudi Arabia, ARC Identifier no. 2610841, CF; "uniquely": Dieter Snell to Pat O'Brien, 1/16/04, "Benomrane Folder," B37, T1A, CF; deported/never interviewed: CR, 515n14; LAPD convinced: Judith Miller, "On the Front Line in the War on Terrorism," Summer 07, www.city-journal.org).

375–8 **photographs:** CR, 515n14; **"barely"/"instructed":** KSM SUBST; **address in CA:** CR, 150, 514n4, *Guardian* (U.K.), 11/12/06, *Telegraph* (U.K.), 11/7/06; **CIA concluded:** CR, 514n4; **"possibly" Long Beach:** CR, 157, 514n7; **language schools LA:** CR, 216; **San Diego directories:** KSM SUBST; **"idea":** ibid.; **Bayoumi 42:** DHS Document Request 3, "Doc Requests, Entire Contents," T5, B9, CF; **rental application:** *San Diego Union-Tribune*, 10/25/01; **Bayoumi employee/ mosque, etc.:** ibid., FBI IG; **"ghost":** CR, 515n18, **Don/trip to LA/consulate/restaurant:** MFR of int. Omar al Bayoumi, 10/16–17/003, "Staff Delegation International Trip, Tab 1," T1A, MFR 04017552, 9/29/03, & MFR 04019254, 4/20/04, CF, FBI 302 of int. Caysan bin Don, 10/8/01, INTELWIRE, CR, 217–, 515n15, 17. Bin Don has also used the name Isamu Dyson. His birth name was Clayton Morgan (CR, 435); **newspaper:** McDermott, 189; **"description"/sought out/apartment:** MFR of int. Bayoumi, MFR 04016481, 1/12/04, National Drug Enforcement Center for the FBI, "265D-NY-280350, TWINBOM-PENTTBOM, Biographical Report,"11/26/01, authors' collection; **pure chance:** MFR 04019254, 4/20/04, MFR 04016231, 11/18/03, CF; **"to pick up":** Report, JI, 173; **contacts imam:** Dieter Snell, et al., to Philip Zelikow, "Summary of Interviews in Saudi Arabia," 2/25/04, MFR, CF; **cell phone:** MFR,

040175541A, 11/17/03, CF, CR, 516n26; **jihad material/salary:** Report, JI, 174; **distinguishing mark:** CR, 516n19; **"We do not":** CR 218; **"very suspicious":** int. Eleanor Hill.

378   **"We firmly":** *Newsweek*, 8/3/03. As noted earlier in this chapter, KSM has denied that there were helpers in place in the U.S. He also specifically denied that he had ever heard of Bayoumi (CR, 516n19, CBS News, 8/3/03); **Aulaqi 29/imam:** FBI Memo, "Ansar Nasser Aulaqi, IT-UBL," 9/26/01, INTELWIRE; **four calls:** MFR 04017541A, 11/17/03 & MFR 04017531, 11/17/03, CF, "Hijackers Timeline [redacted]," 11/14/03, INTELWIRE, CR, 221, 517n33; **attended mosque:** CR, 517n33, MFR 04017542, 11/18/03, CF; **"closed-door":** Report, JI, 178, *NYT,* 5/8/10, Jamie Reno, "Public Enemy #1,"www.sandiegomagazine.com; **Hazmi respected/spoke:** MFR of [name redacted], 4/23/04, CF—since reported to have been Abdussattar Shaikh; **"very calm":** FBI Memo, "Ansar Nasser Aulaqi, IT-UBL," 9/26/01, INTELWIRE; **"spiritual advisor":** Report, JI, 27.

378   **Aulaqi relocated/no contact:** The record seems contradictory on this. The Commission Report quoted Aulaqi as denying having had contact in Virginia with Hazmi or his companion at that point, future fellow hijacker Hani Hanjour. A May 2004 Commission memo, however, states that Aulaqi "admits contact with the hijackers" at both the Virginia and San Diego mosques. ("List of Mosques," MFR 04019202, 5/6/04, CR, 229–, MFR 04019202, 6/6/04).

379   **had investigated/"procurement":** CR, 517n33; **"potentially":** CR, 221; **prison:** *WP,* 2/27/08; **terrorist attacks:** (Fort Hood shooting/bomb on Detroit-bound plane/Times Square car bomb) *Christian Science Monitor,* 5/19/10, Fox News, 10/20/10, CNN, 1/7/10, *Guardian* (U.K.), 10/31/10, MSNBC, 11/1/10; **Harman:** *Christian Science Monitor,* 5/19/10;

379   **KSM suggested:** KSM SUBST; **passes Zoo/SeaWorld:** *LAT,* 9/1/02; **bank accounts/car/ID:** FBI IG, Staff Report, Monograph on Terrorist Financing," CO, MFR.

379–81 **driver's licenses/phone directory:** CR, 539n85, Lance, *Triple Cross,* 349. The two terrorists moved in May 2000 to the home of a man named Abdussattar Shaikh, and—though Mihdhar left that summer—Hazmi stayed until December. Shaikh, the subject of controversy not least because he was an

FBI informant, will be covered in the notes for Ch. 33 (CR, 220, 516n28, MFR of [name redacted], 4/23/04, CF, www.scribd.com, Nawaf al-Hazmi timeline, "Hijacker Primary Documents," B50, T5, CF, Graham with Nussbaum, Shaikh refs., Shenon, 53–); **sociable/"brooding":** Corbin, 174–, *Newsweek*, 6/10/02; **soccer/"psychotic":** CR 220, MFR 04017531, 11/17/03, CF; **"You'll know":** *Newsweek*, 6/10/02; **phone calls/computer/Yahoo:** "Hijackers Timeline [redacted]," 11/14/03, INTELWIRE, Bamford, *Shadow Factory*, 25; **KSM told:** KSM SUBST; **Hazmi enrolled/Mihdhar not start:** ibid., Staff Statement 16, CO, CR, 221, 517n30, 36, FBI 302 of int. Omer Bakarbashat, 9/17/01, INTELWIRE; **flight school/few lessons:** CR, 221–, 517n36; **praying:** Corbin, 174; **"They just"/"Dumb":** *Newsweek*, 6/10/02; **flying not for them:** *WP*, 9/30/01.

381   **dropped out/flew back:** KSM SUBST, CR, 220. Though Mihdhar supposedly went home to rejoin his family, he also went on to travel to Malaysia, Afghanistan, and Saudi Arabia. FBI director Mueller suggested to Congress's Joint Inquiry that his role may have included helping to organize the so-called muscle hijackers. (CR, 222, Statement of Robert Mueller, JI, 9/26/02).

381   **overruled/progressive:** KSM SUBST.

381   **shed clothing/beards:** CR, 167, FBI report, "The 11 September Hijacker Cell Model," 2/03, INTELWIRE.

381   **31 emails/"We are"/"lost"/new passports:** Testimony of George Tenet, 6/18/02, JI, CR, 168, 497n108, Transcript of Jury Trial, *U.S. v. Zacarias Moussaoui*, 3/7/06. Atta had entered a lottery for a U.S. visa as early as October the previous year, perhaps a further indication that he knew something of the bin Laden plan before heading to Afghanistan in November. He applied for and got a visa in the regular way, however, only in May 2000 (MFR 04019351, 12/10–11/03, Staff Report, "9/11 and Terrorist Travel," CO, 15–).

382   **Binalshibh:** Staff Report, 9/11 and Terrorist Travel, CO, 17–, CR, 225, 519n52. Binalshibh applied for a visa three times in the year 2000, each time unsuccessfully; **Shehhi/Atta to NY:** Staff Report, 9/11 and Terrorist Travel, CO, 15; **Bronx/Brooklyn:** Staff Statement 16, CO, Report, JI, 136; **calling card:** "Hijackers Timeline [redacted]," 11/14/03, INTELWIRE, Bamford, *Shadow Factory*, 53; **Jarrah arrives:** Staff Report, 9/11 and Terrorist Travel, CO, 17; **flight**

school: MFR 04019350, 3/18/04, CF, *Herald-Tribune* (Sarasota), 9/10/06; **"He was":** Corbin, 160, & see MFR 04018408, 4/12/04, CF; **"occasional":** Fouda & Fielding, 131; **Private Pilot License/aviation mechanics:** CR, 224, biographical note "Ziad Jarrah," FBI 03212, JICI 4/19/02, www.scribd.com, "Airman Records for Jarrah," B45, T5, CF; **"He wanted":** Corbin, 161; **Oklahoma school/FBI regional office:** Statement of Eleanor Hill re "The FBI's Handling of the Phoenix Electronic Communication and Investigation of Zacarias Moussaoui Prior to Sept. 11, 2001," 9/24/02 (as updated 10/17/02), JI.

384   **toured school:** Title: PENTTBOM, "Summary of Captioned Investigation as of 11/4/01," 11/5/01, authors' collection, CR, 224. The two hijackers' visit was to Airman Flight School, where bin Laden pilot Ihab Ali had trained several years earlier. Zacarias Moussaoui, who was part of KSM's wider operation and would be arrested shortly before 9/11, would also train at Airman, in early 2001 (Ali: CR, 224, "Paving the Road to 9/11," www.intelwire.com; Moussaoui: "Paving the Road to 9/11," www.intelwire.com, CR, 246, 273–).

384   **Huffman:** CR, 224. Daniel Hopsicker, an author who has concentrated on the hijackers' Venice stay, has written extensively about Venice Airport and those who operated flight schools there in 2000. In a 2009 article, he reported having discovered "covert CIA and military operations dating back to at least 1959" involving the airport. Hopsicker has focused on information indicating that the airport has a history of narcotics trafficking. He refers, too, to the seizure in July 2000—the month Atta and Shehhi began flight training—of a Learjet co-owned by Wallace Hilliard, the financier behind Huffman Aviation, with a large shipment of heroin on board. Hilliard maintained that he was the "innocent owner" of the plane. Huffman's Rudi Dekkers, for his part, had what the *St. Petersburg Times* termed "a checkered history" of bankruptcies, business problems, and visa issues (he is a Dutch national). According to the *Times*, he was cited by the FAA in 1999 for several violations, and his pilot's license was suspended. In interviews with a law enforcement official and an aviation executive, the authors got the impression that Venice Airport has indeed seen much illegal activity over the years. A Commission staff memo suggests that Atta and

Shehhi were accepted as students of Huffman without strict adherence to INS regulations—sloppy procedure that had the effect of legitimizing their continued stay in the United States. It may conceivably be of significance that Yeslam bin Laden, one of Osama's half-brothers, had paid for an acquaintance's flight instruction at the school—a bizarre fact that may be no more than a coincidence (Hopsicker: Daniel Hopsicker, *Welcome to Terrorland*, Eugene, OR: MadCow, 2004/2007; CIA: "Big Safari, the Kennedy Assassination, & the War for Control of the Venice Airport," 9/9/09, "The Deep History of the Venice Municipal Airport," 9/21 & 9/24/09, "Venice Was a Quiet Mena, Arkansas," 4/16/10, www.madcowprod.com, Hopsicker, 128–; Hilliard: *Orlando Sentinel*, 8/2/00; Aircraft Bill of Sale, N351WB, U.S. Dept. of Transportation (FAA), World Jet, Inc., to Plane I Leasing—Wallace J. Hilliard, President, filed 11/15/99, Hearing on Motion of Forfeiture Proceedings, *U.S. v. Edgar Javier Valles-Diaz, et al.*, U.S. District Court for the Middle District of FL, 11/3/00; Dekkers: *St. Petersburg Times*, 7/25/04; Commission/legitimizing: Kephart-Robert to Ginsberg, 2/26/04, "Hijacker Pilot Training," B21, T7, CF; interviews: ints. Coy Jacobs & FBI Joint Terrorism Task Force agent; Yeslam: *New Yorker*, 11/12/01).

384–6 **No reliable source:** McDermott, 195; **"had an attitude"/"likeable":** transcript int. Rudi Dekkers, *Four Corners: A Mission to Die For*, 10/18/01, www.abc.net.au; **"When you"/immaculate/"Generally":** int. Mark Mikarts; **no better/another school/failed/argued:** FBI 302 of int. Ivan Chirivella, 9/16/01, INTELWIRE, Corbin, 10–, "Hijackers Timeline [redacted]," 11/14/03, INTELWIRE, CR, 224, *WSJ*, 10/16/01; **"a gesture"/Saudi/cushion:** transcript of int. Ann Greaves, *Four Corners: A Mission to Die For*, 10/18/01, www.abc.net.au; **"I don't want":** "Mohammed Atta's Last Will & Testament, *Frontline*: "Inside the Terror Network," www.pbs.org, *NYT*, 10/4/01; **"We had female":** int. Mark Mikarts; **"very rude":** FBI 302 of Ivan Chirivella, 9/16/01, INTELWIRE; **Outlook bar:** int. Lizsa Lehman. Allegations that several members of the terrorist team—Atta included—indulged in heavy drinking at bars in Florida in the days prior to the attack are covered in Ch. 28, on page 450. Reports of Atta's heavy drinking are probably apocryphal. Lizsa Lehman's firsthand recollection of Atta and Shehhi drinking beer in moderation at the Outlook, however, seems credible.

387 **Jarrah License:** MFR 04021445, 1/13 & 1/25/04, CF, Staff Statement 16, CO; **fall trip/Paris/photographed:** Aysel Sengün statement to Bundeskriminalamt, 9/15/01, authors' collection, Hijackers Timeline [redacted], 11/14/03, INTEL-WIRE, Staff Report, 9/11 and Terrorist Travel, CO, 21–, [Name Redacted] to [Name Redacted], INS, 9/19/01, re Saeed A.A. Al Ghamdi, & attachments, "Inspector Interviews, UA 93, Notes & Memos," B49, T5, CF; **"I love you":** McDermott, 198; **Mitsubishi:** Jarrah timeline, "03009470, Packet 6, Ziad Jarrah chronology," www.scribd.com; **Bahamas:** Report of Investigation, U.S. Customs Service, Case no. TA09FR01TA003, & Letter re plane piloted by Jarrah, N833OU, "Hijacker Primary Docs, UA 93," B51, T5, CF; **Atta/Shehhi licenses:** MFR 04021445, 1/13 & 1/25/04, CF, Staff Statement 16, CO; **Christmas trip:** Aysel Sengün statement to Bundeskriminalamt, 9/15/01, authors' collection, Hijackers Timeline [redacted], 11/14/03, INTEL-WIRE, Staff Report, 9/11 and Terrorist Travel, CO, 21–; **abandoned plane:** MFR 04021445, 1/13 & 1/25/04, CF, Testimony of Rudi Dekkers, Subcommittee on Immigration & Claims, Committee on the Judiciary, U.S. House of Reps., 107th Cong., 2nd Sess., 3/19/02; **videos:** Indictment, *U.S. v. Zacarias Moussaoui*, 12/01; **727 simulator/"They just":** *Daily Record* (Glasgow, Scotland), 9/15/01, *NYT*, 9/14/01, Hijackers Timeline [redacted], 11/14/03, INTELWIRE.

387 **Some have argued:** Skeptics have questioned whether Hani Hanjour had the piloting skill to fly American 77 into the Pentagon at almost ground level. While some flying instructors commented on his inadequacies, however, others recalled having found him competent. One, who flew with Hanjour in August 2001, went so far as to describe him as a "good" pilot. (Skeptics: e.g., Griffin, *New Pearl Harbor*, 78–; inadequacies/competent: e.g., CBS News, 5/10/02, *Newsday*, 9/23/01; "good": MFR 0401840, 4/9/04—citing Eddie G. Shalev. Contrary to an assertion by skeptic Griffin, who questioned the existence of instructor Shalev, 9/11 Commission files contain the record of an interview of him by a commission staffer and an accompanying FBI agent. Shalev, moreover, is listed in various public records. Griffin, *New Pearl Harbor*, 286n99, & see, e.g., www.intelius.com.)

388 **767 simulator:** ibid., Statement of Robert Mueller, JI,

9/26/02, Transcript of Jury Trial, *U.S. v. Zacarias Moussaoui*, Vol. II-A, 3/7/06. Jarrah and Hani Hanjour, the other 9/11 hijack pilots, also trained on simulators (CR, 226–, Testimony of James Fitzgerald, *U.S. v. Zacarias Moussaoui*, 3/7/06).

388 **OBL impatient 2000:** CR, 251. The authors here cite the date used in the Commission Report, which in turn refers to KSM interrogations of 2003 and 2004. The longer account of KSM's statements, the one generally used in this book, states that bin Laden tried in spring 2000 to bring the attacks forward—surely unlikely, as he well knew the hijack pilots had at that time barely embarked on their training (CR 250, 532n177, KSM SUBST).

388–9 **KSM resisted/new candidate:** KSM SUBST, MFR 04019351, 12/10–11/03, CF; **well-to-do:** *BG*, 3/3/02, *WP*, 9/10/02; **back and forth:** Statement of Robert Mueller, JI, 9/26/02, Staff Report, 9/11 and Terrorist Travel, 12, *WP*, 9/10/02; **Hanjour license:** MFR 04021445, 1/13 & 1/25/04, CF, copies of license documents, "Airman Records—Hanjour," B45, T5, CF; **pretending:** *WP*, 9/10/02, *BG*, 3/3/02; **"frail":** FBI 302 of [name redacted], 9/18/01, "FBI 302s of Interest," B17, T7, CF; **"quiet":** MFR 04017517, 1/7/04, CF; **"mouse":** McDermott, 204; **drink/pray:** MFR 04017518, 1/5/04, CF; **in tears:** CR, 520n55; **Afghanistan at 17:** Report, JI, 135, Staff Statement 16, CO; **Atef sent KSM/KSM dispatched/thought:** KSM SUBST; **Hanjour to U.S./Hazmi/flight school:** Staff Report, 9/11 and Terrorist Travel, CO, 19–, Statement of Robert Mueller, JI, 9/26/02, CR, 226; **school owner/"No":** *WP*, 10/21/01, 9/10/02, *Newsday*, 9/23/01; **"content"/"warrior":** *The Times* (London), 9/20/01; " *'Orwah":* Fouda & Fielding, 111.

390–1 **computer/"I went":** transcript of int. Ann Greaves, *Four Corners: A Mission to Die For*, 10/18/01, www.abc.net.au, ints. Mark Mikart; *Cole:* Katz, 269–, Miller & Stone, 226–, Wright, 319–, Graham with Nussbaum, 59–, Fox News, 1/13/09; **OBL deny/praise:** ABC News, 3/1/00; **A destroyer:** *Time*, 9/24/01, Unger, *House of Bush, House of Saud*, 229, Wright, 333; **"With small":** *Newsweek*, 9/24/01.

391–3 **"To those":** Clinton address, 10/18/00, http://usinfo.org; **"Let's hope":** *NYT*, 10/13/01; **"What's it gonna":** Richard Clarke, 224; **"major":** State of the Union address in *WP*, 1/27/00; **"not satisfactory":** CR, 187, Report, JI, 301. National Security Adviser Berger dated this memo as

February 2000. Without giving a clear source, the 9/11 Commission dated it as early March (Report, JI, 301, CR 187, 505n99); **Predator:** Staff Statement 7, CO, CR, 506n118, 513n238; **negotiations:** *CounterPunch*, 1/16/08, 9/9/09, 11/1/04, Reuters, 6/4/04; **U.N. resolution:** Resolution 1333, 12/19/00, http://avalon.law.yale.edu; **Tenet warned:** Tenet, 128.

393 **Pakistani told FBI:** Statement of Eleanor Hill, 9/18/02, JI, NBC News, 7/26/04, *Sunday Times* (London), 2/13/05. The Pakistani was Niaz Kahn, a former waiter from Oldham, near Manchester in the U.K., who apparently became involved in terrorism not because of his ideals but because he needed money. Two men he met in the U.K., he said, encouraged him to go to a camp in Pakistan, where he was given instruction in "conventional" hijackings, not suicide operations. He was eventually flown by a roundabout route to New York, but evaded the contact waiting for him and went to the FBI. Kahn's story was first reported publicly in late 2004 (NBC News, 7/26/04, *Vanity Fair*, 11/04, transcript, int. Niaz Khan, 5/18/04, in collection of Jean-Charles Brisard).

393 **Italian police/"studying":** int. Bruno Megale, Bergen, *OBL I Know*, 281, Miller & Stone, 274–. A U.S. Justice Department official was quoted after 9/11 as saying that a "small cadre of U.S. intelligence experts might have been privy to the Italian surveillance material." On the other hand, other press reporting suggests that the surveillance of the two Yemenis was "not translated by Italian police" until May 2002 (*LAT*, 5/29/02, *Chicago Tribune*, 10/8/02).

394 **Olympics:** *Sydney Morning Herald*, 9/20/01. In October, the Defense Department held a tabletop exercise simulating the crash of an airliner into the courtyard of the Pentagon. Critics have cited this as an indication that the Pentagon received early intelligence of terrorist plans to target the building with an airplane. On the evidence, however, the exercise may simply have been designed to ensure readiness for any possible sort of plane crash into the Pentagon—which is close to Reagan National Airport ("Contingency Planning Pentagon MASCAL Exercise," 11/3/00, www.dcmilitary.com, UPI, 4/22/04).

394 **FBI/FAA downplayed:** In April 2000, an FAA advisory issued to airlines and airports had stated that U.S. airliners could be targeted but that hijacking was "more probable outside the

United States." The advisory would not have been replaced as
of September 11, 2001 (Staff Report, "The Four Flights and
Civil Aviation Security," 8/26/04, CF, 59); **"do not suggest":**
Statement of Eleanor Hill, 9/18/02, JI, Report, JI, 104–;
"imprudent": Report, JI, 334.

394–5 **"Americans would":** CR, 198; **Clinton authorized:** Tenet,
135; **Cheney/Powell/Rice:** Testimony of Sandy Berger,
3/24/04, CO, *Time*, 8/12/02, DeYoung, 344; **"As I briefed":**
Richard Clarke, 229; **"sitting"/"cognizant":** Rice int.,
www.whitehouse.gov, 3/24/04, Testimony, 4/8/04, CO; **did
not know:** Richard Clarke, 31; **"not an amateur":** ibid., 328;
Commission/"on American": Phase III Report, *Road Map
for National Security: Imperative for Change*, U.S. Commission
on National Security, 2/15/01, viii, 6, Tenet, 16, *Columbia
Journalism Review*, Nov/Dec 2001; **pressed to see:** Hurley to
Gorelick, 4/5/04, "Commissioner Prep for Rice," B7, T3, CF;
"did not remember": CR, 199, Ben-Veniste, 302–; **OBL
biggest/"listened":** Clinton, 935–.

CHAPTER 26

396–7 **"We are not":** George W. Bush, Inaugural Address, 1/20/01,
www.bartleby.com, *Time*, 1/20/01; **"empty rhetoric":** *WP*,
1/20/02; **"They ridiculed":** int. of Clinton for Fox News,
9/24/06; **"What we did":** "Report: Rice Challenges Clinton
on Osama," http://wcbstv.com, 9/26/06; **"I'm tired":** CR,
202 & see Testimony of Condoleezza Rice, 4/8/04, CO, CR,
510n185, int. of Stephen Hadley, *60 Minutes*, CBS, 3/21/04;
"just solve": "Transcript: Clarke Praised Bush Team in 02,"
Fox News, 3/24/04.

397 **nothing effective done:** As Rice recalled it, it was in May
that the President told her he was tired of swatting at flies.
Clarke said Bush's directive came to him in March. Bush did
write to President Musharraf in February 2001, emphasizing
that bin Laden was a threat to the United States that "must be
addressed." Though he urged Musharraf to use his influence
with the Taliban over bin Laden, the approach proved
unproductive. So were further Bush administration contacts
with the Pakistanis later in the year (Rice/Clarke: CR,
510n185; Musharraf: CR, 207).

397 **memo/"not some narrow"/"multiple":** Clarke to Rice &
attachments, 1/25/01, www2.gwu.edu. The memorandum
and the December 2000 "Strategy" document have been

released, with some redactions. The September 1998
"Political-Military Plan DELENDA" [a reference to the vow
to destroy Carthage, in the days of ancient Rome] has not
been released (Clarke to Rice, 1/25/01, & Tab A, released to
National Security Archive, www2.gwu.edu, CR, 120, Richard
Clarke, 197–).

397–400 *Cole* **linked al Qaeda:** FBI IG; **"No al Qaeda plan":** *WP,*
3/22/04; **no recommendations:** Testimony of Condoleezza
Rice, 4/8/04, CO; **"Having served":** int. Eleanor
Hill; **no longer member/instead report:** CR, 200, 509n169,
Clarke, 230; **no retaliation for *Cole*:** CR, 201–; **"tit-for-tat":**
Testimony of Condoleezza Rice, 4/8/04, CO & see Ben-
Veniste, 304–; **"ancient history":** MFR 04018415, 12/16/03,
CF; **deputies not meet/April:** CR, 203, Richard Clarke, 231;
Wolfowitz/tetchy: Richard Clarke, 231; **"We are going":**
Benjamin & Simon, 336.

400 **"to be paying":** "Big Media Networks Ignore Gorelick Role,
Highlight Bremer Rebuke of Bush Team," 4/30/04, citing
Bremer int. for CBS News, 2/26/01, www.freerepublic
.com, *LAT,* 4/30/04. Three years later, by which time he had
become U.S. administrator in occupied Iraq, Bremer would
attempt to backtrack and say his 2001 comment had been
"unfair" to Bush, that his speech had reflected frustration that
none of the National Commission's recommendations had
been implemented by either the Clinton or the new Bush
administration. (AP, 5/2/04); **"The highest":** DCI's
Worldwide Threat Briefing, 2/7/01, www.cia.gov; *Le Monde*
scoop: "11 Septembre 2001: Les Français en savaient long,"
Le Monde, 4/16/07.

400 **passed on to CIA:** The DGSE document, one of more than
three hundred pages leaked, is dated January 5, 2001, and
numbered 00007/CT. Its heading reads: "Note de Synthèse—
Projet de Détournement d'Avion par des Islamistes
Radicaux," and it draws on information passed on by the intelligence service of Uzbekistan. The overall dossier leaked is
entitled "Oussama bin Laden" and dated 9/13/01. The
authors have seen the entire dossier. The celebrated French
fortnightly, *Le Canard Enchaîné,* reporting on the material as
early as October 2001, stated that "most" of the reports on bin
Laden had been shared with the CIA and the FBI. *Le Monde,*
in its major story of April 19, 2007, reported as a fact that the
January 5 report was passed to the CIA. *Le Monde* quoted

former senior DGSE official Pierre-Antoine Lorenzi as saying that such information would have been passed to the Agency as a matter of routine. Alain Chouet, former head of the Security Intelligence department, took the same view when interviewed by the authors (attachment, James to Zelikow, 4/14/04, "Motley Submission," B10, T2, CF).

401　**FAA 50 summaries/no action:** Staff Report, "The Four Flights and Civil Aviation Security," CO, Farmer, 96–, *New York Observer,* 6/20/04; **met Tenet almost daily:** Tenet, 137; **40 PDBs:** CR, 254.

401　**Atta January trip:** Staff Statement 16, CO. Atta flew to and back from Europe via Madrid, leaving on January 4 and returning on January 10. There is evidence suggesting he was in Berlin during that period, and the Commission Report states that his purpose in going was to see Binalshibh in Germany. It has been suggested that Madrid was more than a stopover en route to Germany, that at one point in the round-trip from the States Atta paused to meet a contact in Spain. An al Qaeda cell was active in Spain at the time. An allegation that Atta made another trip to Europe in April, during which he met with an Iraqi official in Prague, will be covered in Ch. 34 and related notes (trip: Staff Report, 9/11 & Terrorist Travel, CO, 23–, "Hijackers Timeline [redacted], 11/14/03, INTELWIRE; Binalshibh: CR, 227, 243 Staff Statement 16, CO; contact/cell: *Der Spiegel,* 10/27/03, CR, 530n145; Prague: CR,228).

401　**Shehhi Morocco:** Staff Report, 9/11 and Terrorist Travel, CO, 26–, 215n95; **Jarrah reentered/Aysel to U.S./ Key West/tourist:** Aysel Sengün statement to Bundeskriminalamt, 9/15/01, authors' collection, Hijackers Timeline [redacted], 11/14/03, INTELWIRE, Staff Report, 9/11 and Terrorist Travel, CO, 21–.

401–2　**Atta hurdle/Shehhi referred/"I thought":** Staff Report, 9/11 and Terrorist Travel, CO, 22–, FBI int. [name redacted], Primary Inspector for Atta on 1/10/01, 11/27/01, "Inspector Interviews, AA11" B49, T5, CF & see "The Immigration & Naturalization Service's Contacts with Two September 11 Terrorists," Office of the Inspector General, U.S. Dept. of Justice, 5/20/02. In early May, Atta and two companions—one of whom was probably Jarrah—would go to the Miami Immigration Office to try to get the visa of one of the trio extended to eight months. The inspector not only declined that request but shortened Atta's own permitted stay to six months. Atta left without making a fuss. The second of his companions, the inspector came to suspect after 9/11, had been Adnan Shukrijumah. Shukrijumah, believed to have been an al Qaeda operative reporting to bin Laden, had as of this writing long been on the FBI's Most Wanted List. Though born in Saudi Arabia, he was entitled to live in the United States—his family had moved to Florida in the mid-1990s, but left the country shortly before 9/11. Shukrijumah's late father, an imam, had once served at the al-Farooq mosque in Brooklyn, the hub for jihadi recruiting during the anti-Soviet war. A further alleged Shukrijumah link to the events surrounding 9/11 is reported elsewhere in this edition. See index. (INS visit: [name redacted] Immigration Inspector to Mr. Garofano, 10/23/01, appointment list for May 2, 2001, follow-up interviews, Miami District Office, INS, 4/16/02, & MFR of [name redacted] Customs & Border Protection, 3/25/04, "Inspector Interviews," B49, T5, CF, Staff Report, 9/11 & Terrorist Travel, CO, 30–; Shukrijumah: Staff Report, 9/11 & Terrorist Travel, CO, 216n114, 256n138, CNN, 8/6/10, *NY Daily News*, 8/6/10, "Father Knows Terrorism Best," 10/27/03, www.frontpagemag.com, *Newsweek*, 4/7/04, *NYT*, 9/3/06).

402   **Atta/Shehhi turned up/rented/asked:** Hijackers Timeline [redacted], 11/14/03, INTELWIRE, Counterterrrorism to All Field Offices, 9/15/01, FBI 265A-NY-280350, Serial 2268, released under FOIA to Mike Williams of www.911myths.com, FBI memorandum, PENTTBOM, Summary of captioned investigation as of 11/4/01, 11/5/01, authors' collection, AP, 10/19/01, *WP*, 12/16/01.

402   **optional targets:** KSM SUBST. Separately, there was to be much reference to a claim by Johnelle Bryant, a loan officer for the Department of Agriculture in Homestead, Florida, that Atta came to her office to inquire about a loan to buy a plane for conversion into a crop duster. When told he did not qualify, she said, he made threats, spoke of the destruction of U.S. monuments, and praised bin Laden. Bryant dated the incident as having occurred between late April and mid-May 2000. So far as is known, however, Atta did not arrive in the United States until June 3, 2000 (Timeline Pertaining to Hijackers in Florida, "Timelines 9/11, 2 of 2," B20, T7, CF, ABC News, 6/6/02, Edward Epstein, "The Terror Crop

Dusters," www.edwardjayepstein.com, but see Miller & Stone, 268–).

402–3 **Hanjour certificate:** Hani Hanjour, AA Flight 77, FBI summary 03096, 4/19/02, www.scribd.com, Counter-terrrorism to All Field Offices, 9/15/01, FBI 265A-NY-280350, Serial 2268, released under FOIA to Mike Williams of www.911myths.com, FBI 302 of int. FNU Milton, 4/12/02, INTELWIRE, CR, 226–; **Sporty's video:** Hijackers' Timeline [redacted], 11/14/03, INTELWIRE; **Grand Canyon:** Nawaf al-Hazmi, AA Flight 77, FBI summary 03177, 4/19/02, www.scribd.com; **greet muscle:** Bamford, *Shadow Factory*, 50, Staff Report, 9/11 & Terrorist Travel, CO, 29–.

403 **new arrivals/"The Hour":** CR, 231, *BG*, 3/3/02, 3/4/02. The thirteen were: Satam al-Suqami, Wail al-Shehri, Waleed al-Shehri, Abdul Aziz al-Omari, Ahmed al-Ghamdi, Hamza al-Ghamdi, Mohand al-Shehri, Majed Moqed, Salem al-Hazmi, Saeed al-Ghamdi, Ahmad al-Haznawi, and Ahmed al-Nami—all Saudis—and Fayez Banihammad, from the UAE. Also in the muscle group on 9/11 would be Hamzi and Mihdhar (the latter having arrived back in the United States as of early July). The group included two pairs of brothers, Nawaf and Salem al-Hazmi and Wail and Waleed al-Shehri—though Mohand al-Shehri was unrelated. The three Ghamdis appear to have been not close relatives but merely members of the large Ghamdi tribe. Saudi press reports noted that in Saudi Arabia "the names al Ghamdi and al Shehri are as common as the name Smith in the United States" (CR, 231, 237, *Arab News*, 9/18/01, 9/20/01, 9/22/01, *BG*, 3/3/02).

403–4 **OBL picked:** CR, 235; **5'7":** ibid., 231; **martyr:** ibid., 234; **visa easy/Express:** Staff Report, 9/11 & Terrorist Travel, CO, 32–, 111–, CR, 235, **"teater"/"Wasantwn":** Nonimmigrant Visa Application of Wail al-Shehri, Joel Mowbray, "Visas for Terrorists," *National Review*, archived at www.webcitation.org; **"did not think":** Staff Report, 9/11 & Terrorist Travel, CO, 125, MFR 04016462, 12/5/03, CF; **sky marshals:** CR, 236; **butcher/"to muddy"/told Dubai:** KSM SUBST.

404 **travel pairs/"businessman"/tourists/unsatisfactory:** Staff Report, 9/11 & Terrorist Travel, CO, 29–, Janice Kephart, "The Complete Immigration Story of 9/11 Hijacker Satam al

Suqami," 9/10, www.cis.org. The authors refer here to documentation that was inadequate on its face, but passed muster at Immigration or Customs control. Four of the muscle hijackers, meanwhile, had markers in their passports later understood to have been signs of tampering associated with al Qaeda (Staff Report, 9/11 Terrorist Travel, 29, 33, 34).

405   **prior arrangement:** KSM SUBST; **flew DC/NY:** Staff Report, 9/11 & Terrorist Travel, CO, 29–; **Atta/Hazmi/ money:** CR, 237; **videos/"We left":** *Guardian* (U.K.), 4/16/02, Bruce Hoffman, *Inside Terrorism*, NY: Columbia Univ. Press, 2006, 133, CR 235, 525n104. The first hijacker videotape was released in April 2002 (*Guardian* [U.K.], 4/16/02).

405–8 **Massoud/"If President Bush":** Roy Gutman, *How We Missed the Story*, Washington, D.C.: U.S. Institute of Peace Press, 2008, 246–; Steve Coll, "Ahmad Shah Massoud Links with CIA," 2/23/04, www.rawa.org, *WP*, 1/19 & 20/02; **"gained limited":** Defense Intelligence Agency, cable, "IIR [redacted]/The Assassination of Massoud Related to 11 September 2001 Attack," 11/21/01, as released to the National Security Archive, www.gwu.edu, Schroen, 95–; **"was sending":** Tenet, 156; **Cairo/"We knew":** *NYT*, 6/4/02; **"something big was coming":** MFR 03009296, 11/3/03, MFR 04017179, 10/3/03; **Freeh/Ashcroft/denied:** *Newsweek*, 5/27/02; **briefing documents/"public profile":** Staff Statement 10, CO, Shenon, 151–. The exception is the PDB of August 6, which is covered later in this chapter; **triumphalist speeches:** Bergen, *OBL I Know*, 293–, *Orange County Weekly*, 9/7/02; **"They send":** *The Australian*, 12/21/07, *The Age* (Melbourne), 12/21/07; **"All the people":** *Guardian* (U.K.), 11/28/02; **Mihdhar/"I will make":** Bamford, *Shadow Factory*, 64; **"the success":** CR, 251; **"It's time":** Fouda & Fielding, 166.

408   **Taliban asked:** CR, 251. The Taliban appear to have been concerned not only about U.S. reprisals, but also as to what bin Laden should target. Taliban leader Mullah Omar reportedly favored attacking Jews—not necessarily the United States. Emails found later on the terrorist computer obtained by *Wall Street Journal* reporter Cullison show there was also dissension amongst the terrorists as to whether to give bin Laden full support at this time. "Going on," one writer complained, "is like fighting ghosts and windmills" (CR, 250–, *WSJ*, 7/2/02).

408　**MBC reporter/"some news"/"coffin":** *In the Footsteps of Bin Laden*, 8/23/06, www.cnn.com, Bergen, *OBL I Know*, 284–. According to CIA reporting of KSM's interrogations, KSM and Atef "were concerned about this lack of discretion and urged bin Laden not to make additional comments about the plot." It seems odd then that Atef, normally described as having been professional, should have taken part in the MBC interview. He may have hoped at least to blur the truth by referring to the coming attacks as targeting "American and Israeli interests"—thus avoiding giving away the fact that the attack would be on U.S. territory. If that was his intention, the deception was successful—many in the U.S. had the impression that the attack would take place overseas ("were concerned": KSM SUBST, Atef: CR, refs.; successful: e.g. CR, 256–).

408–9　**impatient/*Cole*:** KSM SUBST, e.g. Mehnaz Sahibzada, "The Symbolism of the Number 7 in Islamic Culture and Rituals," www.wadsworth.com; **dreams:** e.g., Fouda & Fielding, 109, Lacey, *Inside the Kingdom*, 21, *WP*, 9/11/02; **OBL bombarded/Sharon visit/Arafat not invited:** KSM SUBST, *NYT*, 6/20/01; **"big gift":** Bergen, *OBL I Know*, 284–.

409–11　**"like Captain Ahab":** Richard Clarke, 234; **"Clarke was driving":** Conclusions from Review of NSC papers, "Misc. 9/11 Commission Staff Notes About Drafting Final Report," 16095055, CF; **"When these attacks":** CR, 256; **rated a seven:** Tenet, 145–; **was "recruiting"/high alert:** CR, 256–; **"very, very"/Clarke duly:** CR, 257, Bamford, *Shadow Factory*, 55; **July 10 assessment/"There will"/"put his elbows":** Tenet, 150–.

411　**"felt"/"The decision"/"Adults":** Bob Woodward, *State of Denial*, NY: Simon & Schuster, 2006, 49–. It seems clear from this passage—in his 2006 book, *State of Denial*—that he interviewed Cofer Black. Also, perhaps, former CIA director Tenet. While Woodward reported that Tenet left the meeting "feeling frustrated," Tenet stated in his memoir the following year that Black and the head of the Agency's bin Laden unit departed feeling that "at last . . . we had gotten the full attention of the administration." Within two days, a congressional report shows, Tenet went to the Capitol to give a similar briefing to U.S. senators. Only a handful turned up. It was a mystery to him, Tenet wrote, why the 9/11 Commission Report failed to mention the July 10 meeting with Rice—he had told the commissioners about the encounter in closed testimony. It was established that Tenet had indeed told the Commission of the meeting. As others have noted, the Commission's executive director, Philip Zelikow, was closer to Rice and other Bush appointees than was healthy for a man heading a supposedly even-handed investigation—he had even coauthored a book with Rice. According to 9/11 Commissioner Richard Ben-Veniste, Tenet thought Rice "understood the level of urgency he was communicating."

"It is shocking," Peter Rundlet, a former Commission counsel, has written, "that the administration failed to heed such an overwhelming alert from the two officials in the best position to know. Many, many questions need to be asked and answered about this revelation" (meeting: Woodward, *State of Denial*, 50–, Tenet, 151–; congressional report: Report, "Tora Bora Revisited: How We Failed to Get Bin Laden and Why It Matters Today," Committee on Foreign Relations, U.S. Senate, 111th Cong., 1st Sess., U.S. Govt. Printing Office, Washington, D.C., 11/30/09, 4; indeed given: *WP*, 10/3/06; Zelikow: e.g., Shenon, 40–, 65–, 106–, Woodward, *State of Denial*, 52; understood: McClatchy Newspapers, 10/2/06; Rundlet: Peter Rundlet, "Bush Officials May Have Covered Up Rice-Tenet Meeting from 9/11 Commission," http://thinkprogress.org).

411–12 **Black/Scheuer/UBL unit head resignations:** MFR 03009296, 9/3/03, Shenon, 395, CR, 259–; **"The purpose"/Williams concerns/Zubaydah/connected/Hanjour/Williams recommended:** Phoenix, Squad 16 to Counterterrorism, 7/10/01, www.justice.gov, FBI IG, Statement of Eleanor Hill re "The FBI's Handling of the Phoenix Electronic Communication and Investigation of Zacarias Moussaoui Prior to Sept. 11, 2001," 9/24/02 [as updated 10/17/02]. The suspicious activity on the America West flight, which may have been reconnaissance for the 9/11 operation, is described in Ch. 24; **minimal circulation:** *NYT*, 6/10/05, Amy B. Zegart, *Spying Blind*, Princeton: Princeton University Press, 2007, 261n55; **"racial profiling":** Report, JI, 5; **"exercise":** NLETS Message (All Regions), from Counterterrorism, 7/2/01, INTELWIRE; **"I had asked":** Richard Clarke, 236–.

412 **"I don't want":** The Justice Department told the

Commission that Ashcroft, his former deputy, and his chief of staff denied that he had made such a comment to Pickard. Ashcroft himself also denied it in his April 2004 Commission testimony. Pickard, for his part, reiterated his allegation in testimony, in Commission interviews, in a letter to the Commission—and in a later long interview with reporter Philip Shenon. The Commission was unable to resolve the contradictory accounts. It found, though, that—whatever the truth about the Ashcroft/Pickard relationship, "The domestic agencies never mobilized in response to the threat. They did not have direction, and did not have a plan" (Justice Dept./Ashcroft denials: Hearing transcript & Testimony of Ashcroft, 4/13/04, CO; Pickard: CR, 265, 536n52, Shenon, 246, 432n, Ch. 35).

413 **"Fishing rod"/"Frankly":** CBS News, 7/26/01. Ashcroft and senior FBI officials had received recent briefings on the increased terrorist threat level. It is conceivable, however, that the decision that Ashcroft not fly commercial was taken because of threats of a different nature. From early on, reportedly, there had been threats to Ashcroft's personal safety—sparked by his opposition to abortion and gun control (briefings: CR, 258, MFR 04019823, 6/3/04, e.g. Briefing Material, Weekly with Attorney General, 7/12/01, "Ashcroft," B1, Dan Marcus files, CF; threats: Shenon, 243–).

413 **G8 summit:** CR, 258, Shenon, 243–; **slept ships/Pope/airspace:** BBC News, 6/21/01, CNN, 7/17/01, *WP*, 1/19/02, *NYT*, 9/26/01.

413 **Mubarak:** Benjamin & Simon, 342, *Daily Record* (Glasgow), 9/27/01. Warnings of a possible bin Laden attack at Genoa, specifically targeting Bush, also reportedly came from German and Russian intelligence. There were also concerns that violent protest might disturb public order during the summit (BBC News, 6/27/01, CNN, 7/17/01, but see also www.911myths.com/html/genoa_and_mubarak_s_warning.html).

CHAPTER 27

414 **Dubai/passport copied:** *New Yorker*, 7/10/06, Wright, 311, Report, JI, 144, but see Bamford, *Shadow Factory*, 18–.

414 **CIA had not placed:** In spite of the discovery of an internal CIA cable alleging that the visa information had been shared with the FBI, complex investigation did nothing to sub-

stantiate the assertion. Other documents, the 9/11 Commission reported, "contradict" the claim that the visa information was shared with the Bureau. The Commission flatly states that "no one alerted the INS or the FBI" to look for Mihdhar or his traveling companion, Nawaf al-Hazmi (CR, 502n44, 354, & see Tenet, 195).

415   **Mihdhar/visas/July 4:** Staff Report, 9/11 & Terrorist Travel, 33–, 37; **two groups/NJ/Fort Lauderdale:** CR, 230, 240, 248, 253, *WP,* 9/30/01, Hijackers Timeline [redacted], 11/14/03, INTELWIRE; **Mihdhar/crammed:** ibid., CR, 240–, McDermott, 221; **Hazmi bride:** CR, 222, **marriage obligatory:** Fouda & Fielding, 81, & see, e.g., "The Importance of Marriage in Islam," www.sunniforum.com.

415   **Atta:** *Chicago Tribune,* 9/11/04, *Newsweek,* 10/1/01, Bernstein, 105, MFR 04017500, 12/4/03. In a 2004 book, author Daniel Hopsicker gave an account of a supposed relationship, covering periods in 2000 and 2001, between Atta and a young woman named Amanda Keller. Widely circulated on the Internet, the account presents a picture of a deeply unpleasant character who—were the account to prove accurate— frequented sleazy nightspots, beat his girlfriend, and—in one savage incident—killed and dismembered one of her cats and an entire litter of kittens. After lengthy analysis of a tangled scenario, however, the authors concluded that this has been a matter of mistaken identity. A young woman who—according to the Hopsicker account—accompanied Atta and Keller on a trip to the Florida Keys did not recognize pictures of the authentic Atta as the "Mohamed" who made the trip. Keller's mother and sister are reported as having said that her Mohamed was "tall," "lanky," while Atta was only five foot seven. She said early on her boyfriend was French Canadian, and that he told her he had fathered a child in France. That could of course have been a lie—except for another element. According to Keller, the name her Mohamed used at one point to sign a document was "Mohamed Arajaki"—and an official list of men of interest to law enforcement after 9/11 includes a reference to an "Arakj, Mohamad" with a French address.

In the transcript of a long interview with Hopsicker, Keller refers to her sometime boyfriend only as Mohamed, not as Atta or as definitely having been Atta. Press reports of interviews with Keller, moreover, have twice thrown doubt on the notion that her boyfriend was future hijacker Atta. Phone checks, said a counterterrorism agent cited in the second report—in 2006—indicated that the real Atta and Keller never called each other. Keller herself was quoted in that report as saying her Mohamed had been "another flight student not connected to 9/11." If she had given the impression that he was the real Atta, she reportedly said, that had been "my bad for lying. . . . I really didn't think about it until after I did it." The authors did not succeed in reaching Keller for interview. (Hopsicker account: Hopsicker, refs., Keller videotape seen by authors, transcript provided by Hopsicker; trip to Keys: ints. & corr. Linda Lopez; "tall"/"lanky": *Sarasota Herald-Tribune*, 9/24/01; 5'7": Temporary Airman Certificate, "Airman Records," B45, T5, CF; "Arajaki": Hopsicker, 76; list: AP, 10/12/01, list inadvertently released first in Finland, later in Italy, in authors' collection; press reports: *Sarasota Herald-Tribune*, 9/23/01, 9/10/06; in addition, relevant authors' interviews included Elaine Emrich, Stephanie Frederickson, Vicky Keyser, Earle Kimel, Tony & Vonnie LaConca, and Neil Patton).

416   **injections:** *NYT*, 4/25/11; **KSM stipend:** CR, 518n40.

416   **muslimmarriage.com:** MFR of int. [name redacted], 2/23/04, CF. Two of the hijack pilots had married or gone through a form of marriage. As early as 1999, Jarrah and his girlfriend, Aysel, took part in a wedding ceremony at a Hamburg mosque, and—though she would later say she did not consider it binding (the marriage was not registered with the state)—Aysel referred to herself in a letter as Jarrah's "yearning wife." Under pressure from his family, Shehhi had married during a trip back to the United Arab Emirates in early 2000—only to decline to go through with the relationship afterward. Mohamed Atta's father, meanwhile, was to say he found his son a prospective wife who was "nice and delicate, the daughter of a former ambassador." By one account, Atta agreed to get engaged to the woman in 1999— but any prospect of the union becoming a reality vanished with his extended stay in Germany and growing commitment to jihad. One account holds that Atta spoke of marrying a Turk rather than an Egyptian, because he thought Turkish women "more obedient." Binalshibh, for his part, picked up a young woman—believed to have been a Japanese Roman Catholic!—in 2000, and proposed within twenty-four hours.

She would have to dress and behave in the way required of a Muslim wife, he told her, and that their children would have to be brought up to hate Jews. Though they never met again after the initial five-day interlude, Binalshibh later wrote her emails signed: "Your King, Ramzi." Records, meanwhile, indicate that two of the muscle hijackers, Banihammad and Omari, were married (Jarrah: McDermott, 78–; Shehhi: ibid., 54, Corbin, 224, Berlin to Counterterrorism, 12/5/03, FBI 315N-WF-227135, INTELWIRE; Atta: *Newsweek*, 10/1/01, Bernstein, 105, MFR 04017500, 12/4/03, CF; Binalshibh: McDermott, 199–; Banihammad: Riyadh to Counterterrorism, 10/15/01, FBI 265A-NY-280350, Misc. Request 54, "Aliases and Ids," B62, T5, CF; Omari: Visa Application, 6/8/01, www.oldnationalreview.com).

416   **fishing:** Hijackers Timeline [redacted], 11/14/03, INTELWIRE; **Wacko's:** ibid., "Exclusive: 9/11 Hijacker Stayed at Jacksonville Hotel," www.firstcoastnews.com.

416–18 **lap dancing/movies/sex toys:** "Agents of Terror Leave Mark on Sin City," 10/4/01, www.sfgate.com, Hijackers Timeline [redacted], 11/14/03, INTELWIRE, FBI report, "The 11 September Hijacker Cell Model," 2/03, released under FOIA to INTELWIRE. Shehhi's reported visit to a lap dancing club occurred during a trip to Las Vegas, reported later in this chapter. Earlier, in California in 2000, Hazmi and Mihdhar had also reportedly visited strip clubs. The hijacker who visited the Adult Lingerie Center was Majed Moqed (Shehhi: *San Francisco Chronicle*, 10/4/01; Hazmi/Mihdhar: *LAT*, 9/11/02, *Newsweek*, 6/10/02, 10/15/01; Moqed: *Newsday*, 9/23/01, *Newsweek*, 10/15/01, *WP*, 9/30/01, summary re Majed Moqed, JICI, 4/19/02, FBI03135, www.scribd.com).

321–22   **Jarrah to Germany:** Hijackers Timeline [redacted], 11/14/03, INTELWIRE; **Rodriguez/"very humble":** Jeffrey Steinberg, "Cheney's 'Spoon-Benders' Pushing Nuclear Armegeddon," 8/26/05, *Executive Intelligence Review*, eds. *Der Spiegel*, 104–; **fitness classes:** Hijackers Timeline [redacted], 11/14/03, INTELWIRE, "Hijackers' True Name Usage," *U.S. v. Zacarias Moussaoui*, Exhibit 0G0013; **knives:** "Hijacker Knife Purchases," B18, T7, CF; **Hortman:** MFR 04018712, 4/27/04, & MFR 04018407, 4/12/04, CF, Staff Statement 16, CO; **Hanjour Hudson/practice flight DC:** Hijackers Timeline [redacted], 11/14/03, INTELWIRE, Staff Statement 16, CO.

418   **familiarize routine/Vegas, etc.:** "Hijackers' True Name Usage," *U.S. v. Zacarias Moussaoui*, Exhibit 0G0013, Report, JI, 139, MFR, 04016230 [Las Vegas Investigative Summary, undated], MFR 04018564, 1/5/04, MFR 04016240, 1/5/04, & MFR 04016244, 1/5/04, CF. Jarrah was accompanied in Las Vegas by an older fellow Arab. The unidentified Arab resembled the "uncle" who had accompanied him days earlier when he rented a small plane at a Philadelphia airport (MFR 04016240, 1/5/04, MFR 04016239, 1/5/04, CF).

418   **74 times:** McDermott, 222, MFR 04019351, 12/10–11/03, CF; **knives:** MFR 04019351, 12/10–11/03, CF.

418   **needed talk/rendezvous Europe/Spain:** CR, 243–, 530n145. The Commission Report suggests that the pair talked at a hotel not far from Cambrils, near Barcelona, and that Atta rented accommodations in the area until July 19. The experienced author Edward Epstein, who had interviewed prominent Spanish investigating magistrate Baltasar Garzón, wrote in a 2007 article that Atta and Binalshibh "dropped from sight leaving no hotel records, cellphone logs or credit-card receipts" from July 9 to July 16. Judge Garzón reasoned that they spent that time at a prearranged safe house organized by a Spanish-based Algerian accomplice and al Qaeda activists in Spain. Phone intercepts showed that Binalshibh was in touch with the Algerian a few weeks later. Other intercepts indicated that the Germany-based Syrian suspect Marmoun Darkazanli (see Ch. 24) was in Spain at approximately the same time. Binalshibh would claim under interrogation that he met no one but Atta in Spain (Cambrils: CR, 244, 530n145; "dropped"/Algerian accomplice: Edward J. Epstein, "The Spanish Connection," 2/22/07, www.opinionjournal.com, *LAT*, 1/14/03, CNN, 10/31/01; Darkazanli: *LAT*, 1/14/03; Binalshibh: CR, 244).

418–19 **OBL wanted/security/"symbols"/"preferred":** Staff Report, "9/11 & Terrorist Travel," CO, 207, 244; **WH too tough/streets:** CR, 244; **"in the hands":** KSM SUBST; **necklaces/phones:** CR, 245.

419   **Atta admitted:** Staff Report, "9/11 & Terrorist Travel," CO, 38. If the identifications made by witnesses at the Pelican Alley restaurant in Venice, Florida, are accurate, then Atta and Shehhi may have been back in Venice in late July—with a dark-complexioned companion—engaged in what appeared to be a heated argument (ints. Tom & Renee Adorna, Jeff Pritko).

419–20 **drop out?/called Aysel/ticket/"emotional":** CR, 246–, Staff
Statement 16, CO, MFR 04019350, 3/18/04, CR, Hijackers
Timeline [redacted], 11/14/03, INTELWIRE.

420 **Binalshibh told KSM:** How we come to know about this
exchange, which was conducted on the phone, will be discussed in Ch. 30. If meant literally, the reference to cost in the
conversation is odd (and perhaps merely code) unless, as the
Commission was to surmise, KSM was referring to the cost
and trouble of organizing a replacement hijacking pilot. The
notional replacement, the commission thought, was likely
Zacarias Moussaoui, the French-born terrorist who had been
sent to the United States for pilot training early in 2001.
During his conversation with Binalshibh, KSM authorized the
sending of "skirts" to "Sally," an instruction believed to mean
that Binalshibh was to send Moussaoui $14,000. Binalshibh
did so in early August. According to KSM, however, he at no
stage contemplated using Moussaoui as a pilot on the 9/11
operation, but rather in a later "second wave" of attacks. As
will emerge later in this chapter, Moussaoui would be
detained in August because of his suspect behavior at a flight
school in Minnesota (CR, 246–, Indictment, 12/01 &
Superceding Indictment, 7/02, *U.S. v. Zacarias Moussaoui*,
Staff Statement 16, CO).

420–1 **"We spent":** Aysel Sengün statement to Bundeskriminalamt,
9/15/01, authors' collection; **apartment:** Jarrah timeline,
"03009470, Packet 6, Ziad Jarrah chronology,"
www.scribd.com; **"This House":** *Newsweek*, 9/24/01; **"big
planes":** int. Rosmarie Canel by Hannah Cleaver; **GPS:**
Jarrah timeline; **Atta/Hazmi stopped by police:** Hijackers
Timeline [redacted], 11/14/03, INTELWIRE, Mohamed
Mohamed Elamir Awad Elsayed Atta, Enforcement
Operations Division, Texas Service Center, Intelligence
Division, INS, "Hijacker Primary Documents—AA11," B51,
T5, CF, & see Graham with Nussbaum, 36–; **"Every cop":**
MFR of George Tenet, 12/23/03, CF; **"five or six weeks":**
Staff Statement 16, CO, CR, 243; **"Salaam":** McDermott,
225.

422 **warnings:** Chicago attorney David Schippers said soon after
9/11 that he had received information on a coming terror
attack on Manhattan and that—"a month before the bombing"—he had tried to get a warning to Attorney General
Ashcroft. He said he was never able to reach Ashcroft and was

brushed off by Justice Department officials. Schippers's sources, he said, included FBI agents and policemen. In the summer of 2001, Schippers was attorney for Chicago FBI counterterrorism agent Robert Wright, whose book—a "blueprint on how the events of September 11 were inevitable"—was to be suppressed by the FBI. Schippers had also become a vocal advocate for Jayna Davis, an Oklahoma journalist whose research on the bombing of the Alfred P. Murrah building posits a Middle East connection to that attack (see Ch. 22). The warnings Schippers said he attempted to pass on were not just of a coming attack on New York City but also covered Davis's research and information on the infiltration of the United States by the Palestinian group Hamas. The totality of his information, Schippers later concluded, was to lead people to think he was "crazy." Schippers had earlier served as chief investigative counsel to the House Judiciary Committee during the impeachment probe of President Clinton (int. David Schippers, *The Alex Jones Show*, 10/10/01, www.infowars.com, *Indianapolis Star*, 5/18/02, *Chicago* magazine, 10/02, Jayna Davis, *The Third Terrorist*, Nashville: WND, 2004, Foreword).

422 **DGSE:** "Motley Submissions—French Intelligence Passed to the U.S.—Moussaoui—Planes as Weapons Widely Known," B10, T2, CF, "Oussama Bin Laden," leaked DGSE report, 9/13/01, seen by authors.

422 **Russian FSB;** AFP, 9/16/01'; **"20 al Qaeda":** *60 Minutes II: The Plot*, CBS, 10/9/02.

422 **Muttawakil:** Muttawakil's information was given him, according to the emissary, by the head of the Islamic Movement of Uzbekistan, Tahir Yildash. The detail is relevant, for the earliest French intelligence information on bin Laden's hijacking plans came from Uzbek contacts (see p. 400). Following the U.S. rout of the Taliban regime that he had predicted, former Taliban minister Muttawakil surrendered in early 2002, was for some time held in American custody, then freed. His emissary, who told his story on condition of anonymity, stayed on in Kabul—apparently at liberty. U.S. diplomat David Katz declined to discuss the episode when contacted in 2002. The story was reported by the BBC and the British newspaper *The Independent*, based on an interview of the emissary by the journalist Kate Clark (BBC News, *The Independent* [U.K.], 9/7/02).

423–6 **plans postponed:** CR, 259, 534n28; **"will still happen":** ibid., 260, 534n32; **Miller/"very spun-up":** FBI IG; **slow progress/"But the Principals' ":** Testimony of Richard Clarke, 4/8/04, CO; **Bush vacation/"I'm sure":** ABC News, 8/3/01, AP, 8/6/01, *USA Today*, 8/3/01; **Cheney:** *Jackson Hole News & Guide* (Wyoming), 8/15/01; **poll/"too much":** *USA Today*, 8/6/01, "Public Critical of Bush's Vacation Plans," 8/7/01, www.gallup.com, *WP*, 8/7/01. As things turned out, the President was to return to Washington a few days earlier than planned, on August 30 (Public Papers of the Presidents, George W. Bush, 2001, www.gpoaccess.gov, 1569); **CBS re PDB/"bin Laden's":** "What Bush Knew Before September 11," 5/17/02, www.cbsnews.com; **Fleischer/"very generalized":** press briefing, 5/16/02,http://georgewbush-whitehouse.gov; **Fleischer follow-up:** press briefing, 5/17/02, http://georgewbush-whitehouse.gov; **Rice/"not a warning"/"an analytic"/"hijacking"/"could have":** press briefing, 5/16/02, http://georgewbushwhitehouse.archives.gov; **"historical":** ibid., Testimony of Condoleezza Rice, 4/8/04, CO; **struggle:** e.g. Report, JI, 1, Kean & Hamilton, 89–; **"the most highly":** press briefing by Ari Fleischer, 5/21/02, http://georgewbush-whitehouse.gov; **CIA refused:** Report, JI, 1; **several released:** Thomas Blanton, "The President's Daily Brief," National Security Archive, 4/12/04, www.gwu.edu; **leather binder:** Tenet, 31; **"top-secret":** Graham, with Nussbaum, 80; **"news digest":** Blanton, "The President's Daily Brief"; **truly secret/dull:** ibid., Shenon, 220; **Joint Inquiry pressed:** Report, JI, 1; **Commission/"What did":** Kean & Hamilton, 89–, Zelikow to Kean & Hamilton, Proposal for Breaking PDB Impasse, 9/25/03, "Letters & Memos, Negotiations over Access to PDBs," B6, Dan Marcus files, CF; **"blowtorch":** Ben-Veniste, 239; **heading had not read:** *The Washington Post* had reported the correct headline as early as May 19, 2002, two days after Fleischer misstated it. The significance of the press secretary's omission of the word "in," however, got lost in the fog of the subsequent White House effort to minimize the PDB's overall importance ("Press Briefing by Ari Fleischer," 5/17/02, www.gwu.edu, *WP*, 5/19/02, *Nation*, 4/12/04).

426 **Aug. 6 PDB:** released 4/10/04, "Withdrawal Notice re 4–12–04 memo re Aug. 6 PDB, Withdrawal Notice re

5–16–01 Daily UBL Threat," B6, Dan Marcus files, CF. The PDB also referred to the fact that, as indicated by the attacks on the American embassies in Africa in 1998, bin Laden prepared operations "years in advance and is not deterred by setbacks." The PDB also stated that the FBI was currently "conducting approximately 70 full field investigations throughout the U.S." that it considered bin Laden–related. This last assertion turned out to be a CIA misunderstanding of a liaison call to the FBI. Some seventy *individuals* were apparently being investigated by the FBI (Testimony of Thomas Pickard, 4/13/04, CO, Zegart, 109).

426–7 **redacted:** Fact Sheet on Aug. 6, 2001, PDB, Office of the Press Secretary, 4/10/04, www.gwu.gov; **"said nothing"/at own request:** remarks by the President to the Travel Pool [Fort Hood, TX], 4/11/04, www.whitehouse.gov; **Bush/ Commission meeting/Ben-Veniste account:** Ben-Veniste, 293– & see Shenon, 291–, 340–, CR, 260–, Kean & Hamilton, 206–; **Clarke "in writing":** see CR, 255, 263, 535n5; **"I really don't":** Testimony of Condoleezza Rice, 4/8/04, CO.

427–8 **nobody could have foreseen:** Rice acknowledged in her 2004 Commission testimony that she had misspoken in her comment to the press in 2002 that "no one" could have predicted hijackers using planes as missiles. Given the Genoa situation, she said—and given that others had indeed foreseen the possibility—Rice said she ought to have said only that *she* could not have imagined an attack using planes in that way. By contrast, Louis Freeh—FBI director until June 2001—told the Commission that the possible use of planes in suicide missions had in his experience been part of the planning for potential terrorist events (misspoken/*she* could not: Testimony of Condoleezza Rice, 4/8/04, CO, Ben-Veniste, 251, Press Briefing by Condoleezza Rice, 5/16/02, http://georgewbush-whitehouse.archives.gov; Freeh: Testimony of Louis Freeh, 4/13/04, CO).

429 **follow up/discussed with Ashcroft?:** The job of making contact with domestic agencies, Bush told Commissioner Jamie Gorelick, was not Rice's but that of White House chief of staff Andy Card. This assertion was impossible to check because the Commission was bound by yet another condition, not to raise questions arising from the Rice or Bush-Cheney interviews with other White House officials. (Ben-Veniste, 303).

429–30 **Rice in Texas?:** A contemporary *Washington Post* report of the President's activity on August 6 stated that he "held a 45-minute meeting with four senior officials here and talked *by telephone* with National Security Advisor Condoleezza Rice about Macedonia." (authors' italics) (*WP*, 8/7/01, *USA Today*, 8/6/01, 10:24 p.m. update); **doubt/"asked for it":** Ben-Veniste, 300, remarks by the President to the Travel Pool, [Fort Hood, TX], 4/11/04, www.whitehouse.gov; **"All right":** Suskind, *One Percent Doctrine*, 1–, Ben-Veniste, 300, additional information gathered by authors, not for attribution; **"no formal":** Tenet to Kean & Hamilton, 3/26/04, "PDB—letter from Tenet re Aug. 6 PDB," B6, Dan Marcus files, CF; **"none":** Ben-Veniste, 391.

430 **"current"/"pay more":** Shenon, 379, 437n. This account of the August 6 PDB episode is intended by the authors to be not an assessment of the document's quality but a summary of its content—in the context of the way President Bush, National Security Adviser Rice, and press secretary Fleischer described its contents. Author Amy Zegart severely criticized the quality of the PDB in her book *Spying Blind*, on the CIA and the FBI and their role prior to 9/11. She judged it a "tragically shoddy piece of intelligence." Former CIA counterterrorism chief Cofer Black, however, characterized it as a "place-marker" or "reminder" that bin Laden's ultimate objective was "to strike hard against the United States" (Zegart, 108, Testimony of Cofer Black, 4/13/04, CO).

430 **"had written":** Ben-Veniste, 301–.

430–2 **manager alerted/Moussaoui/"goal"/"I am sure"/$6,800:** Stipulation, 3/1/06, *U.S. v. Zacarias Moussaoui*, 3/1/06; **"joy ride":** "Moussaoui, Zacarias, IT—Other," 8/19/01, *U.S. v. Zacarias Moussaoui*, Exhibit 692; **string of questions/ detained/"martyrs"/"unambiguous"/"convinced"/:** CR, 273–, FBI IG, MFR 04019350, 3/18/04, CF, Report, JI, 22–; **KSM would tell/"problematic personality":** KSM SUBST, CR, 247, 531n162; **met Binalshibh/$14,000/telephone number:** Staff Report, "Monograph on Terrorist Financing," CO, MFR, 04019350, 3/18/04, Indictment & Exhibits MN00601, MN00601.1, MN00601.2, *U.S. v. Zacarias Moussaoui*, CR, 225, 520n54.

432 **agents knew nothing:** Had agents been cleared to examine Moussaoui's possessions, they would have discovered letters purporting to show that Moussaoui was acting as consultant in

the States for a company called "InFocus Tech." The signature on the letters was that of Yazid Sufaat, the owner of the Kuala Lumpur condominium in which the terrorist meeting—attended by Mihdhar and Hazmi—had been held in January 2000. The FBI had been aware of that meeting at the time, so—had the Bureau's system been adequately coordinated—discovery of the letters in timely fashion would immediately have linked Moussaoui to al Qaeda. (Report, JI, 26, Exhibit OK01043, *U.S. v. Zacarias Moussaoui*).

432   **appeals/70 messages:** Statement of Eleanor Hill re "The FBI's Handling of the Phoenix Electronic Communication and Investigation of Zacarias Moussaoui Prior to Sept. 11, 2001," 9/24/02 [as updated 10/17/02], JI, *USA Today*, 3/2/06, *Newsday*, 3/21/06, *LAT*, 3/21/06; **"spun up"/"take control":** FBI IG.

433   **"That's not":** Statement of Eleanor Hill. The headquarters failure to respond positively on Moussaoui was to lead to protracted outrage and regret. The wrangle had centered on the complex matter of how legally to get access to Moussaoui's possessions. The options available were either a criminal search warrant or a Foreign Intelligence Surveillance (FISA) warrant—permitted, in this context, if it can be shown that the subject is an agent of an international terrorist group and is engaged in terrorism on behalf of that group. The case agent in Minneapolis, concerned that there was insufficient probable cause for a criminal warrant, favored the FISA option—only to be confronted by legalistic hurdles thrown up by headquarters. The go-ahead was given only on September 11, after the two strikes on the World Trade Center. Evidence and detainee statements were eventually to link Moussaoui to KSM and Binalshibh, and he is now serving a life sentence for conspiracy to commit acts of terror and air piracy. As of this writing, only two other people have been convicted of conspiracy in connection with the 9/11 attacks. One is Syrian-born Imad Yarkas, alleged to have been an al Qaeda member linked to Mohamad Atta. The conviction relating to 9/11, however, was quashed on appeal. The other is Mounir Motassadeq, who is serving fifteen years in Germany. Motassadeq, an associate of the Hamburg-based hijackers, was accused of helping the hijackers prepare for the 9/11 operation. In a lengthy prison interview, Motassadeq told the authors that—while he had certainly been an associate and

friend of the future hijackers in Hamburg—he had had no knowledge whatsoever of what they were plotting. The authors came away from the interview doubting that he was guilty as charged (warrant options: e.g., Graham with Nussbaum, 51; go-ahead: FBI IG; evidence/sentence: Indictment, *U.S. v. Zacarias Moussaoui*, 12/01, AP, 5/4/06, CNN, 4/23/05; Yarkas: *Guardian* [UK], BBC, 9/26/05, www.cbc.ca, CNN, 2/8/08; Motassadeq: *NYT*, 1/9/07, *Der Spiegel*, 1/12/07, *Economist*, 9/3/02, CBS News, 10/22/02, ints. Motassadeq, Udo Jacob, 2009).

433   **second development/New information/Wilshire reconsidered/"Something bad":** CR, 266–,FBI IG. In the 9/11 Commission Report, and in a 2004 review of the FBI's handling of pre-9/11 intelligence information issued by the Justice Department's inspector general, relevant CIA and FBI personnel are referred to by pseudonyms. True names of many of the individuals were revealed in evidence prepared in 2006 for Moussaoui's trial. Others have been asserted by independent writers, notably Lawrence Wright and Kevin Fenton, and the authors have used these identifications in the text. The CIA officer named here as Tom Wilshire is "John" in the official reports. The FBI analyst Margarette Gillespie is "Mary" in reports, while the FBI analyst Dina Corsi appears to be identical with "Jane" in the Commission Report and with "Donna" in the inspector general's review. Steve Bongardt is "Steve B." in the Commission Report and "Scott" in the review. Robert Fuller is "Robert F." in the Commission Report and "Richard" in the review (CR 267–, & 537n63 et seq., FBI IG, McNulty to Troccoli 3/1/06, *U.S. v Zacarias Moussaoui*, Exhibit 952.B, Wright, 311, 340–, 352–, 425n, Kevin Fenton, "Aliases of 9/11 Figures Revealed," 7/15/08, http://hcgroups.wordpress.com).

433–5   **Wilshire suggested to Gillespie:** Lawrence Wright's *The Looming Tower* reads as if it was not Wilshire but CIA supervisor Clark Shannon who assigned Gillespie to this task. Wright's *New Yorker* articles, however, also in 2006, say Wilshire assigned the work. So do other relevant sources (Wright, 340–. CR, 269–, *New Yorker*, 7/10/06, Substitution for the Testimony of "Mary," *U.S. v. Zacarias Moussaoui*, Exhibit 940); **"It all clicked"/"watchlist":** CR, 266–, FBI IG; **not in U.S./FAA not informed:** Report, JI, 15, Staff Report, "9/11 & Terrorist Travel," CO, 42, Staff Statement 2, CO;

Corsi sent email/red tape/misinterpretation: FBI IG; **"Disneyland":** Wright, 353–; **"Someday"/Fuller:** FBI IG; **"assigned no":** CR, 538n77.

435–6   **Tenet fishing:** Breitweiser, 193; **Tenet directed:** Tenet, 159; **Tenet briefed/Aug. 23:** ibid., CR, 275; **seriously/"If this guy":** Tenet, 202–; **"brow furrowed"/"no one ever":** Ben-Veniste, 301; **"I didn't see"/lied:** Testimony of George Tenet, 4/14/04, CO, Shenon, 361–.

436   **Harlow re Aug. 17 & 31:** *Salt Lake Tribune*, *WP*, 4/15/04. Probably because of an informal exchange Bush had with reporters the following day, it has been suggested that Tenet also met with the President on August 24. The wording of one of his answers could be taken to indicate to the press that there had been a Tenet visit on the 24th. The sense Bush intended, however, is not entirely clear and could equally refer to the visit of August 17 (exchange: *Public Papers of the Presidents, George W. Bush, 2001*, www.gpoaccess.gov, 1037; suggested: e.g. Robert Schopmeyer, *Prior Knowledge of 9/11*, Palo Alto, CA: Palo Alto Publishing, 2007, 512, corr. Robert Schopmeyer, 2011).

436   **"to make sure":** Tenet, 159; **"not recall":** CR, 262.

437   **"The question":** *Newsweek*, 5/25/02; **"I do not believe":** Testimony of Condoleezza Rice, 4/8/04, CO; **"an appalling":** *Vanity Fair*, 2/09; **"There was no":** Ben-Veniste, 307– & see 265.

CHAPTER 28

438   **Hello Jenny:** With a few minor changes to ensure verbatim translation from the German, the "Dear Jenny" message is as reported by Al Jazeera reporter Yosri Fouda, drawing on his encounter with Binalshibh in Karachi in 2002 (see pp. 318–19). Binalshibh dated the message as having been sent on or about August 21, 2001. According to Fouda, Binalshibh produced the message "on a floppy disk" and showed it to him "on screen." The 9/11 Commission Report does not reproduce the "Dear Jenny" message, but refers to coded August "communications" between Atta and Binalshibh that were recovered when KSM was captured. These messages included a discussion of targets dated as having occurred on August 3. In a related note, the Commission quotes Binalshibh as claiming that the words "law" and "politics" were both used to refer only to the Capitol—though the

reference was surely in fact to two separate targets (Fouda & Fielding, 138–, *The Australian*, 9/9/02, *Sunday Times* [London], 9/802, CR 248–, 531n 165/166).

439 **August 29 call/Atta riddle:** Reporter Fouda, who learned of the puzzle in 2002 from Binalshibh, rendered it as reproduced in the text. The Commission Report referred to it as "two branches, a slash, and a lollipop." A factor in choosing the date September 11, according to a note found on KSM's computer following his capture, was that the U.S. Congress would be in session in the Capitol by that time (Fouda & Fielding, 140, CR, 249, Staff Statement 16, CO).

440 **Binalshibh passed on:** The Commission Report, drawing on reports of the interrogations of KSM and Binalshibh, states that KSM was informed of the date by Zacaria Essabar, an associate Binalshibh used to carry the message from Germany to KSM in Pakistan. KSM said Essabar brought him the date in a letter, while Binalshibh has said he entrusted Essabar only with a verbal message. Binalshibh has also claimed that he called KSM on the subject. The fact that information was extracted from the prisoners under torture may account for the seeming contradictions. As of this writing, Essabar's whereabouts are unknown (CR249, 531n173, KSM SUBST, Wanted Notice, Bundeskriminalamt Wiesbaden, 2008).

440–1 **inspector doubts/Kahtani/"He started":** MFR 04016447, 11/12/03, CF, CR, 12, 248, 564n33; **"round out":** KSM SUBST; **"like a soldier":** MFR 04016447, 11/12/02, CF.

441 **five rather than four:** Kahtani, who was captured in Afghanistan after 9/11, was one of the prisoners "tortured"— in the words of the retired judge appointed to decide on prosecutions at Guantánamo. The record indicates that he strongly resisted interrogation. He remains a Guantánamo detainee as of this writing. Commission staff identified nine other recruits who were at some point considered for assignment to the 9/11 operation (captured/"tortured": *WP*, 1/14/09; resisted: Interrogation Log, Detainee 063, www.ccrjustice.org, "The Guantánamo Docket," *NYT* website, as of 1/12/11; nine other: Staff Statement 16, CO, CR, 235).

441–2 **Atta at airport:** Staff Statement 16, CO, Mohammed al-Kahtani, "RFBI 03013592, Documents Relating to PENTTBOM Briefing of Dec. 10, 2003, Packet 2, CF; **Atta free/rental cars/flying/hijackers everyday activities:** "Hijackers Timeline [redacted]," 11/14/03, INTELWIRE;

moved out Paterson/flight manuals: MFR 04016237, 11/6/03, CF, *NYT,* 10/28/01; **Valencia/"thought they were gay":** *Die Zeit* (Germany), 10/2/02; **men tugging/retrieve towel:** *St. Petersburg Times,* 9/1/02. Simpson believed the men who tried her door were Ahmad al-Haznawi and Ahmed al-Nami; **Surma:** ibid.; **Warrick:** ibid., *Observer* [U.K.], 9/16/01, int. Brad Warrick.

443 **Longshore/Dragomir:** *WP,* 10/5/01, *Chicago Tribune,* 9/18/01. Though this incident was reported in major newspapers, it is not certain that the men Dragomir remembered were Jarrah and a companion—or indeed that the companion was Atta, as the manager thought he might have been. The date of the incident is also not entirely clear—it was reported both as having occurred on August 30 and in "late August." That said, Jarrah was in the area on August 30, having just returned from Baltimore. He moved out of the accommodations he had been renting for some time on August 31, took another condominium close by—and was apparently using the Internet at a Kinko's in Hollywood—where the reported Longshore Motel incident occurred—on September 3, at a time Atta was also there ("Hijackers Timeline [redacted]," 11/14/03, INTELWIRE, Profile, Ziad Samir Jarrah, ACS Download Documents, Pkt. 6, 03009470, CF).

443–4 **Hazmi phoned:** CR, 223, 249; **Abdullah had known/helped:** CR, 216, 220, 516n20, Los Angeles to Counterterrorism, 1/8/02 , FBI 302 re canvas of hotels, 1/15/02, & FBI 302 re int. instructors Sorbi Flight School, 4/11/02 INTELWIRE, *San Diego Union-Tribune,* 5/26/04, *LAT,* 7/24/04, MSNBC, 9/8/06; **activist/another man/"planes falling":** San Diego to Ottawa, 4/11/02, San Diego, Squad 15, to San Diego, 2/4/03, INTELWIRE, CR, 218–.

444 **"acting"/"nervous":** MFR 04017535, 11/18/03, MFR 04017543, 11/18/03, CF. In detention after 9/11, first as a material witness and then on immigration charges, Abdullah would refuse a 9/11 Commission request to interview him. While in prison, it was alleged, he told other inmates that he had known that Hazmi and Mihdhar were involved in plans for a terrorist attack. According to one inmate, he said he had known the plan was for a 9/11-style attack and that he "found out" three weeks before the attacks occurred. Abdullah, who had arrived in the United States via Canada using a Yemeni

passport identifying him as "al Mihdhar Zaid" but then changed his name, was charged with an immigration offense and deported in 2003. 9/11 Commission executive director Philip Zelikow has described the report's findings on Abdullah as "ominous." In a 2004 interview with *The Washington Post*, however, Abdullah denied having had any foreknowledge of the 9/11 attacks. Reports suggest the possibility that the hijacking references in the notebook found among his possessions may have been written by someone else (refuse: CR, 517n31; involved: ibid., 218–; "Zaid": "Inside I.C.E. [Immigration and Customs Enforcement]," Dept. of Homeland Security, Vol. 4, 5/25–6/7/04, www.ice.gov; "ominous": Zelikow to Shenon, 2/12/07, www.philipshenon.com; denied: *WP*, 8/10/04; notebook: ibid., 516n21, 218).

444 **obtained IDs:** Staff Report, "9/11 & Terrorist Travel," 39, FBI 302 of int. Victor Lopez-Flores, 9/23/01, 9/25/01, 10/06/01, 11/8/01, 11/13/01, "Lopez-Flores," B11, T5, CF, Graham, with Nussbaum, 76; **airline reservations/tickets:** "Hijackers Timeline [redacted]," 11/14/03, INTELWIRE; **frequent flier:** ibid., Staff Report, "Monograph on the Four Flights & Civil Aviation Security," CF, *MH*, 9/18/01; **changed assignments:** "Hijackers Timeline [redacted]," 11/14/03, INTELWIRE; **Muslim meals:** *Time*, 9/24/01; **beyond destinations:** "Hijackers Timeline [redacted]," 11/14/03, INTELWIRE; **transcontinental/fuel/explosive:** ibid., eds. *Der Spiegel*, 32.

445 **Atta thought:** CR, 531n171. As things were to turn out, and as noted in Ch. 2 on pp. 37–8, many Trade Center workers did not reach their place of work before the attacks began. They were delayed by voting in local elections and traffic jams.

445 **shopped knives/Stanley two piece/ Leatherman/Dollar House/folding knife:** Staff Report, "Monograph on the Four Flights & Civil Aviation Security," CF, "Hijackers Timeline [redacted]," 11/14/03, INTELWIRE, witness list, "Hijacker Knife Purchases," B18, T7, CF. The folding knife would be found later in Atta's shipped baggage, which failed to make the transfer to American 11, the plane he hijacked on 9/11 (witness list, "Hijacker Knife Purchases," B18, T7, CF).

445–7 **Principals convened/draft NSPD:** CR, 213–, Farmer, 65–, Richard Clarke, 26; **State had told:** *WP*, 1/20/02; **debate re Predator/dueled:** ibid., Benjamin & Simon, 345–, CR, 214,

Tenet, 160, corr. Miles Kara; **"I just couldn't"**: *Vanity Fair*, 2/09; **reconnaissance**: CR, 214; **"I didn't really"**: Testimony of Richard Clarke, 3/24/04, CO; **"grasp the enormity"**: MFR 04018415, 12/16/03, CF; **"It sounds"**: *New Yorker*, 8/4/03; **strongly worded note**: Staff Statement 8, CO, CR 212–, 343–, 513n247–; **Directive approved**: CR, 213–.

447   **money left over/returned**: Staff Report, Monograph on Terrorist Financing," CO, PENTTBOM, Summary of Captioned Investigation," 11/5/01, authors' collection, Staff Statement 16, CO, Stipulation, *U.S. v. Zacarias Moussaoui*, 3/1/06. The return of funds notwithstanding, it has been alleged that Atta received $100,000 as late as August 2001. A story emerged in the Indian press soon after 9/11, supposedly citing sources in the FBI and Indian intelligence, claiming that the director of the Pakistani ISI, Lieutenant General Mahmoud Ahmed, ordered the supposed wire transfer of the money in either the summer of 2001 or 2000. The FBI told 9/11 Commission staff that there was no evidence Atta received a payment from the Pakistani ISI. Nor, indeed, were there "any unexplained funds at all." One would wonder—if such a payment was made in August 2001—why it was required so late in the operation. Given the long-running enmity between Pakistan and India, the allegation may merely have been Indian propaganda. That said, Pakistani intelligence has had a long involvement with the Taliban, and allegedly with bin Laden. The U.S. government, meanwhile, has never determined the original source of *any* of the money used in the attack, though the mechanics of how it reached the hijackers is known ($100,000: e.g., *Times of India*, 10/9/01, Press Trust of India, 10/8/01, 10/15/01, *WSJ*, 10/10/01; ISI/al Qaeda: e.g., AP, 2/21/02, Fox News, 10/8/01, *Asia Times*, 1/5/02; no evidence: MFR 04019767, CF, Staff Report, "Monograph on Terrorist Financing," CO).

448   **"brothers"**: Fouda & Fielding, 141; **Binalshibh flew/marathon/"The message"**: ibid., MFR 04019351, 12/10–11/03, CF, *Der Spiegel*, 10/27/03, McDermott, 230.

448   **"referred"**: *Sunday Times* (London), 10/7/01; **"information about"**: *NYT*, 6/4/02; **Gary Hart/"preparedness"/Rice "said"**: *Salon*, 9/12/01, *Columbia Journalism Review*, Nov./Dec. 2001, Statement by the President, 5/8/01, http://usgovinfo.about.com, *WP*, 1/20/02, CR, 204; **Bush met Tenet**: *Salt Lake Tribune*, 4/15/04.

449–50 **agent getting started/"security"/tentative feelers/ ChoicePoint:** CR, 270–, FBI IG, Kevin Fenton, *Disconnecting the Dots*, Walterville, OR: TrineDay, 2011, 345–. Another New York FBI agent, who ran an Internet search on September 11 after the attacks, found Mihdhar's San Diego address "within hours." (JI, 43); **traffic policeman/ Hazmi featured, etc.:** "Hijackers Timeline [redacted]," 11/14/03, INTELWIRE. The previous occasions Hamzi had come to the notice of the police are reported on pp. 420–1.

450 **Shuckums:** *Time*, 9/24/01, Hopsicker, 81–, *Newsweek*, 9/24/01, *St. Petersburg Times*, 9/1/02. FBI agents who looked into the Shuckums story evidently thought it occurred on September 6. Atta could not have been there on the 7th, as some press reports had it, as he flew from Fort Lauderdale to Baltimore that day ("Hijackers Timeline [redacted]," 11/14/03, INTELWIRE).

451 **Atta/Jarrah sold cars/headed north:** ibid., Stipulation, 3/1/06 & Exhibit OG0020.2, *U.S. v. Zacarias Moussaoui*, Chronology of Events for Hijackers, Ziad Jarrah chronology, 3/20/02, "03009470 ACS Download Documents, Packet 6," CF, Staff Statement 16, CO. A story would emerge that Atta and Shehhi were at the Holiday Inn at Longboat Key that day, in west Florida and not far from where President Bush would arrive on the eve of 9/11. The authors interviewed Darlene Sievers and Mark Bean, hotel workers who thought they saw them there, but the record indicates that they were mistaken (*Longboat Observer*, 11/21/01, ints. Darlene Sievers, Mark Bean).

451–2 **Sweet Temptations:** MFR 04020636, 2/2/04, "Hijackers Timeline [redacted]," 11/14/03, INTELWIRE; **"the most"/twice:** *Boston Herald*, 10/10/01, 10/11/01; **$100 apiece:** *BG*, 10/10/01, *The Independent* (U.K.), 10/11/01; **porn video:** "Hijackers Timeline [redacted]," 11/14/03, INTEL-WIRE, *WSJ*, 10/16/01; **paid dancer:** *NYT*, 9/27/01, 10/28/01; **Panther Motel/found:** "Hijackers Timeline [redacted]," 11/14/03, INTELWIRE, *St. Petersburg Times*, 9/1/02; **Jarrah ticket:** *NY Daily News*, 1/9/02, Ziad Jarrah chronology, 3/20/02, "03009470 ACS Download Documents, Packet 6," CF; **Jarrah called:** Ziad Jarrah chronology, 3/20/02; **$2,000:** Fisk, *The Great War*, 1051; **sister's wedding/suit:** *LAT*, 10/23/01.

452   **Jarrah package:** Stipulation, *U.S. v. Zacarias Moussaoui*, letter reproduced at http://en.wikepedia.org—Arabic & Turkish translated for the authors by Hans Kippenberg & Tilman Seidensticker, "The Fifth Estate: The Story of Ziad Jarrah," 10/10/01, www.cbc.ca. Jarrah's mind was evidently on his girlfriend, Aysel, a great deal during his last days alive. He called more than usual, she would remember, four times between the Thursday of the week before 9/11 and the morning of the strikes. He appears to have made the final call when he was already at Newark Airport preparing to board United Flight 93. As fate would have it, according to Sengün, she had to cut the call short because it was a busy moment in the hospital where she was working. There had been nothing out of the ordinary about the call, she would remember—Jarrah had said he loved her. Sengün has not given interviews and it is thought German authorities placed her under some form of witness protection (Sengün sworn statement to police in Germany, 9/15/01, in authors' collection).

454   **told later/she would hope:** *LAT,* 1/27/03.

455   **Mihdhar packet:** Stipulation, *U.S. v. Zacarias Moussaoui*, 3/1/06, Bamford, *Shadow Factory,* 81. One FBI document suggests Mihdhar's letter to his wife was in fact sent not by Mihdhar but by Hazmi. This is clearly in error, not least because—unlike Mihdhar—Hazmi had no wife. As reported earlier, he had been attempting and failing to find himself a wife; **Atta had told/called father:** CR, 249; **KSM to Pakistan:** Khalid Sheikh Mohammed, Charge Sheet," 4/15/08, www.findlaw.com; **told disperse/alert:** Bergen, *OBL I Know,* 307–, Fouda & Fielding, 141; **"big plan"/"far"/"My mother":** bin Ladens & Sasson, 279–; **Najwa asked/condition/ring:** ibid., 281–, 312. The children allowed to leave were two-year-old Nour, a boy, four-year-old Rukhaiya, a girl, and Abdul Rahman, a son born in 1978. In the spring of 2002, the Saudi-owned journal was to publish an interview supposedly given by one of bin Laden's wives, identified only as "A.S." Before 9/11, according to her purported interview, bin Laden "came to the house, gave me a telephone, and told me to call my family and tell them we were going somewhere else and that there would be no news of me for a long time." There is much accompanying detail, including a reference to the interviewee's "sons." The authenticity of the interview is dubious. Though the initials match those of

Amal al-Sadah, a seventeen-year-old Yemeni bin Laden married in late 2000 or early 2001, she has reportedly borne him
only a daughter. She could hardly have given birth to sons by
early 2002 (Nour et al.: bin Ladens & Sasson, 282; "A.S.":
BBC, AP, 3/13/02); **"soft-spoken":** bin Ladens & Sasson, 8;
Najwa prayed: ibid., 282.

Part VI: TWENTYFOUR HOURS

CHAPTER 29

459–61 **Fuller search/"Sheraton":** FBI IG, CR, 271–, 539n84–85,
Fenton, 312; **tracks all over:** *Newsweek*, 6/10/06, Lance,
Triple Cross, 349–, CR, 539n85; **Moussaoui detention/
agents begged/blocked/Samitshared/ Harry/Permission:**
FBI IG, Kiser to Samit, 9/10/01, Exhibit 334, *U.S. v. Zacarias
Moussaoui*, ABC News, 3/20/06; **Ashcroft turned down/not
increased:** Staff Statement 9, CO, *Newsweek*, 5/27/02,
Benjamin & Simon, 348; **"very docile":** *NYT*, 6/2/02.

461 **"The Big Wedding"/"aircraft":** John Cooley, a renowned
Middle East specialist, reported in 2002 that the "Big
Wedding" warning came in "late summer," and referred to an
attack within the United States involving airplanes. CNN,
reporting earlier, referred to a Jordanian warning "a few days"
before 9/11—but suggested that it related to a coming attack
not in the United States but on resort hotels in Jordan.
According to CIA director Tenet, "a source we were jointly
running with a Middle Eastern country" went to his foreign
handler on September 10 to say "something big" was about to
happen. He was ignored ("Wedding": Cooley, 229,
International Herald Tribune, 5/21/02, CNN, 11/19/01;
"something big": Tenet, 160).

461 **France passed:** *Le Figaro*, 11/1/01; **Feinstein/"One
of"/"Despite":** *Late Edition*, CNN, 7/1/01, Statement of
Dianne Feinstein, 5/17/01, http://feinstein.senate.gov,
Newsweek, 5/27/02, MSNBC, 9/28/06.

461–2 **Massoud assassinated/"journalists' ":** CR, 214, *Time*,
8/12/02, Burke, *Al-Qaeda*, 197. After 9/11, when U.S. strikes
on Afghanistan had routed Taliban and al Qaeda forces, *Wall
Street Journal* reporter Alan Cullison made remarkable discoveries on a computer that had belonged to the terrorists. The
hard drive contained a letter, apparently crafted by Ayman al-

Zawahiri, purporting to be the "journalists' " request for the Massoud interview (*WSJ*, 12/31/01); **widow:** Bergen, *OBL I Know*, 297–; **O'Neill hadwarned/frustrated/resigned/ "We're due":** Murray Weiss, *The Man Who Warned America*, NY: Regan, 2003, 180–, 320–, 362, 370–, *Frontline:* "The Man Who Knew," PBS, 10/3/02.

462–4 **Putin:** int. of Putin for *Iran & the West: Nuclear Confrontation*, BBC, 2/7/09. While Putin was to say clearly that he spoke with Bush the day before the attack, the former President referred in his 2010 memoir only to a conversation afterward (Bush, 369–); **Massoud assassination/analyzed implications:** Coll, *Holy War Inc.*, 582–, Tenet, 174; **memoir not refer:** e.g. see Bush, 187, 196; **Deputies tinkered/eliminate OBL:** CR, 206, Farmer, 68; **"literally headed":** CBS News, 9/11/02; **"eerie":** int. Rice by Bob Woodward, "Farmer Misc.," B9, NYC files, CF; **PM of Australia:** Sept. 10 entries, *Public Papers of the Presidents, 2001*, www.gpoaccess.gov; **helicopter:** Goldberg et al., Ch. 4; **Bush at Colony:** int. Katie Moulton, *Sarasota Magazine*, 11/01, *Sarasota Herald-Tribune*, 9/10/02; **"soft event":** *WP*, 1/27/02; **"Tomorrow"/"The match":** Report, JI, 32, 205, 375, Graham with Nussbaum, 138–, CBS News, 6/20/02, Bamford, *Shadow Factory*, 92.

464 **Arabs gathered/"finally":** MFR 04017535, 11/18/03, MFR 04017537, 11/18/03, CR 249–; **Dulles/Boston/Newark hotels:** "Hijackers Timeline [redacted]," 11/14/03, INTEL-WIRE, Stipulation, *U.S. v. Zacarias Moussaoui*, 3/1/06.

464–5 **drove Portland/Comfort Inn/ATM/Walmart/Pizza Hut/ phone calls:** What Atta bought at the Walmart, though, according to an FBI document, was a "6-volt battery converter"—a puzzling purchase for a would-be hijacker expecting to go to his death in the morning. "Chronology of Events for Hijackers, 8/16/01," *U.S. v. Zacarias Moussaoui*, Exhibits OG00020.2, FO07011, FO07021, FO07022, FO07023, FO07024, "265D-NY-280350, TWINBOM-PENTTBOM, Biographical Report," 11/26/01, National Drug Intelligence Center for the FBI, authors' collection, FBI press release, 10/14/01, entries for 9/10/01 & 9/11/01, "Hijackers Timeline [redacted]," 11/14/03, INTELWIRE, FBI 302 of [name redacted], 10/15/01, "FBI 302s of Interest," B17, T7, CF, FBI Timeline of 9–11 Hijacker Activity & Movements, "Timelines 9–11, 2 of 2," B20, T7, CF.

465 **Kara:** "Chaos and Ghosts," www.oredigger61.org, corr. Miles Kara, 2010.

465 **Rolince:** "Staff Notes of Int. Michael Rolince, 6/9/04," B70, T5, CF. The authors note that by an FBI account Caysan bin Don, the American Muslim who featured in an episode in January 2000—he was Bayoumi's companion the day he and Bayoumi had their supposedly chance meeting with newly arrived Mihdhar and Hazmi—was in Portland on September 11. It is hard to imagine, though, why Atta could conceivably have needed to meet with bin Don just before 9/11. Other hypotheses to try to explain the Portland expedition include the suggestion (not dissimilar to Miles Kara's) that Atta was worried lest the sight of as many as ten Arabs checking in at Boston for the two targeted flights to Los Angeles attract undue attention. The bottom line is that the trip remains unexplained. As the 9/11 Commission Report noted, "no physical, documentary, or analytical evidence" explains the Portland trip (location of bin Don: MFR 04018561, 11/20/03, MFR 04019254, 4/20/04, & see *National Enquirer*, 11/6/01; met bin Don: "Staff Notes of Int. Michael Rolince, 6/9/04," B70, T5, CF; other hypotheses: AP, 10/4/01, *NYT*, 9/11/02; Commission: CR, 451n1).

466–7 **ritual/"spiritual manual":** FBI report, "The 11 September Hijacker Cell Model," Feb. 03, INTELWIRE. The "spiritual manual" and the ritual it called for is described at length on pp. 161–64; **"noticed large amounts":** MFR 04020636, 2/2/04, CF, "Hijackers Timeline [redacted]," 11/14/03, INTELWIRE. Similar evidence had been found at locations used by the terrorists involved in the bombings of the U.S. embassy in Kenya in 1998 and of the USS *Cole* in 2000 (*New Yorker*, 7/10 & 7/17/06); **"the mutual pledge":** see sources for Ch. 14; **"God willing":** Fouda & Fielding, 109, translation of Binalshibh audiotape by Naouar Bioud, authors' collection; **green:** e.g. *Slate*, 6/9/09, "The Prophet's Mosque," www.sacred-destinations.com.

468 **When the news started:** translation of Binalshibh audiotape by Naouar Bioud, in authors' collection. The tape was obtained by reporter Yosri Fouda, and the material is used with his permission.

Part VII: **UNANSWERED QUESTIONS**

CHAPTER 30

471–2   *Le Figaro* **story/picked up by press/According to report:** *Le Figaro*, 10/21/01, Reuters, 11/14/01, *NYT*, 11/1/01, *Guardian* (U.K.), 11/1/01 int. Alexandra Richard.

472–3   **medical tests:** Rumors long circulated that bin Laden suffered from serious kidney disease requiring dialysis. His son Omar refuted that allegation in the 2009 memoir written with his mother, Najwa—both of whom had intimate contact with bin Laden until well into 2001. Omar conceded, however, that his father—along with others in the extended family—"had a tendency to suffer from kidney stones. Those stones caused immense pain until they had passed out of his body, but his kidneys were strong otherwise." Interviewed by the Pakistani journalist Hamid Mir on November 8, 2001— the only post-9/11 newspaper interview—bin Laden himself said, "My kidneys are all right" (rumors: e.g. Gunaratna, 48, *Eye Spy* magazine, no. 57, 2008; Omar: bin Ladens & Sasson, 172; "all right": ed. Lawrence, 144); **Callaway declined:** *Le Figaro*, 10/21/01; **Koval denied:** *NYT*, 11/1/01; **Mitchell told:** int. Alexandra Richard & authors' int. with Dubai source; **possible OBL did visit Dubai:** In the November 2001 interview cited above, bin Laden said, "I did not go to Dubai last year." The meeting with the CIA, of course, is not alleged to have happened the previous year—2000—but in July 2001 (ed. Lawrence, 144).

473–7   **Chouet:** int. & corr. Alain Chouet, 2009 & 2011, Chouet int. for *Le Monde*, 3/29/07, http://alain.chouet.free.fr. In the furor after initial publication of the story, a *New York Times* article suggested that the allegation of the Dubai meeting was planted by French intelligence "to suggest a continuing covert linkage between the CIA and bin Laden." In her description of how the story developed, however, reporter Alexandra Richard made clear that she first learned of it from a private source she had long trusted—in Dubai. As described in the text, moreover, she firmed it up with further research. Another French journalist, Richard Labévière, meanwhile, told the authors he received corroboration of the Dubai meeting from three other sources. (*NYT*, 11/1/01, *Guardian* [U.K.], 11/1/01, ints. Richard Labévière); **contacts with Taliban/ improved   cooperation/assistance/threats:** *Guardian*

(U.K.), 9/22/01, *Le Monde Diplomatique*, 1/02, *Nation*, 7/12/02, BBC News, 9/18/01; **Simons pressed:** *Guardian* (U.K.), 9/22/01, *Le Monde Diplomatique*, 1/02, *Nation*, 7/12/02, BBC News, 9/18/01; **Rice "whether any":** CR, 204.

477   **major stories re Atta:** e.g. *Chicago Tribune*, 9/16/01; **"had been trailing":** corr. Kate Connolly, 2009; **German intelligence interest/CIA/Joint Inquiry aired:** Report, JI, 29–, 183–; **Commission Report ignored:** CR, 495n81; **sequence of events/Zammar/Darkazanli/card/phone tapped:** ibid., CR, 164, 495n81, McDermott, 71–, *Chicago Tribune*, 10/5/03, "Germany's Imam Mamoun Darkazanli," Vol. 1, No. 8, www.jamestown.org. See earlier references to Zammar and Darkazanli in Chs. 24 and 27 and their related notes; **incoming call/"Marwan"/second/third calls:** "Memorandum, Investigative Proceedings Against Mohmammed Haydar Zammar," 11/19/01, Bundeskriminalamt ST 23–067–256/01, authors' collection, Report, JI, 185–, *Der Spiegel*, 11/23/06, *Frankfurter Allgemeine Sonntagzeitung*, 2/2/03, CR, 495n81; **"particularly valuable"/CIA "didn't sit"/"uncertain":** *NYT*, 22/24/04, 2/25/04, Testimony of George Tenet, Hearings, U.S. Senate Select Committee on Intelligence, 2/24/04, www.intelligence.senate.gov, Report, JI, 185–, Staff Statement 11, CO, Graham with Nussbaum, 61; **Volz:** McDermott, 71–, 75–, 278n11, *Stern* (Germany), 8/3/03, & see *Chicago Tribune*, 11/16/02.

477   **Landesamt:** Landesamt für Verfassungsschutz translates in English as the State Office for the Protection of the Constitution. Each of Germany's sixteen states has such an office, which in turn answer to the Bundesamt für Verfassungsschutz, the federal body. Together, they function as Germany's domestic intelligence service.

477   **"had knowledge"/"turned"/tried approaching:** *Chicago Tribune*, 11/16/02. In an extraordinary episode right after 9/11, German police raided Mamoun Darkazanli's apartment only to find it empty of documents. The raid was followed, however, by the mysterious delivery to the authorities of a bag of Darkazanli's papers—by a man claiming to be a burglar who had stolen them from the suspect. The "burglar's" account, however, appeared to be bogus. In light of the earlier CIA insistence on trying to persuade Darkazanli to become an informant, one German investigator remembered, "We all thought, 'CIA.' " As of this writing, Darkazanli was reportedly

still in Hamburg and at liberty (*Chicago Tribune*, 11/16/02).

478   **Jarrah stopped Dubai/"It was":** Corbin, 179–; **"because his name":** McDermott, 294n3; **learn fly/spread Islam:** Corbin, 180, McDermott, 186; **"What happened":** McDermott, 187.

478   **item redacted:** Ziad Jarrah chronology, "03009470—ACS Download Documents, Packet 6," CF. The FBI's "Hijackers' Timeline [redacted]" has also been heavily censored at that point. Because the episode was first reported as having occurred in January *2001*—not, as was in fact the case, in 2000—U.S. sources were initially able to deny that Jarrah had been questioned at Dubai in response to a CIA request. They also denied ever having been told about it. *Vanity Fair* reported in 2004 that the CIA had merely asked foreign border agencies to "question *anyone* [authors' italics] who may have been returning from a training camp in Afghanistan." While acknowledging that U.S. officials said it was untrue that Jarrah had been stopped specifically because his name was on a U.S.-supplied watchlist, investigative reporter Terry McDermott noted in 2005 that Washington had abandoned its initial denial it had been advised of about the Jarrah stop. "The United States," McDermott wrote, "has acknowledged in internal documents and in communications with German investigators that the Emiratis did contact them. . . . They decline to say what they told the Emiratis" (Timeline: "Hijackers Timeline [redacted]," 11/14/03, INTELWIRE; reported as 2001: CNN, 8/1/02, McDermott, 294n3, Corbin, 179–; deny: CNN, 8/1/02, Statement of Eleanor Hill, 9/20/02, JI; McDermott: McDermott, 186, 294n3).

478–9   **DIA/disquieting claim/four on radar:** Statement of Mark Zaid, U.S. Senate Judiciary Committee, 9/21/05, MFR 04021341, 7/13/04, CF, MFR [names & number redacted], Defense HUMINT Service Officers, Bagram Base, 10/21/03, CF; *WSJ*, 11/17/05, *NYT*, 8/9/05, 8/11/05, Fox News, 8/28/05, Lance, *Triple Cross*, 330–; **"data mining"/"use of high-powered"/visa records:** Anthony Shaffer, *Operation Dark Heart*, NY: Thomas Dunne, 2010, 17–,164–, 245–, 272–, *Bergen Record* (N.J.), 8/14/05.

479   **evidence destroyed:** Though the Able Danger claim had not yet emerged when Congress's Joint Inquiry was at work, its staff did question Major Keith Alexander of the U.S. Army Intelligence and Security Command, and twice visited the unit from which much of the Able Danger material reportedly

originated. On both occasions, asked whether they knew of any evidence that the government had prior knowledge or should have had prior knowledge of the attack, military personnel said they knew of none.

A Defense Department report, and a Senate Intelligence Committee review, were to conclude in 2006 that the Able Danger claims were unsupported by the evidence. It is clear from both documents that witnesses' memories were confused, as one might expect so long after the fact. Relevant documentary material that existed in 2003 now does not. Some was inadvertently destroyed during an office move. Some duplicate documentation Shaffer kept at his office, his attorney told the Committee on the Judiciary, was "apparently destroyed—for reasons unknown—by DIA in spring 2004." The DOD report says no such documentation was found at Shaffer's office (Joint Inquiry: corr. Miles Kara, 2011; claims unsupported: Defense report: "Alleged Misconduct by Senior DOD Officials Concerning the Able Danger Program & Lt. Col. Anthony Shaffer," U.S. Dept of Defense, Office of the Inspector General, 9/18/06; Senate review: Roberts & Rockefeller to colleagues, 12/22/06, www.intelligence. senate.gov; had Commission followed/destroyed?: Statement of Mark Zaid, Judiciary Committee, U.S. Senate, 9/21/05, Shaffer, 164–, 246–, Kean & Hamilton, 114, 294–, MFR 04021341, 7/13/04, CF: Zelikow Afterword, CR (abridged), NY: Norton, 2011, 602–).

479 **Grenzfahndung:** The two known to have been under border watch were Said Bahaji and Mounir Motassadeq (ints. Mounir el-Motassadeq, Motassadeq's lawyer Udo Jacob, Dr. Manfred Murck, Dr. Herbert Müller, McDermott, 73–, 297n23, *Stern* [Germany], 8/13/03, *Frankfurter Allgemeine Sonntagszeitung,* 2/2/03).

480 **officials unhelpful:** The two other organizations that declined interview requests were the Generalbundesanwalt, or Public Prosecutor's Office—which has responsibility for terrorist cases—and the Bundeskriminalamt, the Federal Criminal Police Agency. The latter was the source of most German-related information in the 9/11 Commission Report.

480–1 **Müller "Atta was":** Dr. Müller serves with the Landesamt für Verfassungsschutz Baden-Württemberg—Stuttgart is the state capital of Baden-Württemberg; **"Some countries":** Staff Statement 11, CO; **intermittent friction:** Executive

Summary, "Report on CIA Accountability with Respect to the 9/11 Attacks," Office of the Inspector General, 06/05, Report, JI, 186–, 274–; **Polt:** MFR 04016468, 10/9/03; **"They lied":** int. Dirk Laabs.

481 **coded conversation:** MFR 04019350, 3/18/04 (re Moussaoui team briefing), CF, corr. Kristen Wilhelm, 2011, CR, 245–530n151–152, Staff Statement 16, CO. The exchange was referred to earlier on p. 420.

482 **CIA-FBI wrangling:** www.huffingtonpost.co.uk

482 **intercept by Germans?:** At one stage, in 2000, the Germans had repeatedly discussed applying for clearance to wiretap the Marienstrasse apartment, but at that point decided there was insufficient evidence to justify the request. The 9/11 Commission Report states: "Only after 9/11 would it be discovered that [KSM] had communicated with a phone that was used by Binalshibh . . . the links to Binalshibh might not have been an easy trail to find and would have required substantial cooperation from the German government" (discussed: *Vanity Fair*, 11/04, *NYT*, 6/20/02; "Only after": CR, 277, & see 245).

483 **Berlin visit:** The German officials known to have spoken with the U.S. congressional delegation were Ronald Schill, minister of the interior for Hamburg, Deputy Minister Walter Wellinghausen, Reinhard Wagner, chief of the Landesamt für Verfassungsschutz Hamburg, his deputy Manfred Murck, and Bruno Franz of the Hamburg police. (Contemporary information provided to the authors)

CHAPTER 31

484 **Soon after 1:00 P.M./"Oh, Jesus":** Suskind, *One Percent Doctrine*, 3–, & see Tenet, 167. Tenet's aide Michael Morell, the president's CIA briefer, remembered of the video-conference on the afternoon of 9/11, "They had done name traces on the flight manifests. And when we got to Omaha, and we got to the briefing area, George Tenet briefed the President on the fact that we already knew three of these guys were al Qaeda." Tenet has recalled that, when he told Bush the CIA had been aware of information about Mihdhar and Hazmi he "shot Mike Morell one of those, 'I thought I was supposed to be the first to know' looks." The reference to three, as distinct from two, of the men on the planes being associated with al Qaeda presumably includes Nawaf al-Hazmi's brother Salem (Suskind, 9; Tenet, 169).

484–6 **manifest:** Exhibit P200054, *U.S. v. Zacarias Moussaoui,;*
Tenet claimed/"CIA had multiple": Tenet, 195–, 205;
Tenet on oath/"like a grand": Shenon, 256–; **"We just
didn't believe"/outraged:** *New Yorker,* 11/8/04.

486–7 **NSA identified/Hada/"hub":** Bamford, *Shadow Factory,* 7–,
FBI report, "PENTTBOM, Summary of Captioned
Investigation," 11/5/01, authors' collection, transcript, *Nova:
The Spy Factory,* 2/3/09, www.pbs.org, Wright, 275–; **NSA did
not share:** Report, JI, 145, *Atlantic,* 12/04, Bamford, *Shadow
Factory,* 16, 26–, & see Scheuer, *Marching Toward Hell,* 91–.

487 **Hada phone/FBI/1998 attack/OBL phone/link:** Report, JI,
129, 145, Wright, 277–, 343, Testimony of [unnamed] CIA
Officer [accepted as Wilshire], 9/20/02, JI. Bin Laden stopped
using his satellite phone in September 1998, apparently
because he knew or guessed it was being intercepted (*WP,*
12/22/05, Report, JI, 69).

487 **1999 intercept/"Khalid"/"Nawaf"/Malaysia:** The intercepted conversation also included a reference to "Salem" as
making the trip, too—evidently Hazmi's brother Salem, who
was also to be one of the hijackers. Although the NSA had
access to information indicating that the three first names
were all linked to the surnames Hazmi and Mihdhar, they did
not pass those names to the CIA and FBI—thus making the
CIA's task more difficult than it need have been (CR, 181, JI
Report, 145–, 155–, Staff Statement 2, CO, Bamford, *Shadow
Factory,* 16–).

487–8 **"something more":** CR, 181; **"operational"/"operatives":**
ibid., Report, JI, 144; **passport photographed:** The Dubai
stopover and the copying of Mihdhar's passport was briefly
mentioned earlier in Ch. 27, p. 319. **"This is as good":**
Mayer, 18; **Mihdhar tracked/photographed/pay phones/
computers:** CR, 181–, Staff Statement 2, CO, *Die Zeit,*
10/2/02, FBI IG; **directors/Berger/Clarke:** Staff Statement
2, CO, CR, 181.

488 **Bangkok:** Staff Statement 2, CO. It would later be
established that two suspects who had already, on January 6,
made short trips out of Malaysia—for only a matter of
hours—had also been Attash and Hazmi (Staff Statement 2,
CO, CR, 159).

489–92 **according CIA trail lost/Thai authorities responded/Jan.
15 to LA/cables:** CR, 181–, FBI IG, Staff Statement 2, CO,
Tenet, 196–. The two terrorists flew in aboard UA 002,

arriving at 1:27 p.m. Bin Laden aide Attash had reportedly headed back to Afghanistan via Karachi to report to bin Laden (UA 002: "Hijackers Timeline [redacted]," 11/14/03, INTELWIRE; Attash: CR, 159); **"OBL associates"**: Executive Summary, Report on CIA Accountability with Respect to the 9/11 Attacks, Office of the Inspector General, CIA, 6/05; **"Action Required"**: Report, JI, 147; **"The threat"**: CR, 176, 501n17; **"It is important"**: ibid., CTC Watchlisting Guidance, cited at Report, JI, 1; **CIA did not alert State/FBI**: Report, JI, 40–, 144–, Executive Summary, Report on CIA Accountability with Respect to the 9/11 Attacks, Office of the Inspector General, CIA, 6/05, FBI IG, Graham with Nussbaum, 7–, CR, 355; **"promised to let"**: Staff Statement 2, CO; **"Michelle"/"to the FBI"**: FBI IG, & see Executive Summary, Report on CIA Accountability with Respect to the 9/11 Attacks, Office of the Inspector General, CIA, 6/05; **"James"/"as soon as"/"*in the event*"**: Statement of Eleanor Hill, 9/20/02, JI, Report, JI, 81, FBI IG; **refused interview**: FBI IG; **"Michelle" prevaricated**: FBI IG; **Wilshire/"did not know"**: ibid. In the transcript of a hearing before a U.S. Senate subcommittee, the former deputy chief's name is rendered not as "Wilshire" but as "Wilshere." The authors have used "Wilshire," the spelling most commonly used. ("The Global Reach of al Qaeda," Hearings, Subcommittee on International Operations & Terrorism, Committee on Foreign Relations, U.S. Senate, 107th Cong., 1st Sess., 12/18/01, 7–); **Wilshire deliberately/draft cable/Miller CIR/"pls hold"**: FBI IG, & see Executive Summary, Report on CIA Accountability with Respect to the 9/11 Attacks, Office of the Inspector General, CIA, 6/05.

492   **"Doug came"/"Is this a no go"**: Bamford, *Shadow Factory*, 18–. In a detailed note for his book *Disconnecting the Dots*, published in 2011, author Kevin Fenton would note that Rossini was to resign from the FBI in 2008 after breaching regulations. He had, according to an FBI press release, used Bureau computers to find out information for personal purposes. Fenton argues cogently, however, that the lapse does not detract from Rossini's credibility on the matter of the blocked CIR. The fact of its blocking, and that the agent saw relevant cables in 2000, is well documented (Fenton, proof copy kindly shared with the authors, 2011, 44n26).

492   **"unable to locate"**: FBI IG; **Wilshire int. redacted:** corr.

Kristen Wilhelm, 2011.

492 **Wilshire proposed:** FBI IG. Wilshire's actions in July 2001 were reportedly spurred by his review of the CIA cable and email traffic recording Mihdhar's movements in January the previous year—including the information that Mihdhar had a valid U.S. multiple-entry visa. For reasons unknown, but perhaps because he feared discovery of the fact that he had been in the United States the previous year, Mihdhar had meanwhile obtained a new passport and a new visa in June 2001. He used this new visa when he reentered the United States on July 4. There is no evidence that Wilshire or anyone else at CIA was aware of the new passport and visa at the time the search for Mihdhar was renewed in July 2001 (Wilshire spurred: CR, 267–, FBI IG; new passport/visa: Staff Report, 9/11 & Terrorist Travel, CO, 33–.)

492 **Following a series:** FBI IG, CR, 267–, & re discovered/search see Chs. 27, 28, & 29. Aside from the events described here, the CIA and the FBI disputed each other's versions of events about the identification of Tawfiq bin Attash (referred to in the Commission Report as "Khallad") in the Malaysia surveillance photos. The identification was made by a source the FBI and the CIA shared—a circumstance that led to a prolonged tussle between the agencies. This barely penetrable story is detailed in the Justice Department's inspector general's report. The bottom line is that FBI agents working the *Cole* investigation, who knew of Attash's connection to that attack, would have been far more concerned—and pressed to know all the CIA knew about the Malaysia meeting—had they been told that Attash had been present. As it was, they would learn nothing of Attash's link to Mihdhar and Hazmi until after 9/11. The CIA's performance on this matter notwithstanding, it is evident that once the information on Mihdhar's and Hazmi's likely presence in the United States was passed to the Bureau in August 2001, the FBI fumbled badly. As described in Chapter 27 of this book, the agent at Bureau headquarters who processed the information misinterpreted regulations, with the result that the assignment of looking for Mihdhar and Hazmi was given to an inexperienced intelligence agent, rather than to the experienced criminal agents working the *Cole* investigation (FBI IG, Wright, 340–, *New Yorker*, 7/10 & 17/06).

493 **"The weight":** Staff Statment 2, CO; **"that Mihdhar":** FBI

IG; **CIA summary/acknowledged/accountability board:** Executive Summary, Report on CIA Accountability with Respect to the 9/11 Attacks, Office of the Inspector General, CIA, 6/05; **Goss declined/"amongst the finest":** Director's Statement on Office of Inspector General's Report, "CIA Accountability with Respect to the 9/11 Attacks," 10/6/05, www.cia.gov.

493 **"excessive workload":** Executive Summary, Report on CIA Accountability with Respect to the 9/11 Attacks, Office of the Inspector General, CIA, 6/05; **"nobody read":** *NYT,* 10/17/02; **"All the processes":** Report, JI, 151.

495 **"It is clear":** Fenton, 311, 104. Fenton goes on to suggest that CIA officers may have been aware of the 9/11 plot and "desired the outcome we saw on our television screens." Fenton has done an intriguing analysis, but the authors do not accept that there is sufficient evidence or rationale to accept such a heinous possibility (e.g., Fenton, 95, 239, 281, 241–, 327).

495 **"good operational":** Executive Summary, Report on CIA Accountability with Respect to the 9/11 Attacks, Office of the Inspector General, CIA, 6/05; **Maxwell:** *New Yorker,* 7/10 & 17/06; **"They purposely":** Bamford, *Pretext,* 224.

495 **run operations in U.S.:** For evidence of the CIA having engaged in operations within the United States, readers could consult, for example, the report of the Senate committee that investigated intelligence agency abuses in the wake of the Watergate scandal. That report, published in 1976, details a number of such operations, including four mail-opening programs spanning a twenty-year period, and CHAOS, launched in 1967 to gather information that might reveal foreign government influence on antiwar and civil rights protesters (Final Report, *Supplementary Detailed Staff Reports on Intelligence Activities and the Rights of Americans,* U.S. Senate Select Committee to Study Government Operations with Respect to Intelligence Activities, 94th Cong., 2nd Sess., Washington, D.C.: U.S. Govt. Printing Office, 1976, 559–, 679–).

496–8 **Yousef/"wanted to continue"/"fought":** *New York,* 3/27/95; **some Bureau agents:** Wright, 312; **"Without penetrations"/select group:** Report, JI, 388–. This was the Small Group, which typically included Secretary of State Madeleine Albright, Secretary of Defense William Cohen,

Attorney General Janet Reno, National Security Adviser Sandy Berger, CIA director Tenet, and Chairman of the Joint Chiefs General Hugh Shelton, and counterterrorism co-ordinator Richard Clarke (CR, 119-, 199, Shenon, 255); **Berger episode:** unless otherwise indicated—Biography of Samuel Berger, http://clinton4.nara.gov, Investigative Summary & Exhibits, "Report of Investigation: Samuel R. Berger," Office of the Inspector General, National Archives & Records Administration, www.fas.org, Kean & Hamilton, 183-, 297, Shenon, 1-249-, Fox News, 1/23/07; **MAAR/recommendations:** Clarke, 215-, 219-, CR, 182, 504n78, Farmer, 41; **handwritten notes?:** Farmer, 41; **"desperate":** ibid., 289; **"What information?":** www.usnewswire.com, 7/20/04.

499   **"Michelle" "we need":** Staff Statement 2, CO; **"to determine":** Report, JI, 147; **"believed they were":** KSM SUBST. Ramzi Binalshibh was to tell reporter Yosri Fouda after 9/11, before his arrest, that "Brothers Marwan [Shehhi] and Ziad [Jarrah] were tailed by security officers throughout their reconnaissance flight from New York to California . . . But Allah was with them" (Fouda & Fielding, 135); **Cambone note:** Notes of Stephen Cambone, 9/11/01, released under FOIA to Thad Anderson, www.outragedmoderates.org.

CHAPTER 32

502   **"Had the hijackers":** Kean & Hamilton, 234; **"The terrorists"/"a sensitive":** press briefing, 9/18/01, www.defenselink.mil; **no evidence Iraq;** CR, 66, Staff statement 15, CO.

503   **Iran not know re 9/11:** CR, 241. Iranian contacts with al Qaeda went back at least as far as bin Laden's time in Sudan. Up to ten of the future muscle hijackers traveled through Iran, as did Binalshibh—who said they did so because Iran did not stamp Saudi passports. Numerous al Qaeda operatives fled to Iran following the U.S. invasion of Afghanistan after 9/11, and members of the bin Laden family were given sanctuary there. In 2010, in what was surely a crude exercise in political mischief making, Iran's president, Mahmoud Ahmadinejad, claimed that 9/11 had been merely a "big fabrication" to justify U.S. actions abroad (CR, 240, trial transcript, *U.S. v. Ali Mohamed*, U.S. District Court for the Southern District of NY, 10/20/00, Shenon, 372, int. Thomas

Joscelyn, *FrontPage Magazine*, 9/28/07, ABC News, 2/11/10, *Newsweek*, 8/19/02, Tenet, 244, *The Independent* [U.K.], 3/7/10); **"convincing evidence"**: www.thedailybeast.com, 5/20/11, *Daily Mail* (U.K.), 5/20/11, www.newsmax.com, 5/19/11; **"provided direct"**: *Harlish et al v. Usama bin Laden et al*, U.S. District Court for the Southern District of NY, Case No. 1:03-cv-09848-GBD, Doc. 294, 12/22/11, NYT, 12/16/11.

503–4 **last-minute changes/Snell/Jacobson/De:** Shenon, 398–.

504–6 **Bandar delight/posted:** press statement, 7/22/04, www.saudiembassy.net. Prince Bandar's own name and that of his wife, Princess Haifa—whose name featured in an intriguing part of the investigators' work, described later, in the Notes to Ch. 33—made fleeting appearances in the Report's endnotes, but not in the text (CR, 482n66, 498n123, 557n27, 563n19); **"no evidence"/"problematic"/"a commitment"**: CR, 171, 371–; **Khilewi/"A Saudi citizen"**: *Middle East Quarterly*, 9/98, & see *WP*, 8/25/94, *New Yorker*, 10/22/01; **Khalifa:** see Ch. 20 and related Notes, "In re search of luggage and personal belongings, *Khalifa v. U.S*," 3/6/95 cited in ed. Berger, *Khalifa*, "Top al Qaeda Fundraiser Dead," www.counterterrorismblog.org.

506 **limousine/"high-ranking"/Prince Sultan:** Anonymous, *Through Our Enemies' Eyes*, Washington, D.C.: Brassey's, 2002 [author was in fact Michael Scheuer], 138–, Lance, *Triple Cross*, 166, "Mohammed Jamal Khalifa: Life & Death Secrets," INTELWIRE. *Philippine Daily Inquirer*, 8/11/00. The authors are unaware of any response by or on behalf of Prince Sultan bin Abdul Aziz to the report that he welcomed Khalifa home. Nor have they been able to establish that Khalifa did carry a diplomatic passport.

506–8 **"Since 1994"/" '96 is the key":** *New Yorker*, 10/16/01; **Paris meeting/protection money:** Complaint, *Thomas Burnett et al. v. al Baraka Investment & Development et al.*, U.S. District Court for the District of Columbia, pt. 1080, Trento, 306–, Greg Palast, *The Best Democracy Money Can Buy*, NY: Plume, 2004, 99–; **Kerrey:** *LAT*, 6/20/04; **"It's a lovely":** transcript, *Frontline:* "Saudi Time Bomb," www.pbs.org; **Turki recalled:** *Time*, 8/31/03, int. Turki, *OnLine NewsHour: Inside the Kingdom*, 1/21/02, www.pbs.org, Lacey, *Inside the Kingdom*, 208–, 364, Wright, 266–, 288–, Anthony Cordesman, "Saudi Security & the War on Terrorism," Center for Strategic &

International Studies, 4/22/02, Bergen, 240; **Others say two trips:** Rashid, 48 & see *LAT,* 6/20/04; **Khaksar/deal:** *Guardian,* 3/2/03, *NYT,* 3/24/09 & see *WP,* 1/15/06; **Turki deny:** MSNBC, 9/5/03; **met with OBL:** Reeve, 194—citing interview with U.S. intelligence source; **"at least two"/"The deal was":** *U.S. News & World Report,* 1/6/02; **named the two:** Henderson, formally a journalist with the BBC and the *Financial Times,* later named Naif and Sultan bin Abdul Aziz in this connection in articles in *The Wall Street Journal* and in a paper published by the Washington Institute for Near East Policy. The authors are not aware that Prince Naif or Prince Sultan has commented on the allegation (*WSJ,* 8/3/05, "After King Abdullah: Succession in Saudi Arabia," *Policy Focus 96,* 8/09);"**hundreds"/"Saudi official":** int. & corr. Simon Henderson, *WSJ,* 8/12/02.

509–10 **7,000:** *WSJ,* 2/15/11; **"They would go out":** MSNBC, 9/5/03 & see *WP,* 7/19/07; **"We've got":** *U.S. News & World Report,* 10/11/98; **"an interminable"/"Your Royal Highness":** Tenet, 106–; **Gore/"The United":** CR, 122.

510–11 **"never lifted"/clerics:** Baer, *See No Evil,* 33. The two clerics were Salman al-Awadah and Safar al-Hawali (*National Review,* 3/11/03, Erik Stakelback, "The Saudi Hate Machine," 12/17/03, www.investigativeproject.org); **"the Saudi government":** Report, JI, 110; **"As one of"/"foreign enemy":** Scheuer, *Marching Toward Hell,* 72, 15; **"You've got to be":** Wright, 238.

511 **"All the answers":** Brisard & Dasquié, xxix. The O'Neill conversation was with Jean-Charles Brisard, who began investigating terrorist finances for French intelligence in 1997. After 9/11, he became a lead investigator for the legal firm Motley Rice in connection with the civil action brought by 9/11 victims' families against a list of Saudi-based Islamic charities, a number of financial institutions, and several members of the Saudi royal family. He provided written testimony to the U.S. Committee on Banking, Housing and Urban Affairs in 2003 (ints. Jean-Charles Brisard, Written Testimony, Committee on Banking, Housing & Urban Affairs, U.S. Senate, 10/22/03, www.banking.senate.gov, Brisard & Dasquié, xxvii–, xxi).

511 **longtime head:** Prince Turki had resigned as GID chief, after a quarter of a century, just ten days before 9/11. The reason for the resignation remains unclear. Turki's departure was the

more striking, reportedly, because he had been confirmed in his post as recently as the end of May (Simon Henderson, "A Prince's Mysterious Disappearance," NPR, 10/22/10, Hamel, 237).

511–13 **"At the instruction":** *Arab News*, 9/18/02. On another occasion, in a 2010 CNN interview, Prince Turki said much the same. "From my previous experience, there is a continuous exchange of information between the CIA and the Saudi security agencies" (CNN, 11/17/10); **GID/U.S. understanding:** e.g., Cordesman, "Saudi Security"; **specifically/"What we told":** *USA Today*, 10/16/03, *Salon*, 10/18/03; **Bandar hinted:** transcript of int. Bandar, *Frontline: "*Looking for Answers," www.pbs.org; **Abdullah now king:** Abdullah had succeeded to the throne in 2005, on the death of his long-ailing and incapacitated half-brother King Fahd; **"Saudi security":** ABC News, 11/2/07, CNN, 11/2/07; **"We have sent"/British deny:** John Simpson int. of King Abdullah, BBC News, 10/29/07, CNN, 10/29/07; **denial:** Wright, 448; **silence:** Scheuer, *Marching Toward Hell*, 72–; **"There is not":** *USA Today*, 10/16/03.

513 **Turki stood by/Badeeb:** Wright, 448, 310. A Saudi security consultant, Nawaf Obaid, also told author Lawrence Wright that the terrorists' names were passed to the CIA station chief in Riyadh. Wright believed Turki's 2003 account, and indicated in a *New Yorker* article that the CIA had consulted the Saudi authorities—after learning from an intercept on the Yemen phone "hub" that Mihdhar was headed to Kuala Lumpur (Wright, 310, 376n, 448, *New Yorker*, 7/10 & 16/06).

513 **Scheuer/"fabrication":** Scheuer, *Marching Toward Hell*, 72–; **Bandar/Commission:** MFR of int. Prince Bandar, Access Restricted, Item (3 pages) withdrawn, 10/14/08, CF.

514 **Turki/"I can":** corr. Kristen Wilhelm. This reply to the authors' inquiry is known as a "Glomar Response" to a request under the Freedom of Information Act—so called after the first occasion on which it was used, when the CIA sought to prevent publication of a *Los Angeles Times* story on the agency's operation to raise a sunken Soviet submarine. The U.S. ship that had been intended for use in the operation to raise the sub was called the *Glomar Explorer*. The Glomar Response has been used in cases involving both national security and privacy issues ("The Glomar Response," http://nsarchive.wordpress.com).

514–15 **"penetrated al Qaeda"**: *Seattle Times*, 10/29/01; **returned to Saudi/disclosed**: Report, JI, 131–.

515 **"presented with"**: Staff Report, "9/11 & Terrorist Travel," 12, 15, 37. Before 9/11, according to the Commission's staff report on terrorist travel, neither State Department personnel processing visa applications nor immigration inspectors were aware of such indicators. Even two years after the attacks, the information had "yet to be unclassified and disseminated to the field."

515 **Commission footnote:** The Commission footnote appears to distinguish the cases of Mihdhar, the Hazmi brothers, and two other hijackers from those of the other ten Saudi hijackers. This may reflect the possibility that only the passports of Mihdhar and his named comrades were marked by the Saudi authorities. Absent fuller and clearer information, it is impossible to know (CR, 563n32).

515 **"contained a secret"**: Bamford, *Shadow Factory*, 58; **Trento account/"We had been"**: Joe Trento, "The Real Intelligence Cover-up," 8/6/03 & Joseph Trento & Susan Trento, "The No Fly List," 1/11/10, http://dcbureau.org, & Trento & Trento, refs., conv. Joseph Trento.

516 **Kuala Lumpur "to spy"**: Trento & Trento, 7–. The administrator of the Islamic Center of San Diego, whom Mihdhar and Hazmi asked for assistance following their arrival in early 2000, said after 9/11 that he had "suspected that Mihdhar might have been an intelligence agent of the Saudi government" (CR, 517n29, 220).

516 **Mihdhar multiple-entry visa:** Trento & Trento, 8. According to the Trentos, citing Michael Springmann, who had years earlier served as head of the visa department in the Jeddah consulate, the CIA would have known this fact even sooner—because a CIA officer in the Jeddah consulate "routinely approved visas for Saudi intelligence operatives as a courtesy" (Trento & Trento, 8—see Michael Springmann, "A Sin Concealed—the Visas for Terrorists Program," 12/13/07, http://visasforterrorists.blogspot.com).

516 **"were perceived"**: Trento & Trento, 9; **"Many terrorists"**: ibid, 187; **"because they were"**: Joe Trento, "The Real Intelligence Cover-up," 8/6/03, http://dcbureau.org; **"In fact"**: Trento & Trento, 9.

517 **account bumps facts?:** The Trento account, for example, asserts that the "complacency" of the Bush administration in summer 2001 is explained by CIA assurances that it had high-

level penetration of al Qaeda via the GID. In fact, as documented in this book, the CIA leadership was far from complacent that summer, desperately worried and telling the White House—notably Condoleezza Rice—as much (Trento & Trento, 193; see—re far from complacent—pp. 409–11).

517 **"[name redacted]":** Executive Summary, Report on CIA Accountability with Respect to the 9/11 Attacks, 6/05, www.cia.gov; **"hostile service"/passed to al Qaeda:** Risen, *State of War,* 181–; **"On some occasions":** Report, JI, 274; **Rahman defense:** *New York,* 3/27/95.

517–18 **screen saver:** The intelligence counterparts who told the CIA about bin Laden's picture being used as a screen saver were those of Jordan—apparently in the late 1990s (Risen, 182); **"80% sympathetic":** *The Times* (London), 7/5/04.

CHAPTER 33

519–20 **tens of thousands:** Reuters, 9/11/01; **honked horns:** transcript, *Frontline:* "Saudi Time Bomb," www.pbs.org; **killed camels:** int. of Saad al-Fagih for *Frontline:* "Looking for Answers," www.pbs.org; **screen savers/"somebody":** int. of person in Saudi Arabia who asked to remain anonymous; **Ahmed/"muted"/"So, they lost":** Qanta Ahmed, 395.

520 **survey/Prince Nawwaf:** The survey was conducted by the Saudi GID, the intelligence service, and leaked to *The New York Times* a year later by a U.S. administration official. Prince Nawwaf had become GID chief following the resignation of Prince Turki. In a 2004 interview, Prince Bandar was to claim the situation was very different, that a Zogby poll "showed 91 percent of Saudis said they like America." What the poll actually said was that 91 percent of Saudis said they had "no quarrel with the people of the United States, yet their overall impression of the American people is 70% unfavorable, 24% favorable" (leaked survey: *NYT,* 1/27/02, *Middle East Economic Digest,* 9/14/01; Bandar: int. Bandar, *Meet the Press,* NBC, 4/25/04).

521 **"Almost unanimously":** Kean & Hamilton, 113.

521–2 **Bandar/"not Arabs"/"My God":** *New Yorker,* 3/24/03; **Palestinians celebrating:** There were numerous reports of Palestinians celebrating the attacks. It has been suggested, though, that some news footage of Palestinians supposedly celebrating 9/11 was a distortion—that it in fact showed celebration of something else. For more on the reaction to

9/11 across the Middle East, see Ch. 14, pp. 202–3 (ed. Woods, 12); **"condemned"**: statement, 9/11/01 cied in Cordesman, "Saudi Official Statements on Terrorism, After the Sept. 11 Attacks," Center for Strategic & International Studies, 11/01; **Abdullah fumed/declined/snapped/"I reject"/Bush responded**: *WP*, 2/10/02, *New Yorker,* 3/24/03, Unger, *House of Bush, House of Saud,* 241–, *Online NewsHour: Inside the Kingdom,* www.pbs.org.

522   **Abdullah pulled**: *Atlantic Monthly,* 5/03, Lacey, *Inside the Kingdom,* 232, *WP,* 2/12/02. Though Saudi Arabia at the time produced only some 18 percent of the crude oil consumed by the United States, it has what other oil-producing countries do not have—the world's only surplus production capacity. It means that world oil prices are controlled by Saudi Arabia, according to its decisions as to how much oil to make available at any given time. It had used the oil weapon in 1973, after the Yom Kippur War, by joining with other countries in cutting off the oil supply and in 1990–1991—in reverse—by increasing supply when Iraqi oil was cut off during the Gulf War (*Atlantic,* 2/21/08, *Statistical Abstract of the U.S., 2007,* Washington, D.C.: U.S. Govt. Printing Office, 2007, 821).

523–5   **15 were Saudi**: *Newsweek,* 11/19/01, *New Yorker,* 3/24/03; **"That was a"**: transcript, *Frontline:* "House of Saud," www.pbs.org; **75 royals/Caesars Palace**: Las Vegas to Counterterrorism, 9/25/01, FBI documents obtained under FOIA by Judicial Watch; **One of OBL's brothers**: Unger, 7; **more than 20**: e.g., re International Flight 441 from Boston, 9/17/03, "Ryan Air folder," B70, T5, CF; **Prince Ahmed/yearling**: Jason Levin, *From the Desert to the Derby,* NY: Daily Racing Form Press, 2002, 1, 15, Unger, 7, 255–; **unable to charter/flight on 13th**: MFR of Dan Grossi, "Dan Grossi, Tampa-Lexington Flight," B70, T5, CF, **"his father or his uncle"**: ibid., Unger, 9; **Bandar statement**: press release, 9/12/01, www.saudiembassy.net; **Bush appointment/ welcomed/cigars**: Unger, 7, William Simpson, 315, *New Yorker,* 3/24/03; **assistant rang/Watson/ Clarke**: int. of Bandar, *Meet the Press,* 4/24/04, Staff Report, 9/11 & Terrorist Travel, 171–, MFR 04019823, 6/3/04, CR, 557, Shenon, 287; **photo published**: Woodward, *State of Denial,* facing p. 274; **"not inclined"**: corr. Jodie Steck, George W. Bush Presidential Library, 2011.

525   **Florida/Kentucky flight**: e.g., Unger, 7–. The confusion

about the Tampa charter persisted in part because the FBI accepted, even after having been challenged by journalists, a secondhand report that Prince Ahmed's son and his companions had driven to Lexington. The prince in question, Prince Sultan bin Fahd, had in fact been Ahmed's *nephew*, and the group had *flown*. The FBI's reports moreover, reflected confusion as to when U.S. airspace reopened to charter flights (Final Draft of response to October 2003 *Vanity Fair* article, "Saudi Flights," B68, T5, CF, The Saudi Flights—A Summary, "Saudi Flights," B6, Dan Marcus Files, CF, CTD to Counterterrorism, 9/24/03, FBI 265A-NY-280350, serial 1234567890, *Vanity Fair,* 10/03).

525 **after airspace open:** FAA Notices to Airmen [NOTAM], 1/9817, 1/9832, 1/9853, www.aopa.org, corr. Laura Brown, FAA. The records show that U.S. airspace was open to almost all aircraft—including charter flights—as of 11:00 A.M. EDT on September 13. The exception was for "general aviation" flights—which, contrary to previous reporting, did not include charters such as the Tampa flight. In any event, the Tampa-to-Lexington flight took off at approximately 4:30 P.M.

525–6 **on their way home:** Staff Report, 9/11 & Terrorist Travel, 171–, 270n49/50; **charter:** Judicial Watch press release, 6/20/07, Counterterrorism to Boston, 9/21/01, FBI 265A-NY-280350, serial 1652; **watchlist:** CR, 558, n31; **most not interviewed:** CR, 557n28. It has been reported that one of those interviewed was Prince Ahmed, but there is no evidence of such an interview in FBI files thus far released (The Saudi Flights—A Summary, "Saudi Flights," B6, Dan Marcus Files, CF).

526 **agents interviewed family/Omar:** FBI 302s of ints. Bin Laden family members 9/13–24/01 (inc. Omar Awadh), all in "Ryan Air folder," B70, T5, CF.

526 **Omar shared/briefly investigated:** Coll, *The Bin Ladens,* 483–, 526–, Brisard & Dasquie, 176–, *WP,* 10/2/03. The group, of which Abdullah bin Laden was listed as president, was the World Assembly of Muslim Youth, or WAMY. The U.S. branch was operated by Abdullah, according to *The Washington Post,* until 9/11. Though it has been reported that Abdullah was on a flight with Saudis on board that departed on September 20—Ryan International 441—his name is not on the passenger list supplied by the charter company (Coll,

483–, *WP*, 10/2/03, passenger list in "Saudi Flights, FBI Docs., 3 of 4," B70, T5, CF, Staff Report, 9/11 & Terrorist Travel, 272n94).

526 **"Although":** *NYT*, 3/27/05; **"there is the existence":** CNN, 9/4/03. The reference is to the brother of Adel al Jubeir, mentioned earlier in this chapter (*Washington Report on Middle East Affairs*, 11/07).

527 **public relations firms/Another firm:** The firms initially hired were Burson Marsteller and Qorvis Communications. Patton Boggs was used for the contacts with Congress. On one infamous occasion, Saudi PR maneuvers misfired. New York mayor Giuliani handed back a $10 million donation made to the Twin Towers Fund by Prince Alwaleed bin Talal in light of the press release the prince's staff distributed following the presentation. It read: "We must address some of the issues that led to such a criminal attack. I believe the government of the United States of America should re-examine its policies in the Middle East and adopt a more balanced stance toward the Palestinian cause. . . . Our Palestinian brethren continue to be slaughtered at the hands of the Israelis while the world turns the other cheek." This caused outrage in the United States. Prince Alwaleed, however, has also said: "You have to ask the simple question. Why fifteen Saudis? You can't just say it happened by coincidence. Clearly, there's something wrong with the way of thinking here [in Saudi Arabia], with the way people are raised" (PR firms: *New Internationalist*, 3/1/02, "Terrorism to End Terrorism," fall 2001, www.prwatch.org, *WP*, 3/21/02, *Washington Times*, 12/9/04, Gold, 193; Alwaleed: *Arab News*, 10/14/01; *Irish Times*, 8/3/09, Giuliani, 374–).

527 **"We feel what":** transcript, *Larry King*, CNN, 10/1/01; **Abdullah to ranch/"Yes, I":** Lacey, *Inside the Kingdom*, 284–, Suskind, *One Percent Doctrine*, 104–, Remarks by the President After Meeting with Crown Prince Abdullah, 4/25/02, posted at www.globalsecurity.org, Fox News, 4/26/02.

528 **probably stolen:** *BG*, 9/15/01. The spokesman, Gaafar Allagany, was to say on September 19 that two men with the same names as those of two hijackers, a Salem al-Hazmi and an Abdulaziz al-Omari, had indeed had their passports stolen over the past few years. The two cases cited by Allagany turned out to be cases of mistaken identity—there is no evidence the passports of hijackers Hazmi or Omari had been

stolen. On the issue of hijackers' identity, see also Ch. 14 and its related Notes (*WP,* 9/20/01, 10/7/01, *Telegraph* [U.K.], 9/23/01).

528–9   **"most people":** int. of Hatoon al Fassi for *Frontline:* "House of Saud," www.pbs.org; **"There is no proof":** Gold, 185, citing *Al Hayat,* 10/23/01; **"another power":** *NYT,* 10/23/01; **Naif/"The names":** *USA Today,* 2/6/02; **"It is enough":** Lacey, *Inside the Kingdom,* 231; **"Zionists"/"we put big":** AP, 12/5/02 citing int. Naif by *Al Siyasa* (Kuwait), '*Ain al Yaqeen,* 11/29/02 citing same int.; **"We're getting":** *LAT,* 10/13/01; **"They knew":** *New Yorker,* 10/16/01; **not allowed access:** *Philadelphia Inquirer,* 7/30/03; **"dribble out":** *NYT,* 12/27/01.

529   **blocked attempts:** *U.S. News & World Report,* 1/6/02, Suskind, *One Percent Doctrine,* 109. A State Department spokesman, Richard Boucher, had said in November that Saudi Arabia had been "prominent among the countries acting against the accounts of terrorist organizations . . . in compliance with UN Security Council Resolution 1333." The following month, however, following a visit to Saudi Arabia by Treasury Department assets control chief Richard Newcombe, it was reported that the Saudis "had balked at freezing bank accounts Washington said were linked to terrorists." Working with the Saudis had apparently been "like pulling teeth" (Boucher: State Department briefing, 11/27/01, http://usinfo.org; Newcombe: *U.S. News & World Report,* 1/6/02).

529–31   **"It doesn't look":** *BG,* 3/3/02; **few fluent Arabic:** Report, JI, 59, 245, 255, 336, 358; **men believed to have helped:** For information not particularly cited here, see Ch. 25 and its related Notes; **Thumairy diplomat:** Kean & Hamilton, 308; **"in a Western":** MFR 04019254, 4/20/04; **"uncertain":** MFR of int. Omar al-Bayoumi, 10/18/03, CF; **Bayoumi's income:** Graham with Nussbaum, 167, int. Bob Graham; **three-page section;** Report, JI, 175–; **Graham re payments:** Graham with Nussbaum, 24–, 167–, 224–, int. Bob Graham.

531   **payments originated embassy?:** The 9/11 Commission was to report that it found no evidence that Mihdhar and Hazmi received money from Basnan—or Bayoumi. The public furor around the Basnan money centered on reports that it came to the Basnans in cashier's checks in the name of Saudi ambassador Prince Bandar's wife, Princess Haifa. The royal couple were predictably outraged by the notion that there

could have been a link between the princess and terrorists. Such payments would have been in line, a Saudi embassy spokesman said, with her normal contributions to the needy. 9/11 Commissioner John Lehman surmised that the princess simply signed checks put in front of her by radicals working in the embassy's Islamic Affairs office. *Newsweek* has reported that Saudi wire transfers amounting to $20,000 were made to an individual who was featured in another terrorist case, also in connection with medical treatment for the individual's wife. *Newsweek* made no mention of Princess Haifa in that regard (Commission: CR, 516n24; furor: e.g., *Newsweek*, 11/22/02, 12/9/02, *Washington Times*, 11/26/02; outraged: Fox News, 11/27/02, *LAT,* 11/24/02, *CounterPunch*, 12/3/02, Lehman: Shenon, 185; $20,000: *Newsweek*, 4/7/04, *Daily Times* [Pakistan], 8/8/08).

531–2 **Thumairy "might be":** CR, 217; **Bayoumi attracted/ "connections"/left country:** FBI IG, Report, JI, 173; **Basnan came up:** Report, JI, 176; **party:** ibid., 177; **did more for Islam:** MFR 04017541A, 11/17/03, CF; **"wonderful":** *Newsweek*, 11/22/02; **contact with Binalshibh:** MFR 04017541A, 11/17/03, CF.

532 **agent or spy:** Graham with Nussbaum, 11, 24–, 168–, 224–. At least five people told the FBI they considered Bayoumi to be some sort of government agent. According to Dr. Abdussattar Shaikh, in whose San Diego home future hijackers Hazmi and Mihdhar eventually rented accommodations, one of those who expressed that view was none other than Hazmi himself. In an early interview with *The New York Times* after 9/11, Shaikh said Hazmi and Midhar had been his friends, that their identification as hijackers was perhaps a case of stolen identities. Congressional investigators would later be startled to discover something Sheikh had certainly not revealed to the *Times*—and that the FBI initially sought to conceal from the investigators. Shaikh had long been an FBI informant, and had regularly shared information with a Bureau agent named Steven Butler. Butler had on occasion talked with Shaikh at home while Hazmi and Mihdhar were in a room nearby. According to the agent, Shaikh had mentioned the pair by their first names, saying that they were Saudis. That rang no alarm bells for him, Butler recalled, because "Saudi Arabia was considered an ally." The FBI, backed up by Bush officials, refused to allow Joint

Committee staff to interview Shaikh. A 9/11 Commission memorandum, identifying Shaikh only as Dr. Xxxxxxxxxxx Xxxxxx, makes it clear that 9/11 Commission staff did talk to Shaikh. The memorandum does not say whether Shaikh shared with Agent Butler his belief that Bayoumi, the man who had introduced the hijackers to San Diego, was a Saudi agent. Nor is there evidence that Commission staff queried Shaikh about inconsistencies in his story of how he first met the two future hijackers. Shaikh's simultaneous relationship with both the two terrorists and the FBI just might have led to their being unmasked—an even more glaring might-have-been when one recalls that the CIA had early on identified both men as terrorist suspects, *and* known they had visas for travel to the United States—yet failed to inform the FBI (see pp. 489–80). Much remains to be explained. The former chair of Congress's joint probe, former senator Bob Graham, accepts that the FBI may at first have tried to conceal its relationship with Shaikh simply because it was a "big embarrassment." Graham also raised the possibility, though, that what the FBI tried to hide was that Shaikh knew something that "would be even more damaging were it revealed." What, too, of the report in the press that Agent Butler's interview with congressional investigators had been "explosive," that he "had been monitoring a flow of Saudi Arabian money that wound up in the hands of the two hijackers"? Butler, an official was quoted as having said, "saw a pattern, a trail, and he told his supervisors, but it ended there." As of 2009, Shaikh was still living in San Diego.

Because of agencies' iron rules about the protection of informants—whatever the full story of Shaikh's relationship with the hijackers or with the FBI—there is little likelihood of learning more about him anytime soon. He is virtually invisible in the Commission Report, not even named in the index.

Much the same applies to the Report's handling of Ali Mohamed, a truly significant figure in the sorry story of U.S. agencies' understanding—or lack of it—of al Qaeda. "No single agent of al Qaeda," the author Peter Lance has written, "was more successful in compromising the U.S. intelligence community than a former Egyptian army captain turned CIA operative, Special Forces advisor, and FBI informant" than former Egyptian army major Mohamed. "Mohamed succeeded in penetrating the John F. Kennedy Special Warfare Center at Fort Bragg, while simultaneously training the cell that blew up the World Trade Center in 1993. He went on to train Osama bin Laden's personal bodyguard, and photographed the U.S. embassy in Kenya—taking the surveillance pictures bin Laden himself used to target the [1998] suicide truck bomb."

Though beyond the scope of this book, there is much more to this labyrinthine tale. While the August 6, 2001, CIA brief delivered to President Bush did not mention Mohamed by name, it was shot through with references to him. He was that summer due to be sentenced for his crimes, having pled guilty to multiple terrorist offenses, including his role in the embassy bombings. FBI agent Jack Cloonan, who interviewed Mohamed in prison after 9/11, had the eerie sense that he "knew every detail" of the attacks, in spite of having been in custody for years. As of 2006, though reportedly still a prisoner at an unknown location, Mohamed had yet to be sentenced. There is just one reference to him in the 9/11 Commission Report—and no mention of his relationship with U.S. intelligence agencies (Hazmi view: MFR [unnumbered], 4/23/04, CF; *Times* interview: *NYT,* 10/24/01; investigators startled: Graham with Nussbaum, 159–, ints. Bob Graham, Eleanor Hill; informant/Butler talked: FBI IG, Report, JI, 162, "Conspiracy Theories: The Intelligence Breakdown," www.cbc.ca; "ally": Report, JI, 162; FBI refused: Joint Inquiry, Report, 3, Graham with Nussbaum, 162; Bush officials: "Bush Should Cry Uncle and Release Saudi Info," 6/28/03, www.opednews.com, Report, JI, 3; Commission memorandum: MFR [unnumbered], 4/23/04, CF; inconsistencies: CR, 517n28; might-have-been: Report, JI, 19–; "big embarrassment"/"did know": Graham with Nussbaum, 166; "explosive"/"monitoring": *U.S. News & World* Report, 11/29/02; Shaikh 2009: Miriam Raftery, "Abdussattar Shaikh, Co-Founder of San Diego's Islamic Center, Honored for 50 Years of Service Promoting Religious Tolerance," 10/8/09, www.eastcountymagazine.org; "No single": "A Conversation with Peter Lance," 12/06, www.internetwriting journal.com & see Wright, 179–, Bergen, *OBL I Know,* 142–; Aug. 6 brief: J. M. Berger, "What the Commission Missed," 10/4/06, www.intelwire.com; "knew every": ibid.; pled guilty: J. M Berger, ed., *Ali Mohamed Sourcebook,* INTELWIRE,

2006, 311; unknown location/yet to be sentenced: Bergen, *OBL I Know*, 433, Scott, 348n28, 157, 159; one reference: CR, 68 & see Staff Report, "9/11 & Terrorist Travel, CO, 57).

532   **"incontrovertible":** Report, JI, 395. The document, which Graham dated as August 2, 2002, is partially cited in Congress's Joint Inquiry Report in a passage about a CIA memo that cited "incontrovertible evidence that there is support for these terrorists [words redacted]." The Report goes on to state that "it is also possible that further investigation of these allegations could reveal legitimate, and innocent, explanations for these associations." Senator Graham cast doubt on an FBI finding that Bayoumi and Basnan were neither agents nor accomplices in the 9/11 plot. Former Saudi ambassador Bandar, for his part, described reports that Bayoumi was a Saudi agent as "baseless" (Graham with Nussbaum, 169, 224–, 11n, Bandar press release, "Bayoumi is not a government agent," 7/23/03, www.saudiembassy.net).

532–4 **Commission interviews:** e.g., MFR 04019365, 2/24/04; **Thumairy "deceptive"/denied/prompted/second interview/"say bad"/"implausible":** Snell, De, & Jacobson to Zelikow, 2/25/04, MFR 04019362, 2/23/04, CF; **Bayoumi favorable/stuck to story:** Shenon, 309–, MFR of int. Omar al-Bayoumi, 10/18/03, CF; **Zelikow think not agent:** Zelikow to Shenon, 10/18/07, www.philipshenon.com; **distinguishing mark:** CR, 516n19; **salary approved/picture found:** Report, JI, 174 & see Staff Statement 16, DOCEX 199-HQ-1361032, "Hijacker Primary Docs, PENTTBOM Memo re CD found," B50, T5, CF; **"cleansed"/"deceptive":** MFR 04019367, 2/24/04, Snell, De, & Jacobson to Zelikow, 2/25/04, CF; **"the witness' utter":** MFR int. of Osama Basnan, 10/22/03, CF.

534   **Hussayen/Mosques/in States:** *WSJ*, 2/10/03. In October 2001 the FBI began an investigation of Hussayen's nephew Sami. He eventually became the first person to be charged under the broadened "material support" for terrorism provisions of the then new USA Patriot Act. The government sought to prove that Hussayen used his expertise as an Internet "webmaster" to further the cause of terrorists and promote violent jihad. The hard drive of a computer he had used, according to an agent's testimony, contained "thousands" of photographs, of the World Trade Center, of

the Pentagon, and of planes hitting buildings. Sami Hussayen was eventually found not guilty and returned to Saudi Arabia (Second Superceding Indictment, *U.S. v. Sami Omar al Hussayen*, U.S. District Court for the District of Idaho, AP, 3/12/03, Dept. of Justice press release, "Indictments Allege Illegal Financial Transfers to Iraq; Visa Fraud Involving Assistance to Groups that Advocate Violence," 2/26/03, www.usdoj.gov, *Seattle Times*, 11/22/04).

535–43 **Marriott Sept.10/"muttering"/Paramedics/"faking"/ kitchenette/"I don't":** MFR 04017480, 10/9/03, MFR 04017486, 10/9/03, MFR 04017482, 10/9/03, MFR 04019354, CF, *WSJ*, 2/10/03, *Telegraph* (U.K.), 10/2/03, *WP*, 10/2/03, 3/12/03; **Aulaqi contact/move:** See pp. 291–92; **son of minister:** *Dallas Morning News*, 12/25/09; **preached Capitol:** *NYT*, 5/8/10, Fox News, 11/11/10; **lunched Pentagon:** *NY Daily News*, 10/21/10; **remained U.S.:** *WSJ*, 2/10/03, ABC News, 11/30/09; **phone number/ Binalshibh:** Report, JI, 178; **Fort Hood/Detroit bomb/Times Square/cargo planes:** *Christian Science Monitor*, 5/19/10, Fox News, 10/20/10, CNN, 1/7/10, *Guardian* (U.K.), 10/31/10, MSNBC, 11/1/10; **capture or kill:** *Christian Science Monitor*, 5/19/10, *NYT*, 4/6/10; **"loose end":** McClatchy News, 11/21/09.

Sarasota gated community/al-Hijji: For more than six months, since immediately after the authors' first extended interview with the counterterrorist officer, the authors worked on this part of the story with Florida investigative reporter, and founder of *The Broward Bulldog*, Dan Christensen. We also benefited from the collaboration of Neil Tweedie at *The Daily Telegraph* in the UK. See authors' articles with Christensen in: *Miami Herald*, 9/7/11, *Broward Bulldog*, 9/7/11, 9/16/11, 11/8/11, 2/18/12, 3/13/12, 3/14/12, *Daily Telegraph* [UK], 2/18/12, MSNBC, 3/12/12, 3/13/12 & see 3/14/12, FDLE Investigative Reports released to Dan Christensen, ints. Larry Berberich, Bob Graham; **series of denials**: FBI spokesperson Kathy Wright to Dan Christensen, 9/6/11, Agent Dave Courvertier to Christensen, 9/13/11, Agent Steven Ibison to *St. Petersburg Times*, reported 9/15/11, Section Chief David Hardy to Christensen, 2/7/12, FBI to *The Daily Beast*, reported 3/13/12; **National Archives**: corr. Kristen Wilhelm, 2012, ints./corr. Bob Graham; **Hammoud**: FDLE Investigative Reports, *U.S. v. Wissam Taysir Hammoud*,

U.S. District Court for the Middle District of FL, Tampa Div. Dan Christensen ints./corr. Wissam Hammoud & family members; **Southampton**: al-Hijjis' rental agreement, int. landlord; **al-Hijji replied**: int. by author Summers & Neil Tweedie of *Daily Telegraph* [UK]; **denied**: corr. Neil Tweedie, 2/12; **FBI has said**: e.g. FBI to *St. Petersburg Times*, 9/15/11; **attorney**: Christensen int. Scott McKay; **Beirut**: Warranty Deed, File No. 1027-325924, Sarasota, FL, Circuit Court, Instrument 2003204043, filed 10/7/03. **"most important"**: ibid.. Aside from what is reported in these pages about Saudis allegedly visited by the terrorists in Florida, the authors note one other lead. In a lengthy taped interview, a former Venice Yellow Cab driver named Bob Simpson has described having picked up a "wealthy Saudi businessman" at Orlando Executive Airport and—later the same day—taking him to an apartment building where he had previously picked up Mohamed Atta. After 9/11, Simpson said the FBI questioned him about the Saudi. Simpson did work for Yellow Cab in 2001, but the authors' efforts to trace him were unsuccessful (videotape & transcript in the collection of Daniel Hopsicker).

543   **"that the Saudis"**: int. Bob Graham.

544   **did not name once**: Zelikow Afterword, CR (abridged), NY: Norton, 2011, 504. **"did not find"/"persuasive evidence"**: Zelikow to Shenon, 10/18/07, www.philipshenon.com. The Commission, according to its Report, believed that al Qaeda likely did have "agents" in California, "one or more individuals informed in advance" of Mihdhar and Hazmi's arrival ("agents": CR, 215).

544–6   **page 396**: Report, JI, 395–; **CIA not obstruct**: corr. office of Bob Graham, 2009; **Bush himself**: ibid., Graham with Nussbaum, 228, 215–, 231, *NYT*, 6/24/09, *Salon*, 9/8/04; **Pelosi**: CNN, 7/30/03; **"I went back"**: *Nation*, 7/29/03.

546   **should be made public**: Prince Bandar, then ambassador to Washington, said in 2003 that there was nothing to hide, and Foreign Minister Prince Saud al-Faisal said it was an "outrage to any sense of fairness that 28 blank pages are now considered substantial evidence to proclaim the guilt of a country." The Saudis, it was suggested, saw publication of the classified material as "a chance to clear their Kingdom's name." Senator Graham did not buy it. "It seemed to me," he has written, "that George W. Bush and Prince Bandar were

performing a sort of good cop–bad cop routine, in which Prince Bandar got to claim innocence of behalf of Saudi Arabia, while George W. Bush protected him by being the bad cop who wouldn't release troubling information" (Bandar: "Saudi Ambassador Responds to Reports of Saudi Involvement in 9/11," 7/24/03, www.saudiembassy.net; "outrage": AP, 7/29/03; "a chance": AP, 7/30/03; "It seemed": Graham with Nussbaum, 228–).

546–7   **"I can't tell you":** int. Eleanor Hill; **leaks/details/"central figure"/"very direct"/?"cannot be"/Graham/"apparent":** *Newsweek*, 2/3/03, *LAT*, 8/2/03, Shenon, 50–, 308–, AP, 7/27/03, *NYT*, 8/1/03; **Zubaydah waterboarded June/July:** int. of CIA OIG John Helgerson, *Der Spiegel*, 8/31/09, "Yoo's Legal Memos Gave Bush Retroactive Cover for Torture," 2/23/09, http://pubrecord.org, BBC News, 7/13/09.

547   **Kiriakou/Zubaydah:** As reported, what Kuriakou learned about Zubaydah's references to the princes came to him not firsthand but from those reading the cable traffic. For that reason and because of the passage of time, he told the authors, he is today unsure whether the Zubaydah/princes element first surfaced during interrogation or because he was questioned about something found in the journal Zubaydah had kept.

Refuting suggestions that Zubaydah may not have given good information, or that he may even have been mentally unstable, Kiriakou said he thought the contrary was true, that he did give reliable information and was "not crazy" but "bright, well-read, a good conversationalist."

Kiriakou was indicted in January 2012, accused of having disclosed classified information about Zubaydah to reporters. The complaint also alleged that he had lied to the CIA's Publication Review Board when submitting the manuscript for his memoir.

The Kiriakou interview for this book is first corroboration of the core elements of an account written by author Gerald Posner in 2003, with different detail and citing only anonymous sources. The Posner account, according to Kiriakou, got important detail and chronology skewed. The relevant interrogation of Zubaydah that produced the lead about the Saudi prince did not occur—as Posner wrote—within days of his capture but only months later, after he had been waterboarded. (This would fit with the account of FBI investigator Ali Soufan, who took part in interrogations of Zubaydah until June. During that early period, the link to the Saudi princes did not come up.)

As reported by Posner, Zubaydah was tricked into believing that he had been moved from U.S. to Saudi custody—in hopes that fear of the truly gruesome torture practiced in Saudi Arabia would lead him to start talking. Instead, by the Posner account, he seemed relieved and promptly urged his "Saudi" interrogators to telephone Prince Ahmed bin Salman—even providing the prince's phone numbers from memory. Prince Ahmed, he said, "will tell you what to do." Later, according to Posner's account, he added the names and numbers of the two other princes. Bin Laden, Zubaydah reportedly said, had made a point of letting the Saudi royals know in advance, without sharing details, that there was going to be an attack on the United States on September 11.

Again according to Posner, the CIA decided to share what Zubaydah had said with Saudi intelligence, with a request that it probe further. *New York Times* journalist and author James Risen added a new detail in 2006. When Zubaydah was captured, sources told Risen, he had on his person two bank cards, one from a Saudi bank and another from an institution in Kuwait. American investigators worked through a Muslim financier to check on the accounts, only to be frustrated. There no longer was a way to trace the money that had gone into the accounts, the financier reported, because "Saudi intelligence officials had seized all the records relating to the card from the Saudi financial institution in question; the records then disappeared."

Not only Posner and Risen but also a third writer, Tom Joscelyn, have probed the Zubaydah story. Joscelyn told the authors that one of his interviewees said he had seen the Zubaydah interrogation logs and that they corroborate the Zubaydah/princes scenario. Kiriakou's interview with the authors now becomes the first on-the-record corroboration from a former CIA officer.

Absent the logs, proof positive that Zubaydah did make the claims attributed to him is unobtainable—for the worst of reasons. Though the 2002 interrogations of Zubaydah were videotaped, the Agency has admitted that it has since destroyed the tapes. While the destruction was deplorable, it

may have been done to obscure evidence of brutal interrogation rather than of what Zubaydah said. The waterboarding
of the prisoner occurred weeks before the CIA received formal authority to use that violent measure (Kiriakou: int. John
Kiriakou, BBC News, *NYT*, press release, www.fbi.gov,
1/23/12; Soufan: Testimony of Ali Soufan, 5/13/09,
http://judiciary.senate.gov, corr. Daniel Freedman, the Soufan
Group; 2011 Posner account: Posner, *Why America Slept*,
202–; gruesome torture: e.g., Hollingsworth & Mitchell, 11–,
21–, 56, 62; princes died: AP, 9/2/03, "Prince Ahmed Cited in
New Book on Sept. 11 Attacks," 9/4/03, www
.bloodhorse.com; Risen: Risen, 173–, 187; Joscelyn: conv.
Thomas Joscelyn; destroyed tapes: *WP*, 12/12/07, *NYT*,
3/3/09).

548–50 **not been interviewed:** corr. former FBI Supervisor Robert
Foster, 2012; **"wrongdoing":** *LAT*, 8/1/03; **credible:** int. Bob
Graham; **"assistance":** *Financial Times* (U.K.), 7/25/03; **40
clamored:** CNN, 7/30/03; **"engaged"/"to protect"/"He
has":** Graham with Nussbaum, xv, 231; **"being kept"/"It
was":** ibid., 215–; **"If the 28":** *New Republic*, 8/3/04.

CHAPTER 34

550 **Bush seeded/Cheney said:** In his address to the nation of
October 7, 2002, for example, Bush said: "We know that Iraq
and al Qaeda have had high-level contacts that go back a
decade. . . . After September 11, Saddam Hussein's regime
gleefully celebrated the terrorist attacks on America." The
President mentioned 9/11 eight times at his press conference
just before the invasion of Iraq. "The White House played
endless semantic games on the issue," *The New York Times*'s
Philip Shenon has written. "When pressed, Bush was careful
not to allege that Iraq had any role in the 9/11 attacks, at least
no direct role. But he insisted that if Saddam Hussein had
remained in power, he . . . would have been tempted to hand
over [weapons of mass destruction] to his supposed ally
Osama bin Laden. Vice President Cheney went further . . .
suggesting repeatedly, almost obsessively, that Iraq may in fact
have been involved in the September 11 plot." The Vice
President liked to cite the Czech intelligence report suggesting that hijack leader Atta had met with an Iraqi agent in
Prague. See note below—evidence was developed strongly
suggesting that the report was unreliable (10/7/02 address:

"Address to the Nation on Iraq," www.presidency
.ucsb.edu; mentioned 9/11: *Christian Science Monitor,* 3/14/03;
"White House played": Shenon, 126–, 381–, & see Report,
"Whether Public Statements Regarding Iraq by U.S.
Government Offcials Were Substantiated by Intelligence
Information," U.S. Senate Intelligence Committee, 110th
Cong., http://intelligence.senate.gov).

550   **polls:** The references are to a Pew Research poll of February
2003, a Knight-Ridder poll in January that year, and a
Washington Post poll in September 2003. (*Editor & Publisher,*
3/26/03, *USA Today,* 9/6/03).

552   **Atta/Prague/Iraqi intelligence:** An informant reported to
Czech intelligence after 9/11 that photographs of Mohamed
Atta resembled a man he had seen meeting with an Iraqi
diplomat and suspected spy named Ahmad Khalil Ibrahim
Samir al-Ani in Prague at 11 a.m. on April 9, 2001.
Investigation indicated that neither Atta nor Ani had been in
Prague at the time alleged. Atta was recorded on closed-
circuit TV footage in Florida on April 4, and his cell phone
was used in the state on the 6th, 9th, 10th, and 11th. Atta and
Shehhi, moreover, apparently signed a lease on an apartment
on the 11th. This information, while not certain proof,
strongly suggests that Atta was in the United States on April
9. CIA analysts characterized the alleged Prague sighting as
being "highly unlikely." Nevertheless, the report crept into
prewar intelligence briefings as having been a "known contact" between al Qaeda and Iraq.

In addition to the alleged Atta meeting, rumors have long
circulated that two other hijackers, Mihdhar and Hazmi, had
contact with an Iraqi agent. This was alleged to have been
Ahmad Hikmat Shakir, who acted as a greeter for Arab
visitors in Kuala Lumpur at the time of the terrorist summit
there in 2000. Shakir was captured in 2002. The CIA later
received information that "Shakir was not affiliated with al
Qaeda and had no connections with IIS [Iraqi intelligence]."

(Atta/Prague: CR, 228–, Report, "U.S. Intelligence
Community's Prewar Intelligence Assessments on Iraq," U.S.
Senate, Select Committee on Intelligence, 108th Cong., 2nd
Sess., Washington, D.C.: U.S. Govt. Printing Office, 2004,
340–, "Review of the Pre-Iraqi War Activities of the Office of
the Under Secretary of Defense for Policy," Office of the
Inspector General, U.S. Dept. of Defense, 2/9/07, 5–, but see

Edward Jay Epstein, "Atta in Prague," *NYT*, 11/22/05; Shakir: Report, "Postwar Findings About Iraq's WMD Programs and Links to Terrorism and How They Compare with Prewar Assessments," U.S. Senate Select Committee on Intelligence, 109th Cong., 2nd Sess., Washington, D.C.: U.S. Govt. Printing Office, 9/8/06, 111.)

552   **Mylroie propagated:** e.g. *National Interest*, Winter 95/96, *New Republic*, 9/24/01, CR, 336, 559n73, Laurie Mylroie, *The War Against America*, NY: Regan, 2001, *WSJ*, 4/2/04, "The Saddam-9/11 Link Confirmed," 5/11/04, www.frontpagemagazine.com; **Investigation:** Michael Isikoff and David Corn, *Hubris*, NY: Three Rivers Press, 2007, 72–, and refs., Clarke, 94–, 232; **multiple/"My view":** *Washington Monthly*, 12/03.

552   **"We went back":** int. of Michael Scheuer for *Frontline:* "The Dark Side," www.pbs.org. As described earlier in this book, bin Laden had an antipathy for Saddam Hussein and had sought Saudi government backing to use his fighters to oust Iraqi forces from Kuwait (see p. 279). Though there are reports that bin Laden and Iraqi representatives did meet to discuss possible cooperation as early as 1992, there is no evidence that anything came of the encounters. Reporting in 2004, the Senate Intelligence Committee concluded that prior to the invasion of Iraq, the CIA had "reasonably assessed that there were likely several instances of contacts between Iraq and al Qaeda throughout the 1990s, but that these contacts did not add up to an established formal relationship . . . no evidence proving Iraqi complicity or assistance in an al Qaeda attack" (e.g. Wright, 295–, Report, "U.S. Intelligence Community's Prewar Intelligence Assessments on Iraq," 346–).

552–3   **CIA Report 2003/"no credible"/pressure/"questions":** Report, "U.S. Intelligence Community's Prewar Intelligence Assessments on Iraq," 314, 322, 353, 363, 449–.

553   **Duelfer/senior intelligence officials:** The detainee to whom Duelfer referred was Muhammed Khudayr al-Dulaymi, who had headed the M-14 section of the Mukhabarat, the principal Iraqi intelligence agency. Duelfer noted the episode in a 2009 book and in an interview. The story was reported by Robert Windrem, senior research fellow at New York University's Center on Law and Security and a longtime producer for NBC (Charles Duelfer, *Hide and*

Seek, NY: PublicAffairs, 2009, 416, Robert Windrem, "Cheney's Role Deepens," 5/13/09, www.dailybeast.com).

553–4 **"There were two"/"We were not":** McClatchy News, 4/21/09, Report, "Inquiry into the Treatment of Detainees in U.S. Custody, U.S. Senate Committee on Armed Services," 110th Cong., 2nd Sess. 11/20/08, 72.

554 **Suskind/forgery/brief storm/denials:** Following Ronald Suskind's account of the forgery's origins in his 2008 book, *The Way of the World*, House Judiciary Committee chairman John Conyers wrote letters saying he intended to follow up. As this book went to print, however, there was no sign that he did. The Suskind book suggests that the forgery was hand-written by former Iraqi intelligence chief Tahir Habbush, who began cooperating with the CIA even before the Iraq invasion and was eventually paid off and "resettled." The purported memo was slipped to a British reporter, billed as authentic, by an aide in the Interim Governing Council in Iraq, and pub-lished in late 2003 in Britain's *Sunday Telegraph* (Ronald Suskind, *The Way of the World*, NY: Harper, 2008, 361–, CIA statement, 8/22/08, www.cia.gov, "Statement from Rob Richer," http://suskinsresponse.googlepages.com, "A Note to Readers," www.ronsuskind.com, Letters from Rep. Conyers to Rob Richer, John Maguire, A. B. "Buzzy" Krongard, & John Hannah, 8/20/08, www.judiciary.house.gov).

554–5 **Giraldi:** Philip Giraldi, "Suskind Revisited," 8/7/08, www.amconmag.com; **"manufactured":** int. Paul Pillar for *Frontline:* "The Dark Side," www.pbs.org; **"Unfortunately"/ It's my belief:** press release, 6/5/08, http://intelligence.senate.gov, Report, cited above.

555 **reputable estimates re deaths:** www.iraqbodycount.org, http://icasualties.org. In addition to the American military casualties, more than three hundred non-U.S. troops had died as of early 2012 (Iraq Coalition Casualty Count, www.icasualties.org).

CHAPTER 35

557–8 **"led and financed":** Richard Falkenrath, "The 9/11 Commission Report," *International Security*, Vol. 29, Winter 04; **only three nations:** CR, 122; **"Pakistani mili-tary"/"held the key":** CR, 63–.

558 **financial transactions:** Known 9/11-related money transfers were handled out of Dubai in the UAE. In anticipation of

pursuit in the wake of the attacks, the al Qaeda agents
involved headed for Pakistan.

559   **Rawalpindi, headquarters:** Fouda & Fielding, 181; **Defense
Society:** ibid., 15; **Zubaydah caught:** ibid., 20, int. John
Kiriakou; **"Pakistani people":** Scheuer, *Osama bin Laden*,
121; **"We found":** ed. Lawrence, 71; **"As for Pakistan":**
Rashid, 138; **called on the faithful:** Scheuer, *Osama bin
Laden*, 121.

560   **"the most complicated":** *Sunday Times* (U.K.), 8/1/10;
Kashmir: CR, 58, 63–, Coll, *Ghost Wars*, 292. China also
controls part of Kashmir. The region is a tinderbox.

560–3   **Hamid Gul:** Rashid, 129; **trained in camps:** CR, 67,
Clinton, 799, Rashid, 137, Coll, *Ghost Wars*, 341;
"Whatever": Scheuer, *Osama bin Laden*, 121; **security
system:** Coll, *Ghost Wars*, 341; **"shoehorned":** *Time*,
8/19/08; **"always" support:** *Foreign Policy Journal*, 9/20/10;
"actually were": MFR 03012967, 10/8/03; **additional cash:**
Coll, *Ghost Wars*, 296; **"the most influential":** *Sunday Times*
(U.K.), 8/1/10, *Salon*, 10/18/03, Napoleoni, 82; **"shadow
government":** Coll, *Ghost Wars*, 296, *NYT*, 5/12/11; **"helplessness"/tensions:** MFR 04021470, 12/12/03; **commando
operation:** *WP*, 12/19/01; **Clinton visit/"the moon":** *WP*,
12/20/01, CR, 183, 503n64; **"people who"/"not
persuasive":** *WP*, 12/19/01; **Sheehan:** Benjamin & Simon,
515; **"influential":** Clarke to Rice, 1/25/01; **"loss of
urgency":** Tenet, 139; **"Full Monty":** *NYT*, 5/12/11.

563   **foreknowledge:** The authors have seen no evidence of
Pakistani involvement in 9/11. Soon after publication of the
9/11 Commission Report, however, the distinguished
reporter Arnaud de Borchgrave reported that—according to
an "unimpeachable source"—former Pakistani intelligence
officers knew beforehand all about the September 11 attacks."
This information, de Borchgrave wrote, had reached the
Commission only as its report was being printed. UPI,
8/3/04.

563   **"Stone Age":** Musharraf, 201.

563   **demands:** There are differences between the language of
Washington's demands as rendered in Musharraf's memoir—
seemingly verbatim—and the version reproduced in the 9/11
Commission Report. Musharraf found a demand to help
"destroy" bin Laden illogical, he remembered. How could the
United States be so sure that bin Laden and al Qaeda were

behind 9/11, he wondered, if it was still searching for evidence? Musharraf, 205, CR 331, 558n37.

564 **reservations/cooperated:** CR, 331, Musharraf, 206; **"We have done":** Musharraf, 223; **3,021:** *Sunday Times* (U.K.), 8/1/10; **some 700/369 handed over/bounty:** Musharraf, 237, 369; **Grenier:** *NYT*, 5/12/11; **best-known:** Musharraf, 237–, 220, 240–.

565 **"destroy"/"We have done":** Musharraf, 205, 220.

565–7 **"still visiting":** MFR 03012967, 10/8/03; **McFarland:** Fox News, 1/7/11; **"I'm convinced":** "Whatever Happened to bin Laden?," http://afghanistan.blogs.cnn.com; **"You in the West"/poll:** *Sunday Times* (U.K.), 8/1/10; **S Section:** *NYT*, 5/12/11; **"They were very":** *Sunday Times* (U.K.), 3/8/08; **Better to do/officials:** *Sunday Times* (U.K.), 8/1/10, Fox News, 1/7/11; **"We will kill":** transcript, 2nd presidential debate, 10/7/08; **no statements:** *NYT*, 10/2/10; **"I think":** transcript, *Meet the Press*, NBC News, 8/15/10; **audio messages/still shaped:** *NYT*, 10/2/10; **"senior NATO":** CNN, 10/18/10; **"sightings"/"years":** New York *Daily News*, 10/18/10.

567 **intelligence:** In late November 2010, Saudi Arabia's Prince Turki said in an interview that he thought bin Laden was moving to and fro across the Pakistani/Afghan border, communicating by messenger, and still giving orders. "I think they should find him," Turki said, "I think the United States should call the countries that are of interest, like Saudi Arabia, Pakistan, Afghanistan, Russia, China, and set a plan in motion to capture or—or eliminate him." Transcript, int. of Turki, *Situation Room*, CNN, 11/17/10.

567–72 **"launched":** *Courrier International* (France), 5/5/11; **bulletin/*Post*:** breaking news alerts, *WP*, 5/1/11; **Tonight/Jubilant:** text of Obama address, *Telegraph* (U.K.), 5/2/11, *WP*, 5/2/11; **long article:** *New Yorker*, 8/8/11; **Qadir:** ints./corr. Shaukat Qadir, "Operation Geronimo," draft paper by Shaukat Qadir, *The National* [Pakistan], 3/16/12, *Daily Beast*, 3/30/12; **commission:** CNN, 4/18/12; **Abbottabad:** Musharraf, 39–, *Independent* (U.K.), 5/4/11, *Weekly Standard*, 5/2/11, AP, 5/2/11; **"involved"/"inconceivable"/"whether there":** *Financial Times*, 5/4/11, *Spectator*, 5/7/11, *LAT*, 5/8/11; **"was not anywhere":** *Independent* (U.K.), 5/4/11; **"a bit amazing":** AP, 5/2/11; **Al-Kuwaiti:** e.g. *New Yorker*, 8/8/11; **Musharraf on al-Libi:** Musharraf, 258–, 221; **"made** a": *The National* [Pakistan], 3/16/12; **"It was decided"**: *Irish Times*, 5/5/11; **"a few minutes"**: AP, 5/2/11; **under surveillance?**: *Telegraph* (U.K.), 5/4/11.

573   **Bush/Musharraf deal reported, et seq.:** *Guardian* (U.K.), 5/9/11. The authors were unaware of any response by either the U.S. administration or Prime Minister Gilani to the report that there had been a deal in place. The All Pakistan Muslim League, however, posted a legal notice denying the reported deal by Musharraf (http://www.facebook.com/note.php?note_id=10150198113099339).

573   **Musharraf denial:** *Indian Express*, 5/10/11; **OBL death:** Readers seeking the most up-to-date, authoritative, independent account should consult Peter Bergen's 2012 book *Manhunt: From 9/11 to Abbottabad - the Ten-Year Search for Osama bin Laden*, which reached the authors only as this paperback edition was going to press (London: Bodley Head, 2012)

AFTERWORD

575–81 **"We are sure"**: Miller & Stone with Mitchell, 187; **"the noblest"**: AP, 9/23/09; **"Palestine"**: ed. Lawrence, 9; **"Crusaders' "**: ibid., 17; **"theft"/"paltry"**: ibid., 163; **"have surrendered"**: ibid., 163, 171, and Scheuer, *Osama bin Laden*, 155; **$144:** AP, 9/28/01, *NYT,* 10/14/01; **$100:** ed. Lawrence, 272; **$146:** BBC News, 7/3/08; **"Rage against"**: excerpt from *Rock the Casbah* in *NYT,* 8/1/11; **$103:** *Detroit Free Press*, 4/24/12; **permitted:** Lacey, *Inside the Kingdom*, 291, *Guardian* (U.K.), 4/30/03; **a constant:** see ed. Lawrence, 4, & refs., Scheuer, *Osama bin Laden*, 99, 153, & refs.; **motivation:** see pp. 233, 276–77, and 279–80. **"We wanted"**: Bergen, *OBL I Know*, 225; **bled:** ibid., 316, bin Ladens & Sasson, 177, CR, 191; **"I am rejoicing"**: ed. Lawrence, 208; **90,000 etc.:** BBC, 4/17/12; **second only:** *NYT,* 7/24/10, CNN, 7/20/10; **Brown:** http://costofwar.org; **some believe:** e.g. "Bin Laden Is a Dying Brand," 1/7/10, www.businessinsider.com; **Pew:** "Muslim Publics Divided on Hamas and Hezbollah," 12/2/10, http://pewglobal.org; **Aulaqi:** *Guardian*, 9/30/11; **same fate:** "The Year of the Drone," www.newamericafoundation.net; **were arraigned:** *Observer*, 5/6/12, *Telegraph*, 6/6/12; **"renaissance"/"Tuesday"/"terrified"**: *Guardian* [UK], *International Herald Tribune*, 6/17/11; **pastor/Qur'an:** *NYT,* 4/1, 4/2/11, New York *Daily News*, 4/2/11, *Irish Times*, 4/2,

4/4, 4/6/11; **new tower:** *WSJ*, 3/30/12, inhabitat.com; **mosque:** *Washington Times*, 8/18/10, *WSJ*, 8/15/10, *NYT*, 7/13/10, 8/21/10, 4/1/11, press release, 5/24/10, www.911familiesforamerica.org, "Proposed Muslim Community Center Near Ground Zero," 5/21/10, www.huffingtonpost.com, *Christian Science Monitor*, 9/22/11; **Museum/remains/disagreements:** press release, 12/11/09, National Sept. 11 Memorial Museum, AP, 8/10/10, *NYT*, 4/1/11, 5/12/11, AP, 4/3/11, *NY Daily News*, 3/4/12, *Las Vegas Review-Journal*, 2/10/12, press release, Office of Chief Medical Examiner, 2/12; **Phoenix:** *Arizona Daily Star*, 4/2/11, *Yuma Sun*, 3/29/11; **Aeneid:** *NYT*, 4/1, 4/6, 4/8/11.

SELECTED BIBLIOGRAPHY

This list includes some two hundred books that are cited in the Notes and Sources. It does not include the many other books used for general reference and background only. Nor does it include newspaper and magazine articles or official documents, which are cited in full in the Notes and Sources.

Aaronovitch, David. *Voodoo Histories: The Role of the Conspiracy Theory in Shaping Modern History*. London: Jonathan Cape, 2009.

Ahmed, Nafeez Mosaddeq. *The War on Freedom*. Brighton, U.K.: Media Messenger, 2002.

———. *The War on Truth*. Northampton, MA: Interlink, 2005.

Ahmed, Qanta A. *In the Land of Invisible Women*. Naperville, IL: Source Books, 2008.

Anonymous. *Through Our Enemies' Eyes: Osama bin Laden, Radical Islam, and the Future of America*. Washington, D.C.: Brassey's, 2002.

Ashcroft, John. *Never Again: Securing America and Restoring Justice*. NY: Center Street, 2006.

Atwan, Abdel Bari. *The Secret History of al Qaeda*. Berkeley: University of California Press, 2006.

Aust, Stephan, and Codt Schnibben, and the Staff of *Der Spiegel*, eds. *Inside 9–11: What Really Happened*. NY: St. Martin's, 2002.

Baer, Robert. *See No Evil*. NY: Three Rivers, 2002.

———. *Sleeping with the Devil: How Washington Sold Our Soul for Saudi Crude*. NY: Three Rivers, 2003.

al-Bahri, Nasser, with Georges Malbrunot. *Dans l'Ombre de Ben Laden*. Neuilly-sur-Seine, France: Michel Lafon, 2010.

Ball, Howard; Bush, *The Detainees and the Constitution*. Lawrence, KS: University Press of Kansas, 2007.

Bamford, James. *Body of Secrets*. NY: Doubleday, 2001.

———. *A Pretext for War: 9/11, Iraq, and the Abuse of America's Intelligence Agencies*. NY: Doubleday, 2004.

———. *The Shadow Factory*. NY: Doubleday, 2008.

Barrett, Wayne, and Dan Collins. *Grand Illusion: The Untold Story of Rudy Giuliani and 9/11*. NY: Harper, 2006.

Bawer, Bruce. *While Europe Slept: How Radical Islam Is Destroying the West from Within*. NY: Doubleday, 2006.

Begg, Moazzam. *Enemy Combatant: My Imprisonment at Guantánamo, Bagram and Kandahar*. NY: New Press, 2006.

Benjamin, Daniel, and Steven Simon. *The Age of Sacred Terror*. NY: Random House, 2003.

Ben-Veniste, Richard. *The Emperor's New Clothes*. NY: Thomas Dunne, 2009.

Bergen, Peter L. *Holy War Inc*. NY: Free Press, 2001.

———. *The Osama bin Laden I Know: An Oral History of al Qaeda's Leader*. NY: Free Press, 2006.

Berger, J. M., ed. *Ali Mohamed Sourcebook*. Intelwire, 2006.

———. *Mohammed Jamal Khalifa Sourcebook*. Intelwire, 2007.

Bernstein, Richard. *Out of the Blue*. NY: Times Books, 2002.

Berntsen, Gary, and Ralph Pezzullo. *Jawbreaker: The Attack on Bin Laden and Al-Qaeda*. NY: Three Rivers, 2005.

Bhutto, Benazir. *Daughter of the East*. London: Simon & Schuster, 2008.

bin Laden, Najwa, Omar bin Laden, and Jean Sasson. *Growing Up bin Laden*. NY: St. Martin's, 2009.

bin Ladin, Carmen. *The Veiled Kingdom*. London: Virago, 2004.

Bodansky, Yossef. *Bin Laden: The Man Who Declared War on America*. Roseville, CA: Forum, 1999.

———. *Target America*. NY: SPI, 1993.

———. *Terror: The Inside Story of the Terrorist Conspiracy in America.* NY: SPI, 1994.

Boyd, James. *After September 11.* Saddle River, NJ: Prentice Hall, 2003.

Bradley, John. *Saudi Arabia Exposed.* NY: Palgrave Macmillan, 2006.

Breitweiser, Kristin. *Wake-up Call: The Political Education of a 9/11 Widow.* NY: Warner, 2006.

Brisard, Jean-Charles, and Guillaume Dasquié. *Forbidden Truth: U.S.-Taliban Secret Oil Diplomacy and the Failed Hunt for Bin Laden.* NY: Thunder's Mouth, 2002.

Broeckers, Mathias. *Conspiracies, Conspiracy Theories and the Secrets of 9/11.* Joshua Tree, CA: Progressive, 2006.

Bronson, Rachel. *Thicker than Oil.* NY: Oxford University Press, 2006.

Bugliosi, Vincent. *The Prosecution of George W. Bush for Murder.* Cambridge, MA: Vanguard, 2008.

Burke, Jason. *Al-Qaeda: The True Story of Radical Islam.* London: Penguin, 2004.

———. *On the Road to Kandahar.* London: Allen Lane, 2006.

Bush, George W. *Decision Points.* London: Virgin, 2010.

Carrington, Patricia, Julia Collins, Claudia Gerbasi, and Ann Haynes. *Love You, Mean It.* NY: Hyperion, 2006.

Chomsky, Noam. *Imperial Ambitions: Conversations with Noam Chomsky on the Post-9/11 World.* London: Hamish Hamilton, 2005.

Clarke, Richard. *Against All Enemies.* NY: Free Press, 2004.

Clarke, Torie. *Lipstick on a Pig.* NY: Free Press, 2006.

Clinton, Bill. *My Life.* NY: Alfred A. Knopf, 2004.

Cockburn, Andrew. *Rumsfeld.* NY: Scribner, 2007.

Coll, Steve. *The Bin Ladens.* London: Allen Lane, 2008.

———. *Ghost Wars: The Secret History of the CIA, Afghanistan, and bin Laden, from the Soviet Invasion to September 11, 2001.* NY: Penguin, 2004.

Collins, Aukai. *My Jihad.* Guilford, CT: Lyons, 2002.

Cook, David. *Understanding Jihad.* Berkeley: University of California Press, 2005.

Cooley, John. *Unholy Wars: Afghanistan, America and International Terrorism.* London: Pluto, 2002.

Corbin, Jane. *The Base.* London: Pocket, 2003.

Davis, Jayna. *The Third Terrorist.* Nashville: WND, 2004.

Dean, John W. *Worse than Watergate.* NY: Warner, 2004.

DeYoung, Karen. *Soldier: The Life of Colin Powell.* NY: Alfred A. Knopf, 2006.

DiMarco, Damon. *Tower Stories: The Autobiography of September 11, 2001.* NY: Revolution, 2004.

Duelfer, Charles. *Hide and Seek: The Search for Truth in Iraq.* NY: PublicAffairs, 2009.

Dunbar, David, and Brad Reagan, eds. *Debunking 9/11 Myths: Why Conspiracy Theories Can't Stand Up to the Facts.* NY: Hearst, 2006.

Dwyer, Jim, and Kevin Flynn. *102 Minutes: The Untold Story of the Fight to Survive Inside the Twin Towers.* NY: Times Books, 2005.

Ehrenberg, John, et al., eds. *The Iraq Papers.* NY: Oxford University Press, 2010.

Ehrenfeld, Rachel. *Funding Evil,* Chicago: Bonus, 2003.

Emerson, Steven. *The American House of Saud.* NY: Franklin Watts, 1985.

———. *American Jihad: The Terrorists Living Among Us.* NY: Free Press, 2002.

———. *Jihad Incorporated: A Guide to Militant Islam in the U.S.* NY: Prometheus, 2006.

Esposito, John. *Islam: The Straight Path.* New York: Oxford University Press, 1998.

———. *Political Islam.* Boulder: Lynne Rienner, 1997.

Faludi, Susan. *The Terror Dream.* NY: Metropolitan, 1985.

Fandy, Mamoun. *Saudi Arabia and the Politics of Dissent*. London: Palgrave, 1999.

Farmer, John. *The Ground Truth*. NY: Riverhead, 2009.

Feith, Douglas. *War and Decision*. NY: Harper, 2008.

Fenton, Kevin. *Disconnecting the Dots*. Walterville, OR: TrineDay, 2011.

Fisk, Robert. *The Great War for Civilization: The Conquest of the Middle East*. London: Fourth Estate, 2005.

———. *Pity the Nation*. NY: Thunder's Mouth/Nation Books, 2002.

Fleischer, Ari. *Taking Heat: The President, the Press, and My Years in the White House*. New York: William Morrow, 2005.

Fouda, Yosri, and Nick Fielding. *Masterminds of Terror*. Edinburgh: Mainstream, 2003.

Franks, Tommy, with Malcolm McConnell. *American Soldier*. NY: Regan, 2004.

Freeh, Louis. *My FBI*. NY: St. Martin's, 2006.

Freni, Pamela S. *Ground Stop*. NY: iUniverse, 2003.

Friend, David. *Watching the World Change: Stories Behind the Images of 9/11*. NY: Farrar, Straus & Giroux, 2006.

Frum, David. *The Right Man*. NY: Random House, 2003.

Fury, Dalton. *Kill bin Laden*. NY: St. Martin's, 2008.

Gellman, Barton. *Angler: The Shadow Vice Presidency of Dick Cheney*. London: Allen Lane, 2008.

Gerson, Michael. *Heroic Conservatism*. NY: HarperOne, 2007.

Gertz, Bill. *Betrayal: How the Clinton Administration Undermines American Security*. Washington, D.C.: Regnery, 1999.

———. *Breakdown: The Failure of American Intelligence to Defeat Global Terror*. NY: Plume, 2003.

Gilbert, Martin. *Israel*. London: Black Swan, 1999.

Giuliani, Rudolph W., with Ken Kurson. *Leadership*. NY: Hyperion, 2002.

Gold, Dore. *Hatred's Kingdom*. Washington, D.C.: Regnery, 2003.

Goldberg, Alfred, et al. *Pentagon 9/11*. Washington, D.C.: Office of the Secretary of Defense, 2007.

Gordon, Michael, and Bernard Trainor. *Cobra II*. NY: Pantheon, 2006.

Graham, Bob, with Jeff Nussbaum. *Intelligence Matters*. NY: Random House, 2004.

Graham, Bob, and Jim Talent, eds. *World at Risk*. NY: Vintage, 2008.

Griffin, David Ray. *Debunking 9/11 Debunking*. Northampton, MA: Olive Branch, 2007.

———. *The Mysterious Collapse of World Trade Center 7*. Northhampton, MA: Olive Branch, 2009.

———. *The New Pearl Harbor: Disturbing Questions About the Bush Administration and 9/11*. Gloucestershire, U.K.: Arris, 2005.

———. *The New Pearl Harbor Revisited: 9/11, the Cover-up and the Exposé*. Northampton, MA: Olive Branch, 2008.

———. *The 9/11 Commission Report: Omissions and Distortions*. Gloucestershire, U.K.: Arris, 2005.

———. *9/11 Contradictions*. Northampton, MA: Olive Branch, 2008.

———. *Osama bin Laden: Dead or Alive?* Gloucestershire, U.K.: Arris, 2009.

Griffin, David Ray, and Peter Dale Scott, eds. *9/11 and American Empire: Intellectuals Speak Out*. Northampton, MA: Interlink, 2007.

Gunratna, Rohan. *Inside al Qaeda, Global Network of Terror*. NY: Columbia University Press, 2002.

Gutman, Roy. *How We Missed the Story*. Washington, D.C.: U.S. Institute of Peace Press, 2008.

Halberstam, David. *Firehouse*. NY: Hyperion, 2002.

Hamel, Ian. *L'Énigme Oussama Ben Laden*. Paris: Payot, 2008.

Harris, Sam. *The End of Faith*. London: Free Press, 2004.

Hayes, Stephen. *Cheney*. NY: HarperCollins, 2007.

———. *The Connection*. NY: HarperCollins, 2004.

Henshall, Ian, and Rowland Morgan. *9/11 Revealed: Challenging the*

Facts Behind the War on Terror. London: Robinson, 2005.

Hersh, Seymour M. *Chain of Command: The Road from 9/11 to Abu Ghraib.* NY: HarperPerennial, 2004.

Hicks, Sander. *The Big Wedding: 9/11, the Whistle-Blowers, and the Cover-up.* NY: VoxPop, 2005.

Hilton, Christopher. *The Women's War.* Stroud, U.K.: History Press, 2003.

Hoffman, Bruce. *Inside Terrorism.* New York: Columbia University Press, 2006.

Holden, David, and Richard Johns. *The House of Saud.* NY: Holt, Rinehart & Winston, 1981.

Hollingsworth, Mark, with Sandy Mitchell. *Saudi Babylon.* Edinburgh: Mainstream, 2006.

Hopsicker, Daniel. *Welcome to Terrorland: Mohamed Atta and the 9/11 Cover-up in Florida.* Eugene, OR: MadCow, 2004/2007.

Hufschmid, Eric. *Painful Questions.* Goleta, CA: Self-published, 2002.

Hussain, Ed. *The Islamist.* London: Penguin, 2007.

Hussain, Zahid. *Frontline Pakistan: The Struggle with Militant Islam.* NY: Columbia University Press, 2007.

Isikoff, Michael, and David Corn. *Hubris: The Inside Story of Spin, Scandal, and the Selling of the Iraq War.* NY: Three Rivers, 2006.

Jacquard, Roland. *In the Name of Osama bin Laden.* Durham: Duke University Press, 2002.

Jefferson, Lisa D., and Felicia Middlebrooks. *Called: "Hello, My Name Is Mrs. Jefferson, I Understand Your Plane Is Being Hijacked?"* Chicago: Northfield, 2006.

Katz, Samuel M. *Relentless Pursuit: The DSS and the Manhunt for the al-Qaeda Terrorists.* NY: Forge, 2002.

Kean, Thomas, and Lee Hamilton. *Without Precedent: The Inside Story of the 9/11 Commission.* NY: Alfred A. Knopf, 2006.

Keegan, William, with Bart David. *Closure: The Untold Story of the Ground Zero Recovery Mission.* NY: Touchstone, 2006.

Kepel, Gilles. *Jihad.* Cambridge, MA: Belknap, 2002.

Kessler, Ronald. *The Terrorist Watch*. NY: Crown, 2007.

Kippenberg, Hans, and Tilman Seidensticker, eds. *The 9/11 Handbook*. London: Equinox, 2006.

Labévière, Richard. Trans. Martin DeMers. *Dollars for Terror: The United States and Islam*, NY: Algora, 2000.

Labévière, Richard. *Les Coulisses de la Terreur*. Paris: Bernard Grosset, 2003.

Lacey, Robert. *Inside the Kingdom*. London: Hutchinson, 2009.

———. *The Kingdom*. NY: Avon, 1981.

Lance, Peter. *Cover-up: What the Government Is Still Hiding About the War on Terror*. NY: Regan, 2004.

———, *1000 Years for Revenge: International Terrorism and the FBI*. NY: Regan, 2004.

———. *Triple Cross: How Bin-Laden's Master Spy Pentrated the CIA, the Green Berets, and the FBI—and Why Patrick Fitzgerald Failed to Stop Him*. NY: Regan, 2006.

Landis, Paul. *A Real 9/11 Commission*. Self-published, 2005.

Langewiesche, William. *American Ground: Unbuilding the World Trade Center*. NY: North Point, 2002.

Laurent, Eric. *La Face Cachée du 11 Septembre*. Paris: Plon, 2004.

Lawrence, Bruce, ed. *Messages to the World: The Statements of Osama bin Laden*. London: Verso, 2005.

Levin, Jason. *From the Desert to the Derby*. NY: Daily Racing Form Press, 2002.

Levy, Bernard-Henri. *Who Killed Daniel Pearl?* Hoboken, NJ: Melville House, 2003.

Longman, Jere. *Among the Heroes*. NY: HarperPerennial, 2003.

Margulies, Joseph. *Guantánamo and the Abuse of Presidential Power*. NY: Simon & Schuster, 2006.

Marrs, Jim. *The Terror Conspiracy: Deception, 9/11 and the Loss of Liberty*. NY: Disinformation, 2006.

Mayer, Jane. *The Dark Side: The Inside Story of How the War on Terror Turned into a War on American Ideals*. NY: Doubleday, 2008.

McDermott, Terry. *Perfect Soldiers*. NY: HarperCollins, 2005.

Mearsheimer, John, and Stephen Walt. *The Israel Lobby and U.S. Foreign Policy*. NY: Farrar, Straus & Giroux, 2007.

Meyssan, Thierry. *9/11: The Big Lie*. London: Carnot, 2002.

Miles, Hugh. *Al Jazeera*. London: Abacus, 2005.

Miller, John, and Michael Stone, with Chris Mitchell. *The Cell: Inside the 9/11 Plot, and Why the FBI and CIA Failed to Stop It*. NY: Hyperion, 2002.

Miniter, Richard. *Losing Bin Laden*. Washington, D.C.: Regnery, 2003.

Murphy, Tom. *Reclaiming the Sky*. NY: Amacom, 2007.

Musharraf, Pervez. *In the Line of Fire: A Memoir*. NY: Free Press, 2006.

Mylroie, Laurie. *The War Against America*. NY: Regan, 2002.

Napoleoni, Loretta. *Terror Incorporated*. NY: Seven Stories, 2005.

Nasiri, Omar. *Inside the Jihad: My Life with Al-Qaeda*. NY: Basic Books, 2006.

National Commission on Terrorist Attacks Upon the United States. *9/11 and Terrorist Travel*. Franklin, TN: Hillboro, 2004.

———. *The 9/11 Commission Report*. NY: W. W. Norton, 2004.

O'Clery, Conor. *May You Live in Interesting Times*. Dublin: Poolbeg, 2009.

Ottaway, David. *The King's Messenger*. NY: Walker, 2008.

Picciotto, Richard, with Daniel Paisner. *Last Man Down*. NY: Berkley, 2002.

Palast, Greg. *The Best Democracy Money Can Buy*. NY: Plume, 2004.

Pape, Robert. *Dying to Win*. NY: Random House, 2006.

Pearl, Marianne. *A Mighty Heart*. NY: Scribner, 2003.

Posner, Gerald. *Secrets of the Kingdom*. NY: Random House, 2005.

———. *Why America Slept: The Failure to Prevent 9/11*. NY: Ballantine, 2003.

Posner, Richard. *Not a Suicide Pact: The Constitution in a Time of*

National Emergency. NY: Oxford, 2006.

Pyszcynski, Tom, Sheldon Solomon, and Jeff Greenberg. *In the Wake of 911: The Psychology of Terror.* Washington, D.C.: American Psychological Association, 2003.

Qutb, Sayyid. *Milestones.* New Delhi: Millat Book Centre, undated.

Raimondo, Justin. *The Terror Enigma.* NY: iUniverse, 2003.

Rashid, Ahmed. *Descent into Chaos.* NY: Viking, 2008.

———. *Taliban.* New Haven: Yale University Press, 2001.

Rees, Phil. *Dining with Terrorists: Meetings with the World's Most Wanted Militants.* London: Pan, 2006.

Reeve, Simon. *The New Jackals: Osama bin Laden and the Future of Terrorism.* London: André Deutsch, 1999.

Ressa, Maria. *Seeds of Terror.* NY: Free Press, 2003.

Rich, Frank. *The Greatest Story Ever Sold: The Decline and Fall of Truth from 9/11 to Katrina.* NY: Penguin, 2006.

Ridgeway, James. *The Five Unanswered Questions About 9/11.* NY: Seven Stories, 2005.

Risen, James. *State of War.* NY: Free Press, 2006.

Rove, Karl. *Courage and Consequence: My Life as a Conservative in the Fight.* NY: Threshold, 2010.

Rubinfien, Leo. *Wounded Cities.* Göttingen, Germany: Steidl, 2008.

Rumsfeld, Donald. *Known and Unknown.* NY: Sentinel, 2011.

Ruppert, Michael C. *Crossing the Rubicon: The Decline of the American Empire at the End of the Age of Oil.* Gabriola Island, B.C.: New Society, 2004.

Ruthven, Malise. *A Fury for God.* London: Granta, 2002.

Sageman, Marc. *Leaderless Jihad.* Philadelphia: University of Pennsylvania Press, 2008.

Editors, Salon.com. *Afterwords: Stories and Reports from 9/11 and Beyond.* NY: Washington Square, 2002.

Sammon, Bill. *Fighting Back.* Washington, D.C.: Regnery, 2002.

Scheuer, Michael. *Imperial Hubris: Why the West Is Losing the War on*

Terror. Washington, D.C.: Potomac, 2004.

———. *Marching Toward Hell*. NY: Free Press, 2008.

———. *Osama bin Laden*. NY: Oxford University Press, 2011.

Schindler, John. *Unholy Terror*. Minneapolis: Zenith, 2007.

Schopmeyer, Robert. *Prior Knowledge of 9/11*. Palo Alto, CA: Palo Alto Publishing, 2008.

Schroen, Gary C. *First In: An Insider's Account of How the CIA Spearheaded the War on Terror in Afghanistan*. NY: Ballantine, 2005.

Schultheis, Rob. *Hunting bin Laden*. NY: Skyhorse, 2008.

Schwartz, Stephen. *The Two Faces of Islam*. NY: Doubleday, 2002.

Schwarzkopf, General H. Norman, with Peter Petre. *It Doesn't Take a Hero*. NY: Bantam, 1992.

Scott, Peter Dale. *The Road to 9/11*. Berkeley: University of California Press, 2007.

Shaffer, Anthony. *Operation Dark Heart*. NY: Thomas Dunne, 2010.

Shaler, Robert C. *Who They Were*. NY: Free Press, 2005.

Sheehy, Gail. *Middletown, America*. NY: Random House, 2003.

Shenon, Philip. *The Commission*. NY: Twelve: 2008.

Sifaoui, Mohamed. *Inside Al-Qaeda: How I Infiltrated the World's Deadliest Terrorist Organization*. NY: Thunder's Mouth, 2003.

Simpson, John. *Simpson's World: Dispatches from the Front*. NY: Miramax, 2003.

Simpson, William. *The Prince*. NY: Regan, 2006.

Smith, Dennis. *Report from Ground Zero*. New York: Viking, 2002.

Smucker, Philip. *Al Qaeda's Great Escape: The Military and the Media on Terror's Tail*. Washington, D.C.: Brassey's, 2004.

Spencer, Lynn. *Touching History*. NY: Free Press, 2008.

Strasser, Steven, ed. *The 9/11 Investigations*. NY: PublicAffairs, 2004.

Suskind, Ron. *The One Percent Doctrine: Deep Inside America's Pursuit of Its Enemies Since 9/11*. NY: Simon & Schuster, 2006.

———. *The Price of Loyalty*. NY: Simon & Schuster, 2004.

————. *The Way of the World.* NY: Harper, 2008.

Swanson, Gail. *Behind the Scenes at Ground Zero.* NY: TRAC Team, 2003.

Sylvester, Judyth, and Suzanne Hoffman. *Women Journalists at Ground Zero.* Lanham, MD: Rowman & Littlefield, 2002.

Taheri, Amir. *Holy Terror: The Inside Story of Islamic Terrorism.* London: Sphere, 1987.

Taibbi, Matt. *The Great Derangement.* NY: Spiegel & Grau, 2009.

Tarpley, Webster Griffin. *9/11: Synthetic Terror: Made in USA.* Joshua Tree, CA: Progressive, 2006.

Taylor, John B. *Global Financial Warriors.* NY: W. W. Norton, 2007.

Tenet, George, with Bill Harlow. *At the Center of the Storm: My Years at the CIA.* NY: HarperCollins, 2007.

Thompson, Paul. *The Terror Timeline.* NY: Regan, 2004.

Thorn, Victor. *9/11 on Trial: The World Trade Center Collapse.* State College, PA: Sisyphus, 2006.

Trento, Joseph. *Prelude to Terror: Edwin P. Wilson and the Legacy of America's Private Intelligence Network.* NY: Carroll & Graf, 2005.

Trento, Susan B., and Joseph J. Trento. *Unsafe at Any Altitude.* Hanover, NH: Steerforth, 2007.

Trofimov, Yaroslav. *The Siege of Mecca.* NY: Doubleday, 2007.

Trost, Cathy, and Alicia Shepard. *Running Toward Danger: Stories Behind the Breaking News of 9/11.* Lanham, MD: Rowman & Littlefield, 2002.

Unger, Craig. *The Fall of the House of Bush.* NY: Scribner, 2007.

————. *House of Bush, House of Saud.* London: Gibson Square, 2007.

Ventura, Jesse, with Dick Russell. *American Conspiracies.* NY: Skyhorse, 2010.

Vitug, Marites Dañquilan, and Glenda M. Gloria. *Under the Crescent Moon.* Quezon City, Philippines: Ateneo Center for Social Policy, 2000.

Warde, Ibrahim. *The Price of Fear.* Berkeley: University of California Press, 2007.

Weiner, Tim. *Legacy of Ashes: The History of the CIA*. NY: Doubleday, 2007.

Weiss, Murray. *The Man Who Warned America*. NY: Regan, 2003.

Weldon, Curt. *Countdown to Terror*. Washington, D.C.: Regnery, 2005.

Williams, Eric D. *9/11 101: 101 Points that Everyone Should Know and Consider That Prove 9/11 Was an Inside Job*. Williamsquire, 2006.

———. *The Puzzle of 9/11*. Booksurge, 2006.

Williams, Paul L. *Al Qaeda: Brotherhood of Terror*. Alpha, 2002.

———. *The Day of Islam*. Amherst, NY: Prometheus, 2007.

———. *Osama's Revenge: The Next 9/11*. Amherst, NY: Prometheus, 2004.

Woods, Ian., ed. *9/11: The Greatest Crime of All Time*, Vol. 2. Ontario: Global Outlook, 2006.

Woodward, Bob. *Bush at War*. NY: Simon & Schuster, 2002.

———. *Plan of Attack*. NY: Simon & Schuster, 2004.

———. *State of Denial, Bush at War, Part III*. NY: Simon & Schuster, 2006.

Wright, Lawrence. *The Looming Tower, Al-Qaeda and the Road to 9/11*. NY: Alfred A. Knopf, 2006.

Yoo, John. *War by Any Other Means: An Inside Account of the War on Terror*. NY: Atlantic Monthly Press, 2006.

al-Zayyat, Montasser. *The Road to Al-Qaeda: The Story of Bin Laden's Right-Hand Man*. London: Pluto, 2004.

Zegart, Amy B. *Spying Blind*. Princeton: Princeton University Press, 2007.

Zwicker, Barrie. *Towers of Deception: The Media Cover-up of 9/11*. Gabriola Island, B.C.: New Society, 2006.

PHOTO CREDITS

FIRST SECTION

Second plane approaches Trade Center: Carmen Taylor/AP/Press Association Images. Daniel Lewin: courtesy of Marco Greenberg; Hansons: courtesy of Hanson family; trapped office workers: Jeff Christensen/Reuters; workers make way to safety: Shannon Stapleton/Reuters; Pentagon memorial: Mariana Perez; CeeCee Lyles' ID card: Moussaoui trial exhibit; Barbara Olson: Reuters.

New Yorkers ran: Paul Hawthorne/AP/Press Association Images; Bush is told: Paul J. Richards, AFP/Getty Images; Operations Center: Presidential Materials, U.S. National Archives; firefighters retrieve bodies: Getty Images.

Pentagon façade: U.S. Dept. of Defense; After, in New York: AFP/Getty Images; Wreckage/Voice Recorder: Moussaoui trial exhibits; Investigators search: Tim Shaffer/ Reuters.
Last girder removed: Peter Morgan/Reuters.

SECOND SECTION

Bin Laden acclaimed: (upper) AFP/Getty Images; (lower) Ruth Fremson/*New York Times*/Redux Pictures. Binalshibh: Flashpoint Partners; Zubaydah wounded: authors' collection; nineteen hijackers: Getty Images; poster: used in Birmingham, UK; Young Atta: Getty Images; bearded Atta & Jarrah: AP Photo/*Sunday Times*; "Reward" poster:courtesy of Diplomatic Security Service, Dept. of State. Al-Shehhi & Hanjour: Moussaoui trial exhibits; Jarrah in cockpit & with Sengün: Terry McDermott; al- Mihdhar & al-Hazmi: Moussaoui trial exhibits; Abdullah: Earnie Grafton/Zuma Press; bin Don: Steven Hirsch/Splash News; al-Bayoumi: government of Saudi Arabia; Aulaqi: Washington Post/Getty Images; al-Hussayen: government of Saudi Arabia.

INDEX

Page numbers in *italics* refer to illustrations.

Sinatra: The Life

Anthony Summers & Robbyn Swan

In 1941, at age twenty-five, Sinatra told a friend, 'I'm going to be the best singer in the world'. Two years on, the bobbysoxers were already weeping and screaming for him in their thousands. Half a century on Bono defined him as 'the Big Bang of popular music'.

This the first and last definitive, fully documented, massively researched birth-to-death biography of Frank Sinatra by the bestselling author of *File on the Tsar* and *Goddess: The Secret Lives of Marilyn Monroe*.

'Astonishingly well-researched . . . incredibly well-sourced'
INDEPENDENT ON SUNDAY

'Summers and Swan tell us much that is new, and with panache. Compelling . . . sterling work'
SUNDAY TIMES

'Astonishing book . . . uncovers new evidence'
DAILY EXPRESS

'A definitive, generational work'
VANITY FAIR

'First-rate reporting . . . dense and intimate'
PEOPLE

'Anthony Summers never writes a book that fails to offer accurate material you will find nowhere else . . . No surprise then that *Sinatra: The Life* is one of the very few, bona fide, three-dimensional portraits of an amazingly complex, interesting and sometimes god-awful guy'
NORMAN MAILER